Historical Fiction II

Genreflecting Advisory Series

Diana Tixier Herald, Series Editor

African American Literature: A Guide to Reading Interests
Edited by Alma Dawson and Connie Van Fleet

Historical Fiction: A Guide to the Genre
Sarah L. Johnson

Canadian Fiction: A Guide to Reading Interests
Sharron Smith and Maureen O'Connor

Genreflecting: A Guide to Popular Reading Interests, 6th Edition
Diana Tixier Herald, Edited by Wayne A. Wiegand

The Real Story: A Guide to Nonfiction Reading Interests
Sarah Statz Cords, Edited by Robert Burgin

Read the High Country: A Guide to Western Books and Films
John Mort

Graphic Novels: A Genre Guide to Comic Books, Manga, and More
Michael Pawuk

Genrefied Classics: A Guide to Reading Interests in Classic Literature
Tina Frolund

Encountering Enchantment: A Guide to Speculative Fiction for Teens
Susan Fichtelberg

Fluent in Fantasy: The Next Generation
Diana Tixier Herald and Bonnie Kunzel

Gay, Lesbian, Bisexual, and Transgendered Literature: A Genre Guide
Ellen Bosman and John Bradford; Edited by Robert B. Ridinger

Reality Rules!: A Guide to Teen Nonfiction Reading Interests
Elizabeth Fraser

Historical Fiction II

A Guide to the Genre

Sarah L. Johnson

Genreflecting Advisory Series

Diana Tixier Herald, Series Editor

LIBRARIES

UNLIMITED

A Member of the Greenwood Publishing Group

Westport, Connecticut • London

Library of Congress Cataloging in Publication Data

Johnson, Sarah L., 1969-
   Historical fiction II : a guide to genre / Sarah L. Johnson.
      p. cm. -- (Genreflecting advisory series)
   Includes bibliographical references and indexes.
   ISBN 978-1-59158-624-1 (alk. paper)
1. Historical fiction, American--Bibliography. 2. Historical fiction,
English--Bibliography. I. Title. II. Title: Historical fiction two.
III. Title: Historical fiction 2.
   Z1231.H57J64 2009
   [PS374.H5]
   016.823'08109--dc22   2008045537

British Library Cataloguing in Publication Data is available.

Library of Congress Catalog Card Number: 2008045537
ISBN: 978-1-59158-624-1

First published in 2009

Libraries Unlimited, 88 Post Road West, Westport, CT 06881
A Member of the Greenwood Publishing Group, Inc.
www.lu.com

Printed in the United States of America

The paper used in this book complies with the
Permanent Paper Standard issued by the National
Information Standards Organization (Z39.48–1984).

10   9   8   7   6   5   4   3   2   1

Contents

Acknowledgments

I'd like to thank my husband, Mark, for his support throughout the writing process for this book as well as the previous volume, and for his willingness to ignore the piles of historical novels cluttering up our living room for the past year and a half. Barbara Ittner, my editor at Libraries Unlimited, recognized how much the genre had expanded and changed since publication of the original *Historical Fiction: A Guide to the Genre* and championed the idea of a sequel. Thanks also to my librarian and novelist friends (you know who you are), who offered words of encouragement as well as distractions when needed.

A small number of the annotations in this book appeared previously, in longer versions, either in the *Historical Novels Review* or on my blog, Reading the Past.

All errors and omissions are, of course, my own. If you come across titles you believe should be included in future volumes of this guide, or if you have other comments you'd like to share, please drop me a line via e-mail (sljohnson2@eiu.edu).

Last but not least, I'm grateful to the librarians and readers who took the time to contact me with their thoughts and appreciative words on the previous book. I hope you enjoy this one as much as you did the first, although I make no apology for adding more novels to your to-be-read piles!

Sarah L. Johnson
Booth Library, Eastern Illinois University

Introduction

Purpose and Scope

Historical fiction has truly undergone a renaissance in recent years. Not only are library and bookstore shelves overflowing with new historical novels, but the genre has been steadily gaining respect in the literary community. Historical novels continue to appear regularly on best-seller lists; recent examples include Ken Follett's *World Without End*, Philippa Gregory's *The Boleyn Inheritance*, and Nancy Horan's *Loving Frank*. In addition, they are often recommended as choices for book discussion groups (Lisa See's *Snow Flower and the Secret Fan*, John Shors's *Beneath a Marble Sky*). Older, out-of-print historical novels covering hot topics or by currently popular authors are being reprinted to keep up with reader demand. Between 2000 and 2007, approximately one-third of *Booklist* "Editors' Choice" titles in adult fiction were historical novels.

Now more than ever, librarians and other professionals who work with readers need to develop a greater familiarity with the genre—knowledge of its general characteristics, its appeal to readers, benchmark and representative titles, and publishing trends—or they risk being left behind.

Historical Fiction II: A Guide to the Genre aims to provide guidance in all of these areas. As for the first volume, its primary audience is librarians, both readers' advisors and collection development specialists, curious to learn more about historical fiction and reader interests. Readers and fans of the genre can use it to locate interesting titles and discover more about their own reading tastes. Aspiring historical novelists can read the chapter introductions and annotations to see what's being published by whom, and where their own work might fit into the canon.

Historical fiction overlaps several other genres. For instance, historical romance is a subset both of historical fiction and of romance. Most general readers' advisory tools address historical fiction but place novels in overlapping subgenres, like historical romance or historical mystery, within the other category. Although this may suit readers of other genres just fine, it doesn't work as well for readers who specifically seek out historical settings. This book presents historical fiction, in all its variety, in a single volume to make it easier for librarians and readers to locate worthwhile books.

Most readers' advisors know historical fiction when they see it, though exact definitions are tricky—an issue covered in more detail in Chapter 1. Here "historical fiction" includes novels set prior to the middle of the last century in which the historical backdrop plays a strong role in the story. This guide makes no claims to comprehensiveness, because all-inclusive coverage would mean filling several more volumes.

With these guidelines in mind, selection was done regardless of format, recognizing that an increasing number of titles are published only in paperback. Series titles are listed in full, in their appropriate reading order—which may or may not reflect publication order.

This guide considers historical fiction in its broadest sense, recognizing today's tendency toward "genre-blending." To satisfy as many tastes as possible, subgenres like time-slip novels, alternate history, and historical fantasy each have their own chapters. Although purists may not consider them appropriate, many reader favorites, like Connie Willis's *Doomsday Book* and Marion Zimmer Bradley's *The Mists of Avalon*, to name just two, fall within these categories.

New to This Volume

The existence (and length!) of this second volume of *Historical Fiction* demonstrates the continued and growing interest in the genre. The original volume categorized and described more than 3,800 historical novels published between 1995 and mid-2004, as well as classics and other genre favorites. This updated guide picks up where the first book left off, focusing on English-language novels for adults that were published between 2004 and mid-2008, in particular those commonly found in American public library collections (as indicated in OCLC's WorldCat). It supplements rather than replaces the original volume. It can also work well as a single-volume introduction to recent historical fiction for libraries or readers who don't own the first book.

Within these pages, more than 2,700 historical novels are organized into subgenres, described, and in most cases annotated. More than 2,000 of these, or 75 percent, are new to this book. Old favorites have been included if they continue to be popular, and bibliographic details for earlier (pre-2004) titles in existing series are listed, because many readers will want complete listings of these books at their fingertips. However, because of space limitations, annotations of individual series titles from the first book have not been duplicated here unless it was necessary for comprehension of the continuing storyline. Full-length descriptions of these novels can be found in *Historical Fiction: A Guide to the Genre* (2005).

This book has several new features meant to increase its usefulness to readers' advisors and collection development librarians. ISBNs are listed for every title that has one, as is the format (hardbound or paper), because many new historical novels are being published as paperback originals. (See the section "The Trade Paperback Revolution" in Chapter 1 for more discussion of this important issue.) Keywords reflecting subjects, historical characters, and place or time are included directly after the annotations. Readers can use these keywords, along with the appropriate index in the back of the book, to find other titles that fit these categories. All of the chapter and section introductions have been updated as necessary to reflect the current state of this ever-changing genre. Several new categories ("Religious Thrillers," "Crime Thrillers," and "Viking Romances," for example) have been added or amended to showcase the latest trends; others have been condensed or eliminated.

Organization of This Book

As a genre, historical fiction is incredibly diverse, ranging from the delightful Regency romances of Georgette Heyer to Ken Follett's action-packed World War II adventures. This diversity presents challenges for readers' advisors. Most genre tools arrange historical novels by time period and place, with indexes by subject or theme. This book takes a different approach. Like other volumes in the Genreflecting Advisory Series, this guide is organized by subgenre, which more closely reflects reader interests. For example, while Margaret Mitchell's *Gone with the Wind*, Jeff Shaara's *Gods and Generals*, and Charles Frazier's *Cold Mountain* all take place during the American Civil War, their styles are very different, and readers who enjoy one might not automatically enjoy the others. This guide places each title in its appropriate category: Mitchell with romantic epics, Shaara with other traditional historical novels on the Civil War, and Frazier with literary historical novels set during that time period. The subject index will help omnivorous readers who can't get enough of a particular time period or place, or who wish to access titles that fall into different subgenres.

Each chapter, covering one subgenre within historical fiction, begins by explaining its appeal to readers. Chapters are divided into subcategories or themes, which are based mostly on eras or locales, but not always. The introduction for each theme analyzes common characteristics, which can include historical background that will be useful for readers. Annotations for individual novels include author, title, publisher, original publication date, number of pages, format, and ISBN, followed by a concise plot summary. When novels appear as part of a series, annotations may be provided for the series as a whole rather than for each title.

For the most part, only novels published in the United States, or widely available to American readers, are included. If a book was previously published in another country (usually Great Britain) significantly before the American publication date, this information is indicated. Sometimes an American publisher will discontinue a series even though new volumes continue to appear in Britain. Because readers of a series will want to know what happens next, this book provides information on later titles regardless of where they were published.

The following icons designate special features of novels or series:

🎖 Winner of one or more literary awards, specifics of which are mentioned in the annotation.

✍ Biographical novels, that is, novels in which a historical personage is one of the main characters. These people are listed in the historical character index.

★ Classic or benchmark novels within the subgenre, works to which newly published titles are frequently compared. These may or may not be older novels.

   📖   Novels especially appropriate for reading groups for book discussion. For more information on selecting novels for reading groups, see "Choices for Book Discussions" in Chapter 1.

   YA   Although this book concentrates on novels for adults, some may be suitable for young adults, either because they feature young people or because the subject matter may interest them. This icon denotes these titles.

Although most titles clearly fit within a single subgenre, a selected number may fit into more than one. Full annotations for these titles are placed where, in the author's opinion, they fit most appropriately. "See" and "see also" references appear throughout the book, both within the chapter introductions and the annotations. For example, many thrillers appeal to mystery readers, and fans of traditional historical novels set in ancient Greece may also enjoy historical fantasy novels set during the same period.

Literary historical novels (Chapter 10) deserve special mention here, because some novels in this category can easily fit more than one subgenre. For example, Cormac McCarthy's *Blood Meridian* and Nina Vida's *The Texicans* can be considered literary Westerns, whereas Padma Viswanathan's *The Toss of a Lemon* appeals to readers of both literary fiction and sagas. When works of literary fiction appear outside Chapter 10, they have been given the designation **Literary** at the end of the annotation.

In addition, for a small number of novels listed in Chapter 10 (e.g., Anita Diamant's *The Red Tent*, Tracy Chevalier's *Girl with a Pearl Earring*, Karen Essex's *Stealing Athena*), deciding whether they fit better as literary or traditional historical novels is a judgment call. Dorothy Dunnett's beloved <u>Lymond Chronicles</u>, listed in Chapter 8 alongside other swashbuckling tales, straddles the adventure, literary, and traditional subgenres. For many readers, these special novels seem to have it all: compelling plots, brilliantly described locales, fascinating characters, and lyrical language. Likewise, the novels in Diana Gabaldon's <u>Outlander</u> series have been described as historical romances, traditional historical novels, and even science fiction because of their time-travel aspects. With their widespread appeal, is it any wonder these series are so popular? While consulting this book, readers' advisors should keep in mind the cross-genre appeal of these perennial favorites, most of which are denoted as classic or benchmark titles ★. For these novels, categorization by subgenre, to some degree, can be considered an art rather than an exact science.

Suggestions for Use

Although the organization of this book will be intuitive to most readers, not everyone will be consulting it for the same purpose. Readers' advisors, both in libraries and bookstores, may wish to discover titles of interest to themselves and their patrons. Collection development librarians may use it to fill in gaps or build new collections in areas they haven't covered. Readers looking for what books to read next, or read-alike titles for their favorite novels, can use this book to discover new material. Following are some general guidelines for usage.

1.   The table of contents lists subgenres, themes, and subcategories within themes. Readers searching for a particular type of novel should begin here.

2. To learn about novels similar to ones you or other readers have enjoyed, consult the author/title index at the end of the book to see in what chapter the book is located. Read-alike titles are grouped together within a chapter's subsections, which are based on time period/place or other themes. In addition, use the keywords at the end of each title or series annotation, combined with the indexes, to locate other titles sharing the same subject, theme, locale, or time period.

3. To discover worthwhile books by a certain author, use the author/title index to see where they are located. Some authors write in more than one subgenre, so their novels may be scattered throughout the book. For example, Steven Saylor has written the multi-period epic *Roma* (Chapter 4), as well as his Gordianus the Finder series, set in ancient Rome (Chapter 7). In addition to her Elizabeth I mystery series, Karen Harper has written traditional historical novels set in medieval and Tudor-era England (Chapter 2). Be aware that many authors also have extensive backlists, and this book may not include every novel they have ever written.

4. To find books set during a particular time period and place regardless of subgenre—Victorian England, for instance—use the time/place index to cut across the chapters and locate worthwhile titles.

5. To learn more about overall publishing trends, consult Chapter 1, specifically "Recent Trends in Historical Fiction." For explanations about the appeal of more specific types of novels, like historical mysteries or adventures set during the Age of Sail, see the introductions to chapters and themes. Use the table of contents to locate the section you want. To find more specific subjects or themes (e.g., pirates, artists, epistolary novels), refer to the subject index.

If this book helps you learn more about the vibrant historical fiction genre, or suggests worthwhile titles for you or other readers to consider, it will have served its purpose. Happy reading!

Notes

1. Thomas Mallon, "History, Fiction, and the Burden of Truth," in *Writing Historical Fiction: A Virtual Conference Session* (Albany: Department of History, State University of New York at Albany, 1998). Available at http://www.albany. edu/history/hist_fict/Mallon/Mallons.htm (accessed August 5, 2008).

Chapter 1

The Appeal of the Past

Defining Historical Fiction

At first glance, historical fiction seems an easy genre to define. Although it's true that it basically means "fiction set in the past," this definition brings up a number of questions. For instance, how far back must a novel be set to make it historical—a hundred years, fifty years, ten years? To readers born in the 1960s, novels set during World War II may be considered suitably historical, but older readers who vividly remember the 1940s may not agree.

Even if librarians can agree on a definition, for example, that historical fiction includes any works that are set more than fifty years in the past, whose past are we talking about, the reader's or the author's? Take, for example, F. Scott Fitzgerald's *The Great Gatsby*, both written and set in the 1920s. How about Jane Austen's novels, written during England's Regency period and set slightly beforehand? These works are obviously set in the historical past, and they provide considerable information on customs of the times. By this definition, though, any contemporary novel will become "historical fiction" at some point in the future. When readers ask for historical fiction, this usually isn't what they mean.

In this book, as in the previous volume, "historical fiction" is defined as fictional works (mainly novels) set before the middle of the last century, ones in which the author is writing from research rather than personal experience. This usually means that the novels take place before the author's life and times. Most autobiographical novels wouldn't fit these criteria, but they are included here on occasion if they are newly written works set in the 1940s or earlier.

Some novels written in past centuries or decades (e.g., works by Austen, Fitzgerald, Edith Wharton, and others) may appeal to historical fiction fans, but they must contain enough historical detail to evoke times past. In addition, novels set in the 1950s, 1960s, and even later may fit some people's definitions of historical fiction, especially readers who weren't yet born at the time and who wish to experience what life was like then. In the mainstream press, novels about events as recent as 9/11 have been described as historical fiction, with the reasoning that it was an incident from the (recent) past that caused a significant shift in people's views of the world. These and other such novels are beyond the scope of this book, but readers' advisors in libraries should be aware that readers may not have the same definition of historical fiction that they do, and adjust their advisory interviews accordingly.

A Brief History

Historical fiction is one of the oldest forms of storytelling. Members of long-ago cultures, from Babylonia to ancient Greece and Rome, proudly recounted tales of their forebears' heroism and defeats. Many of these stories have been passed down to us over the years. Early works we consider to be classics—Shakespeare's *Hamlet*, Goethe's *Faust*, even Homer's *Iliad*—were written as fictionalized, embellished retellings of events that occurred long before the author's time. Today's novelists continue to revisit the same characters and themes, proving that the legacy of these ancient tales has endured.

In literary circles, Sir Walter Scott's *Waverley* is generally considered to be the first historical novel. Published anonymously in 1814, *Waverley* was the first novel in Scott's popular series about eighteenth-century Scottish history. What made it unique was Scott's attempt to accurately portray the background and qualities of ordinary people involved in the 1745 Jacobite rebellion against the British crown. With its subtitle, " 'Tis Sixty Years Since," *Waverley* established the original cutoff date for historical fiction. To modern readers its prose seems old-fashioned and cumbersome, but its popularity inspired many devoted followers and imitators. Among other successful historical novels of the nineteenth century are Nathaniel Hawthorne's *The Scarlet Letter* (1850, about Puritan New England), Charles Dickens's *A Tale of Two Cities* (1856, about the French Revolution), and Tolstoy's *War and Peace* (1869, about early nineteenth-century Russia). Considered classics today, they were the best sellers of their era—critically acclaimed yet popular reading.

Historical fiction saw both its highest and lowest points during the twentieth century. Some of the most highly praised and enduring historical novels were written and published during this time, including, among others, Sigrid Undset's <u>Kristin Lavransdatter Trilogy</u>, which helped win her the Nobel Prize for Literature in 1928 and Anya Seton's *Katherine* (1954), which even historians who study the Middle Ages took seriously and recommended for its accurate portrayal of Chaucer's England. The genre also received wide recognition in the form of Westerns, the most prolific subgenre from the early twentieth century through the 1950s. Then historical romances exploded onto the market in the 1970s, with their lavish tales of wild passion and star-crossed lovers set against vividly rendered historical backdrops.

The extreme popularity of historical fiction, in its many guises, contributed to its overall perception as a lowbrow form of literature. All genre fiction has suffered critical disdain to some degree and continues to do so. This should surprise no one. As usually happens when the market is flooded with novels in a certain genre, as was the case with historical fiction in the mid-twentieth century, the overall quality declines. In a 1950 article in *Masses and Mainstream* ("Reply to Critics"), author Howard Fast, a historical novelist himself, wrote, "This is an era of many historical novels, few of them good, and very few indeed which have more than a nodding acquaintance with fact."[1]

His comments were by no means' unique. Over and over again, comments from authors and the media implied that historical fiction was a genre very rarely done well. Either these novels were bad history—costume dramas, in which modern-day characters were dressed up and paraded around in period garb—or bad fiction, in which the author crammed in so much research that it overwhelmed the plot. Many well-known historical novelists first made their mark in the 1950s through 1980s, such as Maurice Druon, Zoé Oldenbourg, John Jakes, Rosemary Sutcliff, and even Howard Fast himself. However, their works were admired as exceptions to the rule.

Things picked up in the mid- to late 1990s, when literary authors started looking back to the past for inspiration. Suddenly their historical novels began winning major literary prizes. Margaret Atwood's novel *Alias Grace*, about a housemaid tried for her employer's murder in 1843, garnered the Pulitzer Prize for Literature in 1996. Appendix A in this guide lists other, more recent examples. However, many works of literary fiction, no matter the time period in which they were set, were typically not considered historical novels by the press, by their publishers, and even by the authors who wrote them, even though they seemed to follow all the rules.

There are many examples. "I rely on the work of great historians, but I'm not a historical novelist," declared Charles Johnson in an interview (1998) with the *Sacramento Bee*, referring to *Dreamer*, his novel about the life of Martin Luther King Jr.[2] Anita Diamant's *The Red Tent* (1997), in which a well-known biblical story is seen through the eyes of the character Dinah, was labeled by its publisher as contemporary women's fiction. *Cold Mountain* (also 1997), which beautifully evokes the pointless loss caused by the Civil War, was more frequently termed literary fiction. If another possible label fit, the book wore it. Historical fiction was everywhere, but nowhere: it had become the genre that dared not speak its name.

By the year 2000, the perception of historical fiction as lowbrow was finally beginning to change (though some labeling problems still persist; see "Of Publishers and Labels," below). It became fashionable again to talk about the historical novel in public. Publishers began actively promoting their books as "upmarket historical fiction"—in other words, novels that one wouldn't be embarrassed to be caught reading on the subway. The success of films like *Gladiator*, *Elizabeth*, *Girl with a Pearl Earring*, and even *Cold Mountain*, the latter two of which were based on novels, demonstrated people's huge and growing interest in historical topics.

As the end of the twenty-first century's first decade approaches, historical fiction's popularity continues to grow. Historical novels now hold a prominent place on library and bookstore shelves. Publishing divisions like Crown (part of Random House), New American Library (Penguin Group USA), and Harper (HarperCollins) are aggressively developing historical fiction lines, with books designed to appeal to a new generation of readers. Historical novels have also become a natural choice for book club discussions (see "Choices for Book Discussions," later in this chapter). The wide following gained by recent cable TV miniseries such as *Rome*, *Into the West*, and *The Tudors* (even as campy and inaccurate as it is!) prove that the public's interest in historical topics is thriving. A 2006 article in *USA Today*[3] calls the merging of historical settings with fictional characters a "winning combination" and cites the incredible success of Elizabeth Kostova's *The Historian*, published in 2005, as one of the catalysts. *Booklist* devotes its April 15 issue each year to historical fiction, and *The Historical Novels Review*, a book review magazine edited by the author of this volume, publishes more than

800 reviews of new historical novels each year. The genre is prolific, healthy, and going strong. Long may it continue.

Literary critics and other publishing industry commentators often speculate on the reasons behind this renaissance in historical fiction. The prevailing opinion seems to be that, in today's post-9/11 world, people are choosing historical novels as a way of temporarily escaping the realities of current world politics and other depressing events reported on the evening news. There is undoubtedly some truth to this statement, for historical novels offer readers the opportunity to slip, if only temporarily, into a world not their own. (So does fiction in general, for that matter.)

However, the related assumption—that historical novels impart a glossed-over, prettified version of the past, providing a window into a time when life was less complicated or more glamorous—does the genre a disservice. The best examples of the genre actually do the opposite. Rather than providing a simplified view of history, historical novels let readers experience the realities of what daily life in past eras was like, in all its complexity and diversity. It's not uncommon for people to finish historical novels with a greater appreciation of the challenges that people living at earlier times had to face. Through historical fiction, today's readers can gain an understanding that decisions made by their forebears were not, in reality, nearly as straightforward as they may seem to us now.

Recent Trends in Historical Fiction

It has been said that historical novels, because they attempt to re-create the past, have a certain timeless quality that novels in other genres don't have. This isn't exactly true. Although some classic titles—like those by Georgette Heyer, Mary Renault, and James Michener—have remained in print almost continuously since their original publication, they are the exceptions that prove the rule. Writing styles change over time, and novels that seemed unique and affecting in years past may seem drab or overly formal today. Even historical novels written as recently as thirty years ago may seem dated, due to changing tastes in subject matter, overly flowery language, or the use of words or phrases that seem politically incorrect. Instead, one might say that because of its reliance on the past, which is fixed and unchanging, historical fiction must keep reinventing itself to remain interesting.

New Angles on Old Topics

Although biographical and wartime novels remain popular, readers and authors continue to look for new angles on familiar historical characters and events. There have been many novels published about Anne Boleyn, but Philippa Gregory's award-winning *The Other Boleyn Girl* was the first major novel to observe her from the viewpoint of her sister Mary—one of Henry VIII's mistresses. Anne Rice's *Christ the Lord: Out of Egypt* and its sequel, *The Road to Cana*, present the early life story of Jesus Christ as a way of simultaneously examining his humanity and divinity. Gregory's and Rice's works are historical novels in the traditional sense, but they look at the historical record, and historical characters, in unique ways. Dan Simmons's *The Terror* turns what could have been a standard novel about the Franklin Expedition's 1840s-era search for the Northwest Passage to the Pacific into a chilling novel of psychological suspense, with more than a hint of supernatural terror.

Social History

Topics chosen for historical novels often reflect trends in history. Beginning in the 1970s, social history came to the forefront in academic circles. A new crop of scholars started to take interest in women's and minorities' roles in history, and relevant programs—women's studies, African American studies—were formed at universities. Historical novels written before then often concerned themselves with the movers and shakers of times past—great men and the countries they ran or conquered. Since that time, there has been more emphasis, both in history and historical fiction, on people and themes that previously remained in the background.

This shift from political to social history uncovered much fertile ground for historical novelists. Although retellings of well-known events and famous people continue to be popular, today's historical novels are just as apt to emphasize more neglected topics, such as common people's daily lives and how they were affected (or not) by major events. An example is Geraldine Brooks's *Year of Wonders*, about how a young widow helps her village survive the plague in seventeenth-century England. In the last decade, there has also been considerably more emphasis placed on women's roles, those of racial minorities, members of the serving class, gays and lesbians, and members of non-Western cultures. Ann Herendeen's *Phyllida and the Brotherhood of Philander*, a self-declared "bisexual Regency romance" that the author originally self-published, was re-released in 2008 by mainstream publisher HarperCollins—proving that times have indeed changed.

The changing appetite among both readers and writers is especially evident in literary historical fiction, where viewpoints seem to have shifted from that of the colonizers—Great Britain in particular—to that of the colonized. One occasionally gets the feeling that writers go out of their way to discover minor historical tidbits worthy of writing a novel about, the more obscure the better. Regardless, the shift to social history, and less familiar subjects, seems to have worked in their favor. As shown in Appendix A, many historical novels of this type have been on the radar of literary prize committees within the last five years.

Focus on Historical Women

Directly related to the two trends above is an increased focus on historical novels with strong female protagonists—which, in terms of marketing, means novels geared heavily toward female readers. Irene Goodman, a literary agent who represents historical novelists Amanda Elyot, Diane Haeger, and Shirley Tallman, among others, expressed her thoughts on the subject in a 2005 article for *Solander*, the Historical Novel Society's literary magazine:

> Another factor in success with historical fiction is that the majority of the readers are women, and they like to read about other women. Much of history is dominated by men, which means you have to look for subjects that include women. The most common device is to take a woman who really lived and to let her tell her own story, free from the

> alleged "misrepresentation" of history. . . . We already
> know the story, or we think we do, but the author gives it a
> delightful new spin. [4]

Examples from the last few years are incredibly easy to come by. Women from the historical record appear as main characters in novels set in many different places and times: first-century Palestine (Marek Halter's *Mary of Nazareth*), ancient Egypt (Michelle Moran's *Nefertiti*), Renaissance Italy (Karen Essex's *Leonardo's Swans*), Tudor England (Vanora Bennett's *Portrait of an Unknown Woman*), and nineteenth-century Massachusetts (Rose MacMurray's *Afternoons with Emily*), to name only a few. Philippa Gregory's groundbreaking *The Other Boleyn Girl* established a trend for novels about female royalty that has yet to abate. Historical novelists have breathed life into historical women previously relegated to the shadows of the famous men they loved. Jude Morgan's *Passion*, for instance, focuses on four women who established close relationships with Romantic poets Byron, Shelley, and Keats; James Tipton's *Annette Vallon* re-creates the little-known life of William Wordsworth's French mistress. Authors have also taken to retelling well-known historical events from a new, feminine viewpoint. Ursula K. Le Guin's *Lavinia* and Jo Graham's *Black Ships*, both historical fantasy novels about the ancient Mediterranean world, accomplish this admirably for Virgil's *The Aeneid*—an epic poem with few female characters, none of whom is given a voice.

Curiously, a related development in cover art has accompanied the movement toward female-oriented historical fiction. As the cliché goes, one can't judge a book by its cover. However, it has become considerably easier for librarians and readers, thanks to publishers' marketing and art departments, to identify this type of historical novel before opening its pages or even reading the blurb. The current trend in jacket art, which shows no signs of fading, presents a woman in authentic period dress—normally an elaborately designed gown. The cover model, whose likeness may have been taken from an authentic painting of the period, often appears with her back to readers, or with her head cropped from the image. Psychologists have speculated that the absence of facial features on historical fiction book covers lets women readers identify more closely with the protagonists. Or perhaps women simply enjoy looking at the gorgeous costumes. Either way, these marketing tactics seem to be working.

Multi-Period Novels

In the past few years, an especially popular trend has been novels that alternate between contemporary and historical subplots, with thematic parallels or other links between the two sections. In Katie Hickman's *The Aviary Gate*, a twenty-first-century researcher travels to Istanbul to look into a mystery relating to a harem woman from late sixteenth-century Constantinople; Christi Phillips's *The Rossetti Letter* uses a similar technique to juxtapose seventeenth-century Venice and the present. Although not all of these novels have historians as protagonists in the modern-day sections, many do. This dual timeline approach lets readers see the parallels—and the differences—between the present and the past more directly. For obvious reasons, these multi-period stories have strong appeal to readers of both contemporary fiction and historical fiction, which broadens their potential audience considerably. Novels of this type have been tagged with the keywords *Multi-period novels* at the end of the annotations, and can be found under this heading in the subject index.

Genre-Blending

The historical fiction genre easily combines with many other genres: mystery, romance, fantasy, thrillers and suspense, even Christian fiction. New historical mystery series still appear regularly from publishers, and historical romance is on the upswing once again, after a decade or more of relative stagnation. Literary historical fiction, which always existed to some degree, got a significant boost with Charles Frazier's 1997 novel *Cold Mountain* and continues to flourish.

Titles that incorporate elements of more than one subgenre are among the most popular of all, for they appeal to the widest possible audience. Take, for example, Diana Gabaldon's Outlander Saga, a best-selling combination of romance, time-travel, and adventure set against a well-researched backdrop of both World War II–era England and eighteenth-century Scotland and America. Literary thrillers like David Liss's *A Conspiracy of Paper* and its sequel, *A Spectacle of Corruption*, mix mystery, action/adventure, suspense, and the intellectual writing style of literary fiction. Even traditional historical novels have been known to add elements of other genres. Manda Scott's four-volume Boudica series adds elements of Celtic spirituality—at least the author's personal version of it—to the exciting life story of Boudica, the first-century queen of the Iceni people who led an uprising against Rome.

Within the past five years, an interesting melding of traditional historical novels and romantic fiction has begun to occur, resulting in a unique type of genre-blending. Much female-centered historical fiction (as described in the previous section), though certainly not all, has a prominent romantic subplot in which the main character sorts out relationships with the man (or men) in her life. Avid readers of genre romance who wouldn't normally choose traditional historical novels may find these works appealing, both for their strong, positive portrayals of female characters and for the romantic story lines.

The growing overlap between the romance and historical fiction genres has resulted in an increased audience for these types of works. It also presented an interesting dilemma when deciding how some novels should be categorized for this second volume of *Historical Fiction*. For instance, should Amanda Elyot's *Too Great a Lady*—biographical fiction about Emma, Lady Hamilton, famous for her all-consuming love affair with naval hero Horatio Nelson—properly be listed with other traditional historical novels (Chapter 2), or with romantic epics (Chapter 4)? Many novels of this type can legitimately fit into both categories, and cross-references between these chapters are provided when appropriate.

Modernizing the Past

Nobody who saw the films *A Knight's Tale* or *Marie Antoinette* can easily forget their directors' attempts to make the historical story lines relevant for modern audiences. Marie Antoinette and her ladies glamming it up to the tune of Bow Wow Wow's "I Want Candy"? Medieval jousting and swordplay unrolling on the screen as 1970s-era rock anthems play in the background? Some historical novelists perform the literary equivalent of these filmmaking techniques, placing very modern slang in their characters' mouths and using deliberate anachronisms. In Suzannah Dunn's *The Queen of Subtleties*, protagonist Anne Boleyn is anything but subtle as she confronts Henry VIII over his promise to marry her one day: "It's all I ever hear! You and your difficult situation! What about *me*? . . . Christ, Henry, just how many years has it been?"[5] Likewise, in *The Last English King*, Julian Rathbone writes unapologetically contemporary prose, and his characters, from King Harold all the way down to his lowly bodyguard, spout four-letter words and tell impressively bad jokes. Reaction to this technique has been mixed; some readers appreciate the authors' attempts to make their characters seem more human and modern, while others find it inaccurate and off-putting. For more discussion on the issue, see the section on dialogue under "Appeal Factors," later in this chapter.

Reissues of Older Titles

One clear sign that historical fiction is undergoing a renaissance is publishers' eagerness to reissue out-of-print titles that fit current reading interests, especially novels about historical women. Karen Harper's *Passion's Reign* (about Mary Boleyn) and *Sweet Passion's Pain* (about Joan of Kent), published as mass-market historical romances in 1983 and 1984 respectively, were recently reissued as traditional historical novels by Three Rivers Press under the new titles *The Last Boleyn* and *The First Princess of Wales*. Other titles brought back into print by Three Rivers include volumes of Jean Plaidy's <u>Queens of England</u> series, as well as popular offerings by Judith Merkle Riley, Karleen Koen, and Rosalind Laker. In the past few years, Chicago Review Press has developed a line of "reissued classics," including old favorites by Anya Seton (*Katherine, Green Darkness, The Winthrop Woman, Avalon*, and more), Pauline Gedge, Gwen Bristow, and others. Librarians interested in replacing dilapidated, heavily circulated hardcover editions with attractive trade (oversized) paperbacks, or those who would like to add longtime reader favorites to their collections, will want to take note of this trend. On the other hand, reissued novels that are given new, more up-to-date titles may deceive librarians into purchasing novels they already own. Jean Plaidy's *The Queen's Devotion*, a biographical novel about Queen Mary II (re-released in paperback in late 2008), was formerly titled *William's Wife* in its original hardcover edition (1993).

The Trade Paperback Revolution

Hardcover fiction has always been a standard and preferred format for library purchases. Librarians should note, however, the recent tendency for debut or mid-list historical novels—highly regarded, profitable books that fall short of best-sellerdom—to be published as trade paperbacks. These books sell at about half the price of hardcovers, which lets avid readers and budget-conscious librarians add more titles to their collections. They are also easily portable, and their pages stay open without difficulty when reading. On the other hand, paperbacks—both trade and mass market—are less likely to be reviewed in major publications like *Publishers Weekly* and *Kirkus*, meaning librarians may need to expend extra effort in keeping up with the newest titles. The books also hold up less well to multiple circulations than hardcovers do.

Regardless of the issues specific to libraries, however, this is a trend that librarians can't afford to ignore. Within the subgenre chapters, this book indicates whenever historical novels are published as paperback originals.

What Do Readers Look For?

Although trends come and go, the overall appeal of historical fiction remains unchanged. Readers seek out authors who evoke or re-create the past by providing detail on all aspects of life in earlier times: customs, food, clothing, religious beliefs, architecture, and much more. This historical frame must be presented as authentically as possible so as not to shatter the illusion, but accuracy in historical facts isn't nearly enough to satisfy readers. If that were the case, they would be content with nonfiction history books. Many avid fiction readers find straight history texts to be dry and lifeless, with their reliance on facts and dates rather than people's personal experiences. The "fiction" part of historical fiction adds emotional intensity, something that straight history can't easily provide. (However, although the subject is beyond the scope of this book, some narrative histories and biographies hold great appeal for historical fiction readers.) The best historical novelists make the history an integral part of the story, but weave it in gradually so that readers aren't overwhelmed.

Readers of historical novels enjoy immersing themselves in the day-to-day lives and mindsets of people who lived in earlier eras. Readers want to learn firsthand about the hopes and dreams of people who lived long ago, marveling at how different their experiences are from those of people today. At the same time, historical fiction makes the unfamiliar seem familiar. Many novels express the same overarching theme: despite changes in politics, culture, and religion over the years, human nature doesn't change.

Most important of all, historical novel readers want to be entertained. They want to be seduced into believing that the historical world an author creates is real. At their best, historical novels bring the past to life, through emotionally involving stories and well-developed, sympathetic characters that reflect their time.

Appeal Factors in Historical Novels

Readers choose and enjoy historical novels based on a variety of factors. In the third edition of *Readers' Advisory Service in the Public Library* (ALA, 2005), Joyce G. Saricks discusses "appeal factors"—qualities that may cause readers to like or dislike a particular novel. Experienced readers' advisors use these features to make recommendations on what patrons might want to read next. Traditionally, bibliographies of historical fiction have been organized by time period and country, but this isn't the only way to match historical novels with readers. In discussing with library patrons what they enjoyed about a particular historical novel, readers' advisors should make note of elements other than era and locale. Appeal factors for individual novels are detailed in the annotations within this guide and are explained further here.

Time Period

Some readers are omnivorous in terms of the eras they want to read about. For example, Civil War buffs may choose to read as many novels as they can about the period, to get as many different perspectives as possible. I know several historical novel buffs who refuse to read anything set after the end of the Tudors' reign in England, as well as others who stick to biographical novels about royalty. For these readers, the index to this book will prove fruitful. These readers will also appreciate comprehensive, book-length bibliographies such as Lynda G. Adamson's *American Historical Fiction* and *World Historical Fiction*, which are organized primarily by locale and era.

Geographic Setting

With historical fiction, geographic setting often goes hand in hand with time period in terms of reader preference. For example, some American readers will avoid American settings in favor of British or European ones, preferring to read about a place that isn't quite so familiar to them. Others will use historical novels about the United States during the antebellum period, the Great Depression, the world wars, etc., to place themselves inside the minds of people—often their own ancestors—who lived during those times.

Amount and Type of Historical Content

How much historical detail do authors include in their novels, and what type of history do they focus on—political, social, economic? Although historical readers often prefer novels in which descriptions of customs, fashion, décor, politics, food, etc., are provided in great detail, others may prefer works in which the background is more lightly sketched. (This book concentrates on the former.) In addition, although some historical novels—such as those by Jeff Shaara, Colleen McCullough, and even Jean Plaidy—focus on major political events and the people who shaped them, others concentrate on an era's social history. Specific historical events rarely figure into the plotlines of Catherine Cookson's British regional sagas or Janette Oke's prairie romances. Instead, these novels focus on female characters' daily lives and how they and their families survived the times. The lack of reference to exact dates and outside events doesn't diminish their value as historical fiction.

Level of Realism

Some historical novel readers prefer a romanticized version of history, one that emphasizes the glory and heroism of past eras. These readers may appreciate traditional stories of knights riding victoriously into battle, the glitz and glamour of royalty, and long, sprawling epics of historical women and men who overcome many obstacles and emerge triumphant. These novels may mention the adverse aspects of life in past eras, but they don't dwell on them.

Other readers will prefer a gritty, more realistic portrayal of history. These readers will appreciate novels that don't gloss over subjects like poverty, fear of religious persecution, serious portrayals of battle, and the struggle to survive during periods of poverty, hunger, and wartime. Much literary fiction falls into this category, as do many mysteries (e.g., Anne Perry's Victorian and World War I–era series) and even traditional historical novels (e.g., Brenda Rickman Vantrease's *The Illuminator*). This is not to say that stories in the latter category are grim and depressing, simply that they present life in historical times with a more authentic flavor. Of course, it's possible for novels to be glorious, romantic, and realistic all at the same time—historical military adventure fiction, for example. (For a related topic, see the section dealing with violence and sexual content, below.)

Author

Historical fiction read-alikes are often chosen with the assumption that authors will stick with the same style from book to book. Strictly within the historical fiction genre, this is often the case, especially with novels in series—but not always. Some authors focus on the period and era in which they have the most expertise: Pauline Gedge writes primarily about ancient Egypt, for example. Some prolific historical novelists like Cecelia Holland are able to master many different historical settings but use a similar style throughout. Within literary historical fiction, authors will likely change themes from novel to novel (e.g., Tracy Chevalier, Isabel Allende, Thomas Mallon), yet they will remain within that particular subgenre. One must be careful with author read-alike suggestions, as they may not always work. For example, recommending Colleen McCullough's hefty Roman political novels to readers who enjoyed her Australian family saga *The Thorn Birds* may not be appropriate.

Pacing

The pacing of historical novels—leisurely, action-packed, or somewhere in between—is often reflected in their subgenre category. This is analyzed in greater detail in the chapter introductions. For example, literary historical novels, many of which are character-centered, unfold their action slowly, and characters' motivations may not be apparent from the outset. Military adventure novels, such as those by Bernard Cornwell, seem to move a mile a minute, with the pace rarely flagging during major battle scenes.

Type of Character

Both historical and fictional characters feature in historical novels, and readers may prefer one over the other. Even when the plot revolves around an actual historical event, one in which royalty or other statesmen may figure, the story may be told from the point of view of a well-known historical character (Susan Holloway Scott's *Royal Harlot*) or a secondary character, real or fictional, who observes the action from a close distance (e.g., Karleen Koen's *Dark Angels*). In recent years, well-known historical stories have been fictionally retold from the viewpoints of fully fleshed out characters few authors had written about before (e.g., Sandra Gulland's *Mistress of the Sun*, about Louise de la Vallière, an early mistress of Louis XIV of France). Readers may also want to read about particular types of characters in earlier societies: royalty, nobility, clergy, merchants, sailors, or soldiers.

Characterization

Different from character type, characterization refers to how well the author has developed his or her characters, and how well the reader gets to know them. Do readers get to know characters' personalities early on, or are they developed throughout the novel? Are they easily recognizable "types," or are they multifaceted? Are the characters easy to sympathize with and understand, or are they presented at a distance?

Subject and Theme

Certain subjects and themes resonate across historical periods and subgenres—race relations, colonialism, political revolutions, art and music, and many more. These are noted in the annotations, and readers can discover read-alikes of this type in the subject index. Other themes are less tangible, such as male–female relationships, women's roles, and the role of religion in historical times. Readers' advisors can develop greater familiarity with these themes by reading relevant novels in the genre.

Dialogue

Considerable debate has raged among authors and readers about how authentic characters' dialogue should be. After all, if novelists were to observe historical accuracy in its purest form, many of their characters would be speaking something other than modern English. To convey authentic atmosphere, authors frequently use slightly more formal dialogue than one would use in casual conversation today. In her romance *For My Lady's Heart* and its sequel, *Shadowheart*, Laura Kinsale has her characters use authentic Middle English phrasings to convince readers of her medieval settings. Regency romances wouldn't be the same without their witty, sparkling dialogue, which reflects the flirtatiousness and propriety of the era. Others (e.g., Lindsey Davis, Simon Scarrow) take the opposite route, having their protagonists speak in modern vernacular. For some readers, this emphasizes the similarities between, for example, the authors' ancient Rome and modern times, because people used slang and raunchy language in all eras. Other readers find that modern use of language in historical fiction throws them out of the period completely.

Language

Language used in a narrative may be lyrical and poetic, as is the case with much literary historical fiction, or it may be more straightforward. It may be descriptive or spare. And as with characters' dialogue, above, the language of a narrative may or may not reflect the historical era. A novel may be told in a slightly formal voice, as if to evoke the language used in earlier times, or it may be modern.

Violence and Sexual Content

Readers often have strong preferences about how much violence or sexual content they want to read about. Nearly all historical novelists deal with these issues to some degree. Battle scenes can be related both on-screen and off, as can bedroom scenes. While some readers find that gritty descriptions of blood and violence give them an authentic feel for the period, they may offend others. The "cozy" versus "hard-boiled" distinction in historical mysteries, mentioned in Chapter 7, reflects the level of violence. Likewise, explicit sexuality in a novel—mainly in romantic fiction, but in other subgenres as well—may be acceptable to some readers. Others will prefer that characters' private lives be kept private.

Determining Historical Accuracy

Historical accuracy is important, if not critical, to readers of historical fiction. Although minor slip-ups may escape their notice, significant blunders will draw readers out of the story, making them suspicious of the novel's overall quality. Mistakes in individual word usage may not matter, but incorrect dates, or placing historical characters in times or places when they weren't really there, aren't nearly as forgivable. The more familiar readers are with the period, the less tolerant they will be of anachronisms or other errors. Although most historical fiction buffs trust certain novelists' research, they read unfamiliar authors with a more critical eye.

What does this mean for readers' advisors who want to assure patrons that a historical novel truthfully reflects its era? In short, there's no easy way to positively determine historical accuracy without personal expertise on the period and people in question—at least as much as the authors know themselves! Readers can develop this familiarity through study of primary or secondary sources, such as historical biographies and narrative histories, or through formal coursework. Many historical novel fans also read biographies and historical nonfiction. But few librarians—and even readers—have the time to do extensive research on any single book. Although any and all background knowledge is helpful, a PhD in history isn't necessary for readers' advisory work.

A more realistic question is how well librarians and readers can judge the amount of research that went into a historical novel. Developing familiarity with benchmark authors and novels is highly recommended. Librarians can also keep up with well-researched novels, and the authors who write them, through discussions with people who read frequently in the genre. Reading published reviews can be helpful, though reviewers may not address historical accuracy. Even if they do, the reviewers—especially those in the popular press—may or may not be history experts.

Historical novelists often provide reader aids that serve as clues to their own research techniques. Because some of them—especially authors' notes, epilogues, and genealogical tables—involve spoilers, readers should be judicious in consulting them before reading. Examples follow:

- *Bibliographies*, which list sources consulted by the author in the writing process, can convince readers of an author's thoroughness. They also provide suggestions for additional reading.

- *Authors' notes*, provided at the end, can provide sources as well as details about where and how the novel diverged from the historical record. It isn't unusual for authors to change minor facts and dates for the story's sake.

Readers can forgive this to some degree, provided the authors don't change history too drastically—and provided they come clean about it.

- *Epilogues* tell readers what happened after the story ends, wrapping up any necessary details on historical characters or events.

- *Genealogical tables*, especially in the case of historical characters, provide names of people, the relationships between them, and dates of birth and death.

- *Glossaries* of unfamiliar or foreign words or phrases used in a novel lend authenticity to the authors' dialogue, language, and depth of research.

- *Photographs* of places and people are usually included in novels based on authors' own family history, like Lalita Tademy's *Cane River*, or novels in which photography is a subject, such as Marianne Wiggins's *The Shadow Catcher*. They may also appear in other biographical novels.

- *Diagrams and maps* of geographic regions accurate to the period in question ("England in the mid-twelfth century"), battlefields, traveling routes, and so forth, provide historical background and help readers follow characters through the story. They are often provided on novels' endpapers.

- *Footnotes* may be used in the novel itself to give historical background on certain people or places. Because they interrupt the story's flow, they aren't very common. Authors are more apt to provide a bibliography instead.

The absence of any of these features doesn't necessarily signify anything. Literary historical novels rarely use them, for example. However, their presence can aid readers and librarians in determining depth of research. Of course, the best way of determining how trustworthy an author's research might be is to *read*—especially works by benchmark authors (as well as nonfiction accounts about the same historical period, for those who are so inclined). Even if authors write in more than one subgenre or historical period, their research techniques tend to stay consistent throughout.

Of Publishers and Labels: Locating Historical Fiction

Although librarians actively select historical fiction for their collections, and current titles are nearly always found in bookstores, historical novels are almost never shelved separately. They are either shelved with other genres—historical mysteries in mystery, historical romance and romantic historicals in romance. Traditional and literary historical novels will likely be found mixed in with the general fiction collection.

Historical fiction is occasionally given useful subject headings in an online catalog, such as "Elizabeth I, Queen of England, 1533–1603—Fiction" for novels about Elizabeth Tudor. While librarians may be used to searching online catalogs in this way, Library of Congress subject headings, especially for anything history-related, are not exactly intuitive. Who would think to look under "United States—History—Revolution, 1775–1783—Fiction" for novels about the American Revolution? It's difficult enough to type, let alone to remember the exact dates. Patrons can't be expected to know these tricks of the library trade.

It doesn't help that relevant novels in publishers' catalogs may not be labeled "historical fiction" even though they are set in the past and seem to fulfill the necessary criteria. Some publishing imprints that actively acquire historical fiction, such as Crown and Harper, will label their novels correctly on the spine. Most won't, however, instead substituting a nonspecific genre label such as plain old "Fiction." The problem is not that historical fiction is too narrow to deserve its own section in libraries and bookstores, but that it's too broad, and it overlaps other genres. Regardless of the category label, blurbs in publishers' catalogs and on the dust jackets will offer a good sense of when and where a novel is set. (For names and addresses of relevant publishers, see Chapter 15.) To get around the shelving issue, some libraries use spine labels that designate fiction with historical settings.

Promoting Historical Fiction Collections

Even though historical fiction rarely has a section of its own, many librarians cater to genre readers by hosting book discussions on relevant titles, developing annotated bibliographies, and creating book displays.

Choices for Book Discussions

Many historical novels make good choices for book discussion groups. Specific titles are noted in this guide. The books chosen should not be unduly lengthy, in order to keep the group's attention. They should also be in print. Literary historical novels tend to be good choices, as do literary historical mysteries (annotated as such in Chapter 7). They speak not only to the time period but also to the human experience, which can raise a lot of discussion points. Because literary novels usually aren't as lengthy as others, this can work to librarians' advantage. Examples include Charles Frazier's *Cold Mountain*, Tracy Chevalier's *Girl with a Pearl Earring*, Nancy Horan's *Loving Frank*, Geraldine Brooks's *Year of Wonders* and *March*, and just about any historical novel by Susan Vreeland.

Other good choices are novels that either feature characters ahead of their time or present social issues resonating with readers today. Examples of these issues are gender roles (e.g., Lisa See's *Snow Flower and the Secret Fan*; Megan Chance's *An Inconvenient Wife*), race (e.g., Barbara Chase-Riboud's *Sally Hemings*; Lalita Tademy's African American family saga *Red River*), or religion (e.g., Brenda Rickman Vantrease's *The Mercy Seller*). Novelist Donna Woolfolk Cross has gone out of her way to market her novel to book discussion groups, and librarians can arrange for her to talk one-on-one with their book groups via her Web site (www.popejoan.com). John Shors, author of *Beneath a Marble Sky*, a love story set in Mughal India, has made good on his promise to speak with any club that chooses his novel (http://www.beneathamarblesky.com/bookclub.html). A good selection of discussion titles may be found at ReadingGroupGuides.com, under Find a Guide, then By Genre, and then Fiction-Historical. These guides are typically supplied by publishers. NoveList also provides detailed book discussion guides for many historical novels, written by literature experts and librarians knowledgeable about readers' advisory.

Bibliographies and Displays

It is important to provide annotations in locally created bibliographies. This is due to the different subgenres a novel may fall into, as well as the appeal factors above. The best annotations will include at least the title, author, original publication date, and number of pages. A brief summary (including when and where the novel takes place) and descriptive commentary should follow. The summary should touch on the book's contents without giving away major plot points ("spoilers") , because that can ruin a book for potential readers. Exceptions can be made in cases where the historical outcome is generally known, for example, that the Union won the Civil War. Librarians should comment on any appeal factors—apparent depth of research, characterization, language, etc.—that distinguish one book from another.

Although it is common to base historical fiction bibliographies around a particular time period and locale, theme-related lists and book displays also make good sense. They may include titles that

- serve as read-alikes for a currently popular historical novel, or related reads for novels or biographies that were recently turned into films (e.g., novels about American presidents to accompany the *John Adams* TV miniseries; historical naval adventure for Patrick O'Brian's *Master and Commander*);

- revolve around an interesting or timely subject or theme (e.g., Islam through the ages, novels on historical women for Women's History Month in March, biographical novels on American presidents for Presidents' Day); or

- describe an interest or cultural heritage shared by many library patrons (e.g., African American historical novels, sagas with family trees for genealogically minded readers).

Because historical fiction is such a diverse genre, the possibilities for displays and annotated lists are almost endless.

Final Recommendations

To cater to readers, librarians should recognize that historical fiction is as valid a genre as romance, mystery, science fiction, or any of the other major fiction genres. Because it's rarely shelved separately, and because publishers may not label historical novels as such, librarians may need to expend extra effort developing and promoting their historical fiction collections. This book can help in that regard. For example, does your library have a readers' advisory Web site that lists other genres but omits historical fiction? This is common, but it's a fault easily remedied. Because historical fiction includes novels of so many different styles, those who enjoy the genre should be able to find something appropriate to both their mood and their reading tastes. Librarians who stay well-informed about historical fiction, in all its great diversity, can only serve their patrons better.

Notes

1. Howard Fast, "Reply to Critics," *Masses and Mainstream* (December 1950): 53–64. Available atwww.trussel.com/hf/reply.htm (accessed July 19, 2008).

2. David Barton, "Facts of Fiction," *Sacramento Bee*, May 5, 1998. Available at http://www.sacbee.com/static/live/lifestyle/bookclub/archives/johnson2.html (accessed July 19, 2008).

3. Carol Memmott, "Historical Settings, Fictional Characters, Winning Combination," *USA Today*, September 11, 2006. Available at http://www.usatoday.com/life/books/news/2006-09-11-hist-fiction-success_x.htm (accessed July 19, 2008).

4. Irene Goodman, "Why Anne Boleyn Is the Poster Girl for Historical Fiction," *Solander: The Magazine of the Historical Novel Society* 9, no. 2 (November 2005): 15.

5. Suzannah Dunn, *The Queen of Subtleties* (New York: HarperPerennial, 2005), 96.

Chapter 2

Traditional Historical Novels

Traditional historical novels are the type of books that readers usually picture when they think of historical fiction. They transport readers to a far-off time and place, and allow them to vicariously experience the past. Their authors are storytellers first and foremost, and their goal is twofold: to portray a historical period as realistically as possible and to entertain. The novels have protagonists readers can root for and strong plotlines that keep readers glued to the pages to find out what happens next. Their appeal lies in the authors' ability to make historical figures and events come alive.

There is no standard pattern to traditional historicals, but for the most part, plots unfold in a straightforward, linear fashion. They tend to be long books, with 300-plus pages as the norm. Although they aren't as action-packed as are adventure novels, the authors keep the plots moving at a nice pace. Most story lines end optimistically, with the protagonist overcoming considerable adversity to reach his or her goals. Even though most traditional historicals don't make use of literary stylistics and multi-layered story lines, the overall quality of the writing is high.

The characters may be real-life historical figures whose lives are imagined against an accurately presented background, or fictional creations placed by the author in a historical period to show how they react to their time. Alternatively, there may be a mix of historical and fictional characters present in the novel, with interaction between them. Traditional historical novels are more likely than those in other subgenres to be biographical, because novels of this type have a predetermined, linear plot: they follow one character through the major events of his or her life. Whether the characters are real or fictional, the history influences the course of events, playing a strong role in the story rather than simply serving as a backdrop.

In the last few years historical novels with strong female protagonists have grown enormously in popularity. A significant number of titles in this chapter fit this category. Many are biographical novels about historical women that also incorporate romantic subplots (Margaret George's novel *Helen of Troy*, for instance). Even though they aren't romances, readers who enjoy historical romantic fiction may find these novels intriguing.

Readers typically look for traditional historicals set in particular places or during specific time periods. The most common settings include ancient Greece and Rome, England/Great Britain, and the United States. In the latter two cases, medieval and Tudor-era England and the American Civil War are among the most popular time periods. (Those set in the historical American West, also a highly popular locale, form a separate subgenre and are covered in Chapter 6.) Novels set in Canada, Africa, Australia, or Central and South America aren't found nearly as frequently, because many publishers feel that traditional historicals with unusual locales are unmarketable, with several exceptions: Indian and Middle Eastern settings are both flourishing (in the latter case, no doubt due to growing interest in the region and its history following 9/11). An even wider variety of settings may be found in literary fiction and adventure novels, however, and North American readers in search of novels set in more distant lands may wish to consult Chapters 8 and 10.

Prehistoric Europe, Asia, and Africa

This section includes novels set in Europe, Asia, and Africa before the time of recorded history. They attempt to re-create life in prehistoric times as accurately as possible, combining archaeological research with a good dose of imagination. Although this was once an incredibly fertile category, spurred originally by Jean Auel's Earth's Children series, prehistoric settings are currently in decline.

Auel, Jean M.

Earth's Children Series. ★

With this series Jean Auel set the standard for prehistoric fiction. Her heroine, Ayla, a young Cro-Magnon woman living in Europe some 30,000 years ago, searches for acceptance and companionship after she is left alone in the world. Auel's novels, all incredibly detailed with plentiful descriptions of flora and fauna, are based on years of anthropological research into prehistoric society. They also have a strong romantic element (including some explicit sex).

Keywords: Ayla; Cro-Magnons; Europe; Neanderthals; Prehistoric civilizations

The Clan of the Cave Bear. Crown, 1980. 468pp. Hardbound, 0517542021.

Ayla, left alone after a disaster kills the members of her tribe, is taken in by the Clan of the Cave Bear, a group of Neanderthals. They distrust her because of her unusual appearance—blue eyes, blond hair, and lack of a flat forehead. Cast out by her adoptive clan, Ayla searches far and wide for others like herself.

The Valley of Horses. Crown, 1982. 502pp. Hardbound, 051754489X.

When Ayla comes upon a fertile valley, she forms a kinship with the horses of the steppe. It is only when a young hunter named Jondalar discovers her cave that she finds human acceptance.

The Mammoth Hunters. Crown, 1985. 645pp. Hardbound, 0517556278.

Ayla and her lover, Jondalar, meet up with people who look like Ayla, the Mamutoi (Mammoth Hunters). Because she was raised by "Flatheads," Ayla doesn't immediately trust them, and they feel the same about her. Ayla and Ranec, master carver of the Mamutoi, are mutually attracted to one another, which arouses Jondalar's jealousy.

The Plains of Passage. Crown, 1990. 760pp. Hardbound, 0517580497.

Jondalar and Ayla journey across the grasslands of Ice Age Europe to his homeland, where Jondalar plans to introduce her to his family.

The Shelters of Stone. Crown, 2002. 749pp. Hardbound, 0609610597.

> At last the pair reach their destination—Jondalar's tribe, the Zelandonii. Ayla fears they won't accept her, even though she's pregnant with Jondalar's child. Some of the Zelandonii are prejudiced against Flatheads and any who associate with them. They don't entirely approve of Ayla and Jondalar's relationship, either.

Barnes, Steven.

Great Sky Woman. **Ballantine/One World, 2006. 347pp. Hardbound, 0345459008.** `YA`

> Thirty thousand years ago, the Ibandis live in peace at the foot of Mt. Kilimanjaro, which they call Great Sky Mountain. When a dangerous tribe threatens them from the south, it is left to two Ibandi youngsters from different camps—a boy called Frog Hopping, and a young orphan, T'Cori, who trains as an herbalist—to scale the mountain and seek assistance from Father Sky. First in a projected two-book series about the history, folklore, and spiritual beliefs of ancient Africa.

> **Keywords:** Coming of age; Mt. Kilimanjaro; Prehistoric civilizations; Tanzania

Dann, John R.

Prehistoric Series.

> A gritty, mystical, and romantic series set in Europe at the time of the last ice age, circa 30,000 years ago.

> **Keywords:** Europe; Prehistoric civilizations

Song of the Earth. Forge, 2005. 380pp. Hardbound, 0765311933.

> This prequel to *Song of the Axe*, published four years later, adds a biblical spin to Dann's take on Ice Age Europe. The progenitor of the prehistoric tribe from the later book was called Grae, and this is his story. Dann relates how young Grae was saved by the seven daughters (by different fathers) of River Woman after a volcano's eruption destroyed their village, and how they repopulated the land after learning they were the only survivors. Guided by spirits, Grae leads three of the women (one of whom is named Lilith—readers may see where this is heading) northward from Africa and into central and eastern Europe. Along the way, and over the next few generations, they fight Neanderthals, hunt native game, and invent things like the knife.

Song of the Axe. Forge, 2001. 479pp. Hardbound, 0312869843.

Biblical

Biblical-era men and women—mostly women, following a recent trend for novels about the "feminine Bible"—are placed in historical contexts. Although religion plays a role in these novels, it is not the focal point; the emphasis is on historical authenticity and the portrayal of societies during biblical times. Biblical settings are also very common in Christian fiction (covered in Chapter 11).

Burton, Ann.

Women of the Bible series. ✍ 📖 **YA**

A four-book series about lesser-known women from the Bible, strong in character and faith, who tell their stories in the first person. Burton is a pseudonym for prolific novelist Sheila Kelly, who writes most frequently as S. L. Viehl.

Abigail's Story. Signet, 2005. 280pp. Paper, 045121479X.

> This novel about Abigail, one of King David's wives, concentrates on her childhood and life before their marriage. To pay her brother's gambling debts and prevent her parents from being sold into slavery, Abigail of Carmel marries Nabal, a greedy, selfish man who forces her to work in his fields. She befriends David, the future king, and successfully intervenes to prevent a war between him and Nabal.
>
> **Keywords:** Abigail (biblical figure); David, King of Israel (historical character); Israel; Kings

Rahab's Story. Signet, 2005. 284pp. Paper, 0451216288.

> Rahab, the God-fearing daughter of a rug seller, is forced to become a prostitute on Jericho's streets when her stepmother casts her out. When two Israelite spies plead with her to hide them from the evil king of Jericho, she courageously agrees.
>
> **Keyword:** Prostitutes; Rahab (biblical figure)

Jael's Story. Signet, 2006. 282pp. Paper, 0451217896.

> Jael, a young Canaanite bride, is devastated when she learns that her new husband, Heber the Kenite, already has one other wife and one concubine. She befriends them and learns that to bear Heber the children he desires, she must risk her life by committing adultery with another man.
>
> **Keyword:** Extramarital affairs; Jael (biblical figure); Polygamy

Deborah's Story. Signet, 2006. 288pp. Paper, 0451219139.

> Deborah, a Hebrew slave and shepherdess in the land of Ephraim, has suffered years of degradation at the hands of her cruel and greedy master, Ybyon. When she saves a traveling merchant, Jeth—a man she has dreamed about for years—from certain death at Ybyon's hands, he saves her life in return, protecting her from Ybyon's wrath and leading her on to her destiny as one of Israel's greatest judges.
>
> **Keywords:** Deborah (biblical figure); Israel; Judges; Prophets; Slaves and slavery

Etzioni-Halevy, Eva.

Etzioni-Halevy, an Austrian native who is now professor emeritus of sociology at Bar-Ilan University in Israel, writes sensual biblical fiction with strong Jewish heroines.

The Garden of Ruth. **Plume, 2006. 293pp. Paper, 9780452286733.** 📖

Osnath, niece of the prophet Samuel, discovers a page of parchment that hints that Ruth the Moabite, King David's great-grandmother, may have had a secret lover. As Osnath, fascinated by Ruth's story, searches for this mysterious man's identity, David's brother Eliab sets out to stop her, for reasons unknown. In the novel's middle section, Ruth reveals her own story in the first person.

Keywords: Israel; Kings; Ruth (biblical figure)

The Song of Hannah. **Plume, 2005. 292pp. Paper, 0452286727.** 📖

Hannah and Pninah grew up as childhood friends, but their relationship is severely tested when Elkanah, husband to Pninah, takes Hannah as his second wife. In despair, Pninah takes a secret lover. Hannah struggles for years with barrenness before she begs God for a son, and she agrees to promise him to the temple if she is granted her wish. Eventually she gives birth to Samuel, destined to be one of Israel's greatest prophets.

Keywords: Friendship; Hannah (biblical figure); Palestine; Polygamy; Prophets

The Triumph of Deborah. **Plume, 2008. 358pp. Paper, 9780452289062.** 📖

In the Bible, Deborah was a prophetess and powerful judge who persuaded the warrior Barak to lead an army against the Canaanite king, Jabin, and his general, Sisra—which united and saved the people of Israel from their oppressors. Etzioni-Halevy's proto-feminist retelling focuses less on the war and more on the love triangle that subsequently develops between Barak and the two beautiful daughters of Jabin—as well as Deborah's own strong attraction to Barak, and his for her.

Keywords: Deborah (biblical figure); Israel; Love triangles; Prophets

Halter, Marek.

Canaan Trilogy. ✍ 📖

The novels in Halter's trilogy of "the feminine Bible"—the lesser-known personal stories of biblical matriarchs, queens, and prophets—were best sellers in France, where they were first published.

Sarah. Crown, 2004. 310pp. Hardbound, 1400052726.

Sarai, daughter of a wealthy Sumerian man in the city-state of Ur, flees an arranged marriage by drinking a potion that makes her barren. For six years she lives as a priestess of Ishtar. When she meets her childhood love Abram again, she escapes and joins his nomadic tribe. Then the familiar biblical story begins to unfold.

Keyword: Priestesses; Sarah (biblical figure)

Zipporah, Wife of Moses. Crown, 2005. 278pp. Hardbound, 1400052793.

Jethro, high priest of Midian, can't find a husband for his adopted daughter Zipporah, a Cushite he rescued as a baby, because of her black skin. Zipporah has always dreamed that an Egyptian prince will rescue her one day, and when she meets a handsome stranger named Moses while drawing water, she knows he is the man chosen for her. Moses, in hiding with the Midianites after killing a man in Egypt, would prefer to stay put, but Zipporah urges him to return home and lead his people.

Keywords: Adopted children; Egypt; Moses (biblical figure); Prophets; Racial conflict; Zipporah (biblical figure)

Lilah: A Forbidden Love, a People's Destiny. Crown, 2006. 258pp. Hardbound, 1400052815.

Lilah, the brave sister of Ezra, dares to speak out against religious fanaticism. Exiled from their native Canaan with their people, Lilah and Ezra live in Babylon, where she falls in love with Antinoes, a Persian warrior. Though he urges her to marry him, she refuses, on the grounds that her brother needs her. After Ezra finally gains permission to reenter the Promised Land and rebuild the Temple of Jerusalem, he heeds the advice of zealots and orders Jewish men to cast off their foreign-born wives. Lilah, still in love with Antinoes, takes a stand against her brother.

Keywords: Babylonia; Brothers and sisters; Ezra (biblical figure); Fanaticism; Israel; Lilah (biblical figure)

***Mary of Nazareth.* Crown, 2008. 303pp. Hardbound, 9780307394835.** 🖋

Most novels about the Virgin Mary speak about her life just before or following the birth of Jesus, but Halter concentrates on her youth in Roman-ruled Palestine. When Miriam (as she's called here) requests the help of the rebel Barabbas to free her beloved father from his wrongful imprisonment, she charts her own path in liberating the Jewish people from the Roman yoke.

Keywords: Mary (biblical figure); Palestine—Roman period

Kohn, Rebecca.

***Seven Days to the Sea.* Rugged Land, 2006. 395pp. Hardbound, 1590710495.** 🖋 📖

Miryam, Moses's elder sister, continues to believe the divine revelation she had as a child: that her brother, not yet born, would grow to be a leader who would save their people. She dedicates her life to ensuring that the prophecy comes true. When Moses flees Egypt for the desert, Tzipporah's narration continues the story. A desert shepherdess who becomes Moses' wife, she struggles to understand God's purpose for him. Following her successful venture into biblical fiction with *The Gilded Chamber*, a novel about Queen Esther, Kohn turns her hand to another ancient tale—that of Moses and the women in his life.

Keywords: Brothers and sisters; Egypt; Miriam (biblical figure); Moses (biblical figure); Prophets; Shepherdesses; Zipporah (biblical figure)

Longfellow, Ki.

***The Secret Magdalene.* Crown, 2007. 426pp. Hardbound, 9780307346667.** 🖋

Longfellow's erudite (it contains a lengthy bibliography) and formally worded novel gives a glimpse into Mary Magdalene's life as an apostle. Mariamne, daughter of a wealthy Jew in Jerusalem, is a learned young woman who happens to have the gift of prophecy. After a family misunderstanding, she and her best friend, Salome, are banished from home. They flee to Egypt, where they disguise themselves as men and absorb as much philosophy, mathematics, and astronomy in the Great Library of Alexandria as they can. When they eventually return to Judea, they encounter two intriguing men, John the Baptizer and his cousin, Yeshu'a. Mariamne shares with Yeshu'a her personal experience with Gnosis—direct communication with God.

Keywords: Apostles; Egypt—Roman period; Judea—Roman period; Mary Magdalene (biblical figure); Prophets

Provoost, Anne.

In the Shadow of the Ark. **Arthur A. Levine, 2004. 368pp. Hardbound, 0439442346.** 📖 **YA**

Fleeing their marshy homeland when the waters rise, Re Jana's family arrives in the desert land of the Rrattika, only to glimpse an enormous ark around which has sprouted a growing little city. Noach, its builder, believes that his god has led him to create this haven, which will save men and animals during the great flood. Re Jana, unsure that Noach's prediction will come true, nevertheless tries to ensure space for herself and her family aboard the boat by forming a romantic attachment to Ham, one of Noach's sons. Their story of forbidden love plays out against the classic Bible story, and tension builds toward the end as people quickly realize that not everyone will be saved. Published as a young adult title in hardcover, this widely read novel was released in trade paperback by Berkley as adult fiction.

Keywords: Noah's ark

Rice, Anne.

Christ the Lord Series. ✍ 📖 **YA**

Readers generally know Anne Rice, author of numerous works of vampire fiction—many of which are historical—as a brave writer. Still, it takes real gumption to write a first-person narrative of the life of Jesus Christ. She bases her series firmly on recent New Testament scholarship and explains her research techniques in a lengthy author's note at the end of the first novel.

Keywords: Divinity; Jesus Christ (historical character); Palestine—Roman period

Christ the Lord: Out of Egypt. Knopf, 2005. 322pp. Hardbound, 0375412018.

As a seven-year-old boy, Yeshua struggles to understand the divine gifts he possesses, while at the same time he marvels at the wonders of the natural world around him.

Christ the Lord: The Road to Cana. Knopf, 2008. 241pp. Hardbound, 9781400043521.

Now in young adulthood, Jesus (Yeshua) struggles to come to terms with God's plan for him: in order to serve his Lord, he must deny himself the pleasures of experiencing personal love with any woman. Rice deals delicately and plausibly with this controversial issue, then traces his life through his baptism, the beginning of his ministry, and the miracle at the wedding at Cana.

Rourke, Mary.

Two Women of Galilee. MIRA, 2006. 244pp. Hardbound, 0778323749. ✍ 📖

Joanna, the consumptive wife of King Herod's chief steward, has been estranged from her cousin Mary's family ever since Joanna's family abandoned traditional Jewish customs in favor of Roman traditions. When the two women reunite and their friendship deepens, Joanna is drawn closely into the circle of Jesus, Mary's son, who fascinates her—and who alone has the power to heal her illness.

Keywords: Cousins; Friendship; Healers; Jesus Christ (historical character); Joanna (biblical figure); Mary (biblical figure); Palestine—Roman period

Other Ancient Civilizations

Carthage

Novels set in this ancient port city in North Africa, which (as legend has it) was settled by Phoenicians from Tyre; over the next several centuries, the Carthaginian Empire rose in power to rival Rome.

Durham, David Anthony.

Pride of Carthage: A Novel of Hannibal. Doubleday, 2005. 568pp. Hardbound, 0385506031. ✍

Durham, previously better known for literary fiction about African American life in nineteenth-century America, turns his hand to the story of the Second Punic War and its star player, Hannibal, Carthage's legendary military leader who dared attack Rome. He vividly describes how Hannibal and his brothers—all of whom play a part—conquer the Roman city of Saguntum, and how that victory propelled them and their 100,000-man army over the Pyrenees in 218 BC and to the gates of Rome itself. But Hannibal and his family members aren't the only main characters here; Durham also lets us see the action from the viewpoint of a humble Carthaginian soldier, Imco Vaca, who falls in love with Aradna, a lowly camp follower.

Keywords: France; Hannibal (historical character); Punic Wars; Soldiers

Raymond, Robert.

Fire and Bronze. Ibooks, 2005. 483pp. Hardbound, 1596871202. ✍

Queen Dido of Carthage, according to legend, was born a princess of Tyre who fled her homeland when a plot against her royal brother failed. Raymond's rousing version of her life begins in her childhood. When Princess Elisha's father dies, her older brother, Pumayyaton, becomes king, and enrages the nobles by befriending Tyre's commoners. Pumayyaton sees her as a rival to his power, so in an attempt to save her own life, she attempts a coup against him—unsuccessfully, alas. Elisha and numerous other exiles flee Tyre aboard ship. They land on the Libyan coast, where she founds the city of Carthage and becomes its queen, adopting the name Dido ("the wanderer") . Details on ancient religions, housing, and shipbuilding give the novel plenty of color.

Keyword: Dido, Queen of Carthage (historical character); Exile; Princesses; Queens; Tyre

Egypt

Ancient Egyptian settings give readers the opportunity to learn about life along the Nile, the polytheistic Egyptian religion, and the politics of the time.

Moran, Michelle.

The Heretic Queen. **Crown, 2008. 383pp. Hardbound, 9780307381750.** ✍ 📖 **YA**

In 1283 BC, Princess Nefertari, daughter of Mutnodjmet from Moran's *Nefertiti*, is the only surviving member of the former Egyptian royal family. She is considered to be tainted because of their heretical beliefs. In the first person, Nefertari describes her slow and difficult rise from palace outcast to beloved wife of Ramses, the handsome young pharaoh. Even after their marriage, however, the court remains suspicious of her, and many enemies—political and personal—stand between her and complete happiness. This briskly paced novel with plentiful historical detail on ancient Egyptian life and times can easily be read without the previous volume.

Keywords: Nefertari, Queen of Egypt (historical character); Pharaohs; Ramses II, King of Egypt (historical character)

Nefertiti. **Crown, 2007. 460pp. Hardbound, 9780307381460.** ✍ 📖 **YA**

Mutnodjmet ("Mutny") , Nefertiti's younger sister by two years, narrates this tale of power, religion, love, and family rivalry set in Egypt in 1351 BC. Nefertiti grows up beloved by the Egyptians, knowing that she's destined to marry the pharaoh. When the pharaoh's elder brother Tutmosis dies, Nefertiti becomes chief wife of the current heir, Amunhotep. However, despite her beauty and popularity, her barrenness threatens her position and her family's continued role at court. Amunhotep abandons Egypt's ancient gods, the priests plot against him, and only Mutny has the courage to warn Nefertiti about it. Then ambitious Nefertiti begins playing political games herself; their sisterly bond is strained when Nefertiti insists Mutny marry someone other than the military man she loves.

Keywords: Mutnodjmet (historical character); Nefertiti, Queen of Egypt (historical character); Pharaohs; Queens; Sisters

Greece

Many historical novels set in ancient Greece are based on epic poems, like the *Iliad* and *Odyssey*, or on figures of the era. Even if the stories are legends, they have the ring of truth.

Bradshaw, Gillian.

The Sun's Bride. **Severn House, 2008. 231pp. Hardbound, 9780727866417.**

In the year 246 BC, when the Rhodian warship *Atalanta* rescues a beautiful woman from her captivity aboard a pirate vessel, its crew takes on much more than they bargained for. They learn that the woman, Dionysia of Miletos, is a concubine of Antiochos, King of the Seleucid Empire, and she seeks passage to Alexandria—Antiochos's greatest enemy. This draws Isokrates, helmsman for the *Atalanta*, into a great war that spans the ancient Mediterranean world.

Keywords: Pirates; Shipboard adventure; Third Syrian War

Clarke, Lindsay.

Troy Series.

Clarke's two-volume series retells, in lucid yet lyrical prose, the stories of Homer's epic poems of ancient Greece: the *Iliad* and the *Odyssey*. They remain faithful to the original, yet they also humanize and render in contemporary language the myths and legends that have surrounded the war fought over the Bronze Age city of Troy. Although the gods on Olympus often serve as catalysts for the characters' actions, Clarke concentrates on the men and women of ancient Greece. This keeps his focus on the history and human drama.

Keywords: Gods and goddesses; Mythology; Trojan War

The War at Troy. **Thomas Dunne, 2004. 452pp. Hardbound, 0312336578.**

Phemius of Ithaca, the elderly Bard of Ithaca and friend of Odysseus, recounts the great story of the Trojan War. Paris, a simple herdsman, learns of his royal birth and is asked to judge a beauty contest among three breathtakingly beautiful goddesses. To win the hand of Helen of Sparta, he chooses Aphrodite, the goddess of love, after which point the traditional Trojan War story plays out. Phemius intersperses this tale with the backstories of some of the myth's major characters, and he allows for variations in Homer's version, too. Phemius also relates alternate versions of Helen's story that he heard in passing.

The Return from Troy. **HarperCollins UK, 2007. 496pp. Hardbound, 000715027X.**

The war at Troy is over, the city destroyed, and victorious Agamemnon, whose journey to rescue the abducted Helen precipitated the war in the first place, returns home to Mycenae, where his angry wife Clytemnestra awaits him—with not exactly a warm welcome. Meanwhile, Odysseus also seeks to return to his wife, Penelope, in Ithaca, but storms at sea carry him far off course and lead him into adventures at the edge of the known world.

Elyot, Amanda.

The Memoirs of Helen of Troy. **Crown, 2005. 320pp. Hardbound, 0307209989.**

Elyot, pseudonym for actress-novelist Leslie Carroll, puts a feminist spin on the traditional Trojan War story. Helen—the beautiful, sensual, and occasionally vain daughter of Queen Leda of Sparta and the god Zeus—writes her memoirs for her only remaining daughter, Hermione, recounting how she became known as Helen of Troy. Married off as a young girl to Menelaus, a worthy yet passionless man, Helen is swept off her feet by Paris, a handsome Trojan prince, with whom she flees back to his homeland. Using Helen's so-called abduction as an excuse, Menelaus's brother, Agamemnon, sees the perfect opportunity to launch an attack against rich, bountiful Troy.

Keywords: Mythology; Trojan War

George, Margaret.

Helen of Troy. **Viking, 2006. 624pp. Hardbound, 0670037788.** 📖
In George's lushly written version of the Trojan War myth, Helen—who narrates her tragic life story—becomes an entirely sympathetic figure, one whose destiny was set in stone from the very beginning. Her parents, King Tyndareus and Queen Leda of Sparta, do their best to hide Helen's beauty from the world and rejoice when Menelaus of Mycenae offers for her hand. But when Helen asks Aphrodite to intervene in her passionless marriage, the goddess's powers focus instead on Paris, a young prince of Troy. Helen and Paris fall in love, precipitating a lengthy and devastating war. George always paints her novels on a broad canvas, and such is the case with her latest fictional biography, which is all the more remarkable because, as George herself states in an afterword, there's no real evidence that Helen ever existed.

Keywords: Mythology; Trojan War

Nicastro, Nicholas.

Empire of Ashes. **Signet, 2004. 369pp. Paper, 0451213661.** ✍
After Alexander the Great's death in 323 BC, his friend and trusted ally, Machon, on trial in Athens for diminishing Alexander's godlike reputation, retells the story of Alexander's rise and fall in order to win back his freedom. Although Alexander is no doubt a brilliant soldier, military tactician, and master in the political arena, he's also extremely reckless and more than a little greedy; Machon's tale reveals the real man in all his flawed humanity. Though more directly told and less lyrical than Pressfield's version of King Alexander's life (*The Virtues of War*), this will no doubt appeal to Pressfield's fans.

Keywords: Alexander the Great (historical character); Kings; Soldiers

The Isle of Stone. **Signet, 2005. 366pp. Paper, 0451217128.**
During the Peloponnesian War, the nearly thirty-year conflict between Athens and Sparta in the fifth century BC, two estranged Spartan brothers, Antalcidas and Epitadas, band together for the first time, to save their lives and their country. Nicastro centers his plot on a little-known historical episode, one of the low points in Spartan history: the siege of the island of Sphacteria in 425 BC, during which a contingent of Spartans were trapped and forced to defend themselves against Athenians and their allies.

Keywords: Brothers; Peloponnesian War

Pressfield, Steven.

The Afghan Campaign. **Doubleday, 2006. 351pp. Hardbound, 038551641X.** ✍

Pressfield's novel of Alexander the Great's invasion of the Afghan kingdoms circa 330 BC has obvious contemporary resonance. Matthias, a Macedonian foot soldier in King Alexander's retinue, narrates the story of their ill-fated Afghan expedition, which lasted for three long years before they withdrew in defeat. Pressfield is at his best when describing war from a minor soldier's viewpoint and the culture clashes of ancient times. His ancient Afghanistan is a vicious, unconquerable place, and the Afghans themselves are canny and inscrutable.

Keywords: Afghanistan; Alexander the Great (historical character); Kings; Soldiers

Gates of Fire. **Doubleday, 1998. 386pp. Hardbound, 0385492510.** ★

In 480 BC, at the Battle of Thermopylae, a brave force of 300 Spartans fought a hopeless battle against the invading armies of Persia's King Xerxes. Though the Spartans all lost their lives, they managed to hold off Persia for seven days, giving the Greeks enough time to rally their forces and repulse a Persian invasion later on. The story is told in flashback by Xeones, a Spartan squire captured by King Xerxes, who recounts his story from boyhood until that fateful day.

Keywords: Soldiers; Squires; Thermopylae, Battle of

Mesopotamia

Barone, Sam.

Empire Series.

The brawny, epic novels in Barone's ongoing series recount how the great walled cities of the ancient world may have been built.

Keywords: Cities; Prehistoric civilizations; Soldiers

Dawn of Empire. Morrow, 2006. 481pp. Hardbound, 0061172502.

It is 3148 BC, on the banks of the Tigris River. The nomad barbarian tribes of the Alur Meriki have their sights set on Orak, a small city populated by farmers and traders they derisively call "dirt eaters." Ten years earlier, Orak was nearly destroyed by the barbarians, but this time, the people of Orak plan to fight back. With the considerable help of Trella, his slave/bedmate, a foreign soldier named Eskkar (a former barbarian himself) decides to lead the defense. Though he's already kept busy building a sturdy wall around Orak and training the city's men in archery, he and Trella also contend with treachery among their own people.

Empire Rising. Morrow, 2007. 465pp. Hardbound, 9780060892463.

Nearly a decade after *Dawn of Empire*, Eskkar and his wife Trella struggle to govern the city now called Akkad, as Akkad's nobles still don't fully accept their leadership. In an effort to further subjugate barbarians outside its walls, and to extend the Akkadian empire, Eskkar and his men leave its borders to pay a visit to distant villages. Chaos erupts in his absence, and Eskkar finds himself tempted by another woman.

Roman Republic and the Roman Empire

Novels set in the Roman Republic (sixth century through first century BC) and in the lands of the Roman Empire (27 BC through AD 476) focus not only on political developments within the city of Rome itself but also on its rulers' conquests of lands throughout Europe. As the soldiers of Rome seek to bring yet more lands under the Empire's umbrella, they clash with the Celtic tribes of Europe and the British Isles, who fight fiercely in defense of their territory.

Bradshaw, Gillian.

Dark North. Severn House, 2007. 315pp. Hardbound, 9780727865243.

In AD 208 an African cavalry scout named Memnon makes the expedition to Britain with the rest of his unit, following Emperor Septimius Severus on his quest to conquer its barbarians once and for all. En route, he saves the life of Lady Athenais, a beautiful attendant to the empress. This brings him into closer proximity to the emperor's inner circle—and a conspiracy that lurks within it. Set in the region we now call Scotland.

Keywords: England; Scotland; Soldiers

Dando-Collins, Stephen.

The Inquest. iBooks, 2005. 384pp. Hardbound, 1416504419.

It is AD 71 in Antioch, capital of the Roman province of Syria; Vespasian sits on the imperial throne. Julius Varro, a Roman questor, is sent to Judea to investigate claims that a Jew rose from the dead after crucifixion in Jerusalem some forty years earlier. His goal, naturally, is to gather enough evidence to debunk the story, for the Nazarene sect has become disruptive to Roman rule in the area. As Varro listens to and evaluates testimony relevant to the case, much of it secondhand, at first it appears the Nazarenes will be completely discredited . . . but then something completely unexpected happens.

Keywords: Inquests; Palestine

Dietrich, William.

The Scourge of God. HarperCollins, 2005. 334pp. Hardbound, 006073499X.

Attila, the "scourge of God," is, in effect, Europe's greatest leader in the year AD 449. The great Roman Empire is finally losing ground—and power—to the Huns and other barbarian tribes. Honoria, the Roman emperor's sister, has been imprisoned for adultery. Believing Attila her only hope for rescue, she sends to him for aid, and Attila, assuming that she's proposing marriage, marches to claim the entire empire as his rightful dowry. But when a Roman plot against Attila's life goes awry, Jonas Alabanda, a diplomat and historian in love with Ilana, a Roman prisoner of the Huns, gets caught in the fray. A fast-moving historical novel based around a comparatively little-known historical incident; all comes to a climax at the bloody Battle of Chalons in AD 451.

Keywords: Attila, the Hun (historical character); Chalons, Battle of; Diplomats; France

Gillespie, Donna.

Light Bearer Series.

A lengthy, passion-filled epic set in ancient times, as the native tribes of Europe in the first century AD clashed with Rome. Although the first volume, *The Light Bearer*, was a best seller when it first appeared in 1994, the second was not picked up by an English-language publisher until twelve years later, even though it had long been a best seller in German translation. A third volume is expected.

Keywords: Auriane; Germany; Senators, Roman; Warriors, women

The Light Bearer. Berkley, 1994. 788pp. Hardbound, 0425143686.

The clash between the might of the Roman Empire and the valiant tribes of Germania circa AD 50 to 90 comes alive in this tale of Auriane, daughter of a Chattian chieftain. She becomes a warrior after Roman invaders murder her people. Word of her exploits reaches as far as Rome, where the Emperor Domitian swears to capture and defeat her. Marcus Julianus, a Roman senator and imperial advisor, grows intrigued by reports of Auriane; he knows that he is destined to meet this remarkable woman.

Lady of the Light. Berkley, 2006. 440pp. paper, 0425212688.

For the past seven years, Auriane and Marcus, happily married with two daughters, have lived peaceably on his estate in a frontier province of Rome. Auriane, however, has never forgotten her position as a warrior of the Chattian tribe, nor her loyalty to her people. Roman law prohibits the Chattians from owning or purchasing weapons, but they desperately need to defend themselves against another invading Germanic tribe. Although Auriane refuses to lead the Chattians herself, she smuggles arms to them behind her husband's back, at risk to herself and her family.

Gold, Alan.

Warrior Queen. NAL, 2005. 366pp. Paper, 0451215257. ✍

In this fairly traditional retelling of the life of Boudica, the warrior queen of the Iceni in the first century AD, Australian novelist Gold portrays her as a Celtic heroine who gave her life for her people. However, he goes beyond the usual limits of biographical fiction by also providing details on Roman culture of the era, as the scenes shift from the lands of the Iceni in Britain to the courts of Claudius and Nero in Rome. Married by arrangement to Prasutagus, a pro-Roman nobleman who was appointed king of the Iceni, flame-haired Boudica can't pay his debts after his death. As a result, she is horribly betrayed by the Romans she had loyally served for years.

Keywords: Boudica (historical character); England; Celts; Warriors, women

Harris, Robert.

Imperium. Simon & Schuster, 2006. 305pp. Hardbound, 074326603X. ✍ **YA**

The life story of Marcus Tullius Cicero, a "new man" from the Roman provinces who rose to Rome's highest office in 64 BC—that of consul—is narrated in lively, fast-paced style by the man who was his confidential secretary/assistant for thirty-six years, a slave named Tiro (a historical figure whose real-life memoirs were unfortunately lost). A consummate orator and politician, Cicero uses his wit to triumph in his first case over Gaius Verres, a corrupt governor of Sicily. He continues to win other high-profile cases throughout his remarkable career. Always detested by Rome's aristocrats for his humble origins, Cicero navigates the convoluted path to power in republican Rome, matching wits (and winning) against well-known political figures such as Caesar and Crassus.

Keywords: Cicero, Marcus Tullius (historical character); Orators; Politicians; Rome; Tiro (historical character)

May, Antoinette.

Pilate's Wife. Morrow, 2006. 368pp. Hardbound, 0061128651. ✍
Little is known of the real Claudia Procula, wife of Pontius Pilate, the first-century governor of Judea who sentenced Christ to death. May imagines Claudia as a clairvoyant, Isis-worshipping daughter of Roman nobility who marries the ambitious Pilate despite her growing love for a gladiator named Holtan. Her friendship with Miriam of Magdala leads her into the circle of Miriam's would-be husband, Jeshua, a religious radical. This provokes violent and disturbing visions of his death—an event Claudia desperately and unsuccessfully tries to prevent. The subtitle ("a novel of the Roman Empire") describes it well, for the Crucifixion plays a small role in the story, and only toward the end. Imaginative and passionately written, but not for biblical literalists.

Keywords: Biblical themes; Judea; Pilate, Pontius (historical character); Procula, Claudia (historical character); Psychics

McCullough, Colleen.

The Masters of Rome. ✍ ★
In her seven novels about the decline of the Roman Republic and the birth of the Roman Empire, McCullough demonstrates her mastery of the politics, culture, and personalities of the era. Erudite and impressively detailed, the novels come complete with maps, glossaries, and black-and-white drawings done by the author. The length of the series as a whole may daunt new readers; the books are best read in order. McCullough's obvious hero is Gaius Julius Caesar, though many of the other historical personages she depicts are equally fascinating.

The First Man in Rome. William Morrow, 1990. 896pp. Hardbound, 068809368X.

The Grass Crown. William Morrow, 1991. 894pp. Hardbound, 0688093698.

Fortune's Favorites. William Morrow, 1993. 878pp. Hardbound, 0688093701.

Caesar's Women. William Morrow, 1996. 695pp. Hardbound, 068809371X.

Caesar: Let the Dice Fly. William Morrow, 1997. 664pp. Hardbound, 0688093728.

The October Horse. Simon & Schuster, 2002. 792pp. Hardbound, 0684853310.

Antony and Cleopatra. Simon & Schuster, 2007. 567pp. Hardbound, 9781416552949.

This seventh and final volume opens in the year 41 BC, several years after Caesar's death. Mark Antony, his "close cousin," and Octavian, his eighteen-year-old great-nephew, reluctantly make provisions to divide Caesar's empire between them. Antony takes charge of the provinces, including the East, whose wealth he desperately seeks to acquire. While in Egypt, Antony runs up against Queen Cleopatra, who entices him into her bed; she plans to use him in her scheme to make Caesarion, her son by Caesar, the sole ruler of the Empire.

Keywords: Caesar, Julius (historical character); Cleopatra, Queen of Egypt (historical character); Egypt; Pharaohs; Rome

Scott, Manda.

Boudica Series. ✍

A four-book series about the Celtic warrior queen Boudica. Her true name is Breaca, while "Boudica" is a title meaning "bringer of victory." Not just a war story, Scott's series has strong elements of Celtic spirituality.

Keywords: Boudica (historical character); Celts; England; Warriors, women

Dreaming the Eagle. Delacorte, 2003. 465pp. Hardbound, 0385336705.

Dreaming the Bull. Delacorte, 2004. 344pp. Hardbound, 0385336713.

Boudica: Dreaming the Hound. Delacorte, 2006. 415pp. Hardbound, 0385336721.

> The proud Roman fighters of Nero's army are winning the fight over the Eceni tribe, led by Breaca, and as their leader she motivates them to action. Although distraught at the banishment of her lover, Caradoc, Breaca leaves the Isle of Mona to rally her people, but in order to strengthen the possibility of victory, she must convince her estranged half-brother Bán, who had turned traitor and fought alongside Rome as "Valerius," to rejoin her side. There is a particularly violent (and historically based) scene toward the end, as Breaca is ordered flogged by the Romans—who also rape her two daughters.

Boudica: Dreaming the Serpent Spear. Delta, 2007. 464pp. Paper, 9780385338356.

> It is now AD 60, and twenty years since the Romans first occupied Britain. Breaca recovers from her injuries, while the Roman governor decides to rid Rome of the Eceni threat once and for all by marching his troops toward the druidic stronghold on Mona. While their capital is undefended, Breaca sees the perfect opportunity to strike back against the Romans.

Watson, Jules.

The Dalriada Trilogy.

Watson's epic series, filled with power struggles, mysticism, and romance, takes place in a comparatively unused locale: first-century Scotland, one of the few lands of Europe not yet conquered by Rome. Though marketed as historical fantasy in the United States, the supernatural elements (Celtic goddess-centered rituals, prophecies, and visions, for the most part) are fairly minor, and the plot is well anchored in Scottish history.

Keywords: Celts; Priestesses; Scotland

The White Mare. Overlook, 2005. 469pp. Hardbound, 1585676209.

> In order to continue the royal line, Rhiann, the priestess sister of the Epidii tribe, is forced into a political marriage with Eremon, an exiled prince from Dalriada in Ireland, after her brother is killed. In exchange for her hand in marriage, Eremon agrees to help the Epidii fight the Romans, who threaten from the south under the all-too-able leadership of Agricola, governor of Roman Britain. But strong-willed Rhiann refuses to consummate their union—she has her reasons—and Eremon's dalliance with a dangerous woman certainly complicates their relationship as well.

The Dawn Stag. Overlook, 2006. 552pp. Hardbound, 1585676217.

> It is AD 81. Together Rhiann and Eremon have forged a romantic and political union that will help their peoples withstand a Roman invasion. However, Agricola doesn't believe the Alban people stand a chance against the might of Rome's armies. The pair also face enemies from within, as warring tribes, enemy druids, and Eremon's old flame, Samana, aim to bring them down.

Song of the North. Overlook, 2008. 403pp. Hardbound, 9782590200506. (Original UK title: *The Boar Stone.*)

> By three centuries after the events in *The Dawn Stag*, circa AD 366, the Dalriadan people have been assimilated into Roman ways. Then Minna, a Roman serving girl left to fend for herself in barbarian Scotland, arrives at the fort of Cahir, King of the Dalriadans; she begins seeing inexplicable visions about Scotland that make her question her loyalties.

The British Isles

In the novels in this section the setting is England unless otherwise indicated in the keywords following the annotations.

Early Middle Ages

These novels take place between the fall of Rome in the fifth century and the Battle of Hastings in 1066, a period commonly known as the Dark Ages. However, historians dislike that term because it implies lack of development and activity—which certainly wasn't true.

King, Susan Fraser.

Lady Macbeth. **Crown, 2008. 340pp. Hardbound, 9780307341747.** ✍

> Drawing her fictional biography not from Shakespeare's tragedy but from historical evidence, King breathes life into a woman about whom little is

known. Gruadh, called Rue, a descendant of the royal line of Scotland, begins her story in the year AD 1025. A skilled swordswoman and an able practitioner of Celtic magic, Rue is first wed to her father's ally, the Mormaer of Moray. Shortly thereafter, widowed with a small son, she is forced to marry his murderer, Macbeth. To her surprise, Macbeth proves to be a man of honor and ambition who's equally willing to preserve her family's legacy.

Keywords: Gruoch, Queen of Scotland (historical character); Macbeth, King of Scotland (historical character); Scotland; Shakespearean themes

Sutcliff, Rosemary.

Sword at Sunset. **Coward-McCann, 1963. 495pp. Hardbound, no ISBN.** ★

Sutcliff's Arthur is the great Romano-Celtic leader who successfully routs the Saxons until his final defeat at Camlann. Her battle scenes are particularly well done. During her lifetime, Sutcliff wrote a number of highly regarded historical novels of Roman Britain for young people. In this, her first adult novel, she reused characters from an earlier work for young adults, *The Lantern Bearers*.

Keywords: Arthurian themes; Celts

Whyte, Jack.

The Camulod Chronicles. (Original series title: A Dream of Eagles.)

Whyte's nine-volume series is placed firmly in the fourth and fifth centuries, as Roman armies are withdrawing from Britain. It can most accurately be called a pre-Arthurian series, as the story begins long before Arthur's birth and foreshadows the coming of the great Briton leader.

Keywords: Arthurian themes; England; Soldiers

The Skystone. Forge, 1996. 352pp. Hardbound, 0312860919.

The Singing Sword. Forge, 1996. 352pp. Hardbound, 0312852924.

The Eagles' Brood. Forge, 1997. 412pp. Hardbound, 0312852894.

The Saxon Shore. Forge, 1998. 496pp. Hardbound, 0312865961.

The Fort at River's Bend. Forge, 1999. 351pp. Hardbound, 031286597X.

The Sorcerer: Metamorphosis. Forge, 1999. 352pp. Hardbound, 0312865988.

Uther. Forge, 2001. 623pp. Hardbound, 0312864434.

The Lance Thrower. Forge, 2004. 527pp. Hardbound, 0312869290. (Original title: *Clothar the Frank.*)

Clothar, a young warrior from Gaul who seeks to avenge his parents' deaths, is sent by his teacher and mentor, Bishop Germanus, to Britain to find his old friend Merlyn. When Clothar arrives, he learns that Merlyn's ward, Arthur Pendragon, is destined to be the first High King of a united Britain. The final two volumes of the Camulod Chronicles, *The Lance Thrower* and *The Eagle*, take readers directly to the traditional Arthurian story; they form a two-book miniseries Whyte calls "The Golden Eagle."

The Eagle. Forge, 2006. 576pp. Hardbound, 0312870078.

> Clothar of Benwick (aka Lancelot) continues his narration in this final volume of Whyte's epic series, detailing how Arthur struggles to unite all of Britain against a Saxon invasion. Two local rulers, jealous of Arthur's success, oppose him. Clothar, fighting his attraction to Arthur's queen, Guinevere, returns to Gaul to help his cousin in his fight against the invading Huns. With so much time spent in Gaul, readers will miss a good deal of what's going on in Camulod, but Clothar returns to Britain at last for the final showdown.

High Middle Ages

This era covers the period between 1066, the year of the Norman Conquest, and 1485, when Richard III's fall at the Battle of Bosworth signaled the ascent of the Tudor monarchs. Novels set during this time cover the lives of England's Plantagenet kings (and their counterparts in Scotland and Wales), feudal societies, and people's relationship with the church.

Chadwick, Elizabeth.

Shadows and Strongholds. **St. Martin's Press, 2006. 568pp. Hardbound, 0312349246.** ✍

> In 1148 ten-year-old Brunin FitzWarin, an awkward introvert, is sent by his despairing father to be fostered with Joscelin de Dinan, lord of Ludlow Castle, and serve as his squire. While there Brunin befriends Hawise, Joscelin's youngest daughter, and grows in confidence. Because of his role in Joscelin's household, Brunin is obliged to help him aid Henry of Anjou (the future Henry II) in his fight to gain England's throne from King Stephen. Brunin's parents also arrange his marriage with Hawise, as this will help ensure Ludlow Castle's defense against the family's rivals. This changes their relationship considerably, and Marion, an orphan living at Ludlow with a major crush on Brunin, is none too happy about it. This prequel to Chadwick's *Lords of the White Castle* tells the story of the parents of Fulke FitzWarin, the medieval outlaw who fought to regain his family's lands.

> **Keywords:** Castles; England; FitzWarin, Fulke "Le Brun" (historical character)

Davenport, Will.

The Sinner's Tale. **Bantam, 2004. 322pp. Paper, 0553802178.** ✍

> In the fourteenth century Sir Guy de Bryan undertakes a dangerous mission to Genoa on behalf of King Edward III. Along the way he tells his life story to his eager squire, a boy named Geoffrey (whom readers may recognize as a certain future author). Guy tells a tale about chivalry, honor, and his passionate love for Elizabeth de Montacute, which causes him immense guilt because she's married to another man. In the present day, Beth Battock, a young British politician who supports her country's public stance on the Iraq War, returns home to Slapton to hide from the fallout of a romantic scandal. She learns about Sir Guy, a man for whom prayers are

still being said in Slapton. Davenport is a pseudonym for James Long, author of the time-slip novels *Ferney* and *Silence and Shadows*.

Keywords: Chivalry; de Bryan, Guy (historical character); Knights; Multi-period novels

Felber, Edith.

Queen of Shadows. NAL, 2006. 304pp. Paper, 045121952X. ✍

Isabella of France, nicknamed the "she-wolf" for her role in deposing her ineffectual, unfaithful husband, Edward II, is the protagonist of this biographical novel. When Isabella arrives in England from France as a twelve-year-old child in 1308 to marry King Edward, she expects to be treated as the princess she is. Instead, over the years, she grows steadily more humiliated at being brushed aside in favor of her husband's male favorites. As Isabella prepares to take action against Edward, her Welsh handmaiden, Gwenith de Percy, steps forward to avenge England's rough treatment of Wales. Felber is better known as Edith Layton, author of numerous historical romances.

Keywords: Gay men; Isabella of France, Queen of England (historical character); Queens

Follett, Ken.

Kingsbridge Series.

Two mammoth novels set in the medieval English town of Kingsbridge, two centuries apart. Epics in every sense but the geographic, they incorporate an array of related subplots involving interesting people from all walks of life. Both are written in Follett's direct, uncomplicated style and can be read independently. Descendants of the characters from *Pillars* populate *World Without End*.

Keyword: Cathedrals

The Pillars of the Earth. Morrow, 1989. 973pp. Hardbound, 0688046592. ★

While the Empress Maud and King Stephen fight a civil war for England's throne, Philip, a monk who becomes prior of the fictional town of Kingsbridge, and Tom, a master builder, join forces to achieve their dream. Divisions in the community mimic the intrigues dividing all of England. Surprisingly, this epic novel of the building of a Gothic cathedral in twelfth-century England was thriller writer Follett's most successful book. Though criticized for the modern outlook of its characters, it has also been praised for the strength of its storytelling. Oprah's Book Club.

World Without End. Dutton, 2007. 987pp. Hardbound, 9780525950073.

In Kingsbridge, England, 200 years after *Pillars of the Earth*, the cathedral designed by Tom Builder still stands. Rather than serving as the story's anchor this time, the Gothic edifice becomes a backdrop and witness of sorts to events occurring in the town between 1327 and 1361. The Hundred Years' War begins, the Black Death descends, and four children of Kingsbridge glimpse a murder (and harbor a secret related to that event) that binds them together and affects each of them differently.

Keywords: Children; Hundred Years' War; Plague

Galland, Nicole.

The Fool's Tale. **Morrow, 2005. 523pp. Hardbound, 0060721502.**

Galland, a screenwriter from the Bay Area, brings more than a touch of drama to this historical novel of loyalty, politics, and romance set in late twelfth-century Wales. King Maelgwyn ap Cadwallon of Maelienydd, known as Noble, has been friends with Gwydion, his court fool, ever since Gwydion saved his life in boyhood. When Isabel Mortimer, niece of Noble's longtime English foe, comes to Maelienydd as Noble's young bride, she and the bawdy fool dislike one another on sight. But an incident that brings them into closer proximity transforms their animosity into unexpected passion. Then a suspenseful tone takes over: what would happen if the king discovered their affair?

Keywords: Jesters and fools; Love triangles; Queens; Wales

Harper, Karen.

The First Princess of Wales. **Three Rivers, 2006. 611pp. Paper, 9780307237910. (First published in 1984 as *Sweet Passion's Pain*.)** ✍

Joan of Kent, a lovely young cousin of King Edward III, comes to court in the mid-fourteenth century. At first she's unprepared for the intrigue that swirls around the royal family, but once she learns that they were responsible for her father's execution, she decides to get closer to Edward, Prince of Wales. Her heart betrays her; they fall in love, but political circumstances keep them apart. She marries another man and bears his children, but she never forgets Edward. Based on a historical story, but inaccuracies appear when this story is compared to the historical timeline of the real-life Joan.

Keywords: Joan of Kent (historical character); Princesses

Kaufman, Pamela.

Alix of Wanthwaite Trilogy.

A trilogy about the adventures of Alix of Wanthwaite, a strong-willed girl from the English–Scots border who comes of age as she accompanies Crusaders to the Holy Land, falls in love and marries, and becomes involved with political events of the time.

Keywords: Crusades and Crusaders; Disguise; Gay men; Magna Carta; Picaresque novels; Richard I, King of England (historical character)

Shield of Three Lions. Crown, 1983. 474pp Hardbound, 0517551284.

Banners of Gold. Crown, 1986. 436pp. Hardbound, 0517561336.

The Prince of Poison. Three Rivers, 2006. 424pp. Paper, 1400080630.

Because King John believes that Alix is carrying the child of his late brother, Richard the Lion Heart, he seeks to have both her and the unborn child killed. Having learned that her Scottish husband, Enoch, was alive, Alix bears her son, a boy named Theo, and eventually makes her way back to England and to Enoch, though she learns he has remarried, believing her dead. She spends most of the rest of the novel traveling across England, avoiding the villainy of King John, and playing a key role in the Magna Carta's development.

Lawhead, Stephen R.

King Raven Trilogy.

Lawhead envisions Robin Hood as Bran ap Brychan, a minor Welsh prince who becomes a folk hero. The author's note at the end of the first book explains his reasoning for setting his novel in late eleventh-century Wales and not, as is traditional, in Sherwood Forest in Nottinghamshire. The usual suspects (Robin Hood's entourage) are all here, too, but in different forms than you'd expect. Although written for a Christian publisher, these novels are quite mainstream. One more volume, *Tuck*, is expected.

Keywords: Outlaws; Princes; Robin Hood; Wales

Hood. WestBow, 2006. 472pp. Hardbound, 1595540857.

In the year 1093 Norman warriors invade the Wye Valley, claiming that King William Rufus granted the land to them. King Brychan ap Tewdwr, lord of Elfael, is killed defending his territory, along with many of his fellow warriors. Bran, his son and heir, takes refuge in the nearby forest, where his following and legend slowly grow. Known to the people as King Raven, Bran abandons his spoiled ways and terrorizes the Norman invaders in his own creative fashion. Action-oriented and occasionally violent, but with a strong element of faith.

🎋 *Scarlet.* Thomas Nelson, 2007. 448pp. Hardbound, 9781596640867.

This second volume continues the story from the viewpoint of Will Scarlet. Will, imprisoned by the men of King William the Red, will be hanged unless he reveals the forest hiding place of King Raven and his followers. While he awaits his death sentence, he speaks of how he came to join Bran's righteous band of merry thieves. Christy Award.

Lord, Elizabeth.

Company of Rebels. **Severn House, 2004. 266pp. Hardbound, 0727861719.**

In the late fourteenth century, the people of England suffer under the burden of the young King Richard II's unpopular poll tax. Some of the peasants in the small village of Fobbing, in Essex, take matters into their own hands by staging a revolt. John Melle and his best friend, Tom Baker, decide to lead a group to London to confront the king directly, but their friendship faces the ultimate test when John embarks on a secret affair with Tom's pretty wife, Marjory.

Keywords: Extramarital affairs; Peasants' Revolt of 1381

Maitland, Karen.

Company of Liars. **Delacorte, 2008. 465pp. Hardbound, 9780385341691.** 📖

In this grim alternative to *The Canterbury Tales*, a band of nine outcasts, forced together by chance, makes their way across southern England on foot in the year 1348 in an attempt to outrun the Black Death. The mismatched group includes a peddler of fake relics (who narrates), an adolescent couple, a maimed storyteller, an Italian musician and his apprentice, a nurse, a traveling magician, and a child rune-reader whose creepy predictions never fail to come true. They all recount tales to entertain the others, yet they also conceal an even darker secret from the past that comes back to haunt them.

Keywords: Peddlers; Plague

Penman, Sharon Kay.

Penman's lengthy, sweeping novels of medieval England make the lives of long-ago royalty and nobility accessible. While most incorporate a romantic subplot, they also include an incredible, though not overwhelming, amount of detail on the politics of the time. All are considered classics of the genre, works against which all other novels of the Middle Ages are measured.

Plantagenet Trilogy. ✍ ★

Intricately detailed novels about the early Plantagenets, their lives, and their loves.

Keyword: Royalty

When Christ and His Saints Slept. Henry Holt, 1995. 746pp. Hardbound, 0805010157.

After the only legitimate son of King Henry I drowns with the White Ship in 1120, the English succession falls into confusion. Maude, King Henry's proud daughter and the widow of the German emperor, is forced by her father to marry Geoffrey of Anjou, a younger man whom she detests and whom England doesn't want as a ruler. Stephen, Henry's nephew, believes that the people will accept him as ruler more readily than Maude and Geoffrey. He quickly has himself crowned king of England after Henry's death. Thus begin twenty years of bloody civil war, a time when people said that Christ and his saints slept. Penman's is one of the few novels to portray the Maude–Stephen relationship as the bitter rivalry it most likely was, rather than as a forbidden romance.

Keywords: Maud, Empress (historical character); Stephen, King of England (historical character)

Time and Chance. Putnam, 2002. 528pp. Hardbound, 0399147853.

Maud's son Henry II, the vigorous young Plantagenet king, finds that his political and religious differences with Thomas Becket cause insurmountable problems. Eleanor of Aquitaine, a beautiful, strong-willed heiress, progresses believably from Henry's beloved queen to his bitter former confidante. And Becket, the king's chancellor and boon companion, suddenly develops a loyalty to the church that sets him against many, Henry most of all.

Keywords: Becket, Thomas (historical character); Eleanor of Aquitaine (historical character); Henry II, King of England (historical character); Saints

Devil's Brood. Putnam, 2008. 734pp. Hardbound, 9780399155260.

> The Henry II–Eleanor of Aquitaine union, which started out so promisingly (as chronicled in *Time and Chance*), disintegrates into bitterness and hatred when Henry's arrogance gets the better of him. His eldest son Hal, crowned but forbidden to exercise any real power, grows resentful; as does Eleanor, shamed by Henry's political schemes regarding her lands and affair with Rosamund Clifford. Along with sons Richard and Geoffrey, they begin forming alliances with the King of France against Henry; the reverberations are felt throughout all of England.
>
> **Keywords:** Eleanor of Aquitaine (historical character); Fathers and sons; Henry II, King of England (historical character)

The Sunne in Splendour. **Holt, Rinehart & Winston, 1982. 936pp. Hardbound, 003061368X.** ✍ ★

Richard III, best known from Shakespeare as the hunchbacked traitor who killed his nephews to steal England's throne, is restored to his proper place in Penman's novel. Here, Richard is both a loyal brother to Edward IV and an intelligent leader himself. Passionately in love with his queen, Anne Neville, with whom he would prefer to have a quiet life, Richard becomes caught up in forces beyond his control as the Wars of the Roses divide families and friends. Penman also tells the story of Richard's elder brother Edward IV, the charming monarch whose ambitious wife costs him some supporters and whose early secret marriage to a noblewoman throws the succession into confusion.

Keywords: Richard III, King of England (historical character); Wars of the Roses

Riley, Judith Merkle.

Margaret of Ashbury Series. ★ YA

Fourteenth-century England is the setting for Riley's novels of early feminism, religion, romance, and medieval family life. All contain liberal doses of humor and supernatural plot twists (which will attract readers of historical fantasy as well). These are reader favorites.

Keywords: Authors, women; Hundred Years' War; Margaret of Ashbury; Midwives

A Vision of Light. Delacorte, 1989. 442pp. Hardbound, 0440501091.

> In 1355 twice-married Margaret of Ashbury hears a mysterious voice advising her to do something unusual and possibly heretical: write a book about her life. Because she is unlettered herself, Margaret enlists Brother Gregory, a Carthusian friar, to take on the task, something he would not have done were he not afraid of starving. Still, he cannot help but become engrossed in Margaret's fascinating life story, which includes midwifery, witchcraft, and the Black Death.

In Pursuit of the Green Lion. Delacorte, 1990. 440pp. Hardbound, 0385300891.

> In this sequel to *A Vision of Light*, twenty-three-year-old Margaret has been kidnapped by her late husband's relatives. She is rescued by Gregory de Vilers, formerly her chronicler Brother Gregory, whose money-grubbing family is equally as odious. Though Margaret and Gregory decide to marry for her protection, there is little affection between them at first. Their love in-

tensifies as she travels to France to rescue him from capture during the Hundred Years' War.

The Water Devil. Three Rivers, 2007. 276pp. Paper, 9780307237897.

It is 1360, and Margaret of Ashbury, weary of adventuring, is ready to settle down in the English countryside with her husband, Gregory, and their noisy brood of children. However, her annoying in-laws won't leave her alone. Gregory's meddlesome father wishes to sell Margaret's daughter, Cecily, in marriage to pay for his debts, which may cause him to lose ownership of some nearby woodlands. As Margaret turns to her old friend Brother Malachi for help, an ancient spirit dwelling in the woodland spring awakens, with an eye on Margaret's son.

Smith, Anne Easter.

Daughter of York. Touchstone, 2008. 570pp. Paper, 9780743277310. ✍ 📖

Margaret of York never expects to figure at all in European politics until her eldest brother comes to England's throne as King Edward IV. At his court, Margaret develops a friendship with Anthony Woodville, brother of Queen Elizabeth, that soon turns into love. Although Margaret does her duty by marrying Charles of Burgundy in an effort to strengthen England's alliances against France, Anthony accompanies her as an escort. Margaret comes to play a major role in international affairs, yet her passion for a man she can never have (an invention of the author) helps her endure her childless marriage and the long years away from her family.

Keywords: France; Margaret, Duchess of Burgundy (historical character); Royalty; Wars of the Roses

A Rose for the Crown. Touchstone, 2006. 649pp. Paper, 0743276876. ✍ 📖

Smith's epic fictional biography of the woman who might have been Richard III's longtime mistress begins in her childhood. Kate Bywood grows up on a prosperous farm on the outskirts of the Kentish market town of Tunbridge in the mid-fifteenth century. Her station in life rises when she joins the household of her mother's cousins, the Hautes, as companion to their daughter. After two unhappy marriages, one to a rich merchant and another to a Haute cousin, Kate meets and forms an immediate connection with Richard, Duke of Gloucester. She becomes his mistress and bears him three children, loving him unreservedly yet realizing all the while that she's not well-born enough to be his wife. Although Richard is obliged to marry another woman, he makes arrangements to bring his children with Kate to court.

Keywords: Kings; Mistresses; Richard III, King of England (historical character); Wars of the Roses

Vantrease, Brenda Rickman.

The Illuminator. St. Martin's Press, 2006. 406pp. Hardbound, 0312331916. 📖

It is 1349, a time of religious unrest in England. To please the local abbot, Lady Kathryn of Blackingham Manor agrees to let an illuminator and his daughter lodge with her, but this adds to her problems. A priest's body is found on her property; her bailiff is cheating her; and Finn, the master illuminator, conceals the manuscripts that reformer John Wycliffe had asked him to illustrate. Finn soon wins over Agnes, Lady Kathryn's cook, and he wins over Kathryn as well; their love affair parallels that of Finn's daughter Rose with Kathryn's gentle son Colin. But when Finn reveals one of his deepest secrets, Kathryn's world unravels, and with it the lives of everyone around her.

Keywords: Illuminators; Lollards; Nobility; Widows

The Tudor Era

The year 1485 marked the ascent of Henry VII, the first Tudor king, to England's throne; the year 1603 saw the death of his granddaughter, Elizabeth I. Most novels set during the Tudor era focus on the royal court, with all its pomp and splendor. Other common subjects include religious dissension, as Henry VIII declares himself head of the Church of England in order to marry Anne Boleyn, as well as the political rivalry between Henry's daughter Elizabeth and her Catholic cousin, Mary, Queen of Scots.

Ashley, Jennifer.

The Queen's Handmaiden. **Berkley, 2007. 323pp. Paper, 9780425217320.** ✍ **YA**

When her father dies, Eloise Rousell joins the household of her aunt, Katherine Ashley, governess to Princess Elizabeth. She becomes Elizabeth's seamstress, friend, and confidante. Eloise and Elizabeth, both born in 1553, find they have much in common despite their vast differences in station. Through Eloise's eyes, we witness Elizabeth's involvement with her stepmother's amorous husband, Thomas Seymour; her troubled relationship with her older sister, Queen Mary; and her gradual progress toward the throne. An uncomplicated coming of age story with a different view of a young Queen Elizabeth; Ashley also wrote *A Lady Raised High* as Laurien Gardner and the <u>Captain Gabriel Lacey</u> mysteries (Chapter 7) as Ashley Gardner.

Keywords: Coming of age; Elizabeth I, Queen of England (historical character); Seamstresses

Bennett, Vanora.

Portrait of an Unknown Woman. **Morrow, 2007. 417pp. Hardbound, 9780061256516.** ✍ 📖 **YA**

British journalist Bennett's first novel vividly evokes the changes wrought by the Protestant Reformation both in England and in the family of Sir Thomas More, Henry VIII's Catholic chancellor, a dangerous position to have when the king was contemplating divorce. Meg Giggs, More's adopted daughter, recounts her courtship with secretive John Clement, her family's former tutor; her dismay at her father's role in rooting out heresy; and her changing relationship with Hans Holbein, the German painter hired to depict her family on canvas. Two paintings done by Holbein of the More household, one in 1527 and the other several years later, craftily reflect how King Henry's changing moods affected them all. The major characters are all historical figures.

Keywords: Artists; Catholicism; Families; Giggs, Meg (historical character); Holbein, Hans (historical character); More, Thomas (historical character)

Cook, Bruce.

Young Will. **St. Martin's Press, 2004. 407pp. Hardbound, 0312335733.** ✍

Cook, who wrote a series of Georgian-era mysteries under the name Bruce Alexander, turns his hand to a part of Shakespeare's life not often told: his coming of age in his native Stratford-upon-Avon and in London. An older Will, revisiting his birthplace in 1616, reminisces about his incredibly successful career as a playwright, but readers will find his confessions about his bawdy youth even more entertaining. In the first person, Will relates his childhood pranks, his love affair with Kit Marlowe, and his admission of being an absentee husband and father. He also struggles to succeed at his craft in London, eking out a living writing sonnets for his patrons. After Cook's death in late 2003, his wife arranged for his final manuscript to be published.

Keywords: Coming of age; Playwrights; Shakespeare, William (historical character)

Erickson, Carolly.

The Last Wife of Henry VIII. **St. Martin's Press, 2006. 326pp. Hardbound, 0312352182.** ✍

Katherine Parr, the sixth and last wife of Henry VIII, recounts her tumultuous life story in lively, dramatic, and occasionally breathless prose. The daughter of a country squire who was named for Katherine of Aragon, Katherine has been twice married and twice widowed when the king's roving eye finally falls on her. They marry, but by then Catherine has fallen in love with rakish Thomas Seymour. Her attraction to the "new learning" at court—Protestantism—leads Henry to arrest her for heresy.

Keywords: Katherine Parr, Queen of England (historical character); Queens

Gardner, Laurien.

The Wives of Henry VIII. ✍ YA

Gardner is a house name used by the publisher specifically for this series. The authors' true identities are, in order, Julianne Ardian Lee, Jennifer Ashley, and Sarah A. Hoyt, all of whom have written other historical novels.

The Spanish Bride. Jove, 2005. 300pp. Paper, 0515140279.

Estrella de Montoya accompanies her mistress, Katherine of Aragon, from Spain to England when Katherine marries Arthur, the Prince of Wales, in 1501. She remains loyal to Katherine through eight years of strife, from Arthur's death to her marriage to his brother, Henry VIII. However, while Estrella eventually grows disillusioned with the ideals of courtly love and court life, Katherine holds steadfast to her dreams, hoping against hope that King Henry will remain true to her.

Keyword: Katherine of Aragon, Queen of England (historical character); Ladies in waiting

A Lady Raised High. Jove, 2006. 299pp. Paper, 0515140899.

> In 1532 Anne Boleyn, grateful to Frances Pierce for protecting her from an angry mob, grants the country girl a place among her ladies in waiting. Frances, who narrates the novel in a lighthearted, entertaining fashion, becomes a court favorite and remains loyal to Lady Anne before and after she becomes queen. But all too soon, both Frances and Anne realize how quickly the mood at court can shift when Henry VIII changes his mind.
>
> **Keyword:** Anne Boleyn, Queen of England (historical character); Ladies in waiting

Plain Jane. Jove, 2006. 342pp. Paper, 0515141550.

> Jane Seymour, plain in looks but strong in character, seizes the opportunity to avoid life in a nunnery by becoming Katherine of Aragon's lady in waiting. When Henry VIII tires first of Katherine and then of his new wife, sharp-tongued Anne Boleyn, his eye falls on Jane. To her surprise and pleasure, Henry makes her his wife, and only she is able to give him what he most desires: a son and heir.
>
> **Keyword:** Jane Seymour, Queen of England (historical character)

George, Margaret.

The Autobiography of Henry VIII. St. Martin's Press, 1986. 932pp. ✍ ★

> Henry himself narrates the story of his life, omitting nothing: the relationship with his six wives, in bed and out; his struggles with the church; the pageantry of the court; and much more. His fool, Will Somers, plays straight man to Henry, interjecting words about the real story behind Henry's narrative. "A whale of a book, about a whale of a king," wrote novelist Mary Stewart about this work, George's first major biographical novel.
>
> **Keywords:** Henry VIII, King of England (historical character); Jesters and fools; Somers, Will (historical character)

Gold, Alan.

The Pirate Queen. NAL, 2006. 358pp. Paper, 0451217446. ✍

> With much swash and buckle, Gold recounts the life story of Grace O'Malley, Irish pirate queen, who commanded a merchant fleet comprising a dozen ships and thousands of sailors. Born the daughter of a trader and pirate from County Mayo in 1530, Grace travels the seas from Ireland to Africa, plundering the ships of her country's enemies, with a particular relish for the vessels of England, and forming liaisons with several men. Her English counterpart, of course, is Queen Elizabeth, with whom she shares a lifelong rivalry and a remarkable affinity of character.
>
> **Keywords:** O'Malley, Grace (historical character); Pirates, women

Gregory, Philippa.

The Boleyn Inheritance. Touchstone, 2006. 518pp. Hardbound, 0743272501. ✍

> Three women share the unfortunate legacy of Anne Boleyn's fall from grace, and each narrates her own story in turn. Anne of Cleves, Gregory's most sympathetic character, knows she's risking her life by marrying Henry VIII, but she's eager to escape her hateful family. She survives numerous court treacheries, a friendless

existence in a foreign court, and her fortunately brief marriage to a husband she cannot please. Katherine Howard, Anne Boleyn's beautiful, naive teenaged cousin, is all too aware of her beauty, yet counts on the king's sexual attraction to her as her salvation. Jane Rochford, Anne Boleyn's jealous and depraved sister-in-law, schemes and spies for whichever party needs her services the most.

Keywords: Anne of Cleves, Queen of England (historical character); Courtiers; Katherine Howard, Queen of England (historical character); Queens; Rochford, Jane (historical character)

The Constant Princess. **Touchstone, 2005. 393pp. Hardbound, 074327248X.** ✍

Catalina of Aragon, the adored youngest daughter of Ferdinand and Isabella, grows up knowing she's destined to be queen of England one day. She eagerly embraces her arranged union with Arthur, Prince of Wales. After a rocky beginning, they share a true and passionate marriage—as well as their dreams for a progressive England. However, when it becomes clear that Arthur will die young, he extracts an oath from his young bride, now renamed Katherine, that she'll pretend their marriage was never consummated, which will allow her to marry his younger brother, Henry. She endures seven years of waiting before Henry is allowed to wed her, and though they're happy for nearly twenty years, her inability to bear a male heir is her downfall.

Keywords: Katherine of Aragon, Queen of England (historical character); Queens

The Other Queen. **Touchstone, 2008. 442pp. Hardbound, 9781416549123.** ✍

Mary, Queen of Scots, remains the center of Gregory's fictionalized version of the early years of her English imprisonment in the 1560s, which switches among three viewpoints. While in the custody of George Talbot, Earl of Shrewsbury, and his redoubtable wife, Bess, Mary uses her feminine wiles to draw George to her side. George finds his loyalties torn between his royal duty and Mary, with whom he's fallen in love; Bess worries that her children's inheritance is being drained in favor of Mary's upkeep. On the side, she spies against Mary for William Cecil, Queen Elizabeth's chief advisor. Though a skillful evocation of the 1569 Rising of the North, the novel is overlong and somewhat repetitive.

Keywords: Hardwick, Bess, Countess of Shrewsbury (historical character); Mary, Queen of Scots (historical character); Talbot, George, Earl of Shrewsbury (historical character); Queens

Harper, Karen.

The Last Boleyn. **Three Rivers, 2006. 585pp. Paper, 0307237907. (First published in 1983 as *Passion's Reign*.)** ✍

Mary Boleyn, elder sister of Anne, travels to France as a young girl to join the retinue of Mary Tudor, Queen of France, Henry VIII's younger sister. At the French court, blonde and attractive Mary becomes embroiled in the sexual and political happenings of the day, and attracts the attention of the new king, François. After returning home to England, she makes an early, unhappy marriage; forms a liaison with King Henry himself; and falls in love with a third man. In the end, out of all the Boleyns, only Mary emerges unscathed from the scandal that follows her family.

Keywords: Boleyn, Mary (historical character); France—Renaissance/Reformation; Mistresses; Queens

Lee, Julianne.

A Question of Guilt. Berkley, 2008. 307pp. Paper, 9780425223512. ✍ **YA**

It is 1587, and Mary, Queen of Scots, has just been executed on the order of her cousin, Queen Elizabeth I, for plotting against her throne. Lady Janet de Ros, a native of Scotland living in London with her English husband, grows increasingly doubtful that Queen Mary was guilty either of treason or of conspiring to murder her second husband, Henry Darnley. Janet travels to Fotheringhay Castle and to Edinburgh, interviewing numerous witnesses to the queen's behavior, in order to determine the truth. Scenes involving Mary and Darnley are related in retrospect. Despite the focus on Janet's investigation, this is more a thoughtful unfolding of facts than a typical historical mystery. Lee has also written novels as Laurien Gardner and J. Ardian Lee.

Keywords: England—Tudor era; Mary, Queen of Scots (historical character); Nobility; Queens; Scotland—16th century

Maxwell, Robin.

Mademoiselle Boleyn. NAL, 2007. 355pp. Paper, 9780451222091.

Annotated under "Europe: The Renaissance and Reformation" in this chapter.

To the Tower Born. Morrow, 2005. 308pp. Hardbound, 0060580518. ✍

The mystery of the lost princes of York—the two young sons of King Edward IV, who disappeared from the Tower of London in 1483—has inspired many works of fiction and nonfiction, with Shakespeare's *Richard III* and Josephine Tey's *Daughter of Time* being the best known examples. Maxwell, author of many biographical novels of Elizabethan England, approaches the story from a new angle. Her protagonist is Nell Caxton, daughter of William Caxton, the first English printer, and the best friend of Princess Elizabeth "Bessie" of York, sister of the lost princes and the future wife of Henry VII. As a well-educated commoner with connections to the royal circle, Nell is in a prime position to see and report on all of the drama at court.

Keywords: Caxton, Nell (historical character); Elizabeth of York, Queen of England (historical character); Princes; Wars of the Roses

Weir, Alison.

Innocent Traitor. Ballantine, 2007. 402pp. Hardbound, 9780345494856. ✍ **YA**

Weir, the author of many popular biographies about medieval and Tudor-era royalty, chose Lady Jane Grey, England's famed nine-day queen, as the subject for her first work of fiction. Jane, a scholarly adolescent forced reluctantly onto England's throne in 1553 by her power-hungry parents, is a realistic and sympathetic heroine for the Protestant cause. Weir recounts her story through the viewpoints of no less than eight people close to her. These include her bitter and ambitious mother,

Frances Brandon, Henry VIII's niece; her kindly nurse, Mrs. Ellen; Queen Katherine Parr, a mother figure of sorts; the future Queen Mary, her Catholic cousin; and John Dudley, Duke of Northumberland, who marries her to his son and uses her for his own ends.

Keywords: Jane Grey, Queen of England (historical character); Queens

The Lady Elizabeth. **Ballantine, 2008. 477pp. Hardbound, 9780345495358.** ✍

From a very young age, Elizabeth knows about her mother's ignominious and tragic end; she strengthens her resolve, vowing to avoid such a fate for herself. Her one weakness proves to be her stepmother's husband, Thomas Seymour. Popular historian Weir proves a fluid storyteller in her multifaceted portrait of a princess who quickly learns how to navigate political quagmires and to weigh her personal desire for love against the more pressing needs of the realm. Many novels have been written about Elizabeth I, but few focus on her childhood and adolescence. Weir admits in the afterword that she strayed from historical fact in one important scene (purists be warned).

Keywords: Elizabeth I, Queen of England (historical character)

The Stuart Era

With the death of Elizabeth I in 1603 came the end of the Tudor era. At this time her cousin James VI of Scotland, the son of Mary Stuart, Queen of Scots, moved south to London and became King James I of both England and Scotland. Thus were the two warring kingdoms united under a single monarch. The end of the Stuart era was marked by the death of Queen Anne in 1714. Historical novels set during this time include depictions of Cromwell's Protectorate, the English Civil War, the restoration of Charles II to the throne in 1660, and the continuing rivalry between Protestants and Catholics.

Dickason, Christie.

The Firemaster's Mistress. **Harper, 2008. 520pp. Paper, 9780061568268.**

Firemaster Francis Quoynt reluctantly gets caught up in the schemes of Robert Cecil, King James's secretary of state. He goes undercover to spy on on Guido Fawkes and his fellow pyromaniacs, without firm assurance that he wouldn't be accused of treason himself if caught. Kate Peach, Francis's former mistress and a secret Catholic, also approaches Francis for help, but whose side is she really on? Although the title will make one think this is a feminine approach to the Stuart era, in reality it's a multifaceted portrait of the complex political atmosphere leading up to the Gunpowder Plot of 1605.

Keywords: Catholicism; Gunpowder Plot; Mistresses

Haeger, Diane.

The Perfect Royal Mistress. **Three Rivers, 2007. 405pp. Paper, 0307237516.** ✍

Pretty, witty Nell Gwynne, an orange seller in the pit of London's King Theatre, quickly learns that the way to ascend society's ladder is with her innate charm and intelligence, rather than by prostitution. She becomes the leading comedic actress of her day, attracting the attention of no less than King Charles II himself. As one of the king's many mistresses, Nell learns to navigate the intrigues of court life. She remains one of his favorites for her irrepressible sense of optimism, quick wit, and remarkable lack of jealousy.

Keywords: Actresses; Gwyn, Nell (historical character); Kings; Mistresses

Hannam, Vanessa.

The Hostage Prince. **Severn House, 2006. 264pp. Hardbound, 0727863312.**

In 1646 England is at war with itself. The family of seventeen-year-old Elizabeth Anne "Lizzie" Jones has always stood loyally by King Charles, despite suffering the burden of his high taxes for years, but headstrong Lizzie has secret Puritan sympathies. After a Roundhead captain appears at her door, commanding her to leave her family to care for the king's youngest son and daughter—who are being held hostage to ensure their father's capitulation to Oliver Cromwell—she changes her mind.

Keywords: English Civil War; Puritans

Koen, Karleen.

Dark Angels. **Crown, 2006. 530pp. Hardbound, 0307339912.**

This "prequel twenty years in the making" to Koen's *Through a Glass Darkly* and *Now Face to Face* presents an unusual heroine, headstrong Alice Verney, who appears as the elderly dowager duchess of Tamworth in the other novels. In 1670 Alice leaves the magnificent but mannered court of Louis XIV's France for England. She quickly regains her previous position as loyal confidante to Charles II's Catholic queen, Catherine of Braganza, and finds herself in the center of intrigue—just where she wants to be. Hearing rumors that King Charles may wish to divorce his barren wife, Alice begins her own investigations into the matter, all the while scheming to marry her former fiancé's rich, elderly uncle. She certainly doesn't count on falling in love with handsome Richard Saylor, commander of the queen's guard, who may be her only real ally. A glorious portrait of the Restoration-era royal court.

Keywords: Courtiers; Ladies in waiting

Peachment, Christopher.

The Green and the Gold. **Thomas Dunne, 2004. 356pp. Hardbound, 0312314507.** ✍

Thomas Marvell, the seventeenth-century English poet and member of Parliament who penned "To His Coy Mistress," narrates this fictionalized story of his life. Though always intrigued by women, he never completely trusts them, and despite his thoughtful and insightful poems about love, Marvell never marries. During the English Civil War he acts as a spy for Cromwell, falls in love with an adolescent girl whom he tutors—the daughter of a Puritan general—and is the man responsible for the Great Fire of London in 1666. His voice, as imagined by Peachment, is opinionated, witty, and frequently sarcastic.

Keywords: English Civil War; Marvell, Thomas (historical character); Poets

Scott, Susan Holloway.

Scott writes mainstream biographical novels under her own name, and she has also authored over thirty well-researched historical romances under the pseudonym Miranda Jarrett.

Duchess. **NAL, 2006. 379pp, Paper, 0451218558.** ✍

Sarah, Duchess of Marlborough, an ancestress of Winston Churchill and Diana, Princess of Wales, comes to vibrant life in Scott's epic fictional biography, told in the first person. Sarah Jennings arrives in London in 1673 as a bright and ambitious thirteen-year-old commoner and, to her surprise, becomes a maid of honor at Charles II's riotous Restoration court. Her friendship with Anne of York, the king's lonely niece who later becomes Queen Anne, ensures Sarah's acceptance into the royal circle. Her marriage to John Churchill, an able military leader, becomes one of her greatest joys in life, and she relies on his strength when her friendship with the aging, stubborn Anne grows more trying.

Keywords: Churchill, Sarah (historical character); Duchesses; Queens

The King's Favorite. **NAL, 2008. 439pp. Paper, 9780451224064.** ✍

From the time she is a young woman, working as a barmaid in London's Drury Lane in 1661, Nelly Gwyn determines to win the heart of King Charles II. Despite her low birth, her bawdy wit and good-natured spirit impress everyone she meets, including noblemen close to the king. She rises to become a leading actress on the London stage and succeeds in becoming the king's mistress, good friend, and confidante.

Keywords: Actresses; Charles II, King of England (historical character); Gwyn, Nell (historical character); Mistresses; Royalty

Royal Harlot. **NAL, 2007. 284pp. Paper, 0451221346.** ✍

Barbara Villiers Palmer, Countess of Castlemaine, narrates her life story from the age of fifteen, when she first arrives in London, a saucy young woman ready to make her fortune. She throws in her lot with the Royalist cause, and when Charles II returns to reclaim his throne in 1660, he's immediately attracted to the voluptuous, sensual, and irresistible Barbara. Both are married to others, but Barbara quickly becomes his closest friend and mistress, a role she keeps for many years, becoming the unofficial queen of his bawdy Restoration court.

Keywords: Charles II, King of England (historical character); Countesses; Mistresses; Palmer, Barbara Villiers (historical character); Royalty

The Georgian Era

England's Georgian Era began in 1714 with the death of Queen Anne and the ascension of her distant cousin, George of Hanover, to the throne; it ended over a hundred years later in 1837 with the ascension of his descendant, Queen Victoria. Many traditional historicals deal with Georgian royalty and the consequences of their personal and political decisions. This includes the American Revolution, a war that George III is blamed for losing.

Bennett, Maggie.

The Tailor's Daughter. **Severn House, 2006. 268pp. Hardbound, 9780727863294.**

In 1771, when they are both children, Tabitha Prewett, a tailor's only daughter, meets Mariette de St. Aubyn, the aristocratic daughter of émigrés from France and the heiress to their wealth. Their friendship sustains them through turbulent times (the Prewetts are Protestant, and the St. Aubyns firm Catholics). But as they grow, the growing religious tension in London can't help but affect them and their families. When rioting breaks out, Tabitha follows Mariette and her Irish husband, Conor, to his homeland, yet finds herself irresistibly attracted to him—and he to her. A gentle novel of women's lives and relationships set in Georgian London.

Keywords: Love triangles; Nobility

Elyot, Amanda.

All for Love. **NAL, 2008. 432pp. Paper, 9780451222978.** ✍ 📖

Readers may know Mary Darby Robinson best as "Perdita," the beautiful actress who became an early mistress of the future George IV. In her biographical novel, Elyot pays equal attention to Mary's renowned literary efforts—she was a noted essayist, poet, and early feminist. Her story begins in Bristol, England, in 1765, after her merchant father abandons her and her mother for his second family. She garners fame as a Drury Lane actress, as well as the romantic attentions of the Prince of Wales. Throughout her life, she's never treated well by any of her lovers, yet Mary emerges as a sympathetic and courageous figure, reinventing herself as necessary and making the most of her innate talents.

Keywords: Actresses; Authors, women; Mistresses; Robinson, Mary Darby (historical character)

Too Great a Lady. **NAL, 2007. 412pp. Paper, 9780451220547.** ✍ 📖

In the first person, Emma Hamilton—half of one of the most famous romantic couples in history—tells her life story, from her poverty-stricken childhood in North Wales, to her time spent as mistress to wealthy English aristocrats, to her marriage with the much older William Hamilton, ambassador to Naples. Their relationship assures her acceptance (to some degree) into Neapolitan society, which leads to her friendship with Maria Carolina, Queen of Naples and Sicily. When England and Italy's war with France throws Horatio Nelson into the Hamiltons' path, he and Emma fall hopelessly in love.

Keywords: Hamilton, Emma (historical character); Italy; Mistresses; Nelson, Horatio (historical character)

Gee, Sophie.

The Scandal of the Season. **Scribner, 2007. 334pp. Hardbound, 9781416540564.** ✍ 📖

Alexander Pope's "The Rape of the Lock," a mock-epic published anonymously in 1712, pokes fun at the ridiculous excesses of aristocratic life. Gee's witty, erudite debut recounts the actual scenario that inspired the poem. Rumors of an illicit love affair between Arabella Fermor, a frivolous coquette, and Robert, Lord Petre, ripple through London society in 1711. Robert's public clipping of a lock of Arabella's hair not only serves as an admission of their involvement, but also of their possible participation in a Jacobite plot, for both of their families are Catholic (as is Pope's).

Keywords: Catholicism; Fermor, Arabella (historical character); Petre, Robert (historical character); Poets; Pope, Alexander (historical character)

Hollingshead, Greg.

Bedlam. **Thomas Dunne, 2006. 312pp. Hardbound, 0312354746.** ✍

In 1797 James Tilly Matthews is incarcerated in London's infamous Bethlem ("Bedlam") Hospital for the insane. Although he has moments of lucidity, he clearly isn't completely stable. Still, both he and his devoted wife, Margaret, believe he was removed to Bethlem for political reasons; he had visited France on a mission of peace during its revolution. Three individuals narrate his story: Margaret, who loves and stands by her husband during his twenty-year stay in Bethlem; James himself; and John Haslam, Bethlem's apothecary and head administrator, who finds himself morally conflicted between the duty to do right and his desire to study his increasingly famous patient. Based on a true story.

Keywords: Matthews, James Tilly (historical character); Mental illness; Psychiatry

Norman, Diana.

Makepeace Burke Series.

Norman, a well-regarded English historical novelist, delivers a tale of politics and romance with her trademark wit. The action moves from colonial America to Georgian-era England.

Keywords: French Revolution; Mothers and daughters; Nobility

A Catch of Consequence. Berkley, 2003. 386pp. Paper, 0425190153.

Taking Liberties. Berkley, 2004. 464pp. Paper, 0425198154.

The Sparks Fly Upward. Berkley, 2006. 423pp. Paper, 0425211584.

In France the Reign of Terror is in full swing, but England's *ton* continues their usual round of parties and social gatherings. Philippa, the independent-minded daughter of Makepeace Hedley (heroine of books 1 and 2), decides to settle into a marriage of convenience when the man she loves weds another. But when Philippa learns that her good friend the marquis de Condorcet has been arrested in Paris, she bravely journeys across the channel to rescue him from the Bastille, at considerable risk to herself. Meanwhile Makepeace, back in London, continues her awareness campaign about the plight of African slaves.

Paisley, Janet.

White Rose Rebel. **Overlook, 2008. 389pp. Hardbound, 9781585679591.** ✍

Anne Farquharson demonstrates, from a young age, her willfulness and fierce determination to fight for her country. In 1745, as the men and women of her native Highlands suffer the tyranny of King George II, she takes the side of the Jacobites and their rightful king, Bonnie Prince Charlie, while her husband, clan chief Aeneas McIntosh, fights for the English. "Colonel Anne," as she is affectionately called, raises a regiment of her own from the men of the McIntosh and Chattan clans and leads them into battle against the English herself. A passionate tale of the woman known as the "female Braveheart" and the "beautiful rebel."

Keywords: Farquharson, Anne (historical character); Jacobite Rebellion; Scotland

Stockley, Philippa.

A Factory of Cunning. **Harcourt, 2005. 335pp. Hardbound, 0151011729.** 📖
In a series of letters and journal entries, a penniless twenty-something French aristocrat calling herself "Mrs. Fox" details her adventures on the run. She and her loyal maid arrive in London from Holland in 1784, where she presided over a notorious whorehouse. She stays one step ahead of her pursuers, scheming to rise to the top of London society as its most exclusive madam and never hiding her true nature: arrogant, sexually avaricious, and greedy. As she squares off against her mortal enemy, the equally notorious English aristocrat Earl Much, she learns she has met her match. In this novel of revenge, dark wit, and even darker morals, little is as it seems.

Keywords: Diaries and journals; Epistolary novels; Madams

The Victorian Era

Queen Victoria gave her name to the years of her reign, the period between 1837 and 1901. These novels either evoke the propriety of the era or contrast it with the plight of the less fortunate. Not to be neglected in favor of England, both Scotland and Ireland figure in this section as well.

Graham, Janice.

The Tailor's Daughter. **St. Martin's Press, 2006. 392pp. Hardbound, 0312349130.**
Graham adds Gothic elements to her otherwise straightforwardly told tale of Victorian class conflicts. Veda Grenfell, attractive and intelligent daughter of a tailor on London's fashionable Savile Row in the 1860s, abandons all hopes of marriage when her mother dies in childbirth and typhoid fever leaves her deaf at the age of sixteen. She develops self-confidence as she proves herself a gifted seamstress in her father's workshop, and to her great surprise she begins to attract suitors—but they don't all have her best interests in mind.

Keywords: Deafness; Gothic novels; Seamstresses

Harris, Jane.

The Observations. **Viking, 2006. 405pp. Hardbound, 0670037737.** 📖
In 1863 Bessy Buckley, a saucy fifteen-year-old Irish girl, stumbles upon a crumbling mansion, Castle Haivers, while making her way from Edinburgh to escape a bad situation. Despite having no domestic skills, she finagles a position as scullery maid to the lady of the house, Arabella Reid, and forms an attachment to her. However, she's puzzled by Arabella's requests that she keep a detailed journal of her daily tasks, among other things. Arabella, as it happens, is writing a book

about servant behavior. When Bessy learns her missus's honest thoughts about her, and about the mysterious disappearance of her predecessor, she crafts a clever and hilarious plan for revenge. Bessy narrates her story in lively, wisecracking fashion, complete with local slang.

Keywords: Diaries and journals; Gothic novels; Maids; Scotland

McNeill, Elisabeth.

Storm series.

A two-book series about a true historical event—a violent storm that devastated the small Scottish fishing village of Eyemouth in 1881—and its aftermath.

Keywords: Families; Scotland; Storms; Widows

The Storm. Severn House, 2006. 236pp. Hardbound, 0727863770.

> Although the weather looks auspicious for a good day of fishing in the Scots border village of Eyemouth in October 1881, its residents could not be more wrong. Nearly 200 men lose their lives when the fleet is destroyed in a horrible and unexpected gale, leaving many of Eyemouth's women without husbands and many of its children fatherless. The women of the village band together to survive and provide for their future, but a corrupt and greedy bureaucrat overseeing charitable contributions stands between them and the money they need.

Turn of the Tide. Severn House, 2007. 167pp. Hardbound, 0727864564.

> Rosabelle Maltman, one of the women who lost their husbands in the gale of 1881, decides to move to London without her son to start a new life, while her sister-in-law, Jessie, finds her own ways of coping with tragedy. Rosabelle's mother-in-law, Effie, bears her grief while helping Eyemouth's villagers plan for the future.

Stace, Wesley.

Misfortune. **Little, Brown, 2006. 531pp. Hardbound, 0316830348.**

> In 1820 Lord Geoffroy Loveall, a wealthy and effeminate aristocrat, spies a baby boy lying in a garbage heap and brings him back to his estate. Needing an heir to inherit his vast fortune and distraught over his sister's recent death, Loveall declares that the baby is a girl and names him Rose. Rose grows up as a proper Victorian young lady, ignorant of her true gender, although certain anatomical differences between her and her friends puzzle her. When her father dies and greedy relatives descend to claim his fortune, Rose's true gender is discovered. This causes a horrible scandal, not least because Rose continues to dress in women's clothing. Stace (better known as musician John Wesley Harding) has written a humorous, gender-bending historical novel set in early nineteenth-century England.

Keywords: Disguise; Heirs and heiresses; Nobility; Transvestites

Twentieth Century

In comparison to literary historicals (Chapter 10) and sagas (Chapter 5) set in the British Isles during the twentieth century, the number of traditional historicals is fairly limited.

Delaney, Frank.

Tipperary. **Random House, 2007. 431pp. Hardbound, 9781400065233.** 📖

Charles O'Brien, an Anglo-Irish country doctor of forty years, meets and falls hopelessly in love with April Burke, a much younger Englishwoman whom he meets in Paris in 1900. She spurns his romantic overtures, but her tales of old, abandoned Tipperary Castle—an estate to which she holds a hereditary claim—convince him to make its restoration his life's purpose. Charles's unrequited passion for April becomes deeply intertwined with his love for the land and Ireland's emergence as a modern nation. His story unfolds by means of an oft-used literary device: Charles's decades-old, handwritten autobiography is found in an old chest many decades later, and the narrator adds commentary on Charles's story.

Keywords: Castles; Ireland

Graham, Laurie.

Gone with the Windsors. **HarperCollins, 2006. 403pp. Hardbound, 0060872713.** ✍

Maybell Brumby, an endearingly dimwitted and wealthy young widow from Baltimore, travels to London after her husband's death in 1931 and meets up with an old school chum, Bessie Wallis "Wally" Simpson, who has not yet obtained a divorce from her second husband. As Maybell tries to break into society, she helps Wally land the bachelor of the century: the Prince of Wales, the future King Edward VIII. Maybell tracks the progress of both women in her diary, leaving nothing out: the royal family's stuffiness, the prince's puppy dog-like devotion to Wallis, and the vacuous nature of the gossipy London social circle. A light, frothy, and chatty historical novel.

Keywords: Diaries and journals; Royalty; Simpson, Wallis (historical character); Socialites

Europe

The Middle Ages

This period roughly covers the years AD 476–1492, from the fall of the Western Roman Empire through Columbus's discovery of the New World. Topics include religious wars of medieval Europe, the origins of the Crusades, and, less commonly, the personal lives of European monarchs and other notables.

Anton, Maggie.

Rashi's Daughters Series. ✍ 📖 **YA**

The first novel in Anton's series about Jewish women's lives in medieval France was originally self-published, but after rave reviews continued to pour in, the series was picked up by a major publisher. Anton is a California-based scholar of medieval history and the Talmud.

Keywords: Fathers and daughters; France; Jews; Rashi (historical character); Scholars

Rashi's Daughters: Book 1, Joheved. **Banot, 2005. 369pp. Paper, 0976305054.**

In 1068, Salomon ben Isaac, the scholar one day to be known as Rashi, leaves his studies in Germany to take over his family's winemaking business in Troyes, France. He teaches his three daughters the Talmud, something unheard of at the time. His eldest child, Joheved, loves to learn but knows it would be dangerous for others to know of it. She even keeps her learning secret from her intended, Meir ben Samuel, which causes trouble in their relationship.

Keyword: Joheved, daughter of Rashi (historical character)

Rashi's Daughters: Book 2, Miriam. **Plume, 2007. 472pp. 9780452288638.**

It is AD 1078, and Rashi's middle daughter, Miriam, strives to begin her life again after her betrothed's death. She uses her medical knowledge, learned from her father, to become both midwife and *mohel* (one who performs circumcisions) for the city of Troyes. She also decides whether to allow a new, mysterious suitor into her well-ordered life.

Keyword: Midwives; Miriam, daughter of Rashi (historical character)

Ball, Margaret.

Duchess of Aquitaine. **St. Martin's, 2006. 377pp. Hardbound, 0312205333.** ✍ **YA**

Unlike most biographical fiction on Eleanor of Aquitaine, Henry II's strong-willed queen, Ball focuses on her early years, when as Aquitaine's ruling duchess she was the greatest unmarried heiress in France. With sparkling prose, Ball describes how fifteen-year-old Eleanor plans for her future after her father's tragic death in 1137. She approaches Louis, the French king's heir, and proposes that they wed. However, Louis turns out to be an overly pious and rather dull husband whom Eleanor overshadows in intelligence and ruling ability. While on crusade with Louis to the Holy Land, Eleanor grows convinced that her destiny lies elsewhere—and so it does.

Keywords: Crusades and Crusaders; Duchesses; Eleanor of Aquitaine, Queen of England (historical character); France; Queens

Bordihn, Maria R.

The Falcon of Palermo. **Grove, 2005. 422pp. Hardbound, 0871138808.** ✍

> Frederick II, Holy Roman Emperor in the early thirteenth century, is known as one of the most enlightened rulers of the Middle Ages. Orphaned as a boy, Frederick, the son of German emperor Henry Hohenstaufen, is plucked from the streets of Muslim-ruled Palermo and raised by the kindly Archbishop Berard, who becomes his lifelong mentor. Tutored by Berard in the arts and sciences, Frederick grows up having remarkable tolerance for religious diversity, and he hopes to make Sicily a kingdom that will rival Rome. As emperor, Frederick deals with many conflicts: the church, with whom he often disagrees; power struggles with his rival monarchs; and his numerous involvements with women, which get him into trouble. The short chapters make this novel more episodic and less of a biographical epic than it could have been, especially given Frederick's strong personality, but it's a fascinating story.
>
> **Keywords:** Emperors; Frederick II, Holy Roman Emperor (historical character); Germany

Cross, Donna Woolfolk.

Pope Joan. **Crown, 1996. 422pp. Hardbound, 0517593653.** ✍ 📖 **YA**

> In the ninth century, as legend has it, a young woman disguised as a man claimed St. Peter's throne and served as pope for two years. Cross's well-researched interpretation of the life of Pope Joan features a young woman, Joan of Ingelheim, who is taught Latin by her brother and takes his place after he is killed in a Viking raid. Disguised as the Christian scholar Brother John Anglicus, Joan heads to Rome, where she becomes a part of the papal inner circle. Her secret is revealed at a most inopportune moment.
>
> **Keywords:** Disguise; Joan, Pope (historical character); Popes, women; Rome

Falcones, Ildefonso.

Cathedral of the Sea. **Dutton, 2008. 611pp. Hardbound, 9780525950486.**

> Arnau Estanyol, a young man of the poorest classes, moves to Barcelona with his family and finds work as one of the "bastaix" who perform the back-breaking task of building the local cathedral. When the Inquisition gets wind of his relationship with a Jewish woman, they pursue him relentlessly. Based on the subject, jacket art, subject, and sheer length, this epic novel, centering on the construction of the Basilica de Santa Maria del Mar in fourteenth-century Barcelona, has obvious similarities to Ken Follett's *Pillars of the Earth*. However, due to its time period and place, its tone is far darker. Like its English counterpart, it was a best seller worldwide.
>
> **Keywords:** Cathedrals; Spain

Galland, Nicole.

Revenge of the Rose. **Morrow, 2006. 452pp. Hardbound, 006084177X.**

> In 1199 Jouglet, the official minstrel of Holy Roman Emperor Konrad (a fictional character based on the emperor in the *Roman de la Rose*), convinces his sovereign to summon Jouglet's good friend Willem of Dole, a poor nobleman, to court. Jouglet

has for years been secretly in love with Willem's beautiful sister, Lienor, who accompanies him. The chivalrous Willem comports himself well, winning many honors for himself, but gets caught up in the dangerous games of intrigue sweeping the realm. Set loosely in Burgundy and throughout Konrad's realm, which encompasses a good part of medieval Europe, this lively, witty tale may offend some historical purists with its fictional emperor (and other liberties), yet Galland has tried to capture the flavor of medieval European courtly life.

Keywords: Chivalry; Europe; Knights; Minstrels; Nobility

Holland, Cecelia.

Corban Loosestrife Series.

The adventures of Corban Loosestrife and his descendants in tenth-century Jorvik (modern York, England), Scandinavia, the Byzantine Empire, across the Atlantic, and back. Holland's latest effort is a projected five-volume series, all told in stark language. As the novels progress, the series grows more mystical in tone, edging closer to historical fantasy. The series will conclude with *The High City.*

Keywords: Byzantium; Iceland; Newfoundland; Russia; Scandinavia; Vikings; Witchcraft

The Soul Thief. Forge, 2002. 300pp. Hardbound, 0312848854.

The Witches' Kitchen. Forge, 2004. 384pp. Hardbound, 0312848862.

The Serpent Dreamer. Forge, 2005. 335pp. Hardbound, 0765305577.

It is 993 by the Christian calendar, although Corban—who escaped Vinland with his mad/bewitched sister Mav after his wife and family were killed—has relocated to precolonized North America and no longer concerns himself with European ways. In this land of warring, savage tribes, Corban undertakes a quest to save his world when his sister's daughter dreams of a serpent-worshipping army that will attack the Wolf clan, his new wife's people.

Varanger. Forge, 2008. 304pp. Hardbound, 9780765305589.

Corban's son and nephew, Conn and Raef, continue Holland's saga into the next generation. Fresh from their war band's defeat at Hjorunga Bay, they find themselves in Novgorod in the dead of winter. To escape their frozen surroundings, they pledge their service to a raider planning an attack on the Byzantine port city of Chersonese.

Janoda, Jeff.

Saga: A Novel of Medieval Iceland. **Academy Chicago, 2005. 359pp. Hardbound, 0897335325.**

Janoda situates his first novel in a unique setting: Iceland circa AD 935, a bleak, barren land whose inhabitants, new arrivals from Norway, are obsessed with hereditary blood feuds and land disputes. When Norse chieftain Arnkel Thorolfsson is denied his rightful inheritance by his wealthy and vindictive father, he initiates a feud with a rival landholder, Snorri

Thorgrimsson, which threatens to destroy everyone caught up in it. In his partial retelling of an ancient Icelandic tale first written down in the thirteenth century, the Eyrbyggja Saga, Janoda vividly evokes the harsh lifestyle and earthy pagan beliefs of his chosen place and period.

Keywords: Eyrbyggja Saga; Heirs and heiresses; Iceland; Neighbors; Paganism

Mailman, Erika.

The Witch's Trinity. **Crown, 2007. 288pp. Hardbound, 9780307351524.** 📖

In the year 1514, the people of Tierkinddorf, Germany, are slowly dying of famine. Desperate to find a scapegoat, Künne, an elderly herbalist, is promptly accused of cursing the townspeople with witchcraft. Güde, Künne's longtime friend, fears for her own life after experiencing perplexing visions. Then her mean-spirited daughter-in-law throws her out of the house in order to have one less mouth to feed. A suspenseful story about the dark side of the human spirit and the irrational power of mass hysteria.

Keywords: Elderly; Germany; Herbalists; Witchcraft

Monroe, Catherine.

Historical and contemporary novelist Paula Paul adopted the pseudonym "Catherine Monroe" for her novels about early female saints.

The Barefoot Girl: A Novel of St. Margaret, Patroness of the Abused. **NAL, 2006. 272pp. Paper, 0451217713.** ✍ **YA**

Margharita, a fifteen-year-old girl, lives with her poverty-stricken family on a farm in San Severino, Italy, in the year 1340. Her unwelcome marriage to Master Domenico Vasari, a gentleman, brings her into a life of wealth but also of cruelty, for he is physically abusive. To protect her unborn child as well as the starving people outside her castle, Margharita prays to the Virgin Mary, who encourages her to strengthen her spirit by helping the less fortunate.

Keywords: Italy; Saints; St. Margaret the Barefooted (historical character)

The King's Nun: A Novel of Emperor Charlemagne. **NAL, 2007. 267pp. Paper, 0451220196.** ✍ **YA**

In the eighth century, Amelia of Ardennes, a seventeen-year-old novice at Münster-Bilzen Abbey, becomes the personal advisor of the much older Charles, King of the Franks, as he was known before he became Charlemagne, Holy Roman Emperor. Charles falls in love with the beautiful and intelligent Amelia, and she with him, which makes her doubt her religious calling.

Keywords: Charlemagne (historical character); Emperors; Germany; Nuns; Saints; St. Amelia (historical character)

Undset, Sigrid.

Kristin Lavransdatter trilogy. ★

First published in 1920–1922 in Norwegian and translated several years later into English, Undset's trilogy spanning the life of one woman in fourteenth-century Norway helped garner the author the Nobel Prize for Literature in 1928. Her heroine, Kristin Lavransdatter, defies her family to marry Erlend Nikulausson, the man she loves beyond reason. She gives him seven sons and manages their estate of Husaby while he is off on political business, but their marriage is not always happy. Besides a love story, Undset's novels provide a detailed picture of life in medieval Norway. Tiina Nunnally's recent translation, less stiff and formal than the original translation, makes the novels accessible to a modern audience. Information on this edition is given below, though there are many others. Undset also completed a four-volume series, The Master of Hestviken, set in medieval Norway.

Keywords: Coming of age; Lavransdatter, Kristin; Married life; Norway

The Wreath. Penguin, 1997. 288pp. Paper, 0141180412. (Alternate title: *The Bridal Wreath.*)

The Wife. Penguin, 1999. 352pp. Paper, 0141181281. (Alternate title: *The Mistress of Husaby.*)

The Cross. Penguin, 2000. 430pp. Paper, 0141182350.

Vantrease, Brenda Rickman.

The Mercy Seller. **St. Martin's, 2007. 432pp. Hardbound, 9780312331931.**

Anna Bookman and her grandfather, Finn, make their living illuminating holy books in fifteenth-century Prague, but their work on heretical texts—English-language versions of the Bible—means danger for them both. Finn sends Anna to his homeland of England for her protection. While en route Anna sets up temporary shop as a bookseller in France, where she meets a Dominican priest, Friar Gabriel, in disguise as a merchant. Anna doesn't realize that Gabriel has been sent to build a case against the heretical Lollards, while Gabriel, very attracted to Anna, is tempted to break his religious vows. This sequel of sorts to *The Illuminator* (listed under "England: High Middle Ages") begins two generations later and continues Vantrease's themes of religious repression and change in medieval Europe.

Keywords: France; Illuminators; Lollards; Priests

The Renaissance and Reformation

The Renaissance in Europe saw many exciting developments in art, literature, and science. During the same time, the Protestant Reformation swept over Europe. These novels cover the period between Columbus' arrival in North America (1492) and the Treaty of Westphalia, which put an end to the political and religious rivalries of many European nations after the Thirty Years War (1618-1648).

Abrams, Douglas Carlton.

The Lost Diary of Don Juan. **Atria, 2007. 307pp. Hardbound, 1416532501.**
In Seville in 1593, at the height of Spain's Golden Age, Juan de Tenario—the man better known as Don Juan, notorious seducer of

women and the world's greatest lover—writes his diary to quash the rumors that have circulated about him for years. Abandoned at birth and raised in a convent, Juan believes he has a religious calling until he falls in love with one of the nuns. The influential Marquis de Mota recruits him as a spy, but when Juan offends a high-ranking nobleman, it sets the Inquisition on his trail. Though he knows and loves countless women, he is never truly content until he meets the one woman, Doña Ana, who makes him want to forsake all others. A swashbuckling, romantic novel about the meaning of love, passion, and fidelity.

Keywords: Inquisition; Lovers; Spain; Spies

Blixt, David.

The Master of Verona. **St. Martin's Press, 2007. 569pp. Hardbound, 9780312361440.** ✍ **YA**

In 1314 seventeen-year-old Pietro Alagheiri arrives in Verona, Italy, with his younger brother and his father, the poet Dante. At the court of "Cangrande" della Scala, Verona's charismatic ruler, Pietro forms a strong bond of friendship with two young men, Mariotto Montecchi and Antonio Capecelatro. They remain inseparable until Mariotto falls in love with Antonio's fiancée, the beautiful Gianozza. Meanwhile, Cangrande causes a scandal by bringing an infant boy to court, a child who may be his illegitimate son. This swashbuckling tale, which imagines the origins of the Montague–Capulet feud from *Romeo and Juliet*, plays out against a vivid, large-scale backdrop of early fourteenth-century Verona, whose off-again, on-again wars with Padua provide for many action-packed moments. Blixt, a Shakespearean actor and director, unites themes and characters from Shakespeare and Dante.

Keywords: Alighieri, Pietro (historical character); Della Scala, Francesco "Cangrande" (historical character); Italy; Shakespearean themes

Gortner, C. W.

The Last Queen. **Ballantine, 2008. 384pp. Hardbound, 9780345501844.** ✍ 📖

Juana, Queen of Castile, has been described down through history as mad, but Gortner makes the strong case that members of her own family had her imprisoned to consolidate their power and steal her rightful inheritance. The daughter of Queen Isabel and King Fernando, the royal couple who vanquished the Moors and united Spain through their marriage, Juana grows up knowing she will marry according to her parents' wishes. Their choice for her is Philip of Flanders, the Hapsburg heir. Juana and Philip's marriage is stormy and passionate, but her world comes tumbling down when only she, among all her siblings, is left to inherit Castile.

Keywords: Heirs and heiresses; Juana, Queen of Castile (historical character); Queens; Spain

Kalogridis, Jeanne.

In her fictional portraits of strong-willed women of the Italian Renaissance, Kalogridis emphasizes the glamour, sexual intrigue, opulence, and decadence of the era.

The Borgia Bride. **St. Martin's Griffin, 2005. 525pp. Paper, 0312341385.** ✍ 📖

Sancha of Aragon, illegitimate daughter of a man who was briefly king of Naples, is wed by her father to Jofre, the youngest son of Rodrigo Borgia, otherwise known as Pope Alexander. After their marriage the couple is sent to rule in Squillace, a remote seaside town, but when Sancha's lecherous father-in-law gets curious about his son's beautiful wife, they are recalled to Rome. There she meets and befriends Lucrezia, her sister-in-law, and falls helplessly in love with her husband's handsome brother, Cesare, with whom she has a steamy affair. Sancha learns of Cesare's cold, calculating, and murderous nature not long after and tries desperately to extricate herself from his web.

Keywords: Borgia, Cesare (historical character); Extramarital affairs; Italy; Nobility; Sancha of Aragon (historical character)

I, Mona Lisa. **St. Martin's Griffin, 2006. 515pp. Paper, 0312341393.** ✍ 📖

At the end of the fifteenth century, Lisa di Antonio Gherardini, better known as Madonna Lisa, the daughter of a rich wool merchant and his wife, falls in love with and marries Giuliano de' Medici, son of the powerful Medici family of Florence. But the history behind her story really began years earlier, in 1478, the year before her birth, when Giuliano's uncle was assassinated by conspirators—which led to the reign of terror of the fanatical, book-burning monk, Savonarola. When Lisa's young husband is killed and her father's life threatened, she must survive as best she can, untangling a web of lies, passion, and intrigue. Her path leads her to the door of painter Leonardo da Vinci.

Keywords: Artists' models; Gherardini, Lisa (historical character); Italy; Mona Lisa; Nobility

Learner, Tobsha.

The Witch of Cologne. **Forge, 2005. 476pp. Paper, 0765314304.**

In 1665 Deutz, Cologne's Jewish quarter, Ruth bas Elazar Saul practices midwifery against her father's wishes. But the Inquisition's interest in her has less to do with her occupation than her birth, for her late mother, a Sephardic Jew, had made a mortal foe of a Dominican friar whose advances she spurned. Imprisoned for witchcraft, Ruth attracts the interest of Detlef von Tennen, a Catholic cleric who secretly yearns to embrace the revolutionary beliefs creeping across Europe from Holland. When Detlef abandons his position to throw in his lot with Ruth, he takes on not just her enemies, but some new ones as well. Australian playwright/novelist Learner delivers an enthralling tale of religious repression, midwifery, and star-crossed romance in an unusual setting.

Keywords: Germany; Inquisition; Jews; Midwives

Martines, Lauro.

Loredana: A Venetian Tale. **Thomas Dunne, 2005. 261pp. Hardbound, 0312347510.**

This is essentially a tale of two cities, both of which can be found in the famed island city of Venice: the upper half, reserved for the nobility, and the lower, suitable only for peasants, pack horses, and other transport. In this epistolary novel set in 1520s Venice, two unlikely lovers—Loredana, a beautiful widow, and Orso, a Dominican friar and revolutionary—write their confessions. Their accounts are interspersed with comments assembled by an archivist seeking to re-create their story 200 years later. Loredana speaks of her horrible marriage to an abusive man, while Orso philosophizes about the possibility of a new, more enlightened Venice. Their affair causes an enormous scandal and brings the wrath of the city's governing body, the Council of Ten, down upon them.

Keywords: Epistolary novels; Italy; Lovers; Multi-period novels; Widows

Maxwell, Robin.

Mademoiselle Boleyn. NAL, 2007. 355pp. Paper, 9780451222091. ✍

Nine years old in the early sixteenth century, Anne Boleyn is sent along with her older sister, Mary, to the French court. She becomes a lady-in-waiting first to Mary Tudor, Henry VIII's younger sister and queen to Louis XII, and, after the death of King Louis, to the new queen, Claude. Surrounded by debauchery and compelled to serve as her ambitious father's spy, Anne sees Mary reluctantly agree to become King François's latest mistress and struggles to hold onto her own virtue.

Keywords: Anne Boleyn, Queen of England (historical character); Coming of age; France

Quinn, Thomas.

The Venetians Series.

A projected trilogy about the fierce rivalry between two families of Renaissance Venice. The third novel is expected to be called *Venice Stands Alone.*

Keywords: Italy; Nobility; Soranzo family; Ziani family

The Lion of St. Mark. St. Martin's, 2005. 326pp. Hardbound, 0312319088.

In 1452, when all of Italy gloried in the Renaissance, its famed island republic, Venice, risks invasion by the infidel Ottoman Turks, who seek some of *La Serenissima*'s bountiful wealth for themselves. Amid the chaos of potential war, two rival nobles and businessmen, naval captain Giovanni Soranzo and marine officer Antonio Ziani, unite to fight their mutual enemy while occasionally battling one another.

The Sword of Venice. St. Martin's, 2007. 304pp. Hardbound, 9780312319106.

The long-standing Soranzo–Ziani feud continues into the next generation, despite the best efforts of family patriarchs Giovanni and Antonio. As Venice faces a new threat from rival Italian city-states, Enrico Soranzo vies with Antonio Ziani's son Constantine for the hand of a senator's daughter, Maria Mocenigo.

Tiffany, Grace.

The Turquoise Ring. Berkley, 2005. 355pp. Hardbound, 0425202488. 📖

Renaissance-era Venice is the setting for Shakespeare professor Tiffany's retelling of *The Merchant of Venice* from the viewpoint of its female characters. Here Shylock the moneylender, whom the Bard had described as a greedy and vengeful Jew, has been transformed into Shiloh ben Gozán, a young merchant who in 1568 flees the Spanish Inquisition in Toledo for Venice, along with his baby daughter, Jessica, and a turquoise ring that belonged to his late wife, Leah. As Jessica grows into a rebellious young woman, rejecting her father's teachings, the turquoise ring changes hands many times, affecting all of the women who own it in succession. A daring, successful portrait of women's roles in an era of religious intolerance.

Keywords: Fathers and daughters; Italy; Jews; Rings; Shakespearean themes

Willocks, Tim.

The Religion. Farrar, Straus & Giroux, 2007. 618pp. Hardbound, 9780374248659.
Annotated in Chapter 8.

Early Modern and Twentieth-Century Europe

The years between the Treaty of Westphalia in 1648 and the early twentieth century saw a number of political and social changes sweep through Europe, including the French Revolution, the Napoleonic Wars, and the Russian Revolution.

Alexander, Robert.

Rasputin's Daughter. Viking, 2006. 304pp. Hardbound, 0670034681. ✍ 📖 **YA**
After the Russian Revolution forces the Romanovs from the imperial throne, a special commission investigates the true story of Grigori Rasputin, the monk said to have had unnatural influence over Empress Alexandra. To do this, they interrogate his daughter, Maria, who relates an engrossing, almost unbelievable story about the holy man's last week of life. As in his first biographical novel, *The Kitchen Boy*, Alexander adds suspense and a surprising, page-turning plot to his fictional narrative of imperial Russia. Russian history buffs will easily recognize the cover photo as that of the beautiful Grand Duchess Tatiana, rather than Maria Rasputin.

Keywords: Bolshevik Revolution; Monks; Rasputin, Gregory (historical character); Russia

The Romanov Bride. Viking, 2008. 306pp. Hardbound, 9780670018819. ✍ 📖 **YA**
The Romanov bride is beautiful Elizabeth (Ella) of Hesse, who takes the name Elisavyeta Fyodorovna when she marries Grand Duke Sergei of Russia in 1884. By 1905 her husband has become the most hated man in Moscow for his uncaring treatment of the lower classes and his recent expulsion of the Jews. Pavel, a young peasant from the country, throws in his lot with the violent revolutionary movement when his wife and unborn child are killed during a peaceful workers' demonstration in St. Petersburg. Alexander delineates Ella's and Pavel's stories simultaneously, as they both lead up to the Bolshevik Revolution of 1917–1918.

Keywords: Bolshevik Revolution; Elisaveta Feodorovna, Grand Duchess of Russia (historical character); Peasants; Russia

Chapman, Myriam.

Why She Married Him. **Other, 2005. 324pp. Hardbound, 1590511751.**

In June 1912 Nina Schavranski, an attractive Russian émigré who fled her homeland with her family on the eve of revolution, weds Abraham Podselver, a socialist fashion illustrator from Lithuania. A seamstress with a sensual nature and an unfulfilled longing for freedom, Nina has her reasons for marrying Abraham, and these are outlined to the reader as Chapman traces her and her family's experiences before and after being forced to leave Russia. Chapman based her novel about Jewish immigrant women's experiences in early twentieth-century Paris on her grandmother's unpublished memoirs.

Keywords: Bolshevik Revolution; France; Jews; Russia; Seamstresses

Charbonnier, Rita.

Mozart's Sister. **Crown, 2007. 322pp. Hardbound, 9780307346780.** ✍ 📖

Maria Anna Walburga Ignatia Mozart establishes herself as a musical child prodigy; at age five, she performs concerts for the public. She and her younger brother Wolfgang enjoy a close relationship as they grow up, but while their ambitious father strongly encourages his musical development, young Nannerl (as Wolfgang nicknames her) is left behind—despite her considerable and possibly greater talent. Though continually frustrated by the supporting role she's forced into, Nannerl takes refuge in her music and in her correspondence with a passionate admirer. Written in a modern, almost conversational style.

Keywords: Austria; Brothers and sisters; Composers; Mozart, Maria Anna (historical character); Musicians

Delors, Catherine.

Mistress of the Revolution. **Dutton, 2008. 451pp. Hardbound, 9780525950547.**

In the year 1815, from the safety of her London home, Gabrielle de Montserrat writes her memoirs of her life before, during, and immediately after the French Revolution as a means of catharsis. Raised far away from Paris, Gabrielle grows up as a member of the minor aristocracy, though she hopes she'll be allowed to marry her childhood love, Pierre-André Coffinhal. It is not to be. Delors traces Gabrielle's life through her marriage to a cruel older cousin, her time at the luxurious court of Louis XVI and Marie Antoinette, and the years leading up to the Terror.

Keywords: France; French Revolution; Nobility

Donn, Linda.

The Little Balloonist. **Dutton, 2006. 206pp. Hardbound, 0525949283.** ✍ **YA**

In this historical fable set in postrevolutionary France, sixteen-year-old Sophie Armont had hoped to wed her childhood sweetheart, André Giroux, but instead agrees to marry a wealthy, renowned balloonist, Jean-Pierre Blanchard, with whom she discovers the joys of flight. Her aeronautical adventures, which bring her considerable fame, attract the attention of Napoleon Bonaparte. After Blanchard's death, André returns to court the woman he never stopped loving, but first she must fight off Napoleon's advances. Donn tells the story of one of the first female aeronauts in spare, lyrical style, alongside drawings and other art of the period.

Keywords: Balloonists; Blanchard, Sophie (historical character); France

Erickson, Carolly.

The Hidden Diary of Marie Antoinette. St. Martin's Press, 2006. 341pp. Hardbound, 0312337086. ✍ **YA**

Imprisoned in the Conciergerie on the eve before her scheduled execution by guillotine, Marie Antoinette concludes writing her life story. Her journal begins with her childhood in Vienna, where as the daughter of Empress Maria Theresa, she knew every privilege. Married off to the stodgy heir to France, the dauphin Louis, for political reasons at age fourteen, Marie Antoinette tries to forget her husband's neglect by throwing extravagant parties; her passionate affair with Swedish count/diplomat Axel Fersen eases her loneliness. Yet despite her growing distance from the feelings of the French people, Marie Antoinette remains a kind, generous person, a loving mother, and a courageous woman who meets her fate bravely.

Keywords: Marie Antoinette, Queen of France (historical character); Diaries and journals; France; Queens

The Secret Life of Josephine. St. Martin's Press, 2007. 328pp. Hardbound, 031236735X. ✍

Josephine Bonaparte, "Napoleon's bird of paradise" per the novel's subtitle, is the subject of Erickson's latest mix of historical fact and whimsy. In her own words, Josephine relates the dramatic story of her childhood in Martinique as a Creole beauty, her time as mistress to powerful revolutionaries in France, and her marriage first to an older nobleman and secondly to Napoleon, who eventually divorces her when she cannot bear him a son. Erickson's author's note acknowledges the many liberties she took with historical fact, including her decision to give her heroine a devoted lover named Donovan. She refers readers to her nonfiction biography, *Josephine: A Life of the Empress*, for those who want the real story without fictional embellishments.

Keywords: Empresses; France; Josephine, Empress of France (historical character); Martinique

Finerman, Debra.

Mademoiselle Victorine. Three Rivers, 2007. 293pp. Paper, 9780307352835. 📖

In 1868 Victorine Laurent, an attractive young woman with few prospects, first meets noted Impressionist painter Edgar Degas at the Paris Opera house, where she is a member of the chorus. Degas introduces her to avant-garde painter Édouard Manet, and she becomes his model and muse, posing for a nude painting that scandalizes the entire city. Her notoriety leads to exclusive invitations to soirees and attracts numerous other men, including the powerful Duke de Lyon, who doesn't approve of her continued association with Manet. Finerman based her first novel on two equally scandalous women of belle époque Paris, courtesan Countess

Virginia de Castiglione and Victorine Meurent, the real-life model for Manet's *Olympia*.

Keywords: Artists; Artists' models; Courtesans; France; Manet, Édouard (historical character); Mistresses

Gulland, Sandra.

Mistress of the Sun. **Touchstone, 2008. 382pp. Hardbound, 9780743298872.** ✍ 📖
Gulland presents Louise de la Vallière as the first and true love of the Sun King. A shy, gentle woman with a talent for taming horses, against all likelihood she becomes the mistress of the most flamboyant, public, important man in France. The story of "Petite," as she's called from a young age, begins in 1650 with her childhood and continues through her entrance into a convent toward the end of her life. Although Louise bears Louis XIV four children, her spirit constantly struggles between her love for him and her desire for a peaceful life away from the hubbub of court.

Keywords: France; La Vallière, Louise de (historical character); Louis XIV, King of France (historical character); Mistresses; Royalty

Michael, Prince of Greece.

The White Night of St. Petersburg. **Atlantic Monthly, 2004. 335pp. Hardbound, 0871139227.** ✍
In 1998, at the ceremony for the reburial of Tsar Nicholas II and his family, Prince Michael (the author) meets a distant cousin who tells him about her grandfather, Grand Duke Nicholas, who was erased from family records. More arrogant than intelligent, Nicholas follows the pattern of all male Romanovs by taking a mistress, but his choice of Hattie Blackford, an American courtesan, scandalizes his family. They flit from city to city, scattering money as they go, until his liberal politics and penchant for women catch him in a trap. The author, a relative of the Romanovs, presents a glittering if somewhat flat portrait of wealth, privilege, passion, and tragedy set against the backdrop of the nineteenth-century European royal courts.

Keywords: Mistresses; Nicholas, Grand Duke of Russia (historical character); Royalty; Russia

Phillips, Christi.

The Rossetti Letter. **Pocket, 2007. 400pp. Hardbound, 9781416527374.**
In this multi-period novel, set partly in seventeenth-century Venice and partly in the present, an American history graduate student crosses paths with a noted British historian on the subject of (fictional) Venetian courtesan Alessandra Rossetti. Claire Donovan's PhD dissertation and future career depend on her assertion that a letter written by Alessandra in 1618 helped save Venice from overthrow by the Spanish government, but Andrew Kent, a professor at Cambridge, believes Alessandra was working secretly for Spain. In a story that parallels the contemporary literary mystery, Phillips provides vivid historical detail on Alessandra Rossetti's chosen life as a courtesan, which she undertook to pull her family out of poverty.

Keywords: Courtesans; Graduate students; Italy; Multi-period novels; Professors

Prince, Peter.

Adam Runaway. Simon & Schuster, 2005. 438pp. Hardbound, 0743271017.

When his family loses their fortune in the South Sea Bubble, twenty-one-year-old Adam Hanaway leaves England for the thriving, cosmopolitan city of Lisbon to serve as apprentice to his uncle Felix, a successful merchant. Unfortunately Adam's attempt to make his way in the world is thwarted by Felix's corrupt clerk and his own personal weaknesses: naïveté, inappropriate social behavior, and cowardice. He has a habit of running away from dangerous situations he creates. While Adam spends time wooing (and bedding) numerous women, his family waits in vain for him to help restore their fortune, and privileged Englishman that he is, he doesn't take the threat of the Inquisition (Portugal remains a very Catholic country) seriously enough.

Keywords: Coming of age; Inquisition; Merchants; Picaresque novels; Portugal

Wallace, Randall.

Love and Honor. Simon & Schuster, 2004. 399pp. Hardbound, 074326519X.

Wallace, screenwriter for the film *Braveheart* (and author of the associated novel), writes a swashbuckling tale about a secret mission undertaken by Virginia cavalryman Kieran Selkirk on the eve of the American Revolution. During a clandestine meeting, Ben Franklin reveals to Selkirk that Russia has agreed to supply 20,000 troops to aid Britain in suppressing the colonists' rebellion. Selkirk travels to Russia disguised as a British mercenary in the hopes of gaining Catherine the Great's favor. En route to St. Petersburg, Selkirk encounters the harsh Russian winter, ferocious wolves, and fearsome Cossacks, not to mention British intrigue aplenty. When he and Catherine finally meet, she sees much in the handsome, honorable American to attract her, and they begin a passionate romance.

Keywords: Catherine II, "the Great," Empress of Russia (historical character); Empresses; Revolutions and revolutionaries; Russia

World Wars I and II

Jacobson, Douglas W.

Night of Flames. McBooks, 2007. 368pp. Hardbound, 9781590131367.

Anna Kopernik, a university professor in Krakow, and her cavalry officer husband, Jan, are separated when the Germans invade Poland in 1939. Over the next five years they each forge separate paths of resistance to the Nazi terror, hoping one day to be reunited. Anna flees to Belgium, where she joins the resistance movement, while Jan works undercover in Poland for the British intelligence service.

Keywords: Belgium—World War II; Poland—World War II; Spies

Lucas, Michele.

A High and Hidden Place. HarperSanFrancisco, 2005. 288pp. Hardbound, 0060740566. 📖

Christine Lenoir, a French journalist on assignment in the United States in 1964, had always believed that her parents died of influenza, leaving her to be raised by nuns. Violent scenes of JFK's assassination on television unlock long-suppressed memories from her childhood, forcing her to remember that she was once Christine of Oradour, survivor of a horrific Nazi massacre of French civilians on June 10, 1944. Lucas intersperses scenes of the modern (1960s-era) Christine with images of the sleepy town of Oradour-sur-Glane, in southwestern France—before, during, and after the massacre in which 642 innocent people died.

Keywords: France—World War II; Multi-period novels; Nazis; Oradour, Massacre at

Russell, Mary Doria.

A Thread of Grace. Doubleday, 2005. 430pp. Hardbound, 0375501843. 📖

In 1943 fourteen-year-old Claudette Blum and her father, Jews from Germany, join thousands of other refugees making their way over the treacherous Alps, where they are welcomed by soldiers to Porto Sant'Andrea, a small village on the northwest coast of Italy. Although they believe they have finally reached safety, Mussolini has just come to power, and the Blums learn they have left one very dangerous situation for another. Russell intertwines many threads: the Blums' struggle to survive, for one, but also the stories of many other characters, all of whom play a role in this tragic tale. Russell, previously better known for her speculative fiction on theological themes (*The Sparrow* and *Children of God*), has written a powerful novel about a little-known event: Italian citizens' underground actions to save the lives of 43,000 Jews during World War II.

Keywords: Italy—World War II; Jews

Shaara, Jeff.

Shaara, best known for his masterful, humanized portraits of the Civil War and its major players, continues his novels of barely fictionalized history; he uses material from real conversations and letters whenever possible. Shaara lets readers experience front-line combat from the points of view of ordinary soldiers in addition to their leaders.

To the Last Man. Ballantine, 2005. 672pp. Hardbound, 0345461347. ✍

Shaara turns his hand to the American experience during World War I, one of the world's most devastating yet most forgotten wars, showing how the United States helped put an end to the fighting overseas. General John J. "Black Jack" Pershing, commander of the American forces in France in 1917–1918, must contend simultaneously with Washington bureaucrats, French and British internal politics, and, of course, the Germans. On the opposite side, flying ace Manfred von Richtofen, better known as the Red Baron, is portrayed honorably and sympathetically. A young Marine experiencing the horrors of trench warfare in France's Argonne Forest and an American flying ace face off against von Richtofen and round out the list of protagonists.

Keywords: France—World War I; Generals; Pershing, John Joseph (historical character); Pilots; von Richtofen, Manfred (historical character)

World War II Trilogy. ✍

A proposed trilogy that will follow a diverse set of characters through the European theater in World War II.

Keywords: Africa, North—World War II; England—World War II; D-Day; Eisenhower, Dwight (historical character); Generals; Patton, George (historical character); Rommel, Erwin (historical character); Tobruk, Battle of

The Rising Tide. Ballantine, 2006. 536pp. Hardbound, 034546141X.

It is May 1942, and the Germans are winning the war in Western Europe against the British. However, Nazi field marshal Erwin Rommel knows the campaign in North Africa will be hard to fight once American forces enter the picture. As things are, he is already dealing with poor supply lines and incompetent Italian leadership. Shaara lets readers see the action of desert warfare through the viewpoints of a few select characters, in particular American generals George Patton and Dwight Eisenhower, "Desert Fox" Erwin Rommel himself, and two lower-ranking American soldiers. The novel concludes just as the Allies begin plotting the Normandy invasion, Operation Overlord.

The Steel Wave. Ballantine, 2008. 493pp. Hardbound, 9780345461421.

Both sides bolster their armies as D-Day approaches, and Shaara takes readers into the minds of many of the men involved. While Dwight Eisenhower works out the details of the Normandy invasion, George Patton frets at his relative inaction, and Erwin Rommel, on the German side, builds the German defenses and deals with Hitler's megalomania. Readers also get to see action from the viewpoints of "ordinary" soldiers such as Sergeant Jesse Adams, an American paratrooper with the 82nd Airborne who drops behind enemy lines.

Young, Sara.

My Enemy's Cradle. **Harcourt, 2008. 365pp. Hardbound, 9780151015375.** 📖

The year is 1941. Life becomes dangerous for Cyrla, a Polish Jew sent to live with her aunt's family in Holland, when the Nazis begin restricting Jews' behavior. Then her cousin, Anneke, reveals that she's pregnant with the child of her lover, a German soldier who's nowhere to be found. In an odd twist of fate, to preserve her safety Cyrla agrees to take Anneke's place in the Lebensborn—a maternity home that, in effect, serves as a breeding institution for German children.

Keywords: Germany—World War II; Jews; Nazis; Netherlands—World War II; Pregnancy

The United States

Pre-Contact Native Americans

These novels re-create the lives of Native Americans before the arrival of white settlers. Most are tales of survival that recount early societies' relations with each other and with the natural world. Even though some take place around AD 1000 or later, they are called "prehistoric" because they are set prior to recorded history. Novels set in prehistoric Europe, Asia, and Africa are annotated at the beginning of this chapter.

Gear, Kathleen O'Neal.

In Me Series.

A trilogy of intrigue, passion, murder, and witchcraft (not to mention erotic love scenes) featuring High Chieftess Sora, the strong-minded leader of the Black Falcon Nation, living in what today is Florida. Set in the fifteenth century AD.

Keywords: Florida; Murderers; Sora; Witchcraft

It Sleeps in Me. Forge, 2005. 254pp. Paper, 0765314150.

High Chieftess Sora learns of the death of her jealous ex-husband, Flint, from Skinner, his good friend, who tells her that Flint's shadow soul now dwells within him. When an enemy nation asks for help and arms from the Black Falcon Nation, and members of her own clan indicate their support, Sora grows suspicious. Captivated by Skinner, whose behavior strongly resembles Flint's, Sora realizes that she no longer knows who she can trust.

It Wakes in Me. Forge, 2006. 268pp. Paper, 0765314827.

Sora has been accused of multiple murders, including that of her friend Skinner, war chief of the Loon People. The problem is that she's unable to defend herself because of blackouts she has suffered since childhood—she can't remember anything about the times the murders were committed. Is it possible she committed them while possessed? Kidnapped by the Loon people, Sora undergoes healing treatment (in a series of erotic ceremonies meant to join her three souls) at the hands of Strongheart, their sympathetic priest.

It Dreams in Me. Forge, 2007. 256pp. Paper, 9780765311672.

The rivalry between Sora's husband Flint and Strongheart, the healer, comes to a head as both seek to heal Sora's wounded soul.

Gear, W. Michael, and Kathleen O'Neal Gear.

The First North Americans. ★ YA

This lengthy series takes readers on visits to various locations throughout prehistoric North America. The Gears, a husband-wife writing team, are archaeologists by profession, and their novels are based on thorough anthropological and ethnographic research. Besides their fascinating story lines, which include a cast of characters appropriate to their time, books in this series include elements of romance and mystery. They can be read in any order.

People of the Wolf. Tor, 1990. 435pp. Paper, 0812507371.

People of the Fire. Tor, 1991. 467pp. Paper, 0812507398.

People of the Earth. Tor, 1992. 587pp. Paper, 0812507428.

People of the River. Tor, 1992. 400pp. Paper, 0312852355.

People of the Sea. Forge, 1993. 425pp. Paper, 0312931220.

People of the Lakes. Forge, 1994. 608pp. Paper, 0312857225.

People of the Lightning. Tor, 1995. 414pp. Hardbound, 0312858523.

People of the Silence. Forge, 1996. 493pp. Hardbound, 0312858531.

People of the Mist. Forge, 1997. 432pp. Hardbound, 031285854X.

People of the Masks. Forge, 1998. 416pp. Hardbound, 0312858574.

People of the Owl. Forge, 2003. 563pp. Hardbound, 0312877412.

🏵 *People of the Raven.* Forge, 2004. 494pp. Hardbound, 076530855X. Spur Award.

People of the Moon. Forge, 2005. 528pp. Hardbound, 0765308568.

In the mid-twelfth century, the Chaco Anasazi live in what is now northwestern New Mexico. Renowned for their skills in construction and road building, they have arrogantly ruled over the First Moon people for hundreds of years. Cold Bringing Woman, the goddess of winter, decides she has had enough of the Chacoans' haughtiness and decides to send Ripple, a young warrior from First Moon Valley, on a mission to bring them down. In retaliation, Leather Hand, the Chacoans' war chief, starts a campaign of terror against Ripple's people.

Keywords: Anasazi; New Mexico

People of the Nightland. Forge, 2007. 576pp. Hardbound, 9780765314406.

In the Great Lakes region circa 13,000 BC, the region's large glaciers are beginning to melt, portending a massive flood. Two warring tribes—the cave-dwelling Nightland people and the lodge-dwelling Sunpath and Lame Bull people—decide to heed the warnings sent by the god Raven Hunter, who sends them a guide, an orphan boy named Silvertip, to lead them to safety through a hole in the ice. The Gears combine their knowledge of anthropology and geology into an imaginative story about an ancient period of global warming and the original formation of the Great Lakes.

Keywords: Great Lakes; Michigan

People of the Weeping Eye. Forge, 2008. 432pp. Hardbound, 9780765314383.

A wanderer named Trader comes upon an old man, Seeker, traveling with a young woman while en route to Split Sky City—a land torn apart by war. All face their respective pasts as an epic battle plays out around them. This is the first volume of a connected set of two dealing with the prehistoric Mississippian cultures. Both are set in and around Alabama's Moundville historic site in the thirteenth century. *People of the Thunder* will conclude the story.

Keywords: Alabama; Native Americans

Wood, Barbara.

Daughter of the Sun. St. Martin's Griffin, 2007. 453pp. Paper, 9780312363680. 📖

Hoshi'tiwa, a young woman of the People of the Sun, lives in what Westerners would one day call New Mexico in the year AD 1150. Stolen away from her home and her handsome fiancé by an army of Toltec warriors, she is brought to their homeland, Center Place. At the court of Jakál, the Dark Lord, she becomes an accomplished potter who, if prophecy holds true, has the power to call the rain; she also becomes romantically involved with Jakál himself, which arouses the jealousy of other women at court. Wood creatively imagines the reasons why the Anasazi abandoned the Chaco Canyon region centuries ago. *Woman of a Thousand Secrets*, annotated later in this chapter, is a loose sequel.

Keywords: Anasazi; New Mexico

Colonial America

Before the United States became a country, it was home to a variety of European settlements. These novels recount early settlers' experiences in the American colonies and their encounters with America's Native American inhabitants.

Cline, Edward.

Sparrowhawk Series.

In this series, Cline fictionalizes the philosophical and political origins of the American Revolution, explaining how it began as a revolution of ideas long before any actual battles took place. It is only natural that the story begins in Britain, with the protagonists meeting up and traveling across the Atlantic later on. Jack Frake, a commoner, grows up in a village in 1740s Cornwall and is sentenced to servitude in the American colonies after being caught smuggling. Hugh Kenrick, born into the nobility, angers his father and uncle when he joins a secret society of free-thinkers, and his family sends him to Philadelphia for his own good. Cline acknowledges the influence of Ayn Rand's novels in his work. Elements of Rand's Objectivist philosophy—of man as a heroic being who values reason above all—are evident. *The Sparrowhawk Companion* (MacAdam/Cage, 2007) serves as a guide to the series.

Keywords: Coming of age; England; Frake, Jack; Friendship; Kenrick, Hugh; Ships; Stamp Act; Virginia

Sparrowhawk: Book One, Jack Frake. MacAdam/Cage, 2001. 360pp. Hardbound, 1931561001.

Sparrowhawk: Book Two, Hugh Kenrick. MacAdam/Cage, 2002. 425pp. Hardbound, 1931561206.

Sparrowhawk: Book Three, Caxton. MacAdam/Cage, 2003. 233pp. Hardbound, 1931561532.

Sparrowhawk: Book Four, Empire. MacAdam/Cage, 2004. Hardbound, 1931561877.

Both Jack Frake and Hugh Kenrick are strongly opposed to the Stamp Act of 1765, in which the British attempt to levy high taxes on the American colonists. As a burgess in the Virginia legislature, Hugh is in a position to do something about it. He uses his ties to friends back in Britain to provide him with advance information that may help the colonists repeal it.

Sparrowhawk: Book Five, Revolution. MacAdam/Cage, 2005. 320pp. Hardbound, 1596921544.

This fifth volume picks up just after *Empire* ended, in June 1765, with fierce debates in the colonies following the repeal of the Stamp Act. Both Jack Frake and Hugh Kenrick attempt to work within the political system to get Parliament to relax its hold on the colonies, but their approaches are becoming increasingly different. Jack is slowly coming to the conclusion that revolution is the only answer to their problems with Britain, while Hugh still believes that a less drastic solution is possible.

Sparrowhawk: Book Six, War. MacAdam/Cage, 2006. 379pp. Hardbound, 1596921986.

It is now 1774, and Jack Frake, continuing to believe war is inevitable, begins stockpiling arms and helps to train a militia. Hugh, still hoping to avoid war, travels to England to meet with Parliament but returns home dejected, for Parliamentarians are holding fast to their position. The colonists are forced to take sides, which leads, ultimately, to the American Revolution. Cline follows the action up until late 1775, though an epilogue ties up loose ends, showing what happened to the characters at the end of the war.

Deane, Pamala-Suzette.

My Story Being This: Details of the Life of Mary Williams Magahee, Lady of Colour. Hardscrabble, 2004. 252pp. Hardbound, 1584653108. ✍

Mary Williams Magahee, a middle-aged African American woman in colonial Rhode Island, records her daily tasks, thoughts, and dreams in her "writing book" beginning in 1771. A gardener, naturopath, and member in good standing of her community, Mary also takes time to record her thoughts on the coming American Revolution and her personal history, including her harrowing road to freedom. An enlightening portrait of a "free woman of color" and day-to-day life in colonial America, written with eighteenth-century prose patterns and spellings.

Keywords: African Americans; Diaries and journals; Magahee, Mary Williams (historical character); Rhode Island

Gaspar de Alba, Alicia.

Calligraphy of the Witch. St. Martin's, 2007. 384pp. Hardbound, 9780312366414.

Concepción Benavidez, the indentured servant who was the assistant to Mexican nun Sor Juana de la Cruz in the author's previous novel, *Sor Juana's Second Dream*, is captured by pirates and forcibly transported to New England in 1683. Sold as a slave to a Boston merchant, Concepción is given a new name, Thankful Seagraves, and discovers that she's pregnant—the result of rape by the pirate ship's captain. As witch hysteria grips Salem Village nine years later, Concepción, a continual outsider in the heavily Puritan colony, finds herself accused of witchcraft by her own daughter.

Keywords: Massachusetts; Mothers and daughters; Puritans; Salem witch trials; Witchcraft

Gunning, Sally.

Bound. Morrow, 2008. 307pp. Hardbound, 9780061240256. 📖

Gunning's second historical explores young Alice Cole's difficult coming of age, a process that teaches her much about freedom and trust. Sold into indentured servitude by her widowed father when they arrive in Massachusetts in 1756, Alice spends her childhood bound to the Morton family; she follows daughter Nabby to a new household when she marries. Unfortunately Alice's beauty attracts the attention of Nabby's husband, which prompts her to escape. A widow from Satucket, Lyddie Berry (first seen in *The Widow's War*) takes her in, but Alice's past life quickly catches up with her.

Keywords: Coming of age; Indentured servants; Massachusetts

The Widow's War. Morrow, 2006. 303pp. Hardbound, 0060791578. 📖

When Lyddie Berry's husband dies in a whaling accident off Cape Cod in 1761, she moves in with her daughter's family, as expected. She soon finds life intolerable, for her hostile son-in-law wants complete control of her money and property. In the hopes of regaining autonomy, she finds herself breaking society's rules, one after another, including moving back into her old home—at least the one-third of it she's now entitled to use. Living as an outcast from friends and family, Lyddie's self-confidence grows, and she discovers two surprising allies: her husband's former lawyer and an Indian neighbor, both of whom have romantic leanings toward her.

Keywords: Massachusetts; Puritans; Widows

Homsher, Deborah.

The Rising Shore: Roanoke. Blue Hull Press, 2007. 273pp. Paper, 9780979051609. ✍

Homsher dramatizes the story of the "lost colony" of Roanoke through the eyes of two historical women who belonged to the original group of settlers in the 1580s: Elenor White Dare, daughter of colony governor John White and mother of Virginia Dare, and Margaret Lawrence, her servant. Both believe that their dreams of exploration and independence will be fulfilled in the New World. When they arrive, they discover instead a land of untamed wilderness and a claustrophobic society that doesn't willingly grant them the freedom they craved.

Keywords: Dare, Eleanor (historical character); Frontier and pioneer life; Lawrence, Margaret (historical character); Roanoke Colony; Virginia

Kent, Kathleen.

The Heretic's Daughter. Little, Brown, 2008. 332pp. Hardbound, 9780316024488. ✍ 📖

Sarah Carrier tells of her complex relationship with her mother, Martha, who was one of the first women hanged as a witch in Salem Village, Massachusetts, in 1692. Kent's novel takes the form of the elderly Sarah's written account of that dark time in history. She sets down her words to tell her granddaughter the whole truth about Martha's brave decision, which ultimately cost her mother her life. Kent is a tenth-generation descendant of Martha Carrier, and she writes with heart and sensitivity.

Keywords: Carrier, Martha (historical character); Carrier, Sarah (historical character); Massachusetts; Salem witch trials; Witchcraft

Minkoff, George Robert.

In the Land of Whispers Series. ✍

A proposed trilogy written as the fictionalized diaries of Captain John Smith, founder of the Jamestown Colony and great admirer of noted Elizabethan adventurer Sir Francis Drake. Minkoff aims for authenticity with his ornate language and descriptions.

Keywords: Diaries and journals; Drake, Francis (historical character); Explorers; Jamestown Colony; Smith, Captain John (historical character); Powhatan Indians; Virginia

The Weight of Smoke. McPherson, 2006. 392pp. Hardbound, 0929701801.

> In May 1607 John Smith lands on the Virginia coast with a motley group of English aristocrats and curiosity seekers, with the goal of establishing an English colony in the New World. His men, not accustomed to the backbreaking labor such a venture demands, look to Smith as their leader, a role he is very happy to assume. Smith vividly describes the hardships they experience—starvation, war with the land's natives, not to mention greed among his own men—as well as the unspoiled beauty of the land and animals they encounter. Interspersed with Smith's narration is that of Jonas Profit, an old sea-dog who had fought alongside Sir Francis Drake against the Spanish Armada.

The Dragons of the Storm. McPherson, 2007. 349pp. Hardbound, 9780929701813.

> John Smith's and Sir Francis Drake's separate but related tales of exploration and discovery continue in this middle volume. Smith tries to get a colony started at Jamestown, but his fellow would-be settlers are restless and argumentative, and he runs into trouble with the Powhatan tribe. While Smith lies ill after being wounded by a stingray, Jonas Profit continues his tale of circumnavigating the globe with Drake and serving alongside him during the Spanish Armada's defeat.

Morrow, James.

The Last Witchfinder. Morrow, 2006. 576pp. Hardbound, 9780060821791. **YA**

> In 1688 England Jennet Stearne, daughter of self-proclaimed "master pricker" (witch hunter) Walter Stearne, takes it upon herself to dissolve the 1604 Parliamentary Witchcraft Act after her father uses it as a basis for condemning her beloved Aunt Isobel, a dabbler in natural science and philosophy, to burn at the stake. Jennet's quest takes her to Salem Village during the famed witch trials, to an Algonquian village, and later to colonial Philadelphia, where she strikes up a professional and romantic partnership with a youthful Ben Franklin. Newton's *Principia Mathematica* (the renowned scientific treatise, which is given a voice here by Morrow) nar-

rates Jennet's story from its unique viewpoint, with lively and often sarcastic asides.

Keywords: England; Franklin, Benjamin (historical character); Massachusetts; Pennsylvania; Picaresque novels; Salem witch trials; Witchcraft

The American Revolution

Novels set between 1775 and 1783, when Americans fought for independence from Great Britain, are action-oriented tales of war and patriotism.

Boggs, Johnny D.

Ghost Legion. **Five Star, 2005. 238pp. Hardbound, 1594141576.**

Though subtitled "a frontier story," *Ghost Legion* takes place not in one of Boggs's traditional Western settings but in late eighteenth-century South Carolina, part of America's southern frontier. Stuart Brodie, a free man of color, joins the Loyalists after his brother's death at the hands of colonial Patriots; Martha McKidrict joins the rebels' "Ghost Legion," striking secretly from the Carolina hills, to evade her abusive husband. Their paths converge at the Battle of Kings Mountain in 1780, an event that proves a turning point in the Revolutionary War.

Keywords: African Americans; Kings Mountain, Battle of; South Carolina

Drinkard, Michael.

Rebels, Turn Out Your Dead. **Harcourt, 2006. 272pp. Hardbound, 0151011192.**

For the members of one family, the American Revolution brings different types of freedom in unexpected ways. Salt, a New York hemp farmer who regularly smokes his own crop, takes off and gets captured by the British when his hotheaded teenaged son James shoots a British officer. Salt's wife Molly, meanwhile, holds down the fort and attracts amorous advances from a general whose troops occupy her father's farm. A fast-paced, rollicking read told in a deceptively light, contemporary style.

Keywords: Families; Farmers; New York

Lake, Deryn.

The Governor's Ladies. **Allison & Busby, 2005. 383pp. Hardbound, 0749082208.** ✍

Thomas Gage, the British governor of Massachusetts in 1775, is torn between his loyalty to his homeland and his love for his American wife, the former Margaret Kemble. Amid the turmoil of the approaching revolution, Thomas finds solace in teaching his slave girl, Sara, to read and write, and the two form an unusual attachment. Lake, the British author of many Georgian-era mysteries, also wrote many historical novels (some of which were biographical) under her real name, Dinah Lampitt.

Keywords: Gage, Thomas (historical character); Governors; Massachusetts; Slaves and slavery

Robson, Lucia St. Clair.

Shadow Patriots. **Forge, 2005. 336pp. Hardbound, 076530550X.**

In 1776 Kate Darby, a young Quaker woman from Philadelphia, is drawn into the American Revolution when her family takes in Major John André, a member of the British army occupying her town. Although she feels very attracted to him, Kate can't help but follow the patriotic lead of her brother, a member of Washington's forces, by becoming a spy for the Patriots. Robson based her novel on the story of a mysterious American female spy known only as "355" in the historical record.

Keywords: Quakers; Pennsylvania; Spies, women

The Early United States

Novels set between the end of the Revolution (1783) and the beginning of the Civil War (1861) tell of the political growth and expansion of the United States. Common themes include fictional biographies of America's presidents, relationships with Native American tribes, and the growth of slavery in the South.

Brown, Amy Belding.

Mr. Emerson's Wife. **St. Martin's Press, 2005. 325pp. Hardbound, 0312336373.**

In 1835 Lidian Jackson meets noted philosopher Ralph Waldo Emerson at a reception in his honor in her hometown of Plymouth, Massachusetts. She is impressed by his brilliance, and he by her independence and strength of character. In her thirties and believing that she would never marry, Lidian accepts Emerson's proposal, fully expecting a partnership of equals, but she quickly learns he's still in love with his late wife, Ellen. Lidian makes the best of her situation, bearing and raising his children, but remains lonely until she becomes friends with his protégé, Henry David Thoreau. The two become close, and she actively fights her attraction to him. A thoughtful novel about marriage and women's roles in early America.

Keywords: Emerson, Lidian (historical character); Married life; Massachusetts; Philosophers; Thoreau, Henry David (historical character)

Chiaverini, Jennifer.

The Sugar Camp Quilt. **Simon & Schuster, 2005. 320pp. Hardbound, 0743260171.**

In Creek's Crossing, Pennsylvania, just before the Civil War, Dorothea Granger's curmudgeonly Uncle Jacob asks her to stitch him a quilt with a very specific pattern. After his unexpected, violent death, Dorothea decodes the symbols on the quilt and discovers it provides a key for slaves escaping along the Underground Railroad. Surprised and pleased to learn of her late uncle's involvement in the abolitionist movement, Dorothea decides to take an active role herself, putting herself at risk. Part of the Elm

Creek Quilts series of mainstream women's fiction (most of which are contemporary novels) centered on master quilter Sylvia Bergstrom Compson of Elm Creek Valley, Pennsylvania, and her ancestors.

Keywords: Abolitionists; Pennsylvania; Quilts; Underground Railroad

Edwards, Geoffrey S.

Fire Bell in the Night. **Touchstone, 2007. 448pp. Paper, 9781416564249.**

On June 30, 1850, *New York Tribune* reporter John Sharp steps off the train in Charleston, South Carolina, to cover the capital trial of Darcy Calhoun, a poor white farmer accused of harboring a runaway slave. Sharp's boss wants him to delve deeply into the social and political ramifications of the trial; he has a feeling it could presage a greater conflict about slavery. As he encounters the diverse opinions held among members of Charleston's plantation society, John discovers that racial tension seethes underneath the city's refined exterior.

Keywords: Journalists and reporters; Racial conflict; Slaves, runaway; South Carolina

Hambly, Barbara.

Patriot Hearts. **Bantam, 2007. 430pp. Hardbound, 9780553804287.** ✍ 📖

In her second mainstream historical novel of early America after *The Emancipator's Wife*, Hambly presents fictionalized portraits of Martha Washington, Abigail Adams, Dolley Madison, and Sally Hemings, each in her own way a founding mother of the United States. Unlike American history books, which center on political happenings and men's public roles, Hambly focuses on the women's domestic and private lives, including their marriages, motherhood, housekeeping duties, and involvement in their men's political activities.

Keywords: Adams, Abigail (historical character); First ladies; Hemings, Sally (historical character); Madison, Dolley (historical character); Slaves and slavery; Virginia; Washington, DC; Washington, Martha (historical character)

MacMurray, Rose.

Afternoons with Emily. **Little, Brown, 2007. 472pp. Hardbound, 9780316017602.** ✍

In Amherst, Massachusetts, in the 1840s, Emily Dickinson is known as a mysterious poet who never leaves the upstairs bedroom of her house. Then Miranda Chase, daughter of a scholar who comes to teach at Amherst College, arrives in town. The two women, though fifteen years apart in age, become friends and confidantes, sharing conversations and dreams in Emily's home every Monday afternoon. Their relationship changes as Miranda grows into adulthood. As she learns more about the world, life, and love, she separates herself more from her reclusive, obsessive friend. MacMurray died in 1997, and her family fulfilled her dreams by finding a publisher for her manuscript.

Keywords: Dickinson, Emily (historical character); Friendship; Massachusetts; Poets, women

Marshall, Jeffrey D.

The Inquest. **University of Vermont/Hardscrabble, 2006. 271pp. Hardbound, 1584655712.** ✍

In 1830 Experience "Speedy" Goodrich died after a botched abortion. This tragedy culminated in an inquiry that affected the entire city of Burlington, Vermont. Three narrators relate their versions of events: Charles Daggett, a medical student accused of performing the abortion and of procuring female bodies for dissection purposes; Stephen Decatur Parker, an undergraduate at UVM who transcribes the inquest as court reporter; and Nancy Goodrich Proctor, Speedy's sister, who provides insight into the victim's mindset at the time. Marshall, university archivist at the University of Vermont, based his novel on a significant case in Vermont's legal history. The public outcry over her death, and the accompanying questions about medical ethics, make this historical tale particularly relevant today.

Keywords: Abortion; Goodrich, Experience (historical character); Inquests; Vermont

Neighbour, Mary E.

Speak Right On: Dred Scott, a Novel. **Toby, 2006. 352pp. Hardbound, 159264144X.** ✍

Before the Civil War, Dred Scott was perhaps the most famous slave in America; his legal challenge to obtain his freedom was denied by the Supreme Court in 1857, sparking a controversy that contributed to the Civil War. Neighbour's biographical novel encompasses Scott's entire life, from his birth in 1799 into slavery, through his time spent working in the cotton fields and as a driver. It ends with his death in 1858, by which point he has been freed by his former owner's sons. Scott recounts his own tale as a traditional African storyteller would, with cadence, rhythm, and local slang.

Keywords: African Americans; Illinois; Scott, Dred (historical character); Slaves and slavery; Wisconsin

Swerling, Beverly.

City of Glory. **Simon & Schuster, 2006. 465pp. Hardbound, 9780743269209.** **YA**

This direct sequel to *City of Dreams*, a multi-period epic about Manhattan's early history as told through the stories of the Turner and Devrey families, picks up the story in 1814, during ten crucial days in America's "second war of independence." The dashing protagonist is Joyful Patrick Turner, a one-armed war hero, ex-surgeon, and businessman determined to save his family's shipping company by establishing trade with China. But his nemesis, trader Gornt Blakeman, has other plans; not only does Gornt plan to steal away Joyful's beautiful Huguenot fiancée, Manon Vionne, but he also hopes to encourage New York to secede from the union and establish a new nation. Swashbuckling action combines with vivid historical detail and a multiplicity of realistic, entertaining characters from all walks of life.

Keywords: New York; Physicians; War of 1812

Wood, Gillen D'Arcy.

Hosack's Folly: A Novel of Old New York. Other Press, 2005. 390pp. Hardbound, 159051162X.

It is the summer of 1820 in Manhattan. Modern medicine is still in its infancy, and the entire city is threatened by yellow fever, a virulent tropical disease. Dr. David Hosack, founder of Bellevue Hospital, and his assistant, Albert Dash, believe it would be in New York's best interest to close off the harbor to incoming ships, but local politicians and businessmen, greedy for the wealth the ships will bring, thwart the physicians' every move. Wood also includes a romantic subplot by introducing Virginia Casey, daughter of a scheming Irish newspaperman, as a love interest for Dr. Dash. A fast-paced historical novel of science, engineering, politics, and the growing pains of an up-and-coming world city.

Keywords: Hosack, David (historical character); New York; Physicians; Yellow fever

The Civil War

Between 1861 and 1865, friends and families were torn apart as people were forced to take sides between the Union and the Confederacy. Many novels cover the actual battles, but others deal with political decisions, social issues such as race and slavery, and the difficulty of conducting daily life during wartime.

Croker, Richard.

No Greater Courage. Morrow, 2006. 416pp. Hardbound, 0060559101. ✍

The Battle of Fredericksburg, fought in and around that Virginia city on December 13, 1862, was a failed attempt by the Union to gain the upper hand against Robert E. Lee and his army. The Union forces, under newly appointed general Ambrose Burnside, make a valiant attempt to surprise the Confederates at Fredericksburg but are confounded by the lack of stable bridges across the Rappahannock, the quickly approaching winter, and General Lee's troops, who are prepared and waiting for them. Croker tells the story of this infamous and blood-soaked Union defeat mostly through the viewpoints of minor characters, though all are based on historical figures. Stonewall Jackson, President Lincoln, and Clara Barton also figure prominently.

Keywords: Fredericksburg, Battle of; Virginia

Gylanders, S. C.

The Better Angels of Our Nature. Random House, 2006. 436pp. Hardbound, 1400065143.

Gylanders (a British novelist) takes the title of her debut novel from President Lincoln's inaugural address, in which he staunchly defended the Union. A young orphan named Jesse Davis appears in General Sherman's camp on the eve of the Battle of Shiloh in 1862, one of the bloodiest encounters of the Civil War. Jesse seems to know Sherman's habits and background uncannily well, which baffles the general, who eventually takes him under his wing. As Jesse's medical skills grow under the camp surgeon's tutelage, it becomes clear that he is hiding something. The action spans the fourteen-month period between Shiloh and Vicksburg.

Keywords: Disguise; Generals; Orphans; Sherman, William Tecumseh (historical character); Shiloh, Battle of; Tennessee

Hambly, Barbara.

The Emancipator's Wife. **Bantam, 2005. 624pp. Hardbound, 0553803018.**

Hambly presents Mary Todd Lincoln, wife of a martyred president, as a sympathetic, flawed, and misunderstood woman whose difficult life the American public would have found hard to imagine. Born a Todd in Lexington, Kentucky, the vivacious Mary grows up knowing every privilege, and though she has many suitors, only Lincoln captures her heart. Their love helps her survive the deaths of two children, the incredible stresses of political life, and her continued fragile mental health. After Lincoln's assassination, Mary is beset by depression, and she struggles to preserve his memory even while her surviving son, Robert, tries to have her declared insane.

Keywords: First ladies; Lincoln, Mary Todd (historical character); Married life; Washington, DC

Hart, Lenore.

Becky: The Life and Loves of Becky Thatcher. **St. Martin's, 2008. 371pp. Hardbound, 9780312373276.**

In Mark Twain's *Tom Sawyer*, Becky Thatcher was Tom's childhood girlfriend, a secondary character who never had her own say. Hart's novel claims that this was thanks to her old friend Sam Clemens, who chose to give Tom the starring role in his book. From old age, Becky looks back on her life. A tomboy in her youth (during which many events from Twain's original are seen in a new light), she grows up to marry Tom's cousin Sid and emerges as a mature, independent woman when she takes her life into her own hands during the Civil War years. As Becky's journey takes her from Missouri to Nevada and San Francisco, she never abandons her passionate love for Tom.

Keywords: Missouri; Tomboys

Jakes, John.

Savannah, or, a Gift for Mr. Lincoln. **Dutton, 2004. 288pp. Hardbound, 0525948031.**

As Union soldiers march on the Confederate city of Savannah, Georgia, during Christmas 1864, planning to make of it a "gift for Mr. Lincoln," widowed Sara Lester hopes to keep her plantation, Silvergrass, safe from destruction by the North as well as forced takeover by an unscrupulous judge. As she and her twelve-year-old daughter, Hattie, take refuge with neighbors, hope arrives from an unexpected source. Famed historical novelist Jakes always conveys a vivid sense of place and era whatever he writes, and *Savannah* is no exception to his classic style, except perhaps in length and tone. Not only is it far shorter than most of his oeuvre, it's also considerably more lighthearted.

Keywords: Georgia; Plantations; Widows

Jakober, Marie.

Sons of Liberty. **Forge, 2005. 315pp. Hardbound, 0765310414.**

During the Civil War the Sons of Liberty were a secessionist force that operated underground and plagued the Union. In 1862, although Baltimore is held by the Union, its sentiments remain widely Confederate. Branden Rolfe, the city's Union provost marshal, fears that the Sons of Liberty will capture this port capital, lending considerable support to the Confederate cause. As Rolfe gathers weapons and spies in an effort to defend Baltimore, the woman he loves risks her life by joining a Union spy network. Meanwhile, nurse Eden Farnswood, a widow, finds a new lease on life by joining the Sons. A unique take on Civil War–era espionage, as seen from both sides.

Keywords: Maryland; Spies; Spies, women

Kantor, MacKinlay.

🐾 *Andersonville.* **World Publishing, 1955. 733pp. Hardbound, no ISBN. ★**

The Andersonville prison camp in southwestern Georgia, infamous for the horrific, inhumane treatment of over 50,000 Union prisoners, is the setting for this gritty novel. The realism of this novel is unremitting, making it at times almost too painful to read. There are some hopeful images, particularly of how war can also bring out the best in basically good people. Pulitzer Prize.

Keywords: Georgia; Prisons

Lerner, Eric.

Pinkerton's Secret. **Henry Holt, 2008. 317pp. Hardbound, 9780805082784.** ✍

Allan Pinkerton, the Scottish native who became America's first private eye, first meets Kate Warne in 1856 when she applies for a position at his Chicago detective agency. Against his better judgment, she convinces him to take her on, stating that some jobs are best handled by a woman. Partners, close confidants, and finally passionate lovers (despite the existence of his wife and family), they team up on cases big and small—most notably to prevent Lincoln's assassination on his first train trip to the nation's capital. Lerner's Pinkerton is a foul-mouthed, irascible creature whose only soft spot proves to be his quick-witted, attractive female counterpart.

Keywords: Detective agencies; Extramarital affairs; Illinois; Pinkerton, Allan (historical character); Scottish Americans; Washington, D.C.

McCaig, Donald.

Rhett Butler's People. **St. Martin's, 2007. 500pp. Hardbound, 9780312262518.** 📖

Promoted as "the other side of the greatest love story ever told," *Rhett Butler's People* removes much of the mystery from Scarlett O'Hara's rogue of a husband (her third) without necessarily lessening his appeal. Rhett Butler is motivated by loyalty and love for his friends (including the overseer's daughter, Belle Watling); his sister Rosemary; the irrepressible Scarlett; and most of all, his own conscience. Beginning with his childhood in South Carolina's Low Country, McCaig tells Rhett's story up through the events in *Gone with the Wind* and continues the narrative after the other novel's ending. With its sharp awareness of the racism and cruelty rampant in the post–Civil War South, its tone is grittier and darker than the original. As the second authorized sequel to *GWTW* (after Alexandra Ripley's *Scarlett*), readers were on high alert at the idea of this novel's publication. General consensus has been that it exceeded expectations, but this should come as no surprise to fans of McCaig, a thorough chronicler of Civil War–era fiction as well as an excellent storyteller.

Keywords: Confederacy; Georgia; South Carolina

Newman, Janis Cooke.

Mary. **MacAdam/Cage, 2006. 705pp. Hardbound, 193156163X.** ✍

Newman's thesis about Mary Todd Lincoln, perhaps our most maligned and enigmatic first lady (a term coined to describe her), is that she was not mad. Rather, as a strong proto-feminist with considerable influence over her husband, she was tragically misunderstood. In 1875, kept awake in Bellevue Asylum by the shrieks of other inmates, Mary sets down a record of her life. She describes her reasons for her unconventional behavior, such as holding séances in the White House and her compulsive shopping expeditions: she was trying to protect her family from further tragedies, which it experienced in abundance. Her sensuality often frightens her husband, though she loves him passionately, and her ambition drives him to succeed.

Keywords: First ladies; Lincoln, Mary Todd (historical character); Married life; New York; Washington, DC

Shaara, Michael, and Jeff Shaara.

Civil War Trilogy. ✍ ★ YA

Like few before them, these novels succeed in bringing readers into the minds of the leaders who fought on both sides of the Civil War. Nearly all of the characters are historical, but the principal players are Confederate general Robert E. Lee, Union commander Ulysses S. Grant, Confederate general Thomas "Stonewall" Jackson, Winfield Scott Hancock (the Union commander at Gettysburg), and Joshua Chamberlain, the Union leader who accepted Lee's surrender at Appomattox. When *The Killer Angels* was first published in 1973, it hardly made waves in the literary world, despite winning the 1975 Pulitzer Prize. Five years after Shaara's death, after the release of the associated film *Gettysburg*, it finally reached best-seller status. At that point Jeff Shaara, Michael's son, took on the project of writing the prequel and sequel to his father's classic novel. A rare coin dealer, Jeff Shaara had no previous writing experience, but all of his novels have become best sellers.

Keywords: Chamberlain, Joshua (historical character); Chancellorsville, Battle of; Fredericksburg, Battle of; Generals; Gettysburg, Battle of; Grant, Ulysses (historical character); Lee, Robert E. (historical character); Longstreet, James (historical character); Pennsylvania; Virginia

Shaara, Jeff.

Gods and Generals. Ballantine, 1996. 498pp. Hardbound, 0345404920.

Shaara's four protagonists—Generals Lee and Jackson in the South, Chamberlain and Hancock in the North—prepare strategies that lead them through the battles of Fredericksburg and Chancellorsville. This novel takes place between 1858 and 1863, ending just before Gettysburg.

Shaara, Michael.

🌹 *The Killer Angels.* McKay, 1974. 374pp. Hardbound, 0679504664.

A dramatic portrait of the Battle of Gettysburg, which killed more men than any other battle on American soil. The entire novel occurs over a very short period, June 29 through July 3, 1863. More literary than Jeff Shaara's two novels, this masterpiece sees the action mostly from the viewpoints of Confederate Generals Robert E. Lee and James Longstreet. Pulitzer Prize.

Shaara, Jeff.

The Last Full Measure. Ballantine, 1998. 560pp. Hardbound, 0345404912.

The trilogy concludes as Lee, Grant, and Chamberlain lead their armies during the last two years of the Civil War. This volume begins as Lee retreats from Gettysburg and follows the armies through 1865. Later chapters reveal each man's fate after the war.

Taylor, Nick.

The Disagreement. **Simon & Schuster, 2008. 360pp. Hardbound, 9781416550655.**

Sixteen-year-old John Alan Muro abandons his dreams of attending medical school in Philadelphia when his home state of Virginia secedes from the Union in 1861. His father sends him to the University of Virginia instead, hoping his schooling will keep him out of combat. Despite his family's thoughts that "the disagreement" won't last long, the war quickly comes to Charlottesville. Casualties begin arriving, supplies at the university hospital run low, and John Alan—a med student ordered to practice as a full-fledged doctor—knows he's in over his head.

Keywords: Coming of age; Physicians; Virginia

Turtledove, Harry.

Fort Pillow. **St. Martin's Press, 2006. 329pp. Hardbound, 0312355203.** ✍

In April 1864 Confederate commander Nathan Bedford Forrest and his men attacked the Union garrison at Fort Pillow, Tennessee. It was a disaster for the Union—barely a third of the garrison survived—as well as a scandal with strong racial overtones, for over half of the fort's defenders were black. Disagreement still rages: Was Forrest motivated by racial hatred? Turtledove revisits the Fort

Pillow Massacre from all sides, demonstrating that, whatever the results of the controversy, it was one of America's least glorious moments.

Keywords: African Americans; Forrest, Nathan Bedford (historical character); Fort Pillow, Battle of; Massacres; Racial conflict; Tennessee

Williams, Philip Lee.

A Distant Flame. **St. Martin's Press, 2004. 309pp. Hardbound, 0312332521.**
YA

In 1914 at a hometown event to celebrate the fiftieth anniversary of the Battle of Atlanta, Charlie Merrill looks back on his experience as a sharpshooter for the Confederacy. An unlikely soldier, Charlie is a frail, bookish youth who, like many in his small Georgia town, is not convinced about either the wisdom of secession or the value of slavery. As Sherman's army begins its march on Atlanta in July 1864, Charlie fights hard for the Confederates even as he doubts the principles on which his side is based. Williams vividly describes the friendships Charlie forms, the action he sees in battle, and the injuries and losses he endures—all of which shape his character. Michael Shaara Award.

Keywords: Atlanta, Battle of; Coming of age; Confederacy; Georgia; Soldiers

Reconstruction and the Gilded Age

The years right after the Civil War were hard on everyone. Both the North and South recuperated from their losses and struggled to rebuild their cities and towns. As the later years of the nineteenth century approached, prosperity was just around the corner. Novels set in 1880s and 1890s America tend to focus on Gilded Age society and its excesses.

Ceely, Jonatha.

Mina series. 📖 **YA**

Ceely evokes mid-nineteenth century Ireland, England, and New York, as seen by an appealing heroine, Irish immigrant Mina Pigot, with big dreams, considerable pluck, and an adventurous spirit.

Keywords: Catholicism; Chefs; Diaries and journals; England; Immigrants, Irish; Ireland; New York; Servants

Mina. Delacorte, 2004. 324pp. Paper, 038533690X.

In 1848, after losing her family to the Irish famine, a fifteen-year-old Irish Catholic girl named Mina disguises herself as a boy and joins the household of an English estate. As a servant, "Paddy" gets to know the ins and outs of the kitchen and gradually befriends Mr. Serle, the estate chef. Mina reveals her true identity to him, telling Mr. Serle about her personal losses and her difficult flight from Ireland to Liverpool.

Bread and Dreams. Delacorte, 2005. 408pp. Hardbound, 0385336896.

In this sequel to *Mina*, Mina Pigot relates her continuing story in journal form, relating how she and her protector/companion, Benjamin Serle, board the sailing ship *Victoria* in search of her brother, Daniel, and a better life in America. While en route they form a culinary partnership that deepens their friendship. In New York Mr. Serle finds work as a hotel's master chef; the Westervelt family, where Mina works as a kitchen servant, values her skills. As Mina struggles with her unwelcome knowledge about the Westervelts' secrets, she finds her romantic feelings toward Mr. Serle—a Jew who is considerably older—difficult to deny.

Chidgey, Catherine.

The Transformation. **Holt, 2005. 306pp. Hardbound, 0805069712.**

Businessmen, wealthy snowbirds, and celebrities gather at the brand new Tampa Bay Hotel, which has one permanent resident: Lucien Goulet III, wigmaker to the rich and famous, who left Paris under suspicious circumstances. He hires Rafael Méndez, a teenage cigar roller from Cuba, to scrounge in garbage dumps for hair clippings. Obsessed with the white-blond hair of Marion Unger, a young widow, Goulet schemes to turn her tresses into the most magnificent "transformation" of his career. The three become unlikely accomplices, not knowing what dire purposes Goulet has in mind. Tampa, Florida, circa 1898, may not seem an exciting setting, but Chidgey (a New Zealand author and past winner of a Betty Trask Award) makes it seem a bustling, exotic place.

Keywords: Florida; Hotels; Wigmakers

Jakes, John.

The Gods of Newport. **Dutton, 2005. 383pp. Hardbound, 0525949763.**

Newport, Rhode Island, in 1893 is the favored summer residence of members of New York's glamorous social elite. Sam Driver, a robber baron and railroad tycoon, had previously found that his "new money" denied him entrance into the fascinating world of yachting, parties, and snobbery, but he is determined to break into Newport's inner circle this time. Then his beautiful daughter, Jenny, falls in love with a poor young Irishman, much to her father's chagrin.

Keywords: Rhode Island; Socialites

O'Brien, Patricia.

Harriet and Isabella. **Touchstone, 2008. 343pp. Hardbound, 9781416552208.** ✍ 📖

Harriet Beecher Stowe and Isabella Beecher Hooker, half-sisters from a famous New England family, take opposing sides when their brother, noted clergyman Henry Ward Beecher, goes on trial for adultery in 1875. When Isabella, who publicly had urged him to admit his guilt, visits Henry on his deathbed in Brooklyn Heights twelve years later, she hopes to mend the breach between them. Feelings from the past come rushing back when she faces Harriet once again. Set in New York City and at the Beecher residence of Nook Farm, in Hartford, during the 1870s and 1880s.

Keywords: Authors, women; Connecticut; Extramarital affairs; Hooker, Isabella Beecher (historical character); New York; Stowe, Harriet Beecher (historical character); Suffragettes

Piercy, Marge.

Sex Wars. **Morrow, 2005. 411pp. Hardbound, 0060789832.** 📖

New York City in the post–Civil War period was a place of contradiction. It symbolized freedom for thousands of European immigrants, and the suffragist movement was in full swing, yet sexual repression pervaded society. While Victoria Woodhull and Elizabeth Cady Stanton fight for women's rights, fundamentalist zealot Anthony Comstock begins a crusade to outlaw pornography and all methods of birth control, which women use to control their own destinies. Piercy interweaves their stories with that of a fictional character, Freydeh Levin, a Russian Jewish immigrant who goes into business selling condoms to earn money to bring her family over from the old country.

Keywords: Feminists; Immigrants, Russian; New York; Suffragettes

Poole-Carter, Rosemary.

Women of Magdalene. **Kunati, 2007. 280pp. Hardbound, 9781601640147.**

Poole-Carter's eerie Southern Gothic tale takes place in and around the Magdalene Ladies' Lunatic Asylum in post–Civil War Louisiana. Dr. Robert Mallory, who joined its staff after an extended stint as a war surgeon, discovers that the dead woman he found in a nearby river was a former Magdalene patient, a fact with which the asylum's director seems unconcerned. As Mallory investigates further, he discovers that most of the Magdalene's residents are not, in fact, insane. As if that's not horrific enough, more bodies keep turning up.

Keywords: Asylums; Gothic novels; Louisiana; Physicians

Twentieth Century

The early twentieth century was a time of cultural and technological discovery, and inventions created during that time were used both in daily life and in war. Most of these novels take place during World War I, the Great Depression, and World War II. Race relations are another popular topic.

Bailey, Tom.

Cotton Song. **Shaye Areheart, 2006. 318pp. Hardbound, 140008332X.** 📖

In Hushpuckashaw County, Mississippi, in 1944, a mob of angry townspeople lynches a young black nanny, Letitia Johnson, for supposedly drowning her young charge, a wealthy white couple's baby daughter, in her bath. Baby Allen, a social worker assigned to the case of Letitia's twelve-year-old daughter, Sally, cares for the girl. She decides to uncover the truth, but in trying to clear Letitia's name she learns that the case is more complex than anyone suspected.

Keywords: African Americans; Mississippi—World War II; Racial conflict; Social workers

Blake, James Carlos.

The Killings of Stanley Ketchel. **Morrow, 2005. 312pp. Hardbound, 0060554363.** ✍

Stanley Ketchel, the middleweight boxing champion whose raging temper and racist, misogynistic tendencies were as great as his success in the ring, escapes from his violent childhood home at age fifteen. He lives a hobo's life, riding the rails, ending up in Butte, Montana—where he wins his first big fights—and turns pro out in San Francisco, where he encounters heavyweight champ Jack Johnson and determines to best him. A grim, action-packed portrait of Ketchel's short and tragic life, from his adolescence through his murder at age twenty-four.

Keywords: Boxers; California; Ketchel, Stanley (historical character); Montana

Broder, Bill.

Taking Care of Cleo. **Handsel, 2006. 349pp. Hardbound, 1590512138.**

In this suspenseful coming of age story, Rebecca Bearwald is the eighteen-year-old daughter of the only Jewish family in Charlevoix, a small lake resort town on the shores of Lake Michigan at the height of Prohibition in 1928. Worried her family will require her to take care of her elder, autistic sister, Cleo, for the rest of her life, Rebecca yearns for greater things. But Cleo has other plans for herself as well. When Cleo accidentally discovers a bootlegging ring operating in town, she decides to sell the liquor herself, in order to earn Rebecca sufficient funds to attend the University of Michigan. Cleo's actions attract the attention of the Purple Gang, Jewish gangsters from Detroit, with dangerous results for the family.

Keywords: Autism; Coming of age; Jews; Michigan; Prohibition; Sisters

Brownstein, Gabriel.

The Man from Beyond. **Norton, 2005. 298pp. Hardbound, 0393051528.**

It is 1922, and Molly Goodman, fresh out of Vassar and struggling with possible lesbian inclinations, joins the staff of a New York City tabloid, on the beat of local celebrities and their antics. An interview with famed magician Harry Houdini draws her into his circle and that of his friend and sometime adversary, Sir Arthur Conan Doyle. While Doyle firmly believes in spiritualism, the latest trend to hit society, Houdini firmly believes all mediums are charlatans. At a séance on the Jersey shore, the famous medium "Margery" decides to contact Houdini's late mother, with hopes of turning him into a believer, but what happens there changes the men's friendship forever.

Keywords: Doyle, Arthur Conan (historical character); Houdini, Harry (historical character); Journalists and reporters; Magic and magicians; New York; Séances

Dalessandro, James.

1906. **Chronicle, 2004. 361pp. Hardbound, 0811843130.**

In 1906 Annalisa Passarelli, reporter and music/opera critic for the *Evening Bulletin*, is secretly working undercover for Byron Fallon, San Francisco's head police detective, on a mission to rid the city of corruption. Byron had hoped to arrest a number of unsavory government officials, including the mayor and city attorney, but when he is killed in the line of duty, his rebellious son, Hunter, forms an alliance with Annalisa and takes up where his dad left off. They continue to pursue justice, even as a horrible earthquake strikes and San Francisco erupts in flames. Suspenseful, and based on newly uncovered facts about the great San Francisco earthquake of 1906.

Keywords: California; Cities; Fires; Journalists and reporters; Politicians; San Francisco earthquake

Dallas, Sandra.

New Mercies. **St. Martin's Press, 2005. 301pp. Hardbound, 0312336195.**

In 1933 Nora Bondurant, a recent divorcee, comes to Natchez, Mississippi, from Denver to learn more about an aunt she never knew she had, "Miss Amalia" Bondurant, who was recently killed in a murder/suicide and who left Avoca, her crumbling estate, to Nora. Although she tries to learn more about Amalia and her own murky family history, Nora runs into brick walls everywhere, at least until she becomes more familiar with the community, and the community with her. She befriends two former slaves on Amalia's plantation, Ezra and his mother, Aunt Polly, who gradually reveal to her some of Avoca's secrets. A leisurely paced, gentle read with some old-fashioned Gothic touches. WILLA Award.

Keywords: Families; Gothic novels; Heirs and heiresses; Mississippi; Plantations

Despres, Loraine.

The Bad Behavior of Belle Cantrell. **Morrow, 2005. 338pp. Hardbound, 0060515244.**

Belle Cantrell, a young widow in the small town of Gentry, Louisiana, in 1920, decides that she's had enough of society's expectations. After a year and a half of proper mourning, Belle decides to make something of her life: she bobs her hair, joins the local group of suffragists (and gets arrested for going swimming with them in an indecent bathing outfit), and takes on her neighbors' nasty prejudices. Both humorous and sexy on the surface, this novel also explores deeper realities, such as religious bigotry, racial violence, women's growing roles in political life, and what it means to be a lady. This sassy Southern tale about a woman breaking free of society's rules is a prequel of sorts to *The Scandalous Summer of Sissy LeBlanc*, which featured Belle Cantrell's equally feisty granddaughter.

Keywords: Louisiana; Racial conflict; Suffragettes; Widows

Hamamura, John Hideyo.

The Color of the Sea. **Thomas Dunne, 2006. 306pp. Hardbound, 0312340737. YA**

Isamu "Sam" Hamada grows up in Hawaii, the son of a plantation worker of Japanese birth. He learns the martial arts, a skill he's passionate about, but he relocates to California as a young man in search of a better life. There he meets Keiko, but their love is thwarted by her parents' plans for her—an arranged marriage back in Japan—and Japan's attack on Pearl Harbor in 1941. Because of his knowledge of Japanese, Sam is recruited by the U.S. Army, which sends him on a secret mission, while members of Keiko's family are detained in internment camps. Hamamura, a Japanese

American born during World War II, writes sparely and passionately about a man caught between cultures at a time of war. Alex Award.

Keywords: California—World War II; Hawaii—World War II; Internment camps; Japan; Japanese Americans; Pearl Harbor

Hamill, Pete.

North River. **Little Brown, 2007. 341pp. Hardbound, 9780316340588.** 📖 **YA**

During the winter of 1934 Jim Delaney, a physician wounded in body and spirit, tends to the poor of Greenwich Village. New problems arise when his teenaged daughter, Grace, leaves her two-year-old son, Carlito, on his doorstep, and he saves the life of an old war buddy with mob connections. Delaney hires Rose, a Sicilian immigrant, to be his housekeeper, and the trio becomes, in its own unlikely way, a new family. A gritty yet warmhearted story of New York during the Depression.

Keywords: Grandparents and grandchildren; Great Depression; New York; Physicians

Henderson, Genie Chipps.

A Woman of the World. **Berkley, 2004. 372pp. Paper, 0425199134.**

Henderson loosely based her heroine on early twentieth-century photojournalist Margaret Bourke-White, an ambitious and adventurous woman who dared step into a man's profession. Kate Goodfellow—strong-willed, beautiful, and independent—embodies the same qualities. Stranded on a lifeboat off the coast of North Africa in 1942, Kate looks back on her whirlwind life and career, including her love affair with author Hopper Delaney. An involving epic about social changes and gender roles in America, mostly in New York City, during the 1920s and 1930s.

Keywords: Africa, North; New York; Photojournalists

King, Kevin.

All the Stars Came Out That Night. **Dutton, 2005. 415pp. Hardbound, 0525949054.** ✍

From the grave, famed newscaster Walter Winchell narrates this exuberant, picaresque epic about the American game of baseball and the best game never officially played—an all-star match-up in Fenway Park, circa 1934, in which an all-white team including Babe Ruth, Shoeless Joe Jackson, and Joe DiMaggio faced off against the best players of Satchel Paige's Negro League. At that time, members of the Negro teams were forbidden to play against anyone from the Majors. The entire venture is funded by Henry Ford, an auto entrepreneur known for his racist attitudes. The journey to Fenway is at least half the fun, though, with many cameo appearances from famous 1930s-era personalities.

Keywords: African Americans; Baseball; Great Depression; Massachusetts; Racial conflict; Winchell, Walter (historical character)

Landvik, Lorna.

Oh My Stars. **Ballantine, 2005. 400pp. Hardbound, 0345472314.** 📖

Eighteen-year-old Violet Mathers has had a hard life, growing up with family troubles in the hinterlands of Kentucky during the Depression; she feels especially unwanted and unattractive after losing her right arm in the sewing factory where she worked. Distraught, she boards a bus west to San Francisco, where she plans to commit suicide by jumping off the Golden Gate Bridge. When their bus breaks down in North Dakota, two local musicians rescue her, and—together with the brother of one of them—they fill in for the scheduled act at a local carnival. Successful beyond their expectations, the band goes on the road as the Pearltones, with Violet as their savvy manager.

Keywords: Great Depression; Kentucky; Musicians; North Dakota

Lowy, Jonathan.

The Temple of Music. **Crown, 2004. 336pp. Hardbound, 0609608193.** ✍ 📖

In 1901 President William McKinley was assassinated while attending the Pan-American Exposition in Buffalo, New York. Little is known about his killer, Leon Czolgosz, an anarchist and son of Russian-Polish immigrants from Detroit. In his retelling of the events leading up to this tragedy, Lowy re-creates the tumultuous social and political changes that rocked turn-of-the-century America, bringing to life personalities such as anarchist Emma Goldman; William Jennings Bryan, McKinley's biggest political rival; and newspaper mogul William Randolph Hearst.

Keywords: Assassination; Czolgosz, Leon (historical character); McKinley, William (historical character); New York; Presidents; World's Fair

Preston, Caroline.

Gatsby's Girl. **Houghton Mifflin, 2006. 320pp. Hardbound, 0618537252.** ✍

F. Scott Fitzgerald scholars have named Ginevra King, a Chicago debutante who was his first love and who cruelly rejected him after an extended romance and correspondence, as the model for Daisy Buchanan and several other female characters from his novels. In Preston's version his muse is Ginevra Perry, a self-centered socialite who meets him in 1916, when she is sixteen. Despite his devotion, she jilts him for a dashing aviator, whom she marries, though their union is hardly blissful. Ginevra keeps tabs on Scott's life from afar, through the time of his death in 1940.

Keywords: Authors; Fitzgerald, F. Scott (historical character); Illinois; Socialites

Shamp, Dawn.

On Account of Conspicuous Women. **Thomas Dunne, 2008. 306pp. Hardbound, 9780312379971.**

In 1920, the beginning of the Prohibition years, four young women from Roxbury, North Carolina, become friends and change the social fabric of their small Southern town. Bertie, her cousin Guerine, tomboy/farm girl Doodle, and socialite Ina, Roxbury's new schoolteacher, form an unlikely quartet, but they have more in common than they initially believe. In her portraits of four unique women and their changing times, Shamp touches on issues as diverse as racism, women's suffrage, poverty, and other things of concern to Americans at the time.

Keywords: Friendship; North Carolina; Prohibition; Suffragettes

Sickels, Noëlle.

The Medium. **Five Star, 2007. 427pp. Hardbound, 9781594146183.**

Helen Schneider never wanted to be a medium. As a German American teenager growing up in northern New Jersey, Helen had ignored her uncanny ability to foretell the future. But when war touches America in 1941, Helen uses her psychic abilities for the good of servicemen's families, who desperately seek to make contact with their deceased loved ones. Although she gradually comes to terms with her gift, it affects her relationship with her fiancé, Billy Mackey, who strongly disapproves of it.

Keywords: German Americans; Mediums; New Jersey—World War II; Séances

Latin America, the Hispanic Southwest, and the Caribbean

These novels are set in early Mexico and other Spanish territories in North America. The difference between these and Western historical novels featuring Native Americans (Chapter 6) can be slight.

Manrique, Jaime.

Our Lives Are the Rivers. **Rayo, 2006. 352pp. Hardbound, 0060820705.** ✍

Manuela Sáenz, mistress of the brilliant revolutionary and Colombian president Simón Bolívar, was one of South America's earliest feminists and greatest patriots. She narrates her life story starting with her childhood schooling at a convent in Quito. The nuns' cruel treatment of her, the illegitimate daughter of a wealthy *criolla* by a Spanish nobleman, turns her against Catholicism for life. Disdainful of the cruel Spanish, she grows up admiring Bolívar and his ideals. Although her father recognizes her at last, he forces her to marry a wealthy Englishman. Her relationship with the legendary Bolívar, the great love of her life, is the culmination of her dream to unite with the revolutionary cause. Manrique articulates the vibrant color of colonial South America: its flowering plants, wild fauna, and horrible violence.

Keywords: Bolívar, Simón (historical character); Colombia—19th century; Ecuador; Mistresses; Revolutions and revolutionaries; Sáenz, Manuela (historical character)

Wood, Barbara.

Daughter of the Sun. **St. Martin's Griffin, 2007. 453pp. Paper, 9780312363680.**

Annotated under "Pre-Contact Native Americans," previously in this chapter.

Woman of a Thousand Secrets. **Thomas Dunne, 2008. 482pp. Paper, 9780312363697.**

Twenty-one years ago, Tonina's adoptive grandparents found her as an infant floating in a basket near their Caribbean island home. When it becomes clear she'll never fit into their society, they invent a reason for her to seek out her own people on the mainland. Her adventure takes her throughout the lands of fourteenth-century Mesoamerica, from the burgeoning metropolis at Mayapan to the rainforest jungles of Tikal (modern-day Guatemala) and finally westward to the Mexican interior. Her destiny intertwines with that of Kaan, a ballplayer of common birth who disdains his outsider origins to gain acceptance by the Mayans.

Keywords: Adopted children; Mayan Indians; Guatemala—14th century; Mexico —14th century; Pre-contact Native Americans

The Middle East and North Africa

Fictional drama set in long-ago times and in distant lands: Byzantium at its zenith (fifth through ninth centuries), the time of the Crusades to the Holy Land, and the inner lives of harem women in the later Ottoman Empire.

Amirrezvani, Anita.

The Blood of Flowers. **Little, Brown, 2007. 376pp. Hardbound, 9780316065764.** 📖

> In the 1620s the fourteen-year-old narrator, left unnamed in the tradition of Iran's anonymous artisans, is forced to leave her small village for Isfahan with her mother when her father dies unexpectedly. They settle into the household of her father's half-brother, Gostaham, but his wife treats them like servants. Seeing her obvious skill and ambition, Gostaham teaches the narrator the art and craft of rug design, but his wife, seeing a way to get rid of an unwanted burden and to better the family's finances at the same time, arranges a temporary marriage for her with a wealthy horse trader. Her innocence sold away, her hopes for a good marriage gone, she slowly regains her dignity in a world where women have little say in their own lives.
>
> **Keywords:** Persia—17th century; Rug designers

Bradshaw, Gillian.

Alchemy of Fire. **Severn House, 2004. 247pp. Hardbound, 0727860976.**
> In Constantinople in AD 672, Anna supports her daughter, Theodosia, through her work as a perfume manufacturer. Few people know that Theodosia was the result of a liaison between Anna and the late Prince Theodosius, but this is about to change when Kallinikos, a Syrian engineer, comes to her shop to purchase distilling equipment. When an Arab invasion threatens, Kallinikos's work on a new and deadly weapon is put to the test. Anna and Kallinikos's friendship slowly turns to love, while Theodosia—her heritage now revealed—adjusts to her new life as an imperial heiress. Bradshaw, a trained classical historian, is in top form in this novel about the development and use of "Greek fire."
>
> **Keywords:** Byzantium—Middle Ages; Concubines; Greek fire; Weapons

Galland, Nicole.

Crossed: A Tale of the Fourth Crusade. **Harper, 2008. 640pp. Paper, 9780060841805.**
> The ill-fated Fourth Crusade forms the backdrop of Galland's third novel, another rollicking adventure with entertaining characters. An unnamed English musician and vagabond, under the protection of the pious knight Gregor of Mainz, decides to accompany Gregor, his father-in-law

Boniface of Montferrat, and the rest of their rambunctious company on their crusade from Venice to the Holy Land. Before leaving, the musician rescues Jamila, a Jewess in disguise as an Arab princess, and secretly plans to help return her to her homeland. Their plans fall apart en route to Constantinople, as money problems crop up and the Crusaders' moral fervor sinks into greed and depravity.

Keywords: Byzantium—Middle Ages; Crusades and Crusaders

Hickman, Katie.

The Aviary Gate. **Bloomsbury USA, 2008. 339pp. Hardbound, 9781596914759.** 📖

While conducting research in the Bodleian Library at Oxford, Elizabeth Stavely finally finds what she's been seeking: a captivity narrative about Celia Lamprey, a British sea captain's daughter who was rescued from a shipwreck and brought to live in the harem of Sultan Mehmet III of Constantinople, circa AD 1599. Paul Pindar, a member of the British ambassador's entourage and Celia's betrothed, learns that she may in fact be alive when he arrives at the Ottoman palace bearing a gift for the sultan. Meanwhile, Celia gets entangled in harem intrigues involving the sultan's devious mother, Safiye.

Keywords: Byzantium—16th century; Diplomats; Harems; Multi-period novels; Pindar, Paul (historical character); Safiye, consort of Sultan Murad II (historical character)

Holeman, Linda.

The Moonlit Cage. **Three Rivers, 2007. 496pp. Paper, 0307346498.**

Daryâ, a young Muslim girl in Afghanistan in 1845, has spirit and personality to spare, which doesn't earn her points in her repressive, patriarchal society. Sold to an abusive husband by her father's cruel second wife, Daryâ escapes her troublesome life and is rescued by David Ingram, an enigmatic Englishman (and the son of Linny Gow from Holeman's earlier novel, *The Linnet Bird*). He brings her to Bombay, and she falls in love with him en route, but David denies his feelings and returns alone to Victorian London. Missing him terribly, Daryâ decides to follow him but discovers that life for an unmarried, poor young woman in London is more dangerous than she'd imagined.

Keywords: Afghanistan—19th century; England—Victorian era; India—19th century; Muslims

Johnson, Jane.

The Tenth Gift. **Crown, 2008. 385pp. Hardbound, 9780307405227. (Published in the UK as** *Crossed Bones.***)**

After their relationship ends, Julia Lovat's ex-lover gives her an odd parting memento: a seventeenth-century embroidery book which, as Julia discovers, also served as the diary of Catherine Tregenna, who documented her extraordinary adventure from Cornwall to Morocco. After being kidnapped by Muslim pirates while attending church services in Cornwall in 1625, Cat saves the life of their leader after a brutal sea battle. Intrigued by Cat's story, Julia follows her trail to North Africa, where she finds their lives are entwined in ways she couldn't have predicted. Romantic adventure set in the world of the white slave trade and based on the life of the author's ancestor.

Keywords: Diaries and journals; Embroidery; Morocco—19th century; Multi-period novels; Pirates; Slaves and slavery

Russell, Mary Doria.

Dreamers of the Day. **Random House, 2008. 255pp. Hardbound, 9781400064717.** 📖

Agnes Shanklin, a forty-year-old spinster schoolteacher from Cleveland, visits Egypt after her entire family dies during the great influenza epidemic of 1918. Drawn into the circle of T. E. Lawrence ("Lawrence of Arabia") , a friend of her late sister, she meets luminaries such as Gertrude Bell, Winston and Clementine Churchill, and others who drew up the boundaries of the modern Middle East during the Cairo Peace Conference of 1921. A straight-talking, astute narrator, Agnes undergoes a personal awakening in Cairo and Jerusalem, and she can't help but fall hard for a charming man who may be a German spy. Though her tone veers toward the didactic, Russell makes it clear how the disorder and bloodshed in present-day Iraq was set in motion more than eighty years ago.

Keywords: Churchill, Winston (historical character); Egypt—20th century; Iraq—20th century; Lawrence, T. E. (historical character); Spinsters

Whyte, Jack.

The Templar Trilogy.

Whyte, a Canadian novelist of Scottish birth, is best known for his popular Camulod series about the forebears, rise, and fall of King Arthur. In this trilogy (the final volume has not yet appeared) he covers the founding of the Knights Templar, a mysterious order of warrior monks cloaked in mystery. The history of the Order intertwines with that of the Crusades, meaning readers experience all of the blood, gore, adventure, and religious conflict of the era along with the protagonists.

Keywords: Crusades and Crusaders; Jerusalem, Kingdom of—Middle Ages; Knights Templar; Treasure

Knights of the Black and White. Putnam, 2006. 548pp. Hardbound, 0399153969. ✍

In 1088 Sir Hugh de Payens (the historical founder of the Templars) becomes an initiate of the Order of the Rebirth of Sion, a secretive religious organization made up of men from many noble families. While on crusade to Jerusalem, Hugh grows so horrified at the slaughter that he resolves to serve only God from that day forth. But the Order has other plans. Along with other French knights, including his own cousin, Hugh is charged with finding and retrieving the Order's hidden treasure, buried within the Temple Mount of Jerusalem.

Keywords: de Payens, Hugh (historical character)

Standard of Honor. Putnam, 2007. 614pp. Hardbound, 9780399154294.

Family drama plays out on an epic scale as the Templars' story picks up in the year 1187. Scottish knight Alec Sinclair saves his life by going into hiding in the deserts of the Holy Land after his fellow Templars are executed following the Battle of Hattin. Two years later Richard I of England asks Sir Henry Sinclair to join him on Crusade as his master-of-arms. As the Third Crusade moves south and east toward Jerusalem, three men find their loyalties tested: Alec, a member of the secret Brotherhood of Sion; Henry, who distrusts King Richard's motives; and Henry's son André, a newish member of the Temple Order who idolizes his cousin Alec.

Asia, Africa, and the Antipodes

These novels make the exotic seem familiar—either via Western protagonists who discover new lands and peoples, or by telling the stories of sympathetic characters from faraway countries. There are still comparatively few traditional historical novels set in Asia or the South Pacific, and even fewer in Africa. Because of this, some older titles are listed below. For additional titles with non-Western settings, readers should investigate literary historical novels (Chapter 10) and the Romance chapter (Chapter 4) under romantic epics.

Ali, Thalassa.

Paradise Trilogy. `YA`

An involving saga of court intrigue, romance, and adventure set in India and Afghanistan during the British Raj.

Keywords: Afghanistan—19th century; Children; First Afghan War; Hostages; India—19th century; Interracial romance

A Singular Hostage. Bantam, 2002. 349pp. Paper, 0553381768.

A Beggar at the Gate. Bantam, 2004. 301pp. Paper, 0553381776.

Companions of Paradise. Bantam, 2007. 319pp. Paper, 9780553381788.

In 1841, on the eve of the First Afghan War, Mariana resides at the British cantonment near Kabul, miserable about causing a misunderstanding that forced her to flee from her husband, Hassan Sahib, her adopted son Saboor, and the city of Lahore—as she has come to love all three. The British in Kabul don't recognize her marriage to Hassan, and they and her family pressure her to marry a British officer. Mariana takes her life in her hands by secretly visiting a Sufi mystic in search of answers; meanwhile, Afghan tribesmen are closing in on British-held Kabul.

Hantover, Jeffrey.

The Jewel Trader of Pegu. Morrow, 2008. 227pp. Hardbound, 9780061252709. 📖

Abraham, the jewel trader of the title, leaves Venice in 1598 to venture to the distant Burmese kingdom of Pegu to find beautiful gems prized by wealthy noblemen back home. A widower who lost his wife and son in childbirth, he finds himself enjoying his new life away from the constraints of Venice's Jewish ghetto, as well as his burgeoning friendship with Win, his broker. Although initially horrified by the local tradition that foreign traders deflower new brides, he begrudgingly accepts his responsibility in order to continue doing business—and unexpectedly falls in love with Mya, a young Peguan woman widowed on her wedding night. A gentle romance in an exotic setting that coincides with a man's search for what matters most.

Keywords: Interracial romance; Jews; Merchants; Pegu—17th century; Widowers

Holeman, Linda.

The Linnet Bird. **Crown, 2005. 416pp. Hardbound, 1400097398.**

Catherine Cookson meets *The Far Pavilions* in Holeman's first novel for adults, a compelling read about a woman's search for her place in the world. Linny Gow, orphaned at a young age, is sold by her stepfather into prostitution in 1823, when she's eleven, and forced to survive on the rough streets of Liverpool. Through a combination of luck and sheer determination, she meets people who help her rise above her station, and a friendship with a merchant's daughter lands her a place on a ship bound for India, where the young women plan to find wealthy husbands. With her marriage to Somers Ingram, a rich British officer, Linny hopes to assure her place in society, but Somers keeps his own secrets, and Linny's past soon catches up with her. Holeman's *The Moonlit Cage*, listed under "The Middle East," is a partial sequel.

Keywords: England—Victorian era; India—19th century; Prostitutes; Socialites

McNeill, Elisabeth.

The Lady of Cawnpore. **Severn House, 2005. 384pp. Hardbound, 9780727874719.**

The action of this novel shifts deftly between 1857 and 1919, with the tragedy of the Sepoy Mutiny—a violent Indian uprising against British rule—overshadowing everything. Emily Maynard lost nearly all of her family, except her husband and nephew, in the mutiny at Cawnpore in 1857. Rescued by one of her father's servants, Emily falls in love with him and lives with him as his Indian wife in Cawnpore, although she's still married. Decades later, in 1919, a doctor named Jenny Garland comes to Cawnpore after losing her husband in World War I and meets an elderly woman. They become friends and learn they have much in common.

Keywords: Friendship; India—19th and 20th centuries; Sepoy Mutiny

Shors, John.

Beneath a Marble Sky. **McPherson, 2004. 324pp. Hardbound, 0929701712.**

Jahanara, the beloved eldest daughter of Emperor Shah Jahan and his wife, sees her world shatter when her mother dies in childbirth. With her father incapacitated by grief, her cruel brother Aurangzeb begins destroying the fragile peace between the country's Muslims and its Hindu majority; her older brother Dara, the heir, never sees him as a threat until it's too late. As Shah Jahan arranges to construct the magnificent Taj Mahal as a memorial to his wife, Jahanara uses her cunning and diplomatic skills to survive the empire's wars of succession. She also finds the love of her life in Isa, the Taj Mahal's chief architect, and they begin an exciting but forbidden relationship. A lyrical novel set in India's Mughal Empire in the mid-seventeenth century.

Keywords: Architects; India—17th century; Jahanara, Princess (historical character); Muslims; Princesses; Taj Mahal

Beside a Burning Sea. **NAL, 2008. 424pp. Paper, 9780451224927.** 📖

This novel takes place over an eighteen-day period. On September 23, 1942, the navy hospital ship *Benevolence* is hit by a torpedo while making its way through the South Pacific. Nine survivors swim to a nearby island in the Solomons, among them Joshua, the ship's captain; his wife, Isabelle; Isabelle's sister, Annie; and Akira, a wounded, English-speaking Japanese soldier who saved Annie from drowning. Annie and Akira grow closer while sharing their mutual love for poetry, while the other castaways adjust to their situation, forming new relationships with one another and doing much soul-searching.

Keywords: Interracial romance; Shipwrecks; Soldiers; South Pacific—World War II

Speed, John.

Temple Dancer Series.

Sensual historical fiction set in seventeenth-century India during a time of political and religious unrest: the gradual decline of the Mogul Empire and the concurrent rise of the Marathis.

Keywords: Dancers; India—17th century; Muslims

The Temple Dancer. St. Martin's, 2006. 366pp. Hardbound, 0312325487.

It is 1657 in the Portuguese colony of Goa. To ensure that their trading rights in Goa remain unimpeded, the family of spoiled heiress Lucinda Dasana decide to send a bribe to the dissolute vizier of Bijapur: Maya, a Hindi slave and temple dancer with a mysterious past. Joining Maya on her journey across the treacherous Western Ghats to Bijapur are Da Gama, a settlement man sent by the Dasanas; Pathan, the grand vizier's man; Lucinda's handsome cousin Geraldo; a sneaky Muslim eunuch named Slipper; and Lucinda herself. Their journey is marked by adventure, bandit attacks, the growing friendship between the two women, and forbidden romance.

Tiger Claws. St. Martin's, 2007. 436pp. Hardbound, 9780312325510.

Speed sets his sequel firmly in the midst of the Muslim–Hindu civil wars of the mid-seventeenth century. Prince Aurangzeb, a fanatical Muslim with little sympathy for the country's Hindu majority, conspires to overthrow his father, Emperor Shah Jahan, who loses himself in opium dreams; his elder brother Dara, he believes, is a nonentity. Meanwhile Shivaji, son of a minor Hindu chieftain, begins consolidating his power. Temple dancer Maya, kidnapped from her caravan by Shivali, plays a minor role in this novel.

Williams, Adam.

The Palace of Heavenly Pleasure. **St. Martin's Press, 2004. 624pp. Hardbound, 031231566X.**

In 1899 China is on the brink of the Boxer Rebellion, yet Helen Frances Delamere, a convent-educated English girl in the fictional city of Shishan, remains completely unaware of these political undercurrents. But as peasants from the Chinese countryside slowly amass and make their way toward the city, Helen Frances and her fellow foreigners—including a crazed American missionary; Edward Airton, a compassionate Scottish physician; and Henry Manners, a British secret agent whose love affair with Helen Frances is passionate and complicated—find themselves in grave danger. At the center of it all is the titular Palace of Heavenly Pleasure, a brothel run by the wicked madam, Mother Liu.

Keywords: Boxer Rebellion; Brothels; China—19th century

Zimler, Richard.

Guardian of the Dawn. **Delta, 2005. 403pp. Hardbound, 0385338813.** 📖

From his prison cell in the Indian port city of Goa in 1592, Tiago Zarco tells his life story while awaiting his trial for heresy. He grows up secure in the affections of his loving father, his younger sister, Sofia, and their Hindu cook. Their forebears had fled Portugal decades earlier to escape forced conversions to Christianity; they now reside on a plantation just outside Goa, for Jews cannot live inside Portuguese territory. When the siblings are older, Ti's adopted cousin Wadi, a Moor, destroys the close relationship between him and Sofia. Soon after, the Inquisition carts Ti's father off to prison, setting him on the path to discover who betrayed him and his family. This luminous reinterpretation of *Othello* is the third volume in Zimler's loosely linked series about Jews of the Iberian Peninsula (others include *The Last Kabbalist of Lisbon* and *Hunting Midnight*).

Keywords: India—16th century; Inquisition; Jews; Shakespearean themes

Chapter **3**

Multi-Period Epics

Novels in this chapter can be called epic in every sense of the word. Through them, readers can view a culture from its beginnings in the distant past until today. Most take the form of a series of chronological snapshots, which demonstrate how characters in a number of different time periods react to the eras in which they live. Other novels focus on an object, legacy, or faith that is passed down through the centuries, affecting a number of people over the years. Taken in their entirety, multi-period epics give us a comprehensive picture of a civilization or geographic area, showing how the land and its people have changed over time. Although character development of these novels' human inhabitants is not always their strong point, the setting itself may be the most important character of all.

Multi-period epics may not only be hard to put down, but they can also be difficult to pick up. Literally, that is, because these hefty tomes can easily number well over 500 pages, typically in miniscule type. Meticulously researched, they are packed to the brim with words, characters, and history. Though this still isn't a large subgenre, it is an important one, for the process of historical change as told through fiction is what historical novels are all about.

Because some multi-period epics focus on the generations of one particular family over a thousand years or more, they can be thought of as the ultimate family saga, though their scope is broader than most books that fall into this category. Genealogical charts are occasionally included. Readers who enjoy these novels may also want to investigate sagas (Chapter 5), in particular those that belong to a multi-part series.

Ancient Rome

Saylor, Steven.

Roma. **St. Martin's Press, 2007. 555pp. Hardbound, 0312328311.**
Saylor, best known as the author of the <u>Roma Sub Rosa</u> mystery series featuring Gordianus the Finder, covers 1,000 years of Roman history in slightly over half as many pages. Beginning in 1000 BC, he traces the development of Rome as a city from its earliest beginnings as a minor trading post along an early salt trail to the founding of the Roman Empire, circa 44 BC, through the stories of two of its early families, the Pinarii and the Potitii. He dramatizes major events in Roman history appropriately: the founding of the city by Romulus and Remus, its capture by the

Gauls, political struggles, and Julius Caesar's assassination. Over the years, a mysterious golden talisman depicting a winged phallus is passed down from generation to generation.

Keywords: Rome—ancient/prehistoric and multi-period

The British Isles

Long novels exploring the fascinating history of the British Isles from their pagan, prehistoric past through today, concentrating on cities in England and Ireland.

Delaney, Frank.

Ireland. **HarperCollins, 2005. 559pp. Hardbound, 0060563486.**

In 1951, when Ronan O'Mara is nine years old, an itinerant storyteller (or *seanchai*) appears at his home and regales his family with entrancing tales from various periods in Ireland's history. A blasphemous comment leads Ronan's mother to send the old man on his way, but Ronan never forgets him. Ronan spends the next few decades traversing the cities and green hills of Ireland in search of the storyteller and the truth behind the larger-than-life tales he told. In lilting prose that never turns mawkish, Delaney alternates the *seanchai*'s stories with those from the O'Mara family, forming a folkloric yet real epic portrait of Ireland and its oral tradition.

Keywords: Ireland—multi-period; Storytellers

Rutherfurd, Edward.

With his lengthy, epic sagas of the history of England, Rutherfurd can be called the British heir to James Michener, but without the strong social agenda of his predecessor.

The Dublin Saga.

This two-volume series encompasses the entire known history of Dublin, Ireland, from its prehistoric past through the twentieth century. Family trees included.

The Princes of Ireland. Crown, 2004. 776pp. Hardbound, 0385502869.

Beginning in pre-Christian Ireland and continuing through the sixteenth century, Rutherfurd introduces a wide cast of characters who interact with one another and the land. Historical periods include the times of the great High Kings of Tara, the coming of St. Patrick, Viking raids and the founding of Dublin in the tenth century, the glory of Brian Boru's leadership, the Norman invasion in the twelfth century, and Henry VIII's desecration of Dublin's churches and monasteries. Throughout it all, Ireland's political and religious struggles with England loom large.

Keywords: Ireland—multi-period; Vikings

The Rebels of Ireland. Crown, 2006. 800pp. Hardbound, 0385512899.

Descendants of the families from *The Princes of Ireland* continue Rutherfurd's epic tale, beginning in Elizabethan times (which saw Ireland colonized by the English) and continuing to the founding of the Irish Republic in 1922. Principal themes here are Ireland's complicated, rebellious, often tragic relationship with England, and the growing religious and cultural divisions within Ireland itself. Rutherfurd's multifaceted characters, both Catholic and Protestant, come from all walks of life, presenting a well-rounded and instructive portrait of the city of Dublin.

Keywords: Ireland—multi-period; Revolutions and revolutionaries

London. **Crown, 1997. 829pp. Hardbound, 0517591812.** ★

From its Roman origins through the signing of the Magna Carta and up to the modern day, Rutherfurd recounts the history of London through a series of interconnected stories that detail the lives of its inhabitants. Some of the families from *Sarum* (see below) who left the countryside for the big city make an appearance here.

Keywords: England-multi-period

Sarum. **Crown, 1987. 897pp. Hardbound, 051756338X .** ★

Sarum is the old Roman name for Salisbury, England, the home of Stonehenge. In a series of interconnected vignettes, this area's history over 10,000 years is seen through the eyes of five families living on the Salisbury Plain from the last ice age until the 1980s.

Keywords: England—multi-period; Stonehenge

Europe

Religious and social conflicts, prevalent throughout European history, are the themes of these novels.

Baumgold, Julie.

The Diamond. **Simon & Schuster, 2005. 307pp. Hardbound, 0743264819.**

In this relatively short but richly written epic, Baumgold tells the story of the famed Régent diamond from its discovery in India in 1701 through the late nineteenth century. The Comte de las Cases, a nobleman who joined Napoleon in exile on St. Helena, narrates the novel's first part, in which Thomas Pitt, governor of the East India Company, buys the jewel in India. His son sells it to the Duc d'Orléans, whose descendants would become the Bourbon kings of France. It passes through the hands of the Bourbons and their wives, ending up finally in the Louvre in Paris, where it remains today. "Abraham," a fictional character, continues this glittering tale in an epilogue set after the death of Las Cases.

Keywords: Diamonds; Europe—multi-period; France—multi-period; Royalty

Rutherfurd, Edward.

Russka. **Crown, 1991. 760pp. Hardbound, 0517580489.** ★

In the author's only epic with a non-British setting, he continues to write on a broad canvas, this time telling the story of Russia and its people from the first century AD until the present. Three rival families—the noble Babrovs, the merchant Suvorins, and the peasant Romanovs (later, revolutionaries and rulers)—vie for supremacy as their descendants rise and fall in power with the times.

Keywords: Merchants; Nobility; Peasants; Russia—multi-period

The United States

Written by Americans, these epics demonstrate pride in the authors' national heritage.

Martin, William.

Peter Fallon Series.

An evolving series of American epics with a touch of mystery and suspense. Peter Fallon and his girlfriend, Evangeline Carrington, trace the histories of colonial-era artifacts over centuries of New England history. Martin is a native Bostonian and Harvard graduate.

Keywords: Fallon, Peter; Graduate students; Historians; Manuscripts

Back Bay. Crown, 1979. 437pp. Hardbound, 0517536021.

Harvard graduate student Peter Fallon's hunt for a lost Paul Revere tea set begins a chase that takes him through the entire history of Boston. As he traces the history of the powerful Pratt family over six generations, from colonial America to the present, he learns of the longstanding family curse that each member has had to deal with.

Keywords: Massachusetts—multi-period; Tea sets

Harvard Yard. Warner, 2003. 580pp. Hardbound, 0446530840.

Martin's most recent novel speaks to the history of New England and America as much as it does to Harvard University in Cambridge, Massachusetts. Historian and antiquarian book dealer Peter Fallon, older and maybe a little wiser than he was during his first appearance in *Back Bay*, learns about the hidden existence of a long-lost Shakespearean play, one possibly given by the Bard himself to Harvard's founder. To discover its current whereabouts, Fallon sorts through documentation belonging to the Wedge family, the play's original guardians, down through the generations. His searches reveal 300 years of Harvard's history, from the time of the witch hunts through the 1960s. A combination epic and bibliomystery.

Keywords: Massachusetts—multi-period; Universities

The Lost Constitution. Forge, 2007. 512pp. Hardbound, 9780765315380.

Peter Fallon and Evangeline Carrington must find the whereabouts of an early, rare, annotated draft of the U.S. Constitution, which disappeared around the time of the constitutional convention in Philadelphia in 1787. Notes left on the margins of the document supposedly reveal what may be the founding fathers' original intent for the Bill of Rights. On the hunt for yet another early American treasure, and in a race against their competitors, Peter and Evangeline trace the history of the Pike family all over New England, from the White Mountains of New Hampshire to historic Fenway Park on the first night of the World Series.

Keywords: Constitution; New England—multi-period

Michener, James A.

James Michener's panoramic historical novels are meticulously re-searched presentations of the history of a place as seen through the eyes of its inhabitants. Many include family trees on the endpapers, detailing the genealogy of the families involved in the story from beginning to end. Though entertaining, Michener's epics don't shrink from exploring seri-ous themes, such as the repression of one race or people by another. Michener is so well associated with this subgenre that the term "Micheneresque" is frequently used to describe all other novels written in this style. Three of his most popular titles are listed below.

Alaska. **Random House, 1988. 868pp. Hardbound, 0394551540.** ★

From prehistory to the Klondike Gold Rush to its successful bid for state-hood in 1959, Michener retells the history of America's forty-ninth state in epic form. In essence, *Alaska* is a saga of exploitation and neglect, both of the land's native peoples and of its natural resources.

Keywords: Alaska—multi-period; Gold Rush; Native Americans

Hawaii. **Random House, 1959. 937pp. Hardbound, no ISBN.** ★

The great Pacific melting pot that is America's fiftieth state is shown in in-credible detail in this novel, which takes us from prehistory until the mid-dle of the twentieth century. Hawaii's growth from a volcanic island paradise through statehood in 1959 is shown through the eyes of the eth-nic groups who contributed to its development and exploitation, includ-ing the English, Americans, Japanese, Chinese, and native Hawaiians.

Keywords: Hawaii—multi-period; Multiculturalism

Texas. **Random House, 1985. 1096pp. Hardbound, 0394541545.** ★

Among Michener's "big books," at over 1,000 pages this is the grandfather of them all. A Governor's Task Force composed of Texans from a variety of ethnic backgrounds comes together to decide on an appropriate curric-ulum for a required seventh-grade history class. Each chapter retells a story describing a different period in Texas history, from its beginnings as a Spanish colony in the sixteenth century through the middle of the 1980s. The state of Texas is presented as colorful, vivid, and larger than life.

Keywords: Texas—multi-period

Latin America and the Caribbean

Novels about the culturally diverse and occasionally violent history of countries located south of the American border.

Michener, James A.

Caribbean. **Random House, 1989. 672pp. Hardbound, 0394565614.** ★

In the first sentence, Michener describes the chief character of his novel as the alluring Caribbean Sea, and in doing so begins a tale of the islands and people who inhabit them from the year 1310 to the 1980s. Sixteen vignettes illustrate the history of the Caribbean and its invasions by a variety of European cultures, including the Spanish, English, and French.

Keywords: Caribbean—multi-period; Colonialism

Mexico. **Random House, 1992. 625pp. Hardbound, 0679416498.** ★

Norman Clay is an American journalist, born in Mexico, who returns to his homeland after twenty years' absence to report on a showdown between two famous bullfighters. One of them is of Indian ancestry, the other Spanish. In the process, Norman gets caught up in the story of his own Mexican ancestors, who come from three different ethnic groups: Mexican Indian, Spanish, and English. The stories, taking place over a 1,500-year period, range from the gory sacrifices of the native Mexican tribes, to the coming of the Spaniards, to the war with the United States in the mid-nineteenth century.

Keywords: Journalists and reporters; Mexico—multi-period

Chapter 4

Romancing the Past

Romantic historical novels involve readers emotionally with engaging stories that celebrate the love between two people—most typically a woman and a man. Readers enjoy romances because they provide a means of escaping from their day-to-day lives into a world where love takes center stage. Romances set in the past let readers live vicariously through the experiences of lovers from earlier periods of history, which makes the sense of escapism even more paramount. While being entertained, readers can see how the political atmosphere, social factors, and everyday life of the times influence the actions of the heroes and heroines.

Although traditional romance novels conclude with happily-ever-after endings, the novels in this chapter don't always follow this formula. Historical romantic fiction can be divided into three categories, depending on the scope of the novel and also on whether the history or the romance is more prominent in the story line. The eras, geographical settings, and pace used by the authors of historical romantic fiction also differ for each subcategory.

Romantic epics feature sweeping drama, vividly described and colorful settings, and star-crossed romances. They play out on a wide canvas, and their heroes and heroines often get caught up in major political events from history. A classic example is Margaret Mitchell's *Gone with the Wind*. *Romantic historicals*, set on a smaller scale than romantic epics, strike a balance between the romance and the historical content; both are equally important to the story line. Both romantic epics and romantic historicals tend to be long books, and the couples in these novels may or may not have a happy ending.

Historical romances, on the other hand, follow the formula of the romance genre in that the romance ends happily. The romantic story also forms the major plotline of the book; although historical details are important, major political events occur in the background. These novels tend to be shorter than romantic epics or romantic historicals, though there are exceptions. People who enjoy reading family sagas with a romantic aspect should also investigate "Romantic Sagas" (Chapter 5). In addition, many novels in Chapter 2 incorporate a strong romantic plotline, particularly those featuring female protagonists.

Romantic Epics

Romantic epics are novels in which a protagonist, usually female, searches for love in a vibrantly described historical setting. These lengthy novels contain sweeping drama, lush historical imagery, and larger-than-life characters who waltz in and out of history, typically interacting with many real-life characters and events. Romantic epics feature star-crossed lovers who take on the world in order to stay together, though they are continually forced apart—by duty, circumstance, or choice. The heroines are bright, beautiful, and courageous, while the heroes are attractive, dashing, and intriguing. The pair may or may not be perfect for each other, though they find themselves passionately drawn together, often against their better judgment.

Exotic settings are common to these novels, and many romantic epics are set in more than one location, as the heroine and hero undertake dangerous voyages or are forced to live their own lives when they are separated from one another. The brilliantly described locale, painted on a broad canvas yet illustrated down to the last detail, plays into the dramatic impact of these novels, as if to emphasize that these are extraordinary people living in extraordinary times.

Many of these novels take place against a wartime setting or a period of political upheaval, which adds to the drama and tension. The historical events in these novels usually play a strong role both in keeping the hero and heroine apart and in bringing them back together. Social factors, such as class barriers between the pair, can also serve as a challenge to the protagonists.

There is no standard pattern to the plot of romantic epics. Both the hero and heroine may find love with more than one partner, although only one of them is typically his or her true soul mate. Although these novels usually end optimistically, the hopeful conclusion may or may not refer to the romance. In most romantic epics, the heroine emerges triumphant, confident that the decisions she's had to make were the best ones for her, given the tumultuous times she was forced to live in.

Readers who appreciate the broad sweep of history in romantic epics may also appreciate multi-period epics (Chapter 3) as well as traditional historical novels (Chapter 2) written on a broad canvas, such as those written by Jules Watson and Margaret George. Some historical fantasy novels (Chapter 14), such as Marion Zimmer Bradley's *The Mists of Avalon*, also appeal to fans of romantic epics, as they follow a strong-willed heroine on a romantic, magical journey.

Donati, Sara.

Wilderness Series. ★

Sequels of sorts to James Fenimore Cooper's *The Last of the Mohicans*, Sara Donati's novels sweep from the New York frontier and Canada in the late eighteenth century to Louisiana and the Caribbean during the War of 1812. Donati also writes fiction under her real name, Rosina Lippi.

Keywords: Bonner family; French Antilles—19th century; Louisiana—early United States; Mixed heritage; Mohawk Indians; New York—early United States; Physicians, women

Into the Wilderness. Bantam, 1998. 691pp. Hardbound, 0553107364.

In 1792 Englishwoman Elizabeth Middleton, a twenty-nine-year-old spinster, comes to her father's lands in New York State ostensibly to become a schoolteacher. Soon she discovers that her father has plans to marry her off to wealthy doctor Richard Todd. However, the man she loves is Nathaniel Bonner, a rough outdoorsman who is the son of "Hawkeye" Bonner, the hero of Cooper's classic novel. Elizabeth's future inheritance—her father's lands—is the source of the rivalry among Nathaniel, Todd, and the Mahican tribespeople, who believe the land to be their own.

Dawn on a Distant Shore. Bantam, 2000. 463pp. Hardbound, 0553107488.

Elizabeth and Nathaniel are happily married with twins, but fate keeps them apart. To rescue his father, Nathaniel travels to Montreal, but when his own life is in jeopardy, Elizabeth bundles up her children and takes them on a frozen journey north.

Lake in the Clouds. Bantam, 2002. 613pp. Hardbound, 0553801406.

In 1802 Hannah Bonner, Nathaniel's daughter by his Mahican first wife, struggles with her mixed-race identity and her decision to pursue a career in medicine. While nursing a runaway slave back to health, she puts her family in danger, but the bounty hunter assigned to recapture the slave turns out to be Hannah's childhood sweetheart, Liam Kirby.

Fire Along the Sky. Bantam, 2004. 624pp. Hardbound, 0553801465.

This latest volume picks up the Bonners' story ten years after *Lake in the Clouds* ends. Hannah Bonner comes home to Paradise a changed person, and war with Britain is on the horizon. Elizabeth and Nathaniel's son Daniel itches to head to war, while his sister Lily lives her own life in Montreal.

Queen of Swords. Bantam, 2006. 576pp. Hardbound, 055380149X.

It is 1814 in the French Antilles, where Jennet Scott Huntar, the fiancée of the Bonners' son, Luke, is being held captive. Luke and his half-Mohawk sister, Hannah, free her, but Jennet has a secret: she gave birth to Luke's son while imprisoned and was forced to give him up to Honoré Poiterin, an untrustworthy man, to save the child's life. The trio journey to New Orleans to find and reclaim the boy, only to discover that his new family plans on keeping him.

Donnelly, Jennifer.

Tea Rose Series.

Two connected novels about ambitious women in the late nineteenth and early twentieth centuries who throw off societal strictures to pursue their own dreams of independence.

The Tea Rose. Thomas Dunne, 2002. 544pp. Hardbound, 0312288352.

Fiona Finnegan is an Irish working-class girl in East London in 1888. After her father's murder she is torn from her lover, Joe Bristow, and flees to America with her younger brother to avoid being hunted down by the tea baron responsible for her father's death. It takes ten years of hard work, but Fiona builds a tea empire of her own from the ground up—always dreaming of the day when she can return home and take revenge on the man who destroyed her family.

Keywords: Businesswomen; England—Victorian era; Immigrants, Irish; New York—Reconstruction/Gilded Age; Tea

The Winter Rose. Hyperion, 2008. 720pp. Hardbound, 9781401301033.

In 1900 India Selwyn Jones, a recent medical school graduate, puts her safety at risk by tending to the poor in London's East End, where her services are desperately needed. Her aristocratic family and ambitious fiancé, Freddie Lytton, are less than pleased by her decision. India grows unexpectedly close to gangster Sid Malone—the brother of Fiona from *The Tea Rose*, in his guise as an underworld crime boss—when he becomes her patient. However, Freddie will stop at nothing to marry her; he needs her promised dowry to finance his political career. The action moves, in the course of this lengthy novel, from London's squalid Whitechapel district to African coffee plantations to the California coast.

Keywords: England—20th century; Gangsters; Nobility; Physicians, women; Poverty

Furnivall, Kate.

The Red Scarf. **Berkley, 2008. 480pp. Paper, 9780425221648.**

Furnivall's second epic love story opens in a Siberian labor camp in 1933, at the height of Stalinist Russia. In these wretched conditions, two young women, Sofia and Anna, form a strong bond of friendship, with Anna telling Sofia stories about her love for Vasily, a fervent revolutionary. When Anna becomes ill, Sofia risks her life to help her—escaping and traveling great distances across Siberia to track down Vasily. In a remote village populated by gypsies, Sofia finds Mikhail Pashin, whom she finds disturbingly attractive—and who she comes to believe is Vasily in disguise. A gritty romantic novel that also evokes women's friendships.

Keywords: Communism; Friendship; Gulags; Gypsies; Love triangles; Russia—20th century

The Russian Concubine. **Berkley, 2007. 517pp. Paper, 9780425215586.**

Junchow, China, in 1928 is a city divided by both race and class: the Westerners of the International Settlement don't mix with the Chinese, whom they consider far beneath them. Red-haired Lydia Ivanova, a recent Russian émigré who fled with her mother after the Bolshevik Revolution, challenges these boundaries when she falls in love with Chang An Lo, a Chinese member of the Communist party. But Chiang Kai Shek's troops are on the way, prepared to kill all Communists, and Lydia dares not tell anyone about her romance, not even her mother.

Keywords: China—20th century; Communism; Immigrants, Russian; Interracial romance; Racial conflict

Gabaldon, Diana.

Outlander Series. ★

The combination of time travel, epic romance, and plentiful historical detail make Gabaldon's novels difficult to pigeonhole. They are enjoyed by numerous romance fans but are meatier than most works in the genre. The story begins as Claire Randall, a former combat nurse during World War II, goes back in time to eighteenth-century Scotland, where she falls in love with Scotsman Jamie Fraser. But Claire is married, and she remains torn between her present-day husband and the romantic Scotsman who lived two centuries earlier. In the series Claire and Jamie try to prevent the loss of Scottish lives at the Battle of Culloden in 1745, and, much later, try to ride out the trouble that the American Revolution will bring to the colonies and to England. Claire's certain knowledge of what the future holds, though, is only of so much help when the pair are forced to live through it all. A nonfiction work by Gabaldon, *The Outlandish Companion* (Delacorte, 1999), provides background to the series.

Keywords: Culloden; Battle of; Fraser, Claire; Fraser, Jamie; Scotland—18th century; Time travel

Outlander. Delacorte, 1991. 627pp. Hardbound, 0385302304.

Claire Randall, back from her stint in World War II and on her second honeymoon with her husband in Scotland, touches a boulder in an ancient stone circle. This takes her back in time to 1743 Scotland, where she becomes caught up in a world filled with spies, rebellions, and a handsome red-haired Scotsman named Jamie Fraser. RITA Award.

Dragonfly in Amber. Delacorte, 1992. 743pp. Hardbound, 0385302312.

In 1968, twenty years after her adventures in *Outlander*, Claire's husband Frank has died. Claire and her adult daughter Brianna journey to Scotland, hoping to learn what happened to Claire's eighteenth-century husband, Jamie, after she left him to return to the present. Claire revisits her past adventures with Jamie, in which the pair do all they can to prevent Bonnie Prince Charlie from returning to Scotland in 1745. In a contemporary story, Claire puzzles over the best way to tell Brianna about her true paternity.

Voyager. Delacorte, 1994. 870pp. Hardbound, 0385302320.

After discovering that Jamie survived the 1745 Battle of Culloden, Claire travels back into the past to find her lost love. After reuniting passionately with him, the pair escape the wrath of the English by fleeing to the West Indies, where Jamie's nephew has been taken prisoner aboard a pirate ship.

Keywords: West Indies—18th century; Pirates

Drums of Autumn. Delacorte, 1997. 880pp. Hardbound, 0385311400.

Claire and Jamie turn up in 1760s Charleston, South Carolina, where they live among unhappy expatriate Scots and try to prevent the

American Revolution. Their daughter Brianna, romantically involved with a man from the present day, travels back into the past herself to try to prevent Claire's and Jamie's deaths.

Keywords: South Carolina—Colonial period

The Fiery Cross. Delacorte, 2001. 979pp. Hardbound, 0385315279.

In the Carolinas in 1771, the American Revolution will soon be under way, and Claire knows that war is unavoidable. Brianna and her husband Roger are happily married with a son, but all of their lives will be threatened if Jamie fights against England in the upcoming war.

Keywords: North Carolina—American Revolution

A Breath of Snow and Ashes. Delacorte, 2006. 979pp. Hardbound, 9780385324168.

It is 1772, and the colonial governor of North Carolina asks Jamie Fraser, living happily on Fraser's Ridge in the backcountry with his wife, Claire, to defend the land for king and country. But thanks to his time-traveling wife, Jamie knows that war will break out within a few years. He also realizes that, thanks to a newspaper clipping from the *Wilmington Gazette*, he and his family may die in a fire four years hence.

Keywords: North Carolina—American Revolution

Gilchrist, Michaela.

The Fiercer Heart. **Simon & Schuster, 2005. 374pp. Hardbound, 0743222822.** ✍

Using letters and papers relating to the pair, Gilchrist based her second novel (after *The Good Journey*) on the tumultuous relationship between two historical individuals: Diana Bullitt, a vivacious Southern belle from Kentucky, and Lt. Philip Kearny, the wealthy Northerner she marries in 1841. They begin their life together promisingly in Washington, D.C., but his military career takes him around the world, and his service during the Mexican War cripples him for life. Meanwhile, although she loves him, Diana must decide whether to put up with his infidelities or create a new life for herself.

Keywords: Kearny, Diana Bullitt (historical character); Kearny, Philip (historical character); Soldiers; Washington, D.C.—early United States

Givens, Kathleen.

On a Highland Shore. **Pocket, 2006. 384pp. Paper, 1416509909.**

It is 1263 on Scotland's western shore, and laird's daughter Margaret MacDonald prepares for her wedding to Lachlan Ross, a man she's known since childhood. She changes her mind when she learns of his affair with her best friend, Fiona, a woman not of her class. Then Vikings attack her family's settlement of Somerstrath, destroying her home, killing her parents, and kidnapping her younger brother. She and her remaining siblings owe their lives to Gannon MacMagnus, a half-Norse, half-Irish warrior, who vows to find the raiders responsible for attacking both Somerstrath and his own home back in Ireland. Though she doesn't entirely trust him, Margaret and Gannon fall in love, but Lachlan refuses to give her up.

Keywords: Scotland—high Middle Ages; Vikings

Rivals for the Crown. **Pocket, 2007. 414pp. Paper, 9781416509929.**

This sequel to *On a Highland Shore* begins in 1290, as numerous competitors vie for Scotland's throne. Childhood friends Rachel de Anjou and Isabel de Burke are separated after King Edward I expels all Jews from England. Rachel heads north to Scotland, where Highlander Kieran MacDonald intrigues her. Isabel remains behind, becoming a lady-in-waiting to Queen Eleanor in London. When the friends reunite in Scotland, they have some tough decisions to make, both romantically and politically.

Keywords: Friendship; Jews; Ladies in waiting; Scotland—high Middle Ages

Koen, Karleen.

Through a Glass Darkly Series.

Adventure and romance in wildly decadent London and Paris in the eighteenth century, and later, in pre-revolutionary America.

Dark Angels. Crown, 2006. 530pp. Hardbound, 0307339912.

This prequel to the series is annotated in Chapter 2, under "The British Isles: The Stuart Era."

Through a Glass Darkly. Random House, 1986. 738pp. Hardbound, 0394553780.

As fifteen-year-old Barbara Alderley grows to womanhood, her grandmother, the duchess of Tamworth, plans for her to marry her late husband's friend, Roger Montgeoffry. Although Barbara easily falls in love with the much older Roger, and he is intrigued by the husky-voiced Barbara, he loves her mainly for the lands he acquires through their marriage. This isn't the only secret that Roger is keeping from her, either.

Keywords: England—Georgian era; Gay men; Nobility

Now Face to Face. Random House, 1995. 733pp. Hardbound, 0394569296.

In the sequel to *Through a Glass Darkly*, Barbara Montgeoffry, Countess Devane, is a twenty-year-old widow in 1721. She sails to Virginia to make something out of her family's tobacco plantation. She steadily grows stronger and more mature, not hesitating to take action against the evils of slavery. Barbara returns home only when the timing is right, and becomes romantically involved with a Jacobite spy.

Keywords: Plantations; Slaves and slavery; Virginia—colonial period; Widows

Martin, James Conroyd.

Push Not the River series. ✍ 📖

An epic set around Poland's failed quest in pursuit of stability and a democratic government in the late eighteenth century. Martin based his novels on the actual diary of Polish countess Anna Maria Berezowska, which for a time was sealed in wax to hide its scandalous contents from the eyes of later generations. They should be read in order.

Keywords: Berezowska, Anna Maria (historical character); Cousins; Napoleonic Wars; Nobility; Poland—early modern era; Revolutions and revolutionaries; Third of May Constitution

Push Not the River. Thomas Dunne, 2003. 432pp. Hardbound, 0312311508.

Countess Anna Maria Berezowska, a noblewoman in late eighteenth-century Poland, fights for herself and her country during a time of great upheaval in Polish history: the rise and fall of the Third of May Constitution, a document that promised democratic reform for the Polish people. Sent away to live with her Aunt Stella after her parents' deaths, Anna falls in love with Jan Stelnicki, a patriot who fights for his country's independence, but their romance is stalled by war and the romantic manipulations of Anna's beautiful, selfish cousin Zofia. Through it all, Anna emerges as an indomitable heroine.

Against a Crimson Sky. Thomas Dunne, 2006. 384pp. Hardbound, 0312326823.

Poland was dissolved in 1794, but the Stelnicki family continue to fight for their country's independence from Russia. Anna and Jan Stelnicki are married and live happily with their children on her country estate. When Napoleon begins making war against Poland's enemies, Jan and his friend Pawel, the longtime suitor of Anna's cousin Zofia, join his forces. The novel concludes with Napoleon's famously ill-fated march on Moscow in 1812.

Mercury, Karen.

Karen Mercury writes dramatic, passionate, humor-laced tales about adventurous men and women in precolonial Africa. Explicit sex scenes.

The Four Quarters of the World. Medallion, 2006. 505pp. Paper, 9781932815443.

Tewodros II, the mostly mad Christian king of Abyssinia (modern-day Ethiopia) in 1866, aims to unite his country under one ruler and one god, so he parades his army from one province to another in the hopes of displaying his power and quashing rebellions. Captain Ravinger Howland, an American adventurer who becomes Tewodros's right-hand man and favored companion, accompanies him on his travels. All changes when American doctor Delphine Chambliss arrives in the kingdom. Tewodros believes she's the reincarnation of his ancestor Makeda, the biblical Queen of Sheba. Ravi, who has come to believe that Tewodros is insane, falls in love with Delphine while Abyssinia falls apart around them.

Keywords: Adventurers; Ethiopia—19th century; Physicians, women; Theodore II, Negus of Ethiopia (historical character)

The Hinterlands. Medallion, 2005. 389pp. Paper, 1932815112.

In 1896 American anthropologist Elle Bowie travels to the ancient kingdom of Benin, in the Niger Delta, to study the native people and their customs. Accompanying her is Rip Bowie, a rowdy Texan photographer who pretends to be her husband. Brendan Donivan, an American adventurer heavily involved in local trade, is recommended to her as a source of information for her research. In the harsh jungle atmosphere, he and Elle become sexually and romantically involved. The real suspense begins when Britain begins encroaching on the region, for Brendan fiercely protects his adopted homeland.

Keywords: Adventurers; Anthropologists; Colonialism; Nigeria—19th century

Strangely Wonderful. **Medallion, 2007. 451pp. Paper, 9781933836027.**

Tomaj Balashazy first meets Dagny Ravenhurst in 1827, when he rescues her from drowning in his lagoon. Tomaj, a former member of the U.S. Navy, is a pirate hiding out from his enemies on his tropical plantation at Mavasarona Bay in Madagascar. Dagny, an American naturalist studying the island paradise's exotic and rare animal species, feels strongly attracted to the Hungarian count. Her jealous patron/lover, French industrialist Paul Boneaux, is not the only obstacle to their happiness. Madagascar's bloodthirsty Queen Ranavalona doesn't want competition for her affections, either.

Keywords: Madagascar—19th century; Naturalists; Pirates

Mitchell, Margaret.

🎗 *Gone with the Wind.* **Macmillan, 1936. 1037pp. Hardbound.** ★

Margaret Mitchell's epic of the Old South during the Civil War and Reconstruction—later made into a popular film—features raven-haired heroine Scarlett O'Hara, a Southern belle on a Georgia plantation who can't figure out which man is truly best for her until it's too late. Though debonair Rhett Butler is her soul mate, she only discovers this after mooning for years over Ashley Wilkes, a classic Southern gentleman and dreamer who's not free to return her love. Some sections, particularly the portrayal of blacks, are seen today as racially offensive, though the historical context of the time in which Mitchell was writing should be taken into account. Even after over seventy years, her classic remains an absorbing read. Pulitzer Prize.

Keywords: Confederacy; Georgia—Civil War and Reconstruction/Gilded Age; Plantations

Moore, Ann.

Gracelin O'Malley Trilogy. 📖

Moore's trilogy follows a young Irishwoman's romantic yet tear-filled journey from 1840s Ireland to the Pacific Northwest.

Gracelin O'Malley. New American Library, 2001. 398pp. Paper, 0451202996.

In Ireland at the time of the potato famine, young Protestant Gracelin O'Malley is married off to Bram Donnelly, the lord of the manor, to save her family from starvation. He turns out to be an abusive drunk, though his wealth helps her provide for the starving poor of the local countryside. She finds her true love in her brother's Catholic friend Morgan, who believes as passionately in social change as she does.

Keywords: Abusive relationships; Ireland—19th century; Potato famine; Revolutions and revolutionaries

Leaving Ireland. New American Library, 2002. 378pp. Paper, 0451207076.

More somber than *Gracelin O'Malley*, this sequel sees Gracelin on a journey to America via Liverpool with her daughter, because she is wanted for murder back in Ireland. After surviving a difficult sea voyage, Gracelin arrives in New York City in 1849 only to confront anti-Irish sentiment and unsanitary living conditions.

Keywords: Immigrants, Irish; New York—early United States

Til Morning Light. New American Library, 2005. 416pp. Paper, 0451214048.

After accepting sea captain Peter Reinders's marriage proposal, Gracelin moves with her children to his home city of San Francisco, in hopes that a doctor there will cure her daughter Mary Kate's illness. Dr. Wakefield is destined to change her life and those of others around her. Moore also ties in the stories of two other men from Gracelin's past and their struggles to reunite with her in America.

Keywords: Immigrants, Irish; California—early United States

Sawyer, Cheryl.

New Zealand-born novelist Sawyer writes adventure-filled, intricately plotted romantic epics about people who fall in love at transformative times in history.

The Chase. **Signet Eclipse, 2005. 435pp. Paper, 0451215664.**

Only the testimony of Lady Sophia Hamilton can save the life of Jacques Decernay, a captured French soldier who turned traitor by joining the British army. Accused of desertion, he risks death by firing squad. Despite her hatred of all things French, Sophia, a beautiful Englishwoman who lost her husband in the Napoleonic Wars, knows that telling the truth is the right thing to do. Sophia flees to Sussex, afraid of what her fellow countrymen will do to her for aiding the enemy, and when Jacques follows her, they find it difficult to deny their mutual attraction. A lush romantic story set during the Hundred Days before the Battle of Waterloo in 1815.

Keywords: England—Regency era; France—early modern era; Napoleonic Wars; Soldiers; Widows

The Code of Love. **Signet Eclipse, 2006. 378pp. Paper, 0451218388.**

Delphine Dalgleish, a loyal Bonapartist, lives on the French island of Mauritius, off the African coast, while the Napoleonic Wars rage across Europe. At a reception one evening she meets Sir Gideon Landor, an English naval officer and French prisoner; soon after he manages to escape. They meet again in England, where Delphine is working as a spy for Napoleon himself. He finds her cold and empty-headed, while she believes he's a double agent working for France and despises him for it. Both their initial impressions are wrong.

Keywords: England—Regency era; France—early modern era; Mauritius—19th century; Napoleonic Wars; Spies

Siren. **Signet Eclipse, 2005. 520pp. Paper, 045121377.** ✍

As rumor has it, pirate's daughter Léonore Roncival was a beautiful siren who lured men to the wealthy Caribbean island paradise of San Stefan and chose only a select few to be her lovers. When pirate Jean Laffite invades San Stefan, hoping to make away with the treasure supposedly hidden there, he finds he has met his match in Léonore. Their adventures, together and apart, culminate at the Battle of New Orleans in 1815.

Keywords: Caribbean; Laffite, Jean (historical character); Louisiana—early United States; New Orleans, Battle of; Pirates

The Winter Prince. **NAL, 2007. 400pp. Paper, 9780451220448.** ✍

> Mary Villiers, Duchess of Richmond and Lennox, is the witty and beautiful ward of King Charles I and considers him a second father. But even she refuses to countenance his insistence on declaring war on Parliament and, therefore, on his own people. Mary secretly takes measures to preserve England while simultaneously keeping the peace within the Stuart royal family. However, she runs into trouble when she falls in love with Rupert of the Rhine, the king's handsome nephew, nicknamed the "winter prince." Set in the mid-seventeenth century at the very beginning of the English Civil War, and based loosely on a true story; Mary and Rupert are historical characters.
>
> **Keywords:** England—Stuart era; English Civil War; Royalty; Rupert, Prince (historical character); Villiers, Mary (historical character)

Sedley, Kate.

For King and Country. **Severn House, 2006. 416pp. Hardbound, 0727864068.**

> Prior to the beginning of the English Civil War in the mid-seventeenth century, Cornishwoman Lilias Pengelly flees her home with her father, a loyal Puritan, to avoid religious persecution. They plan to sail to America, but tragedy changes the course of her life. She eventually marries Richard Pride, the city of Bristol's member of Parliament, and loyally supports both him and the Puritan cause. That is, until she meets Priam Lithgow, the Earl of Chelwood, a Royalist whom she risks her life to save. When Oliver Cromwell comes to power, Lilias has some tough decisions to make. Originally published in 1984 as *The Lofty Banners* by Brenda Clarke.
>
> **Keywords:** England—Stuart era; English Civil War; Puritans

Seton, Anya.

Avalon. **Houghton Mifflin, 1965. 440pp. Hardbound.** ★ **YA**

> In this poignant love story Merewyn, a Cornish peasant girl, and Rumon de Provence, a French prince, begin an adventure that takes them from the coast of Cornwall to Iceland, Greenland, the North American coast, and finally to the royal court of tenth-century England.
>
> **Keywords:** England—early Middle Ages; Iceland—10th century; Nobility

Katherine. **Houghton Mifflin, 1954. 588pp. Hardbound.** ✍ ★ **YA**

> Katherine de Roet, a poor commoner, grows up in a convent and marries knight Hugh Swynford, by whom she has two children. Her sister Philippa weds the poet Geoffrey Chaucer. When Katherine's path brings her into the royal circle, she meets John of Gaunt, Duke of Lancaster and King Edward III's third son, with whom she falls passionately in love. Their romance must wait until the deaths of both their spouses, but by then John is forced to marry for political reasons. For the rest of their lives, Katherine and the duke remain devoted to each other, and their illicit union (and four illegitimate children) causes scandals to ripple through fourteenth-century England. Meticulously researched and based on historical

figures, Seton's classic romance has served as the inspiration for many of today's romance novelists.

Keywords: England—high Middle Ages; John of Gaunt (historical character); Mistresses; Royalty; Swynford, Katherine (historical character)

Sundaresan, Indu.

The Splendor of Silence. **Atria, 2006. 403pp. Hardbound, 0743283678.**

Sam Hawthorne, a captain in the U.S. Army, arrives in the (fictional) small kingdom of Rudrakot, India, in May 1942, ostensibly to recover from an injury he suffered while fighting in Burma. In reality, he's a spy with the newly formed OSS who is in Rudrakot to find his brother, Mike, who disappeared while serving with an undercover group working for India's independence. When Sam falls in love with Mila, daughter of the local political agent, it complicates his mission considerably. The novel opens in 1963, as Sam and Mila's daughter, Olivia, goes through her parents' personal effects and learns about their passionate affair.

Keywords: India—World War II; Spies

Romantic Historical Novels

Romantic historicals are historical novels with a strong romantic element. Historical events and characters are integral to the plot of romantic historicals, so much so that these novels could not realistically take place in any other location or time. Although they take place on a smaller scale than romantic epics, their background is nonetheless realistically drawn.

Although the romance has played a strong role in the development of the story line and characters, it is not always the most important. The protagonist may have other problems to contend with, such as saving the family name or fortune, protecting herself and her land against invaders, or avoiding political controversy or capture. These elements may play as much of a part in the story as does the romance.

Many authors of romantic historicals (e.g., Diane Haeger, Sandra Worth) were inspired by the real-life romantic tales of historical figures, such as British or European royals and nobles. Others create believable fictional characters who interact with one another against a well-realized historical background. With approximately equal weight given to the historical setting and the romance, romantic historicals give readers a realistic feel for the courtship practices of past eras. Medieval settings are common, as are novels set in the American West, Victorian England, and Europe during wartime. While some authors write exclusively in one historical period, others write novels set in a variety of locations and eras.

Unlike historical romances, romantic historicals may or may not end on an optimistic note. Historical fiction readers find this unpredictability to be appealing, for it keeps them turning the pages to discover whether the heroine and hero will end up together. The protagonist may also have more than one love interest within the novel, as might his or her partner. Many older romantic historicals, written before the happily-ever-after ending and single-partner elements became the norm in romances, are considered classics of the romance genre today.

Fans of romantic historicals may also enjoy traditional historical novels (Chapter 2) with a strong romantic element, such as those written by Jean Auel, Susan Holloway Scott, and John Shors. Romantic Westerns, novels of the American West with a romance story line, are found in Chapter 6.

The Roman Empire

Iverson, Kimberly.

Liberty. HQN, 2006. 490pp. Paper, 0373771347.

Rhyddes, a flame-haired Celtic slave, is compelled to perform for the Romans as a gladiatrix in Londinium's arena after her family sells her into captivity. Marcus Calpurnius Aquila, son of Britannia's Roman governor, incurs his family's wrath by fighting in the arena himself, although he agrees to give up his hobby and marry the senator's daughter his ambitious family chooses for him. Even after she gets over her natural abhorrence to all things Roman, Rhyddes knows a future with Aquila is impossible. Political forces ensnare both of them in a plot to assassinate Emperor Marcus Aurelius, making their burgeoning romance not as important as mere survival. Iverson has written mainstream historical fiction as Kim Headlee.

Keywords: Celts; Gladiators; Gladiators, women; Rome

Europe and the British Isles

The Middle Ages

Here, romances develop between members of opposing political and cultural groups in medieval times (circa the fifth through fifteenth centuries AD): the Normans and the Saxons, the lower and upper classes of medieval England, and lovers on opposite sides of the Wars of the Roses. These novels are all set in England.

Graeme-Evans, Posie.

Anne Trilogy.

A trilogy about Anne de Bohun, secret illegitimate daughter of Lancastrian King Henry VI and secret lover of Yorkist King Edward IV. An unlikely historical occurrence, admittedly—Henry VI wasn't exactly a womanizer—but the romance and intrigue of fifteenth-century England will sweep readers along.

Keywords: Belgium; Edward IV, King of England (historical character); Herbalists; Illegitimate children; Mistresses; Peasants; Wars of the Roses

The Innocent. Atria, 2004. 406pp. Paper, 0743272226.

Anne de Bohun, a beautiful young peasant girl, is raised in secrecy in the forests of fifteenth-century England after political foes kill her mother. In 1465 Anne arrives at the London court of King Edward IV. With her knowledge of herbs, she saves the life of Edward IV's queen and quickly becomes the royal healer. Before Anne knows it, she and the king are caught up in a passionate affair.

The Exiled. Atria, 2005. 407pp. Paper, 074344373X.

Anne raises her son, Edward, the product of her affair with Edward IV, in the politically enlightened city of Brugge and supports him by becoming a merchant. But her jealous fellow businessmen believe it's unnatural for a woman to succeed in business. If they discover her son's true parentage—something the king himself doesn't even know—it would destroy them both.

The Uncrowned Queen. Atria, 2006. 465pp. Paper, 0743443748.

Anne has abandoned her former existence and now lives peacefully as an herbalist in the country on the outskirts of Brugge. As the Wars of the Roses continue to rage, Anne is called back to help her former lover. Then Edward is sent into exile himself, and Anne becomes the only one he trusts to help broker an alliance between him and his brother-in-law, the Duke of Burgundy. Originally titled *The Beloved* in Graeme-Evans's native Australia.

Lane, Janet.

Coin Forest Series.

Historical romantic adventures set in mid-fifteenth-century England, a time when the gypsies (Romani people) roamed freely throughout the British Isles and Europe.

Keywords: Chalices; Gypsies; Knights

Tabor's Trinket. Five Star, 2006. 335pp. Hardbound, 9781594145421.

In 1435, during the tumultuous reign of Henry VI, Baron Tabor takes refuge in a gypsy camp in Somerset after sustaining wounds in a castle siege. Enchanted by the beauty of Sharai, a young Romani woman, he falls in love with her. Despite belonging to a group of hereditary nomads, Sharai has always longed for a permanent home. She gladly returns his love, not knowing the financial burden and responsibility that accompany his noble title.

Emerald Silk. Five Star, 2007. 324pp. Hardbound, 9781594146824.

Kadriya, the half-gypsy girl whom Sharai has raised, agrees to honor her Romani heritage by marrying Teraf, a handsome gypsy tribal king. At the Applewood horse fair in Somerset in 1448 where they plan to announce their betrothal, Teraf is accused of stealing an emerald chalice. In the course of trying to prove his innocence, Kadriya crosses paths with a bigoted knight, Sir John Wynter.

Worth, Sandra.

Lady of the Roses. Berkley, 2007. 404pp. Paper, 9780425219140. ✍

Isobel Ingoldesthorpe, a fifteen-year-old ward of Lancastrian Queen Marguerite d'Anjou in England in 1456, only has eyes for Sir John Neville, a Yorkist knight. Their families are hereditary enemies, yet Queen Marguerite permits their marriage. Isobel narrates the story of their lifelong passion, which endures despite the ongoing war between the houses of Lancaster and York.

Keywords: Ingoldesthorpe, Isobel (historical character); Knights; Neville, John (historical character); Wars of the Roses

The Rose of York Series. ✍

Worth describes the marriage between Richard, Duke of Gloucester—later King Richard III—and his wife, Anne Neville, as a star-crossed romance comparable to that of Romeo and Juliet. As one of the suspects in the murders of the princes in the Tower, Richard III hasn't received great press over the years, but Worth goes far in reestablishing his good name.

Keywords: Anne Neville, Queen of England (historical character); Richard III, King of England (historical character); Royalty; Wars of the Roses

The Rose of York: Love and War. End Table, 2003. 340pp. Paper, 0975126407.

> During the Wars of the Roses, Richard of Gloucester, a thoughtful and lonely young man often overshadowed by his strong-willed elder brother Edward IV, falls in love with his cousin, Anne Neville, daughter of the powerful Earl of Warwick.

The Rose of York: Crown of Destiny. End Table, 2006. 176pp. Paper, 0975126482.

> After numerous separations and trials, Richard and Anne are finally wed. Then Edward IV dies, forcing Richard to leave country life in northern England and return to court. He struggles mightily with his conscience but comes to realize that war could be prevented if he took over the throne himself, rather than guarding it for his young nephew.

The Rose of York: Fall from Grace. End Table, 2007. 272pp. Paper, 0975126490.

> As king, Richard strives to rule wisely and do justice for the common man. His beloved wife, Anne, stands by him, but he can only watch helplessly as she grows more and more ill on their travels through England. The death of their son, Ned, adds even more to Richard's burden.

The Renaissance and Reformation

Romances set amid political and courtly intrigue in France, Italy, Scotland, and England during the sixteenth century.

Abrams, Douglas Carlton.

The Lost Diary of Don Juan. Atria, 2007. 307pp. Hardbound, 1416532501.
Annotated in Chapter 2.

Bennett, T. J.

The Legacy. Medallion, 2007. 458pp. Paper, 9781933836362.

To escape imprisonment by her tyrannical adoptive father, Baronesse Sabina von Ziegler agrees to wed Wolfgang Behaim, a widowed printer, in a marriage of convenience. Wolf, for his part, is being blackmailed by the baron into marrying Sabina. Their union ripens into something more, but it can't flourish until they discover the truth behind the baron's machinations. Set in 1525 in Wittenberg, Germany, at the time of Martin Luther's religious reforms.

Keywords: Germany; Marriages of convenience; Nobility; Printers

Carroll, Susan.

Daughters of the Earth Novels. ✍

A sweeping historical and romantic series, with a touch of fantasy. Carroll sets the scene in Brittany, Paris, and England in the late sixteenth century, during the time of Catherine de Medici, dowager queen of France, mistress of political intrigue and—as rumors have it—black magic. In the first three novels, which form a loose trilogy, the protagonists are the Cheney sisters, "daughters of the earth" renowned for their wisdom and healing skills. In this dangerous time, they risk being accused as witches. The scene then shifts to Elizabethan England, where wars between Protestants and Catholics continue.

Keywords: Catherine de Medici, Queen of France (historical character); England; France; Henry IV, King of France (historical character); Magic and magicians; Sisters; Witchcraft

The Dark Queen. Ballantine, 2005. 533pp. Paper, 0345437969.

Ariane Cheney, the eldest Cheney sister, is widely known as "the lady of Faire Isle" (which is somewhere in Brittany) due to her skills in healing and earth magic. When a wounded stranger arrives in her land with evidence that Catherine de Medici may have murdered her rival queen, Jeanne of Navarre, with a pair of poisoned gloves, Catherine sends her men to Faire Isle, bent on revenge. To save her life, Ariane forges an alliance with a powerful nobleman, the Comte de Renard, who is determined to marry her.

The Courtesan. Ballantine, 2005. 560pp. Paper, 0345437977.

It is now 1575, and Gabrielle Cheney, the middle sister, has established herself in Paris as a courtesan. She hopes to secure her future by becoming the mistress of Henry, King of Navarre, but Captain Nicolas Rémy, an old flame she believed was dead, returns—and he has other plans for her. They aim to put an end to Catherine and the black arts she practices.

The Silver Rose. Ballantine, 2006. 515pp. Paper, 0345482514.

Ten years after the events in *The Courtesan*, the youngest and most powerful Cheney sister, Miri, takes center stage. As the only sister still remaining in France, Miri arrives in Paris from the Faire Isle in Brittany to defend her country against Catherine de Medici's most dangerous rival, a woman known only as the Silver Rose. To do so she turns to Simon Aristide, a former witch-hunter who had persecuted her family for years.

The Huntress. Ballantine, 2007. 490pp. Paper, 9780345490612.

It is 1586, and the Protestant Queen Elizabeth I faces challenges from rebellious Catholics who seek to put Mary, Queen of Scots on England's throne. Amid this political and religious turmoil, Catriona "Cat" O'Hanlon, a pagan Irishwoman accused of witchcraft, takes up the fight against the coven of the Silver Rose. It's up to her to find the mysterious young girl who may possess the power to bring down Catherine de Medici, the Dark Queen.

Haeger, Diane.

The Ruby Ring. **Three Rivers, 2005. 384pp. Paper, 1400051738.** ✍

Raphael, one of the greatest painters of the Italian Renaissance, unexpectedly finds his muse and greatest love in Margherita Luti, a humble baker's daughter, and she poses for many of his paintings of the Madonna. Haeger tells her story from Margherita's viewpoint, beginning after Raphael's death in 1520, when she hopes to retire to a convent. Before the Mother Superior will grant permission, she asks Margherita to remove the ruby ring Raphael once gave her.

Keywords: Artists; Italy; Luti, Margherita (historical character); Raphael (historical character)

The Secret Bride. **NAL, 2008. 398pp. Paper, 9780451223135.** ✍

Princess Mary, her older brother Henry, and his good friend Charles Brandon grow up as childhood companions. The three are drawn together in sorrow and hope after Mary's eldest brother Arthur dies in 1502, which leaves Henry as heir to the throne. Although wed in a political match to the old, sickly Louis XII of France, Mary always remembers her brother's promise: that she'll be allowed to choose her second husband herself. To Henry's chagrin, she sets her sights on Charles, and his are on her—despite his being a commoner with two previous marriages. A lush, romantic story based on fact.

Keywords: Brandon, Charles (historical character); England; France; Mary Tudor, Queen of France (historical character); Princesses

Scott-Turner, Caitlin.

The Queen's Fencer. **Five Star, 2005. 297pp. Hardbound, 1594143021.**

Ardys Trevallon, daughter of Elizabeth I's fencing master, has clearly inherited her father's skills, and she's devastated when he collapses after a tournament. On her way back home to Cornwall, Irish pirate Desmond Kirkconnell captures her ship, not realizing she can easily best him with a sword. They become passionately involved, and when Desmond's rival, François de la Roche, abducts her, Desmond pursues them all the way to the Caribbean.

Keywords: Caribbean; England; Fencers; Pirates

Seventeenth Century

The English Civil War and the Restoration (mid-seventeenth century) are common settings for romantic historicals; European settings are much less frequent.

Herries, Anne.

English Civil War trilogy.

Star-crossed lovers in the mid-seventeenth century, as the Roundheads and Royalists battle for control of England. The novels, which feature members of the Saunders and Mortimer families, are best read in order.

Keywords: England; English Civil War; Families; Quakers

Lovers and Enemies. Severn House, 2005. 256pp. Hardbound, 9780727862686.

Caroline Saunders always expected to marry ne'er-do-well Harry Mortimer, son of her parents' friends. But when civil war threatens, Lord Mortimer sides with the king, while the Saunders family, though not Puritans, believe in justice for the people. This leaves Caroline free to acknowledge her attraction to Harry's younger brother, Nicolas, who joins Cromwell's army. Sent away to Oxford when her father falls ill, Caroline and her Quaker cousin, Mercy, find themselves in the center of Royalist activity. Caroline risks much to be with Nicolas, while Mercy, hopelessly attracted to Harry, makes an impulsive decision fated to change all their lives.

Love Lies Weeping. Severn House, 2006. 256pp. Hardbound, 9780727863584.

After the Battle of Naseby, quiet Elizabeth Bellingham risks much when she tends to Rupert Saunders, a wounded Cavalier soldier (and brother of Caroline from the previous book), who shows up at her family's door. Unfortunately he only has eyes for her beautiful, spoiled cousin Sarah.

The Seeds of Sin. Severn House, 2006. 256pp. Hardbound, 9780727863898.

The Civil War is over, Charles II is back on the throne, and Herries concludes her trilogy with the next generation of Saunderses and Mortimers. Angelica Saunders has always loved her cousin Hal and hopes to win him over once her other cousin, Claire, turns down his proposal. Distraught at losing Claire, Hal takes up with a loose gypsy girl, repeating the mistakes his father made decades earlier.

Nineteenth Century

The political and economic changes sweeping Britain and Europe in the nineteenth century once more take center stage in these novels of lovers kept apart by political and religious differences or social circumstance.

Davis, Anna.

The Shoe Queen. Pocket, 2007. 399pp. Paper, 9781416537359.

In the decadent, bohemian world of haute couture Paris in the 1920s, would-be poet Genevieve Shelby King's hunger to acquire the gorgeous lace slippers adorning her archrival's feet is matched only by her desire for Paolo Zachari, the Italian designer who created them. Zachari's refusal to accede to her whims increases her obsession with the pair of unobtainable shoes she covets. Heedless of the consequences, she throws her marriage to her wealthy Bostonian husband into disarray.

Keywords: France; Shoes; Socialites

Herendeen, Ann.

Phyllida and the Brotherhood of Philander. Harper, 2008. 532pp. Paper, 9780061451362.

Andrew Carrington, a dashing nobleman in Regency London, knows he needs to marry and beget an heir. Even knowing that he's gay, Phyllida Lewis agrees to his proposal. She has only one condition: that she be able to continue her secret romance writing career. Andrew finds himself surprisingly attracted to his new wife, and his fellow members of the Brotherhood of Philander—an exclusive gay men's club—begin taking bets about her possible pregnancy. Phyllida even proves amenable to Andrew's simultaneous relationship with another man, but an embezzler in Andrew's household proves their downfall. A unique love story (with explicit love scenes) that takes a witty look at the gay subculture of Regency England.

Keywords: Authors, women; Bisexuality; England—Regency era; Gay men

James, Syrie.

The Lost Memoirs of Jane Austen. Avon A, 2007. 303pp. Paper, 9780061341427. ✍ 📖 **YA**

Discovered in the attic of Chawton House in Steventon, England, during renovations, Jane Austen's lost memoirs reveal her passionate midlife romance with a certain Frederick Ashford, a gentleman she meets while visiting the seaside resort village of Lyme in the early 1800s. James, knowing Jane Austen's numerous fans would have liked to see their favorite author get her own happy ending in real life, imagines her as the heroine in her own love story. Although the romance is fictional, she also gives insight into customs of the era and Austen's life as an author.

Keywords: Austen, Jane (historical character); Austen themes; Authors, women; England—Georgian era

Morgan, Jude.

Indiscretion. St. Martin's Press, 2006. 378pp. Hardbound, 0312362064.
Annotated in Chapter 10.

Richman, Alyson.

The Last Van Gogh. Berkley, 2006. 308pp. Paper, 042521267X. ✍

It is the summer of 1890, and Vincent van Gogh spends his final months in the care of Dr. Paul Gachet, a homeopathic physician in the country village of Auvers-sur-Oise, France. Dr. Gachet's twenty-one-year-old daughter, Marguerite, narrates the story of her relationship with the despairing, disheveled artist, as she poses for several of his paintings and gradually falls in love with him—a feeling eventually returned. Van Gogh's stay in Auvers is historically based, as are his paintings, but his love affair with Marguerite is fictional.

Keywords: Artists; Artists' models; France; Van Gogh, Vincent (historical character)

Robards, Elizabeth.

With Violets. Five Star, 2005. 317pp. Hardbound, 1410402223. ✍

In Paris in 1868 Berthe Morisot, one of the few women painters associated with the Impressionist movement, is introduced to Édouard Manet for the first time. She has always placed her avocation before romantic relationships, but she cannot deny her attraction to Manet and his for her, although he is already married. Afraid of the scandal that would blacken their names should their relationship become known, Berthe marries Manet's brother, Eugène. Robards (pseudonym of Nancy Robards Thompson) imagines a passionate love affair between the two Impressionist painters based on Morisot's correspondence, some of which is reproduced within the novel. The paperback edition of *With Violets* (Avon A, 2008) was rewritten using present-tense rather than past-tense verbs, which gives it a more literary feel.

Keywords: Artists; France; Love triangles; Manet, Édouard (historical character); Morisot, Berthe (historical character)

Willig, Lauren.

Pink Carnation Series. YA

An entertaining historical romp, set in the modern day and during the Napoleonic Wars. Harvard graduate student Eloise Kelly gradually uncovers the true identity of the Pink Carnation, a dashing, elusive spy who helped save England from the French, as she finishes work on her dissertation. Swashbuckling adventure, light romance, witty dialogue, and emphasis on women's lives give this series the flavor of chick lit with a historical twist. When Willig began her series she was a PhD candidate and history graduate student at Harvard; she now practices law and writes novels.

Keywords: Archivists; England; France; Graduate students; Multi-period novels; Napoleonic Wars; Spies, women

The Secret History of the Pink Carnation. Dutton, 2004. 388pp. Hardbound, 0525948600.

> For her PhD dissertation, Eloise Kelly travels to London to research the real identities of the Pink Carnation and Purple Gentian, successors to the Scarlet Pimpernel. She butts heads with archivist Colin Selwick, who tries to deny her access to relevant papers, but she gains access to a trunk of early nineteenth-century letters and diaries that give her clues. In a parallel story, Amy Balcourt, a refugee from the French Revolution residing in rural England, decides to avenge her father's death at the hands of the French by joining the League of the Purple Gentian, aka Lord Richard Selwick, an English nobleman and spy. Not surprisingly, sparks fly between them.

The Masque of the Black Tulip. Dutton, 2005. 416pp. Hardbound, 0525949208.

> Fresh upon discovering who the Pink Carnation really was, Eloise Kelly travels to France to learn more about the Black Tulip, France's most dangerous spy and the Pink Carnation's French counterpart during the Napoleonic Wars. In early nineteenth-century London, Henrietta Uppington and Miles Dorrington try to prevent the Black Tulip, newly arrived in England, from killing the Pink Carnation.

The Deception of the Emerald Ring. Dutton, 2006. 400pp. Hardbound, 0525949771.

> As Eloise Kelly continues her PhD studies, as well as her infatuation with handsome British archivist Colin Selwick, her nineteenth-century research subjects Letty Alsworthy and Lord Geoffrey Pinchingdale-Snipe are forced to wed after Geoff abducts her by mistake. Under orders from England Geoff, a secret spy bent on suppressing an Irish rebellion, makes his way to Ireland, Letty following close behind.

The Seduction of the Crimson Rose. Dutton, 2008. 400pp. Hardbound, 9780525950332.

> Raven-tressed Mary Alsworthy, whose suitor was accidentally stolen by her sister Letty in the previous book, agrees to help Lord Vaughn capture a French spy, the notorious Black Tulip—a man who has a known weakness for dark-haired women.

Twentieth Century

Love blossoms during wartime all throughout twentieth-century Europe. Just like in real life, not all of the stories end happily. See also "Wartime Sagas" (Chapter 5).

Capella, Anthony.

The Wedding Officer. Bantam, 2007. 423pp. Hardbound, 9780553805475.

> It is 1944 in occupied Naples, where Captain James Gould has been assigned to discourage weddings between British soldiers and local Italian women. Unfortunately for the women, he's very good at his job. Therefore, they encourage him to hire Livia Pertini, a former restaurant chef and widow from Vesuvius, as his cook. Livia's culinary delights distract him from his job, and her fiery personality captures his heart.

> **Keywords:** Cooks; Italy—World War II

Di Michele, Mary.

Tenor of Love. Touchstone, 2005. 329pp. Paper, 0743266927. ✍

> In this novel of passion, betrayal, and ambition, English professor Mary di Michele tells the story of opera singer Enrico Caruso's three great loves. It is 1897, and Caruso has arrived in Livorno, Italy, where he will perform on the summer stage with soprano Ada Giachetti, at whose family home he is living. A love triangle, which lasts for the first two decades of the twentieth century, forms among Caruso, Ada, and her younger sister, Rina, who wants to take Ada's place on stage and in his bed. Caruso's widow, Dorothy, imagines their story.

> **Keywords:** Caruso, Enrico (historical character); Italy; Love triangles; Opera singers

Jenoff, Pam.
World War II Series.

Two interconnected novels about women's survival, loves, and heartbreak during World War II.

The Kommandant's Girl. MIRA, 2007. 395pp. Paper, 9780778323426. 📖

> Emma and Jacob Bau, a young Jewish couple, have been married only three weeks when the Nazis invade Poland. Jacob is forced to disappear underground with the resistance, while Emma, only nineteen, escapes the Jewish ghetto with their help. She takes shelter with Jacob's elderly, Catholic aunt and assumes the new identity of Anna Lipowski. When Emma (as Anna) is introduced to Kommandant

Georg Richwalder, a high-ranking Nazi leader, he is captivated immediately and hires her to work as his assistant. To help Jacob's cause, Emma accepts, but their unexpected chemistry challenges her role.

Keywords: Jews; Nazis; Poland—World War II

The Diplomat's Wife. MIRA, 2008. 360pp. Paper, 9780778325123. 📖

Marta Nederman, a member of the Polish resistance (and good friend of Emma from *The Kommandant's Girl*), barely survives a Nazi prison camp. A caring American soldier nurses her back to health, but their future happiness is derailed when he dies in a plane crash. She finds contentment anew with Simon Gold, a British diplomat whom she marries, but she returns to her homeland as a spy when an anti-Communist mission proves too tempting to resist. *The Diplomat's Wife* picks up where the first book left off, but it can also be read independently.

Keywords: England—World War II; Poland—World War II; Spies, women

Simoni, Lina.

The Scent of Rosa's Oil. **Kensington, 2008. 259pp. Paper, 9780758219244.**

Rosa, the sixteen-year-old orphaned daughter of a prostitute in Genoa, Italy, in 1910, grows up in the Luna brothel, but the house's women—particularly its proprietor, Madam C—keep its true purpose a secret. One evening, while wearing alluring scented oil created by her friend Isabel, an elderly neighbor who has a perfume shop, naïve Rosa attracts the attention of the mayor. Thrown out on the street by a jealous Madam C, Rosa flees to Isabel's home and becomes her apprentice, taking care to hide her scandalous past from her new beau, Renato.

Keywords: Brothels; Illegitimate children; Italy; Perfume; Prostitutes

Zacharius, Walter.

Songbird. **Atria, 2004. 291pp. Hardbound, 0743482115.** 📖

Mia Levy, a Jewish teenager from Poland, loses her family and her entire way of life when Nazis take over her homeland. With the help of the resistance, she escapes to America, where she falls in love with a young musician. But even their romance can't prevent her from returning to war-torn Poland as a spy, to avenge the deaths of her family.

Zacharias, the founder of Kensington Publishing and its former CEO, decided to write his debut novel at age eighty, after a friend convinced him to share a very personal story from his World War II experience. Published in paperback as *The Memories We Keep.*

Keywords: Jews; Poland—World War II; Spies, women

The United States

Colonial America

Love stories set in the wild and as-yet-untamed American colonies in the seventeenth century.

Holman, Anne.

The Mantua-Maker's Beau. **Five Star, 2006. 299pp. Hardbound, 1594144524.**
In Bath, England, in 1774, Clementina Willoby's employer, Mrs. Elizabeth Hunter, has just died—without changing her will to formalize Clementina's inheritance of her dress shop. She tracks down the woman's heir in Philadelphia and journeys there as a lady's companion to convince him to let her keep the shop. Then she learns that he owns the vessel she's traveling on, a ship that also transported indentured servants to the colonies under horrible conditions.

Keywords: Pennsylvania; Seamstresses

The Nineteenth Century

Romantic novels set during America's early growth as a nation—just before, and during, the U.S. Civil War (1861–1865). Romantic Western novels, those set on the American Western frontier in the nineteenth century, are featured in Chapter 6.

Herries, Anne.

My Lady, My Love. **Severn House, 2005. 224pp. Hardbound, 9780727861832.**
Justin St. Arnaud, visiting New Orleans in the early nineteenth century to find the wife and son of his late friend, meets Estelle LeBrun, daughter of a French Creole gentleman who's deep in debt. He makes a bargain with Estelle: if she'll spend the night with him, he'll pay off what her father owes. She accepts—she has no choice—and Justin, who sails the Caribbean as a privateer, can't get her off his mind.

Keywords: Louisiana; Privateers

Mackey, Mary.

The Notorious Mrs. Winston. **Berkley, 2007. 340pp. Paper, 9780425215128.**
In 1861 abolitionist Claire Winston feels trapped in her new marriage to an older man she doesn't love, but takes pride in her abolitionist beliefs—she feels her country needs her. When her husband's nephew, John Taylor, reciprocates her interest, they begin a passionate affair that endures, despite his dedication to the Confederate cause. She loves John so much that when he leaves to join Morgan's Raiders, Claire leaves her husband to follow him, disguised as a male soldier.

Keywords: Abolitionists; Disguise; United States—Civil War

Murphy, Kim.

Promise and Honor Trilogy.
A romantic yet gritty trilogy about two Virginia sisters, Amanda Graham and Alice McGuire, who are swept into the maelstrom of the Civil War.

Keywords: Sisters; Virginia—Civil War and Reconstruction/Gilded Age

Promise and Honor. Coachlight, 2004. 252pp. Paper, 0971679029.

> At the start of the Civil War, Amanda Graham's husband John is killed in battle, leaving her without any means of support. Lieutenant Wil Jackson, a man with a reputation as a womanizer, pays her for smuggling medical supplies for the Confederacy. Sam Prescott, a Union soldier and the widower of Amanda's best friend Kate, makes it clear he wants Amanda for himself.

Honor and Glory. Coachlight, 2005. 269pp. Paper, 0971679061.

> Amanda has married her Yankee beau, Sam Prescott, but Alice McGuire, Amanda's younger sister, sides with the Confederacy, because she can't forget how Union troops destroyed her home. The sisters find themselves on opposite sides, especially when Alice begins seeing Wil Jackson and helping him with his smuggling activities.

Glory and Promise. Coachlight, 2006. 272pp. Paper, 0971679088.

> Although the Civil War has theoretically ended, resentment still remains on both sides, and the reconstruction of the South—Virginia in particular—has a long way to go. Both Amanda and Alice, married to soldiers formerly on opposite sides, struggle with their relationships with one another, their husbands, and the newly reunited country.

Schoenecker, Mary Fremont.

Four Summers Waiting. **Five Star, 2006. 247pp. Hardbound, 1594144753.** ✍

> At an abolitionist meeting, judge's daughter Maria Onderdonk meets Henry Simms, a medical student who is a conductor on the Underground Railroad. As the Civil War breaks out and they are separated over four long years, Maria and Henry communicate their growing love through letters. Set in Long Island and Washington, D.C.. Based on the ancestors of the author's husband.

> **Keywords:** Abolitionists; New York; Onderdonk, Maria (historical character); Simms, Henry (historical character); Underground Railroad; Washington, D.C.

Twentieth Century

Like novels of the same time period in Europe, most works in this section feature stories of wartime romances.

Bostwick, Marie.

Glennon Series. 📖

> Poignant novels about passionate women and men living and loving during the early years of aviation in America.

> **Keywords:** Coming of age; Great Depression; Lindbergh, Charles (historical character); Oklahoma; Pilots; Pilots, women; Women's Air Service Pilots

Fields of Gold. Kensington, 2005. 314pp. Paper, 0758209908.

> Evangeline "Eva" Glennon grows up in the farming town of Dillon, Oklahoma, in the 1920s, content to live quietly with her loving parents. She realizes that with her lame leg, romance just won't be in the cards. Then a handsome young aviator calling himself Slim makes an unexpected landing in her family's wheat field. They spend one romantic night together that

leaves her pregnant with his son. Slim and Eva stay in touch through the years, and she never forgets him, even after word arrives—via the newspapers—that Slim has married another woman. Eva finds peace only years later, when she learns how the world has changed him.

On Wings of the Morning. Kensington, 2007. 288pp. Paper, 9780758222565.

Young Morgan Glennon, Charles Lindbergh's illegitimate son, has a passion for flight, just like his famous father. As he begins a career in aviation, he meets Georgia Carter, a beautiful divorcee who becomes a WASP (Women's Air Service Pilot). Their relationship deepens during America's involvement in World War II.

River's Edge. **Kensington, 2006. 357pp. Paper, 0758209916.** 📖

In the late 1930s Elise Braun's father sends her to live with distant cousins in America, the Mullers, when it becomes clear that Germany will soon be at war. Elise, an accomplished pianist, settles into a new life in a Massachusetts village, taking solace in her music, and she falls in love with one of the Mullers' sons, Junior. But she regularly faces prejudice from other Americans because of her German name and heritage, and when Junior decides to enlist, she misses him terribly.

Keywords: Fathers and daughters: Massachusetts—World War II; Pianists; Prejudice

Steffen, Kathy.

First, There Is a River. **Medallion, 2007. 356pp. Paper, 9781932815931.**

When Emma Perkins's abusive husband, Jared, sends their two children away to work on a nearby farm, she summons up all that's left of her remaining courage and flees to safety aboard her uncle Quentin's riverboat. Aboard the *Spirit* as it travels up and down the Ohio River, Emma grows close to Gage, the riverboat's engineer, who opens up to her about his scarred past.

Keywords: Abusive relationships; Ohio—20th century; Riverboats

Historical Romances

In novels of historical romance, the love story takes center stage. Historical events, customs, and values are present in the story and may serve to advance the plot, but they function primarily as a background to the romance. If any battles or political developments occur within the novel, for the most part they take place offstage. This keeps the focus on the main characters and their growing relationship. As a rule, historical romances have an optimistic, happily-ever-after ending.

Historical romances vary considerably in terms of how much period detail the author weaves into the story, and reader preferences will vary as well. People who simply want to read a well-written love story in a non-modern setting may not want to be overwhelmed with historical details. Other readers will want exactly the opposite.

After spending nearly a decade as the unpopular stepsister of contemporary romances, historical romances are finally seeing a resurgence of reader interest—something that their fans appreciate. Within the subgenre, paranormal subplots have become more prevalent. Readers who enjoy romantic novels with a dash of the supernatural should pay attention to authors such as Naomi Bellis, Joy Nash, Patricia Rice, and Sandra Schwab.

Despite the unfortunately commonly held perception that historical romances incorporate modern characters in fancy dress, many historical romance authors today do considerable background research for their novels. They take care to ensure that their facts are correct and that their characters behave in ways appropriate to their era. There is some controversy about whether romances featuring feisty, freethinking heroines should automatically be considered anachronistic. Those who disagree mention that historical novels in general are written about characters who stand apart from the norm (Eleanor of Aquitaine is frequently used as an example), and they have a point. The debate will no doubt continue.

Some settings in historical romance are more common than others. In novels taking place in the British Isles, Regency-set novels command the widest audience; also popular are medieval settings, the Georgian period, Victorian times, and Scottish settings in general. Among American settings, the frontier West is perhaps the most popular. Historical romance novels set in other times or locations—such as ancient times, the American Revolution and Civil War, and Asia and Australia—are harder to come by. Bloody battle scenes, after all, have little appeal for the romance reader, and some publishers feel that unusual settings deflect attention from the love story. (Librarians interested in learning why some settings are more popular than others should read Kristin Ramsdell's "Getting Behind Reader Taboos: What's Wrong with France," published in the July 2002 issue of *Romance Writers Report*.) Other unpleasant aspects of life in times past, while they certainly existed, are not dwelt upon in most historical romances.

On the other hand, some readers, seeing the overabundance of novels about aristocratic British lords and ladies, have demanded more diversity in their romances, and publishers are beginning to listen. Readers interested in discovering romances in more out-of-the-way settings should consult the catalogs (and Web sites) of publishers such as Harlequin, Dorchester, and Medallion Press. This chapter aims to strike a balance, providing information on romances set in common locales as well as those that are more unusual, such as ancient Rome; medieval Ireland; Renaissance Italy; and even Australia, China, and India.

After spending nearly a decade as the unpopular stepsister of contemporary romances, historical romances are finally seeing a resurgence of reader interest—something that their fans appreciate. Within the subgenre, paranormal subplots have become more prevalent. Readers who enjoy romantic novels with a dash of the supernatural should pay attention to authors such as Naomi Bellis, Joy Nash, Patricia Rice, and Sandra Schwab.

Authors listed in this section do their best to create characters and plotlines that faithfully reflect their time periods. With so many historical romances published each month, comprehensiveness is next to impossible; the following list provides a selected bibliography. Only authors' most significant or newest titles are provided here, but many writers have a lengthy backlist of titles that would be equally appropriate for readers who enjoy a good dose of history with their romance. (Not all of these authors limit themselves to historical romance titles, however.) Also, publishers frequently bring older paperback titles by popular authors back into print so that they can reach a new audience—and so that readers and librarians can purchase fresh copies for their collections.

Novels in this section are categorized chronologically. Historical romance novels listed in the previous volume of *Historical Fiction* indicated levels of sexual content/sensuality. However, because explicit sex is now the norm within the genre, readers can assume that the following romances—unless stated otherwise —may be described as "sensual."

Ancient Civilizations

Few romance novels are set during ancient times, though they do exist. With their long-ago setting, larger-than-life heroes and heroines, and compelling plots, these romances read like ancient legends.

Allen, Louise.

Virgin Slave, Barbarian King. **Harlequin, 2007. 294pp. Paper, 9780373294770.**
Julia Livia Rufa, a sheltered Roman virgin dragged away from her home by marauding Goths, is forced to become a household slave for Wulfric, one of the invaders—who turns out not to be as barbaric as his reputation. Readers who can manage to ignore the cheesy title will find an entertaining (if fanciful) romance in an unusual setting: Rome after its sacking by the Visigoths in AD 410.

Keywords: Rome—5th century; Slaves and slavery; Visigoths

Nash, Joy.

Druids of Avalon Series.
A paranormal historical romance series set in Roman-era Scotland, and echoing the Arthurian legends. *Silver Silence* will be the next volume.

Keywords: Arthurian themes; Celts; Druids; Holy Grail; Scotland—Roman period; Swords

Celtic Fire. LoveSpell, 2005. 309pp. Paper, 0505526395.
In AD 116 Rhiannon, queen of her Celtic tribe, longs to drive the Romans from their land, but regrets that the druids chose to sacrifice one of them to their god. A year later Lucius Aquila is visited by the ghost of his brother Aulus, the Roman killed by the druids, who begs him to come to Britannia to rescue him from a deathless limbo.

The Grail King. LoveSpell, 2006. 324pp. Paper, 0505526832.
Owein, younger brother of Rhiannon from *Celtic Fire*, has had visions of a beautiful Roman maiden who begs him to use his Sight to help her find a mystical object, a grail with healing powers that was stolen from her family.

Deep Magic. LoveSpell, 2008. 372pp. Paper, 9780505527165.

> The druidess Gwendolyn, a guardian of Avalon, joins forces with Marcus Aquila, a Roman blacksmith, to create the fearsome sword known as Exchalybur.

Randal, Lyn.

Warrior or Wife. **Harlequin, 2007. 291pp. Paper, 9780373294374.**

> In Rome in the year AD 106, while attending the gladiatorial games, Marcus Flavius Donatus is shocked to recognize Leda, the star gladiatrix, as Lelia, the senator's daughter whom he used to love.

> **Keywords:** Gladiators; Rome—ancient/prehistoric

Styles, Michelle.

The Gladiator's Honor. **Harlequin, 2006. 295pp. Paper, 0373294174.**

> Julia Antonia, a Roman noblewoman, should know better than to be attracted to Gaius Gracchus Valens, a gladiator in Rome's arena in 65 BC, but she has some scandal in her own past.

> **Keywords:** Gladiators; Rome—ancient/prehistoric

The Roman's Virgin Mistress. **Harlequin, 2007. 296pp. Paper, 9780373294589.**

> In the Roman resort town of Baiae in 69 BC, Silvana Junia is rescued from the sea by Lucius Aurelius Fortis, a high-ranking Roman. They fall in love, but she hides a secret that could change their relationship.

> **Keywords:** Rome—ancient/prehistoric

Viking Romances

Romances about fierce Viking warriors and the maidens they love, set in early medieval Britain and Europe. The voyages undertaken by the heroes and heroines give these novels a sweeping, epic quality.

Groe, Diana.

Erinsong. **Leisure, 2006. 326pp. Paper, 0843957891.**

> When Brenna of Donegal and her sister, Moira, find a blond stranger washed up on Ireland's shores, Brenna names him Keefe, "handsome," for he has amnesia. After Keefe proves himself to their family, their father, the chieftain of Donegal, chooses him as Brenna's handfast husband. As time passes, Keefe remembers his past involvement in Viking raids, making him an enemy of Brenna's people.

> **Keywords:** Ireland—early Middle Ages; Vikings

Maidensong. **Leisure, 2005. 326pp. Paper, 0843957107.**

> In tenth-century Scandinavia, Rika is as powerful a skald—singer of ancient Norse legend—as her father, but when he is killed in a Viking raid on her homeland, she is dragged away as a captive of Bjorn the Black, younger brother

of Gunnar, Jarl of Sogna. But when Gunnar sees how entranced Bjorn is by his thrall, he conceives a plan to sell her as a wife to a Muslim merchant in Constantinople.

Keywords: Byzantium—10th century; Norway; Singers; Slaves and slavery; Vikings

Silk Dreams. **Leisure, 2007. 326pp. Paper, 9780843958690.**

Valdis Ivorsdottir, a young woman from Scandinavia in the tenth century, has the "falling sickness" (epilepsy), which gives her visions and leads her family to sell her into slavery. While at the slave market in Constantinople she catches the eye of Erik, an exiled Viking working for the Byzantine emperor.

Keywords: Byzantium—10th century; Epilepsy; Slaves and slavery

Kirkman, Helen.

Forbidden. **Harlequin, 2004. 352pp. Paper, 0373836295.**

When Lady Rowena buys Wulf of Northumbria, a muscular, dangerous-looking barbarian, in the slave market in AD 716, she expects to use him to avenge her father's murder.

Keywords: England—early Middle Ages

Warriors of the Dragon Banner Series.

This action-packed romantic series, written in a simple style with short sentences and paragraphs, features warrior heroes who swear an oath under the Dragon Banner to defend Wessex and its young king, Alfred, against Viking invaders.

Keywords: England—early Middle Ages; Vikings

A Fragile Trust. HQN, 2005. 377pp. Paper, 0373770774.

In AD 872 along the Mercian border, Lady Gemma discovers Ash, a wounded English warrior raised among Vikings, and risks her life to safe his.

Destiny. HQN, 2006. 384pp. Paper, 0373770545.

Berg, an exiled East Anglian warrior (and a prince in disguise who was horribly scarred while fighting Vikings years ago), rescues Elena from a Viking leader who had used her as his sex slave.

Fearless. HQN, 2006. 384pp. Paper, 0373771193.

In AD 875 Princess Judith of East Anglia journeys to King Alfred's court to find a hero worthy of defending her land from the Vikings. She believes she has found him in Einhard of Frisia, captain of a fleet of ships.

Keywords: Princesses

Untamed. HQN, 2006. 385pp. Paper, 0373771657.

For some time Aurilia, a beautiful healer, has been experiencing visions of Macsen, an English warrior, and he of her. They meet at last when Macsen brings a wounded boy, her cousin, to her home of Wytch Heath for her to heal.

Keywords: Healers

Captured. HQN, 2007. 376pp. Paper, 9780373772377.

Rosamund, a Mercian princess held captive by the enemy, succeeds in winning custody of the warrior Boda from his Viking captors, but both are keeping secrets about their past from the other. Set in AD 876.

Keywords: Princesses

Mathis, Jolie.

The Sea King. **Berkley Sensation, 2006. 295pp. Paper, 0425210650.**

In Anglo-Saxon England, Princess Isabel of Norsex had once risked her life to free Viking warrior Kol Thorleksson from bondage. When he returns to Norsex later to seek revenge against his captors, he is stunned to discover she's the sister of the man responsible for his captivity.

Keywords: England—early Middle Ages; Princesses; Vikings

Styles, Michelle.

Taken by the Viking. **Harlequin, 2008. 281pp. Paper, 9780373294985.**

After Vikings sack and loot the monastery at Lindisfarne in AD 793, Annis of Birdoswald finds a surprising protector in Haakon Haroldson, who takes her back to Norway as his captive and bedmate.

Keywords: England—early Middle Ages; Norway—8th century; Vikings

Medieval Romances

Most medieval romances are chivalrous love stories featuring knights and their ladies. They are set between the fifth and fifteenth centuries in the British Isles or elsewhere in Europe. While most medieval noblewomen had a fair amount of independence, arranged marriages were the norm. They often serve as catalysts for the romance. See also "Viking Romances," above. Unless otherwise stated, all take place in England.

Banning, Lynna.

Crusader's Lady. **Harlequin, 2007. 304pp. Paper, 0373294425.**

In Jerusalem in 1192 Soraya al-Din, a young Arab woman disguised as a boy while spying for Saladin, accompanies Marc de Valery, a war-weary knight on the Third Crusade, as he follows King Richard across Europe back to England. She has revenge in mind, for Marc killed her uncle.

Keywords: Crusades and Crusaders; Disguise; Jerusalem—Middle Ages; Knights

Dain, Claudia.

The Fall. **Leisure, 2004. 374pp. Paper, 0843952210.**

In England in 1165 Juliane of Stanora has been known throughout the land as a cold, passionless woman because her would-be husband was unable to consummate their marriage. Ulrich of Caen, a landless knight with a reputation as a womanizer, accepts a bet that he can seduce her.

Keywords: Knights

Gellis, Roberta.

The Roselynde Chronicles. ★

A panoramic, classic series of romantic novels set between the reigns of Richard the Lion Heart and his nephew Henry III (late twelfth through early thirteenth centuries), featuring a beautiful, strong-willed woman—Alinor of Roselynde—and her children and grandchildren. The political history of England, Wales, and indeed all of Europe plays a major role in the plotline of the series. All of Gellis's historical romances, most of which are set in medieval England, are recommended for their impeccable research and skillful storytelling.

Keywords: Families; Nobility

Roselynde. Playboy Press, 1978. 495pp. Paper.

Lady Alinor Devaux, mistress of Roselynde at the beginning of King Richard's reign, defies her namesake and queen by marrying Sir Simon Lemagne, the warden of her estates, who is thirty years older and not of her station.

Alinor. Playboy Press, 1978. 558pp. Paper.

Following the death of her great love, Simon, Lady Alinor Lemagne surprises herself with her attraction to her late husband's handsome former squire, Ian de Vipont.

Joanna. Playboy Press, 1978. 560pp. Paper.

Beautiful red-haired Joanna, daughter of Alinor and Simon, lets her passions rule her except when it comes to love. She turns down suitor after suitor until she meets a knight named Geoffrey.

Gilliane. Playboy Press, 1979. 494pp. Paper.

At the time of King John's death in 1204, Gilliane, forced for political reasons to marry a man she hates, becomes the prisoner—and the star-crossed lover—of Adam Lemagne, Alinor and Simon's son.

Rhiannon. Playboy Press, 1982. 381pp. Paper.

Simon de Vipont, one of medieval England's most eligible bachelors, fights for the hand of Rhiannon, daughter of a Welsh prince.

Sybelle. Jove, 1983. 404pp. Paper.

Sybelle, daughter of Joanna and Geoffrey and the heiress to Roselynde, vows to wed no man—that is, until she meets a knight named Walter de Clare.

Desiree. Harlequin, 2004. 358pp. Paper, 0373836414.

> After her aging husband is struck with apoplexy, Desiree of Exceat needs help defending their lands from possible French invaders. Coming to her rescue is Sir Alexander Baudoin, nephew of Simon Lemagne (from the first novel, *Roselynde*).

Gifford, Blythe.

The Harlot's Daughter. Harlequin, 2007. 296pp. Paper, 9780373294701.

> Lady Joan, the illegitimate daughter of the late King Edward III and his mistress, arrives at the court of his successor, Richard II, in 1386 in search of funds to support her family. Lord Justin Lamont tries to prevent her from succeeding.

Keywords: Illegitimate children

Innocence Unveiled. Harlequin, 2008. 281pp. Paper, 9780373295029.

> In 1337 in Flanders, Lady Katrine de Gravere, a nobleman's daughter, hides her true identity by working as a weaver. To get the wool she needs to earn her living, she grants shelter to a mysterious stranger who is keeping his own identity hidden.

Keywords: Belgium; Weavers

Johns, Deborah.

Maiden of Fire. Zebra, 2004. 347pp. Paper, 0821774786.

> Claire of Foix was raised by a renegade Templar knight who was the last of the Cathars, a heretical Christian sect destroyed by forerunners of the Inquisition. In Montsegur, France, in 1331, it's up to her to free a prisoner held by the new lord of Montsegur, Aimery dei Conti di Segni, but she and Aimery find themselves passionately attracted to each other.

Keywords: Cathars; France

Maguire, Margo.

Conqueror Series.

> Maguire sets her medieval romances in an earlier period than most: the 1070s, as Normans from France begin to settle throughout England. Relations between the Normans and native Saxons, not to mention the Scots up north, are frosty at best, violent at worst.

Keywords: Nobility

Saxon Lady. Harlequin, 2006. 296pp. Paper, 0373293984.

> After receiving ownership of Lady Aelia of Ingelwald's family's lands from William the Conqueror, Norman knight Mathieu Fitz Autier brings her to London. Their budding romance is thwarted not only by the king, but by the father of the Norman lady he is promised to.

The Bride Hunt. Avon, 2006. 384pp. Paper, 0060837144.

> Not long after the Battle of Hastings, noblewoman Isabel Louvet is captured into slavery when the Scots raid her Northumberland castle. Anvrai d'Arques, a disfigured warrior who was a guest at her castle, does his best to rescue her.
>
> **Keywords:** Disfigurement

The Perfect Seduction. Avon, 2006. 384pp. Paper, 0060837322.

> Kathryn de St. Marie, a Norman baron's daughter kidnapped by Scottish raiders from her family's home, is rescued by a Saxon lord, Edric of Braxton Fell. So that he won't treat her badly because of her origins, she claims to be a lowly serving maid.

McCall, Mary Reed.

The Templar Knights Series.

In the early fourteenth century, three Knights Templar flee to England from France after they are labeled heretics; their order is disbanded, their fellow knights tortured and killed.

Keywords: Knights Templar

Beyond Temptation. Avon, 2005. 384pp. Paper, 0060593687.

> Sir Richard de Cantor's wife Eleanor has been mentally ill for years, and though he feels badly for her, he can't prevent his attraction to her younger cousin, Lady Margaret Newcomb, a fallen noblewoman who has become Eleanor's de facto nurse and caretaker.

Sinful Pleasures. Avon, 2006. 400pp. Paper, 0060593741.

> Lady Alissende de Montague and Sir Damien de Ashby once loved one another, but he was a landless second son and commoner. She was obliged to marry someone of her station, while he became a Templar Knight. Now her husband is dead, and Damien has returned to England.

The Templar's Seduction. Avon, 2007. Paper, 978006117044.

> Sir Alexander de Ashby's reputation isn't exactly shiny after he's caught trying to steal Templar gold. He'll win his freedom if he agrees to impersonate a recently deceased Scottish lord, the Earl of Marston, whom he strongly resembles, in order to spy for the English. First he must convince the earl's wife, Lady Elizabeth, that he really is the man she married.
>
> **Keywords:** Disguise

Willingham, Michelle.

MacEgan Brothers Series.

Willingham incorporates an unusual setting for historical romance: twelfth-century Ireland and England. She writes about three brothers, brave Irish warriors all, and the women who love them.

Keywords: Ireland; Warriors

The Warrior's Touch. Harlequin, 2007. 299pp. Paper, 9780373294664.

> After Connor MacEgan's hands are damaged in battle, he's forced to rely on Aileen Ó Duinne, a healer, for assistance. Set in Ireland in AD 1175.

Her Irish Warrior. Harlequin, 2007. 300pp. 9780373294503.

> To escape marriage to a hateful man, Norman maiden Genevieve de Renalt throws herself on the mercy of Bevan MacEgan.

Her Warrior King. Harlequin, 2008. 297pp. 978037394824.

> Patrick MacEgan, a warrior king of Ireland, is blackmailed into marrying Isabel de Godred, the gentle daughter of the man who invaded his territory.

The Renaissance and Reformation

Romance intertwines with political matters—international intrigue and clan warfare—from the late fifteenth through the very early seventeenth centuries. Despite the popularity of this time period for traditional historical novels, it isn't a common setting for romances.

McCabe, Amanda.

Renaissance Trilogy.

A loosely connected series of historical romances set in Renaissance-era Italy, France, and England. One more will follow.

A Notorious Woman. Harlequin, 2007. 290pp. Paper, 9780373294619.

> Rumors of witchcraft and poison swirl around Venice in 1525. Julietta Bassano, the secretive proprietor of a perfume shop, finds her match in Marc Antonio Velasquez, a man sworn to destroy her.
>
> **Keywords:** Italy; Perfume

A Sinful Alliance. Harlequin, 2008. 282pp. Paper, 9780373294930.

> Marguerite Dumas, a spy for the king of France known as the Emerald Lily, discovers her longtime enemy, Nicolai Ostrovsky, in the dissolute court of England's Henry VIII.
>
> **Keywords:** England; Spies, women

McCarty, Monica.

Highlander Series.

Handsome and virile Highland warriors find their matches in strong-minded, beautiful women as clan wars rage on the Isle of Skye. Although some of the love stories are heavily fictionalized, all of McCarty's heroes and heroines are historical figures.

Keywords: Scotland; Warriors

Highlander Untamed. Ballantine, 2007. 385pp. Paper, 9780345494368.

> It is 1599. Rory MacLeod, chief of the MacLeods on the Isle of Skye, doesn't want to wed Isabel MacDonald, but he agrees to a handfast marriage for

duty's sake. They fall passionately in love, although Isabel is charged to discover his secrets and betray him to her clan. A dramatization of the MacLeod–MacDonald conflict known as the War of the One-Eyed Woman.

Keywords: MacDonald, Isabel (historical character); MacLeod, Rory (historical character)

Highlander Unmasked. Ballantine, 2007. 420pp. Paper, 9780345494375.

In 1605 Alex MacLeod becomes a mercenary whose covert mission is to defend his clan against King James. When he rescues Meg Mackinnon from outlaws, she throws his plans into disarray.

Keywords: Mackinnon, Margaret (historical character); MacLeod, Alexander (historical character); Mercenaries

Highlander Unchained. Ballantine, 2007. 367pp. Paper, 9780345494382.

Lachlan Maclean, a clan chief cursed by his late wife's dying words, abducts Flora MacLeod and plans to wed her in order to bring peace to his people. Set in 1607.

Keywords: Curses; Kidnapping; Maclean, Lachlan (historical character); MacLeod, Flora (historical character)

Seventeenth Century

The English Civil War in the seventeenth century was a time of intense political and religious rivalry, as Royalists fought against Roundheads (Puritans) for control of England. Romances set during the Civil War and Restoration vividly contrast the plain Puritan lifestyle with that of the more glamorous Royalists. Not surprisingly, most of this era's romantic heroes fall into the latter group. All in this current category are set predominantly in England.

Cornick, Nicola.

Lord Greville's Captive. Harlequin, 2006. 296pp. Paper, 0373294271.

The betrothal of Simon, Lord Greville, and Anne Grafton, both of Oxfordshire, was broken after their families found themselves on opposite sides during the English Civil War. Now Simon comes to Grafton Manor aiming to claim it for Parliament, but Anne refuses to yield it to him.

Keywords: English Civil War

O'Brien, Anne.

Puritan Bride. Harlequin, 2004. 297pp. Paper, 0373293623.

To cement his claim to Winteringham Priory in 1663, Marcus, Viscount Marlbrooke, agrees to marry Katherine Harley, a Puritan woman whose family was given ownership of his lands during the English Civil War. Both are surprised by the unexpected passion stirred up by their arranged union.

Keywords: Arranged marriages; English Civil War; Puritans

Thornton, Claire.

City of Flames Trilogy.

A trilogy about three cousins who find love in England and Europe in the mid-seventeenth century. The Great Fire of London in 1666 serves as a backdrop and gives the series its title.

Keywords: Cousins; Great Fire of London

The Defiant Mistress. Harlequin, 2006. 297pp. Paper, 0373294263.

Eight years ago Athena Fairchild was blackmailed into leaving her betrothed, Gabriel Vaughan, at the altar. Now, after a chance meeting at the ambassador's palace in Venice, Gabriel only wants revenge—and demands that Athena, in need of safe passage to England, accompany him as his mistress.

Keywords: Italy

The Abducted Heiress. Harlequin, 2007. 304pp. Paper, 0373294344.

Lady Desire Godwin, a reclusive young heiress who prefers her rooftop garden on the Strand to society life, barely escapes being abducted by brigands. Saving the one surviving would-be abductor from being lynched by her servants, she has him carted to prison instead. In the confusion of the Great Fire of London, he escapes—and saves her life in return.

The Vagabond Duchess. Harlequin, 2007. 304pp. Paper, 0373294468.

After both survive the Great Fire, Temperance Challinor, a draper's daughter, shares a night of passion with wandering poet Jack Bow, not knowing he's really a duke in disguise. Soon after she hears he has been killed. Left pregnant, Temperance pretends to be his widow and travels to his hometown to raise the child—only to meet his mother, who informs her that Jack is very much alive.

Westin, Jeane.

Restoration Romance Series.

An adventurous romantic series filled with intrigue, featuring rakish highwaymen, spies, and the women who love them. Set in bawdy Restoration England.

Lady Anne's Dangerous Man. Signet Eclipse, 2005. 346pp. Paper, 0451217365.

Lady Anne Gascoigne overhears her fiancé, Edward, offering her virtue to the Merry Monarch, Charles II, in an attempt to curry favor with him. She flees home, and until her betrothal can be annulled, her father places her under the protection of "Gentleman Johnny" Gilbert, a notorious highwayman.

Keywords: Highwaymen

Lady Katherne's Wild Ride. Signet Eclipse, 2006. 335pp. Paper, 045121921X.

Lady Katherne Lindsay, a price on her head after assaulting her cousin's cruel husband (who had tried to rape her), barely escapes Bournely Hall with her maid, Martha. Along their route to London they take shelter with a traveling band of actors led by Jeremy Hughes. As Jeremy's leading lady on stage, Katherne discovers she has an unexpected talent for the dramatic life.

Keywords: Actresses

Lady Merry's Dashing Champion. Signet Eclipse, 2007. 310pp. Paper, 9780451221926.

> Meriel St. Thomas, the orphaned ward of a rich benefactor, bears a striking resemblance to Lady Felice, the cold, unfaithful wife of Lord Giles, Earl of Warborough, who has been spying for the Dutch. When the king's spymaster notices this, he compels her to take Felice's place, so that she might discover whether Giles has turned traitor as well.

> **Keywords:** Imposters; Spies

Georgian Romances

The majority of these romances are set in England during the reign of George III in the 1760s, before his madness made him unable to rule. Others are set in the late eighteenth and very early nineteenth centuries—the early Napoleonic era—and feature heroes who are spies, highwaymen, and the like. Like romances set in the Regency period, Georgian romances tend to feature members of the upper classes. Some of them fit into the Regency romance style (below), with light, witty dialogue and banter. Others reflect the treacherous and often erotic undercurrent hidden beneath the propriety of English society.

Archer, Zoe.

Love in a Bottle. **Leisure, 2006. 326pp. Paper, 0843957387.**

> It is 1763 in Wiltshire, England, and Sophie Andrews's beloved Uncle Alforth, the only other person who understands her preoccupation with botany, has just been kidnapped by highwaymen. Ian Blackpool, a roguish peddler who hawks love potions, joins forces with Sophie to get him back.

> **Keywords:** Botanists; Peddlers

Bellis, Naomi.

Draw Down the Darkness. **Signet Eclipse, 2007. 308pp. Paper, 9780451220950.**

> Helen Barrett, a proper young lady in London in 1798, breaks off her long engagement to Nicholas Saville, Viscount Redfern, because of his unexplained absences. Nicholas, for his part, secretly serves as a spy for King George, but when Helen unexpectedly falls into danger, Nicholas leaves his dangerous mission to save her.

> **Keywords:** Nobility; Spies

Step into Darkness. **Signet Eclipse, 2006. 314pp. Paper, 0451219384.**

> In 1793, at the height of the French Revolution, viscount's daughter Sarah Leaford searches London's dingiest taverns for Gentleman Jack, a notorious thief, who may be her only hope for rescuing her father from a dungeon in Paris. She doesn't realize that her father was the one responsible for framing Jack for murder years ago. Set in England and France, with light paranormal elements.

> **Keywords:** French Revolution; Thieves

Theft of Shadows. **Signet Eclipse, 2008. 310pp. Paper, 9780451223289.**

Gabriel D'Aubrigny, returning to England from France in 1799, must return to his old life of espionage after his purse and horse are stolen by a lady thief. He earns his keep by spying on a mysterious gentleman reputed to be practicing dark magic, but little does he know that the thief herself, Anne Tremaine, has a grudge against the same man.

Keywords: Magic and magicians; Thieves

Beverley, Jo.

Malloren Series.

Beverley's Malloren novels, about an aristocratic family of four brothers and two sisters, are set in 1760s Georgian England—when highwaymen roamed the roads in search of adventure. The most recent entries, which feature members of their extended group of friends, are annotated.

Keywords: Malloren family; Nobility

My Lady Notorious. Avon, 1993. 380pp. Paper, 0451206444

Tempting Fortune. Zebra, 1995. 444pp. Paper, 0821748580.

Something Wicked. Topaz, 1997. 374pp. Paper, 0451407806.

Secrets of the Night. Topaz, 1999. 338pp. Paper, 0451408896.

Devilish. Signet, 2000. 372pp. Paper, 0451199979.

Winter Fire. Signet, 2003. 311pp. Paper, 0451210654.

A Most Unsuitable Man. Signet, 2005. 370pp. Paper, 0451214234.

Damaris Myddleton, an incredibly wealthy heiress whose plans to marry the Marquess of Ashart were thwarted at the end of *Winter Fire*, starts up a flirtation with Octavius "Fitz" Fitzroger, Ashart's friend, despite his being a penniless commoner.

Keywords: Heirs and heiresses

A Lady's Secret. Signet, 2008. 416pp. Paper, 9780451224194.

While disguised as a nun named Sister Immaculata, Petra d'Averio travels to England in 1764 in the company of Robin Fitzvitry, Earl of Huntersdown, to find her long-lost father.

Keywords: Disguise; Nuns

Bourne, Joanna.

Bourne's suspenseful Napoleonic-era romances incorporate twisting plots, authentic historical atmosphere, and dialogue that reflects the characters' nationalities.

My Lord and Spymaster. **Berkley Sensation, 2008. 380pp. Paper, 9780425222461.**

To prove her father is innocent of treason against England, Jess Whitby travels deep into the London underworld in search of the real culprit. Captain Sebastian

Kennett, who saves her from being attacked on the docks, may be just the man she's seeking.

Keywords: Napoleonic Wars; Spies

The Spymaster's Lady. **Berkley Sensation, 2008. 373pp. Paper, 9780425219607.**
Annique Villiers, the expert French spy known by the code name "Fox Cub," has been imprisoned by her own countrymen, who believe she knows more than she's telling. British spymaster Robert Grey is determined to free her and use her knowledge for England's purposes. They form an uneasy, unlikely, and temporary truce while fleeing France for England, with enemies in close pursuit.

Keywords: France; Napoleonic Wars; Spies, women

Cornick, Nicola.

Unmasked. **HQN, 2008. 384pp. Paper, 9780373773039.**
In 1805 Mari Osborne risks her freedom and her very life by riding the North Yorkshire countryside as one of the Glory Girls, a group of highwaymen out to right society's wrongs. Britain's home secretary charges Nick Falconer with the task of bringing these notorious women to justice.

Keywords: Highwaymen

Feather, Jane.

Almost Series.

Romance and adventure in late eighteenth- and early nineteenth-century England (and on the high seas), and featuring older, independent-minded heroines.

Keywords: Napoleonic Wars

Almost a Bride. Bantam, 2005. 435pp. Paper, 0553587552.
> To avenge himself against the man who sent his sister to the guillotine, Jack Fortescu, Duke of St. Jules, decides to ruin Frederick Lacey. After Lacey commits suicide, Jack pays a visit to Lacey's half-sister, Arabella, and proposes marriage. She's not inclined to accept.

Almost a Lady. Bantam, 2006. 453pp. Paper, 0553587560.
> Meg Barrett, aged twenty-nine, feels she's too independent for the strictures of marriage, though she yearns for passion and adventure. Her wish is granted when a privateer named Cosimo mistakes her for someone else, kidnaps her, and tries to use her in a mission against Napoleon.
>
> **Keywords:** Privateers; Spinsters

Heyer, Georgette.
Though best known for her Regencies, Heyer also wrote several well-regarded Georgian romances.

The Black Moth. **HQN, 2008. 326pp. Paper, 9780373773398.**

In the 1750s Jack Carstares, returning from exile, becomes a highwayman in order to remain in England undetected. Jack first meets beautiful Diana Beauleigh when he rescues her from abduction by the notorious Duke of Andover—aka the Black Moth. Originally published in 1921.

Keywords: Highwaymen

These Old Shades. **HQN, 2008. 384pp. Paper, 9780373773404.**

Heyer transforms the wicked rake from *The Black Moth* into Justin Alastair, Duke of Avon, called "Satanas" for his devilish ways. While roaming pre-revolutionary Paris one evening, he comes across Léon, a starved, red-haired child whom he rescues from the streets. But Léon is really Leonie, and she bears a mysteriously strong resemblance to one of Justin's longtime enemies. Set partly in Paris, partly in aristocratic England.

Keywords: Disguise; France; Nobility

Hoyt, Elizabeth.

Legend of the Four Soldiers Series.

Like Hoyt's previous <u>Prince Series</u> (see below), these novels are set in England in the 1760s. In this case, the four heroes of this anticipated quartet are all veterans of the French and Indian War. Future volumes include *To Beguile a Beauty* and *To Redeem a Rogue.*

Keywords: French and Indian War; Nobility; Soldiers

To Taste Temptation. Grand Central, 2008. 368pp. Paper, 9780446406918.

Samuel Hartley, a Boston merchant raised in the colonial wilderness, comes to London to seek out the man who betrayed his regiment. In London he meets Lady Emeline Gordon, a widow whose brother was killed in the massacre, and asks her to chaperone his younger sister into fashionable society.

To Seduce a Sinner. Grand Central, 2008. 368pp. Paper, 9780446406925.

Melisande Fleming weds Lord Vale, the man she has always loved, after his fiancée leaves him at the altar. To get her to open up to him, both body and soul, Vale must come clean about his past deeds in the colonies.

Prince Series.

A witty historical romance series set in London and in the English countryside in the 1760s, featuring three men, good friends, who belong to the Agrarian Society. They meet at a London coffeehouse regularly to argue, commiserate with one another, and (of course) drink coffee. The novels' titles are taken from fairy tales excerpted at the start of each chapter.

The Raven Prince. Warner, 2006. 378pp. Paper, 0446618570.

Anna Wren of Little Battleford, England, a young widow living with her mother-in-law, has been finding it hard to make ends meet, so she agrees to become the secretary of Edward de Raaf, Earl of Swartingham, whose face was marred during a childhood smallpox epidemic. Due to the difference in their social status, they don't orally acknowledge their mutual attraction. When Edward travels to London to visit a brothel in an attempt to assuage his lust for Anna, she follows him, adopts a disguise, and secretly becomes his lover.

Keywords: Disfigurement; Disguise; Widows

The Leopard Prince. Warner, 2007. 345pp. Paper, 9780446618489.

Lady Georgina "George" Maitland, a wealthy landowner, hires Harry Pye to be the steward on her estates. Someone has been poisoning her neighbor's sheep, and signs point to Harry. He has a disreputable past, but George loyally defends him.

Keywords: Nobility

The Serpent Prince. Warner, 2007. 362pp. Paper, 9780446400534.

In the countryside of Maiden Hill, England, in 1760, Lucy Craddock-Hayes's peaceful life is disturbed when she finds a nude, unconscious man on her property. In nursing Simon, Viscount Iddesleigh, back to health, she learns about his dangerous plan to take revenge against his brother's murderer.

Keywords: Nobility

Hughes, Kalen.

Rakes of London Series.

Novelist and costume historian Hughes writes well-researched romances about gorgeous aristocratic women who scandalize Georgian society with their outspoken ways.

Keywords: Nobility

Lord Sin. Zebra, 2007. 301pp. Paper, 9780821781494.

Georgianna "George" Exley enjoys many lovers, but forbids them more than one night in her bed. Then her old flame Ivo Dauntry comes back to London, demanding one night for every year he spent in exile on her behalf.

Lord Scandal. Zebra, 2008. 285pp. Paper, 9780821781500.

All of London society gasped when Imogen Mowbray posed for an indecent portrait. Gabriel Angelstone courts even more scandal when he decides to seduce the woman known as the "Portrait Divorcée."

James, Eloisa.

Desperate Duchesses Series.

James was already a popular Regency novelist when she revealed her real identity: Mary Bly, a professor of Shakespearean literature and the daughter of poet Robert Bly. She writes witty romances that also emphasize the strong bonds between women. Here she moves from the Regency to the earlier, bawdier Georgian period with her series about the secret desires of aristocratic ladies in 1780s London. Several couples' stories are told, in alternating sections, within each book, though each has its distinct hero and heroine. A proposed sextet.

Keywords: Duchesses; Married life; Nobility

Desperate Duchesses. Avon, 2007. 382pp. Paper, 9780060781934.

> Roberta St. Giles—eager to marry a man as unlike her poetry-obsessed, overly emotional father as possible—has her heart set on the Duke of Villiers. She asks her cousin Jemma, Duchess of Beaumont, to help her achieve her goals. Jemma's brother Damon has other ideas.

An Affair Before Christmas. Avon, 2007. 386pp. Paper, 9780061245541.

> The Duke of Fletcher ("Fletch") and his wife Perdita ("Poppy") still love each other, though their marriage is fraught with communication problems—both in and out of the bedroom. He resorts to desperate measures to win back his wife's affection.

> **Keywords:** Married life

Duchess by Night. Avon, 2008. 384pp. Paper, 9780061245572.

> It is 1784 and Harriet, Duchess of Berrow, is tired of being a widow. To bring some excitement back into her life, she dons breeches, disguises herself as a man, and heads to the scandalous soiree at Lord Strange's country estate.

> **Keywords:** Disguise; Widows

Rice, Patricia.

Magic Series.

A six-book series, set in mid-eighteenth-century Scotland and England, about women of the Malcolm family, their psychic gifts (all of which are different), and the men they adore (most of whom come from the very scientifically minded and rational Ives family). Historical romance with a touch of the paranormal.

Keywords: Families; Magic and magicians; Malcolm family; Scotland

Merely Magic. Signet Eclipse, 2000. 384pp. Paper, 0451200497.

> In 1750 Ninian Malcolm, a young woman known to be a witch and healer, lives just outside the village of Wystan and remains distant from society. Drogo Ives, whose family has always clashed with the Malcolms, can't resist her charms.

> **Keywords:** Witchcraft

Must Be Magic. Signet Eclipse, 2002. 363pp. Paper, 0451206754.

> Lady Leila Staines, a Malcolm daughter and a widow, has yet to discover her magical gift; she believes she may not have one. She does have a keen sense of smell, though, and she hires agronomist Dunstan Ives, desperately in need of cash, to help her grow a flower garden.

The Trouble with Magic. Signet Eclipse, 2003. 364pp. Paper, 0451209478.

> Felicity Malcolm Childe gets psychic impressions from objects and people she touches, which disturbs her greatly. She and her sister run away to Edinburgh to find a book that may control her gifts' en route they run into Ewan Ives, the only person whom Felicity can touch without sensing him.

> **Keywords:** Psychics

This Magic Moment. Signet Eclipse, 2004. 368pp. Paper, 0451212649.

> Christina Malcolm Childe, an eccentric young woman who can communicate with ghosts, has long been betrothed to super-rational Harry of Sommersville, though no wedding plans have been arranged. This all changes once Harry needs Christina's dowry to pay off mounting debts.

Much Ado About Magic. Signet Eclipse, 2005. 359pp. Paper, 0451215915.

> In London in 1755 Lady Lucinda Malcolm Pembroke, a gifted artist, manages to paint a realistic portrait of a man she's never seen, Sir Trevelyan Rochester. As if that wasn't bad enough, her painting makes him look like a killer, which causes a great scandal.

Keywords: Artists, women

Magic Man. Signet Eclipse, 2006. 371pp. Paper, 0451218965.

> After her adoptive parents' deaths, Mora Abbott travels to Scotland in 1757 to find out more about people who may be her birth family after a spellbook reveals their names. There she meets Aidan Dougal, a relative of the Ives family with magical gifts of his own, whose ownership of his hereditary lands is in jeopardy.

Keywords: Adopted children

Regency-Era Romances

Romances set during England's Regency period (1811–1820), when the Prince of Wales (later George IV) ruled in his mad father's stead, are typically novels of manners. Most of these lighthearted love stories are set among the upper crust in London, though the scene can shift to the nearby countryside during the summer as members of the aristocracy leave the city. Regency authors are meticulous about their research, thoroughly checking all of their facts, from their characters' titles down to their garments, jewelry, and mannerisms. Fans revel in the characters' sparkling dialogue, reminiscent of that of the great Jane Austen, and also in the obligatory happy ending. The "Regency" label often appears on novels set just before or following the Regency, due to a similarity of writing style and content. Even though it isn't technically accurate from a historical standpoint, romances that closely fit this category are included here as well.

Regency novels can be divided into two categories, depending on the level of physical intimacy between the couple. In the first category, *Regency romances*, the stories tend to be fairly "sweet," with little more than kisses exchanged by the pair, and the focus is on the romantic pair and their acceptance by society. Exceedingly few of these novels are being published in today's marketplace. In the second category, *Regency historicals*, stories are considerably more sensual and take place not just in Society, but in the world at large.

The late Georgette Heyer, though she wrote in other historical periods as well, is the grande dame of the Regency romance, and her work continues to be popular in libraries. Most Regency authors are prolific; following is a selected bibliography of their novels.

Balogh, Mary.

Balogh is a Welsh-born, multi-published historical romance novelist who now resides in Canada.

Simply Quartet.

A quartet of novels centering on four women, close friends, who teach at Miss Martin's School for Girls, a private academy for genteel young ladies in Bath. This series has loose connections to Balogh's previous series about the Bedwyn family, and some Bedwyns make appearances in these novels. They are regency historicals, but with more formal, less risqué language than most romances in this category.

Keywords: Friendship; Nobility; Teachers

Simply Unforgettable. Delacorte, 2005. 434pp. Hardbound, 0385338228.

Frances Allard, a music teacher with a secret past, finds herself stranded in a country inn with a stranger, Lucius Marshall, during a horrible snowstorm. They share a passionate encounter, but Frances, who has not yet begun her teaching assignment at Miss Martin's School for Girls, believes she must forget him to preserve her reputation.

Simply Love. Delacorte, 2006. 320pp. Hardbound, 038533883X.

Anne Jewell, a single mother, reluctantly agrees to spend the summer at the Welsh estate of the Duke of Bewcastle, a relative of the father of her nine-year-old son David. Scandal has always followed Anne because of her unwed state. Sydnam Butler, the reclusive Bewcastle steward, lost an eye and right arm in the Peninsular Wars, and he doesn't believe that the beautiful Anne could have any romantic interest in a scarred war veteran.

Keywords: Disfigurement

Simply Magic. Delacorte, 2007. 326pp. Hardbound, 9780385338233.

When teacher and gentleman's daughter Susanna Osbourne, a very independent-minded young woman, is first introduced to Peter Edgeworth, Viscount Whitleaf, she finds him irresistibly handsome. She also hopes he doesn't remember that they had met before; she believes his connection to a traumatic event from his childhood will derail their relationship.

Simply Perfect. Delacorte, 2008. 343pp. Hardbound, 9780385338240.

Claudia Martin, the school's headmistress, finds a romance of her own in this final volume. Though she had resigned herself to being a spinster, she can't resist her feelings for Joseph, Marquess of Attingsborough, despite the difference in their social station.

Keywords: Spinsters

Beverley, Jo.

Company of Rogues Series.

An ongoing and lengthy series about men belonging to the Company of Rogues, a group of young men who formed a brotherhood of protection against bullies at their boarding school. Later in life, as fully grown men, they embody the same honorable qualities. When Jo Beverley, an Englishwoman now living in Canada, first began this series, the "Regency historical" label didn't exist, but she based her novels on those of Georgette Heyer, Lois Burford, and Dorothy Dunnett, whose works she greatly admires. The newer titles are annotated fully. **Regency historicals.**

Keywords: Nobility

An Arranged Marriage. Zebra, 1999 (©1991). Paper, 0821764012.

An Unwilling Bride. Zebra, 2000 (©1992). 351pp. Paper, 0821767240.

Christmas Angel. Zebra, 2001 (©1993). 352pp. Paper, 0821768433.

Forbidden. Zebra, 2003 (©1998). 384pp. Paper, 0821775995.

Dangerous Joy. Zebra, 2004 (©1995). 384pp. Paper, 0821773461.

Three Heroes. NAL, 2004. 688pp. Paper, 0451212002.

Hazard. Signet, 2002. 384pp. Paper, 0451205804.

St. Raven. Signet, 2003. 384pp. Paper, 0451208072.

Skylark. Signet, 2004. 384pp. Paper, 0451211839.

> Laura Gardeyne, "Lady Skylark," refuses to relinquish her young son's care to his late father's nasty relatives. She reluctantly asks an old friend, Stephen Ball, for help, remembering how she rejected his marriage proposal years earlier.

The Rogue's Return. Signet, 2006. 384pp. Paper, 0451217888.

> Simon St. Bride leaves England for Canada to track misspent government funds and fight the Americans during the War of 1812. Though his family wants him home, he is forced to remain to defend the honor of Jane Otterburn, a young woman he barely knows.
>
> **Keywords:** Canada—19th century

To Rescue a Rogue. Signet, 2006. 432pp. Paper, 0451220010.

> Lord Darius "Dare" Debenham, wounded at Waterloo, doesn't believe that his friend's impetuous sister, Lady Mara St. Bride, can do anything to lift his spirits.

Lady Beware. Signet, 2007. 432pp. Paper, 0451221494.

> Horatio Cave, the new Viscount Darien, hopes to rehabilitate his long-tarnished family name by winning over Lady Thea Debenham, sister of Dare from *To Rescue a Rogue*.

Carlyle, Liz.

Sins, Lies, and Secrets Trilogy.

A trilogy about the MacLachlan brothers and their friend, who all appeared in Carlyle's earlier novel, *The Devil to Pay*. Carlyle is a prolific Regency novelist. **Regency historicals.**

Keywords: MacLachlan family; Nobility

One Little Sin. Pocket Star, 2005. 384pp. Paper, 0743496108.

> Sir Alasdair MacLachlan, womanizer and man-about-town, finally gets his comeuppance when Miss Esmée Hamilton shows up on his doorstep all the way from Scotland, carrying her infant half-sister Sorcha, whom she claims is his daughter.

Keywords: Illegitimate children

Two Little Lies. Pocket Star, 2005. 384pp. Paper, 0743496116.

> Quin, Earl of Wynwood, ended his liaison with Italian opera singer Viviana Alessandri nine years ago, in 1821. When she returns to London as a widow, she brings her family along, and one of the children bears a striking resemblance to him.

Keywords: Opera singers; Widows

Three Little Secrets. Pocket Star, 2006. 384pp. Paper, 0743496124.

> Lady Madeleine Bessett's husband, Merrick MacLachlan, eloped with her thirteen years ago, then deserted her on their honeymoon. Told that her marriage had been annulled, Madeleine remarried. Now she's back in London as a widow and having to deal with Merrick once again.

Keywords: Widows

Chase, Loretta.

Carsington Brothers Series.

Romance and adventure in the Regency period and just afterward, featuring the sons of the Right Honorable Edward Junius Carsington, Earl of Hargate. A very witty series set in England and Egypt. **Regency historicals.**

Keywords: Carsington family; Nobility

Miss Wonderful. Berkley Sensation, 2004. 342pp. Paper, 0425194833.

> In 1817 Alistair Carsington, the third son, sojourns in Derbyshire to escape the temptations (particularly women and expensive tailor bills) of London and to assist his best friend in building a canal through the area. Here he comes up against Miss Mirabel Oldridge, daughter of Derbyshire's largest landowner, who's dead set against his engineering plans.

Mr. Impossible. Berkley Sensation, 2005. 312pp. Paper, 0425201503.

> It is April 1821 when Rupert Carsington, the fourth and most troublesome son of the Earl of Hargate, ends up languishing in a Cairo jail as a result of his latest escapade. Naturally he can't resist the proposal of Daphne Pembroke, scholar and Egyptologist, when she asks him for help in rescuing her missing brother.

Keywords: Egypt; Egyptologists

Lord Perfect. Berkley Sensation, 2006. 293pp. Paper, 0425208885.

> Benedict Carsington always acts in a manner befitting the Earl of Hargate's heir: dutifully, respectably, and honorably. He even has a set of rules that he obligingly follows. Then Bathsheba Wingate's young daughter, Olivia, in-

volves Benedict's nephew in a rash treasure-hunting scheme, prompting their elders to pursue them throughout the country.

Keywords: Treasure

Not Quite a Lady. Avon, 2007. 384pp. Paper, 0061231231.

Darius Carsington, the youngest brother, is an expert on agriculture with a reputation of being cold and heartless. His neighbor's daughter, Lady Charlotte Hayward, is a spinster who closed off her heart after being seduced (and left pregnant) at age sixteen.

Keywords: Spinsters

Cornick, Nicola.

Deceived. HQN, 2006. 376pp. Paper, 0373771649.

To save herself from debtors' prison, Princess Isabella Di Cassilis, widow of an Italian prince, agrees to wed John Ellis, a resident of Fleet Prison, because her debts would become his upon their marriage. Then she learns Ellis is really Marcus Stockhaven, the Earl of Stockbridge, a man she jilted years earlier. **Regency historical.**

Keywords: Nobility; Princesses

Lord of Scandal. HQN, 2007. 384pp. Paper, 0373772114.

Catherine Fenton, an heiress promised in marriage to a man she hates, desperately needs rescuing. Ben, Lord Hawksmoor, a noted fortune hunter, may be her only hope of escape. **Regency historical.**

Keywords: Heirs and heiresses

Dain, Claudia.

Courtesan Series.

Ex-courtesan Sophia Dalby, who gained a title through her marriage, delights in helping other worthy young ladies make successful matches. Set in London in 1802. **Regency historicals.**

Keywords: Courtesans; Matchmakers; Mothers and daughters; Nobility

The Courtesan's Daughter. Berkley Sensation, 2007. 327pp. Paper, 9780425217207.

Lady Caroline Dalby, Sophia's daughter, can't find a suitable husband because her mother's scandalous past is too well known. Wealthy Sophia finagles a match between Caroline and Lord Ashdon, an earl who has accumulated too much debt at the gaming tables, but Caroline finds the idea insulting.

The Courtesan's Secret. Berkley Sensation, 2008. 312pp. Paper, 9780425221365.

In helping Lady Louisa Kirkland get her family's pearls back from the aloof Marquis of Dutton, Sophia Dalby also helps Louisa see that her true love lies with another man—Lord Henry Blakesley.

Feather, Jane.

Cavendish Square Trilogy.

Prolific historical romance writer Feather has written about many historical periods. She sets her latest trilogy in London's fashionable Cavendish Square during the pre-Regency period and focuses on the romances of three women friends. **Regency historicals.**

Keywords: Friendship; Nobility

A Wicked Gentleman. Pocket, 2007. 474pp. Paper, 9781416525516.

Lady Cornelia Dagenham can't understand why Harry, Viscount Bonham, is expressing so much curiosity about buying the dilapidated Cavendish Square house her friend Livia has recently inherited. His interest may relate to his secret role as spy and code-breaker.

To Wed a Wicked Prince. Pocket, 2008. 496pp. Paper, 978-1416525523.

Livia Lacey is taken aback when Alexander Prokov, a Russian prince, pursues her relentlessly. She accepts his proposal, but he has hidden motives for marrying her—plus, he turns out to have a domineering side.

Keywords: Princes

Foley, Gaelen.

The Knight Miscellany.

A Regency-set series about the five sons and one daughter of late eighteenth-century noblewoman Georgiana Knight, known as the "Hawkscliffe Harlot" because of her many lovers. Her children, most of whom have different fathers, inherited her unconquerable spirit and wild ways. Family tree included. **Regency historicals.**

Keywords: Families; Knight family; Nobility

The Duke. Ballantine, 2000. 400pp. Paper, 0449006360.

Robert Knight, the Duke of Hawkscliffe, agrees to be the protector of Belinda "Bel" Hamilton, a notorious courtesan, in order to save her life.

Lord of Fire. Ballantine, 2002. 432pp. Paper, 0449006379.

Lord Lucien Knight does hold orgies at his country estate, but he uses them to gather intelligence for the British government. When naïve Alice Montague arrives there, looking for her sister-in-law, Lucien makes her an offer she finds hard to refuse.

Lord of Ice. Ballantine, 2002. 417pp. Paper, 0804119732.

Damien Knight, Earl of Winterley, has suffered flashbacks ever since he fought at Waterloo. After his friend Jason dies, he becomes the guardian of Jason's illegitimate niece, Miranda FitzHubert, who is a real troublemaker.

Keywords: Post-Traumatic Stress Disorder

Lady of Desire. Ballantine, 2003. 412pp. Paper, 0804119740.

Lady Jacinda Knight, the eighteen-year-old pampered and only daughter of the Knight family, runs away to avoid an arranged marriage and finds herself in the back alleys of London, in the middle of a war between gangs of thieves. Her rescuer, Billy Blade, leader of one of the gangs, is much more than he seems.

Devil Takes a Bride. Ballantine, 2004. 469pp. Paper, 0804119759.

In order to get Devlin "Devil" Kimball, Viscount Strathmore, to visit his elderly aunt Augusta, her companion, Lizzie Carlisle, sends him a message implying that Augusta is dying.

One Night of Sin. Ballantine, 2005. 471pp. Paper, 0345480090.

Lord Alec Knight, a notorious bad boy among the London social set (he had become a noblewoman's kept man to pay off his gambling debts), decides he needs to settle down. He may have found his perfect match in Miss Becky Ward, a woman on the run after witnessing a murder.

His Wicked Kiss. Ballantine, 2006. 431pp. Paper, 0345480104.

While in Venezuela to help support Simon Bolivar's revolution, Lord Jack Knight, a pirate turned shipowner, meets Eden Farraday on his travels through the country. Eden, who has lived with her physician father in the Venezuelan jungle for years and longs to return to London, stows away on Jack's ship when he refuses to take her back there himself.

Keywords: Shipboard adventure; Venezuela

The Spice Trilogy.

A spin-off of Foley's <u>Knight Miscellany</u> series, featuring Knight cousins who were raised in British-ruled India and relocate to London. **Regency historicals.**

Keywords: India—19th century; Knight family; Nobility; Soldiers

Her Only Desire. Ballantine, 2007. 453pp. Paper, 9780345480118.

In 1817 in Calcutta Georgiana Knight, namesake of her scandalous aunt, ruins the diplomatic mission that Ian Prescott, Marquess of Griffith, had traveled from London to work on. Sent back to London with her two brothers in disgrace, she realizes en route that she had better shape up.

Her Secret Fantasy. Ballantine, 2007. 448pp. Paper, 034549668X.

Lily Balfour must make a good match to rescue her family from poverty, but Major Derek Knight, just returned from fighting for Britain in India, thwarts all her plans.

Her Every Pleasure. Ballantine, 2008.

After she turns twenty-one Sophia, a princess of the Greek island country of Kavros, plans to return home from London to reclaim her throne. Ambushed en route to a meeting with Britain's Foreign Office, Sophia disguises herself as a peasant girl and goes into hiding —until she is discovered, by accident, by Major Gabriel Knight, a soldier injured in India.

Keywords: Disguise; Princesses

Gaston, Diane.

Gaston's romances examine the dark side of Regency life. She also writes under her real name, Diane Perkins. **Regency historicals.**

Innocence and Impropriety. **Harlequin, 2007. 293pp. Paper, 9780373294404.**

Jameson Flynn, an Irishman serving as secretary to the Marquess of Tannerton, becomes entranced by the beautiful voice of Rose O'Keefe, a singer at Vauxhall Gardens whom the Marquess desires for his mistress.

Keywords: Nobility; Singers

The Mysterious Miss M. **Harlequin, 2005. 299pp. Paper, 0373293771.**

Lord Devlin Steele, a veteran of Waterloo, first meets Madeleine in 1812, when as "the Mysterious Miss M" she is the beautiful, masked prize that Lord Farley offers to men who win big at his elite, dissolute London gambling hall. Three years later Devlin returns and finds himself responsible for Maddy and her young daughter, who are in danger from the Regency underworld.

Keywords: Nobility; Prostitutes

🎗 *A Reputable Rake.* **Harlequin, 2006. 304pp. Paper, 037329400X.**

Cyprian Sloane, gambler, smuggler, former spy, and all-around rogue, decides to improve his reputation, and courting respectable Hannah Cowdlin is part of his plan. He doesn't count on his attraction to Hannah's cousin, Morgana Hart, whose own reputation is in jeopardy after it becomes known she's helping ladies of the evening become courtesans. RITA Award.

The Vanishing Viscountess. **Harlequin, 2008. 299pp. Paper, 9780373294794.**

When Adam "Tanner" Vickery, Marquess of Tannerton, rescues Marlena Parronley from certain death during a shipwreck, she doesn't tell him the whole truth: that she was brought back from Ireland as a prisoner accused of killing her husband. A spin-off novel from *Innocence and Impropriety.*

Keywords: Nobility

Hern, Candice.

Merry Widows Series.

A series about five friends, wealthy young widows all, who are widely believed to be fine, respectable Society ladies, but who all agree to take lovers to fulfill their physical needs. None expects to fall in love. **Regency historicals.**

Keywords: Nobility; Widows

In the Thrill of the Night. Signet Eclipse, 2005. 304pp. Paper, 0451217845.

Marianne Nesbitt, a board member of the Benevolent Widows Fund, speaks lightly with her friends about her desire to take a lover. Intrigued by the possibility, she asks her good friend Adam Cazenove—who is already betrothed, and thus unavailable—how best to attract such a man.

Just One of Those Flings. Signet Eclipse, 2006. 306pp. Paper, 0451219201.

Beatrice Campion, Lady Somerfield, finds an ideal lover in Gabriel, Marquess of Thayne, whom she first encounters at a masked ball. Unfortunately her headstrong niece, a young lady attending her first London season, desires him herself.

Lady Be Bad. Signet Eclipse, 2007. 307pp. Paper, 0451221915.

Grace Marlowe, a bishop's prim and proper widow, is secretly attracted to John Grayston, Viscount Rochdale, known as the most infamous rake in London. She doesn't realize his initial interest in her was the result of a bet to entice a beautiful woman into his bed.

Heyer, Georgette.

With her well-researched and witty portrayals of all classes of life in Regency England, Heyer set the standard by which other Regency romances are measured. Many of her earlier works have been reissued in trade paperback with striking new covers; a selection is presented below. For a complete list of titles, see the Georgette Heyer Web site (www.georgette-heyer.com). **Regency romances.**

False Colours. **Sourcebooks, 2008. 352pp. Paper, 9781402210754.**

Evelyn, the Earl of Denville, has been missing for days. To preserve his twin brother's betrothal to a rich heiress, Cressy Stavely, young army officer Kit Fancot agrees to impersonate him during his anticipated meeting with Cressy's redoubtable grandmother. Originally published in 1963.

Keywords: Heirs and heiresses; Imposters; Nobility; Twins

Faro's Daughter. **Sourcebooks, 2008. 304pp. Paper, 9781402213526.**

Deborah Grantham, hostess at her aunt's gaming house, needs to marry to improve their station, but neither of her two suitors has great appeal. Max Ravenscar, convinced that she's after his nephew's fortune, is prepared to pay her off to leave them alone. Originally published in 1941.

Friday's Child. **Sourcebooks, 2008. 432pp. Paper, 9781402210792.**

Lord Sherington, spurned by the woman he wanted for his bride, makes the impulsive decision to marry Hero Wantage, a childhood friend who has no experience whatsoever with London Society. Originally published in 1944.

Keywords: Nobility

The Spanish Bride. **Sourcebooks, 2008. 496pp. Paper, 9781402211133.** ✍

The real-life love story of Brigade-Major Harry Smith, a soldier in Wellington's army, and his young Spanish bride, Juana, unfolds against the backdrop of the Peninsular Wars. Both characters are historical people. Originally published in 1940.

Keywords: Napoleonic Wars; Smith, Harry (historical character); Smith, Juana (historical character)

Hunter, Madeline.

Rothwell Brothers Series.

An interlinked series about the three Rothwell brothers—Christian, Hayden, and Elliot—as well as the daughter from another family, the

Longworths, whose tale is told in the background of the Rothwells' love stories. *The Sins of Lord Easterbrook* will conclude the series. **Regency historicals.**

Keywords: Brothers; Nobility; Rothwell family

The Rules of Seduction. Bantam, 2006. 416pp. Paper, 0553587323.

Alexia Welbourne blames Lord Hayden Rothwell for her family's ruin and reluctantly agrees to wed him only to improve her circumstances.

Keywords: Marriages of convenience

🏵 *Lessons of Desire.* Bantam, 2007. 386pp. Paper, 9780440243946.

At her father's deathbed, Phaedra Blair, a freethinking intellectual and early feminist, promises to publish his memoirs. Elliot Rothwell negotiates with her to stop their publication, because revelations within them could destroy his parents' reputations. RITA Award.

Keywords: Feminists

Secrets of Surrender. Bantam, 2008. 372pp. Paper, 9780440243953.

Roselyn Longwood, mistress of Lord Norbury, is auctioned off to the highest bidder at a drunken party at Norbury's country estate. Kyle Bradwell, a self-made businessman, buys her, but he doesn't fully know all the details of her ruined past.

Keywords: Mistresses

Seducer Series.

The heroes of the first five novels in this early nineteenth-century romance series, set in the aftermath of the Napoleonic Wars, are members of the Hampstead Dueling Society, a group of men proficient in the art of the duel, political intrigue, and seduction. For the rest of her novels, a spin-off series from the earlier books (some of the earlier characters reappear), Hunter looks at the private lives of English and Scottish aristocrats. **Regency historicals.**

Keywords: Duelists

The Seducer. Bantam, 2003. 419pp. Paper, 0553585894.

The Saint. Bantam, 2003. 432pp. Paper, 0553585908.

The Charmer. Bantam, 2003. 400pp. Paper, 0553585916

The Sinner. Bantam, 2004. 372pp. Paper, 0553585924.

The Romantic. Bantam, 2004. 416pp. Paper, 0553587293.

Julian Hampton, a thoughtful London solicitor, has always loved his best friend's sister Penelope, Countess of Glasbury, from afar. He risks everything to save her from an abusive husband.

Keywords: Abusive relationships

Lord of Sin. Bantam, 2005. 406pp. Paper, 0553587307.

Ewan McLean, a reckless spendthrift, inherits an earldom in Scotland, where he meets his latest responsibility: four unmarried sisters who need a guardian. Bride Cameron, the eldest, tells him they don't need his help.

Keywords: Scotland; Sisters

Lady of Sin. Bantam, 2006. 405pp. Paper, 0553587315.

> Charlotte, Baroness Mardenford, had attended a masked orgy and had a forbidden encounter with defense attorney Nathaniel Knightridge while both were in disguise. Now the very proper Charlotte approaches Nathaniel at his home, demanding his help in the women's rights movement.
>
> **Keywords:** Disguise; Nobility; Suffragettes

James, Eloisa.

Essex Sisters Series.

A quartet about the four strong-willed Essex sisters, who, after their father dies, move from Scotland to London to become the wards of Rafe Jourdain, the Duke of Holbrook—a kindly wastrel who has no idea how to marry them off. **Regency historicals.**

Keywords: Essex family; Nobility; Sisters

Much Ado About You. Avon, 2005. 376pp. Paper, 0060732067.

> Tess Essex, the eldest daughter, wants to set a proper example for her three younger sisters by marrying her guardian's friend, the Earl of Mayne, but she can't resist the charms of untitled Lucius Felton.

Kiss Me, Annabel. Avon, 2005. 400pp. Paper, 0060732105.

> Miss Annabel Essex does her best to ensnare a rich English husband, because memories of life with her dissolute father in Scotland aren't exactly appealing— but then she unexpectedly finds herself sharing a carriage en route to Scotland with an impoverished, handsome Scottish earl.

The Taming of the Duke. Avon, 2006. 394pp. Paper, 0060781580.

> Imogen Maitland, the third sister, lost her beloved husband Draven after a mere two weeks of marriage. Time has passed, and, feeling lonely, she decides to take a lover. Who better than Gabe Spencer, her guardian's illegitimate half-brother? Then her growing closeness to Rafe himself—she's helping him overcome an alcohol addiction— makes her think twice about him.
>
> **Keywords:** Alcoholism; Widows

Pleasure for Pleasure. Avon, 2006. 416pp. Paper, 0060781920.

> Josie Essex, the youngest sister, believes no man will look at her twice because of her plumpish figure. Garret, Earl of Mayne, feeling sorry for her, decides to help her gain a beau—but grows jealous of the men she attracts.

Kelly, Carla.

Beau Crusoe. **Harlequin, 2007. 298pp. Paper, 9780373294398.**

> Susannah Park, a beautiful widow shunned by society after her scandalous elopement, lost her husband to a cholera epidemic in India seven years earlier. James Trevenen, a lifelong sailor, has just returned from

London after spending five years stranded on a deserted South Pacific island. When Susannah's godfather invites James for a visit to discuss their mutual interest in the South Seas, he hopes to make a match between him and Susannah. But James hides a secret that makes him unsuitable for marriage. **Regency historical.**

Keywords: Post-Traumatic Stress Disorder; Shipwrecks; Widows

Mullany, Janet.

The Rules of Gentility. **Avon A, 2007. 268pp. Paper, 9780061229831.**

This gentle spoof (of sorts) of Regency romances features the romance between Philomena Wellesley-Clegg, a fashionable middle-class miss obsessed with finding the perfect hat, and Inigo Linsley, the handsome brother-in-law of her best friend. To please her family, they pretend that they're betrothed, and their courtship includes nearly every element of the classic Regency romance—twisted just a bit. Philomena and Inigo reveal their thoughts in the first person in alternating passages. **Regency romance.**

Keywords: Parodies and spoofs

Rosenthal, Pam.

The Slightest Provocation. **NAL, 2006. 352pp. Paper, 0451219473.**

Nine years earlier, Mary Penley and Kit Stansell had eloped, displeasing their relations, because their families had been enemies in Derbyshire for some time. They spent one year of wedded bliss together before their innate restlessness took hold; they quarreled, parted, and have been living separate lives ever since. Now they encounter one another again, find their passion undiminished, but they're on opposite sides of the political spectrum: Mary considers herself a liberal free-thinker and reformer, while Kit believes strongly in the existing British government. **Regency historical** that verges on erotic.

Keywords: Married life

Jane Austen Sequels

Authors envision their own retellings and continuations of Jane Austen's classic romance novels. A very popular category.

Aidan, Pamela.

Fitzwilliam Darcy, Gentleman Trilogy.

Aidan's trilogy, previously self-published, retells the events from *Pride and Prejudice* from Darcy's viewpoint, with new insights into his character as well as others from the original novel, such as Charles Bingley, Darcy's sister Georgiana, and his clever valet, Fletcher. **Regency romances.**

Keywords: Austen themes

An Assembly Such as This. Touchstone, 2006. 246pp. Paper, 0743291344.

Duty and Desire. Touchstone, 2006. 280pp. Paper, 0743291360.

These Three Remain. Touchstone, 2007. 464pp. Paper, 9780743291378.

Aston, Elizabeth.

<u>Darcy Series.</u>

More sequels to *Pride and Prejudice*, featuring the five imagined daughters of Fitzwilliam and Elizabeth as well as members of the extended Darcy family. Especially toward the end of the series, the resemblance between Aston's and Austen's creations is remote, yet these are lively romances. **Regency romances.**

Keywords: Austen themes; Darcy family

Mr. Darcy's Daughters. Touchstone, 2003. 360pp. Paper, 0743243978.

In 1818, while Mr. and Mrs. Darcy are on a diplomatic mission to Constantinople, their lively daughters remain at home in London with Darcy's cousin. Many romantic entanglements ensue.

The Exploits and Adventures of Miss Alethea Darcy. Touchstone, 2005. 353pp. Paper, 0743261933.

Alethea Darcy, the youngest and most rebellious daughter, flees an abusive marriage by disguising herself as a man and heading to Venice with her maid, in the hopes of asking her sister Camilla for support.

The True Darcy Spirit. Touchstone, 2006. 341pp. Paper, 074327490.

Cassandra Darcy, the eldest daughter of Anne de Bourgh, strives to make her own living in London with her talent in painting, but must contend with an unwanted suitor.

Keywords: Artists, women

The Second Mrs. Darcy. Touchstone, 2007. 300pp. Paper, 9780743297295.

Octavia, the widow of Captain Christopher Darcy, returns from India and prepares to claim the fortune she has inherited. She frequently squares off against Lord Sholto Rutherford, an arrogant and powerful man who can easily match wits with her.

The Darcy Connection. Touchstone, 2008. 287pp. Paper, 9781416547259.

Eliza Collins, daughter of Elizabeth Bennet's good friend Charlotte Collins, is the wit of the family, while her older sister Charlotte is the beauty. Eliza accompanies her sister to London for the season and finds her match there.

Berdoll, Linda.

<u>Darcy Series.</u>

Berdoll's bawdy and rather over-the-top sequels to *Pride and Prejudice* (the first of which, in its original 1999 self-published version, *The Bar Sinister*, became an underground classic) focus on the growing intimate relationship between the couple. Her love scenes most decidedly do not stop at the bedroom door. She also, wisely, doesn't try to copy Austen's style, which results in rollicking, adventuresome romances. **Regency historicals.**

Keywords: Austen themes; Darcy family

Mr. Darcy Takes a Wife. Sourcebooks, 2004. 465pp. Paper, 1402202733.

Darcy & Elizabeth: Nights and Days at Pemberley. Sourcebooks, 2006. 429pp. Paper, 1402205635.

Grange, Amanda.

Grange, a prolific British novelist, retells Jane Austen's classic romantic novels from the viewpoint of Austen's heroes. Conversations from the originals are occasionally reproduced verbatim, but shown from a new perspective. **Regency romances.**

Captain Wentworth's Diary. **Berkley, 2007. 293pp. Paper, 9780425223529.**

Captain Frederick Wentworth, veteran of the Napoleonic Wars, fell in love with Miss Anne Elliot while on shore leave, but her godmother disapproved of the match. When their paths cross again in 1806, she has grown older, but her wit is as refreshing as ever. A retelling of *Persuasion.*

Keywords: Austen themes; Diaries and journals

Mr. Darcy's Diary. **Sourcebooks, 2007. 329pp. Paper, 9781402208768.**

Grange makes her American debut with Fitzwilliam Darcy's imagined diary, in which he records his thoughts about contemporary society, Elizabeth Bennet, and more. A retelling of *Pride and Prejudice.*

Keywords: Austen themes; Diaries and journals

Mr Knightley's Diary. **Berkley, 2007. 294pp. Paper, 9780425217719.**

Mr. Knightley, who has just started thinking that it's getting to be time for him to marry, doesn't know what to make of Emma Woodhouse, whose matchmaking shenanigans are the talk of the village of Highbury. He details his ongoing thoughts in his diary. A retelling of *Emma.*

Keywords: Austen themes; Diaries and journals; Matchmakers

Victorian and Edwardian Romances

Life in Victorian England (1837–1901) is normally thought of as prim and proper, and many Victorian romances include heroines or heroes who rebel against the strict rules of conduct imposed by society. Rather than focusing primarily on the upper classes, as do most Georgian and Regency romances, these works feature the rich, the working class, and the poor—and the differences between them. Romances set during the brief Edwardian period (1901–1910), when Victoria's son Edward was on the throne, are similar in tone.

Archer, Zoe.

Lady X's Cowboy. **Leisure, 2006. 325pp. Paper, 0843956666.**

It is 1883. Lady Olivia Xavier, who took over ownership of a London brewery after her husband's death, is a secret and passionate reader of Western dime novels. Nobody is more surprised than she when Will Coffin, a real-life cowboy from Colorado, rescues her from the nefarious schemes of a business rival.

Keywords: Businesswomen; Cowboys

Blair, Annette.

Scoundrel in Disguise. **Five Star, 2006. 287pp. Hardbound, 1594144834.**
Lady Jade Smithfield, a compassionate woman who oversees a home for abused and unwanted women and children in the East Sussex countryside in 1847, has very good reasons for wanting to prevent a railroad from being constructed on her property. Marcus Fitzalan sets out to discover what she's hiding and why.

Keywords: Railroads

Joyce, Lydia.

Joyce writes dark, edgy historical romances set in the mid- to late nineteenth century. For additional novels by Joyce, see the next section, "Early Modern Europe."

The Veil of Night. **Signet Eclipse, 2005. 302pp. Paper, 0451214838.**
In the year 1864, to save her family from ruin, Lady Victoria Wakefield, a thirtyish spinster, agrees to become the mistress of Byron Stratford, Duke of Raeburn, a reclusive nobleman with many secrets to hide. They share many passionate encounters by night, but she always wonders why he avoids the daylight.

Keywords: Gothic novels; Mistresses; Nobility; Spinsters

Shadows of the Night. **Signet Eclipse, 2008. 284pp. Paper, 9780451223425.**
On their wedding night Fern Radcliffe and her new husband Colin experience passion of a kind that surprises and energizes them. They know their behavior would shock Victorian society, but continue exploring their desires, until a secret from Colin's past reaches out to touch them both.

Keywords: Married life

Voices of the Night. **Signet Eclipse, 2007. 299pp. Paper, 0451220773.**
Maggie King, a girl from the London slums, will do anything to improve her family's livelihood. When Charles, Lord Edgington, spies her auditioning for an opera, he sees the perfect opportunity to win a bet with his sister to successfully transform a street girl into a lady. Learning of Charles's predicament, Maggie accepts his offer and agrees to be tutored in proper ladylike behavior. A retelling of sorts of *Pygmalion*, set in London in 1864.

Keywords: Nobility; Poverty

Kleypas, Lisa.

Wallflower Series.

A quartet about four young ladies of early Victorian England who, tired of being snubbed by men among the London social set, band together to help each other snag husbands.

Keywords: Heirs and heiresses; Nobility

Secrets of a Summer Night. Avon, 2004. 384pp. Paper, 0060091290.

> Gently born aristocrat Annabelle Peyton must marry a peer to help recoup her family's wealth, she decides, but Simon Hunt, a proud commoner who made his fortune in business, seeks to change her plans.

It Happened One Autumn. Avon, 2005. 391pp. Paper, 0060562498.

> Lillian Bowman, an American heiress from a nouveau riche New York City family, is thought to be strong-willed, arrogant, and uppity. She clashes immediately with Marcus Marsden, Earl of Westcliff, who has the same reputation.

The Devil in Winter. Avon, 2006. 374pp. Paper, 006056251X.

> Sebastian, Lord St. Vincent, is a degenerate rake and doesn't care who knows it, but financial reasons compel him to seek a wife. Heiress Evie Jenner needs a husband and figures that if Sebastian agrees, she'll ignore his indiscretions with other women.

Scandal in Spring. Avon, 2006. 384pp. Paper, 0060562536.

> Daisy Bowman, sister of Lillian from *It Happened One Autumn*, has been on the shelf for far too long. Her father, despairing that she'll ever marry, decides that she'll marry his prize employee, Matthew Swift, a man who has loved her for years.

Quick, Amanda.

Quick, the pseudonym used by author and former librarian Jayne Ann Krentz for her historical romantic suspense novels, writes witty historical romances with a touch of mystery, set mostly in nineteenth-century England.

Lie by Moonlight. **Putnam, 2005. 400pp. Hardbound, 0399152881.**

> Concordia Glade, a tutor for rich orphaned young heiresses at Aldwick Castle, flees with her four charges to London, starting a fire to hide their escape once she discovers that they're all in danger. En route she meets the mysterious Ambrose Wells, private detective extraordinaire, and he champions their cause.

Keywords: Detective stories

The Paid Companion. **Putnam, 2004. 464pp. Hardbound, 0399151745.**

> Arthur Lancaster, Earl of St. Merryn, needs someone to pose as his fiancée for a few weeks, just so husband-hunting women will leave him alone while he searches for his uncle's murderer. He believes Elenora Lodge, an attractive, sensible woman in impoverished circumstances, is the perfect choice.

Keywords: Detective stories

The River Knows. **Putnam, 2007. 368pp. Hardbound, 9780399154171.**

> In the late nineteenth century, a businesswoman decides she needs to start a new life for herself, so she fakes her death by pretending she has thrown herself into the Thames. Nobody would ever suspect that Louisa Bryce, a dowdy widow, is working as an undercover reporter for a sensational newspaper. She and Anthony Stalbridge wonder whether other recent drownings were really suicides, so they join forces to find out.

Keywords: Detective stories; Disguise

Second Sight. **Putnam, 2006. 400pp. Hardbound, 0399153527.**

Late in Queen Victoria's reign, spinster Venetia Milton is chosen to photo-graph a collection of mysterious artifacts previously owned by the Arcane Society, a 200-year-old secret association of alchemists and the like. At his Gothic mansion, she shares a night of passion with the collection's care-taker, Gabriel Jones, but is devastated to hear of his death soon afterward. She poses as his widow and embarks on a lucrative photography career—her own second sight helps her capture people's likenesses well—but then Gabriel shows up again, very much alive. Part of the <u>Arcane Society</u> series of novels (which includes two contemporary titles as well as *The Third Circle*, below).

Keywords: Photographers; Psychics

The Third Circle. **Putnam, 2008. 352pp. Hardbound, 9780399154843.**

Leona Hewitt, a woman gifted in crystal reading, and Thaddeus Ware, whose voice has the power to mesmerize, meet up unexpectedly while both are trying to steal the mysterious aurora stone from the private col-lection of Lord Delbridge. They band together to stop a serial killer with psychic abilities who is attracted to the stone's power. Part of the <u>Arcane Society</u> series of novels.

Keywords: Psychics; Serial killers

Wait Until Midnight. **Jove, 2005. 368pp. Paper, 0515138622.**

Caroline Fordyce, who writes sensational novels, and Adam Hardesty, who's being blackmailed by an unknown person, have secrets from the past they're trying to hide. They decide to work together to uncover the killer of a medium with connections to them both.

Keywords: Authors, women; Detective stories

Silver, Eve.

Dark, suspenseful Victorian romances written in the classic Gothic tradition.

Dark Desires. **Zebra, 2005. 349pp. Paper, 0821779664.**

Someone is killing women on the streets of Whitechapel in Victorian Lon-don. In desperate need of money and safety, Darcie Finch approaches a disreputable-looking brothel, but the madam sends her elsewhere—to the home of Dr. Damien Cole, who runs a very unusual laboratory.

Keywords: Gothic novels

Dark Prince. **Zebra, 2007. 352pp. Paper, 0821781286.**

In late nineteenth-century Cornwall, Jane Heatherington, a beautiful yet crippled young woman sold into indentured servitude by her abusive innkeeper father, struggles to understand the man to whom she owes her loyalty: Aidan Warrick, a privateer who recently purchased shadowy Trevisham House.

Keywords: Gothic novels

His Dark Kiss. **Zebra, 2006. 352pp. Paper, 0821779672.**

Emma Parrish, a poor relation living with two unpleasant aunts, has no choice but to become the governess of her late cousin's children. At the forbidding mansion called Manorbrier, she learns that her cousin's husband, Lord Craven, may have thrown his wife down the stairs. And what's with all the dead bodies that arrive at Manorbrier at night?

Keywords: Gothic novels; Governesses

Tarr, Hope.

Men of Roxbury House Trilogy.

Novels of romance and redemption, featuring a trio of men who struggle to overcome their poverty-stricken pasts.

Vanquished. **Medallion, 2006. 368pp. Paper, 1932815759.**

In order to win back money lost at the gaming tables, photographer Hadrian St. Claire agrees to seduce Caledonia "Callie" Rivers, a suffragette leader of unimpeachable virtue, photograph her in a compromising position, and blackmail her with the resulting pictures.

Keywords: Photographers; Suffragettes

Enslaved. **Medallion, 2007. 376pp. Paper, 9781933836126.**

Gavin Carmichael and Daisy Lake grew up in the orphanage of London's Roxbury House in the 1870s. When Gavin next sees Daisy, after a separation of over ten years, she's the featured act at a supper club in the squalid East End.

Untamed. **Medallion, 2008. 377pp. Paper, 9781933836171.**

Lady Katherine Lindsey, a spinster, agrees to wed Patrick O'Rourke, a wealthy businessman, in a marriage of convenience. At his castle in the Scottish Highlands, he tries to romance her using techniques from Shakespeare's *The Taming of the Shrew.*

Keywords: Marriages of convenience; Scotland

Thomas, Sherry.

Delicious. **Bantam, 2008. 432pp. Paper, 9780440244325.**

In November 1892, when the master of Fairleigh Park in Yorkshire dies, Verity Durant assumes the duties of executive chef for his brother, Stuart Somerset, a lawyer who is a rising political force in the House of Commons. Her presence in his household reminds him of a passionate night he spent with a stranger ten years earlier.

Keywords: Chefs

Private Arrangements. **Bantam, 2008. 351pp. Paper, 9780440244318.**

The marriage between Gigi Rowland and Camden Saybrook, Lord Tremaine, derailed after their wedding night, after he learned of her betrayal. Now, in 1893, she asks him for a divorce, which he will only grant if she agrees to give him an heir.

Keywords: Divorce; Nobility

Early Modern Europe

Historical romances set predominantly in the nineteenth century, but elsewhere in Europe rather than in Britain.

Allen, Louise.

A Most Unconventional Courtship. **Harlequin, 2007. 304pp. Paper, 0373294492.**
In 1817 Benedict Chancellor, Earl of Blakeney, visits the Greek island of Corfu during his Grand Tour. Alessa Meredith, an Englishman's daughter stranded on Corfu after the Napoleonic Wars, falls in love with him at first sight, and he with her.

Keywords: Greece; Nobility

Cree, Ann Elizabeth.

The Venetian's Mistress. **Harlequin, 2005. 296pp. Paper, 0373293968.**
Cecily Renato, the English widow of an Italian nobleman, learns that her stepdaughter's proposed marriage to Simon, Viscount Ballister, may rekindle a long-standing family feud. Nico, the Duke of Severin and Simon's guardian, vehemently opposes the match, and makes no bones about telling Cecily so. Romantic suspense with a Regency feel, set in early nineteenth-century Venice.

Keywords: Italy; Nobility

Joyce, Lydia.

The Music of the Night. **Signet Eclipse, 2005. 297pp. Paper, 0451217063.**
Sebastian Grimsthorpe, Lord Wortham, longs to avenge the rape of his young illegitimate daughter. After a horrible accident that disfigures him and forces him to wear a mask, he fakes his death, leaving him time and opportunity to fulfill his goal. He follows the perpetrator, Bertrand de Lint, to Venice, where he spies his mother's companion, Sarah Connolly, and mistakenly assumes she was the whore present at his daughter's rape.

Keywords: Disfigurement; Gothic novels; Italy

Whispers of the Night. **Signet Eclipse, 2006. 329pp. Paper, 0451218973.**
Alcyone "Alcy" Carter, daughter of a wealthy businessman who hasn't had many marriage prospects despite her beauty and intelligence (she's a skilled mathematician), agrees to marry Baron Benedak of Hungary at her father's request. When she arrives at the baron's home, she learns that Dumitru Constaninescu, a Rumanian nobleman in need of money, has taken her fiancé's place.

Keywords: Mathematicians; Nobility; Romania

Schwab, Sandra.

Castle of the Wolf. LoveSpell, 2007. 320pp. Paper, 9780505527202.

In order to inherit Wolfenbach Castle, Celia (Cissy) Fussell travels to Germany to marry its former master, Fenris—a mysterious man with a dark secret. Historical paranormal romance set in the legendary Black Forest region in the early nineteenth century.

Keywords: Germany; Gothic novels

Americana Romances

Although historical romances set in the United States are less common than those set in England, a number of prominent authors use American history as a backdrop. Most use small-town or rural settings and reflect day-to-day life in early America. Romances set in the American West in the nineteenth century are listed in a separate section, later in this chapter.

Blake, Jennifer.

Masters at Arms Series.

A continuing series about skilled *maîtres d'armes*, who instruct New Orleans' young aristocrats in the art of sword-fighting, and the women they love. Set in mid-nineteenth-century New Orleans.

Keywords: Duelists; Louisiana—early United States; Swordsmen

Challenge to Honor. MIRA, 2005. 416pp. Paper, 0778321703.

When Celina Vallier's brother challenges notable swordsman Rio de Salva to a duel, she makes a bargain with Rio: if he spares her brother's life, she'll become his mistress.

Dawn Encounter. MIRA, 2006. 409pp. Paper, 0778322130.

Caid O'Neill had killed Lisette Moisant's hateful husband in a duel to avenge his sister, so he can't refuse when she falls into danger and turns to him for help. Then their enemies begin spreading rumors about her virtue, suggesting that it was their plan to kill her husband all along.

Rogue's Salute. MIRA, 2007. 512pp. Paper, 0778324052.

Juliette Armant, pledged to the religious life since childhood, agrees to marry in order to inherit an ancient marriage chest and protect her family heritage from her greedy twin sister, Paulette. She and fencing master Nicholas Pasquale make a deal about it, as he needs a mother for his young ward.

Guarded Heart. MIRA, 2008. 416pp. Paper, 9780778324546.

In 1844 Madame Ariadne Faucher, a statuesque widow, demands that Gavin Blackford instruct her in the art of sword-fighting: she wishes to challenge an old enemy to a duel herself.

Keywords: Widows

Clare, Pamela.

Ride the Fire. **Leisure, 2005. 356pp. Paper, 0843954876.**

Elspeth Stewart's husband died, leaving her pregnant and alone on the Ohio frontier in 1763. Nicholas Kenleigh, a fur trapper recently freed after being held captive by the Wyandot, comes upon Elspeth in her cabin, waiting to give birth. Each helps the other make peace with the past.

Keywords: Frontier and pioneer life; Ohio—colonial period; Pregnancy

MacKinnon's Rangers Series.

A continuing series about the three MacKinnon brothers of Scotland, Jacobites in exile who were trained in the arts of war by Native Americans and who were forced to fight alongside the British army in the French and Indian War. Romantic yet gritty, with occasional scenes of violence. *Untamed* will be the next entry.

Keywords: Brothers; French and Indian War

Surrender. Leisure, 2006. 355pp. Paper, 0843954884.

In the 1750s Iain MacKinnon rescues Lady Anne Burness-Campbell from Abenaki soldiers who raid her home. In order to survive, Annie accompanies him back to his camp.

Garlock, Dorothy.

1920s Missouri Series.

Realistic romances set in rural Missouri during Prohibition and shortly afterward.

Keywords: Great Depression; Missouri—20th century

The Edge of Town. Warner, 2001. 370pp. Paper, 0446527696.

High on a Hill. Warner, 2002. 385pp. Paper, 044652946X.

A Place Called Rainwater. Warner, 2003. 400pp. Paper, 0446529508.

River Rising. Warner, 2005. 388pp. Paper, 0446693944.

April Asbury, a nurse, arrives in Fertile, Missouri, in the 1930s from the big city, looking for a calmer, more rural place to live. Joe Jones, the local playboy, rescues her when her car breaks down, and she settles into a job at Dr. Poole's office. However, she grows steadily more uncomfortable with staying at the home of Mrs. Poole, because Mrs. Poole's brother seems to be a peeping Tom.

Train from Marietta. **Warner, 2006. 373pp. Paper, 0446695319.**

In 1933, as she makes her way from New Orleans to San Francisco to take a nursing job, Katherine "Kate" Tyler is kidnapped in Texas. Her wealthy father hires Tate Castle, a horse rancher, to find her.

Keywords: Great Depression; Kidnapping; Texas—20th century

A Week from Sunday. **Grand Central, 2007. 384pp. Paper, 9780446695336.**

> To avoid marriage to her late father's creepy lawyer, who vows that she must marry him "a week from Sunday" to claim her inheritance, Adrianna Moore flees—and promptly crashes her car into a vehicle owned by Quinn Baxter. Set in the small town of Lee's Point, Louisiana, during the Depression.
>
> **Keywords:** Great Depression; Heirs and heiresses; Louisiana—20th century

Jenkins, Beverly.

House of Le Veq Series.

Jenkins writes realistically about strong-willed African-American men and women who fall in love during America's Reconstruction years.

Keywords: African Americans; LeVeq Family

Through the Storm. Avon, 1998. 384pp. Paper, 0380798646.

> Sable Fontaine, a mulatto slave, escapes into freedom after being horribly mistreated by a new owner during the Civil War. At one of the contraband camps along the route North, Sable steals money from Raimond le Veq, the Union major in charge. They meet again in New Orleans after the war, and Raimond discovers his mother has arranged for him to marry her.
>
> **Keywords:** Louisiana—Civil War; Slaves and slavery

Winds of the Storm. Avon, 2006. 366pp. Paper, 006057531X.

> During the Civil War, a beautiful female spy known only as "Butterfly" rescued Archer le Veq from hanging. Now it is 1871, and Zahra Lafayette, a laundress from South Carolina, has been recruited back into espionage by Harriet Tubman herself. While posing as a high-class New Orleans madam named Domino in order to sniff out information on white supremacists, Zahra encounters Archer again.
>
> **Keywords:** Louisiana—Reconstruction/Gilded Age; Madams; Spies, women

Joyce, Brenda.

Francesca Cahill Novels.

A romantic mystery series set in Gilded Age Manhattan, featuring heiress Francesca Cahill as heroine and sleuth. As she leaves her elegant Fifth Avenue abode to solve crimes in the most grimy, decadent areas of the city, she struggles with her affections for two different men: handsome police commissioner Rick Bragg and his half-brother and rival, Calder Hart.

Keywords: Detective stories; Heirs and heiresses; New York—Reconstruction/Gilded Age

Deadly Love. St. Martin's, 2001. 338pp. Paper, 0312977670. (As B. D. Joyce.)

Deadly Pleasure. St. Martin's, 2002. 359pp. Paper, 0312977689.

Deadly Affairs. St. Martin's, 2002. 358pp. Paper, 0312982623.

Deadly Desire. St. Martin's, 2002. 371pp. Paper, 0312982631.

Deadly Caress. St. Martin's, 2003. 384pp. Paper, 0312989431.

Deadly Promise. St. Martin's, 2003. 341pp. Paper, 0312989873.

Deadly Illusions. MIRA, 2005. 377pp. Paper, 077832138X.

Deadly Kisses. MIRA, 2006. 480pp. Paper, 0312977689.

Lane, Elizabeth.

On the Wings of Love. **Harlequin, 2008. 288pp. Paper, 9780373294817.**
Rafe Garrick's biplane crashes on the Long Island coastline in 1911, during an elaborate dinner party hosted by Alexandra Bromley's wealthy parents. She nurses him back to health, and his pioneering spirit encourages her to escape from her overbearing father's clutches.

Keywords: New York—20th century; Pilots

Langan, Ruth Ryan.

Ashes of Dreams. **Berkley Sensation, 2005. 278pp. Paper, 0425201511.**
Amanda Jeffrey's dream of running a horse farm in 1880s Kentucky shattered when her husband, Shane, was killed; now she lives with her three sons and father-in-law, Mordechai, and tries to make ends meet. When Mordechai takes ill, it's fortunate that drifter Cole Donnelly and his son, Irish immigrants, come by the ranch looking for work.

Keywords: Immigrants, Irish; Kentucky—Reconstruction/Gilded Age

Duchess of Fifth Avenue. **Berkley, 2006. 320pp. Paper, 0425208893.**
After her best friend Siobhan is murdered in 1890s New York City, Lana Dunleavy, an Irish immigrant, knows the only way she'll get to obtain custody of Siobhan's young son is if she impersonates an English lady. She hires a known con artist, Jesse Hanover, to help her with the transformation.

Keywords: Disguise; Immigrants, Irish; New York—Reconstruction/Gilded Age

Heart's Delight. **Berkley Sensation, 2007. 293pp. Paper, 9780425216330.**
Molly O'Brien, a twenty-nine-year-old spinster and recent immigrant from Ireland, takes pride in raising orphans on her own in Delight, Wisconsin, in 1890. Then two strangers with gunshot wounds arrive in town. She tends to them both, not knowing which one is U.S. Marshal Hodge Egan and which is the outlaw he's trying to capture.

Keywords: Immigrants, Irish; Wisconsin—Reconstruction/Gilded Age

Paradise Falls. **Berkley Sensation, 2004. 304pp. Paper, 0425194841.**
In the 1890s Fiona Downey, the daughter of Irish immigrants who settled in Massachusetts, takes a position as schoolteacher in Paradise Falls, Michigan, after her father dies suddenly. She boards with the Haydn family, whose two sons, Grayson and Fleming, are both intrigued by her.

Keywords: Irish Americans; Michigan—Reconstruction/Gilded Age; Teachers

Schaller, Mary.

Beloved Enemy. **Harlequin, 2004. 296pp. Paper, 0373293011.**

> When Julia Chandler, daughter of a proud Confederate family, meets Yankee major Robert Montgomery at a masked ball in Alexandria, Virginia, in 1863, she innocently asks him to "ruin her" (not knowing what this means) so that she can get out of marrying her distasteful cousin, Payton. Schaller also writes romances under the pseudonym Tori Phillips.
>
> **Keywords:** Confederacy; Virginia—Civil War

St. Giles, Jennifer.

> St. Giles writes Gothic historical romance in the tradition of Victoria Holt and Daphne du Maurier: mysterious haunted houses, secrets from the past, and dangerously attractive men.

The Mistress of Trevelyan. **Pocket, 2004. 375pp. Paper, 0743486250.**

> In 1873 in San Francisco, Ann Lovell agrees to become the governess of Benedict Trevelyan's two young sons, ignoring whispers that nefarious deeds had happened at Trevelyan Manor.
>
> **Keywords:** California—Reconstruction/Gilded Age; Gothic novels; Governesses

His Dark Desires. **Pocket, 2005. 304pp. Paper, 0743486269.**

> Widow Juliet Bucheron, keeper of a boarding house in New Orleans in 1874, tries to ignore the rumors that the dwelling is haunted—and may have been the scene of a murder. Her new tenant, handsome Stephen Trevelyan, only adds to her feeling of disquiet.
>
> **Keywords:** Gothic novels; Innkeepers; Louisiana—Reconstruction/Gilded Age

Frontier and Western Romances

Romances set in the Western United States and Canada during the nineteenth century include freethinking female heroines and men as wild and untamed as the Western frontier. Following is a selection. "Prairie romances," a phrase more often used to describe Christian-centered romances set on the Western frontier, are annotated in Chapter 11.

Banning, Lynna.

Loner's Lady. **Harlequin, 2006. 304pp. Paper, 0373294069.**

> It is 1872, and for three long years Ellen O'Brian has struggled to run her Oregon farm after her husband, Dan, took off for parts unknown. Then Jess Flint, a cowboy, comes by, and ends up staying after Ellen breaks her leg.
>
> **Keywords:** Cowboys; Farmers; Oregon—Reconstruction/Gilded Age

The Ranger and the Redhead. **Harlequin, 2005. 304pp. Paper, 0373293739.**

> Charlotte Greenfield travels to Oregon by wagon train to take a teaching position, and ranger Will Bondurant serves as her guide and protector as they make their way through hostile Indian Territory.
>
> **Keywords:** Oregon—Reconstruction/Gilded Age; Teachers; Wagon trains

Bridges, Kate.

Bridges is a prolific author of romantic novels set on the Canadian Western frontier.

The Commander. **Harlequin, 2006. 304pp. Paper, 0373294107.**

Julia O'Shea, a widow and newspaper owner in Calgary in 1895, decides to post an ad for a gentleman husband. When Ryan Reid, a commander in the Mounties, returns to town after ten years' absence, he hopes Julia will forgive him for leaving her, but she won't consider it.

Keywords: Alberta—19th century; Mounties; Widows

Klondike Doctor. **Harlequin, 2007. 304pp. Paper, 9790373294480.**

Elizabeth Langley, a newly graduated doctor in British Columbia in 1898, determines to get to the Klondike any which way she can—even if it means accompanying North-West Mounted Police sergeant Colten Hunter, with whom she has always clashed.

Keywords: British Columbia—19th century; Mounties; Physicians, women

Davidson, Carolyn.

Haven. **HQN, 2007. 384pp. Paper, 0373771797.**

It is 1878. Susannah Carvel fled Washington, D.C., for Ottawa Falls, Colorado, after her wealthy senator husband was murdered. Now calling herself Anna Whitfield, she works as a hospital nurse and tends to the wounds of Sheriff Aaron McBain after he is shot by a bank robber. He's sure he's seen her face somewhere before.

Keywords: Colorado—Reconstruction/Gilded Age; Disguise; Lawmen

Redemption. **Harlequin, 2006. 384pp. Paper, 0373771495.**

Jake McPherson, disabled and withdrawn after the Civil War (he's a double amputee), doesn't exactly welcome Alicia Merriwether, a schoolteacher who stops by his Kansas home to check on him and his son, Jason, who has been running wild at school.

Keywords: Amputees; Kansas—Reconstruction/Gilded Age; Teachers; Veterans

Ihle, Sharon.

Dear Penelope. **Leisure, 2005. 342pp. Paper, 0843955996.**

Lucy Preston arrives in Emancipation, Wyoming, in 1896 from Kansas City, expecting to meet her fiancé at the train station. When she discovers he has jilted her for another woman, she takes a job at Sebastian Cole's saloon and secretly begins writing a newspaper advice column called "Dear Penelope." When she proposes a marriage of convenience, Seb surprisingly accepts.

Keywords: Advice columnists; Marriages of convenience; Wyoming—Reconstruction/Gilded Age

McKade, Maureen.

Forrester Series.

Gentle romances about the three courageous and handsome Forrester brothers, making their way in the post–Civil War West.

Keywords: Forrester family

A Reason to Live. Berkley Sensation, 2006. 293pp. Paper, 0425212203.

During the Civil War Laurel Covey, a young widow, served as a nurse, caring for wounded soldiers and comforting them in their last moments. When traveling to Tennessee from Virginia to inform one family of their son's death, she is rescued from a band of ruffians by Texas gunslinger Creede Forrester and has to inform him that his son also died in battle.

Keywords: Gunfighters; Nurses; Virginia—Reconstruction/Gilded Age

A Reason to Believe. Berkley Sensation, 2007. 277pp. Paper, 0425216624.

Dulcie McDaniel, a young Texas widow with a four-year-old daughter, offers shelter and work to Rye Forrester, a drifter who offers to help harvest the crops. Things become romantic, though both are hiding secrets—in Rye's case, his role in the death of her husband.

Keywords: Texas—Reconstruction/Gilded Age; Widows

A Reason to Sin. Berkley Sensation, 2008. 296pp. Paper, 9780425220597.

To Slader Forrester, a faro dealer at the Scarlet Garter saloon in Oaktree, Kansas, it's clear that their new hurdy-gurdy dancer doesn't fit in. The woman calling herself Glory Bowen is really Rebecca Colfax, whose no-good husband disappeared with her son and her inheritance.

Keywords: Dancers; Disguise; Kansas—Reconstruction/Gilded Age

To Find You Again. **Berkley Sensation, 2004. 352pp. Paper, 0425197093.**

After seven years of living with the Lakota people, Emma Hartwell is rescued by the U.S. Cavalry but finds it hard to adjust to her old life again. Her parents don't know that she had a son by her Lakota husband, who was killed in a raid, and Emma longs to know whether her son is still alive. When Emma sets out to return to her adopted family, her father hires Ridge Madoc to bring her back.

Keywords: Indian captives; Lakota Sioux Indians

Miller, Linda Lael.

McKettrick Cowboys Series.

The first three novels in Miller's Western series form a trilogy about the three squabbling McKettrick brothers in 1880s Arizona Territory. Their father, Angus, states that he'll deed ownership of the Triple M Ranch to the first son who marries and gives him a grandchild, which sets them on a race to find the right woman. The final two novels feature members of the same family. Miller has written other McKettrick novels not listed here, contemporary romances with descendants of the nineteenth-century McKettrick couples as protagonists.

Keywords: Arizona—Reconstruction/Gilded Age; Cowboys; McKettrick family; Ranchers

High Country Bride. Pocket, 2002. 435pp. Paper, 0743422732.

> Rafe McKettrick, ordered to wed by his father in order to inherit the ranch, sends away for a mail-order bride. He expects Emmeline Harding to be calm and biddable, but she's quite the opposite.
>
> **Keywords:** Mail-order brides

Shotgun Bride. Pocket, 2003. 432pp. Paper, 0743422740.

> Kade McKettrick follows in Rafe's footsteps by requesting a mail-order bride, but none of the women who reply suit his tastes. Instead, he's attracted to Mandy Sperrin, a spirited woman who, for some reason, has disguised herself as a nun.
>
> **Keywords:** Mail-order brides

Secondhand Bride. Pocket, 2004. 433pp. Paper, 0743422759.

> With his older brothers already married, Jeb McKettrick is feeling the pressure, for he desperately wants to inherit the ranch. He weds schoolteacher Chloe Wakefield in haste, then finds out she's already married.
>
> **Keywords:** Bigamy; Teachers

Sierra's Homecoming. Silhouette, 2006. 248pp. Paper, 0373247958.

> In this multi-period story Sierra McKettrick, a modern-day single mom, moves to the Triple M Ranch with her son, Liam, and gets glimpses of the house's past residents. Back in 1919 Sierra's ancestor, Hannah McKettrick, struggles with her feelings for her brother-in-law, Doss.
>
> **Keywords:** Multi-period novels

McKettrick's Choice. HQN, 2005. 448pp. Paper, 0373771010.

> Holt McKettrick, oldest son of Angus (and raised away from his brothers), leaves his mail-order bride at the altar in Arizona, heading back to Texas to save his partner from the gallows and rescue the man who raised him from land-grabbers. When he reaches San Antonio he runs right into Lorelei Fellows, who sets fire to her wedding dress in the middle of the town square.
>
> **Keywords:** Texas—Reconstruction/Gilded Age

Stone Creek Novels.

Romance, adventure, and plenty of Western action, all set in small Arizona towns. These novels can stand alone.

Keywords: Arizona—20th century; Lawmen

The Man from Stone Creek. HQN, 2006. 336pp. Hardbound, 0373771150.

> In the small town of Haven in Arizona Territory in 1903, ranger Sam O'Ballivan goes undercover as a schoolteacher to catch outlaws who have been robbing trains. Postmistress Maddie Chancelor's younger brother turns out to be one of his more troublesome pupils.

A Wanted Man. HQN, 2007. 347pp. Hardbound, 9780373772360.

In Stone Creek, Arizona, in 1905, both marshal Rowdy Rhodes and school-marm Lark Morgan have secrets they're hiding from one another: he's a wanted man, and she's in hiding from an abusive husband.

Keywords: Abusive relationships; Teachers

St. John, Cheryl.

The Lawman's Bride. Harlequin, 2007. 304pp. Paper, 0373294352.

Sophie Hollis, tired of living her life as a con artist, yearns to change her ways and settle down. Clay Connor, the marshal of the small town of Newton, Kansas, may be just the man to help her—if she can finally put the past behind her.

Keywords: Kansas—Reconstruction/Gilded Age; Lawmen

Prairie Wife. Harlequin, 2005. 304pp. Paper, 0373293399.

Amy and Jesse Shelby run Shelby Station, Kansas, a wagon train stopping point on the route west. Amy has shut down emotionally ever since the death of her two-year-old son, Tim, and Jesse doesn't know how to help her. Grieving as well, but feeling very alone, Jesse turns to the bottle.

Keywords: Alcoholism; Kansas—Reconstruction/Gilded Age; Married life

The Preacher's Daughter. Harlequin, 2007. 304pp. Paper, 9780373294510.

Twenty-one-year-old Lorabeth Holdridge, a preacher's daughter in Newton, Kansas, in 1894, longs to escape from her overly strict father's home. He finally grants permission for her to take a job as housekeeper to a lively family; it's here that she meets Ben Chaney.

Keywords: Housekeepers; Kansas—Reconstruction/Gilded Age

Thomas, Jodi.

Thomas, a fifth-generation Texan, is a prolific author of Western historical romances, all of which are set in Texas. She also writes mainstream women's fiction.

Whispering Mountain Series.

The characters of this 1850s-set romance series, the McMurray siblings, are all associated with the Whispering Mountain Ranch in Texas.

Keywords: McMurray family; Ranchers; Texas—early United States

Texas Rain. Berkley, 2006. 384pp. Paper, 0425212793.

Travis McMurray, a half-Irish Texas Ranger, is a strong and silent type who, with his two brothers, helped raise his young sister, Sage, after their parents' deaths. At a local dance Rainey Adams attempts to steal a horse and distracts Travis's attention with a kiss.

Keywords: Texas Rangers

Texas Princess. Berkley, 2007. 368pp. Paper, 9780425218259.

When Tobin McMurray, a horse breeder on the Whispering Mountain Ranch, delivers a horse to senator's daughter Liberty Mayfield, he discovers that she's nowhere near the spoiled rich girl he imagined. Even more, she and her father need his help.

Keywords: Horses

World Wars I and II

Romantic intrigue and suspense during wartime, in both London and Germany.

McKendrick, Elspeth.

Perfidia. **Leisure, 2007. 321pp. Paper, 9780505527394.**
After a failed romance, Sophie de Havilland leaves London for her Aunt Augusta's house in Berlin, where she quickly becomes absorbed by the local nightlife. Sophie gets a wake-up call to the evils of the Third Reich eventually, but is it too late for her to escape? Baron Klaus von Richten, a half-American SS officer, may be her only hope. (McKendrick is a pseudonym for Morag McKendrick Pippin, below.)

Keywords: Germany—World War II; Nazis

Pippin, Morag McKendrick.

Blood Moon Over Britain. **Leisure, 2005. 323pp. Paper, 0843955821.**
It's 1942, and Cicely Winterbourne works at Bletchley Park as a file clerk. Many messages between the Germans pass through her hands, and the German Enigma Code has just been broken. She knows her life is in danger—other code-breakers have been killed—but doesn't dare trust even Alistair Fielding, war hero and inspector from Scotland Yard.

Keywords: England—World War II

Romance in Non-Western Cultures

A mélange of historical romances set in unusual, out-of-the way places: China, India, Egypt, Africa, Australia, and even nineteenth-century Mexico.

Chase, Loretta.

Mr. Impossible. **Berkley Sensation, 2005. 312pp. Paper, 0425201503.**
Annotated with others in her Carsington Brothers series, in the "Regency" section.

Duran, Meredith.

The Duke of Shadows. **Pocket, 2008. 371pp. Paper, 9781416567035.**
Emmaline Martin arrives in Delhi in 1857, the lone survivor of a shipwreck in which her parents drowned. At her engagement party she meets Julian Sinclair, the handsome heir to the Duke of Auburn and her fiancé's cousin. Julian courts scandal due to his part-Indian heritage, and Emma's outspokenness and haunted eyes attract him. They fall in love but are torn

apart during the violent Sepoy Mutiny; when their paths cross again in London years later, both are different people. Duran's debut won Gather.com's first romance writing contest.

Keywords: India—19th century; Mixed heritage; Sepoy Mutiny

Jones, Marjorie.

The Lighthorseman. **Medallion, 2006. 430pp. Paper, 1932815457.**

Devastated by the death of his younger brother, Joel, in the great charge at Beersheeba during World War I, Dale Winters returns home to Western Australia riddled with guilt for surviving. Then Emily Castle, formerly of Arizona, travels to Australia to help run the half of the sheep station she inherited after her uncle's death. She has always looked forward to meeting Dale, whom her uncle had raised, but finds him a broken man.

Keywords: Australia—20th century; Ranchers

Krahn, Betina.

The Book of the Seven Delights. **Jove, 2005. 327pp. Paper, 0515139726.**

Librarian Abigail Merchant is chagrined to take a lowly cataloging position at the British Museum, but she takes what she can get. Startled by an amazing discovery in a batch of donated papers—the existence of ancient scrolls that may be all that remains of the Library of Alexandria—she takes off for Morocco, where rakish adventurer Apollo Smith rescues her from danger.

Keywords: Librarians; Morocco—19th century

🐾 *The Book of True Desires.* **Jove, 2006. 352pp. Paper, 0515141704.**

Before he agrees to fund her latest expedition to Africa, Cordelia O'Keefe's grandfather, rich millionaire Samuel Blackburn, insists she travel to Mexico and find three Mayan stone carvings for him. An intrepid adventurer, Cordelia agrees, even when she learns Blackburn's butler, Hartford Goodnight, will be accompanying her. RITA Award.

Keywords: Butlers; Mexico—19th century

Lee, Jade.

Tigress Series.

A loosely connected series of romances about the union of male and female sexuality—yin and yang—in pre-revolutionary (1890s) Shanghai, China. Though some characters appear in multiple novels, they can be read in any order.

Keywords: China—19th century; Interracial romance

White Tigress. Leisure, 2005. 354pp. Paper, 0843953934.

Englishwoman Lydia Smith travels to Shanghai in 1897 to pay a surprise visit to her fiancé, Max, but is taken captive en route and transported to a brothel—from which Cheng Ru Shan, a Chinese man seeking immortality through sex, buys her.

Keywords: Brothels

Hungry Tigress. Leisure, 2005. 353pp. Paper, 084395504X.

After ten years living in China among the Chinese, Joanna Crane tries to help her adopted people by joining the Boxer Rebellion. Not surprisingly, they don't accept a Westerner in their company. Zou Tan, a Manchu prince who studies Taoism, rescues her.

Keywords: Boxer Rebellion

Desperate Tigress. Leisure, 2006. 342pp. Paper, 0843955058.

Shi Po, a teacher of tantric sex (part of her Taoist beliefs) in 1898 Shanghai, feels like a failure when two of her Western students manage to achieve what she cannot, and sees no reason to continue living. Her husband, Kui Yu, helps her out of her depression.

Burning Tigress. Leisure, 2006. 337pp. Paper, 0843956887.

Charlotte Wicks, an English spinster in 1898 Shanghai, discovers erotic scrolls left behind by her friend Joanna after her elopement. When Ken Jin, her family's handsome Chinese servant, learns that Charlotte found them, he tries to convince her to return them to where they belong.

Cornered Tigress. Leisure, 2007. 337pp. Paper, 0843956895.

Little Pearl takes over management of the Tigress House when her master and mistress, the Tans, are taken captive. Captain Jonas Storm seeks out his Chinese business partner, Tan Kui Yu, when his cargo goes missing, and he and Little Pearl band together to rescue them.

Tempted Tigress. Leisure, 2007. 368pp. Paper, 0843956909.

Anna Marie Thompson, an Englishwoman orphaned in late nineteenth-century China, begins running drugs for her adoptive father, an opium dealer, and gets addicted to the dreadful poppy herself. Zhi-Gang, who combats drug trafficking on behalf of the Emperor, may be the only one who can save her from herself.

Keywords: Opium

Nichols, Therese.

Sunburst's Citadel. **Medallion, 2006. 443pp. Paper, 1932815619.**

In fifteenth-century India, Shamsi, a young Hindu woman haunted by her past, now entertains the masses as a veiled exotic dancer. Karim, a Moghul nobleman, rescues her from unwanted male attention at a performance, and desires her for himself.

Keywords: Dancers; India—15th century

Pippin, Morag McKendrick.

Blood Moon Over Bengal. **Leisure, 2004. 337pp. Paper, 0843954523.**

Elizabeth Mainwarring arrives in Calcutta in 1933, during the last years of British rule, to make amends with her long-estranged father, a colonel in the British army in Bengal. She feels immediately attracted to Major Nigel Covington-Singh, an Anglo-Indian officer in her father's regiment, though socialization between whites and the native Indians is strictly forbidden. Meanwhile, Nigel is occupied with solving a series of murders—women who become involved with Indian men are being strangled.

Keywords: Detective stories; India—20th century; Mixed heritage

Chapter 5

Sagas

Historical novels that focus on characters' domestic lives and family relationships over time comprise the subgenre of sagas. Most sagas follow several generations of one family or of multiple families, revolving around a matriarchal or, less frequently, a patriarchal figure who serves as a dominant and guiding force in the lives of family members. Alternately, sagas may follow groups of friends from their younger days through middle or old age.

Because they tell involved stories, or series of stories, sagas tend to be long books. They often appear in multiple volumes, which gives readers a sense of continuity and a feeling that life continues to unfold throughout the march of history. Some sagas include family trees to aid readers in sorting out the names and relationships of the numerous characters and their descendants. The plots of sagas commonly include a good deal of romance and adventure; readers of romantic historicals, romantic epics, and multi-volume historical romance series, such as those by Eloisa James (Chapter 4), may enjoy these books as well.

Sagas allow their readers to feel emotionally invested in the characters and to see how the changing times affect the characters' lives. The emphasis is usually on social and economic rather than political history. The protagonists don't necessarily serve as instruments of change for large-scale historical events, but they find their lives greatly affected by sweeping changes around them. Although historical events may not always be at the forefront, the background of sagas is nonetheless accurately presented.

Lengthy single-volume novels are often labeled as "sagas" in publishers' blurbs, though most of these don't fit the saga definition. The popularity of sagas peaked in the 1970s and 1980s, with benchmark series such as R. F. Delderfield's Swann Family Saga and John Jakes's North and South trilogy appearing during this time. Sagas still command a devoted readership, particularly among older women, but this is a declining genre; comparatively few are still being published. There are exceptions, of course. Many of the novels in this chapter are published by British companies such as Severn House, a hardcover library publisher, which has new sagas among its regular offerings. Literary sagas, especially those based on the author's cultural heritage, also appear regularly. (Sagas written in a literary style are tagged with the word **Literary** in bold at the end of the annotation.) Family sagas are also frequently published for the Christian market, and these are annotated in Chapter 11.

Classic Sagas

These sagas are classic stories of family life through history, complete with strong men, courageous women, domestic squabbles, and class conflict. Illicit romance and black sheep are often thrown in as well. The appeal of these stories often hinges on character as well as setting, and these novels usually also contain minor elements of adventure.

The British Isles

Classic British sagas, very popular in the 1970s and 1980s, portray the domestic side of life in the British Isles.

Anand, Valerie.

The Exmoor Saga.

Anand, best known for her six-volume <u>Bridges Over Time</u> series and her Elizabethan mysteries written as Fiona Buckley, returns with a multi-volume saga set on Exmoor, the rolling countryside and woodlands around Somerset, England. She keeps the focus on several related families, their trades, and local customs; political matters are a mostly distant backdrop, especially in the first volume.

Keywords: Lanyon family; Sweetwater family

The House of Lanyon. MIRA, 2007. 586pp. Hardbound, 9780778325024.

Richard Lanyon swears to improve his family's station enough to put their landlords, the Sweetwaters, to shame. He begins by arranging his son Peter's marriage to Liza Weaver, the daughter of a neighboring family in the wool trade. Peter and Liza abandon hopes of marrying the people they love, but they form a strong marital bond nonetheless and raise a small family, doing their best to ignore Richard's social ambitions. Richard, for his part, closely guards a secret that could destroy everything he's built. Set between 1458 and 1504.

Keywords: England—high Middle Ages; Wars of the Roses

The House of Allerbrook. MIRA, 2008. 537pp. Paper, 9780778326014.

Because Jane Sweetwater refuses to become Henry VIII's mistress, she returns home to Allerbrook House in disgrace and is married off to Harry Hudd, an older tenant farmer of lower social standing. Making the best of her depressing situation, she takes comfort in remaining on Exmoor, the land she loves. She gradually rises again in social status, becoming a matriarch of sorts, and finds that the religious and political climate in faraway London has a way of reaching out and touching her family. Set between 1535 and 1587.

Keywords: England—Tudor era

Delderfield, R. F.

Swann Family Saga. ★

In 1858, British army officer Adam Swann returns from service in India with a determination to succeed in commerce. He marries Henrietta, a mill owner's daughter, and together they raise a brood of children, all of whom have their own romantic adventures. The final novel sees the Swann clan at the beginning of World War I, as they and England itself are gradually moving into the modern age.

Keywords: England—Victorian era; Swann family

God Is an Englishman. Simon & Schuster, 1970. 687pp. Hardbound, 0671205021.

Theirs Was the Kingdom. Simon & Schuster, 1971. 798pp. Hardbound, 0671210246.

Give Us This Day. Simon & Schuster, 1973. 767pp. Hardbound, 0671216589.

Graham, Winston.

Poldark Saga. ★

The twelve-volume <u>Poldark Saga</u>, completed in 2002, is an extended family saga set in Graham's trademark location, the bleak Cornwall coast in the late eighteenth and early nineteenth centuries. The initial volume, first published in 1945 in Britain, begins as Captain Ross Poldark, returning home from fighting in the American Revolution, finds his sweetheart engaged to his cousin and his crumbling estate in need of repair. He takes as his wife Demelza, daughter of a brutal local miner, and transforms her into a woman suited to his station. The two have a stormy relationship, complicated by class differences and their passing affections for others. Poldark's archenemy is neighbor George Warleggan, and their two families continue to vie for power throughout most of the series. Readers who are looking for scenes of drama, romance, class conflict, family troubles, and, of course, illegal smuggling along the rocky Cornish coast, will find plenty of it here. The <u>Poldark Saga</u> was later dramatized in several installments by the BBC. Graham died shortly after publication of the last volume, at age ninety.

Keywords: England—Georgian era; Poldark family

The Renegade. Doubleday, 1951. 344pp. Hardbound. (Original title: *Ross Poldark*.)

Demelza. Doubleday, 1953. 320pp. Hardbound.

Venture Once More. Doubleday, 1954. 283pp. Hardbound. (Original title: *Jeremy Poldark*.)

The Last Gamble. Doubleday, 1955. 347pp. Hardbound. (Original title: *Warleggan*.)

The Black Moon. Doubleday, 1974. 424pp. Hardbound, 0385001118.

The Four Swans. Doubleday, 1977. 479pp. Hardbound, 0385123388.

The Angry Tide. Doubleday, 1978. 476pp. Hardbound, 038513682X.

Stranger from the Sea. Doubleday, 1982. 445pp. Hardbound, 0385179677.

The Miller's Dance. Doubleday, 1983. 372pp. Hardbound, 0385184050.

The Loving Cup. Doubleday, 1985. 440pp. Hardbound, 0385198345.

The Twisted Sword. Carroll & Graf, 1991. 510pp. Hardbound, 0881846937.

Bella Poldark. London: Macmillan, 2002. 530pp. Hardbound, 0333989236.

Madoc, Gwen.

Mothers and Daughters. **Severn House, 2007. 234pp. Hardbound, 9780727865236.**

In Edwardian times, Lucy Chandler only discovers the illegality of her parents' marriage after her father dies; the realization leaves her family impoverished, with her father's first (and only legal) wife inheriting everything. While Lucy searches for any work she can get, her younger sister, Eva, falls into the hands of a charming loan shark.

Keywords: Bigamy; England—20th century; Poverty

Matthews, Beryl.

The Forgotten Family. **Severn House, 2006. 284pp. Hardbound, 0727864270.**

In 1890, when Queenie Bonner is two years old, her parents—unable to care for their large brood of children—sell her to Albert and Mary Warrender, an upper-class couple who have longed to adopt a child. They rename her Eleanor, take her away from the slums in London's Whitechapel district, and bring her up as their own daughter on their large country estate. Ellie slowly forgets her first family, but her adoptive father reveals her true history when she turns fifteen—which compels her to find her siblings again.

Keywords: Adopted children; England—Victorian era

Morton, Kate.

The House at Riverton. **Atria, 2008. 469pp. Hardbound, 9781416550518.**

Grace Bradley, ninety-eight years old in 1999, receives an unexpected missive from a documentary filmmaker interested in knowing about her past: specifically, the years when Grace was a maidservant for the Ashbury family of Riverton Manor in the English countryside. Grace Reeves joins the Ashbury household in 1914 and observes the interactions among siblings Hannah, Emmeline, and David. All four grow up just as the ebullient Edwardian period gives way to the more sobering prewar years. A mystery lies at the novel's center, for only Hannah, Emmeline, and Grace know the truth about a young poet's alleged suicide at Riverton in 1924. Morton pays homage to du Maurier's *Rebecca*, which should be clear after reading the novel's first two lines.

Keywords: England—20th century; Gothic novels

The United States

These novels depict the widespread political and social changes sweeping through American history, as seen from the point of view of a single family.

Baker, Ellen.

Keeping the House. **Random House, 2007. 544pp. Hardbound, 9781400066353.**

The small town of Pine Rapids, Wisconsin, is the setting for two parallel stories of marriage, family, and rediscovery of the past. Dolly Magnuson comes to Pine Rapids in 1950 as a new bride. Unable to have children, she does her best to keep her husband happy—even if it means giving up some of her dreams. When she learns about the old Mickelson house on the hill, she grows obsessed with learning more about its previous inhabitants. These include Wilma Mickelson, who married a lumberman's son right out of college, moved to town, and promptly fell in love with her husband's brother. The Mickelsons' story continues over the next two generations, with Wilma's son, Jack, a World War I veteran, and his son, JJ.

Keywords: Multi-period novels; Wisconsin—20th century

Fast, Howard.

The Immigrants. ★

Twenty years in the making, this saga by the late historical novelist Howard Fast focuses on the Lavette family of California, beginning with Italian immigrant Dan Lavette, who survives the San Francisco earthquake of 1906 and becomes a businessman to be reckoned with. The heroine of the following five books is his daughter Barbara, a noted foreign correspondent whose journeys abroad give her an education in life and love. *An Independent Woman*, which ends in the modern day, shows Barbara as her family's beloved matriarch, still fighting for what she believes in.

Keywords: California—20th century; Immigrants, Italian; Lavette family

The Immigrants. Houghton Mifflin, 1977. 389pp. Hardbound, 0395256992.

Second Generation. Houghton Mifflin, 1978. 441pp. Hardbound, 0395264839.

The Establishment. Houghton Mifflin, 1979. 365pp. Hardbound, 0395281601.

The Legacy. Houghton Mifflin, 1981. 359pp. Hardbound, 0395312604.

The Immigrant's Daughter. Houghton Mifflin, 1985. 321pp. Hardbound, 0395393817.

An Independent Woman. Harcourt Brace, 1997. 252pp. Hardbound, 0151002711.

Sagas with a Sense of Place

In these family sagas, the sense of place feels so strong that it becomes almost a character of its own. The lives of the novels' characters are intimately tied to the region where they live.

British Regional Sagas

British regional sagas are heartwarming tales that deal with the realities of working-class life in England, Scotland, and Wales, mostly in the nineteenth and early twentieth centuries. Their protagonists, nearly all female, struggle to create better lives for themselves and their families through hard work, education, and marriage with people of higher social standing. However, for those women who decide to "marry up," class differences often cause as many problems as they solve, to their frequent disappointment. The benchmark novelist in this category is Catherine Cookson, whose "clog and shawl" sagas (nicknamed for the outfits worn by the women on her novels' covers) remain immensely popular in Britain today. See also the section on romantic sagas.

Cook, Gloria.

Harvey Family Saga.

An ongoing series about the Harvey family of Ford Farm, Cornwall, over two generations (so far), from the advent of World War I through the late 1940s.

Keywords: England—20th century; Harvey family

Touch the Silence. Severn House, 2003. 282pp. Hardbound, 0727858947.

Moments of Time. Severn House, 2003. 262pp. Hardbound, 0727859781.

From a Distance. Severn House, 2004. 288pp. Hardbound, 0727861549.

Never Just a Memory Severn House, 2005. 250pp. Hardbound, 0727862529.

A Stranger Light. Severn House, 2006. 217pp. Hardbound, 0727863991.

A Whisper of Life. Severn House, 2007. 220pp. Hardbound, 0727864513.

Meryen Series.

Family disputes, romantic intrigue, and power struggles in the copper-mining village of Meryen, Cornwall, during the Victorian era. Cook doesn't stint on describing the lives of those family members, both women and men, whose livelihoods depend on the ore.

Keywords: Copper mining; England—Victorian era

Keeping Echoes. Severn House, 2005. 256pp. Hardbound, 0727863096.

Out of Shadows. Severn House, 2007. 224pp. Hardbound, 9780727865311.

All in a Day. Severn House, 2008. 240pp. Hardbound, 9780727866196.

Cookson, Catherine.

The late Catherine Cookson (1906–1998), the originator of the British regional saga, wrote over a hundred novels of family, romance, hard work, and triumph, mostly set against a well-researched backdrop of industrial northeast England and the surrounding countryside in the nineteenth century. Her compelling stories frequently begin with one woman's journey from poverty to happiness and continue to focus on her family, friends, and descendants. Cookson based many of her novels on her own background, growing up as the illegitimate daughter of a poverty-stricken woman in Tyne Dock, Northumberland. Many British authors follow in Cookson's immensely popular style. Three of her best known series are listed below.

Kate Hannigan Series. ★

These two books, Cookson's first published novel and her last, are partly autobiographical, loosely following the life stories of Cookson's mother Kate and Cookson herself. Both take place in the slums of Tyneside's "fifteen streets" in the Edwardian period.

Keywords: England—20th century; Hannigan, Kate; Illegitimate children; Poverty

Kate Hannigan. Simon & Schuster, 2004. 305pp. Hardbound, 0743237730. (Originally published in Britain in 1950.)

> Lovely Kate Hannigan falls in love with Dr. Rodney Prince, the well-to-do doctor who delivers her illegitimate daughter, Annie. Their long-term affection causes her neighbors (and Rodney's mean-spirited wife) to gossip spitefully about her.

Kate Hannigan's Girl. Simon & Schuster, 2000. 287pp. Hardbound, 0743212525.

> This sequel to *Kate Hannigan* picks up with Kate's daughter Annie in the 1920s. Despite her mother's happy and prosperous marriage, Annie is humiliated by her own illegitimate birth. She faces the same religious prejudice that her mother faced. Even worse, she must compete for everything, including mathematician Terence Macbane, with the scheming Cathleen Davidson. Originally written much earlier than 2000, *Kate Hannigan's Girl* was originally rejected by Cookson's publisher for its controversial content, but was later accepted and released as her 100th published novel.

The Mallen Trilogy. ★

The Mallens are a family accursed, as shown by the white streak of hair borne by the sons of the ruthless Thomas Mallen, squire of High Banks Hall, who loses his fortune amid scandal in the 1850s. Not even his illegitimate, deaf daughter Barbara is immune from his tyrannical legacy, as demonstrated by the effect the Mallen curse has on her three sons.

Keywords: Curses; Deafness; England—Victorian era; Mallen family

The Mallen Streak. Dutton, 1973. 282pp. Hardbound, 0525150757.

The Mallen Girl. Dutton, 1973. 282pp. Hardbound, 0525150722.

The Mallen Lot. Dutton, 1974. 309pp. Hardbound, 0525150730. (Original title: *The Mallen Litter.*)

Tilly Trotter Trilogy.

Beginning in 1836, Matilda Trotter, called Tilly, learns the hard way that beauty can be both a gift and a curse. Growing up with her grandparents in Tyneside in County Durham, as Cookson did herself, Tilly falls on hard times. Accused of witchcraft and barely escaping with her life, she comes to work at the local mill. Mistress to a rich, married man for years, after he dies she is forced out of their home by his jealous daughter. At this point the ever-resourceful Tilly heads to America, where she becomes a frontier wife. Her frontier adventures over at the ripe old age of thirty-five, Tilly heads back to her homeland. Popular British saga novelist Rosie Goodwin has recently penned a sequel to the trilogy, *Tilly Trotter's Legacy*, with the approval of Cookson's estate.

Keywords: England—Victorian era; Trotter, Tilly

Tilly. Morrow, 1980. 372pp. Hardbound, 0688037151. (Original title: *Tilly.*)

Tilly Wed. Morrow, 1981. 310pp. Hardbound, 0688001882. (Original title: *Tilly Trotter Wed.*)

Tilly Alone. Morrow, 1982. 1982. Hardbound, 0688004555. (Original title: *Tilly Trotter Widowed.*)

Johnson, Jeannie.

Where the Wild Thyme Blows. **Severn House, 2007. 264pp. Hardbound, 9780727864994.**

During the years between the two world wars, Beth Dawson, whose family depends on the boating trade for their livelihood, becomes involved with the local labor movement—and with Anthony Wesley, a local union agitator.

Keywords: England—20th century; Unions

Kirkwood, Gwen.

Kirkwood, a popular Scottish saga writer, has written over a hundred novels (mostly published only in Britain) under various pseudonyms as well as her own name, Jean Saunders.

Heather Series.

Romantic entanglements in an upstairs-downstairs setting, on a rural estate in southwestern Scotland between the two world wars. *When the Heather Blooms* will continue the series.

Keywords: Farmers; Scotland—20th century

Secrets in the Heather. Severn House, 2007. 256pp. Hardbound, 9780727864901.

When her great-grandmother dies, Victoria becomes a cook's assistant to the Pringle family, who are tenants to the Laird of Darlonachie. While trying to survive her arduous duties, she tries to decide whether Andrew Pringle is the man for her, and deals with secrets in her past that have newly come to light.

Call of the Heather. Severn House, 2008. 256pp. Hardbound, 9780727865649.

Libby Pringle, daughter of Andrew and Victoria, shares her family's love for the Scottish glens, as does her new friend, Billy Lennox. Billy's life changes after his grandfather's death, when he realizes that he was illegitimate. Set beginning in 1939.

Lochandee Saga.

Love, troubles, and family life on a dairy farm, Lochandee, in 1930s through 1980s rural Scotland.

Keywords: Farmers; Maxwell family; Scotland—20th century

The Laird of Lochandee. Severn House, 2002. 314pp. Hardbound, 0727858777.

> In 1930s Scotland, Connor Maxwell takes in young Rachel O'Brien after her father dies, but his wife treats her worse than a servant. When she falls in love with Ross, the son of the house, and becomes pregnant, the pair must face his parents' wrath if they are to stay together.

A Tangled Web. Severn House, 2003. 288pp. Hardbound, 0727859862.

> At the end of World War II, Ross and Rachel are married, but secrets from the past threaten their happiness.

Children of the Glens. Severn House, 2004. 304pp. Hardbound, 9780727861221.

> The 1950s have brought considerable change to the farming industry and to the Maxwells in particular. Rachel Maxwell has become the proud family matriarch, but her brood's happiness may be destroyed by Gerda Fritz-Allan, a gold digger who has her sights on Rachel's youngest son, Ewan.

Home to the Glen. Severn House, 2006. 304pp. Hardbound, 9780727863263.

> Cousins Paul and Ryan Maxwell, the fourth generation of Maxwells to run Lochandee, aim to restore the family's fortunes by developing a pedigreed dairy farm.

Lord, Elizabeth.

To Cast a Stone. **Severn House, 2007. 288pp. Hardbound, 9780727865137.**

Ellie and Dora Jay, daughters of an alcoholic father in London's East End at the turn of the twentieth century, accept help from a local doctor after their mother dies, to improve their lot in life.

Keywords: Alcoholism; England—20th century; Poverty

Matthews, Beryl.

Webster Series.

A London-based family raises themselves out of poverty; their story covers a good part of the twentieth century.

Keywords: England—20th century; Poverty; Webster family

The Open Door. Severn House, 2004. 464pp. Hardbound, 9780727860811.

> Rose Webster knows that the only way out of the London slum where she lives with her family is by obtaining an education. She pursues this chance, but fears the man she loves, Bill, may not wait for her.

Wings of the Morning. Severn House, 2004. 480pp. Hardbound, 9780727861436.

> Annie Webster, Rose's younger sister, grows up contentedly in a close-knit family environment. When World War II begins, her brothers sign up with the army, and Annie joins the Women's Auxiliary Air Force.

> **Keywords:** Pilots, women

A Time of Peace. Severn House, 2005. 440pp. Hardbound, 0727862219.

In the 1960s, Rose's daughter, Kate, moves to London to become a photographer.

Keywords: Photographers

Stirling, Jessica.

The Conways Trilogy.

An urban family saga set in Glasgow, Scotland, primarily during the Great Depression and World War II.

Keywords: Conway family; Great Depression; Mothers and daughters; Poverty; Scotland —20th century and World War II; Sisters

Prized Possessions. St. Martin's Press, 2001. 412pp. Hardbound, 0312280572.

In Depression-era Glasgow, Lizzie Conway fights to keep her three teenaged daughters out of poverty, hoping that one day they'll be able to move out of the slums. It doesn't help that she has to keep paying off the money her deceased husband stole from the Mafia. Babs and Polly, strong-willed girls both, get involved with the wrong men and learn about their mother's mistakes the hard way.

Sisters Three. St. Martin's Press, 2002. 443pp. Hardbound, 0312305230.

Still in the Gorbals slums of Glasgow on the eve of World War II, Polly and Babs raise their own families and try to keep their gangster husbands out of trouble. Trouble brews when Rosie, the deaf youngest sister, becomes romantically involved with a policeman.

Wives at War. St. Martin's Press, 2005. 475pp. Hardbound, 0312340249.

Rosie, Babs, and Polly, all wives with families in the year 1940, work tirelessly for the war effort in Glasgow, knowing and fearing that the Germans will be attacking Britain soon.

Summers, Rowena.

Elkins Family Series.

The lively story of the Elkins family of Braydon, a coastal town near Bristol, who run a popular seaside hotel in the mid- to late 1930s.

Keywords: Elkins family; England—20th century; Hotels

Shelter from the Storm. Severn House, 2005. 220pp. Hardbound, 0727862294.

Charlotte, Josie, and Milly are the three teenaged daughters of Donald and Ruth Elkins, and help them run The Retreat, a hotel on the Somerset coast. Their lives turn upside down when their beloved and eccentric grandmother dies, and after a violent storm floods the hotel. Bones are discovered in the cellar soon afterward.

Monday's Child. Severn House, 2005. 218pp. Hardbound, 0727863215.

It's now 1937, and the Elkins' hotel has been renovated after the storm. The three Elkins daughters become romantically entangled with young men; Charlotte has second thoughts about marrying her blacksmith beau, and Josie proves her worth to a handsome lad she meets at the local fair.

American Regional Sagas

These sagas give readers a good feel for family life in different regions of the United States: New England, the Midwest, the South, and the West.

New York

Barton, Emily.

Brookland. **Farrar, Straus & Giroux, 2006.**
   Annotated in Chapter 10.

Gilmore, Jennifer.

Golden Country. **Scribner, 2006. Hardbound, 0743288637.**
   Annotated under "Jewish Sagas."

Groff, Lauren.

The Monsters of Templeton. **Voice, 2008. 361pp. Hardbound, 9781401322250.**

Templeton, New York, a thinly disguised analogue of Cooperstown, hides many secrets related to Wilhelmina Upton's family history. Willie, an archaeology graduate student who just terminated an affair with her married professor, returns home in disgrace, only to learn from her ex-hippie mother that her real father is a resident of Templeton—exactly who, she's not telling, but he's a member of the Temple family. As Willie combs through the branches of the Temple family tree all the way up to Marmaduke Temple, the town's founder, she amasses evidence related to her mission. In intervening chapters, various Temple family members pop in to reveal their own stories.

Keywords: Graduate students; New York—Multi-period

Lustbader, Victoria.

Hidden. **Forge, 2006. 463pp. Hardbound, 0765315564.**
Jed Gates, eldest son of a wealthy Manhattan family whose elegant Fifth Avenue apartment overlooks Central Park, forms an unlikely friendship with David Warshinsky, a first-generation Jewish American from the Lower East Side, while serving in the army during World War I. When they return home, wounded but alive, Jed insists his family take in David, who sees association with the Gateses as a way to better himself. Knowing he has the brains to become a successful financier, he begins going by David Shaw, cutting himself off from his family and hoping his Jewish heritage never comes to light. Meanwhile, Jed ignores his latent homosexuality in an effort to become the son his parents always wanted. Lustbader (wife of novelist Eric) also vividly portrays the working lives of Jed's and David's siblings. An entertaining depiction of a city on the cusp of economic and social change.

Keywords: Businessmen; Gay men; Jews; New York—World War I

Trevanian.

The Crazyladies of Pearl Street. **Crown, 2005. 384pp. Hardbound, 14000080363.**

This coming of age story is set in the slums of Albany, New York, beginning in 1936 and continuing through the end of World War II. Jean-Luc LaPointe, six years old, and his three-year-old sister Anne-Marie move with their mother to Pearl Street in downtown Albany, hoping to live as a family with their frequently absent father. Unfortunately, their dad heads out to the store one day and never comes home. The "crazyladies" of the title are the eccentric Irish American women whom Jean-Luc observes with affection as they, too, struggle to create lives for themselves and their families. Trevanian's novel is highly autobiographical, as he himself grew up on Pearl Street in Albany.

Keywords: Coming of age; Irish Americans; Great Depression; New York—World War II; Poverty

Widmer, Eleanor.

Up from Orchard Street. **Bantam, 2005. 389pp. Hardbound, 0553804006.**

Annotated under "Jewish Sagas."

The South

Agee, Jonis.

The River Wife. **Random House, 2007. 416pp. Hardbound, 9781400065967.** 📖

When pregnant Hedie Rails moves to Jacques Landing, Missouri, in 1930 to become the bride of Clement Ducharme, she doesn't know she's also marrying into his disturbing family legacy. As Hedie reads the diaries of Annie Lark, crippled in the 1811 New Madrid earthquake and rescued from Mississippi flooding by French fur trapper Jacques Ducharme, she starts to notice eerie parallels between Annie's life and hers. Annie is only the first of several "river wives," women associated with Jacques over the next 120 years; the others include Omah, a freed slave who joins him as a river pirate; Laura, his fortune-hunting second wife; and their daughter, Little Maddie, who becomes Clement's mother. Classic Southern gothic. **Literary.**

Keywords: Earthquakes; Gothic novels; Great Depression; Missouri—early United States

Caldwell, Wayne.

Cataloochee. **Random House, 2007. 352pp. Hardbound, 9781400063437.** 📖

In the tradition of *Cold Mountain*, Caldwell (whose debut novel boasts an endorsement from Charles Frazier) writes about three generations of Wrights and Carters, two families from the mountain town of Cataloochee, North Carolina. The novel begins in the 1880s, as Ezra Banks escapes his abusive family to settle down in Cataloochee with Hannah Carter, a local girl, and raise a family. Over four generations, the Carters, Banks, and Wrightses emerge into the twentieth century, squabbling with one another, and gradually lose their ancestral lands as the federal government moves in to claim them. A gentle saga, replete with local folklore, set in the region that later became the Great Smoky Mountains National Park.

Keywords: Mountains; North Carolina—Reconstruction/Gilded Age

Cook, Jacquelyn.

Sunrise. BelleBooks, 2008. 300pp. Paper, 9780976876090. ✍

Cook echoes Eugenia Price in her gentle, nostalgic look back on the life of Anne Tracy, an heiress and Southern belle from Macon, Georgia. With the recent death of her father in 1849, twenty-year-old Anne has nowhere to turn, so she agrees to marry a railroad entrepreneur, William Butler Johnston, who is twenty years her elder. To her pleasant surprise, she and William fall deeply in love. Their story is not without hardship, as the Civil War and the deaths of several children bring pain and tragedy to their lives, yet Anne—with the help of her strong faith and Sidney Lanier's poems—learns to make peace with her troubles. Their family mansion, Hay House, figures strongly in the story and is a National Historic Landmark today.

Keywords: Georgia—Civil War; Johnston, Anne Tracy (historical character); Mansions

Craig, Gretchen.

Always and Forever series.

Marketed as historical romances, these old-fashioned and absorbing Creole sagas focus on two generations of the same extended family, members of which live along the Louisiana bayou between the 1820s and the Civil War period.

Keywords: Abolitionists; Creoles; Louisiana—early United States; Mixed heritage; Plantations; Slaves and slavery

Always and Forever. Zebra, 2006. 414pp. Paper, 0821780190.

Beginning in 1823, Josie Tassin and her slave, Cleo, grow up together on her family's plantation, though Josie never realizes until much later that Cleo is her half-sister. Adolescence, personal tragedies, and financial crises etch new lines onto their personalities. Despite the closed world she inhabits, Josie remains a good person, and as she matures, she adjusts her relationships with everyone around her. These include her sharp-eyed Grandmère, Emmeline, who struggles to teach Josie how to run the plantation; handsome Phanor, whose poor Cajun heritage makes him an unacceptable suitor; and her elegant second cousin, Bertrand, whose sensuality attracts her, but whose roving eye follows Cleo.

Ever My Love. Zebra, 2007. 384pp. Paper, 0821780204.

Just prior to the Civil War, Louisiana plantation owner's daughter Marianne Johnston has her heart in the right place: she nurses slaves back to health after slavers catch them and bring them back home. When Yves Chamard first meets Marianne, he sees a beautiful Southern belle who's out of his reach, while she believes him to be a typical Creole slave owner; she doesn't realize he regularly helps slaves to freedom along the Underground Railroad. Then Yves's black half-brother Gabriel, a physician, is kidnapped and sold back into slavery, forcing them, their family, and friends to take action. A gripping family saga with large dollops of romance and some scenes of racial brutality, featuring the children of the characters from *Always and Forever*.

Payne, David.

Back to Wando Passo. Morrow, 2006. 435pp. Hardbound, 0060851899.

After a short separation, ex-rock star Ransom "Ran" Hill joins his wife, Claire, and their children on her South Carolina family plantation, Wando Passo. However, Claire seems to have taken more than a platonic interest in Marcel Jones, a black musician who's an old friend. This modern love triangle echoes that of two of Claire's Civil War–era ancestors, Harlan and Addie DeLay. Payne tells their story, and that of Addie's love for Harlan's black half-brother, Jarry, in alternating chapters. Elements of the romance, mystery, and traditional ghost story mingle in this classic Southern saga.

Keywords: Ghosts; Love triangles; Multi-period novels; Plantations; Rock musicians; South Carolina—Civil War

Price, Eugenia.

Over her lifetime, the late Eugenia Price wrote a number of best-selling historical novels set in the Deep South before, during, and after the Civil War. Her meticulously researched novels are family sagas and sentimental love stories, all based on the lives of real people—so-called average citizens who manage to triumph over heartbreak, war, and other adverse circumstances. Price took inspiration from names she saw on gravestones and took it upon herself to discover the stories of these people who had passed on. Her portrayals of charming characters and her heartwarming evocations of days gone by appeal to all age groups. Many of her historical novels, gentle reads originally published by the mainstream press, have been reissued for the Christian market. These are her best-known sagas.

Georgia Trilogy. ✍ ★

Anne Couper Fraser of St. Simons Island, Georgia, and her Scottish soldier-husband, John, are the protagonists of this extended romantic saga beginning during the War of 1812 and ending during the Civil War.

Keywords: Fraser, Anne Couper (historical character); Georgia—early United States

Bright Captivity. Doubleday, 1991. 631pp. Hardbound, 0385267010.

Where Shadows Go. Doubleday, 1993. 646pp. Hardbound, 0385267029.

Beauty from Ashes. Doubleday, 1995. 627pp. Hardbound, 0385267037.

St. Simons Island Trilogy. ✍ ★

Beginning in post-revolutionary Maine and ending on St. Simons Island, Georgia, just after the Civil War, James Gould, James's son Horace, and northerner Anson Dodge make the South their home, renew their faith, and discover love. Price wrote the volumes of this trilogy in the opposite order of their chronology.

Keywords: Dodge, Anson (historical character); Georgia—Civil War; Gould, James (historical character)

Lighthouse. Lippincott, 1971. 342pp. Hardbound.

New Moon Rising. Lippincott, 1969. 281pp. Hardbound.

The Beloved Invader. Lippincott, 1965. 284pp. Hardbound.

Savannah Quartet. ★ ✍

Beginning with Philadelphian Mark Browning, who arrives in Savannah as a young man, the Browning, Mackay, and Stiles families of antebellum Georgia interact with one another, find romance, and find themselves divided on the issue of slavery.

Keywords: Browning, Mark (historical character); Georgia—early United States

Savannah. Doubleday, 1983. 595pp. Hardbound, 0385152744.

To See Your Face Again. Doubleday, 1985. 546pp. Hardbound, 0385152752.

Before the Darkness Falls. Doubleday, 1987. 455pp. Hardbound, 0385230680.

Stranger in Savannah. Doubleday, 1989. 755pp. Hardbound, 0385230699.

Rubio, Gwyn Hyman.

The Woodsman's Daughter. **Viking, 2005. 402pp. Hardbound, 0670033219.**
📖

In the piney flatlands of southern Georgia in the 1880s, Dalia Miller, the beautiful older daughter of a turpentine farmer with a drinking problem, struggles to help herself and her family rise above the shameful secret her father always strived to keep hidden. Rubio recounts Dalia's journey, and that of her descendants, over three generations. Classic Southern gothic complete with a flawed family, its disturbing legacy, and a well-rendered, distinct Georgia setting, all overlaid with a tragic air. **Literary.**

Keywords: Georgia—Reconstruction/Gilded Age; Gothic novels; Turpentine farming

Scully, Helen.

In the Hope of Rising Again. **Viking, 2004. 312pp. Hardbound, 1594200254.**
📖

Scully's debut novel, published when she was in her mid-twenties, deals with her own ancestors, in particular Regina Riant, daughter of a proud Confederate veteran in turn-of-the-century Mobile, Alabama. Like the South itself, Regina's family struggles to rise again after the Confederacy's defeat decades earlier, but never quite manages to do so. To escape her emotionally distant mother and lazy brothers, Regina decides to marry Charles Morrow, a handsome but weak-willed man, but has to rely on her own strength to save her family from poverty. **Literary.**

Keywords: Alabama—Reconstruction/Gilded Age; Confederacy; Poverty

The West

Western sagas are annotated in Chapter 6, "Westerns Historical Novels."

African Sagas

Smith, Wilbur.

The following adventure-filled series are annotated in Chapter 8.

Ballantyne Novels.

Courtney Family Saga.

Australian Sagas

McCullough, Colleen.

The Thorn Birds. **Harper & Row, 1977. 533pp. Hardbound, 0060129565.** ★

Paddy Cleary and his wife Fiona arrive from New Zealand with their family in the 1940s to run Drogheda, a large sheep station in the Australian outback owned by Paddy's rich sister, Mary Carson. Despite their responsibilities, Mary continually treats her brother's family like poor relations, suitable for hard work but not much else. Paddy and Fiona's only daughter, Meggie, grows up admiring the family's itinerant priest, Father Ralph de Bricassart. Despite Ralph's avowed celibacy, Mary wants him for herself. Meggie's growing love for Ralph causes them nothing but pain over the years, as he's continually torn between Meggie and the Church. His choice has immense repercussions for the next generation of Clearys. This passionate multigenerational saga was made into a popular yet controversial television miniseries.

Keywords: Australia—20th century; Extramarital affairs; Priests; Sheep ranchers

Romantic Sagas

Romantic sagas are family stories that also incorporate a strong romantic element. Readers who enjoy novels of this type should also investigate romantic epics and romantic historicals (Chapter 4).

Aitken, Rosemary.

Cornish Sagas.

A series of novels set in the Cornish tin mining town of Penvarris circa 1910. All but the first two can stand alone, though there are some overlapping characters among the rest. Aitken also writes Roman-era mysteries as Rosemary Rowe.

Keywords: England—20th century; Tin mining

Stormy Waters. Severn House, 2001. 216pp. Hardbound, 0727857282.

The Silent Shore. Severn House, 2002. 208pp. Hardbound, 0727857436.

The Granite Cliffs. Severn House, 2003. 250pp. Hardbound, 0727858548.

Against the Tide. Severn House, 2004. 224pp. Hardbound, 9780727860293.

> In 1914 in Cornwall, fisherman Stan Hunkin rules over his family, in-cluding his strong-minded twin daughters, Winnie and Dora. He doesn't like Dora hanging out with Tom Trewin, a local miner's son, because he thinks she can do better.
>
> **Keywords:** Twins

The Tregenza Girls. Severn House, 2006. 250pp. Hardbound, 0727863967.

> Helena Tregenza—beautiful, intelligent, and an accomplished pia-nist—knows that no man will ever marry her due to her blindness. Her younger sister, Lucy, flighty and ambitious, believes she loves her childhood friend, James, but Helena has always carried a torch for him, too. Then World War I arrives, changing all of their lives. Set in Penzance in Edwardian times.
>
> **Keywords:** Blindness; England—World War I; Pianists

From Penvarris with Love. Severn House, 2008. 224pp. Hardbound, 9780727866271.

> Maud Olds and Belinda Richards, apprentice seamstresses in Penzance, both hope to find husbands before the area's men are forced to head off to fight in World War I.
>
> **Keywords:** England—World War I; Seamstresses

Bacon, Margaret.

Northrop Hall Series.

After the horrors of World War I, life at the magnificent family residence of Northrop Hall won't ever be the same. The three-volume saga takes readers through both world wars.

Keywords: Arndale family; England—World War I and World War II

Northrop Hall. Severn House, 2003. 256pp. Hardbound, 0727859412.

> When war breaks out in Europe in 1914, and Lady Arndale of Northrop Hall dies in an accident, her son Charles takes over man-agement of the estate. Daughters Diana and Laura take on more grown-up roles. The social fabric of their world is changing, as the roles of master and servant are occasionally swapped, and the women of the family find themselves taking on greater responsibili-ties—and gaining respect for it.

The Years Between. Severn House, 2003. 256pp. Hardbound, 0727859676.

> After the war, Diana and her husband James work tirelessly to trans-form Northrop Hall into a home for wounded soldiers, but their mar-riage feels the strain. Then Sebastian, Diana's first love from when she was a teenager, comes back into her life.

For Better, for Worse. Severn House, 2005. 224pp. Hardbound, 9780727862334.

Sebastian Crawley of Yorkshire has always been in love with Diana Arndale, yet was forced to marry Celia. After the end of World War II, Felicity, one of Sebastian and Celia's daughters, determines to reunite her father with his first love.

Donati, Sara.

Wilderness Series.

Annotated in Chapter 4, under "Romantic Epics."

Douglas, Anne.

The Girl from Wish Lane. Severn House, 2008. 320pp. Hardbound, 9780727866134.

Eva Masson, a girl from the wrong side of the tracks in Dundee, Scotland, in the 1920s, falls in love with Nicholas North, son of the man who owns the mills where her family works. Their relationship is fraught with misunderstandings on the part of both families, as well as Eva's growing interest in the local labor movement.

Keywords: Mill workers; Scotland—20th century; Unions

Gellis, Roberta.

The Roselynde Chronicles.

Annotated in Chapter 4, under "Historical Romances."

Gregory, Philippa.

Wideacre Trilogy. ★

Like an eighteenth-century version of the television show *Dynasty*, this saga overflows with greed, drama, and desperate scheming, but the historical research behind it is well done, and it has more substance than most works of this type. Gregory's trilogy features three strong-willed women who strive to succeed in a world that mistreats members of the female sex. As they find to their detriment, excessive greed comes at a great price.

Keywords: England—Georgian era; Gypsies; Heirs and heiresses; Incest; Lacey family

Wideacre. Simon & Schuster, 1987. 556pp. Hardbound, 0671634623.

Beatrice Lacey is obsessed with her ancestral home of Wideacre Hall, but as an eighteenth-century woman, her rights are ignored in favor of her brother. Harry, though, is no match for the determined Beatrice, who will resort to anything—incest, blackmail, and other corrupt acts—to ensure that she'll never have to leave.

The Favored Child. Pocket, 1989. 472pp. Hardbound, 0671679104.

Beatrice Lacey's greed has ruined Wideacre, her former Sussex estate. Her two heirs, cousins Julia and Richard, grow up in innocence in the nearby dower house, not knowing that they're more closely related than they've been told.

Meridon. Pocket, 1990. 439pp. Hardbound, 0671701517.

> The lost Lacey heir, a young gypsy called Meridon, joins a traveling circus, but mysterious dreams keep calling her home.

Laker, Rosalind.

To Dance with Kings. **Doubleday, 1988. 564pp. Hardbound, 0385242735.**

Four generations of women of Versailles feature in this romantic family saga. It begins in 1664 as peasant Jeanne Dremont, a fan maker, makes a promise to her newborn daughter Marguerite that she will not grow up in poverty. Marguerite, her daughter Jasmin, Jasmin's daughter Violette, and Violette's daughter Rose grow up alongside the palace, where the Bourbon kings (from Louis XIV, the Sun King, through Louis XVI) reign in splendor—at least until the Revolution, which affects Rose, companion to Marie Antoinette, most of all. Reprinted in paperback by Three Rivers in 2007.

Keywords: France—early modern era; Fan makers; French Revolution; Royalty

Glitz, Glamour, and Riches

Sagas featuring families involved in the glamorous worlds of show business and high finance.

Bradford, Barbara Taylor.

Ravenscar Trilogy.

Bradford transplants the story of King Edward IV and the York–Lancaster rivalry from England's Wars of the Roses to the Edwardian period and afterward. A soap opera-style saga with compelling characters, political and financial intrigue, and plenty of juicy bits. The final volume, *Being Elizabeth*, will take the Deravenels through the end of the twentieth century.

Keywords: Businessmen; England—20th century; Heirs and heiresses; Ravenscar family; Wars of the Roses

The Ravenscar Dynasty. St. Martin's Press, 2006. 484pp. Hardbound, 0312354606.

> It is 1904, and eighteen-year-old Edward Deravenel turns his hand to commerce when his father, brother, uncle, and cousin all die in a mysterious fire. Edward and another cousin, Neville, believe the fire was deliberately set, so they band together to find the truth and retake control of their family's trading empire, which has been run by the Grants, a distant branch of the family, for sixty years. Henry Grant (think Henry VI) isn't completely sane, so his wife Margot (aka Margaret of Anjou) runs the business in his stead. Reminiscent of the original War of the Roses saga, Edward is a handsome playboy-type caught between duty and sexual attraction to a dangerous woman.

The Heir. St. Martin's Press, 2007. 470pp. Hardbound, 9780312354626.

> Edward Deravenel has lost much in the First World War, but his immediate family remains intact, and business couldn't be better. Little by little, various strands of the family empire, Deravenels, begin to unravel. Edward's infidelities anger his jealous wife, and his brother George betrays the family. After Edward's sudden death, his savvy daughter, Bess, is left to pick up the pieces, marry, and bear a male heir to inherit the Deravenel fortune.

Lustbader, Victoria.

Hidden. **Forge, 2006. 463pp. Hardbound, 0765315564.**

> Annotated under "American Regional Sagas: New York."

Palmer, Elizabeth.

The Distaff Side. **St. Martin's Press, 2004. 279pp. Hardbound, 0312325398.**

> In 1917 in London, Bertie Langham is forced to break his engagement with wealthy Mai Binnington when his controlling mother, Augusta, learns that Mai is a feminist and suffragette. Mai decides to wed her childhood friend, dull Ned Fielding, while Bertie gets drawn into the web of enigmatic Russian princess Zhenia Dashkova, who hides the fact that she's a thief who stole her previous employer's identity. Shenanigans amid London's upper crust form the subject of Palmer's satirical and witty British saga.
>
> **Keywords:** Disguise; England—World War I

Parker, Una-Mary.

Granville Sisters Trilogy.

> Annotated under "Wartime Sagas."

Vincenzi, Penny.

Spoils of Time Trilogy.

> Vincenzi, a best-selling author in Britain, made her American debut with this family saga set in England during the belle époque of the Edwardian era, the First World War, and the twenties. Later volumes take the family all the way through the 1950s.
>
> **Keywords:** Businesswomen; England—20th century; Newspaper publishing

No Angel. Overlook, 2003. 640pp. Hardbound, 1585674818.

> Celia Lytton, a woman of aristocratic birth and bearing, is used to getting her way. This shows in her dealings with her husband Oliver, a publishing magnate; her own children; Sylvia Miller, whose daughter comes to live with the Lyttons; and a children's book author who falls under Celia's influence.

Something Dangerous. Overlook, 2004. 710pp. Hardbound, 1585674826.

> Venetia and Adele Lytton, eighteen-year-old twins in 1928, are fully confident about their emerging beauty and more concerned with the London social scene than their family's publishing business. Celia Lytton's greatest hope for the future may be Barty Miller, the Lyttons' foster child, now a

young woman with keen business sense. Then, as England begins to feel the threat of Nazi Germany, the Lyttons learn that their privileged upbringing hasn't prepared them for its dangers.

Keywords: England—World War II; Socialites; Twins

Into Temptation. Overlook, 2005. 654pp. Hardbound, 1585677086.

It's now 1953, and Celia Lytton stuns the family by announcing her retirement from Lytton's to marry a younger man, her husband having died the previous year. Barty Miller heads up the business's New York office, though back in London the Lyttons fear she'll make a rash business decision.

Sagas of Ethnic and Cultural Heritage

These sagas focus on the cultural heritage of a family or families that has been passed down through the generations. They are about cultural identity as much as they are about family ties. These novels can deal with stories of immigrant life and the adjustments made by older members of a family after their arrival in the United States long ago, or they can use the form of a saga to illustrate how ethnic groups' experiences have changed over the years. Many authors of these family sagas belong to the ethnic group they write about and use their works to celebrate the cultural legacy left to them by their forebears.

African

Forna, Aminatta.

Ancestor Stones. **Atlantic Monthly, 2006. 317pp. Hardbound, 0871139448.** 📖

Abie, a young woman from an unnamed African country (assumed to be Sierra Leone, the author's homeland) now living in London with her Scottish husband and their children, receives a letter from her cousin Alpha, bequeathing her the family's coffee plantation and implying she should return to claim it. When Abie comes home, her four aunts—Asana, Mary, Hawa, and Serah, all daughters of different wives of her grandfather—unfold their life stories in succession, speaking of village life, folklore, their lives as co-wives, and the development of Sierra Leone from 1926 through the present. **Literary.**

Keywords: Aunts; Bigamy; Multi-period novels; Plantations; Sierra Leone—20th century

African American

These novels depict the struggles and triumphs of African American families in American history, from the early days of slavery through the civil rights era, and their complicated relationships with members of white families.

Alers, Rochelle.

Best Kept Secrets. **Kimani, 2006. 352pp. Paper, 1583146709.**

Alers has written many contemporary romances about members of the extended Cole family in her <u>Hideaway</u> series; *Best Kept Secrets* is the story of the family matriarch and patriarch. Set in Cuba and Florida from the mid-1920s through the mid-1940s, the story illustrates the difficulties of maintaining an interracial marriage in the early twentieth century. Samuel Cole, a black would-be entrepreneur, meets Marguerite-Josefina (MJ) Diaz on his first business trip to Havana in 1924 and is immediately smitten. Thus begins their romance, as well as the Cole-Diaz family dynasty; many secrets concealed within the later books are revealed here.

Keywords: African Americans; Cuba—20th century; Florida—20th century; Interracial romance

Baker, Calvin.

Dominion. **Grove, 2006. 368pp. Hardbound, 0802118291.**

This literary saga about three generations of African American men begins in the late seventeenth century and continues through the revolutionary period. In colonial times, Jasper Merian, a freed slave from Virginia, settles in South Carolina and, in the untamed wilderness, raises a family and builds a home he names Stonehouses. He also struggles to earn enough money to purchase the freedom of the slave family he left behind. The novel continues with the stories of his sons and grandson, who fight the land and for their people's freedom in their own ways. **Literary.**

Keywords: African Americans; Slaves, former; South Carolina—colonial period

Haley, Alex.

🐾 *Roots.* **Doubleday, 1976. 688pp. Hardbound, 0385037872.** ✍ ★

Haley's classic saga of African Americans' journey from their African homeland through years of slavery and discrimination in America and finally to freedom is considered a masterpiece of social history. It was also the subject of one of the most watched TV miniseries of all time. The story begins with Kunta Kinte, Haley's distant ancestor in 1750s Africa, who is captured by slavers and brought to America; it concludes six generations later with Haley's father. Haley's novel convinced thousands if not millions of people, both black and white, to pursue genealogy as a hobby. *Roots*, a fictionalized biographical saga, was originally marketed as nonfiction but is now—after considerable controversy over whether certain scenes in the book were real or fictionalized—considered more along the lines of a historical novel. Pulitzer Prize.

Keywords: African Americans; Ghana—18th century; Haley, Alex (historical character); Kinte, Kunta (historical character)

Tademy, Lalita.

<u>Cane River Series.</u> ✍ ★ 📖

Tademy left her high-powered Silicon Valley job to write novels about her ancestors' lives—with very successful results.

Keywords: African Americans; Tademy family

Cane River. Warner, 2001. 418pp. Hardbound, 0446527327.

> This saga of four successive generations of African American women living on a Creole plantation along Louisiana's Cane River is the most similar to *Roots* in its initial concept (based on the author's own ancestors), scope, and emotional impact. It begins with Elisabeth, a slave on a Virginia plantation who is sold south to Louisiana, and ends four generations later with Tademy's great-grandmother Emily, a light-skinned, beautiful former slave. The women live side by side with white men of French ancestry, bearing their children—sometimes willingly, sometimes not. All must fight for their and their children's rights in a society where mixed-race relationships are never formalized, and illegitimate black children of white men are ignored in favor of their legitimate white half-siblings. Oprah's Book Club.

> **Keywords:** Concubines; Creoles; Fredieu, Emily (historical character); Illegitimate children; Louisiana—early United States; Mixed heritage; Slaves and slavery

Red River. Warner, 2007. 420pp. Hardbound, 0446578983.

> In 1873, the newly freed blacks of Colfax, Louisiana, gather at the local courthouse to defend their citizenship and rights to vote and own land. In one of Southern America's most deadly examples of racial violence, over 100 black men are massacred by white supremacists who refused to honor those rights. Along with other black families of Colfax, over the next seventy years the Tademys and the Smiths find the strength to persevere. They survive racial oppression and yet more violence as they raise their families and set up businesses in town, making it clear that they plan to not only stay but prosper.

> **Keywords:** Colfax riots; Louisiana—Reconstruction/Gilded Age; Racial conflict

Asian

Chinese

The stories of Chinese and Chinese American families, both in Asia and in the United States. Many of these families struggle to find a balance traditional Chinese values and more modern ways of life.

Chang, Lan Samantha.

Inheritance. **Norton, 2004. 302pp. Hardbound, 0393059197.**

> In China in 1931, sisters Junan and Yinan rely heavily on one another after their mother's suicide. Their father promises Junan to Li-Ang, a soldier, in an arranged marriage, and despite her cool demeanor, she falls in love with him. But when the Japanese invade China, the couple is separated; Junan sends her sister to join his household, setting in motion a betrayal that echoes down to the next generation in China and America.

> **Keywords:** China—20th century; Chinese Americans; Extramarital affairs; Sisters

Choy, Wayson.

Jade Peony Series.

Choy, born in Vancouver of Chinese ancestry, centers his novels on three siblings in a family of recent immigrants living in Vancouver's Chinatown during the 1930s and 1940s. Both novels were Canadian best sellers. A lyrical set of coming of age stories replete with Chinese folklore, customs, and ghosts. **Literary.**

Keywords: British Columbia—20th century; Brothers and sisters; Chen family; Coming of age; Immigrants, Chinese

The Jade Peony. Picador USA, 1997. 238pp. Paper, 0312155565.

The years before World War II prove transformative for three siblings in a Chinese Canadian family, the Chens. Jook-Liang, the only daughter in a family with three boys, idolizes Shirley Temple. Her adopted brother, Jung, who struggles with his sexual identity, is drawn to boxing, while her sickly youngest brother Sekky begins to doubt the reasons behind the war.

All That Matters. Other Press, 2007. 432pp. Paper, 9781590512159.

Choy retells events from *The Jade Peony* through the viewpoint of Kiam-Kim Chen, First Son, who arrives in Vancouver in 1925 with his father and grandmother, Po-Poh.

Indian

Viswanathan, Padma.

The Toss of a Lemon. Harcourt, 2008. 619pp. Hardbound, 9780151015337. 📖

Sivakami, a girl of the Brahmin caste in Tamil Nadu, India, marries at age ten, in 1896, and is widowed eight years later—fulfilling astrologers' predictions. For the rest of her long life, she must adhere strictly to the rules prescribed by her culture: wearing a white sari, shaving her head, and touching no one during daylight hours, not even her young children. Sivakami raises them as best she can, though her decision to give her son Vairum a secular education puts him at odds with his mother, who builds her life around honoring and obeying Brahmin ways. **Literary.**

Keywords: Brahmins; India—20th century; Widows

Japanese

Tsukiyama, Gail.

Street of a Thousand Blossoms. St. Martin's, 2007. 416pp. Hardbound, 9780312274825. 📖

Hiroshi and Kenji Matsumoto, two young orphaned brothers in pre–World War II Tokyo, are raised by their devoted grandparents. After war breaks out, their lives, and those of the neighboring Tanaka family, are changed forever. Hiroshi, strong-minded and a natural leader, grows up to become a sumo wrestler, while gentle Kenji becomes a mask-maker for the Noh Theater. The novel, spanning the years 1939 to 1966, expresses how people's and a country's dreams change after unimaginable devastation. **Literary.**

Keywords: Brothers; Japan—World War II; Noh Theater; Sumo wrestlers

European

Eastern European

Stefaniak, Mary Helen.

The Turk and My Mother. **Norton, 2004. 320pp. Hardbound, 0393059243.**
Stefaniak used tales from her Croatian heritage to craft this charming collection of three interlocking stories about Croatian immigrants who settle in Milwaukee, Wisconsin, after World War I. As George Iljasic, the first child of the family born in America, lies on his deathbed, he recounts stories about his life in 1930s Milwaukee and his mother and grandmother in the Old Country. Points of view shift to characters from older generations as Stefaniak reveals how George's mother, Agnes, fell in love with a Serbian prisoner of war (who she and her family assumed was Turkish), as well as how his grandmother, the family matriarch known as Staramajka, befriended a blind violinist in her village.

Keywords: Immigrants, Croatian; Prisoners of war; Wisconsin—20th century

Irish

Family sagas about Irish heritage and the Irish American immigrant experience.

Moore, Ann.

Gracelin O'Malley Series.
Annotated in Chapter 4, under "Romantic Epics."

O'Keeffe, Patrick.

The Hill Road. **Viking, 2005. 240pp. Hardbound, 0670033987.**
In a series of four interconnected novellas, O'Keeffe writes not about the Irish who left their homeland and traveled overseas to America, but about those left behind. Life in the small rural parish of Kilroan, on Ireland's southwestern coast, is difficult; to survive this harsh existence, its residents take comfort in one another, a fleeting chance at love, and the natural beauty of the landscape. **Literary.**

Keywords: Immigrants, Irish; Ireland—20th century

Shaw, Maura.

The Keeners. **Medallion, 2005. 278pp. Hardbound, 1932815155.**
Seventeen-year-old Margaret Meehan, a keener for the dead in County Clare, Ireland, in 1846, is forced to leave her beloved home when the potato crops fail and the country's people begin starving. Her friends and family destroyed by the cruelty of the English landholders, Margaret escapes Ireland for a new life in America with her longtime love, Tom Riordan, who has become a wanted man. They settle down and begin

anew in Troy, New York, where they become involved with the local labor movement and raise their own family.

Keywords: Immigrants, Irish; New York—early United States; Potato famine; Unions

Italian

The lives of close-knit Italian and Italian American families in the early twentieth century.

Bernardi, Adria.

Openwork. **Southern Methodist University Press, 2006. 344pp. Hardbound, 0870745107.** 📖

The voice of Imola Bartolai, a woman living in the Tuscany mountains at the end of the nineteenth century, begins this multi-generational, multi-family tale of emigration, family ties, longing, and desire. Imola's brother leaves Italy for America in search of a better life, yet in the coal mines of New Mexico, he finds mostly class struggles and misery. His childhood friend, Antenore Gimorri, fights on his and others' behalf for labor rights. The novel comes full circle with Antenore's fully American granddaughter, Adele, living in Chicago in the present day. **Literary.**

Keywords: Coal mining; Immigrants, Italian; New Mexico—20th century; Unions

Gaudé, Laurent.

The House of Scorta. **MacAdam/Cage, 2005. 289pp. Hardbound, 1596921595.** 📖

Over nearly a hundred years in the small village of Montepuccio in southern Italy, from 1870 through the 1980s, members of the Scorta family struggle to overcome their progenitor's criminal past, with mixed results. The story begins as Luciano Mascalzone, a petty criminal last seen in Montepuccio fifteen years earlier, leaves prison and returns to town, bent on revenge. He sets his sights on Filomena Biscotti, the woman he loves, not noticing that the woman he encounters is her sister, Immacolata. She gives birth to their bastard son, Rocco, who leaves a devastating family legacy of his own. A lyrical yet completely unsentimental look at how secrets, lies, and wealth—or lack thereof—can transform a family. **Literary.**

Keywords: Italy—early modern and 20th century; Organized crime

Hornby, Simonetta Agnello.

The Marchesa. **Farrar, Straus & Giroux, 2007. 326pp. Hardbound, 9780374182458.** 📖

In Sicily in the late nineteenth century, Costanza Safamita is the apple of her father's eye but an outcast in her family due to her bright red hair. Her life changes when her father makes her the sole heir to his fortune, rejecting her brothers. In Palermo, she marries a poverty-stricken nobleman who wants her mostly for her dowry; predictably, he's an unfaithful spendthrift. Over the course of her life, Costanza finds the strength within herself not only to survive, but to triumph. A prequel of sorts to Hornby's earlier *The Almond Picker.*

Keywords: Heirs and heiresses; Italy—19th century; Nobility

Mazzucco, Melania.

Vita. **Farrar, Straus & Giroux, 2005. 433pp. Hardbound, 0374284954.** ✍ 📖

In 1903, cousins Vita and Diamante Mazzucco, ages nine and twelve, arrive at Ellis Island aboard the steamship *Republic* and begin their journey to becoming Americans. Forced to endure degrading conditions at Vita's father's Prince Street boardinghouse, the pair quickly learn that life in the new country is even harsher than it was in their rural Italian village. Diamante, in love with Vita from adolescence on, works hard to earn enough to marry her, but he's swept into servitude working on the railroads. Vita endures their years apart by cooking, cleaning, and eventually opening a restaurant. Based on the author's family history, with chapters detailing her search for her ancestors. **Literary.**

Keywords: Cousins; Immigrants, Italian; Mazzucco, Vita (historical character); New York—20th century

Jewish

These novels express the strong ties between Jewish families, whose members pass on religious and cultural traditions from the Middle East, Eastern Europe, and America to subsequent generations.

Arkin, Frieda.

Hedwig and Berti. **Thomas Dunne, 2005. 258pp. Hardbound, 0312333544.**

Hedwig Kessler, a tall Valkyrie of a woman, and her husband (and first cousin) Berti, shy and diminutive, are an unlikely married couple. Neither ever expected to leave their small German village, but when the Nazis take over, they (for they are Jewish) show up on the doorstep of their London cousin, Harry, who takes them in, but not without surprise. They leave London for New York and then Kansas; meanwhile their daughter, Gerda, travels Europe as a concert pianist.

Keywords: Germany—World War II; Jews; Married life

Gilmore, Jennifer.

Golden Country. **Scribner, 2006. Hardbound, 0743288637.** 📖

Gilmore traces the Brodskys, the Verdoniks, and the Blooms from when they settle in Brooklyn in the 1920s through the 1960s, as their lives are affected by Prohibition, World War II, the invention of television, and the city's underworld of organized crime. The families' lives intertwine when door-to-door salesman Joseph Brodsky's daughter marries Seymour Bloom's son, and when Joseph invents a powerful cleaning solution he decides to advertise on television. Frances Verdonik, renamed Frances Gold, becomes the product's first spokesperson. An ambitious novel about the American dream, namely how three Jewish immigrants and their families shape the history of a city and a country.

Keywords: Jews; New York—20th century

Lustbader, Victoria.

Hidden. Forge, 2006. 463pp. Hardbound, 0765315564.
   Annotated under "Sagas with a Sense of Place: American Regional Sagas: New York."

Widmer, Eleanor.

Up from Orchard Street. Bantam, 2005. 389pp. Hardbound, 0553804006. 📖
   Widmer brings to life the bustling atmosphere and close relationships among three generations of Roths, recent immigrants from Odessa living in the Jewish ghetto on New York's Lower East Side in the 1930s. Elka Roth, nine years old, narrates this affecting story, focusing primarily on her bubby (grandmother), Manya, the family matriarch whose mouthwatering dinners transform their kitchen into a paradise. Widmer, a first-time author at the age of eighty, died one month after final revisions on her manuscript were complete.

   Keywords: Immigrants, Ukrainian; Jews; New York—20th century

Yellin, Tamar.

The Genizah at the House of Shepher. Toby, 2005. 345pp. Hardbound, 1592640850.
   Shula, a biblical scholar living in England, returns to her family's home in Jerusalem when a mysterious codex is found in the attic. Unsure of its value, either monetary or genealogical, she delves deeply into her family's ancestry going back four generations and learns about her great-grandfather's journey across the Middle East to find the ten lost tribes of Israel. Shula's tale unfolds in piecemeal fashion, telling of both the present and the past as she uncovers successive portions of the Shephers' history. **Literary.**

   Keywords: Codexes; Israel—19th and 20th century; Jews

Latin American

These family sagas celebrate Latin American culture and society, both in the United States and in the authors' native countries.

Allende, Isabel.

The House of the Spirits. Knopf, 1985. 368pp. Hardbound, 0394539079. ★ 📖
   The Truebas, a close Chilean family with supernatural interests and talents, is at the heart of Allende's best-known novel. Their matriarch is the spiritual Clara del Valle, mute since a young age, who breaks her silence to announce that she'll soon be marrying her late sister's former fiancé, Esteban Trueba. Together they raise two sons, Jaime and Nicolas, and daughter Blanca, who enrages her father by falling in love with his foreman. The story continues into the next generation, as the entire family, including Blanca's daughter Alba, becomes more politically involved while Chile moves toward Pinochet's military coup of 1973. The author is a relative of the assassinated former president of Chile, Salvador Allende. **Literary.**

   Keywords: Chile—20th century; Magical realism

Baca, Ana.

Mama Fela's Girls. **University of New Mexico, 2006. 318pp. Hardbound, 0826340237.**

Mama Fela, the aging matriarch of the Romero family, lives in Santa Lucia, a dusty small town in northeastern New Mexico, during the Great Depression with her daughter, son, daughter-in-law, and six-year-old granddaughter, Cipriana, who delights her grandmother with her liveliness and her love for Shirley Temple movies. Readers will glimpse the life of a hard-working Mexican American family through Cipriana's eyes, as she watches her parents argue over money and her caring aunt get wrapped up in her friends' and neighbors' problems.

Keywords: Great Depression; Mexican Americans; New Mexico—20th century

Guerin, Gene.

Cottonwood Saints. **University of New Mexico, 2005. 344pp. Paper, 0826337244.**

This literary saga, based on the life of the author's mother, spans most of the twentieth century, focusing on Margarita Juana Galvan, born in 1913 to poverty-stricken parents in northern New Mexico and given to her great-aunt and -uncle to raise. She grows up in a loving home environment, thanks to a caring Indian nanny, yet she always yearns for something more—a hope that rules her decisions. Her youngest son, Michael, narrates the story of his mother's life: her disappointment in marriage and her children, and her strength in coping with the difficulties life has thrown her way. Guerin interweaves Margarita Juana's story with that of New Mexico itself. **Literary.**

Keywords: New Mexico—20th century; Poverty

Rodriguez, Luis.

Music of the Mill. **Rayo, 2005. 308pp. Hardbound, 0060560762.**

In 1943, Procopio Salcido and his wife-to-be, Elaida, leave Mexico for a better life in the United States. They settle in Los Angeles and raise their family there, alongside the Nazareth steel mill. This factory employs numerous Mexicans, African Americans, and poor whites, yet despite the economic prosperity of the postwar period, its employees live in a state of racial disharmony, and the backbreaking labor threatens to destroy their hopes of achieving the American dream. This novel of industrial strife and labor struggles in Southern California spans three generations. **Literary.**

Keywords: California—20th century; Immigrants, Mexican; Mill workers; Racial conflict

Wartime Sagas

During wartime, when separation and loss become a way of life, families and communities band together for comfort and strength. Wartime sagas express both the stresses and the joys of these difficult times. Some of the novels under "Romantic Sagas," previously in this chapter, also take place during times of war.

Europe and the British Isles

War disrupts family life in Britain during World Wars I and II, yet it also brings people closer together. Romances blossom, but when couples are forced to separate, the women left behind rely on support from their parents, siblings, and friends. Because these novels are told from a woman's perspective, they will appeal most to female readers. The two world wars are a perennially popular subject for British sagas. Several books that fall within multi-volume sagas found in other sections of this chapter ("British Regional Sagas," "Romantic Sagas") occur during wartime.

Johnson, Jeannie.

Mary Anne Randall Series.

One working-class woman's struggles to create a safe home life for herself and her children during World War II. Set in Bristol, England.

Keywords: Abusive relationships; Businesswomen; England—World War II; Pawnshops; Poverty

Loving Enemies. Severn House, 2007. 256pp. Hardbound, 0727864475.

In 1939, Mary Anne Randall runs a secret pawn-broking business from the back of her overcrowded home in Bristol. She contends with constant poverty and the demands of her abusive husband. She immediately feels threatened by Michael Maurice, a foreigner who inherits a nearby pawnshop, but wartime forces them to work closely together, and they discover they have more in common than they realized.

Secret Sins. Severn House, 2007. 288pp. Hardbound, 9780727865540.

Mary Anne does her best to keep her family together, although her lover, Michael, has gone off to fight the war, her home has been bombed, and someone—perhaps her estranged husband—has been taking revenge against her.

Lively, Penelope.

Consequences. **Viking, 2007. 258pp. Hardbound, 9780670038565.** 📖

In 1935, Matt Faraday, of a modest tradesman's background, meets upper-class Lorna Faraday in St. James's Park, London; they fall in love despite their class differences. They marry and move to Somerset to raise their daughter, Molly; Lorna is left alone when Matt is killed during World War II. Though Lorna finds happiness again with another, their life together doesn't last. Lively picks up the story again with Molly, in 1960s London, and Molly's daughter Ruth brings the story full circle as she investigates her grandmother's past. Lively compresses three generations of women's lives and seventy years of history into a comparatively short number of pages, so readers should expect more of a quick sweep through history than most sagas of this type provide.

Keywords: England—World War II; Mothers and daughters

Matthews, Beryl.

A Flight of Golden Wings. **Severn House, 2007. 256pp. Hardbound, 9780727865007.**

As a civilian member of the Air Transport Auxiliary in 1939, Ruth Aspinall honors her pilot brother's memory by qualifying as a pilot herself and delivering aircraft to bases around Britain. She falls in love with a handsome American pilot, Jack Nelson, though he's reluctant to commit to their relationship. Later, she is devastated when he's reported missing in action over France.

Keywords: England—World War II; Pilots, women

Parker, Una-Mary.

Granville Series.

The complicated love lives of five sisters from a high society family in 1930s to 1940s London.

Keywords: Blitz; England—World War II; Granville family; Sisters; Socialites

The Granville Sisters. Severn House, 2005. 236pp. Hardbound, 0727862588.

Rosie, Juliet, Louise, Amanda, and Charlotte Granville, five gorgeous sisters, enjoy a life of privilege in 1930s Mayfair, and the two eldest compete with one another for beaus. Then World War II hits, throwing their lives into disarray. Louise falls in love with a man outside her class, and Amanda turns into a social liberal.

The Granville Affaire. Severn House, 2005. 224pp. Hardbound, 9780727863034.

To protect his family during wartime, Henry Granville moves them all away from Mayfair, but his socially conscious wife, Liza, still holds out hope that her daughters will follow in her footsteps. The Blitz changes the way each of them looks at the world.

The Granville Legacy. Severn House, 2006. 252pp. Hardbound, 9780727864123.

It is now 1946, and although the war is over, postwar rationing restricts the Granvilles from regaining the same level of luxury they enjoyed before the war. With the four eldest daughters dealing with their own romantic and family complications, Liza Granville pins her remaining hopes on Charlotte, the youngest, but Charlotte disappoints her mother with her desire to become a model.

Steel, Danielle.

Echoes. **Delacorte, 2005. 325pp. Hardbound, 0385336349.**

In one of her rare historical offerings, prolific women's fiction author Steel turns to Switzerland and France during both world wars. In 1915, Beata Wittgenstein, a young Jewish woman, falls in love with a French nobleman, Antoine de Vallerand. They marry, though this alienates them from their families; Beata converts to Catholicism and raises her daughter,

Amadea, in her new faith. A generation later, Amadea has become a Carmelite nun, yet this doesn't keep her, her family, or her friends safe from the evils of the Third Reich.

Keywords: France—World War II; Jews; Nazis; Nuns; Switzerland—20th century

Taylor, Michael.

Linden Woods. **Severn House, 2007. 256pp. Hardbound, 9780727865175.**

At the beginning of World War II, Linden Woods, an intelligent, attractive working-class girl living in England's industrial Black Country region, gets a job as an assistant secretary at the local steelworks. She falls in love with Edward Burgayne, son of her employer, and despises his older brother, Hugh—who goes to outrageous lengths to win her over when Edward leaves for the front lines. Taylor has written many other sagas for British publishers, all set around his hometown of Dudley; this is his first novel readily available in American libraries.

Keywords: England—World War II

The United States

Portrayals of family life on the American home front during wartime.

The Civil War

Jakes, John.

North and South Trilogy. ★

Jakes's epic family saga of life in America before, during, and after the Civil War tells the story of two families—the Mains and the Hazards—over three generations, beginning in 1842 and lasting through Reconstruction. The prologue introduces both families' progenitors by showing their individual arrivals in America from England and France in the 1680s, and sows the seeds for their future leadership in the iron and rice industries. At West Point, the Hazards from Pennsylvania meet and befriend the Mains of South Carolina. When the Civil War begins, members of the two families find themselves on opposite sides. During Reconstruction, the families struggle to rebuild themselves as well as their country. Jakes's characters interact with historical figures such as John Brown and George Custer, and play major roles in well-known historical events. Perhaps best of all, Jakes never romanticizes the war or its aftermath. The first book of this saga was made into one of the most successful TV miniseries of all time.

Keywords: Pennsylvania—Civil War; South Carolina—Civil War

North and South. Harcourt Brace Jovanovich, 1982. 740pp. Hardbound, 0151669988.

Love and War. Harcourt Brace Jovanovich, 1984. 1019pp. Hardbound, 0151544964.

Heaven and Hell. Harcourt Brace Jovanovich, 1987. 700pp. Hardbound, 0151310750.

Hallam, Livia, with James Reasoner.

Palmetto Trilogy.

A projected three-volume series set during the Civil War, centering on two young men from Charleston, their friends, and their families. It begins around the time when South Carolina secedes from the Union. It has strong romantic elements. Hallam and Reasoner are husband and wife.

Keywords: Confederacy; South Carolina—Civil War

Call to Arms. Cumberland House, 2005. 350pp. Hardbound, 1581824793.

Despite their differing social backgrounds, Robert Gilmore, of a rural farming family, and Allard Tyler, from a family of wealthy shipbuilders, become good friends while studying at The Citadel. Then, on December 20, 1860, South Carolinians sign an ordinance of succession from the Union. While Robert and Allard eagerly sign on with the military to defend the South's interests, the women they're involved with worry about their well-being and survive as best they can.

War Drums. Cumberland House, 2006. 351pp. Hardbound, 1581825315.

While Robert Gilmore rises in the ranks of the Hampton Legion, his good friend Allard, a sailor with the Confederate navy, continues to prey on Union merchant ships around Nassau. Meanwhile, back on the home front, Robert's brother Cam, a new arrival at The Citadel, becomes romantically entangled with Allard's sister, Lucinda.

Rosen, Elisabeth Payne.

Hallam's War. Unbridled, 2008. 473pp. Hardbound, 9781932961492. 📖

Rosen's debut centers on the Hallams—Hugh, Serena, and their children—of Palmyra Farm in rural West Tennessee, the land to which they relocated with the family's slaves in the years just before the Civil War. Hugh treats his slaves well, but doesn't give the concept of slavery sufficient thought until he, along with many thousands of other Southern farmers, is forced to take sides in the war. Fighting for the Confederacy puts his morals to the test; meanwhile, Serena struggles with running the family's farm on her own. **Literary.**

Keywords: Confederacy; Farmers; Slaves and slavery; Tennessee—Civil War

World War II

Berg, Elizabeth.

Dream When You're Feeling Blue. Random House, 2007. 276pp. Hardbound, 9781400065103. 📖

In Chicago at the time of World War II, the three daughters of the Irish American Heaney family write to men overseas in order to keep their spirits up. Louise pens letters to her fiancé; Kitty writes to her boyfriend, Julian; and their younger sister Tish exchanges notes with men she meets at local USO dances. A heartwarming portrait of life on the American home front, and how wartime changed one particular family.

Keywords: Illinois—World War II; Irish Americans; Sisters

Haigh, Jennifer.

Baker Towers. **Morrow, 2005. 334pp. Hardbound, 0060509414.** 📖

Bakerton, in western Pennsylvania, is a company mining town named for the mine, not the other way around; Haigh tells us this important fact early on. Life in Bakerton revolves around the coal industry, symbolized by the tall black piles of coal dirt known as Baker Towers. The five Novak siblings, raised on Polish Hill and of Italian Polish heritage, grow up during the Second World War, discovering life beyond the company house where they live. Over the next twenty years, readers watch as some siblings move away for good, while others, like daughter Dorothy, discover they're unprepared for city life and return home to Bakerton. **Literary.**

Keywords: Coal mining; Pennsylvania—World War II; Polish Americans

Chapter 6

Western Historical Novels

Western historical novels are defined not only by a time period and place but also by several overarching themes: freedom, opportunity, and strength of character, all of which symbolize the American Western experience. They are novels of adventure, discovery, and survival. On the other hand, they are also novels of civilization and its effects, for they demonstrate the impact that settlement and exploration has had on the lands of the Western frontier and their native peoples.

Novels of the historical American West can be divided into two categories: *historical Westerns* and *traditional Westerns* (also known simply as "Westerns"). It's important for readers' advisors to know the difference between the two, but the dividing line between them isn't always clear. This chapter deals primarily with historical Westerns, though a select number of traditional Westerns with significant historical detail and a strong sense of place are included.

A typical plot for a traditional Western goes something like this. A tough but morally upright man rides alone into a Western scene, fights off Indians or outlaws, and proceeds to save the day—after which he mysteriously rides off into the sunset, literally or figuratively. These novels, usually fairly short, are set somewhere west of the Mississippi River, although the exact locale is not always given. They take place sometime between the end of the Civil War (1865) and the Massacre at Wounded Knee (1890), the horrific event that finally ended the U.S. government's Indian wars and signaled the end of the American frontier. Traditional Westerns evoke a strong sense of time and place with their brilliant descriptions of the unspoiled Western landscape. Setting is extremely important to traditional Westerns, as "the West" is seen as the place where freedom can be found, where simple moral goodness triumphs, and where characters find their destinies. However, specific historical events and locales tend not to figure in the story, although there are exceptions.

Although traditional Westerns still command a devoted audience, the genre as a whole has evolved into something new. Today's Western novels have been relabeled as historical Westerns, historical fiction, frontier fiction, or simply "novels of the West." These descriptions reflect their wide-ranging content. Historical Westerns tend to be longer than traditional Westerns, with a meatier, more detailed plot. Though many are still adventure stories at heart, they may or may not be fast-paced. Character development is important, and the protagonists' moral dilemmas aren't nearly as black and white as traditional Westerns made them out to be.

Historical Westerns require an accurate historical setting; historical fiction fans won't be satisfied without it. The time frame is also broader, covering the entire experience of Western exploration and settlement. This ranges from the mid-sixteenth century, when Spanish explorers first encountered the Plains Indian tribes of the Southwest, all the way through the first few decades of the twentieth century. In between, historical events commonly portrayed include the settlement of the Western frontier (as told from both male and female points of view); the U.S. government's Indian wars; the westward expeditions of Lewis, Clark, and their contemporaries; the California Gold Rush; and the fight to win Texas from Spain.

In comparison to traditional Westerns, historical Westerns offer more diverse subjects. They don't hesitate to take on complex social issues, such as race relations, white settlers' poor treatment of the Indians, and the hard lives of women eking out a living on the Western frontier. The most recent examples are less stereotypical in their portrayals of white settlers and Native Americans than those written decades earlier. Traditional Westerns rarely had female, Native American, or African American protagonists, but these characters are common to historical Westerns. Because they try to be true to the era in which their works are set, novelists in this genre strive to be historically accurate, which is why terms like "Indian" appear in their pages. On the other hand, Western historical novelists often take a balanced point of view, showing Native–white relations from both sides.

Over the past five years, historical Westerns have declined in popularity. Forge Books, which used to publish new voices in Western fiction frequently, now sticks mainly to established authors such as Richard Wheeler, Win Blevins, and Elmer Kelton. Historical Westerns appear only occasionally from other major trade publishers. Five Star, in addition to reissuing classic Westerns first published in the early twentieth century, holds down the fort with Westerns by new and familiar authors. Westerns also appear regularly from university presses located in Western states. Leisure, the Western imprint of Dorchester, publishes mainly traditional Westerns but also some historical Westerns.

Although some of the novels mentioned in this chapter are apt to be found in "Western" collections in libraries or bookstores, others will be found mixed in with the rest of the fiction, as is the case with most historical novels. Two major organizations for Western writers, Western Writers of America (WWA, founded 1953) and Women Writing the West (WWW, founded 1994), actively promote the field and their authors' works to readers and the media. Both groups sponsor awards for excellence in Western writing, the Spur and the Willa Cather Award (or WILLA), respectively.

This chapter divides historical Westerns by theme, rather than by specific era or locale. Because many include elements of adventure, readers who enjoy that aspect of Western historicals may wish to investigate Chapter 8 for additional historical adventure titles. In addition, readers interested in other novels of Native American history, such as those set in prehistoric North America and in colonial times, will find them primarily in Chapters 2 and 10.

Traditional Westerns

These action-packed, mostly male-centered novels tell of independence and survival in the historical American West. They may feature outlaws and lawmen fighting each other and the Indians; other common topics include cattle drives, ranching, shootouts, treasure hunts, and male camaraderie. Although most are told from the viewpoint of white settlers, the novels listed here are more culturally sensitive than most traditional Westerns. They also have better character development and use an accurate historical backdrop. Most take place during the usual time frame for Westerns, the late 1860s through the 1890s. A sampling is presented.

Blakely, Mike.

Honore Greenwood Series.

Unlikely hero Honore Greenwood, whose life spans a century, takes part in nearly every major conflict in the history of the nineteenth-century American West.

Keywords: Comanche Indians; Greenwood, Honore; New Mexico—Civil War; Picaresque novels

Moon Medicine. Forge, 2001. 416pp. Hardbound, 0312867042.

In the 1840s intellectual Honore Greenwood fled Paris, France, after dueling with a swordsman over a woman, but his escapades have only begun. He traipses through the Wild West on a variety of adventures—fighting Indians, dangerously falling in love with a beautiful New Mexican señorita, and rescuing children from raids. Called Plenty Man by the Comanche, Honore recalls everything from the viewpoint of old age.

Come Sundown. Forge, 2006. 479pp. Hardbound, 0312867050.

Greenwood continues the story of the Wild West adventures of his youth, as he moves easily from the world of his adoptive family, the Comanche, to his life as a Civil War soldier fighting in the battles of Valverde and Glorieta Pass in New Mexico Territory. Torn between two cultures, Greenwood finally decides to return to the Comanche, even though it means taking their side against his good friend, scout Kit Carson.

Boggs, Johnny D.

Doubtful Cañon. **Five Star, 2007. 212pp. Hardbound, 9781594145575.**

In 1881 three youngsters from Shakespeare, New Mexico, don't know whether to believe Whitey Grey's story of buried gold coins out at Doubtful Cañon on the Arizona border, the result of a stagecoach robbery gone wrong twenty years earlier. The elderly albino promises them a steep reward for their efforts in helping him, but they don't really trust him, and furthermore, the group has competition. A quirky, fast-paced Western adventure narrated in an authentic, slang-filled voice.

Keywords: New Mexico—Reconstruction/Gilded Age; Treasure

The Hart Brand. **Five Star, 2006. 213pp. Hardbound, 1594143994.**

Caleb Hart, speaking thirty years after the events in the novel, relates his experiences growing up on the ranch of his uncle, Captain Frank Hart, which turned him into a real-life cowboy. Captain Hart has a tried-and-true way of dealing with cattle rustlers himself, but his fellow ranchers want them tried in a court of law. Set in New Mexico Territory in 1896.

Keywords: Cowboys; New Mexico—Reconstruction/Gilded Age; Ranchers

Walk Proud, Stand Tall. **Five Star, 2006. 238pp. Hardbound, 159414348X.**

An aged lawman looks back on his Wild West adventures and begins a new one in this detailed character study. As the twentieth century dawns, Lin Garrett (no relation to Pat), left injured after a run-in with a trio of hoodlums, fears he has nowhere left to go. Then his longtime enemy Ollie Sinclair, released from Yuma Penitentiary, starts rustling up trouble again.

Keywords: Arizona—Reconstruction/Gilded Age; Lawmen; Outlaws

Brooks, Bill.

Dakota Lawman Series.

Fleeing his medical practice after being falsely accused of murder, Jake Horn takes refuge in the small town of Sweet Sorrow in the Dakota Territories, where he's named as the local marshal. Trouble finds him soon enough, in the form of local outlaws, not to mention a bounty hunter from his past who is hot on his trail.

Keywords: Horn, Jake; Lawmen; Outlaws; South Dakota—Reconstruction/Gilded Age

Last Stand at Sweet Sorrow. HarperTorch, 2005. 309pp. Paper, 0060737182.

Killing Mr. Sunday. HarperTorch, 2005. 300pp. Paper, 0060737190.

The Big Gundown. HarperTorch, 2005. 242pp. Paper, 0060737220.

The Journey of Jim Glass.

After way too many encounters with danger and the law (and often both at the same time), drifter Jim Glass would prefer to live a quiet life in New Mexico Territory, but after he takes a job with Marshal Bronson in the little town of Coffin Flats, he gets entangled in his employer's messy and very personal business. That's only the beginning of his problems.

Keywords: Glass, Jim; Lawmen; New Mexico—Reconstruction/Gilded Age

Rides a Stranger. Harper, 2007. 273pp. Paper, 9780060885960.

A Bullet for Billy. Harper, 2007. 243pp. Paper, 9780060885977.

The Horses. Harper, 2008. 246pp. Paper, 9780060885984.

Champlin, Tim.

Cold Cache. **Five Star, 2007. 222pp. Hardbound, 9781594144974.**

On his way home to Minnesota from Ontario, Kent Rasmussen, a former officer for the North-West Mounted Police, gets drawn into a long-standing family feud.

The prize is the "cold cache"—a lump of treasure reportedly buried in New Mexico during the Civil War, which is meant to finance a new Confederate nation.

Keywords: Minnesota—Reconstruction/Gilded Age; Treasure

Geoffrion, Alan.

🏵 *Broken Trail.* **Fulcrum, 2006. 244pp. Paper, 1555916058.**
This traditional Western with a twist begins as Prentice "Print" Ritter, a silver-haired former cowboy, teams up with his late sister's son, Tom, to make their fortune by driving horses out to Wyoming, where they'll be bought for a fair price. While en route, the pair comes across a group of five young Chinese girls with bound feet who have been kidnapped and are destined for a life as prostitutes. Though the girls don't understand English nor the cowboys Chinese, the men risk their lives to free them. Spur Award; Western Heritage Award.

Keywords: Immigrants, Chinese; Kidnapping; West—Reconstruction/Gilded Age

Grey, Zane.

Dorn of the Mountains. **Five Star, 2008. 360pp. Hardbound, 9781594146213.**
Milt Dorn, a loner living contentedly in the Arizona wilderness, gets wind of a scheme to kidnap and murder Helen and Bo Rayner, nieces of a wealthy local rancher. Dorn foils the plot before their stage arrives in town, bringing them to safety at his mountain retreat—but danger follows even there. This is a restored version of Grey's original text, which was serialized in magazines during 1917–1918.

Keywords: Arizona—Reconstruction/Gilded Age; Mountain men

Hall, Russ.

Bent Red Moon. **Five Star, 2005. 243pp. Hardbound, 1594141355.** **YA**
In 1870s Texas Hill Country, a land swarming with dangerous Indians and treasure seekers, two teenagers band together to find the same man, Bill Hinton—the long-lost uncle of one of them, and the longtime enemy of the other.

Keywords: Texas—Reconstruction/Gilded Age

Luckey, William A.

Burn English. **Five Star, 2008. 207pp. Hardbound, 9781594145032.**
Burn English had always had a way with wild horses, but never one with women; despite his being in love with Katherine Hildahl for years, she married a friend of his, a fellow rancher. Now, at the age of forty-five, Burn decides to make a new life for himself, leaving his beloved ranch for a place where he can finally find peace. His presence in the land called Salt Valley arouses curiosity in the local townspeople.

Keywords: Ranchers; West—Reconstruction/Gilded Age

Murdock, Mackey.

War Relic. **Five Star, 2007. 235pp. Hardbound, 9781594145209.**

"Bones" Malone, nicknamed for his penchant for collecting the sun-whitened buffalo bones that hunters leave behind, lost his fiancée, Sassy, to his cousin Wade while Bones was off fighting the Civil War. Now it's eighteen years later, and a family reunion at Wade's Texas ranch dredges up hard feelings and regrets on all sides.

Keywords: Texas—Reconstruction/Gilded Age

Parker, Robert B.

Appaloosa Trilogy.

Best known for his detective fiction, Parker also brings his terse, sharp writing style to the Western genre—first with *Gunman's Rhapsody* (2001), a novel about Wyatt Earp, and second with this duology about partners Virgil Cole and Everett Hitch, itinerant lawmen hired to keep the peace in various towns in the Old West. Legendary gunfighter Cole is more the strong, silent type, while Hitch, Cole's friend and longtime deputy, looks back on their adventures.

Keywords: Cole, Virgil; Gunfighters; Hitch, Everett; Lawmen; West—Reconstruction/ Gilded Age

Appaloosa. Putnam, 2006. 276pp. Hardbound, 0399152776.

Virgil Cole and Everett Hitch stumble into Appaloosa and discover the town in thrall to one of its wealthiest landowners, a rancher named Bragg whose cronies have taken control (and who murdered the previous marshal). Bragg refuses to play by any rules whatsoever, which challenges Cole's black-and-white notions of right and wrong.

Resolution. Putnam, 2008. 304pp. Hardbound, 9780399155048.

Hitch, hired by the Blackfoot Saloon in the town of Resolution to enforce the peace, finds his partner's help comes in handy when a no-good mine owner stirs up trouble with the local ranchers.

Stone, R. W.

Trail Hand. **Five Star, 2006. 217pp. Hardbound, 1594143900.**

Owen Burke signs on for what he thinks will be easy work—a trail hand guiding horses from south of the border to California for a Mexican rancher whose daughter he covets. When Mexican banditos steal most of the herd, Burke goes after the thieves himself so that he, a gringo, won't be blamed for the crime by the ranch's ramrod.

Keywords: California—Reconstruction/Gilded Age; Cowboys; Mexico—19th century; Trail guides

Wister, Owen.

The Virginian: A Horseman of the Plains. **Dover, 2006. 296pp. Paper, 0486449041.**
★

In the rangeland surrounding Medicine Bow, Wyoming, a rancher known only as "the Virginian" takes justice into his own hands. Over time the enigmatic young

Southerner goes from ranch tenderfoot to ranch foreman. New England schoolmarm Molly Stark loves the morally upright cowboy, but given his violent past, she knows he'd never fit in with her family back home. This classic is said to have established the literary "code of the West," a path of honor that all cowboys should follow. Originally published in 1902; frequently reprinted.

Keywords: Ranchers; Teachers; Wyoming—Reconstruction/Gilded Age

Celebrity Characters

These biographical novels fictionalize the lives of famous characters from the Old West, both male and female. Among historical happenings featuring legendary outlaws and lawmen, two events loom large. One is the 1881 showdown at the O.K. Corral in Tombstone, Arizona, where the Earp brothers and Doc Holliday fought the Clanton gang. The other is the bloody Lincoln County War of the late 1870s, when two rival factions—one of which included William Bonney, aka Billy the Kid—fought over control of military contracts in Lincoln County, New Mexico.

Braun, Matt.

🏅 *Dakota.* **St. Martin's, 2005. 306pp. Paper, 0312997833.** ✍

After the deaths of his mother and his first wife, who passed away on the same night in February 1884, Theodore Roosevelt leaves New York politics temporarily behind to seek solace in the wide open spaces of Dakota Territory. He rejuvenates his spirit by building a ranching empire and having the adventure of a lifetime in the West. Spur Award.

Keywords: Presidents; Ranchers; Roosevelt, Theodore (historical character); South Dakota—Reconstruction/Gilded Age

Dodge City. **St. Martin's, 2006. 308pp. Paper, 0312938160.**

Harry Gryden, counsel for the defense in Dodge City, Kansas, has a job few men would envy. Determined to see the accused parties receive a fair and just trial, he regularly clashes with local lawmen and their comrades, such as the Earp brothers and Doc Holliday, who'd rather pursue their own type of frontier justice.

Keywords: Kansas—Reconstruction/Gilded Age; Lawyers

Boggs, Johnny D.

Northfield. **Five Star, 2007. 230pp. Hardbound, 9781594145049.** ✍

One day in September 1876 the James-Younger gang—made up of notorious outlaw Jesse James, his brother Frank, and the Younger brothers—set out on a supposedly easy raid: robbing the First National Bank in Northfield, Minnesota. It proves to be a big mistake. In two dozen chapters, each of which is narrated by a different character, Boggs takes a kaleidoscopic

yet intimate approach to fictionalizing the most ill-fated bank robbery in American history.

Keywords: Bank robberies; James, Frank (historical character); James, Jesse (historical character); Minnesota—Reconstruction/Gilded Age

Coleman, Jane Candia.

Tombstone Travesty. **Five Star, 2004. 248pp. Hardbound, 1594140111. (Alternate title: *Tumbleweed.*)**

Allie Earp, the petite, feisty, and loving wife of Virgil Earp, narrates an action-filled tale of adventure, local politics, family loyalty, and betrayal from the viewpoint of old age. Orphaned at her mother's death, Allie spends her childhood in boardinghouses and whorehouses. At her sister's Iowa home she meets "Virge" Earp for the first time. Declaring themselves married, they travel west, never staying anywhere long, until they hear about a great opportunity down in Tombstone. The real travesty, in Allie's mind, is how the surviving Earps and Doc Holliday were treated after the showdown at the O.K. Corral: talked up as crooks by a reporter who got their story wrong. Based on the historical Allie's memoirs. WILLA Award.

Keywords: Arizona—Reconstruction/Gilded Age; Earp, Allie (historical character); Married life

Wheeler, Richard S.

The Honorable Cody. **Sunstone, 2006. 256pp. Paper, 086534521X.**

After the death of Buffalo Bill Cody in 1917, those who knew him, or thought they did—both friends and enemies—share anecdotes of their dealings with the famous showman, from his youth as a scout for the U.S. Cavalry to his time with his Wild West Show and on through his old age, when his estranged widow tells us what she really thought of him. In the end, Cody rises above all the petty squabbling among his associates, emerging as a well-meaning, honest man whose press, to his amusement, made a legend out of him.

Keywords: Cody, William "Buffalo Bill" (historical character); West—Reconstruction/Gilded Age

Trouble in Tombstone. **Pinnacle, 2004. 284pp. Paper, 045121370X.**

Wyatt Earp tells readers exactly why things went so wrong in Tombstone, Arizona, culminating in the famous shootout at the O.K. Corral. Charged with keeping the peace in a town filled with outlaws, a corrupt sheriff, and a press that clearly didn't take his side, Earp admits that the cards were stacked against him. He does his best to defend his actions and those of his family members.

Keywords: Arizona—Reconstruction/Gilded Age; Earp, Wyatt (historical character)

Frontier and Pioneer Life

These novels portray the day-to-day lives of both men and women during the Westward Expansion. In the mid- to late nineteenth century, men, women, and families make their way westward from the United States to the Western frontier in search of open land and new opportunities. They travel in wagon trains across the prairie, making do with minimal comfort. Their journeys are fraught with hardship, in the form of the harsh landscape, conflicts with their fellow settlers, and Indian raids. After their difficult journey ends, pioneers settle down and begin their lives anew. They band together to form communities, setting up businesses, saloons, and newspapers, hoping the railroad will come to town and connect them with the wider world. For frontier novels told from a feminine viewpoint, see "Women on the Frontier," later in this chapter.

Estleman, Loren D.

🎗 *The Undertaker's Wife.* **Forge, 2005. 284pp. Hardbound, 065309130.**

One afternoon in 1900 railroad magnate Elihu Warrick commits suicide aboard the Michigan Central as it makes its way between Chicago and New York. Panicked at the thought of an economic disaster, Warrick's associates persuade retired undertaker Richard Connable to work some magic of mortuary science and disguise the true cause of death. So begins a look back into the past for Richard's long-suffering wife, Lucy, who reluctantly accompanies him west to San Francisco in the post–Civil War years, and later to Hays City, Kansas, where Wild Bill Hickok's shootouts keep him in business. As Richard's fortunes rise and fall, the couple relocate as necessary. Their marriage frequently strains near breaking point, but Lucy tenaciously stands by him. Spur Award.

Keywords: Kansas—Reconstruction/Gilded Age; Married life; Undertakers

McMurtry, Larry.

Telegraph Days. **Simon & Schuster, 2006. 289pp. Hardbound, 0743250788.**

McMurtry's most recent effort can be read either as a seriously over-the-top, improbable account of a brother-sister pair who encounter nearly every trope of the typical Western and come out winning, or as an enjoyable spoof of the genre he knows so well. After their parents' deaths, circa 1876, Marie Antoinette ("Nellie") Courtright and her younger brother, Jackson, settle down in the frontier town of Rita Blanca in Oklahoma Territory, where Jackson becomes a most unlikely deputy sheriff, and Nellie a telegraph operator. As plucky Nellie grows famous for writing a dime novel about her brother's unintentional success in shooting up outlaws, she travels throughout the West on Buffalo Bill Cody's dime, meeting nearly every famous Western icon (and having sex with many of them).

Keywords: Oklahoma—Reconstruction/Gilded Age; Parodies and spoofs; Telegraph operators

Means, Laurel.

The Long Journey Home. **Academy Chicago, 2008. 319pp. Paper, 9780897335690.**

Henry Morton brings his son Wilson, injured in the Civil War, home to Winona, Minnesota, only to learn from his other son that his wife died of consumption a year earlier. Then he learns he's been given a grant to land 200 miles north, on the Minnesota prairie, as a reward for his military service. A one-night stand with a young barmaid, Agnes, results in her pregnancy and their unlikely marriage. Henry's hasty actions from that point forward lead to their separate, and equally dangerous, journeys westward. Agnes believes he deserted their family, while Henry tries desperately to find her. **Literary.**

Keywords: Minnesota—Reconstruction/Gilded Age

Russell, Sheldon.

🎗 *Dreams to Dust: A Novel of the Oklahoma Land Rush.* **University of Oklahoma, 2006. 285pp. Hardbound, 0806137215.**

Russell unfolds the epic story of Guthrie Station, Oklahoma—the state's original capital—beginning with its birth during the Land Rush of 1889. Creed McReynolds, the half-Kiowa son of a U.S. Cavalry doctor, is one of the multitudes of settlers seeking to make his name and fortune in Oklahoma. As he amasses wealth in the lumber business and forms relationships with many others with the same dreams, he gets drawn into the path of an unscrupulous, power-hungry newspaperman. Russell, who lives in Guthrie, based his fictional characters on historical personages. Langum Prize; Oklahoma Book Award.

Keywords: Kiowa Indians; Oklahoma Land Rush of 1889; Oklahoma—Reconstruction/Gilded Age

Vida, Nina.

The Texicans. **Soho, 2006. 295pp. Hardbound, 1569474346.**

Described in the "Texas and Mexico" section.

Western Explorers and Adventurers

The daring exploits of the men and women who were among the first to explore the Western frontier. The novels in this section tend to be fast-paced, action-packed adventures.

Mountain Men

White men in search of adventure head west as fur trappers, living on their own in the Rocky Mountains and trading with Indians for supplies. The ultimate survival stories, these novels feature independent souls who live off the land, becoming as free and untamed as the wilderness that surrounds them. Most are set in the 1820s through 1850s, before the arrival of settlers.

Blevins, Win.

Rendezvous Series.

A projected six-book series about white-haired mountain man Sam Morgan, fur trapper and trader: his journey across the Western plains to California and Mexico, his encounters (both peaceful and violent) with native tribes, and his love affairs with several different women.

Keywords: California—early United States; Crow Indians; Morgan, Sam; Mountain men; New Mexico—early United States; Trappers

🎗 *So Wild a Dream.* Forge, 2003. 398pp. Hardbound, 0765305739.

Sam Morgan yearns for a more adventurous life than Morgantown, Pennsylvania, can offer. In 1822 he takes off down the Ohio River, learns the fur trade, and befriends Indian guides and legendary mountain men—whose dream of freedom he follows. Spur Award.

Beauty for Ashes. Forge, 2004. 302pp. Hardbound, 0765305747.

After a brief trip back home, after which he vows never to return, Sam Morgan heads back out West on his own, determined to find Meadowlark, the Crow woman he fell in love with, once again. He faces competition for her hand and must learn Crow ways himself in order to win her.

Dancing with the Golden Bear. Forge, 2005. 303pp. Hardbound, 0765305755.

Sam and Meadowlark, now married, bring along their coyote pup when they follow famed mountain man Jedediah Smith on an expedition across the Rockies to California in 1826.

Heaven Is a Long Way Off. Forge, 2006. 302pp. Hardbound, 0765305763.

Devastated by Meadowlark's death in childbirth, Sam and the rest of Jedediah Smith's band of mountain men are made to leave Mexican California, but Sam is determined to reclaim his baby daughter, Esperanza, whom he was forced to leave behind. In Santa Fe, he has an affair with a beautiful widow, Doña Paloma.

A Long and Winding Road. Forge, 2007. 352pp. Hardbound, 9780765305770.

It's now 1828, and Sam's love life takes another downturn. His lover, Paloma, is slowly dying of breast cancer. He finds purpose in rescuing two new Mexican brides taken captive by Navajo raiders.

Johnston, Terry C.

The late Terry C. Johnston (1947–2001) is best known for two series, <u>Titus Bass</u> and <u>The Plainsmen</u> (earlier this chapter). His novels of the early Western frontier are enhanced by thorough historical research and his personal experience roaming the Western mountains and plains. Johnston died of cancer just after completion of *Wind Walker*.

<u>Titus Bass Series</u> (also called <u>Mountain Man Series</u>). ★

Johnston's Western adventures about Titus "Scratch" Bass—fur trapper, fearless mountain man, and all-around survivor—are hardly politically correct, but they reflect an important part of American history. Titus's story begins in the early 1800s, as he grows up as a Kentucky farm boy, and run through the 1850s, when he settles down with his Crow family in the Rocky Mountains. In between, Titus hunts buffalo, fights off Indians, endures numerous hardships, and tries to prevent white settlers from taking over the West. The books, written as a set of three trilogies, are listed in historical order.

Keywords: Bass, Titus; Crow Indians; Mountain men; Trappers

Dance on the Wind. Bantam, 1995. 517pp. Paper, 0553090712.

Buffalo Palace. Bantam, 1996. 405pp. Paper, 0553090747.

Crack in the Sky. Bantam, 1997. 481pp. Paper, 055309078X.

Carry the Wind. Green Hill, 1982. 571pp. Paper, 0898031060.

BorderLords. Jameson, 1985. 455pp. Paper, 0915463113.

One-Eyed Dream. Jameson, 1988. 432pp. Paper, 0915463385.

Ride the Moon Down. Bantam, 1998. 427pp. Paper, 0553090828.

Death Rattle. Bantam, 1999. 429pp. Paper, 0553090844.

Wind Walker. Bantam, 2001. 461pp. Paper, 0553090909.

Wheeler, Richard S.

Skye's West Series.

Barnaby Skye, legendary mountain man and guide from the 1820s through the 1870s, has an unlikely past. A reluctant seaman pressed into service with Britain's Royal Navy, Skye saw his chance at freedom at Fort Vancouver and jumped ship. His penchant for getting into trouble continues to follow him. "Mister Skye," as he prefers to be called, makes his living fur trapping and escorting missionaries and settlers to various locations out West. Over time he acquires two wives—Many Quill Woman of the Crow tribe, whom he calls Victoria, and a younger Shoshone woman named Mary—as well as an ugly, bad-tempered horse named Jawbone. The cultural differences between Skye and his wives, as well as their odd domestic arrangement, are both touching and funny. The novels, numbered as given in the order below, can be read in almost any order, though *Rendezvous* takes Skye back to his early days—his military past. By the time of the sixteenth volume (*Virgin River*), Wheeler has traced nearly the entire history of the Western frontier through Skye's experiences. The series is expected to continue in future volumes with Skye's half-Shoshone son, North Star, as protagonist.

Keywords: Mountain men; Shoshone Indians; Skye, Barnaby; Trail guides

Sun River. Tor, 1989. 314pp. Paper, 0812510739.

Bannack. Tor, 1989. 314pp. Paper, 0812510712.

The Far Tribes. Tor, 1990. 313pp. Paper, 0812510690.

Yellowstone. Tor, 1990. 312pp. Paper, 0812508947.

Bitterroot. Tor, 1991. 356pp. Paper, 0812513053.

Sundance. Tor, 1992. 346pp. Paper, 0812513061.

Wind River. Tor, 1993. 342pp. Paper, 0812521420.

Santa Fe. Forge, 1994. 345pp. Paper, 0812521447.

Rendezvous. Forge, 1997. 349pp. Hardbound, 0312863195.

Dark Passage. Forge, 1998. 318pp. Hardbound, 0312865260.

Going Home. Forge, 2000. 315pp. Hardbound, 0312873107.

Downriver. Forge, 2001. 304pp. Hardbound, 0312878451.

The Deliverance. Forge, 2003. 318pp. Hardbound, 0312878443.

The Fire Arrow. Forge, 2006. 320pp. Hardbound, 0765313235.

The Canyon of Bones. Forge, 2007. 330pp. Hardbound, 9780765313249.

Virgin River. Forge, 2008. 320pp. Hardbound, 9780765307095.

Lewis and Clark

In the early nineteenth century, explorers Meriwether Lewis and William Clark mapped the Western frontier and opened it up for further settlement. Some of these biographical novels take a revisionist stance, portraying these American legends in a less than heroic light. Others take their familiar stories and retell them from the point of view of others in their party.

Cleary, Rita.

Calling the Wind. **Five Star, 2005. 224pp. Hardbound, 1594141533.** ✍

Cleary has written several novels about the 1803–1806 Lewis and Clark expedition, all with a slightly different perspective. Her earlier *River Walk* told the story from the viewpoint of John Collins, a member of their expedition; *Charbonneau's Gold* speaks about the perilous journey westward. *Calling the Wind* details the remainder of their passage from the Pacific and back over the treacherous mountains—a trip they barely survived on the route west.

Keywords: Clark, William (historical character); Lewis, Meriwether (historical character)

Hunter, Frances.

To the Ends of the Earth: The Last Journey of Lewis and Clark. **Blind Rabbit, 2006. 386pp. Paper, 0977763625.** ✍

Less a wild adventure story than a well-rounded character study, the debut novel from Hunter (pseudonym of sisters Liz and Mary Clare) begins in 1809, three years after the pair completed their expedition. The authors explore the reasons behind Meriwether Lewis's depression and gradual decline into mental illness; his relationships with Clark and other associates; and their theory about his death: he was found shot along the Natchez Trace while en route to the nation's capital.

Keywords: Lewis, Meriwether (historical character)

Native Americans

In contrast to traditional Western novels, in which Indians are portrayed as hostile, violent, or unintelligent, these novels depict Native Americans sympathetically and/or relate the story from their point of view. They introduce readers to the customs and history of different Native American tribes, presenting America's westward movement from a very different viewpoint than traditional Westerns. The authors write with sensitivity, relating the degradation and extreme hardship that Indians suffered at the hands of white men. Some novels are told from the point of view of white men "adopted" into Indian tribes rather than that of Native Americans themselves. The two series by Robert Conley and Don Coldsmith begin several centuries earlier than most, telling about Indians' day-to-day lives in the sixteenth and seventeenth centuries and how their lives changed upon their first encounters with Spanish settlers. Additional novels of Native American life can be found in Chapter 2.

Agonito, Rosemary, and Joseph Agonito.

🦃 *Buffalo Calf Road Woman: The Story of a Warrior at the Little Bighorn.* **TwoDot, 2006. 242pp. Paper, 0762738170.** ✍

Based on detailed research into the mysterious presence of a Cheyenne woman at the Battle of the Rosebud in 1876, the Agonitos reconstructed and fictionalized the life of Buffalo Calf Road Woman. Calf, as she's called here, is credited for swooping in and rescuing her wounded brother during the battle; controversy currently rages over whether she was the one to strike the final blow against Custer before his death a week later at the Little Big Horn. A unique fictional account of a Cheyenne woman warrior who takes action when her people's way of life is threatened. Western Heritage Award.

Keywords: Buffalo Calf Road Woman (historical character); Cheyenne Indians; Little Big Horn, Battle of the; Montana—Reconstruction/Gilded Age; Rosebud, Battle of the

Boggs, Johnny D.

Killstraight. **Five Star, 2008. 226pp. Hardbound, 9781594146220.**

On his way back home from the Carlisle Indian School in Pennsylvania, Daniel Killstraight, of the Comanche nation, passes by Fort Sill, Arkansas, and witnesses the hanging of his old friend Jimmy Comes Last for murdering a white couple. Jimmy's distraught mother, Naséca, asks Daniel's help in determining whether her son really was guilty.

Keywords: Arkansas—Reconstruction/Gilded Age; Comanche Indians; Murderers

Coldsmith, Don.

Spanish Bit Series. ★ YA

In the sixteenth century, the Elk-Dog People (an amalgam of Plains Indian tribes) come upon a lost Spanish conquistador named Juan Garcia. The encounter changes their entire way of life. As the Spaniard (renamed "Heads Off") adapts to The People's ways, he introduces them to the horse. This transforms them from a wandering hunter-gatherer society to a race of warriors. Heads Off becomes their chief, and later volumes of this saga detail the lives of his descendants through the late eighteenth century. In these short character-centered novels, the family stands at the heart of Plains culture, and readers will appreciate the genealogical tables. Common elements include vision quests, encounters with other tribes, trade with French and Spanish traders, and bits of native myth and legend.

Keywords: Families; Plains Indians

Trail of the Spanish Bit. Doubleday, 1980. 180pp. Hardbound, 0385151780.

The Elk-Dog Heritage. Doubleday, 1981. 181pp. Hardbound, 0385175019.

Follow the Wind. Doubleday, 1983. 192pp. Hardbound, 0385175027.

Buffalo Medicine. Doubleday, 1981. 183pp. Hardbound, 0385159706.

Man of the Shadows. Doubleday, 1983. 183pp. Hardbound, 0385180918.

Daughter of the Eagle. Doubleday, 1984. 178pp. Hardbound, 0385180926.

Moon of Thunder. Doubleday, 1985. 179pp. Hardbound, 0385189230.

The Sacred Hills. Doubleday, 1985. 179pp. Hardbound, 0385189249.

Pale Star. Doubleday, 1986. 176pp. Hardbound, 0385232276.

River of Swans. Doubleday, 1986. 176pp. Hardbound, 0385232284.

Return to the River. Doubleday, 1987. 181pp. Hardbound, 0385235208.

Medicine Knife. Doubleday, 1988. 187pp. Hardbound, 0385235216.

The Flower in the Mountains. Doubleday, 1988. 188pp. Hardbound, 038524231X.

Trail from Taos. Doubleday, 1989. 176pp. Hardbound, 0385242328.

Song of the Rock. Doubleday, 1989. 178pp. Hardbound, 0385245750.

Fort de Chastaigne. Doubleday, 1990. 180pp. Hardbound, 0385245769.

Quest of the White Bull. Doubleday, 1990. 180pp. Hardbound, 0385263015.

Return of the Spanish. Doubleday, 1991. 179pp. Hardbound, 0385263023.

Bride of the Morning Star. Doubleday, 1991. 176pp. Hardbound, 0385263031.

Walks in the Sun. Doubleday, 1992. 240pp. Hardbound, 0553082620.

Thunderstick. Doubleday, 1993. 182pp. Hardbound, 0385470266.

Track of the Bear. Doubleday, 1994. 180pp. Hardbound, 0385470290.

Child of the Dead. Doubleday, 1995. 245pp. Hardbound, 0385470290.

Bearer of the Pipe. Doubleday, 1995. 258pp. Hardbound, 0385470304.

Medicine Hat. University of Oklahoma Press, 1997. 266pp. Hardbound, 080612959X.

The Lost Band. University of Oklahoma Press, 2000. 260pp. Hardbound, 0806132264.

Raven Mocker. University of Oklahoma Press, 2001. 253pp. Hardbound, 0806133163.

The Pipestone Quest. University of Oklahoma Press, 2004. 255pp. Hardbound, 080613612X.

Conley, Robert J.

Real People Series. ★

An authentic, continuing series set among the Cherokee (the "Real People"), based on Native lore and legend. The time line begins before European contact (1500s), during a dark period when the Cherokee revolt against their priests. Later volumes cover contact with the Spaniards and the tragedy of the Trail of Tears (1838), when the American government forcibly relocated the Cherokee to Oklahoma. Loosely connected, they can be read in any order. Technically, not all of these books are Westerns, because many take place in the southeastern United States. However, they deal with the history of the Cherokee Nation (of which the author is a member), and most readers consider them Westerns—in style, if not completely in substance. The novels are also issued in paperback from the University of Oklahoma Press.

Keywords: Cherokee Indians; Oklahoma—early United States; Trail of Tears

The Way of the Priests. Doubleday, 1992. 177pp. Hardbound, 0385419325.

The White Path. Doubleday, 1993. 183pp. Hardbound, 0385419341.

The Dark Way. Doubleday, 1993. 179pp. Hardbound, 0385419333.

The Way South. Doubleday, 1994. 176pp. Hardbound, 0385426208.

The Long Way Home. Doubleday, 1994. 182pp. Hardbound, 0385426216.

The War Trail North. Doubleday, 1995. 183pp. Hardbound, 0385472528.

The Dark Island. Doubleday, 1995. 181pp. Hardbound, 0385426224.
Spur Award.

War Woman. St. Martin's Press, 1997. 357pp. Hardbound, 0312170580.

The Peace Chief. St. Martin's Press, 1998. 339pp. Hardbound, 0312193149.

Cherokee Dragon. St. Martin's Press, 2000. 289pp. Hardbound, 0312208847.

Spanish Jack. St. Martin's Press, 2001. 210pp. Hardbound, 0312262310.

Sequoyah. St. Martin's Press, 2002. 217pp. Hardbound, 031228134X.

Fergus, Jim.

The Wild Girl: The Notebooks of Ned Giles, 1932. **Hyperion, 2005. 355pp. Hardbound, 1401300545.** 📖

Set later than most Westerns in this category, Fergus's follow-up to *A Thousand White Women* focuses on conflicts between whites and Native Americans that still simmered along the Arizona border during the Depression. In 1999 an elderly Ned Giles looks back on the summer of 1932, when he, a Chicago youth of seventeen, signed on with the Great Apache Expedition as a photographer. Their goal: rescue the young son of a rich Mexican rancher kidnapped by Apaches and spirited away to somewhere in the Sierra Madres of Mexico. Their plan to trade a wild

Apache girl, captured by them into brutal submission, for the missing boy doesn't turn out as planned.

Keywords: Apache Indians; Coming of age; Great Depression; Kidnapping; Mexico—20th century; Photographers

Hill, Ruth Beebe.

🌱 *Hanta Yo*. **Doubleday, 1979. 834pp. Hardbound, 0385135548. ★**
This mammoth novel, meant to be a fictionalized ethnographic study, describes the life of the Sioux from the 1790s to the 1830s (before the arrival of white settlers) as seen through the eyes of two families. To achieve authenticity, Hill translated her novel from English to Dakotah and then back to early American English. However, this controversial novel was denounced by some Native Americans as inauthentic and disrespectful of their way of life, because (among other things) it focuses on characters' individual strengths, à la Ayn Rand, rather than on their togetherness. Western Heritage Award.

Keywords: Lakota Sioux Indians

Marshall, Joseph M., III

Hundred in the Hand. **Fulcrum, 2007. 375pp. Paper, 9781555916534.**
The Battle of Hundred in the Hand, called the Fetterman Massacre by historians, was fought on December 21, 1866, and ended with Captain William Fetterman and seventy-nine of his men—all of the U.S. soldiers involved—being killed by Lakota warriors. Marshall recounts events leading up to the battle from the viewpoint of the Lakota, including Red Cloud and his wife, other members of their family, and a young Crazy Horse. Their daily lives, recounted with depth, clarity, and precision, are based on oral tradition. Hardly any historical novels about the Native American experience are written by members of the tribes they depict; this novel from Lakota author Marshall is a welcome exception.

Keywords: Fetterman Massacre; Lakota Sioux Indians; Nebraska—Reconstruction/ Gilded Age; Red Cloud's War

Meyers, Harold Burton.

🌱 *The Death at Awahi*. **Texas Tech University Press, 2007. 226pp. Hardbound, 9780896725997.**
Quill Thompson, the white principal of a school at the (fictional) New Mexico pueblo of Awahi in 1923, faces an ethical dilemma when another white man is found dead on Indian land. Quill and his nurse wife, Jane, outspoken opponents of the federal government's policies to "Christianize and civilize" Indians, must decide whether to let the whites or the Awahi—who have held steadfast to their culture—mete out justice. Despite the title, Meyers' short novel is more a morality tale about the clash of cultures than a standard murder mystery. New Mexico Book Award.

Keywords: Murderers; Native Americans; New Mexico—20th century; Pueblos; Racial conflict

O'Brien, Dan.

Contract Surgeon series. ✍

O'Brien's duology explores the relationships among Valentine McGillycuddy (a historical figure), a contract surgeon for the army, and two high-profile leaders of the Lakota Sioux—Crazy Horse and Red Cloud—during a critical time in U.S.–Indian relations.

Keywords: Army; Great Sioux War; Lakota Sioux Indians; McGillycuddy, Valentine (historical character); South Dakota—Reconstruction/Gilded Age; Surgeons

🌳 *The Contract Surgeon.* Lyons, 1999. 316pp. Hardbound, 1558219323.

In 1877 the great Sioux chief Crazy Horse died a suspicious death while in the hands of the U.S. Army. Valentine McGillycuddy, a mostly untried physician contracted to the army as a surgeon during the Great Sioux War, befriends the famed warrior while trying to save his life. Through his experiences, McGillycuddy loses his youthful idealism, disregarding his belief that the government really has the Indians' best interests at heart. Based on a true story. Western Heritage Award.

Keywords: Crazy Horse (historical character)

The Indian Agent. Lyons, 2004. 281pp. Hardbound, 159228244X.

Sixteen months after the death of Crazy Horse, thirty-year-old McGillycuddy is named as the new agent for the Pine Ridge Indian Reservation (in present-day South Dakota), where the U.S. government forced members of the Oglala Lakota tribe to relocate. Red Cloud, their war leader, couldn't be more different from the Protestant Irish McGillicuddy, and their relationship is fraught with tension, but they also discover they share some sentiments—not the least of which is a love for the land.

Keywords: Red Cloud (historical character)

Robson, Lucia St. Clair.

🌳 *Ride the Wind.* **Ballantine, 1982. 562pp. Paper, 034529145X.** ✍ ★ 📖

In 1836 Cynthia Ann Parker is nine years old. When Comanches raid her family's camp on the Texas frontier, killing most of the men and animals and raping the women, they take Cynthia and several other children back with them. Cynthia grows up with the Comanche, slowly accepting their ways, adopting the name Naduah, and becoming the wife of a Comanche warrior named Wanderer. Her son Quanah Parker, loyal to his Comanche heritage, grows up to be the tribe's last free war chief. Robson's novel, replete with descriptions of Comanche culture and religion, is based on a true story. Spur Award.

Keywords: Comanche Indians; Indian captives; Kidnapping; Parker, Cynthia Ann (historical character)

Schlesier, Karl H.

Trail of the Red Butterfly. **Texas Tech University Press, 2007. 288pp. Hard-bound, 9780896726178.**

A Cheyenne warrior named Whirlwind has gone missing while raiding horses in New Spain in 1807, prompting his brother, Stone, head of the Cheyenne Kit Fox, to gather up a small band to rescue him. Their party, composed of warriors, their women, and children from the Cheyenne and other tribes, scour the lands of present-day Colorado, Texas, and New Mexico. Forced to make their way into unfamiliar and potentially danger-ous territory, the group risks much to follow Whirlwind's trail.

Keywords: Cheyenne Indians

Texas and Mexico

A whole mythology has grown up around the history of Texas: the bloody conflicts with Indian tribes, the battle for statehood, and perhaps most of all, the 1836 siege of the Alamo, where over 200 Texians lost their lives in a hope-less attempt to wrest territory from Mexican control. (The term "Texians" re-fers to the early Anglo settlers of Texas.) Many novelists have attempted to humanize the history of this great state, but in the end, Texas remains larger than life. The Mexican–American War of 1846–1848, which followed closely upon the annexation of Texas by the United States, figures in a smaller number of novels.

Bass, Rick.

The Diezmo. **Houghton Mifflin, 2005. 208pp. Hardbound, 0395926173.**

A "diezmo" is literally a tithe, or a tax of one-tenth. It's 1842, and Texas has existed as a republic separate from Mexico for seven years, something many Mexicans are unwilling to accept. On the order of Sam Houston, a party of soldiers later known as the Mier Expedition heads south to patrol the Texas–Mexico border. Finding less excitement than they'd hoped for, they cross the Rio Grande to raid Mexican villages—a fatal mistake. After killing hundreds of Mexicans at the town of Mier, the militia band is forced to surrender to Santa Anna, one of whose commanders arbitrarily executes one-tenth of the Texans. Fifty years after the event, James Alexan-der, a lucky survivor, details the group's foolish journey (which chal-lenged his own morals), their arduous imprisonment, and the aftermath.

Keywords: Mexico—19th century; Mier Expedition

Bauman, Jon R.

Santa Fe Passage. **Truman Talley, 2004. 323pp. Hardbound, 031233348X.**

Matt Collins, an enterprising young man, takes full advantage of the Brit-ish appetite for beaver-skin hats as he makes his way back and forth along the Santa Fe Trail between St. Louis and Santa Fe—which is still a part of Mexico—beginning in 1826. Matt comes to love his adopted land and the local culture, and his marriage to Celestina Mendoza, daughter of a *hacendado* (wealthy landowner), further cements his ties to Mexico. Two decades later President Polk asks him to help the United States annex Celestina's homeland. A novelization of the years leading up to the Mexican–American War.

Keywords: Mexico—19th century; Santa Fe Trail; Trappers

Chappell, Henry.

Blood Kin. **Texas Tech University Press, 2004. 298pp. Hardbound, 0896725308.**

Isaac Webb, a teenager who joins the Texas Rangers in 1836 during the height of the Texas Revolution, grows up alongside Texas's growth as a republic. His friendship with a young Comanche warrior leads him to an unexpected understanding of their ways, but their bond is tested by Texan settlers' hunger for land and the Comanches' continued raids. He faces heartbreaking choices in his love life, as well, for the woman he loves doesn't share his positive opinion of the Comanche.

Keywords: Comanche Indians; Coming of age; Texas—early United States; Texas Rangers

Harrigan, Stephen M.

🔥 *The Gates of the Alamo.* **Knopf, 2000. 581pp. Hardbound, 0679447172.** ★ 📖

At the seventy-fifth anniversary of the siege of the Alamo, Terrell Mott, aged ninety-one in 1911, reminisces about the events leading up to that fateful day. At the center of Harrigan's story are three proud individuals. Edmund McGowan, a naturalist, finally gets up the courage to stand for what he believes in. Mary Mott, Terrell's widowed mother, maintains an inn along the Gulf Coast. Her son, sixteen-year-old Terrell, has a tragic love affair that drives him into the heart of the conflict. Historical personages like David Crockett, James Bowie, Sam Houston, and Mexican General Santa Anna play secondary roles but are well characterized nonetheless. Harrigan strips the mythology from the 1836 siege of the Alamo in this historically based account. Spur Award; Western Heritage Award.

Keywords: Alamo, Battle of the; Texas—early United States

Kelton, Elmer.

Kelton, described as the best living Western writer, is a seven-time winner of the Spur Award.

Texas Rangers Series.

An ongoing series dealing with the beginning of the Texas Rangers, a group of volunteers who banded together to protect settlers from the Comanche Indians. It also covers Texans' role during the Civil War and Reconstruction. The first three novels were republished as the paperback omnibus *Lone Star Rising* (2003) and the next three as *Ranger's Law* (2006).

Keywords: Texas—Reconstruction/Gilded Age; Texas Rangers

The Buckskin Line. **Forge, 1999. 287pp. Hardbound, 0312865228.**

Davy "Rusty" Shannon, a young red-haired Texas Ranger, was taken in and raised by the man who rescued him from a Comanche raid. When his adoptive father, Mike Shannon, is killed for his political views, Rusty vows revenge.

Badger Boy. Forge, 2000. 286pp. Hardbound, 0312873190.

Rusty leaves the Rangers to start up his own ranch. When he encounters Badger Boy, a young white boy who was captured by the Comanche as a baby, Rusty gets the chance to reexamine his past.

Keywords: Indian captives

🎗 *The Way of the Coyote.* Forge, 2001. 283pp. Hardbound, 0312873182.

Ten-year-old Andy Pickard, formerly known as Badger Boy, makes the effort to adapt to white civilization. Rusty tries hard to make a success of his ranch, and Comanches kidnap the son of Rusty's former flame. Spur Award.

Ranger's Trail. Forge, 2002. 287pp. Hardbound, 0765305712.

In 1874 Rusty prepares to marry his sweetheart, Josie Monahan, but she is murdered by an outlaw out for revenge on her family. In tracking down her killer, Rusty discovers he may be following the wrong man.

Texas Vendetta. Forge, 2004. 301pp. Hardbound, 0765305720.

With his companion Farley Brackett, Texas Ranger Andy Pickard aims to deliver killer Jayce Landon to the courthouse for trial, but their prisoner escapes.

Jericho's Road. Forge, 2004. 288pp. Hardbound, 0765309556.

During the 1870s Andy and his partners are reassigned to the Texas–Mexico border. They get caught up in an ongoing battle between a Texas cattle baron and a Mexican rancher, both of whom have scores to settle.

Hard Trail to Follow. Forge, 2008. Hardbound, 9780765315229.

Andy, who has traded his badge as a Texas Ranger for the farmer's life, reluctantly becomes a lawman once more when an escaped outlaw kills Andy's good friend, Sheriff Tom Blessing.

Kelton, Elmer, et al.

Noah's Ride: A Collaborative Novel. **Texas Christian University Press, 2006. 176pp. Paper, 9780875653341.**

An experiment in collaborative serial writing designed by the editors at TCU Press results in this short novel about a runaway plantation slave, Noah, who escapes to Texas after the Civil War, establishes a ranch and sees his past catch up with him. With each chapter (thirteen in all) written by a different Texas author, each of whom picked up the story from where his or her predecessor left off, the story is an unpredictable, wild ride through late nineteenth-century Texas history. The authors are Elmer Kelton, Judy Alter, Carlton Stowers, Phyllis Allen, James Reasoner, Mary Rogers, Mike Blackman, Mike Cochran, Mary Dittoe Kelly, Jane Roberts

Wood, James Ward Lee, Jeff Guinn, and Mary Dittoe Kelly (who won a contest to become the final contributing author).

Keywords: Collaborative novels; Slaves, runaway; Texas—Reconstruction/Gilded Age

Sanderson, Jim.

Nevin's History: A Novel of Texas. **Texas Tech University Press, 2004. 277pp. Hardbound, 0896725189.**

Sanderson's historical epic about the brutal Texas–Mexico border wars and their aftermath is set firmly in the lower Rio Grande Valley beginning in the 1870s. Andrew Nevin, a reporter for the *Brownsville Sentinel*, readily admits that he's a coward, but when necessary he proves worthy of the demanding task his uncle, retired Texas Ranger Rip Ford, sets before him. In an effort to stop border banditry once and for all, thus avoiding a potential war with Mexico, Ford directs Nevin to join Lee McNelly's band of Rangers and send regular reports back to him. Nevin is one of the few fictional characters in this tightly written novel about the development and growth of southern Texas in the late nineteenth and early twentieth centuries.

Keywords: Texas—Reconstruction/Gilded Age; Texas Rangers

Thom, James Alexander.

Saint Patrick's Battalion. **Ballantine, 2006. 279pp. Hardbound, 0345445562.**

The historical Saint Patrick's Battalion, or the "San Patricios" en español, comprised a motley group of Irish and German immigrants. Under the leadership of charismatic Irishman John Riley, they fought for Mexico, a Catholic country, against the United States in the Mexican–American War of 1845–1846. Through his diary, American camp-boy Paddy Quinn reveals his thoughts about the rough, racist treatment he and his fellow soldiers endured first in the American army (where their superiors were mostly Protestant) and then when fighting for Mexico, where they faced death for treason if Mexico lost (which they did). In his novel about a little-known episode of American history, Thom redefines the meaning of loyalty to one's country and people.

Keywords: Catholicism; Immigrants, Irish; Mexican–American War; Mexico—19th century; Racial conflict; Traitors

Vida, Nina.

The Texicans. **Soho, 2006. 295pp. Hardbound, 1569474346.** 📖

In her novel about the last years of the Texas Republic and its transition to statehood, Vida focuses on ethnic groups and individuals not often mentioned in other novels on the same topic. Aurelia Ruiz, a part-Mexican, part-Anglo young woman with an uncanny talent for healing, takes refuge with the Comanches after her Texas Ranger husband is killed. At the same time, Henry Castro travels south with a wagon train of Alsatian immigrants with whom he will found the city of Castroville. En route he picks up Joseph Kimmel, a Jewish schoolteacher from Missouri who is heading for San Antonio, and convinces him to join their group. Joseph obsessively fixes his sights on Aurelia, despite the presence of Katrin, the Alsatian woman he marries. Vida turns the tables on commonly held opinions of the Texas Rangers, portrayed here (in some cases) as cruel bullies rather than brave lawmen. **Literary.**

Keywords: Comanche Indians; Frontier and pioneer life; Immigrants, German; Jews; Mixed heritage; Texas—early United States

Wier, Allen.

Tehano. **Southern Methodist University Press, 2006. 716pp. Hardbound, 0870745069.**

Wier presents an epic history of Texas, from the early Civil War years through 1875, when Quanah Parker, last chief of the Comanche, surrendered to the U.S. Army at Fort Sill, Oklahoma. The stories of a multitude of pioneers, explorers, runaway slaves, recent immigrants, Mexicans, Native Americans, and others all thread through the narrative. All seek places for themselves in Texas at a particularly tumultuous time in its history. All also cross paths with Gideon Jones, a Western traveler, itinerant journalist, and frontier undertaker who jots their stories down in his letters and journals. They form a loosely woven tapestry that celebrates the diversity and history of Texas in the late nineteenth century.

Keywords: Frontier and pioneer life; Texas—Reconstruction/Gilded Age; Undertakers

The Army in the West

Historical novelists re-create real-life battles fought by the U.S. Army on the Western frontier, and the Americans don't always come out looking like heroes. During the Civil War the U.S. Army went west to prevent the Confederacy from gaining ground. After the Civil War American soldiers headed westward to control the rebellious Native tribes—who were, of course, only defending their lands against white settlers. Custer's Last Stand, the legendary Battle of the Little Big Horn in Montana, is the most common topic. It was in this battle—fought on June 25, 1876—that General George Armstrong Custer led the officers of the 7th Cavalry in a doomed charge against a much larger army of Cheyenne and Lakota Sioux Indians. Its story has been retold in fiction again and again, each time with a slightly different perspective. Like the 1836 siege of the Alamo, readers seem to never tire of it. (For more novels of the frontier army, see the Texas and Mexico section.)

Boggs, Johnny D.

🎗 *Camp Ford.* **Five Star, 2005. 264pp. Hardbound, 1594141290.**

Boggs demonstrates that baseball is not only a great American pastime, it can mirror sentiments already brewing on the American political and social scene. Win MacNaughton, a ninety-nine-year-old army veteran and former baseball player, is invited by a national sports newspaper to attend the 1946 World Series, which causes him to recollect the most dramatic baseball game he's ever seen played. Back during the Civil War, when he was a POW in the rough Confederate prison at Camp Ford, Texas, he and fellow Union soldiers challenged their guards to a baseball game. It proved a learning experience for all involved. Spur Award.

Keywords: Baseball; Prisoners of war; Texas—Civil War

Haycox, Ernest.

Bugles in the Afternoon. **Little, Brown, 1944. 306pp. Hardbound.** ★

There's dissent within General Custer's famed 7th Cavalry. Private Kern Shafter, a soldier under Custer's command, discovers that his former rival has been appointed his superior. Haycox's classic novel is refreshingly free of sentimentality. Reissued by the University of Oklahoma Press in 2003, with a foreword by the author's son.

Keywords: Little Big Horn, Battle of the; Montana—Reconstruction/Gilded Age; Soldiers

McCaig, Donald.

Canaan. **Norton, 2007. 428pp. Hardbound, 9780393062465.**

Annotated in Chapter 10.

Wheeler, Richard S.

An Obituary for Major Reno. **Forge, 2004. 318pp. Hardbound, 0765307081.**

In 1889, prior to undergoing surgery for tongue cancer, Major Marcus Reno grants a final interview to Joseph Richler, a *New York Herald* reporter, and gets Richler to promise to restore his honor. Richler approaches his assignment cynically, not wanting to listen to the last words of a man whom history had condemned as a traitor. Reno, one of Custer's high-ranking officers at the Little Bighorn in 1876, had reportedly failed to go to Custer's aid during his last stand. After Reno's death, Richler dutifully interviews the major's former compatriots and reads relevant documents about the battle; they leave Richler, to his surprise, believing that Reno was a scapegoat created to cover Custer's own tragic mistakes.

Keywords: Generals; Little Big Horn, Battle of the; Montana—Reconstruction/Gilded Age; Reno, Marcus (historical character)

Women of the West

Some of the most popular Western historical novels have female protagonists. When men head westward in search of new lands to settle, their wives and families accompany them. The women bring a touch of civilization to the Wild West frontier, though most find their new way of life to be quite an adjustment. Despite their apparent physical frailty, frontier women possess an inner strength that helps them survive the harsh conditions both along the trail and at their final destination. The cramped living conditions en route make them reevaluate their relationships with the men in their lives. Other independent-minded women make their way westward on their own, taking their destinies into their own hands. They take on roles and occupations traditionally held by men, including doctor, cattle rancher, businesswoman, and explorer.

All of these female-centered stories explore the social issues women faced on the Western frontier: early suffrage, finding friends on the isolated prairie, raising families, and learning how to work the land. Many inspirational novels (Chapter 11) fit this same theme, as do novels in the "Romantic Westerns" section of this chapter.

Bristow, Gwen.

Jubilee Trail. **Chicago Review, 2006. 564pp. Paper, 1556526016.**

In 1844 eighteen-year-old Garnet Cameron, a recent graduate of a young ladies' finishing school in Manhattan, meets fur trader Oliver Hale on one of his trips east to buy merchandise. She marries him shortly thereafter, agreeing joyfully to accompany him to his home in California, a place she had never previously heard of. Bristow details their adventurous yet grueling expedition in bountiful detail, showcasing Garnet's disarming enthusiasm as she comes of age en route. In New Orleans they meet Florinda, a former "dancehall performer" (a 1950s euphemism for a prostitute), after which the novel becomes the tale of two strong women's journeys, both individually and together, of self-discovery. A popular classic about women's lives in the American West, its readability hasn't diminished since its publication in 1950.

Keywords: Coming of age; Friendship; Frontier and pioneer life; Prostitutes; West—early United States

Cather, Willa.

Cather's novels of immigrant pioneer life on the majestic Nebraska prairie in the late nineteenth century, replete with poetic descriptions of the native landscape, have been reprinted many times.

My Ántonia. **Houghton Mifflin, 1918. 418pp. Hardbound.** ★ 📖

Jim Burden, an orphaned ten-year-old boy, comes to live with his grandparents in Black Hawk, Nebraska, at the same time that Ántonia Shimerda, the free-spirited daughter of a Bohemian immigrant family, arrives in town. Obviously smitten with her, Jim describes Ántonia's fascinating life through his own eyes. They remain friends throughout adulthood, despite physical separation and Ántonia's marriage to another, and learn to respect each other's personal and social differences.

Keywords: Immigrants, Bohemian; Nebraska— Reconstruction/Gilded Age

O Pioneers! **Houghton Mifflin, 1913. 308pp. Hardbound.** ★ 📖

Alexandra Bergson, a young Swedish woman in the small town of Hanover, Nebraska, inherits her family farm after her father's death—to her younger brothers' consternation. Despite their disapproval, she decides to make a go of it, struggling with the elements and ignoring the pressure to sell the farm and move to the city.

Keywords: Farmers; Immigrants, Swedish; Nebraska—Reconstruction/Gilded Age

Fisher, Karen.

A Sudden Country. **Random House, 2005. 366pp. Hardbound, 1400063221.** ✍ 📖
Lucy Mitchell, a remarried widow and mother still grieving for her first husband, reluctantly agrees to accompany her new husband, Israel, on the Oregon Trail heading westward in 1847. Her family encounters James MacLaren, a Scottish trapper whose children died of smallpox and whose Nez Perce wife ran off with another man; MacLaren is on a mission of revenge. His decision to join their small band as a guide changes all of their lives. Avoiding commonly held stereotypes—the self-reliant, feisty woman, the wild mountain man—Fisher humanizes and reimagines both the journey through the American frontier West and the region's early settlers. Based on an account of the Oregon migration written by Emma Ruth, Lucy's daughter and the author's ancestor. **Literary.**

Keywords: Frontier and pioneer life; Mitchell, Lucy (historical character); Oregon Trail; Trail guides; Trappers; West—early United States

Gloss, Molly.

The Hearts of Horses. **Houghton Mifflin, 2007. 289pp. Hardbound, 9780618799909.** 📖
During November 1917 nineteen-year-old Martha Lessen shows up at the eastern Oregon ranch belonging to George and Louise Bliss, quietly offering to help the couple break in horses. Though their friends are amused by the thought of a female "bronco-buster," the Blisses need as much help as they can get, with most of the area's men off fighting in World War I. Gloss's lyrical novel traces Martha's life during the harsh winter of 1917–1918, showing how her gentle ways gradually win over both horses and the hearts of the local townsfolk despite her innate shyness and reserve. **Literary.**

Keywords: Horse tamers; Oregon—World War I

Hershon, Joanna.

The German Bride. **Ballantine, 2008. 320pp. Hardbound, 9780345468451.** 📖
After an illicit relationship (and the resulting tragedy) destroys her matrimonial chances, Eva Frank leaves 1860s Berlin with her new husband, Abraham Shein—a German merchant she barely knows—for Santa Fe, New Mexico. In her new home Eva grows from a naïve adolescent into a strong, confident woman as she adjusts to a completely unfamiliar life. Finally, frustrated with Abraham's penchant for gambling and whoring, she debates taking off on her own, in search of a better life than the two she left behind in succession. Hershon elegantly illuminates the lives of Jews in the nineteenth-century Southwest, not a common topic. **Literary.**

Keywords: Immigrants, German; Jews; New Mexico—Reconstruction/Gilded Age

Lyon, Suzanne.

A Heart for Any Fate. **Five Star, 2005. 295pp. Hardbound, 1594143293.** ✍
Virginia-born Hannah Allison marries William Temple Cole in 1790, after which the couple gradually migrate westward in search of opportunity and suitable farmland. They travel to the hills of Kentucky and finally settle their growing family in Missouri, where they encounter treacherous weather and Indian attacks.

Throughout her life (the novel follows her faithfully through to her death in 1843), Hannah keeps a diary in which she addresses her thoughts to Dolley Madison, a cousin of her husband's, who gave her the journal after her wedding. Lyon based her biographical novel of Hannah Cole, Missouri's "pioneer mother," on the life story of her four times great-grandmother.

Keywords: Cole, Hannah (historical character); Diaries and journals; Frontier and pioneer life; Missouri—early United States

Mailman, Erika.

Woman of Ill Fame. **Heyday, 2007. 257pp. Paper, 9781597140515.**

San Francisco during the Gold Rush of 1849 is a hotbed of frenzied activity, from prospectors in search of instant wealth in the mines to the tragically exploited Chinese sex workers, forced to sell their bodies and kept compliant with opium. Nora Simms, an enterprising young Bostonian, refuses to be a victim; rather, she willingly starts at the lower ranks among the city's prostitutes, knowing she'll have it made if she works her way up the ladder. When a trunk of her clothing vanishes and her garments start turning up on the dead bodies of her fellow hookers, Nora tracks down a serial killer.

Keywords: California—early United States; Detective stories; Gold rush; Prostitutes; Serial killers

Turner, Nancy E.

Sarah Agnes Prine Series. ✍ 📖 **YA**

Turner's ongoing series about Sarah Agnes Prine, an outspoken, strong-minded Texas pioneer, is based on the life of her great-grandmother. Sarah records her experiences in her diary.

Keywords: Diaries and journals; Frontier and pioneer life; Prine, Sarah Agnes (historical character); Ranchers, women

These Is My Words: The Diary of Sarah Agnes Prine, 1881–1901. ReganBooks, 1998. 384pp. Hardbound, 0060392258.

Sarah Agnes Prine, eighteen years old as she begins her diary in 1881, lives with her family on the frontier settlement near Tucson. Unable to bear the unremitting heat of the Arizona desert, Sarah and her family pack up their wagon and head to Texas. Through many deprivations and hardships, the resourceful Sarah embodies the family's strength and spirit, and her writing and poise mature throughout the novel. Initially she resists her attraction to Captain Jack Elliott, the army man assigned to protect the settlers, but their blossoming romance soon takes over her diary and heart.

Keywords: Arizona—Reconstruction/Gilded Age

Sarah's Quilt. St. Martin's, 2005. 402pp. Hardbound, 0312332629.

Sarah picks up her journal four years after the events in *These Is My Words*. It's 1906 and Sarah, twice widowed, struggles through painful drought conditions on her southern Arizona cattle ranch. Her desperate mother hires a water witch whose behavior proves alarming; her grown sons drop out of college and come home, trying her patience; and amid her other turmoil at home, Sarah travels to San Francisco to help out her brother, who lost everything in the earthquake.

Keywords: Arizona—20th century; Widows

The Star Garden. St. Martin's, 2007. 320pp. Hardbound, 9780312363161.

The trials and tribulations of Sarah Agnes Prine Elliott continue, with more family-related woes, one untrustworthy neighbor seeking to make amends for nearly sabotaging her ranch, and another neighbor, Udell Hanna, proposing to marry her. Used to her independence, Sarah isn't convinced she needs or wants a husband.

Keywords: Neighbors

Romantic Westerns

These are romantic historicals (Chapter 4) set in the American West, mostly during the nineteenth century. The romance and the history play equal roles in the plot, and happily-ever-after outcomes aren't guaranteed (though they are frequent). Like novels in the previous section, romantic Westerns are written by women for female readers. Readers should also investigate "Western Romances" in Chapter 4; they have similar subjects but focus more on the romance than on history.

Admirand, C. H.

Irish Western Series.

An ongoing series about the experiences of Irish émigrés in the American West. Set in the small ranching town of Emerson, Colorado, in the 1870s and 1880s.

Keywords: Colorado—Reconstruction/Gilded Age; Lawmen; Ranchers

The Marshal's Destiny. Avalon, 2001. 186pp. Hardbound, 0803495110.

U.S. Marshal Joshua Turner rescues Margaret Mary Flaherty, who is wounded in the arm when her stagecoach is attacked by Indians. Joshua and Maggie fall in love at first sight, but their romance is complicated by his ongoing lawman duties, her slow recuperation, and her pressing need to get word to her brother that she can prove he owns his ranch.

The Rancher's Heart. Five Star, 2007. 299pp. Hardbound, 9781594145742.

James Ryan lives peacefully on his Colorado ranch, hoping nobody will uncover an unpleasant secret from his past. Then he catches Mick O'Toole trying to steal his cattle. Feeling sorry for the boy and his ill mother, Bridget, James takes the pair of them in; neither knows that the husband who deserted her years before has turned to crime and is coming to town.

Pearl's Redemption. Five Star, 2008. 351pp. Hardbound, 9781594147005.

Pearl Lloyd, proud owner of a large ranch, has the unfortunate habit of shooting first and asking questions later. When a committee of local do-gooders underhandedly sells her ranch to Bostonian Davidson Smythe, they're the ones to regret it when Pearl and David team up against them.

Keywords: Ranchers, women

Breene, Leslee.

Leadville Lady. **Five Star, 2006. 271pp. Hardbound, 1594145466.**

Cody Cassidy, a U.S. Marshal in Leadville, Colorado, during the height of the silver mining era (circa 1880), does his best to catch claim-jumpers himself, his deputy Ned having just eloped. Then Sky Saunders, Ned's beautiful cousin, arrives in town from Ohio, in search of investment opportunities and to escape her abusive husband.

Keywords: Colorado—Reconstruction/Gilded Age; Lawmen; Silver mining

Duncan, Alice.

Cactus Flower. **Five Star, 2006. 303pp. Hardbound, 1594144567.**

Eulalie Gibb, born into a family of performers from New York City, comes to Rio Peñasco in New Mexico Territory to sing at the local opera house, but discovers the establishment is better known for less savory activities. Even worse, a stalker from back East has followed her to town. Nick Taggart, a local blacksmith, vows to protect Eulalie and her sister, despite her prickly attitude and ferocious temper.

Keywords: Blacksmiths; New Mexico—Reconstruction/Gilded Age; Opera singers

Galloway, Shelley.

Suddenly, You. **Five Star, 2007. 249pp. Hardbound, 9781594145711.**

Quentin Smith, a retired Texas Ranger now working for the railroads, comes to Cedar Springs, Colorado Territory, in 1872 to track down the mastermind behind a train robbery and murder. Though attracted to Jasmine Fairchild, a barmaid at the local saloon, he worries about putting her in danger.

Keywords: Barmaids; Colorado—Reconstruction/Gilded Age; Detective stories; Railroads

Grady, Erin.

These are both annotated in Chapter 12.

Echoes. **Berkley, 2004. 355pp. Paper, 0425200736.**

Whispers. **Berkley, 2006. 343pp. Paper, 0425209636.**

Jacobs, Linda.

Lake of Fire. **Medallion, 2007. 540pp. Paper, 9781933836218.**

Cord Sutton, a hotel owner of part Nez Perce heritage, and Laura Fielding, a woman he rescues from a stagecoach robbery, take each other's measure as they travel together through rough wilderness while making their way to luxurious Lake Hotel in Yellowstone Park in 1900. Neither learns the other's true identity until they arrive: Laura's wealthy father, a Chicago banking magnate, is backing Cord's principal rival for ultimate ownership of the hotel.

Keywords: Businessmen; Hotels; Mixed heritage; Nez Perce Indians; Yellowstone National Park

Kraft, Bridget.

Fields of Gold. **Five Star, 2005. 285pp. Hardbound, 1594143625.**

In this sweet, unconventional romance, set in rural northern California in 1882, two potential rivals discover they need to work together to achieve their goals. Guin Talbot, owner of a small family hop farm, refuses to allow Kellen O'Roarke, a neighboring landowner, access to her property, which he needs in order to build a hot springs resort. Kellen, for his part, sees his development project as the way to take revenge against the man who forced his family into poverty.

Keywords: California—Reconstruction/Gilded Age; Hop farmers; Neighbors

MacQuigg, Donna.

MacQuigg, a New Mexico native, writes gritty, action-packed romantic Westerns that showcase the history and beauty of her home state.

The Doctor's Daughter. **Five Star, 2007. 273pp. Hardbound, 9781594145964.**

In 1880 Rebeccah Randolph reluctantly heeds her mother's deathbed request that she leave England to visit her estranged father, a frontier doctor living near the mountains of Santa Fe, New Mexico. Colonel Sayer MacLaren, a cavalry officer, rescues her when her stagecoach is ambushed by Indians. She denies their attraction, as she is already engaged and believes all Western men are uncivilized anyway.

Keywords: New Mexico—Reconstruction/Gilded Age; Physicians

Honorable Intentions. **Five Star, 2008. 301pp. Hardbound, 9781594146961.**

Lydia Randolph, sister of Rebeccah from *The Doctor's Daughter*, stands to inherit a fortune from her family back in England. While in Santa Fe visiting her father at his ranch, she becomes convinced that wounded Mexican nobleman Miguel Estrada, a temporary resident of the local jail, is really notorious outlaw Antonio Garcia. She nurses him back to health. Miguel has the chance to repay the favor later, though it means deceiving her about his identity once more.

Keywords: Heirs and heiresses; New Mexico—Reconstruction/Gilded Age; Nobility; Outlaws; Ranchers

The Price of Pride. **Five Star, 2006. 327pp. Hardbound, 1594144648.**

Sarah Brighton, a journalist from back East who believes in women's suffrage, gets involved in investigating the supposedly accidental deaths of a young couple in a recent fire—to the chagrin of the male victim's brother, U.S. Marshal Ira Farrell. Set in the Sangre de Cristo Mountains outside Santa Fe in the 1880s.

Keywords: Detective stories; Journalists, women; Lawmen; New Mexico—Reconstruction/Gilded Age; Suffragettes

Nowak, Pamela.

Chances. **Five Star, 2008. 327pp. Hardbound, 9781594146374.**

In Denver in 1876, ardent suffragette Sarah Donovan, a telegraph operator for the Kansas Pacific line, first meets undertaker Daniel Petterman when she delivers a telegram to the wrong person by mistake. Though attracted to her, Daniel fears her outspoken ways will be a bad influence on his two daughters.

Keywords: Colorado—Reconstruction/Gilded Age; Suffragettes; Telegraph operators; Undertakers

Sundell, Joanne.

A . . . My Name's Amelia. **Five Star, 2007. 295pp. Hardbound, 9781594145650.**

Eighteen-year-old Amelia Anne Polley, deaf since age twelve, proudly works in the hearing world at the local newspaper office in Colorado Springs in 1880. One day Aaron Zachary buys a classified ad requesting a mail-order bride, and the handsome rancher piques Amelia's interest. After a little creative scheming, Amelia answers the ad herself. The strangers become husband and wife, yet communication becomes a major barrier to their relationship.

Keywords: Colorado—Reconstruction/Gilded Age; Deafness; Mail-order brides; Ranchers

Matchmaker, Matchmaker. **Five Star, 2006. 315pp. Hardbound, 1594144117.**

Zoe-Esther Zundelevich, a recent graduate of a Philadelphia medical school, faces obstacles out West because of her sex, background (she is a Russian immigrant), and religion (Jewish). In 1867 she and her father, Yitzhak, relocate to Golden City, Colorado, in hopes of improving his tubercular condition. Saloon owner Jake Whiskey intrigues her, but he doesn't exactly live a clean lifestyle, and her papa wants her to marry a good Jewish boy.

Keywords: Colorado—Reconstruction/Gilded Age; Immigrants, Russian; Jews; Physicians, women

6

Mining Boomtowns and the Gold Rush

After 1848, when miner James Marshall discovered gold at Sutter's Mill in California, people rushed west to California in droves. For fortune seekers around the globe, it was the American dream come to life. In these novels, as men and women head westward with visions of gold and silver, rough frontier communities spring up where they land. Fortunes are won and lost in these bustling mining towns, but the thrill doesn't last forever. When the ore runs out, it leaves behind only disappointment and heartache.

Allende, Isabel.

Daughter of Fortune. HarperCollins, 1999. 399pp. Hardbound, 006019491X.
   Annotated in Chapter 10.

Cunningham, M. Allen.

The Green Age of Asher Witherow. Unbridled, 2004. 275pp. Hardbound, 1932961003.
   Annotated in Chapter 10.

Parker, Ann.

Silver Rush Mysteries.
   Annotated in Chapter 7.

Wheeler, Richard S.
   Wheeler is at his best when describing the frenetic atmosphere of Western mining boomtowns and the courageous men and women who came in search of wealth and ended up staying. His novels of the American West are complex psychological portraits of Western towns and their people. Ignore the stereotypical gunfighter paintings on his novels' covers, for they don't match the content in the least.

The Bounty Trail. Pinnacle, 2004. 304pp. Paper, 0786015950.
   C. P. Raines, a good-looking swindler, sees the potential for gold in the near-abandoned mining town of Pearlygates, Nevada. He teams up with a hard-edged, sexy divorcee to cook up a scheme to put money back in his pockets and Pearlygates back on the map.

   Keywords: Gold mining; Nevada——Reconstruction/Gilded Age

Seven Miles to Sundown. Pinnacle, 2005. 288pp. Paper, 0786015977.
   When a prospector dies in the street of Rio Blanco, his last words about gold in the Lost Doubloon mine prompt the remaining residents of the dying town to hunt for the lost treasure.

   Keywords: Gold mining

🎗 *Vengeance Valley.* Pinnacle, 2004. 287pp. Paper, 0786015969.
   "Hard Luck" Yancey, a bookish mining engineer, got his nickname after being swindled out of a fortune in silver mining (and the town that bears his name) in the San Juans. When he discovers black telluride gold hidden underneath the land where a nuns' mining hospital now stands, he and the Sisters of Charity contend with corrupt miners desperate for the mother lode. Spur Award.

   Keywords: Colorado—Reconstruction/Gilded Age; Gold mining; Nuns

The Mythic West

This is the West as it never was, but perhaps as it should have been. These novels take traditional Western tales and turn them on their heads, which may not be all that much of a stretch given all of the other legends evoked by this period and place. Some of these novels retell old legends using a Western setting, and others create new ones. The characters' wacky and sometimes fantastical picaresque adventures are entertaining, humorous, and touching.

Berger, Thomas.

Little Big Man Series. ★

A fictional autobiography of Jack Crabb, presented as the only white man to survive Custer's Last Stand. Behind his tall-tale adventures and self-deprecating humor lies a serious tone, for this was one of the first novels to look behind the image of the "noble savage" and reveal Native Americans' humanity. Berger presents this theme in an entertaining, nondidactic way.

Keywords: Cheyenne Indians; Little Big Horn, Battle of the; Picaresque novels

🎗 *Little Big Man.* Dial, 1964. 440pp. Hardbound.

At 111 years old, Jack Crabb has seen and done it all. Born to a white couple but adopted into the Cheyenne, Jack doesn't belong to either group, and he feels guilty whenever he considers the brutality that whites inflict on the American Indians. Between the 1840s and the Battle of the Little Big Horn in 1876, Jack tries a variety of careers: drunkard, hustler, mule-skinner, and more. He meets many famous names along the way and doesn't hesitate to name-drop. Western Heritage Award.

The Return of Little Big Man. Little, Brown, 1999. 432pp. Hardbound, 0316098442.

Crabb, who died at the end of *Little Big Man* at age 112, admits he faked his own death to get out of an unfair publishing contract. He resumes his life story after the Battle of the Little Big Horn and proceeds to meet more famous historical characters like Annie Oakley, Wyatt Earp, and Doc Holliday. Then he joins Buffalo Bill Cody's Wild West show, which already has Sitting Bull as a headliner.

Estleman, Loren.

The Adventures of Johnny Vermillion. **Forge, 2006. 269pp. Hardbound, 0765309149.**

While the Prairie Rose Repertory Company are putting on productions for eager audiences in various towns in the Old West in the 1870s, other members of Johnny Vermillion's theater troupe perform the company's real function: robbing banks. When rival thieves get wind of the competition, and a clever Pinkerton detective sets out to foil both rackets, it results in a rip-roaring Western adventure that never takes itself too seriously—in keeping with the jaunty spirit of handsome Johnny and his likeable group of rogues.

Keywords: Actors; Outlaws; West—Reconstruction/Gilded Age

Hannan, Chris.

Missy. **Farrar, Straus & Giroux, 2008. 304pp. Hardbound, 9780374199838.**

Hannan, a playwright from Glasgow, somehow manages to inhabit the body and spirit of nineteen-year-old Dol McQueen, a "flash girl" in 1862 California who's thoroughly addicted to liquid opium, or "missy." Her outrageous adventures begin when a pimp stashes a crate of opium under her bed while she's on a road trip heading east with a bunch of friends. After she saves him from suicide, he isn't properly grateful and decides to take revenge—forcing her to go on the run from all of the crate's previous owners.

Keywords: Opium; Picaresque novels; Prostitutes

Hockensmith, Steve.

Amlingmeyer Series.

This Western mystery series is annotated in Chapter 7.

Liebmann-Smith, Richard.

The James Boys. **Random House, 2008. 262pp. Hardbound, 9780345470782.**

Humorist Liebmann-Smith imagines that the two younger brothers of noted intellectuals William and Henry James, tired of being overshadowed by their elders' fame, reinvented themselves, emerging as the notorious Western outlaws Frank and Jesse James. The four reunite after Frank and Jesse happen to rob the train that Henry is riding from Kansas City to St. Louis in 1876. Their histories—real, invented, and mingled—unfold in this inventive romp through the nineteenth-century West (and East).

Keywords: Brothers; James, Jesse (historical character); James, William (historical character); Outlaws; Picaresque novels; West—Reconstruction/Gilded Age

McMurtry, Larry.

Telegraph Days. **Simon & Schuster, 2006. 289pp. Hardbound, 0743250788.**

Annotated previously in this chapter, under "Frontier and Pioneer Life."

Warren, Spring.

Turpentine. **Black Cat, 2007. 418pp. Paper, 9780802170361.**

Sent from his Connecticut home to the Nebraskan plains in the hopes of curing his tuberculosis, young Edward Turrentine Bayard III becomes a buffalo skinner when the sanitorium where he was sent to recover turns out to be a rickety outpost. He's called back East for employment, but after he and two unlikely friends are wrongly accused of inciting anarchy (and worse), the trio heads on a circuitous route back out West, from Chicago to Indian country, encountering a wide variety of colorful characters.

Keywords: Picaresque novels; West—Reconstruction/Gilded Age

The Real Wild West

These gritty novels don't pull any punches about life on the Western frontier. They subvert the romantic mythology of the Wild West and focus on the bloody, violent reality. Here there are no good guys or bad guys, just people struggling to stay alive as best they can—even if it means abandoning all morality. With their emphasis on gore, degradation, and physical brutality, these novels aren't for the faint of heart. See also the "Crime Thrillers" section of Chapter 9.

Adamson, Gil.

The Outlander. Ecco, 2008. 400pp. Hardbound, 9780061491252.
   Annotated in Chapter 10.

Brandvold, Peter.

Rogue Lawman Series.

After his young son is killed and his wife hangs herself in her grief, Deputy U.S. Marshal Gideon Hawk abandons the law and turns vigilante, throwing aside caution to go after the man responsible. Of course this forces his former fellow lawmen to hunt him down. A brutal Western series about a determined antihero, one which challenges the usual Western dichotomy of right and wrong.

Keywords: Outlaws

Rogue Lawman. Berkley, 2005. 203pp. Paper, 0425205231.

Deadly Prey. Berkley, 2006. 200pp. Paper, 0425209156.

Cold Corpse, Hot Trail. Berkley, 2007. 216pp. Paper, 9780425214794.

Bullets Over Bedlam. Berkley, 2008. 200pp. Paper, 9780425220665.

Cobb, Thomas.

Shavetail. Scribner, 2008. 384pp. Hardbound, 9781416561194.
   Ned Thorne from Connecticut, aged seventeen, signs up with the U.S. Army in 1871 to escape a shameful episode in his past, but he is ill prepared for the violence he will encounter. Nicknamed a "shavetail," slang for a young, untrained mule, Ned takes up his place in the desert country of southern Arizona, where he undergoes a brutal initiation into his new rank. His commanding officer, Capt. Robert Franklin, also seeks atonement for past mistakes, and seeks to right them in attempting to rescue a woman presumed kidnapped by Apache warriors into Mexico. More a character study of Ned's painful coming of age than a traditional action-packed Western. **Literary.**

Keywords: Arizona—Reconstruction/Gilded Age; Army; Coming of age; Indian wars; Soldiers

Estleman, Loren.

The Undertaker's Wife. **Forge, 2005. 284pp. Hardbound, 065309130.**
Annotated under "Frontier and Pioneer Life" in this chapter.

McCarthy, Cormac.

Blood Meridian, or, The Evening Redness in the West. **Random House, 1985. 337pp. Hardbound, 0394400275.** ★

The Kid, a fourteen-year-old boy from Tennessee, gets a real education in how the West really lives when he joins a band of bounty hunters set on obtaining Apache scalps along the Texas–Mexico border in the 1850s. The crimson sunsets, combined with the bloody carnage and the red desert landscape, present nothing less than hell transferred to a Western setting. Lyrically written, but intensely dark and grim; it may be one of the most violent books ever written. **Literary.**

Keywords: Apache Indians; Bounty hunters; Indian wars; Texas—early United States

Swarthout, Glendon Fred.

🌶 *The Homesman.* **Weidenfeld & Nicolson, 1988. 239pp. Hardbound, 1555842356.** ★

The realities of the Western frontier—with its harsh winters, lack of comforts, and isolation—prove to be more than some women can handle. Mary Bee Cuddy, a plain-faced schoolmarm, serves as a "homesman," agreeing to escort four young wives from Missouri back home to Iowa after life out West drives them into madness. A ruthless land-grabber, whom Mary saves from a lynching, unwillingly accompanies them all. Spur Award; Western Heritage Award.

Keywords: Mental illness; Missouri—early United States; Teachers

The Early Twentieth-Century West

Life on the Western frontier was never easy, but the early twentieth century was particularly tough for individuals and families. These novels deal with social issues out West during the first decades of the last century: racial tension, religious prejudice, organized crime, and the overwhelming poverty of the Great Depression. Readers who don't believe that this occasionally grim setting can work in a romance should investigate Dorothy Garlock's homespun Americana romances (Chapter 4).

Askew, Rilla.

🌶 *Harpsong.* **University of Oklahoma, 2007. 243pp. Hardbound, 9780806138237.** 📖

The Joads from Steinbeck's *Grapes of Wrath*, a family of Okies driven away from their home following drought and crop failure, have become ingrained in America's mythology of the Dust Bowl era. Askew's *Harpsong* presents a folksy, lyrical counterpoint portrait of the Oklahomans who remained behind. Harlan Singer, a charming, harmonica-playing hobo, seduces fourteen-year-old Sharon Thompson away from her family, after which the young couple ride the rails throughout the Great Plains. While Harlan becomes known as a local folk hero, Sharon grows increasingly frustrated with their never-ending travels, doubting they'll ever find their way home. Oklahoma Book Award; Western Heritage Award. **Literary**.

Keywords: Great Depression; Hoboes; Oklahoma—20th century; Picaresque novels

Dallas, Sandra.

🏵 *Tallgrass*. **St. Martin's Press, 2007. 305pp. Hardbound, 9780312360191.** 📖
YA

Dallas continues in her tradition of describing the landscapes of small Western towns and the people who inhabit them. Just after Pearl Harbor, the U.S. government establishes an internment camp for Japanese Americans, Tallgrass, on the outskirts of the remote farming town of Ellis, Colorado. The viewpoint character is thirteen-year-old Rennie Stroud, a young girl who grows in wisdom as she juggles her loyalties between the bigoted residents of Ellis and the Japanese people her family hires to work their farm. Tensions rise to a climax when one of Rennie's friends is found murdered. Spur Award.

Keywords: Colorado—World War II; Coming of age; Internment camps; Japanese Americans; Prejudice

Doig, Ivan.

🏵 *The Whistling Season*. **Harcourt, 2006. 345pp. Hardbound, 0151012377.** 📖
Widower Oliver Milliron gets much more than he bargained for when he responds to a "work wanted" ad offered by would-be housekeeper Rose Llewellyn, a Minnesota woman who, as she writes, "can't cook but doesn't bite." Rose, who has a penchant for whistling, takes up residence at the Milliron home in Marias Coulee in rural eastern Montana in 1909, bringing along her scholarly brother, Morris—who deftly and brilliantly replaces the local schoolteacher, who has eloped and left town. Paul, the oldest of Oliver's three sons, narrates the story years later, looking back on a vanished era that had a distinct charm. **Literary**. ALA Notable Book, Alex Award.

Keywords: Cooks; Families; Montana—20th century; Teachers; Widowers

Harris, Fred.

Following the Harvest. **University of Oklahoma, 2004. 282pp. Hardbound, 0806136367.** **YA**

Will Haley, Harris's sixteen-year-old narrator, learns more about people, social issues, and life in general during the summer of 1943, when he accompanies his father and an odd mix of friends, relatives, and other folks north from Oklahoma to North Dakota as part of an itinerant wheat-harvesting crew. On their journey, Will's dad fights an ongoing battle with the bottle (which he frequently loses), while Will and other crew members deal with their own problems, both weather-related and personal.

Keywords: Alcoholism; Coming of age; North Dakota—World War II; Wheat harvesters

Jiles, Paulette.

Stormy Weather. **Morrow, 2007. 342pp. Hardbound, 9780060537326.** 📖 **YA**

Jeanine Stoddard's father Jack is an itinerant oil worker during the Great Depression, dragging her, her sisters Mayme and Bea, and their mother, Elizabeth, along as he travels from town to town in East Texas looking for employment on the pipelines. Unfortunately, he also has a weakness for gambling, women, and liquor, and his accidental death leaves his family impoverished. But the Stoddard women are resilient, choosing to go back to Elizabeth's childhood homestead, which had been abandoned for years. The family struggles through hard times, holding onto the promise of better days and pinning their last hopes on an investment scheme that just might make their fortune. **Literary.**

Keywords: Families; Great Depression; Sisters; Texas—20th century

Leonard, Elmore.

Carl Webster Series.

Annotated in Chapter 9, under "Crime Thrillers."

Wyman, Willard.

🏵 *High Country.* **University of Oklahoma Press, 2005. 359pp. Hardbound, 0806136979.**

Wyman's multi-award winning novel (garnering two Spurs, for Best First Novel and Best Novel of the West in 2006) traverses forty-odd years in the life of mule packer Ty Hardin, who guides travelers through otherwise impenetrable passes in Montana's Swan Range and farther south into California's Sierra Madres. His story begins during the Depression, when an adolescent Ty apprentices himself to an experienced packer who's a legend in the field. The novel's center is Ty's ever-developing relationship with (and respect for) the natural landscapes of the region—from the mules and other animals he partners with to the lands of the High Country itself, whose beauty, strength, and rhythms sink deep into his blood. Spur Award.

Keywords: Great Depression; Montana—20th century; Mountains; Mule packers; Trail guides

Western Sagas

The harsh life on the Western frontier can bring families together, but it can also force them apart. These family sagas, set between the nineteenth century and the present, are told from a variety of viewpoints: newly arrived immigrants, ranchers, Native Americans, Mexicans, and more.

Chiaverini, Jennifer.

The Quilter's Homecoming. **Simon & Schuster, 2007. 336pp. Hardbound, 9780743260220.** 📖

Longtime readers of Chiaverini's Elm Creek Quilts series may already feel at home with her characters, but newcomers shouldn't find it difficult to read this volume (tenth in that series) by itself. It focuses on longtime protagonist Sylvia Bergstrom Compson's older cousin, Elizabeth, who leaves Pennsylvania in 1925 with her new husband, Henry Nelson, for a ranch in southern California's Arboles Valley. When they arrive they learn that Henry's deed to the property had been faked, but the ranch's real owners give the proud newlyweds (who are ashamed to return home) jobs as hired hand and housemaid, respectively. Flashbacks about the ranch's original owners, the Rodriguez family, lead back to the 1870s; the two plot threads eventually converge.

Keywords: California—20th century; Married life; Multi-period novels; Quilters; Ranchers

Crook, Elizabeth.

🏆 *The Night Journal.* Viking, 2006. 451pp. Hardbound, 0670034770.

Meg Mabry, a biomedical technician in Austin, Texas, has never bought into the mythology of her family history, as was painstakingly revealed in journals written by her great-grandmother, Hannah Bass, a Harvey Girl and railway wife in Las Vegas, New Mexico, in the 1890s. These accounts were published to wide acclaim by Claudia Bass, aka "Bassie," Hannah's historian daughter. When Meg accompanies a now-elderly Bassie, a woman with whom she's always clashed, back to her great-grandmother's property, Meg finally breaks down and reads the famous journals. As both women revisit the past, they discover secrets that turn the family legacy they thought they'd known upside down. A multigenerational story that ties the present closely to the past and reveals, through Hannah's literary efforts, the candid experiences of a young woman with a spirit as exuberant as the landscape she comes to love. Spur Award; WILLA Award.

Keywords: Diaries and journals; Harvey Girls; Multi-period novels; New Mexico —Reconstruction/Gilded age

Doig, Ivan.

Montana Trilogy. ★ 📖

The continuing saga of two Scottish immigrant families in Montana's rural Two Medicine Country and the ways they adjust to pioneer life out West. Doig overlays the innate tragedy of Western frontier life with rewarding and human qualities. Set over a hundred-year period in Montana's history, beginning in 1889.

Keywords: Frontier and pioneer life; Immigrants, Scottish; Montana—Reconstruction/Gilded Age and 20th century; Sheep ranchers

Dancing at the Rascal Fair. Atheneum, 1987. 405pp. Hardbound, 0689117647.

Friends Angus McKaskill and Rob Barclay arrive in Montana from Scotland in 1889 with plans to set up homesteads. They each build up flocks of sheep to raise, but the harsh land and stark winters prove difficult to master. Over the next thirty years their friendship is strained by both men's stubbornness and Angus's marriage to Rob's sister, whom he only marries after the loss of his first love.

✤ *English Creek*. Atheneum, 1984. 339pp. Hardbound, 0689114788.

Jick McKaskill, age fourteen in 1939, grows into maturity and wisdom. From his family's ranch in Two Medicine Country, Jick watches his older brother leave to become a cowboy, defying his parents. A dangerous forest fire threatens his community that summer, and as a result, Jick discovers his proper place. Western Heritage Award.

Ride with Me, Mariah Montana. Atheneum, 1990. 324pp. Hardbound, 0689120192.

In 1989, the year of Montana's centennial, Jick McKaskill's daughter Mariah, a news photographer, takes him (and an enterprising reporter) on a whirlwind tour of the state's history.

Henderson, William Haywood.

Augusta Locke. Viking, 2006. 419pp. Hardbound, 0670034916. 📖

Henderson's third novel spans six decades in the life of a woman who seeks a place for herself amid the wildness and solitude of the American West in the early and mid-twentieth centuries. Born in rural Minnesota in 1903, the unexpectedly plain daughter of attractive parents, Gussie moves with her mother to Greeley, Colorado, when she's a teenager. Her new stepfather's desire to transform her into a proper lady leads her to run away. In the lands of Wyoming's Wind River Valley she creates a new life for herself and her daughter, Anne—conceived during a passionate one-night stand—and makes her own way in the world, working men's jobs and never remaining anywhere for long. Anne grows up to follow her mother's example, abandoning her just as Gussie deserted her own family. Most memorable, aside from his vivid characterization of feisty Gussie, are Henderson's soaring descriptions of the Wyoming mountains and the peaceful, invigorating sense of isolation they provide. **Literary**.

Keywords: Colorado—20th century; Mothers and daughters; Mountains; Wyoming—20th century

Kittredge, William.

The Willow Field. Knopf, 2006. 342pp. Hardbound, 1400040973.

Essayist and short story writer Kittredge's first novel spans nearly the entirety of the twentieth century and pays tribute to a steadily vanishing way of life. Teenaged Rossie Benasco's first job as a horse wrangler takes him from his Nevada ranch home to the plains of Alberta. His thousand-mile trek leads him ultimately to the love of his life, Eliza Stevenson, the pregnant daughter of a wealthy Scots businessman. Despite the difference in their lifestyles, the couple settle on her family's farm in Montana's Bitterroot Mountains and raise a family together. The remainder of the novel picks up speed, touching Rossie's family's World War II experiences and his ventures into local politics. **Literary.**

Keywords: Montana—20th century; Mountains; Ranchers

L'Amour, Louis.

Sackett Family Series. ★

1

At the beginning of this seventeen-book series, Barnabas Sackett travels to the New World after being exiled from Elizabethan England. Over the next ten generations, Sackett descendants settle and conquer the American frontier, from the mountains of Tennessee to the plains of the American West. The first four novels take place between 1600 and 1620, after which the saga jumps to the 1840s and continues straight on to the 1870s. Among this close extended family, readers will find cattle drivers, sharp-shooters, gold seekers, explorers, and ranchers—all prototypes of the men and women who won the West. L'Amour's *The Sackett Companion* explains his inspiration for the series and serves as a guide to characters, relationships, plots, and commonly used terms. Titles are listed in historical order.

2

Keywords: Sackett family

Sackett's Land. Saturday Review, 1974. 198pp. Hardbound, 0841503427.

3

To the Far Blue Mountains. Saturday Review, 1976. 176pp. Hardbound, 0841504229.

The Warrior's Path. Bantam, 1980. 226pp. Paper, 0553142070.

Jubal Sackett. Bantam, 1985. 375pp. Paper, 0553256734.

4

Ride the River. Bantam, 1983. 184pp. Paper, 055323742X.

The Daybreakers. Bantam, 1960. 204pp. Paper.

Lando. Bantam, 1962. 122pp. Paper.

Sackett . Bantam, 1961. 151pp. Paper.

5

Mojave Crossing. Bantam, 1964. 150pp. Paper.

The Sackett Brand. Bantam, 1965. 120pp. Paper.

The Sky-liners. Bantam, 1967. 151pp. Paper.

6

The Lonely Men. Bantam, 1969. 140pp. Paper.

Mustang Man. Bantam, 1966. 137pp. Paper.

Galloway. Bantam, 1970. 156pp. Paper.

Treasure Mountain. Bantam, 1972. 187pp. Paper.

7

Ride the Dark Trail. Bantam, 1972. 176pp. Paper.

Lonely on the Mountain. Bantam, 1980. 194pp. Paper, 0553242032.

Lott, Bret.

8

Ancient Highway. **Random House, 2008. 241pp. Hardbound, 9781400063741.**
📖

Lott's literary saga situates itself in the star-studded world of Hollywood during most of the twentieth century. Earl's adolescent wish for a life away from his family's farm in sleepy Hawkins, Texas, propels him on to southern California, where dreams of fame are created. There he observes the glitter-filled and disillusioning film industry firsthand; the tale continues over the next two generations, through to his grandson's tale of self-discovery in 1980s Los Angeles. **Literary.**

Keywords: California—20th century; Film industry

McMurtry, Larry.

Lonesome Dove Saga. ★ YA

In this classic saga of Western heroism and tragedy, McMurtry details the adventures, lives, and loves of two former Texas rangers, Augustus "Gus" McCrae and Woodrow F. Call, in the barren Texas landscape. Epic in scope and told in plain language, these character-centered dramas have proven to be hits with thousands of readers. The partnership between Gus, easygoing and sensitive, and Woodrow, a gruff workaholic, is a study in contrasts. Their friendship carries them through many tough times: Indian attacks, periods of drought and hunger, and arguments among their entourage. McMurtry patterned his protagonists on legendary cattle drivers Oliver Loving and Charles Goodnight.

Keywords: Call, Woodrow; Cowboys; McCrae, Gus; Texas—early United States and Reconstruction/Gilded Age; Texas Rangers

Dead Man's Walk. Simon & Schuster, 1995. 477pp. Hardbound, 068480753X.

Woodrow Call and Gus McCrae, two young and untried Texas Rangers, head to Santa Fe to recapture the city from the Mexicans. Crazed Comanche Indians and deadly forces of nature meet them at every turn, and the treacherous Dead Man's Walk proves to be their greatest challenge. McMurtry portrayed the early lives of the *Lonesome Dove* protagonists in this prequel.

🐾 *Comanche Moon.* Simon & Schuster, 1997. 752pp. Hardbound, 0684807548.

Another prequel to *Lonesome Dove*, set in pre–Civil War Texas. Call and McCrae, still relatively young men, get their feet wet wresting control of Texas from the Comanche. Their primary foes are Comanche warrior Buffalo Hump and his son, Blue Duck, who discovers the deadly power of gunfire. Spur Award.

🐾 *Lonesome Dove.* Simon & Schuster, 1985. 843pp. Hardbound, 0671504207.

In the 1870s former Texas lawmen Gus and Woodrow co-own the Hat Creek Cattle Company in the small town of Lonesome Dove. Though content with their carefree life, another ex-ranger speaks in glowing terms of the Montana grasslands, ideal ranching ground that's still unclaimed. The men pull together a herd of Mexican cattle and proceed to drive them north. The problem is, a bunch of other people insist on coming along for the ride. Pulitzer Prize.

The Streets of Laredo. Simon & Schuster, 1993. 589pp. Hardbound, 0671792814.

The railroad hires Captain Woodrow Call, practically a living legend, to find Joey Garza, a Mexican bandit and train robber. Raised by Apaches, Garza has been impossible to track down. With the help of Pea Eye, Call's former deputy, Call gives it his best shot.

Todd, Jack.

Sun Going Down. **Touchstone, 2008. 367pp. Hardbound, 9781416550488.** 📖
Between the post–Civil War period and the Great Depression, the Paint family of Dakota Territory (later South Dakota) endures considerable hardship, experiences some domestic joys, and watches the sun go down on Native Americans' time-honored ways and the traditional ranching way of life. Family patriarch Eb Paint relocates from the Mississippi Delta to the Western High Plains in 1863, marrying a twice-widowed, half-Lakota woman with whom he raises two sons, Eli and Ezra, who couldn't be more different. The story of Eli's troubled daughter Velma carries the final part of the novel. Based on the author's family history. **Literary.**

Keywords: Lakota Sioux Indians; Mixed heritage; South Dakota—Reconstruction/Gilded Age and 20th century

Williams, Jeanne.

Beneath the Burning Ground Trilogy.

In the late 1850s tomboy Christy Ware and Irish immigrant Dan O'Brien, both teenagers, discover an underground cave that later serves as a hiding place along the Underground Railroad. So begins an epic saga of several families' struggles to survive the Civil War years along the Kansas/Missouri border. The Wares are against slavery, though their wealthy Missouri neighbors, the Jardines, are longtime slave owners. When one of the Jardines' slaves escapes, the Wares risk their lives to shelter him in the cave. Romance develops between Christy and Dan, while Christy's brother Charlie reluctantly sides with the Confederacy when he marries a Jardine daughter. The tone becomes darker throughout the series, with fearsome scenes of war and the devastation wrought by Quantrill's Raiders. The author describes the Civil War experience from all possible angles: Union and Confederate; black, white, and Indian; rich and poor; in battle and on the home front. The series reads as one long novel.

Keywords: Missouri—Civil War; Slaves and slavery; Underground Railroad

The Underground River. Five Star, 2004. 224pp. Hardbound, 1594140030.

The Hidden Valley. Five Star, 2004. 214pp. Hardbound, 1594140162.

The Trampled Fields. Five Star, 2005. 219pp. Hardbound, 1594141215.

Chapter 7

Historical Mysteries

Historical mysteries present readers with a puzzle to solve—most typically, figuring out who committed a murder or murders. Readers combine their interest in times past with an intellectual challenge, one in which they can try to figure out "whodunit" by delving through clues along with the protagonist. As in Gary Warren Niebuhr's *Make Mine a Mystery* (Libraries Unlimited, 2003), the works covered in this chapter are mystery novels in their most traditional sense. That is, they are works of historical fiction in which detectives try to serve justice by solving crimes.

Today, historical mysteries form one of the most popular subgenres of historical fiction, and the trend shows no signs of slowing down. Most historical mysteries occur in series, which gives readers the chance to get comfortable with the characters, the era, and the physical setting. Readers who enjoy historical mysteries in series find that over time, even unfamiliar settings such as ancient Egypt or feudal Japan can feel like home.

The subgenre is not new, though its current popularity might make readers think otherwise. Agatha Christie's ancient Egyptian mystery *Death Comes at the End* (1944) was an early entry, as were Lillian de la Torre's short story collections starring Dr. Samuel Johnson as detective. Josephine Tey's *Daughter of Time* (1951), about a modern Scotland Yard detective who becomes intrigued by a portrait of England's Richard III, was one of the first modern novels to get readers thinking about historical crimes. Although Tey's novel takes place in the present, it is still beloved by historical mystery fans. In the late 1970s and early 1980s Ellis Peters started a trend with her popular Brother Cadfael medieval mysteries, which are still widely read. Peters set the bar for the subgenre with her suspenseful plots and historical accuracy.

Many series that first got their start in the 1980s and early 1990s, such as Lindsey Davis's <u>Falco</u> and Steven Saylor's <u>Roma Sub Rosa</u>, are still going strong, with new volumes appearing nearly every year. Long-running paperback series, such as those by Margaret Frazer and Robin Paige, grew so popular that their publisher made the transition to hardcover. On the other hand, the newest volumes in other series that began as hardcovers (e.g., Boris Akunin's <u>Erast Fandorin</u>, I. J. Parker's <u>Sugarawa Akitada</u>) are appearing in trade paperback, which may encourage new readers to pick them up due to the lower cost. New series spring up regularly, as do new stand-alone titles. Many well-known romance writers—such as Roberta Gellis, Patricia (P.B.) Ryan, Jennifer Ashley (writing as Ashley Gardner)—have successfully made the transition to historical mystery, to the delight of readers who enjoy novels in both genres. These crossover titles also gain the historical mystery subgenre many new converts.

On the other hand, the sheer number of titles appearing today may make librarians wonder if publishers are choosing quantity over quality. The market may become saturated at some point, but this hasn't happened yet. Only time will tell which new series will survive to become classics. Two major awards in the mystery genre are devoted specifically to historical mysteries: the Sue Feder Historical Mystery Award and the CWA Ellis Peters Historical Award (the Bruce Alexander Historical Mystery Award has ceased). This demonstrates the prevalence and the popularity of this subgenre within the larger mystery field.

In contrast to mysteries set in contemporary times, protagonists in historical mysteries are challenged to solve murder cases without employing modern forensic methods. Instead, they must use whatever tools and clues their era and setting make available. For the protagonists, this means not only being an astute observer of people and personalities, but also being well versed in the era's political and social realities, because these factors are frequently motives for murder. Some historical mystery sleuths have their own investigative specialties as well. For example, Kathy Lynn Emerson's Elizabethan amateur sleuth, Susanna, Lady Appleton, is an expert in herbalism, which means that she's familiar with the effects of plant-based poisons.

Readers have different degrees of tolerance for mysteries featuring historical characters as sleuths, even though traditional biographical novels (covered in Chapter 3) are generally well accepted. The main issue here is plausibility, because the pretext of these novels runs contrary to known historical facts. Did the historical Queen Elizabeth I disguise herself as a servant and sneak out of her castle at night to solve crimes, as in Karen Harper's novels? Did the real Pliny the Younger track down murderers when he wasn't busy serving as a Roman statesman? However, if the setting, dialogue, and other factors seem historically authentic, many readers willingly suspend their disbelief long enough to enjoy the story. Other readers, those who take a more purist view of historical truth, will want to stick with mysteries in which fictional characters do all the sleuthing.

This chapter is organized by historical setting (place and period), as this is of great interest to readers who specifically look for historical mysteries, but there are other factors that will appeal to readers. The mystery genre uses standard terms to define two of these characteristics.

The personal qualities of the main character, as well as some secondary characters, can make or break a mystery for a reader. This is especially true because most historical mysteries occur in series, and the detective must be someone readers are willing to stick with through multiple cases. People may prefer to read about protagonists who are either male or female, of a particular personality type, or with a certain career or role in society. These characteristics are noted in the annotations. Readers enjoy solving crimes along with the detective, and the way they go about doing so is determined by the official role the detective has in the investigation, if any. Common terms describing the main character in mysteries are discussed below. For readers who look for historical mysteries featuring a particular type of detective, these terms are listed in boldface at the end of each title or series annotation.

Public detectives. In the case of historical mysteries, these novels feature members of the local police force, who investigate crimes with the authority of the state behind them. In these novels, which can also be called "police procedurals" (though this term is more often used for modern police detective mysteries), members of a crime-solving team follow official police procedure in solving crimes. These detectives may depend on one another for support or go out on their own. Examples are Thomas Pitt (as written by Anne Perry, Victorian England) and Sir John Fielding (Bruce Alexander, Georgian England).

Private detectives. These investigators work on their own, for hire. They may have their own investigative agencies. Examples are Cyrus Barker (Will Thomas, Victorian England) and Marcus Didius Falco (Lindsey Davis, ancient Rome).

Amateur detectives. This is the most common type of protagonist in historical mysteries. Individual members of society get dragged into their first investigation by chance, usually when someone either physically nearby or emotionally close to them is murdered. Over time word of their success gets around, and people ask them to help solve crimes. Authors must take special care to make these characters' actions believable, because average people tend not to stumble upon murders as often as public or private detectives might. These sleuths also have to be very creative in gathering evidence, because they rarely have an official role in an investigation. Likewise, they may run into opposition from local law enforcement officers, who resent outsiders' interference in police matters. Examples of amateur detectives are Sister Frevisse (Margaret Frazer, medieval England) and Gaius Petreius Ruso (Ruth Downie, Roman Britain).

In historical mysteries the type of detective isn't always obvious, because an official "police force" may not have existed at the time the novel is set. However, most eras had judges or other arbiters of law who fulfilled these roles for society. In this book, legal professionals who investigate on behalf of the government and whose word has the force of law are listed as public detectives. A series of this is Peter Tremayne's <u>Sister Fidelma Series</u>. On the other hand, Sharon Kay Penman's <u>Justin de Quincy Series</u>, which involves an untrained young man asked by Eleanor of Aquitaine to look into crimes, is listed as an amateur detective series.

The level of action and violence in historical mysteries serves as another appeal factor for readers. Novels in this chapter will be identified with one of the following terms, placed in bold at the end of the title or series annotation, as appropriate.

Hard-boiled. These action-packed mysteries follow lone private detectives who solve brutal murders in the heart of the inner city. They are dark, violent, and suspenseful, with crime scenes graphically described. These aren't common in historical mystery, because hard-boiled novels practically require modern settings. Examples are Valentine St. Cyr (David Fulmer, 1900s Louisiana) and the <u>Bernie Gunther series</u> (Philip Kerr, 1940s Germany).

Cozy (also called "soft-boiled") . These lighthearted mysteries use comfortable settings such as English country houses, rural villages, or small towns—places that would normally be pleasant to live in, were it not for the murders that take place nearby. There is no graphic violence or even much blood; death normally occurs offstage, with the characters discussing it after it happened. Most cozy mysteries use amateur detectives. Examples are Victorian Mysteries (Robin Paige) and the Daisy Dalrymple series (Carola Dunn, 1920s England).

Traditional. A term used by Gary Warren Niebuhr in *Make Mine a Mystery* to describe mysteries that fall between "hard-boiled" and "cozy." The level of violence is realistic, but not gratuitously so. Most historical mysteries fit this category.

Other appeal factors in historical mysteries are language (appropriate to the period, or modern), pacing (fast-paced or leisurely), and overall theme. These are delineated in the annotations in this chapter.

Traditional Westerns (in general, as well as the historical Westerns in Chapter 6) may appeal to historical mystery readers, especially those that involve lawmen of the Wild West who track down outlaws in pursuit of justice. And because many historical thrillers also involve crimes, readers may wish to investigate the novels listed in Chapter 9, which emphasize danger and suspense. One might argue that some of these novels could be described as either thrillers or mysteries. The Mystery FAQ on the ClueLass home page (http://www.cluelass.com), an excellent overview of the mystery genre in general, provides more detail on the mystery/thriller/suspense distinctions as well as a glossary of terms frequently used within the mystery genre.

Ancient Civilizations

Egypt

Mysteries of ancient Egypt blend the unusual with the familiar. Their dry desert setting, colorful character names, and polytheistic religion will seem exotic, but the situations the characters find themselves in—family squabbles and political rivalry—are similar to those found in mysteries with more traditional settings.

Geagley, Brad.

Semerket Series.

In the year 1153 BC, Semerket, Clerk of Investigations and Secrets, is an ancient Egyptian private eye. As readers will quickly learn in these fast-paced mysteries, Semerket has much in common with many of his modern-day counterparts: he's down on his luck, drinks heavily, and spends too much time brooding over his ex-wife. He also has a reputation, well-earned, for always telling the truth regardless of the consequences. These novels are similar in tone to those in Lindsey Davis's Falco series. **Private detective/Traditional.**

Keywords: Semerket

Year of the Hyenas. Simon & Schuster, 2005. 291pp. Hardbound, 074325080X.

The two mayors of Thebes hire Semerket to solve the murder of an old priestess, and he reluctantly accepts, but it soon becomes clear that the authorities expect him to fail. As he looks into the case more thoroughly, he uncovers a plot of treason against the pharaoh.

Keywords: Priestesses

Day of the False King. Simon & Schuster, 2006. 254pp. Hardbound, 0743250818.

> Semerket's ex-wife, Naia, has been banished to Babylon, a land in the throes of revolution, as an indentured servant, and he is worried for her safety. Then Ramses IV decides to send him on a mission there in order to bring a sacred statue back to Egypt.

> **Keywords:** Babylonia—ancient/prehistoric; Ex-wives; Statues

The Roman Empire

The Senate, that group of men who dominated the political landscape of ancient Rome, takes center stage in these mysteries. As such, most of the murders are politically motivated. The detectives are well aware of this, though because of the Senate's power, it doesn't make the crimes any easier to solve.

Bell, Albert A., Jr.

Pliny the Younger Series. ✍

Pliny the Younger, the well-known Roman senator and letter-writer, narrates his own crime-solving adventures in the first century AD. As a narrator, Pliny is a bit stuffy and priggish, but he freely admits to these faults. **Amateur detective/Traditional**.

Keywords: Pliny the Younger (historical character); Rome—ancient/prehistoric; Senators, Roman

All Roads Lead to Murder. High Country, 2002. 246pp. Hardbound, 097130453X.

> In AD 83, Pliny the Younger heads to Rome in a caravan along with the historian Tacitus and some other travelers. When one among their number ends up murdered after spending the night in Smyrna, Pliny takes the case, with Tacitus's help. Things become complicated after Pliny learns that he himself might have been the intended victim.

> **Keywords:** Tacitus (historical character)

The Blood of Caesar. Ingalls, 2008. 257pp. Hardbound, 9781932158823.

> Emperor Domitian approaches Pliny in secret, worried about the security of his throne. He asks Pliny to look into possible rival claimants. Do any other blood descendants of Agrippina, Nero's mother, still survive?

> **Keywords:** Domitian, Emperor of Rome (historical character); Heirs and heiresses

Boast, Philip.

Septimus Severus Quistus Series.

Septimus Severus Quistus, a family man and senator of Rome during Nero's reign, is completely devastated when his wife and eight of his children are brutally murdered. The problem is that seeing the murderer brought to justice, according to Roman tradition, will mean the death of over a thousand innocent slaves. An action-packed series with numerous plot twists. **Amateur detective/Traditional.**

Keywords: Quistus, Septimus Severus; Rome—ancient/prehistoric; Senators, Roman; Slaves and slavery

The Third Princess. Severn House, 2005. 220pp. Hardbound, 0727863223.

> While attempting to discover whether his only daughter and seventh son, twins, are still alive, Quistus is forced to obey the emperor's orders to escort Claudia, a Christian princess from Britannia, back to her homeland on a peace mission.

> **Keywords:** Princesses

The Son of Heaven. Severn House, 2007. 251pp. Hardbound, 9780727864987.

> In the year AD 64 the young heir of the Chinese imperial throne trusts only Quintus to secretly bring him back home. Along the way, Quintus unmasks a murderer.

> **Keywords:** Heirs and heiresses; Princes

Davis, Lindsey.

Marcus Didius Falco Series. ★ YA

Davis's detective/narrator is Marcus Didius Falco, a wisecracking, bumbling private investigator in ancient Rome during the reign of Vespasian (circa AD 70). Though originally from the lower classes, Falco somehow manages to capture the heart of a Roman senator's daughter, Helena Justina, an intelligent woman who becomes his ideal mate. With a combination of witty dialogue, idiomatic phrasings, fast pace, and likable characters (imagine the typical cast of 1940s private eye novels, but dressed in togas), the author brings the period to life without taking it (or herself) too seriously. **Private detective/Traditional.**

Keywords: Falco, Marcus Didius; Rome—ancient/prehistoric

The Silver Pigs. Crown, 1989. 258pp. Hardbound, 0517573636.

Shadows in Bronze. Crown, 1990. 341pp. Hardbound, 0517576120.

Venus in Copper. Crown, 1991. 277pp. Hardbound, 0517584778.

The Iron Hand of Mars. Crown, 1992. 305pp. Hardbound, 0517592401.

Poseidon's Gold. Crown, 1994. 336pp. Hardbound, 051759241X.

Last Act in Palmyra. Mysterious Press, 1996. 476pp. Hardbound, 0892966254.

Time to Depart. Mysterious Press, 1997. 400pp. Hardbound, 0892966262.

A Dying Light in Corduba. Mysterious Press, 1998. 428pp. Hardbound, 0892966645.

Three Hands in the Fountain. Mysterious Press, 1999. 351pp. Hardbound, 0892966912.

Two for the Lions. Mysterious Press, 1999. 390pp. Hardbound, 0892966939. Ellis Peters Historical Dagger.

One Virgin Too Many. Mysterious Press, 1999. 304pp. Hardbound, 0892967161.

Ode to a Banker. Mysterious Press, 2001. 372pp. Hardbound, 0892967404.

A Body in the Bathhouse. Mysterious Press, 2002. 354pp. Hardbound, 0892967714.

The Jupiter Myth. Mysterious Press, 2002. 323pp. Hardbound, 0892967773.

The *Accusers. My*sterious Press, 2003. 368pp. Hardbound, 0892968117.

Scandal Takes a Holiday. Mysterious Press, 2004. 352pp. Hardbound, 0892968125.

See Delphi and Die. Minotaur, 2006. 300pp. Hardbound, 0312357656.

> In the year AD 76 Falco and wife Helena Justina investigate the deaths of two female tourists who met their demise while on a tour of Olympia, Greece, that was run by the shady Seven Sights tour company.
>
> **Keywords:** Tourists

Saturnalia. Minotaur, 2007. 324pp. Hardbound, 9780312361297.

> In Rome during the wild celebration of debauchery that is the annual Saturnalia holiday, Falco is asked to find the murderer of Gratianus Scaeva. The victim was a nobleman whose brother-in-law had been holding Veleda, a German rebel leader, captive. Perhaps not coincidentally, Veleda managed to escape around the same time the murder happened.
>
> **Keywords:** Saturnalia

Downie, Ruth.

Ruso Series.

Downie introduces Gaius Petreius Ruso, a new Roman sleuth with a wry, likable attitude and an excellent sense of comic timing. Set in second-century Britain. **Amateur detective/Traditional.**

Keywords: England—Roman period; Physicians; Ruso, Gaius Petreius; Slaves and slavery

Medicus. Bloomsbury USA, 2007. 386pp. Hardbound, 9781596912311.

> During the end of Trajan's reign, Ruso, a recently divorced doctor (medicus) encumbered with multiple debts, travels to Britain with the Roman army in search of fortune and excitement. What he finds instead is a filthy military outpost, bad weather, and long hours; his decision to rescue a mute slave girl named Tilla from her abusive owner causes him only trouble. Ruso reluctantly looks into the murders of two young prostitutes at a local bordello while pondering how he—a man once celebrated for saving the emperor's life—could have fallen so low. Previously published in the UK as *Medicus and the Disappearing Dancing Girls*.

Terra Incognita. Bloomsbury USA, 2008. 400pp. Hardbound, 9781596912328.

> Anxious to clear his head after his first crime-solving adventure, Ruso attaches himself to a contingent of the Roman army, the Batavians, that is heading to Roman Britannia's northernmost border. This happens to be the very place where his slave/lover/housekeeper, Tilla, grew up. When a Batavian soldier is found beheaded, his fellow Romans look for a scapegoat from among the locals—pagans who are chafing under Roman rule. Published in the UK as *Ruso and the Demented Doctor.*

Finnis, Jane.

Aurelia Marcella Mysteries.

In AD 91 many Roman citizens choose to make their homes in the frontier province of Britannia, but the native Britons want them gone. Aurelia Marcella, who runs a guesthouse (*mansio*) along the road to York with her sister Albia, roots out the person (or persons) responsible for a series of murders. **Amateur detective/Traditional.**

Keywords: Aurelia Marcella; England—Roman period; Innkeepers

Get Out or Die. Poisoned Pen, 2003. 350pp. Hardbound, 1590580753.

A Bitter Chill. Poisoned Pen, 2005. 341pp. Hardbound, 1590581938.

> During the brutal winter of the year AD 95, Aurelia's family is threatened with devastating (and false) rumors, and a band of rowdy guests demands to stay at her *mansio* during Saturnalia. Amid this chaos, the banquet celebrating the holiday culminates in murder, and her sister Albia becomes the prime suspect.

> **Keywords:** Saturnalia

Buried Too Deep. Poisoned Pen, 2008. 349pp. Hardbound, 9781590584002.

> Aurelia and her twin brother Lucius, who run the *mansio* together in AD 98, learn that the violent death of a local farmer may be related to pirates from Gaul who have been conducting raids along the coast.

> **Keywords:** Pirates; Twins

Pastor, Ben.

Aelius Spartianus Series.

In AD 304 Aelius Spartianus, a former cavalry officer, serves as historian to Emperor Diocletian and does his diplomatic bidding on various excursions to far-flung regions of the ever-expanding Roman Empire. Readers who want to learn more about the complicated politics of the time should enjoy these novels. Pastor, an Italian woman born in Rome, is better known internationally than in the States. **Amateur detective/Traditional.**

Keywords: Aelius Spartianus; Historians

The Water Thief. Thomas Dunne, 2007. 350pp. Hardbound, 9780312353902.

> While writing a biography of Emperor Hadrian, who reigned 200 years earlier, Aelius becomes intrigued by the supposed drowning death in the Nile of

Antinous, one of Hadrian's young male favorites. He travels to Egypt on Diocletian's behalf, both on a research mission and to look into the current trials against Christians. Things become even more curious when one of his sources also drowns in the Nile. If Aelius can find Antinous's grave, he may also uncover the roots of a conspiracy against the Roman Empire.

Keywords: Egypt—Roman period; Gay men

The Fire Waker. Thomas Dunne, 2008. 320pp. Hardbound, 9780312353919.

On a diplomatic mission to Trier (in modern Germany) on behalf of Diocletian, Aelius receives word of a mysterious "fire waker" in that town, a Christian preacher named Agnus who has brought a man back from the dead. Then the resurrected man himself is found murdered.

Keywords: Germany—Roman period; Preachers; Resurrection

Roberts, John Maddox.

SPQR Series.

SPQR, Senatus QuePopulus Romanus, translates as "the Senate and People of Rome." Roberts's series traces the often stormy relationship between the two. His detective, Senator Decius Caecilius Metellus the Younger, doesn't hesitate to plunge into mysteries involving the lower classes if it means that justice will be served. His adventures are amusing. Metellus enjoys a good time as much as anyone, and his playboy attitude usually gets him into trouble. **Amateur detective /Traditional.**

Keywords: Metellus; Senators, Roman; Rome—ancient/prehistoric

SPQR I: The King's Gambit. Minotaur, 2001 (©1990). 274pp. Paper, 0312277059.

SPQR II: The Catiline Conspiracy. Minotaur, 2001 (©1991). 278pp. Paper, 0312277067.

SPQR III: The Sacrilege. Thomas Dunne, 1999 (©1992). 245pp. Paper, 0312246978.

SPQR IV: The Temple of the Muses. Thomas Dunne, 1999 (©1992). 231pp. Hardbound, 0312246986.

SPQR V: Saturnalia. Minotaur, 1999. 275pp. Hardbound, 0312205821.

SPQR VI: Nobody Loves a Centurion. Minotaur, 2001. 276pp. Hardbound, 031227257X.

SPQR VII: The Tribune's Curse. Minotaur, 2003. 248pp. Hardbound, 0312304889.

SPQR VIII: The River God's Vengeance. Minotaur, 2004. 290pp. Hardbound, 0312323190.

SPQR IX: The Princess and the Pirates. Minotaur, 2005. 198pp. Hardbound, 031233723X.

SPQR X: A Point of Law. Minotaur, 2006. 253pp. Hardbound, 0312337256.

SPQR XI: Under Vesuvius. Minotaur, 2007. 211pp. Hardbound, 9780312370886.

Saylor, Steven.

Roma Sub Rosa Series. ★ 📖

Both more serious and more suspenseful than Lindsey Davis's novels, Saylor's series begins nearly a hundred years earlier (circa 80 to 48 BC), just before the Roman Republic became the Roman Empire. Gordianus the Finder, a private investigator, is a fairly average Roman citizen—gray-haired and slightly past middle age—but unusual in that high-profile patrons such as Pompey and Cicero request his services. Gordianus's choice of wife—Bethesda, a freed Egyptian-Jewish slave from his household—is also out of the ordinary. Saylor takes on many complicated issues, such as slavery and other traditional Roman values, without moralizing. The novels mix fictional with historical characters to good effect. **Private detective/Traditional.**

Keywords: Gordianus the Finder; Rome—ancient/prehistoric

Roman Blood. St. Martin's Press, 1991. 357pp. Hardbound, 0312064543.

The House of the Vestals. St. Martin's Press, 1997. 260pp. Hardbound, 0312154445.

Arms of Nemesis. St. Martin's Press, 1992. 304pp. Hardbound, 0312081359.

Catilina's Riddle. St. Martin's Press, 1993. 430pp. Hardbound, 0312097638.

The Venus Throw. St. Martin's Press, 1995. 308pp. Hardbound, 0312119127.

A Murder on the Appian Way. St. Martin's Press, 1996. 304pp. Hardbound, 031214377X.

🎖 *Rubicon.* St. Martin's Press, 1999. 276pp. Hardbound, 0312205767. Herodotus Award.

Last Seen in Massilia. Minotaur, 2000. 277pp. Hardbound, 0312209282.

A Mist of Prophecies. Minotaur, 2002. 270pp. Hardbound, 0312271212.

The Judgment of Caesar. Minotaur, 2004. 290pp. Hardbound, 0312271190.

A Gladiator Dies Only Once. Minotaur, 2005. 269pp. Hardbound, 0312271204.

These nine short stories date from Gordianus's early detective career; chronologically, this collection fits just following Saylor's previous short story collection, *The House of the Vestals.*

The Triumph of Caesar. Minotaur, 2008. 311pp. Hardbound, 9780312359836.

Rome's civil war is over, and Julius Caesar has clearly triumphed. However, although the Senate has appointed him dictator, political plots against his life continue to crop up. The aging Gordianus, although formally retired, returns from Egypt with his wife, Bethesda, and agrees to do some detecting work for Calpurnia, Caesar's wife. She hires him to discover who's behind the latest conspiracy against Caesar.

Keywords: Caesar, Julius (historical character)

Stanley, Kelli.

Nox Dormienda: A Long Night for Sleeping. **Five Star, 2008. 320pp. Hardbound, 9780312359836.**

In Londinium (London) in the year AD 83, Arcturus—the half-native personal physician to Agricola, governor of Britannia—investigates the mysterious murder of a Syrian spy while trying not to be overly dazzled by the beautiful blonde who was the spy's unwilling fiancée. The subtitle of Stanley's debut mystery, which is written in a dark, edgy style she terms "Roman Noir," deliberately echoes Raymond Chandler's *The Big Sleep.* **Private detective/Traditional-Hard Boiled.**

Keywords: England—Roman period; Physicians; Spies

Todd, Marilyn.

Claudia Series.

Claudia Seferius, an ex-prostitute in ancient Rome, attempts to make herself respectable by marrying a rich wine merchant but continues offering "services" to men on the side. Later, as a beautiful young widow, trouble continues to find her, as does murder. Her insistence on traveling to disreputable areas of the city doesn't help her reputation; neither do her looming, ever-increasing gambling debts. A coarse and irreverent heroine who lives on the edge of danger, Claudia is impossible not to root for. The first six volumes were published only in Britain. **Amateur detective/Traditional**.

Keywords: Prostitutes; Rome—ancient/prehistoric; Seferius, Claudia; Widows

I, Claudia. Macmillan UK, 1995. 310pp. Hardbound, 0333650220.

Virgin Territory. Macmillan UK, 1996. 342pp. Hardbound, 0333652975

Man Eater. Macmillan UK, 1997. 375pp. Hardbound, 0333716582.

Wolf Whistle. Macmillan UK, 1998. 345pp. Hardbound, 0333743083.

Jail Bait. Macmillan UK, 1999. 346pp. Hardbound, 0333765982.

Black Salamander. Macmillan UK, 2000. 327pp. Hardbound, 0333766717.

Dream Boat. Severn House, 2002. 278pp. Hardbound, 0727858181.

Dark Horse. Severn House, 2002. 282pp. Hardbound, 0727858610.

Second Act. Severn House, 2003. 282pp. Hardbound, 0727860089.

Widow's Pique. Severn House, 2004. 280pp. Hardbound, 0727861174.

Stone Cold. Severn House, 2005. 236pp. Hardbound, 0727861875.

Sour Grapes. Severn House, 2005. 249pp. Hardbound, 0727863177.

Scorpion Rising. Severn House, 2006. 248pp. Hardbound, 0727863754.

The British Isles

The Middle Ages

Both politics and religion play strong roles in medieval mysteries, and the two are frequently interrelated. Common causes of death include religious differences and feudal disputes. All are set in England unless otherwise stated.

Ash, Maureen.
Templar Knight Mysteries.

Bascot de Marins, a former Templar Knight who returned wounded after eight years' imprisonment in the Holy Land, recuperates in the town of Lincoln, but trouble seems to be following him. A very well-researched new series, set just following the Crusades in the early thirteenth century.

Keywords: de Marins, Bascot; Knights Templar

The Alehouse Murders. Berkley Prime Crime, 2007. 288pp. Paper, 9780425217658.

> Dame Nicolaa de la Haye, the feisty castellan of Lincoln Castle, asks Bascot to investigate the murders of several people found dead in a local alehouse.

Death of a Squire. Berkley Prime Crime, 2008. 256pp. Paper, 9780425219591.

> Bascot's second investigation begins when he finds the body of a young squire hanging from a tree in the forest. Was it suicide, or does the death relate to an upcoming meeting between the English and Scottish kings at nearby Lincoln Castle?

> **Keywords:** Squires

Beaufort, Simon.

Sir Geoffrey Mappestone Mysteries.

Sir Geoffrey Mappestone survives the First Crusade to Jerusalem in the early twelfth century, but his adventures have only begun. After the Crusaders return to England, he reluctantly takes on criminal investigations, both in his homeland on the Welsh border and back in the Holy Land. See also the anthologies from The Medieval Murderers, below. **Amateur detective/Traditional.**

Keywords: Counterfeiters; Crusades and Crusaders; Mappestone, Sir Geoffrey

Murder in the Holy City. St. Martin's Press, 1998. 280pp. Hardbound, 0312195664.

A Head for Poisoning. St. Martin's Press, 1999. 378pp. Hardbound, 031220549X.

The Bishop's Brood. Severn House, 2003. 348pp. Hardbound, 0727859838.

The King's Spies. Severn House, 2004. 320pp. Hardbound, 0727860399.

The Coiners' Quarrel. Severn House, 2005. 345pp. Hardbound, 0727861093.

> In 1102, while preparing to head out on Crusade again, Sir Geoffrey gets annoyed when he's summoned to court; he is ordered to look into counterfeiting activities in the city of Bristol.

Frazer, Margaret.

Joliffe Series. 📖 **YA**

Simon Joliffe, a traveling player (and sometime spy) in 1430s England, first made his appearance in Frazer's novel *The Clerk's Tale*. His fellow thespians and companions on the road include playmaster Thomas Basset; his daughter Rose, seamstress and costumer; her young son Piers; and Ellis, an actor who has an on-off relationship with Rose and would marry her in a minute if not for her inconveniently absent husband, who deserted her and Piers years earlier. Over the course of the series, Joliffe and company obtain official patronage, which gives them respect and regular work. In exchange, they are occasionally asked to look into suspicious activities at the households where they perform. These delightful slice-of-life mysteries give an excellent picture of the Oxfordshire countryside and theatrical life in medieval England.

Keywords: Actors; Joliffe, Simon; Plays; Spies

A Play of Isaac. Berkley Prime Crime, 2004. 312pp. Paper, 0425197514.

> Joliffe and company are asked to perform *Isaac and Abraham*, a mystery play, at the Corpus Christi festival in Oxford in 1434. Master Penteney, a local merchant, also requests they perform for his household, but when a man is found murdered on his property, the players risk being blamed unless they can find the true culprit.

> **Keywords:** Festivals; Merchants

A Play of Dux Moraud. Berkley Prime Crime, 2005. 273pp. Paper, 0425204340.

> Joliffe and his players, now under the patronage of Lord Lovell, travel to Deneby Manor to perform at the wedding of Mariena Deneby. Lord Lovell asks Joliffe to investigate Mariena's previous betrothed, a healthy man who inexplicably died just before they were wed.

> **Keywords:** Weddings

A Play of Knaves. Berkley Prime Crime, 2006. 288pp. Paper, 0425211118.

> Lord Lovell asks the strolling players to visit the small town of Ashewell, where three prominent families are squabbling among themselves.

A Play of Lords. Berkley Prime Crime, 2007. 295pp. Paper, 9780425216682.

> It's autumn in the year 1435 when the players travel to London to perform for Bishop Beaufort. While there, Joliffe and company are sent to spy on members of the royal family.

> **Keywords:** Royalty

Sister Frevisse Medieval Mysteries. 📖 **YA**

Sister Frevisse, a sharp-witted Benedictine nun at St. Frideswide's in Oxfordshire during the reign of Henry VI (1430s and 1440s), serves as amateur sleuth. Though she chose a religious vocation of her own free will, Frevisse's background as the niece-by-marriage of Thomas Chaucer

(Geoffrey's son) gives her entrance into the world beyond the convent. Frevisse's no-nonsense attitude makes her hard to get to know, but her astute knowledge of human behavior stands her in good stead. Like Ellis Peters's novels, the works of Margaret Frazer (pseudonym for Mary Monica Pulver/Kuhfeld and Gail Frazer, and after the sixth novel, Frazer alone) don't dwell on the unpleasant aspects of medieval life. The plots unfold slowly, and they alternate points of view between Frevisse and the title character. The titles echo verses from Chaucer's *Canterbury Tales*. **Amateur detective/Traditional.**

Keywords: Frevisse; Nuns

The Novice's Tale. Berkley Prime Crime, 1992. 229pp. Paper, 042514321X.

The Servant's Tale. Jove, 1993. 234pp. Paper, 0515111635.

The Outlaw's Tale. Jove, 1994. 217pp. Paper, 0425151190.

The Bishop's Tale. Berkley Prime Crime, 1994. 198pp. Paper, 0425144925.

The Boy's Tale. Berkley Prime Crime, 1995. 233pp. Paper, 0425148998.

The Murderer's Tale. Berkley Prime Crime, 1996. 230pp. Paper, 0425154068.

The Prioress' Tale. Berkley Prime Crime, 1997. 246pp. Paper, 0425159442.

The Maiden's Tale. Berkley Prime Crime, 1998. 245pp. Paper, 0425164071.

The Reeve's Tale. Berkley Prime Crime, 1999. 274pp. Paper, 0425172325.

The Squire's Tale. Berkley Prime Crime, 2000. 277pp. Hardbound, 0425176789.

The Clerk's Tale. Berkley Prime Crime, 2002. 312pp. Hardbound, 0425183246.

The Bastard's Tale. Berkley Prime Crime, 2003. 309pp. Hardbound, 0425186490.

The Hunter's Tale. Berkley Prime Crime, 2004. 336pp. Hardbound, 0425194019.

The Widow's Tale. Berkley Prime Crime, 2005. 266pp. Hardbound, 0425200183.

Cristiana Helyngton, a recent widow forced into St. Frideswide's nunnery by her late husband's relatives (who seek control of her lands and children), is determined to earn back her freedom. She confides to Frevisse a secret her husband told her on his deathbed, which could have drastic political implications.

Keywords: Widows

The Sempster's Tale. Berkley Prime Crime, 2006. 339pp. Hardbound, 0425207668.

In the summer of 1450 Frevisse helps her cousin, the duchess of Suffolk, recover funds that her late husband, the duke, had sent out of England before he died. Daved Weir, a merchant from the Low Countries, returns the gold, yet his presence in England is a constant worry for him and his lover, seamstress Anne Blakhall, because Jews are forbidden to set foot in the country. Then his friend's son is found murdered in a London church, his body mutilated with Hebrew letters.

Keywords: Alice, Duchess of Suffolk (historical character); Jews

The Traitor's Tale. Berkley Prime Crime, 2007. 372pp. Hardbound, 9780425213704.

> Frevisse rejoins her old partner in sleuthing, traveling player Simon Joliffe (star of Frazer's other series) in this entry, set toward the end of the Hundred Years' War. Joliffe, on a mission for the exiled duke of York, tries to locate a letter that lists English noblemen who are traitors to the realm.
>
> **Keywords:** Actors; Hundred Years' War; Joliffe, Simon

The Apostate's Tale. Berkley Prime Crime, 2008. 307pp. Hardbound, 9780425219249.

> Sister Cecely—who had left St. Frideswide's in disgrace nine years ago with her lover—returns with her bastard son, claiming to be repentant. Then three men, relatives of the boy's late father, stop by the nunnery, laying claim to both her son and property they say that she stole.
>
> **Keywords:** Illegitimate children

Gellis, Roberta.

Magdalene La Bâtarde Mysteries.

An unlikely mystery heroine, Magdalene la Bâtarde runs a high-class whorehouse in London's Southwark district in the mid-twelfth century. Despite her choice of profession (and a past she'd prefer to hide), Magdalene is a woman of integrity. Her women all have physical disabilities that disqualify them for marriage—one is blind, another deaf, another mute—but this doesn't interfere with their work. The bishop of Winchester, whose guesthouse Magdalene rents, silently accepts their presence on his property. One of the bishop's knights, Sir Bellamy "Bell" of Itchen, grows ever more fascinated with the still-beautiful Magdalene as the series continues. **Amateur detective/Traditional.**

Keywords: Madams; Magdalene la Bâtarde; Prostitutes

A Mortal Bane. Forge, 1999. 350pp. Hardbound, 0312870000.

A Personal Devil. Forge, 2001. 316pp. Hardbound, 0312869983.

Bone of Contention. Forge, 2002. 431pp. Hardbound, 0765300192.

Chains of Folly. Five Star, 2006. 320pp. Hardbound, 1594144729.

> The battered body of a fellow prostitute, Nelda Roundheels, is found in the bedroom of the bishop of Winchester, Sir Bellamy's patron. Believing that someone is trying to incriminate the bishop, Magdalene and Bell work together to find the killer.

Gregory, Susanna.

Chronicles of Matthew Bartholomew.

Matthew Bartholomew, a physician and university lecturer in Cambridge in the aftermath of the Black Death in mid-fourteenth-century England, uses his knowledge of medicine and human nature to solve murders. The world-renowned university at Cambridge is the centerpiece for these tales, and as in any university locale, town–gown relations are less than perfect. Volumes appear in their correct order below.

Keywords: Bartholomew, Matthew; Physicians; Universities

A Plague on Both Your Houses. St. Martin's Press, 1998. 406pp. Hardbound, 0312193181.

An Unholy Alliance. St. Martin's Press, 1996. 208pp. Hardbound, 031214752X.

A Bone of Contention. St. Martin's Press, 1997. 375pp. Hardbound, 031216792X.

A Deadly Brew. Trafalgar Square (Little Brown UK), 1998. 360pp. Hardbound, 0316640573.

A Wicked Deed. Trafalgar Square (Little Brown UK), 1999. 392pp. Hardbound, 0316646393.

A Masterly Murder. Trafalgar Square (Little Brown UK), 2000. 406pp. Hardbound, 0316646261.

An Order for Death. Trafalgar Square (Little Brown UK), 2001. 470pp. Hardbound, 0316856797.

A Summer of Discontent. Trafalgar Square (Little Brown UK), 2002. 520pp. Hardbound, 0316859524.

A Killer in Winter. Trafalgar Square (Little Brown UK), 2003. 496pp. Hardbound, 0316860115.

The Hand of Justice. Trafalgar Square (Little Brown UK), 2004. 536pp.

The Mark of a Murderer. Trafalgar Square (Time Warner UK), 2005. 469pp. Hardbound, 0316726400.

The Tarnished Chalice. Trafalgar Square (Time Warner UK), 2006. 502pp. Hardbound, 0316726419.

To Kill or Cure. Trafalgar Square (Time Warner UK), 2007. 436pp. Hardbound, 9781847440327.

The Devil's Disciples. Trafalgar Square (Time Warner UK), 2008. 487pp. Hardbound, 9781847440815.

Jecks, Michael.

Medieval West Country Mysteries.

Jecks's series focuses on the peasants of medieval England and their relationship with the land. The detectives are Simon Puttock, Bailiff of Lydford Castle in Devon, and his friend, Sir Baldwin Furnshill, Keeper of the King's Peace. The fourteenth century was a turbulent time for England: the Knights Templar were disbanded, the Hundred Years' War began, and the Black Plague hit hard. Even Simon and Baldwin's quiet village sees its share of feudal disputes, religious strife, violence, and murder. **Public detective/Traditional.**

Keywords: Furnshill, Sir Baldwin; Knights Templar; Puttock, Simon

The Last Templar. Trafalgar Square (Headline UK), 1995. 375pp. Paper, 0747250618.

The Merchant's Partner. Avon, 2005 (©1995). 374pp. Paper, 0060763469.

A Moorland Hanging. Avon, 2005 (©1996). 378pp. Paper, 0060763477.

The Crediton Killings. Avon, 2006 (©1997). 386pp. Paper, 0060846542.

The Abbot's Gibbet. Avon, 2006 (©1998). 400pp. Paper, 0060846569.

The Leper's Return. Avon, 2006 (©1998). 397pp. Paper, 0060846585.

Squire Throwleigh's Heir. Trafalgar Square (Headline UK), 1999. 337pp. Paper, 0747259526.

Belladonna at Belstone. Trafalgar Square (Headline UK), 1999. 327pp. Pa**per, 0747274029.**

The Traitor of St. Giles. Trafalgar Square (Headline UK), 2000. 335pp. Paper, 0747274037.

The Boy-Bishop's Glovemaker. Trafalgar Square (Headline UK), 2000. 331pp. Paper, 0747272476.

The Tournament of Blood. Trafalgar Square (Headline UK), 2001. 362pp. Hardbound, 0747266123.

The Sticklepath Strangler. Trafalgar Square (Headline UK), 2001. 366pp. Hardbound, 074726919X.

The Devil's Acolyte. Trafalgar Square (Headline UK), 2002. 395pp. Hardbound, 0747269203.

The Mad Monk of Gidleigh. Trafalgar Square (Headline UK), 2002. 460pp. Hardbound, 0755301684.

The Templar's Penance. Trafalgar Square (Headline UK), 2003. 364pp. Hardbound, 0755301714.

The Outlaws of Ennor. Trafalgar Square (Headline UK), 2004. 320pp. Hardbound, 0755301722.

The Tolls of Death. Trafalgar Square (Headline UK), 2004. 392pp. Hardbound, 0755301749.

The Chapel of Bones. Trafalgar Square (Headline UK), 2004. 334pp. Hardbound, 0755322959.

The Butcher of St. Peter's. Trafalgar Square (Headline UK), 2005. 416pp. Hardbound, 0755322975.

A Friar's Bloodfeud. Trafalgar Square (Headline UK), 2005. 416pp. Hardbound, 0755322991.

The Death Ship of Dartmouth. Trafalgar Square (Headline UK), 2006. 395pp. Hardbound, 0755323017.

The Malice of Unnatural Death. Trafalgar Square (Headline UK), 2006. 399pp. Hardbound, 0755332768.

Dispensation of Death. Trafalgar Square (Headline UK), 2007. 364pp. Hardbound, 9780755332793.

The Templar, the Queen and Her Lover. Trafalgar Square (Headline UK), 2007. 391pp. Hardbound, 9780755332823.

The Prophecy of Death. Trafalgar Square (Headline UK), 2008. 352pp. Hardbound, 9780755344147.

Knight, Bernard.

Crowner John Mysteries.

In the twelfth century Sir John de Wolfe, a former Crusader appointed as the first coroner, or "crowner," for the county of Devon, solves crimes within his jurisdiction. The novels are listed in chronological order, though the American publication dates vary. Bernard Knight, CBE, is a retired professor of forensic pathology who has also written numerous texts on medicine and forensics. See also The Medieval Murderers, below. **Public detective/Traditional.**

Keywords: Coroners; de Wolfe, Sir John

The Sanctuary Seeker. Severn House, 2003 (©1998). 320pp. Hardbound, 0727859137.

The Poisoned Chalice. Severn House, 2003 (©1998). 384pp. Hardbound, 0727860097.

Crowner's Quest. Severn House, 2004 (©1999). 352pp. Hardbound, 0727860542.

An Awful Secret. Pocket, 2004 (©2000). 335pp. Paper, 0743492080.

The Tinner's Corpse. Pocket, 2001. 330pp. Paper, 0671029665.

The Grim Reaper. Pocket, 2002. 351pp. Paper, 0671029673.

Fear in the Forest. Pocket, 2003. 410pp. Paper, 0743449908.

The Witch Hunter. Pocket, 2004. 400pp. Paper, 0743449894.

Figure of Hate. Pocket, 2005. 374pp. Paper, 0743492145.

The Elixir of Death. Simon & Schuster UK, 2006. 347pp. Hardbound, 0743259513.

The Noble Outlaw. Simon & Schuster UK, 2007. 344pp. Hardbound, 9780743294980.

The Manor of Death. Simon & Schuster UK, 2008. 368pp. Hardbound, 9780743294997.

Maitland, Karen.

Company of Liars. **Delacorte, 2008. 465pp. Hardbound, 9780385341691.**
Annotated in Chapter 2.

McDuffie, Susan.

A Mass for the Dead. **Five Star, 2006. 239pp. Hardbound, 1594144893.**

In Scotland in 1373, Muirteach, the eldest (and illegitimate) son of Crispinus, the Prior of Oronsay, is asked by the lord of the Isles to find out who killed his father and left his strangled body in the tidal strand separating the isles of Colonsay and Oronsay. His relationship with Crispinus had always been strained, yet Muirteach does his duty, even though he himself is considered a suspect. **Amateur detective/Traditional**.

Keywords: Illegitimate children; Priests; Scotland

McIntosh, Pat.

Gil Cunningham Murder Mysteries.

In Glasgow, Scotland, in the 1490s, during the reign of James IV, new lawyer Gilbert (Gil) Cunningham doesn't particularly want to train for the priesthood, but he wishes to please his family. He quickly abandons that career choice after meeting a young woman named Alys in the first book. As a questioner for the local archbishop, Gil's investigations take him all around Glasgow: its religious houses, universities, almshouses, and the shores of the Clyde. McIntosh incorporates Scots dialect and slang into her novels, which add authenticity but can make them a challenge to get into. **Public detective/Traditional.**

Keywords: Lawyers; Scotland

The Harper's Quine. Carroll & Graf, 2004. 300pp. Hardbound, 0786713496.

The Nicholas Feast. Carroll & Graf, 2005. 288pp. Hardbound, 0786715707.

While attending a performance by players from his old university in celebration of the Nicholas Feast, Gil learns that one of the youthful actors has been found murdered in the coal house. He investigates with the help of Alys, his betrothed, and her father, Pierre, the French mason from *The Harper's Quine*.

Keywords: Actors; Festivals

The Merchant's Mark. Carroll & Graf, 2006. 302pp. Hardbound, 0786717416.

Gil and his friend Augie Morison, a merchant, discover a severed head and a packet of valuable jewels in a barrel used to import books from the Low Countries. When Augie is arrested for the man's murder, Gil seeks to clear his name.

St. Mungo's Robin. Carroll & Graf, 2007. 301pp. Hardbound, 9780786719037.

Just before Gil's wedding to Alys, his two sisters pay a visit. It's not particularly good timing for dealing with family problems, as Gil is already occupied with solving the murder of the warden of St. Serf's almshouse.

The Rough Collier. Soho Constable, 2008. 302pp. Hardbound, 9781569475072.

While Gil and Alys are visiting his mother, local peat-cutters find a dead man in a nearby coal mine, his face no longer recognizable. The couple believes the body belongs to a local man who has gone missing; others aren't so sure. Then Gil faces accusations of having killed the man by witchcraft.

Keywords: Witchcraft

Medieval Murderers, The.

The "Medieval Murderers" are five prolific British authors of historical mysteries who band together both to promote their books and write novels. They include Michael Jecks, Susanna Gregory, Bernard Knight, Ian Morson, Philip Gooden, and Simon Beaufort (who is really Gregory, again, under a pseudonym). In these jointly written novels, each author writes part of the book. These shorter tales are full-fledged mysteries in themselves, starring the authors' usual protagonists. Taken together, the individual stories interlink to trace a larger mystery through time.

The Tainted Relic. **Simon & Schuster UK, 2005. 502pp. Paper, 0743267958.**

This set of interlinked murder mysteries begins in the year 1100, in Jerusalem, where Simon Beaufort's hero Geoffrey Mappestone is entrusted with a fragment of the True Cross that happens to be cursed. The relic leaves havoc (and murders) in its wake over the next 500 years and leads to investigations by Bernard Knight's Crowner John (mid-twelfth-century Glastonbury), Ian Morson's William Falconer (1269 Oxford), Michael Jecks's Sir Baldwin Furnshill (1323 Exeter), Susanna Gregory's Matthew Bartholomew (1350s Cambridge), and Philip Gooden's Nick Revill (Elizabethan London).

Keywords: Collaborative novels; Relics

Sword of Shame. **Simon & Schuster UK, 2006. 406pp. Paper, 074328545X.**

An accursed sword, created by a Saxon swordsmith and first brought to England with William the Conqueror, passes from hand to hand as it travels Europe over the next 300 years, bringing bad luck wherever it goes. The sword makes appearances (resulting in interlinked mysteries, naturally) in 1066 England, thirteenth-century Venice, and 1356 Poitiers, among others.

Keywords: Collaborative novels; Swords

Morgan, Philippa.

Geoffrey Chaucer Series. ✍

In the 1370s future poet Geoffrey Chaucer traipses across England and the continent on diplomatic errands on behalf of his monarch, King Edward III, who persists in waging war against France. Chaucer uses his ready wit to solve mysteries when he comes across them. Light, entertaining, and occasionally satirical, just as his own *Canterbury Tales* are. Morgan is the pseudonym of Philip Gooden, author of the Nick Revill Series (see below, under "Tudor Era," and also under Medieval Murderers, above).

Keywords: Chaucer, Geoffrey (historical character); Diplomats

Chaucer and the House of Fame. Carroll & Graf, 2004. 341pp. Hardbound, 0786714662.

> In 1370 Chaucer crosses the channel to Aquitaine on behalf of John of Gaunt, Duke of Lancaster, to convince a French nobleman, the comte de Guyac, to remain loyal to England. When the comte is killed while out hunting wild boar, Chaucer suspects murder.
>
> **Keywords:** France; Nobility

Chaucer and the Legend of Good Women. Carroll & Graf, 2005. 299pp. Hardbound, 0786715987.

> Chaucer arrives in the lively city of Florence in 1373, planning to meet with Italian banker Antonio Lipari, who will help finance King Edward's campaign against France. Some members of the Lipari family oppose the arrangements, and shortly thereafter Antonio is killed.
>
> **Keywords:** Bankers; Italy

Chaucer and the Doctor of Physic. Carroll & Graf, 2006. 298pp. Hardbound, 0786718242.

> Edward III sends Chaucer to the English seaport of Devon to find out who stole the cargo of the *San Giovanni*, a ship arriving from Genoa. While the ship's captain and Dartmouth's mayor squabble among themselves, Chaucer also contends with a murder occurring at the house of his local host, Dr. Richard Storey.
>
> **Keywords:** Physicians

Penman, Sharon Kay.

Justin de Quincy Series.

During the reign of Richard the Lion Heart in the late twelfth century, young Justin de Quincy, the unacknowledged bastard son of a bishop, becomes the unexpected ally of Eleanor of Aquitaine, the elderly queen dowager, and does her bidding on his travels throughout the British Isles. The crimes he solves are deeply rooted in the politics of medieval Europe. Though lighter and considerably shorter than her epic novels of medieval royalty (Chapter 2), Penman's fun and entertaining mysteries feature many of the same historical characters: the Plantagenets and their political rivals, the native Welsh princes. **Amateur detective/Traditional.**

Keywords: De Quincy, Justin; Illegitimate children

The Queen's Man. Henry Holt, 1996. 291pp. Hardbound, 080503885X.

Cruel as the Grave. Henry Holt, 1998. 242pp. Hardbound, 0805056084.

Dragon's Lair. Putnam, 2003. 322pp. Hardbound, 0399150773.

Prince of Darkness. Putnam, 2005. 326pp. Hardbound, 0399152563.

> In 1193 the Prince of Darkness himself, aka Prince John, asks Justin to help clear him from involvement in a plot to kill King Richard, who still languishes in a European prison.
>
> **Keywords:** John, King of England (historical character)

Peters, Ellis.

Brother Cadfael Series. ★

During the civil wars that engulf England in the mid-twelfth century, as King Stephen and his cousin, the Empress Maud, vie for control of the country, not even the Benedictine monastery of St. Peter and St. Paul in the Welsh border town of Shrewsbury remains unaffected. Peters's detective, Brother Cadfael, possesses expertise in both herbal lore and human nature that works well with his crime-solving abilities. A former Crusader who joined the monastery late in life, Cadfael has an unusual history that is revealed gradually throughout the series. The author's version of medieval English life is calm, unrushed, and slightly romanticized; although unpleasantries aren't hidden, they're not dwelled on, either. Her novels proceed at a leisurely pace and are filled with beautiful descriptions of cloister life as well as the English and Welsh countryside. (Peters is a pseudonym for English novelist Edith Pargeter, who died in 1995.)

Keywords: Monks

A Rare Benedictine. Mysterious Press, 1988. 118pp. Hardbound, 0892963972.

A Morbid Taste for Bones. William Morrow, 1977. 191pp. Hardbound, 0688033741.

One Corpse Too Many. William Morrow, 1980. 191pp. Hardbound, 0688036309.

Monk's-Hood. William Morrow, 1981. 223pp. Hardbound, 0688004520.

St. Peter's Fair. William Morrow, 1981. 219pp. Hardbound, 0688006671.

The Leper of St. Giles. William Morrow, 1982. 223pp. Hardbound, 0688010970.

The Virgin in the Ice. William Morrow, 1983. 220pp. Hardbound, 0688016723.

The Sanctuary Sparrow. William Morrow, 1983. 181pp. Hardbound, 0688022529.

The Devil's Novice. William Morrow, 1984. 191pp. Hardbound, 0688032478.

Dead Man's Ransom. William Morrow, 1984. 189pp. Hardbound, 0688041949.

The Pilgrim of Hate. William Morrow, 1984. 190pp. Hardbound, 0688049648.

An Excellent Mystery. William Morrow, 1986. 190pp. Hardbound, 0688062504.

The Raven in the Foregate. William Morrow, 1986. 201pp. Hardbound, 0688065589.

The Rose Rent. William Morrow, 1986. 190pp. Hardbound, 0688069827.

The Hermit of Eyton Forest. Mysterious Press, 1988. 224pp. Hardbound, 0892962909.

The Confession of Brother Haluin. Mysterious Press, 1989. 164pp. Hardbound, 0892963492.

The Heretic's Apprentice. Mysterious Press, 1990. 186pp. Hardbound, 0892963816.

The Potter's Field. Mysterious Press, 1990. 230pp. Hardbound, 0892964197.

The Summer of the Danes. Mysterious Press, 1991. 251pp. Hardbound, 0892964480.

The Holy Thief. Mysterious Press, 1992. 246pp. Hardbound, 089296524X.

Brother Cadfael's Penance. Mysterious Press, 1994. 292pp. Hardbound, 0892965991.

Royal, Priscilla.

Eleanor of Wynethorpe Series.

When Eleanor of Wynethorpe becomes prioress at Tyndal Priory in East Anglia in the year 1270, during the reign of Henry III, she faces prejudice from the nuns and monks she is meant to lead, not just because of her youth (she's considerably younger than most of her flock) but because hers was a political appointment. Tyndal, like many religious houses of the time, is a "double house," for both men and women. Eleanor eventually earns their grudging respect, particularly after she solves her first crime. The tone is fairly serious throughout, even dark in places, and thus very reminiscent of Ellis Peters's Brother Cadfael Series. **Amateur detective/Traditional**.

Keywords: Eleanor of Wynethorpe; Monks; Nuns; Prioresses

Wine of Violence. Poisoned Pen Press, 2003. 228pp. Hardbound, 1590580885.

Eleanor of Wynethorpe, a nun of some twenty-odd years, has just been installed as prioress of Tyndal, to the resentment of nearly everyone, especially Sister Ruth, who wanted the job for herself. Shortly thereafter the beloved monk Brother Rupert is found dead in Tyndal's cloister gardens. Brother Thomas a young, new priest recently punished for homosexual acts, comes to the priory to investigate their finances.

Tyrant of the Mind. Poisoned Pen Press, 2004. 241pp. Hardbound, 1590581350.

Eleanor travels with her friend and fellow nun, Lady Anne, and Brother Thomas home to Wynethorpe Castle, where her brother Robert stands accused of killing his betrothed's brother.

Sorrow Without End. Poisoned Pen Press, 2006. 232pp. Hardbound, 1590582144.

In 1271 Eleanor permits Ralf the Crowner to bring the murdered body of a soldier to Tyndal's chapel for repose while he tries to find the killer. Then others at Tyndal are subsequently murdered, putting Eleanor and Ralf on the trail of a serial killer.

Keywords: Serial killers

Justice for the Damned. Poisoned Pen Press, 2007. 229pp. Hardbound, 9781590583302.

Prioress Eleanor, recovering from a near-fatal illness, gladly accepts the invitation of her aunt Beatrice, head of novices at Amesbury Priory, to find out whether there's a real ghost, or a suspicious human being, haunting the abbey.

Forsaken Soul. Poisoned Pen, 2008. 256pp. Hardbound, 9781590585214.

During the summer of 1273 Eleanor fights her intense attraction to Brother Thomas while providing emotional support to her friend, Ralf the Crowner, whose wife recently died in childbirth. She also has to contend with her new anchoress, who has been receiving visitors at night, and with solving the murder of Martin the Cooper, a cruel man who may have been poisoned by a local whore.

Sedley, Kate.

Roger the Chapman Mysteries.

Roger the Chapman, an English peddler living during the Wars of the Roses (1470s), finds that his insatiable curiosity serves him well as a sleuth. After discovering that monastic life doesn't suit his personality, Roger turns to selling miscellaneous household wares door to door throughout the English countryside. He recounts his youthful adventures from the viewpoint of old age. Historically sound, with an engaging protagonist. **Amateur detective/Traditional.**

Keywords: Peddlers; Roger the Chapman

Death and the Chapman. St. Martin's Press, 1992. 190pp. Hardbound, 0312069456.

The Plymouth Cloak. St. Martin's Press, 1993. 192pp. Hardbound, 0312088752.

The Weaver's Tale. St. Martin's, 1994. 248pp. Hardbound, 031210474X. (Original UK title: *The Hanged Man.*)

The Holy Innocents. St. Martin's Press, 1995. 280pp. Hardbound, 0312118236.

The Eve of Saint Hyacinth. St. Martin's Press, 1996. 280pp. Hardbound, 0312143311.

The Wicked Winter. St. Martin's Press, 1999. 282pp. Hardbound, 0312206259.

The Brothers of Glastonbury. Minotaur, 2001. 279pp. Hardbound, 0312272820.

The Weaver's Inheritance. Minotaur, 2001. 247pp. Hardbound, 0312276842.

The Saint John's Fern. Minotaur, 2002. 246pp. Hardbound, 0312276834.

The Goldsmith's Daughter. Severn House, 2001. 214pp. Hardbound, 0727857320.

The Lammas Feast. Severn House, 2002. 250pp. Hardbound, 072785867X.

Nine Men Dancing. Severn House, 2003. 252pp. Hardbound, 0727859773.

The Midsummer Rose. Severn House, 2004. 249pp. Hardbound, 072786078X.

The Burgundian's Tale. Severn House, 2005. 252pp. Hardbound, 0727862162.

The Prodigal Son. Severn House, 2006. 252pp. Hardbound, 0727863371.

The Three Kings of Cologne. Severn House, 2007. 252pp. Hardbound, 9780727864819.

The Green Man. Severn House, 2008. 251pp. Hardbound, 9780727866172.

Tremayne, Peter.

Sister Fidelma Series. ★

Sister Fidelma, a young red-haired Irish "religieuse" at St. Brigid's in Kildare, was born the daughter of the king of Cashel in AD 636. Her training in the Brehon law and her role as court advocate make her a perceptive sleuth, especially in matters of politics and law. She's not as adept at matters of the heart, as shown in her affectionate but awkward relationship with Brother Eadulf, a Saxon. As Tremayne (pseudonym for Celtic scholar Peter Beresford Ellis) reveals, early medieval Ireland was the cradle of civilization and hardly deserving of the term "Dark Ages." In particular, women could serve as judges, political leaders, and lawyers, and nuns and priests were allowed to marry. Tremayne lays the history lesson on a bit thick in places, which can make his novels challenging, yet they can't be beat for a detailed portrait of ancient Ireland. **Public detective/Traditional.**

Keywords: Fidelma; Ireland—early Middle Ages; Lawyers; Nuns

Hemlock at Vespers. Minotaur, 2000. 398pp. Hardbound, 0312252889.

Absolution by Murder. St. Martin's Press, 1996. 274pp. Hardbound, 0312139187.

Shroud for the Archbishop. St. Martin's Press, 1996. 340pp. Hardbound, 0312147341.

Suffer Little Children. St. Martin's Press, 1997. 339pp. Hardbound, 0312156650.

The Subtle Serpent. St. Martin's Press, 1998. 339pp. Hardbound, 0312186703.

The Spider's Web. St. Martin's Press, 1999. 325pp. Hardbound, 0312205899.

Valley of the Shadow. St. Martin's Press, 2000. 269pp. Hardbound, 0312209398.

The Monk Who Vanished. Minotaur, 2001. 272pp. Hardbound, 0312242190.

Act of Mercy. Minotaur, 2001. 268pp. Hardbound, 0312268645.

Our Lady of Darkness. St. Martin's Press, 2002. 270pp. Hardbound, 0312272952.

Smoke in the Wind. St. Martin's Press, 2003. 267pp. Hardbound, 0312287801.

The Haunted Abbot. Minotaur, 2004. 298pp. Hardbound, 0312287690.

Whispers of the Dead. Minotaur, 2004. 370pp. Hardbound, 0312303823.

Badger's Moon. Minotaur, 2005. 265pp. Hardbound, 0312323417.

> After a lengthy partnership, Fidelma and Eadulf are the proud parents of a young son. Not accustomed to domestic life and eager to continue using her legal knowledge for the greater good, Fidelma is somewhat relieved when her cousin Becc, chieftain of the Cinel na

Aeda, requests her help in finding the killer of three young girls from his village—all of whom died during a full moon.

The Leper's Bell. Minotaur, 2006. 252pp. Hardbound, 0312323433.

In AD 667 Fidelma's investigations grow intensely personal as her baby son, Alchú, goes missing, and his nurse is found in the nearby woods, brutally murdered.

Keywords: Infants; Nurses

Master of Souls. Minotaur, 2006. 306pp. Hardbound, 0312348320.

Fidelma and Eadulf travel to the Abbey of Ard Fhearta—located in the heart of Cashel's enemies, the Uí Fidgente—to look into the death of Abbess Faife, who had been leading a pilgrimage when she was killed. Her death may be connected to several other inexplicable murders.

Keywords: Abbesses

A Prayer for the Damned. Minotaur, 2007. 320pp. Hardbound, 9780312348335.

In the year 668 Fidelma and Eadulf are to be formally wed at last, yet the celebration threatens to be disrupted when one of the guests, Abbot Ultan, is killed in his chamber. The king of Connacht, accused of the murder, asks Fidelma's help in his defense.

Keywords: Weddings

The Tudor Era

Murder and mayhem at the court of the Tudor monarchs: Henry VIII, Mary I, and Elizabeth I. In this unstable political climate, where loyalty to the wrong monarch or religion could cost you your position or even your head, tracking down a killer can be dangerous work.

Emerson, Kathy Lynn.

Susanna, Lady Appleton Mysteries. `YA`

Susanna, Lady Appleton, is an Elizabethan noblewoman-by-marriage with a talent for sleuthing. Most of the victims die by poison, so her knowledge of herbs comes in handy. The novels, set in the 1550s and 1560s, present a lively picture of Elizabethan England's numerous residents, from high-ranking courtiers and royalty to local villagers. **Amateur detective/Cozy-Traditional.**

Keywords: Herbalists; Susanna, Lady Appleton

Face Down in the Marrow-Bone Pie. St. Martin's Press, 1997. 218pp. Hardbound, 0312151233.

Face Down upon an Herbal. St. Martin's Press, 1998. 295pp. Hardbound, 0312180926.

Face Down Among the Winchester Geese. St. Martin's Press, 1999. 244pp. Hardbound, 0312205422.

Face Down Beneath the Eleanor Cross. Minotaur, 2000. 280pp. Hardbound, 0312205449.

Face Down Under the Wych Elm. Minotaur, 2000. 250pp. Hardbound, 0312265891.

Face Down Before Rebel Hooves. Minotaur, 2001. 261pp. Hardbound, 031228036X.

Face Down Across the Western Sea. Minotaur, 2002. 227pp. Hardbound, 0312288239.

Murders and Other Confusions. Crippen & Landru, 2004. 229pp. Paper, 1932009213.

Eleven short stories featuring Susanna, Lady Appleton.

Face Down Below the Banqueting House. Perseverance, 2005. 232pp. Paper, 1880284715.

> As Susanna readies her home, Leigh Abbey, for a visit by Queen Elizabeth on her progress through the countryside in 1573, two men—one the manservant of the queen's man, Brian Tymberley—meet their ends.

Face Down Beside St. Anne's Well. Perseverance, 2006. 231pp. Paper, 1880284820.

> In 1575 Susanna investigates the death of her stepdaughter Rosamund's French tutor, who has drowned in St. Anne's Well.

Face Down O'er the Border. Perseverance, 2007. 216pp. Paper, 9781880284919.

> Susanna travels to Scotland in search of her friend, Catherine, who has gone missing after her mother-in-law's murder.

> **Keywords:** Scotland—16th century

Gooden, Philip.

Nick Revill Series.

In the hectic world of Elizabethan theater, Nick Revill belongs to an elite company of actors: Lord Chamberlain's Men, a troupe partially owned by famed playwright William Shakespeare. His witty adventures and investigations in and around the Globe Theatre make for fun reading. **Amateur detective/Traditional.**

Keywords: Actors; Revill, Nick

Sleep of Death. Carroll & Graf, 2000. 310pp. Paper, 0786707623.

Death of Kings. Carroll & Graf, 2001. 310pp. Paper, 0786708751.

The Pale Companion. Carroll & Graf, 2002. 280pp. Hardbound, 078671008X.

Alms for Oblivion. Carroll & Graf, 2003. 281pp. Hardbound, 0786711426.

The Mask of Night. Carroll & Graf, 2004. 281pp. Hardbound, 0786713127.

An Honorable Murderer. Carroll & Graf, 2005. 282pp. Hardbound, 0786715286.

It's now 1604. James I is on the English throne, and the Spanish have arrived in London to celebrate a recent peace treaty with England. Nick Revill and his company, now called the King's Men, are asked to put on a play in celebration, but one of the courtiers playing a role in his production is killed in a stage accident. Uncovering the murderer reveals a wide-ranging political conspiracy.

Keywords: England—Stuart era

Harper, Karen.

Queen Elizabeth Mystery Series. ✍ YA

In the early years of Elizabeth I's reign, when Catholics loyal to the late Queen Mary are devising plots against her life, Elizabeth forms an impromptu Privy Council among her trustworthy household servants. The novels humanize the young Elizabeth, who sneaks out of her castle in disguise and investigates crimes herself in order to serve justice. (Harper used to write historical romance and now writes contemporary suspense and historical mysteries; two of her historical romances featuring royalty have been republished as traditional historicals and appear in Chapter 2.) **Amateur detective/Traditional.**

Keywords: Elizabeth I, Queen of England (historical character); Queens

The Poyson Garden. Delacorte, 1999. 310pp. Hardbound, 0385332831.

The Tidal Poole. Delacorte, 2000. 290pp. Hardbound, 038533284X.

The Twylight Tower. Delacorte, 2001. 289pp. Hardbound, 038533477X.

The Queene's Cure. Delacorte, 2002. 273pp. Hardbound, 0385334788.

The Thorne Maze. Delacorte, 2003. 290pp. Hardbound, 0312301766.

The Queene's Christmas. Thomas Dunne, 2003. 320pp. Hardbound, 0312301758.

The Fyre Mirror. Thomas Dunne, 2003. 273pp. Hardbound, 0312326920.

It is 1565, and Elizabeth is having her portrait painted at Nonsuch Castle in Surrey. One of her protégés, Gil Sharpe, a young artist just returned from Italy, is accused of killing two of his fellow portraitists.

Keywords: Artists

The Fatal Fashione. Thomas Dunne, 2006. 286pp. Hardbound, 0312338856.

The woman responsible for starching Queen Elizabeth's ruffs is found dead in a vat of starch.

Keywords: Washerwomen

The Hooded Hawke. Thomas Dunne, 2007. 272pp. Hardbound, 9780312338879.

In 1569, as Queen Elizabeth makes her summer progress through the southern English countryside, a deadly arrow kills her falconer while Elizabeth is standing right beside him.

Keywords: Falconers

Harrison, Cora.

Burren Mysteries.

Mara, Brehon of the Burren on the remote western seaboard of Ireland, uses her considerable legal knowledge to solve crimes in the late sixteenth century. With a female Irish judge and lawgiver as sleuth, Harrison's series has obvious similarities to Peter Tremayne's Sister Fidelma mysteries, but Mara is, refreshingly, an original. Harrison has also written many children's novels set in modern and historical Ireland. **Public detective/Traditional**.

Keywords: Festivals; Ireland—16th century; Judges, women

My Lady Judge. Minotaur, 2007. 368pp. Hardbound, 9780312368364.

In 1509 at the annual feast of Beltaine, Colman, Mara's assistant, is murdered atop the mountain of Mullaghmore.

A Secret and Unlawful Killing. Minotaur, 2008. 336pp. Hardbound, 9780312372682.

As residents of the Burren gather for the local Michaelmas Fair, the celebrations are interrupted by the murder of Ragnall MacNamara, steward of the MacNamaras, who was killed while out gathering his clan's Michaelmas tribute to their lord. (UK title: *Michaelmas Tribute*.)

Marston, Edward.

Nicholas Bracewell Series. YA

Nicholas Bracewell, book holder for the acting troupe Lord Westfield's Men, does his best to keep his thespians in line and out of trouble. He's not always successful. Like the novels of Simon Hawke (see volume 1 of *Historical Fiction*) and Philip Gooden, Marston's Bracewell novels are set in the world of the Elizabethan stage, circa 1580s–1590s. In comparison, though, Marston's works are both more serious and more politically involved. The Catholic threat to Elizabeth's throne and the Puritan threat to Elizabethan drama are always in the background. Edward Marston is a pseudonym of Keith Miles. **Amateur detective/Traditional.**

Keywords: Actors; Bracewell, Nicholas

The Queen's Head. St. Martin's Press, 1988. 236pp. Hardbound, 0312029705.

The Merry Devils. St. Martin's Press, 1989. 236pp. Hardbound, 0312038631.

The Trip to Jerusalem. St. Martin's Press, 1990. 222pp. Hardbound, 0312051743.

The Nine Giants. St. Martin's Press, 1991. 235pp. Hardbound, 0312064268.

The Mad Courtesan. St. Martin's Press, 1992. 252pp. Hardbound, 0312082592.

The Silent Woman. St. Martin's Press, 1994. 312pp. Hardbound, 0312111150.

The Roaring Boy. St. Martin's Press, 1995. 260pp. Hardbound, 0312131550.

The Laughing Hangman. St. Martin's Press, 1996. 248pp. Hardbound, 0312143052.

The Fair Maid of Bohemia. St. Martin's Press, 1997. 229pp. Hardbound, 0312156065.

The Wanton Angel. St. Martin's Press, 1999. 279pp . Hardbound, 0312203918.

The Devil's Apprentice. Minotaur, 2001. 273pp. Hardbound, 0312265743.

The Bawdy Basket. Minotaur, 2002. 262pp. Hardbound, 0312285019.

The Counterfeit Crank. Minotaur, 2004. 272pp. Hardbound, 0312319495.

The Malevolent Comedy. Minotaur, 2005. 245pp. Hardbound, 0312342837.

> Nicholas Bracewell's company, Lord Westfield's Men, has fallen on hard times, and hires a playwright to bring in some new business. Their plans go awry when a young actor in their new play is poisoned on opening night.

The Princess of Denmark. Minotaur, 2006. 230pp. Hardbound, 0312356188.

> After a fire destroys their Queen's Head Theatre, the members of Lord Westfield's Men sail for Denmark for the wedding of their patron, Lord Westfield, to a beautiful Danish woman he's never met, but whose portrait in miniature he admires. In the remote city of Elsinore, Lord Harling, Westfield's business agent and the intermediary who arranged his betrothal, is murdered.
>
> **Keywords:** Denmark—16th century

Peterson, Audrey.

Murder in Stratford. **Five Star, 2005. 213pp. Hardbound, 1594142734.** ✑

> This novel recounts the private lives of Anne Hathaway and Will Shakespeare in addition to presenting a murder mystery. Anne tells not only about her experience with detection—clearing her husband Will from the murder of a family friend in their garden in Stratford-upon-Avon— but also about their courtship and her life spent raising their children while he pursues his dreams as an actor and playwright in London. **Amateur detective/Traditional**.
>
> **Keywords:** Hathaway, Anne (historical character); Married life; Playwrights; Shakespeare, William (historical character)

Pilkington, John.

Thomas the Falconer Series.

> Thomas Finbow, falconer to Sir Robert Vicary in 1580s and 1590s England, investigates crimes on behalf of his master and proves surprisingly good at it. Along the way, readers of these atmospheric period mysteries will learn not only about falconry but also about country life in Elizabethan times. **Amateur detective/Traditional**.
>
> **Keywords:** Falconers; Thomas the Falconer

The Ruffler's Child. London: Robert Hale, 2002. 224pp. Hardbound, 0709070578.

A Ruinous Wind. Severn House, 2003. 230pp. Hardbound, 0727860313.

The Ramage Hawk. Severn House, 2004. 234pp. Hardbound, 0727860879.

The Mapmaker's Daughter. Severn House, 2005. 250pp. Hardbound, 0727861603.

The Maiden Bell. Severn House, 2005. 218pp. Hardbound, 0727862936.

The Jingler's Luck. Severn House, 2006. 215pp. Hardbound, 0727863738.

The Muscovy Chain. Severn House, 2007. 203pp. Hardbound, 9780727865434.

The Stuart Era

Murder mysteries of the Stuart era focus almost exclusively on the Restoration period (late seventeenth century), after Charles II returned to claim the English throne. Their gaudy, bawdy atmosphere reflects the times as well as the character of the Merry Monarch himself. A sparse category for new titles.

Gregory, Susanna.

Thomas Chaloner Series.

Gregory, best known for her <u>Matthew Bartholomew series</u> set in medieval Cambridge (see previously in this chapter), begins a new series set three centuries later. Thomas Chaloner, a former government spy, returns to London from Holland after Charles II resumes his throne in 1660. Needing employment, Chaloner takes a position spying for his ex-boss John Thurloe, an ex-Parliamentarian who's now secretary of State. **Public detective/Traditional.**

Keywords: Chaloner, Thomas; Spies

A Conspiracy of Violence. Trafalgar Square (Time Warner UK), 2006. 502pp. Hardbound, 0316731102.

Blood on the Strand. Trafalgar Square (Time Warner UK), 2007. 457pp. Hardbound, 9781847440020.

The Butcher of Smithfield. Trafalgar Square (Time Warner UK), 2008. 503pp. Hardbound, 9781847440624.

The Georgian and Regency Eras

Mysteries set during the Georgian period (1714–1837, which includes the Regency) juxtapose two different sides of English society. They can either re-create the witty dialogue and fashion-conscious world of the upper classes, as Regency romances do, or they can contrast the modes of London's upper crust with the dingy, poverty-stricken side of the city. Some do both.

Alexander, Bruce.

Sir John Fielding Series. ✍

Sir John Fielding, the half-brother of novelist and magistrate Henry Fielding, took over his sibling's duties as chief of London's first police force, the "Bow Street Runners," from 1754 to 1780. What made his accomplishments all the more remarkable was that he was completely blind. Alexander's mystery series re-creates the activities of the real-life "Blind Beak" in rooting out criminals in a city overrun with prostitutes, gangs of pickpockets, highwaymen who preyed on travelers, and slum children with no good way to earn a living. Yet Fielding is also a compassionate judge of character, as he proves in the first book when he gives young Jeremy Proctor a break. Alexander, a pseudonym for Bruce Alexander Cook, died in 2003; his wife, Judith, assisted in the completion of his final novel. **Public detective/Traditional.**

Keywords: Blindness; Fielding, Sir John (historical character); Policemen; Proctor, Jeremy

Blind Justice. Putnam, 1994. 254pp. Hardbound, 0399139788.

Murder in Grub Street. Putnam, 1995. 276pp. Hardbound.

Watery Grave. Putnam, 1996. 265pp. Hardbound.

Person or Persons Unknown. Putnam, 1997. 279pp. Hardbound, 0399143092.

Jack, Knave and Fool. Putnam, 1998. 279pp. Hardbound, 0399144196.

Death of a Colonial. Putnam, 1999. 275pp. Hardbound, 0399145648.

The Color of Death. Putnam, 2000. 279pp. Hardbound, 0399146482.

Smuggler's Moon. Putnam, 2001. 247pp. Hardbound, 0399147748.

An Experiment in Treason. Putnam, 2002. 247pp. Hardbound, 0399149236.

The Price of Murder. Putnam, 2003. 257pp. Hardbound, 0399150781.

Rules of Engagement. Putnam, 2005. 243pp. Hardbound, 0399152423.

> Lord Lammermoor, an old school chum of the Lord Chief Justice, plunges to his death from Westminster Bridge in full view of many witnesses. It's up to Fielding and his protégé, Jeremy Proctor, to prove that he was, in fact, murdered, possibly through hypnosis.

Barron, Stephanie.

Jane Austen Mysteries. ✍ YA

Jane Austen (1775–1817), whose novels of early nineteenth-century English society and manners were the inspiration for many Regency romance writers, does some investigating of her own. The novels are set in late Georgian England (early nineteenth century), primarily in Bath, where Austen lived. Written in Austen's own style—complete with witty dialogue, formal phrasings, leisurely pacing, and lengthy digressions—Barron's novels let readers experience Austen's keen psychological insight firsthand. Jane narrates each novel, paying attention to even the smallest historical details. Footnotes about the real-life Austen's life and acquaintances are interspersed throughout the text. (The pseudonym "Stephanie Barron" uses the middle and maiden names of mystery novelist Francine Mathews.) **Amateur detective/Cozy.**

Keywords: Austen, Jane (historical character); Authors, women

Jane and the Unpleasantness at Scargrave Manor. Bantam, 1996. 289pp. Hardbound, 055310196X.

Jane and the Man of the Cloth. Bantam, 1997. 274pp. Hardbound, 0553102036.

Jane and the Wandering Eye. Bantam, 1998. 262pp. Hardbound, 0553102044.

Jane and the Genius of the Place. Bantam, 1999. 290pp. Hardbound, 055310733X.

Jane and the Stillroom Maid. Bantam, 2000. 277pp. Hardbound, 0553107348.

Jane and the Prisoner of Wool House. Bantam, 2001. 291pp. Hardbound, 0553107356.

Jane and the Ghosts of Netley. Bantam, 2003. 294pp. Hardbound, 0553802224.

Jane and His Lordship's Legacy. Bantam, 2005. 384pp. Hardbound, 0553802259.

In 1809 Jane and her mother move to Chawton in the Hampshire countryside. Jane is surprised to find that Lord Harold Trowbridge, her good friend who died in *Jane and the Ghosts of Netley*, has left her a collection of his personal papers. She plans to write his biography, but before she can do so she finds the body of a murdered man in the cellar of her cottage.

Jane and the Barque of Frailty. Bantam, 2006. 304pp. Hardbound, 0553802267.

"Barque of frailty" is the contemporary (circa 1811) nickname for a courtesan, and in this latest case of Austen's, it's a Russian princess who meets her death outside the home of a well-known Tory politician. Jane, visiting her brother Henry in London while preparing *Sense and Sensibility* for printing, finds that she and her sister-in-law are accused of murder after the princess's jewels are found in their possession.

Keywords: Courtesans; Princesses

Bebris, Carrie.

Mr. & Mrs. Darcy Mysteries. `YA`

Elizabeth Bennet and Fitzwilliam Darcy, the happy couple from Jane Austen's *Pride and Prejudice*, have been married in a double ceremony with Elizabeth's sister Jane and her fiancé, Charles Bingley. Bebris continues their story in these quasi-sequels, though here Elizabeth and Darcy have become detectives. Regency mysteries with Gothic elements; *The Matters at Mansfield* will be the fourth volume. **Amateur detective/Cozy.**

Keywords: Austen themes; Bennet, Elizabeth; Darcy, Fitzwilliam; England—Regency era; Gothic novels; Married life

Pride and Prescience. Forge, 2003. 287pp. Hardbound, 0765305089.

Suspense and Sensibility. Forge, 2005. 304pp. Hardbound, 0765305097.

> In 1813 Elizabeth's sister Kitty experiences her first London Season, with Elizabeth and Darcy as sponsors. When Harry Dashwood expresses a romantic interest, the Darcys eventually give their approval to the match, but then Harry begins acting very strangely.

North by Northanger. Forge, 2006. 320pp. Hardbound, 076531410X.

> Elizabeth Darcy, thrilled about her first pregnancy, discovers an unusual letter written by her late mother-in-law in which she mentions a lost family heirloom.

Gabaldon, Diana.

Lord John Grey Novels.

Lord John Grey began as a minor character in the author's <u>Outlander</u> novels (annotated in Chapter 4). A high-ranking officer in His Majesty's Army in the 1750s, Major Grey, a secret homosexual, solves crimes for the crown and tries to keep his private life from being discovered. With its darker tone and its vivid depictions of the gay subculture in Georgian England, these well-written mysteries may surprise readers who expect more of Gabaldon's romantic adventure stories. **Amateur detective/Traditional.**

Keywords: Gay men; Grey, Lord John; Spies

Lord John and the Private Matter. Delacorte, 2003. 305pp. Hardbound, 0385337477.

Lord John and the Brotherhood of the Blade. Delacorte, 2007. 494pp. Hardbound, 9780385337496

> In 1758 Grey comes across evidence from seventeen years prior—a page from the diary of his late father, the duke of Pardloe—that suggests he may not have killed himself from shame after being accused of being a Jacobite spy. Grey teams up with an old enemy, Jamie Fraser from Gabaldon's <u>Outlander</u> novels, to discern the truth.

Lord John and the Hand of Death. Delacorte, 2007. 302pp. Hardbound, 9780385311397.

> A collection of three novellas (*Lord John and the Hellfire Club, Lord John and the Succubus, Lord John and the Haunted Soldier*) about Gabaldon's detective hero, Lord John Grey. Characters from her <u>Outlander</u> series make occasional appearances.

Gardner, Ashley.

Captain Gabriel Lacey Series.

A series starring Captain Gabriel Lacey, a veteran of the Peninsular Campaign against Napoleon. Lacey narrates the novels, which encompass all classes of people in Regency England. (Gardner is a pseudonym of Jennifer Ashley, who writes romances and traditional historical novels under her own name; she has also written as Laurien Gardner.) **Amateur detective/Traditional.**

Keywords: England—Regency era; Lacey, Captain Gabriel; Napoleonic Wars; Soldiers

The Hanover Square Affair. Berkley Prime Crime, 2003. 262pp. Paper, 0425193306.

A Regimental Murder. Berkley Prime Crime, 2004. 248pp. Paper, 0425196127.

The Glass House. Berkley Prime Crime, 2004. 249pp. Paper, 0425199436.

> In 1817 one of the female regulars at the "Glass House," a place where members of Society indulge in exotic vice, is found dead in the Thames. Lacey discovers her true identity as a barrister's wife.

The Sudbury School Murders. Berkley Prime Crime, 2005. 295pp. Paper, 0425203611.

> In order to look into mysterious deaths there, Lacey takes a position as secretary to the headmaster of the Sudbury School, an institution of education for the sons of wealthy Englishmen.
>
> **Keywords:** Schools

A Body in Berkeley Square. Berkley Prime Crime, 2005. 252pp. Paper, 0425207285.

> Lacey has always had an awkward relationship with his former commanding officer, Colonel Brandon, yet chooses to stand by him when he's accused of murder.

A Covent Garden Mystery. Berkley Prime Crime, 2006. 282pp. Paper, 0425210863.

> Lacey faces several professional and personal crises: street girls are disappearing from Covent Garden, his long-estranged wife seeks a divorce, and his daughter, Gabriella, has vanished.

Harris, C. S.

Sebastian St. Cyr Regency Mystery Series.

Harris delves into the dark side of Regency England as her dashing hero, Sebastian St. Cyr, Viscount Devlin, uses his experience in espionage during the Napoleonic Wars to good effect. Because of his social status as the only surviving son of the earl of Hendon, Sebastian ably moves between refined, upper-crust society and the Regency underworld to solve crimes. The novels, replete with political intrigue and rich historical detail, provide a nearly comprehensive picture of early nineteenth-century British life, in all its glamour and depravity. Harris, who has a PhD in European history, formerly wrote historical romances as Candice Proctor. **Amateur detective/Traditional**.

Keywords: England—Regency era; Nobility; St. Cyr, Sebastian

What Angels Fear. NAL, 2005. 341pp. Hardbound, 0451216695.

> In 1811 a sexton discovers the body of a brutally murdered young actress, Rachel York, near the altar of the Church of St. Matthew of the Fields. A pistol at the scene connects Sebastian to the crime, forcing him to find the real murderer in order to clear his name.
>
> **Keywords:** Actresses

When Gods Die. NAL, 2006. 352pp. Hardbound, 0451219686.

> With King George III incapacitated, England's populace worries about the stability of the realm with the dissolute Prince of Wales as regent. This is especially true when he is discovered with the body of a beautiful dead marchioness in his arms; Sebastian investigates.

Keywords: Princes

Why Mermaids Sing. NAL, 2007. 342pp. Hardbound, 9780451222268.

> The sons of some of London's wealthiest, most well-established families are being murdered in grisly fashion. Their bodies are found mutilated, and stuffed in their mouths are an odd collection of items relating to one of John Donne's poems.

Keywords: Serial killers

Wynn, Patricia.

Blue Satan Mystery Series.

It is 1715, and George, Elector of Hanover, has become King George I of England. Falsely accused of killing his father, Gideon Fitzsimmons, Viscount St. Mars goes into hiding and reemerges as the highwayman Blue Satan. Hester Kean assists with his investigations. **Amateur detective/Traditional.**

Keywords: Blue Satan; Highwaymen; Jacobites; Nobility; Printers

The Birth of Blue Satan. Pemberley Press, 2001. 325pp. Hardbound, 0970272707.

The Spider's Touch. Pemberley Press, 2002. 390pp. Hardbound, 097027274X.

The Motive for the Deed. Pemberley, 2007. 378pp. Hardbound, 0977191338.

> In 1715 supporters of the Jacobites launch a rebellion against the crown, and a result all Catholics are banished from London. Hester Kean's brother, Jeremy, is sent to Newgate Prison for printing seditious pamphlets; he is also accused of murdering the bookseller who employed him.

The Victorian Era

The social lives of men and women of all classes dominate the plots of murder mysteries set in Victorian times (1837–1901). Death strikes both the rich and the poor in equal numbers. If nothing else, these mysteries prove that the wealthier a person is, the more secrets he or she has to hide. In this category, the first pastiches of Conan Doyle's Sherlock Holmes stories begin to appear.

Alexander, Tasha.

Emily Ashton Series.

Lady Emily Ashton, a beautiful Victorian widow, discovers newfound independence after the early death of her aristocrat husband, Philip, a man she barely got a chance to know. She loves to read and also conceives a passion for classical antiquities after learning more about her late husband's interests. Light, witty dialogue, Greek archaeology, romance, and dark suspense. **Amateur detective/Traditional.**

Keywords: Archaeology; Ashton, Emily; Imposters; Nobility; Widows

And Only to Deceive. Morrow, 2005. 310pp. Hardbound, 0060756713.

Emily Bromley decides to marry Viscount Philip Ashton to escape her overbearing mother's pressure to marry. Several months later he dies while on safari in Africa, leaving Emily a wealthy widow who's not exactly overwhelmed with grief. With plenty of time on her hands during her forced mourning period, she begins learning more about Philip's interest in the *Iliad* and ancient Greek artifacts, of which he had amassed a large collection. To Emily's surprise, she learns how much Philip had loved her; she also discovers that some of the artifacts he donated to the British Museum may have been forgeries.

A Poisoned Season. Morrow, 2007. 320pp. Hardbound, 9780061174148.

With her penchant for port and reading ancient Greek literature in the original, Emily has become known for her unconventional behavior. When she arrives in London for the latest Season, she grows curious about the identity of a stranger claiming to be descended from Marie Antoinette. Then several objects once owned by the late queen are stolen.

A Fatal Waltz. Morrow, 2008. 304pp. Hardbound, 9780061174223.

With reluctance, Emily agrees to attend a country house party on the estate of Lord Fortescue, whom she dislikes (the feeling is mutual). Things worsen when Emily learns that her fiancé's former paramour, the Countess von Lange, was also invited. When Fortescue is murdered, Emily stops at nothing to clear the name of her best friend's husband, who was seen arguing with him just before his death. The investigation takes her to Vienna and forces her to work closely with the countess.

Brandreth, Gyles.

Oscar Wilde Murder Mysteries.

Oscar Wilde, the Irish dramatist with the devastating wit, takes center stage in this new series of classic murder mysteries set in fin de siècle London. **Amateur detective/Traditional.**

Keywords: Authors; Playwrights; Prostitutes; Wilde, Oscar (historical character)

Oscar Wilde and a Death of No Importance. Touchstone, 2008. 368pp. Hardbound, 9781416551744. (UK title: *Oscar Wilde and the Candlelight Murders.*)

In 1889 Oscar and his friend Arthur Conan Doyle investigate the death of a teenaged boy whose nude body was found surrounded by candles. This leads them to uncover a ring of male prostitution.

Keywords: Conan Doyle, Arthur (historical character)

Oscar Wilde and a Game Called Murder. Touchstone, 2008. 288pp. Hardbound, 9781416575795. (UK title: *Oscar Wilde and the Ring of Death.*)

By 1892 Oscar has become a successful playwright. A dinner party game played by him and his literary luminary friends—one in which they playfully name individuals they wouldn't mind killing, if they could get away with it—turns deadly when one of their "victims" is murdered for real.

Carr, Caleb.

The Italian Secretary. **Carroll & Graf, 2005. 263pp. Hardbound, 0786715480.**
Another investigation of Sherlock Holmes and company: Holmes, Watson, and Holmes's brother Mycroft investigate the deaths of two builders who had been renovating Queen Victoria's royal palace of Holyrood in Edinburgh. The deaths of the two men call to mind David Rizzio, the music teacher/secretary of Mary, Queen of Scots, stabbed to death 300 years earlier by supporters of Elizabeth I. Carr's most recent novel (he's also the author of *The Alienist*, one of the first historical thrillers) was commissioned by Sir Arthur Conan Doyle's estate. **Private detective/Traditional.**

Keywords: Musicians; Scotland; Sherlock Holmes retellings and themes

Dickinson, David.

Lord Francis Powerscourt Mysteries.
Murder surrounds the British royal family in the last years of Queen Victoria's reign and the early years of the Edwardian era. Lord Francis Powerscourt, an Irish peer with a talent for espionage, tries to protect the royal family's interests. **Amateur detective/Traditional.**

Keywords: Nobility; Powerscourt, Lord Francis

Goodnight, Sweet Prince. Carroll & Graf, 2002. 314pp. Hardbound, 0786709456.

Death and the Jubilee. Carroll & Graf, 2003. 344pp. Hardbound, 0786711108.

Death of an Old Master. Carroll & Graf, 2004. 314pp. Hardbound, 0786713062.

Death of a Chancellor. Carroll & Graf, 2005. 313pp. Hardbound, 0786714921.
In 1901 Powerscourt returns to England after an espionage mission in South Africa during the Boer War and is hired by the sister of the late chancellor of Compton Cathedral to look into his suspicious death.

Death Called to the Bar. Carroll & Graf, 2006. 288pp. Hardbound, 0786716967.
During a formal dinner one of Powerscourt's fellow barristers falls face-down into his bowl of borscht Romanov, leading Powerscourt on a chase to find out who poisoned him.

Keywords: Lawyers

Death on the Nevskii Prospekt. Carroll & Graf, 2007. 256pp. Hardbound, 0786718978.
In 1904, after some time spent in other, less dangerous pursuits at the request of his concerned wife, Lucy, Powerscourt journeys to Russia to investigate the murder of a British diplomat.

Keywords: Diplomats; Russia—20th century

Death on the Holy Mountain. Soho Constable, 2008. 312pp. Hardbound, 9781569475034.

>Powerscourt travels to Ireland in 1905 to find out why portraits of Protestant aristocrats are being stolen. A simple case of art theft turns grisly when the paintings' subjects begin showing up dead.
>
>**Keywords:** Ireland—20th century; Portraits

Finch, Charles.

Charles Lenox Chronicles. `YA`

Charles Lenox, a wealthy aristocrat and armchair adventurer in London in 1865, solves murders alongside his good friend and neighbor, Lady Jane Grey. This leisurely paced series boasts an attractively scholarly sleuth and enough twists and turns in the plot to keep readers guessing. **Amateur detective/Traditional.**

Keywords: Lenox, Charles; Nobility

A Beautiful Blue Death. Minotaur, 2007. 320pp. Hardbound, 9780312359775.

>Charles is called in to solve the murder of Lady Jane's former maid, whose poisoning death was set up to look like suicide.
>
>**Keywords:** Maids

The September Society. Minotaur, 2008. 320pp. Hardbound, 9780312359782.

>A recent crime in London, circa 1866, has direct connections to an earlier murder that took place in India nearly twenty years ago. Lady Annabelle Payson, a widow, asks Lenox to find her missing son George, an undergraduate student at Oxford, whose dorm room reveals a murdered cat and a note bearing reference to the "September Society."
>
>**Keywords:** Students

Granger, Ann.

The Companion. **Minotaur, 2007. 320pp. Hardbound, 9780312363376.**

Elizabeth "Lizzie" Martin, daughter of a poor country doctor in 1864, relocates to London to take a position as companion to her wealthy Aunt Parry, her aunt's previous companion having eloped—or so she believes. Lizzie works closely with one of her friends from childhood, Inspector Benjamin Ross of Scotland Yard, once the pair discovers that her predecessor was in fact murdered, her body found in an abandoned house scheduled to be demolished. (UK title: *A Rare Interest in Corpses.*) **Amateur detective/Traditional.**

Keywords: Companions

Gray, John MacLachlan.

Edmund Whitty Series.

Fleet Street journalist Edmund Whitty finds subjects for his lurid stories (and crimes) in perhaps the likeliest of places: Victorian London's dark alleyways, slums, gaming clubs, and houses of prostitution. **Amateur detective/Traditional.**

Keywords: Journalists and reporters; Whitty, Edmund

The Fiend in Human. Minotaur, 2003. 352pp. Hardbound, 0312282842.

White Stone Day. Minotaur, 2005. 304pp. Hardbound, 0312282931.

> Two story lines cross and overlap: in his journalistic guise, Whitty attends a séance, where his dead brother's spirit supposedly contacts him. Meanwhile, at his Oxfordshire estate a creepy minister (based on Lewis Carroll) delights in taking photographs of young girls.
>
> **Keywords:** Séances

Marston, Edward.

Inspector Robert Colbeck Mysteries.

The prolific Marston (pseudonym of Keith Miles, who writes historical mysteries set in many different historical periods) sets this series in Victorian England. His detective, Robert Colbeck of the newly formed Metropolitan Police in London, is charged with solving murders connected to Britain's railways, one of the country's primary means of transport. Marston also writes mysteries as Conrad Allen and military historical novels (Chapter 2) as David Garland. **Public detective/ Traditional.**

Keywords: Policemen; Railroads

The Railway Detective. Allison & Busby, 2004. 261pp. Hardbound, 0749006331.

The Excursion Train. Allison & Busby, 2005. 270pp. Hardbound, 0749083921.

The Railway Viaduct. Allison & Busby, 2006. 269pp. Hardbound, 0749081805.

The Iron Horse. Allison & Busby, 2007. 334pp. Hardbound, 9780749080808.

Myers, Amy.

Tom Wasp and the Murdered Stunner. **Five Star, 2007. 247pp. Hardbound, 9781594145933.**

> Tom Wasp, a chimney sweep in England in 1862, is distraught when the body of his good friend Bessie Barton, a beautiful artists' model, washes up on the bank of the Thames. As he and his eleven-year-old apprentice Ned track her killer, their path winds through some of the most disreputable and poverty-stricken areas of London and leads ultimately to one person: the Moonman, the mysterious someone whose presence Bessie had fled years earlier. Tom narrates the story in his own lively voice. **Amateur detective/Traditional.**
>
> **Keywords:** Artists' models; Chimney sweeps

Paige, Robin.

Victorian Mysteries/Edwardian Mysteries.

Kathryn (Kate) Ardleigh, an outspoken Irish American author of penny-dreadfuls (dime novels), hardly fits the image of a proper Victorian gentlewoman. After serving as companion to an aunt she hadn't known she had, Sabrina Ardleigh of Bishop's Keep in Essex, Kate later inherits her estate. There Kate meets Sir Charles Sheridan, a peer of the realm and an amateur scientist, who becomes her sleuthing partner and husband. Cozy mysteries featuring famous people from Victorian times, from literary figures to royalty. The novels take place from the late Victorian (1890s) through the early Edwardian (1903) periods, hence the double series title. ("Robin Paige" is the pseudonym of married authors Susan Wittig Albert and William Albert.) **Amateur detective/Cozy.**

Keywords: Authors, women; Nobility; Sheridan, Kate

Death at Bishop's Keep. Avon, 1994. 266pp. Paper, 0425164357.

Death at Gallows Green. Avon, 1995. 267pp. Paper, 0425163997.

Death at Daisy's Folly. Berkley Prime Crime, 1997. 274pp. Paper, 0425156710.

Death at Devil's Bridge. Berkley Prime Crime, 1998. 274pp. Paper, 0425161951.

Death at Rottingdean. Berkley Prime Crime, 1999. 290pp. Paper, 0425167828.

Death at Whitechapel. Berkley Prime Crime, 2000. 276pp. Paper, 0425173410.

Death at Epsom Downs. Berkley Prime Crime, 2001. 292pp. Hardbound, 0425178072.

Death at Dartmoor. Berkley Prime Crime, 2002. 324pp. Hardbound, 0425183424.

Death at Glamis Castle. Berkley Prime Crime, 2003. 338pp. Hardbound, 0425188477.

Death in Hyde Park. Berkley Prime Crime, 2004. 304pp. Hardbound, 0425194191.

Death at Blenheim Palace. Berkley Prime Crime, 2005. 309pp. Hardbound, 0425200353.

> While visiting the duke and duchess of Marlborough at Blenheim Palace in the course of researching one of her novels, Kate looks into the disappearance of Kitty, one of the estate's housemaids.
>
> **Keywords:** Maids; Vanderbilt, Consuelo (historical character)

Death on the Lizard. Berkley Prime Crime, 2006. 328pp. Hardbound, 042520779X.

This final entry in the series focuses on the advent of new technology, circa 1903, proving that some things never change. In Cornwall, Lord Charles hurriedly investigates a number of incidents of sabotage surrounding Marconi's wireless telegraph company, in the hopes that he'll solve the mystery before the Prince and Princess of Wales come by to observe the telegraph in action.

Keywords: Telegraph

Peacock, Caro.

A Foreign Affair. **Avon A, 2008. 331pp. Paper, 9780061445897.**

In 1837, the very first year of Victoria's reign, there are some who would prefer to see their own candidates on England's throne rather than the current young queen. Liberty (Libby) Lane, a spirited young woman grieving over her beloved father's recent death in a duel in France, vows to discover whether he was deliberately murdered. The trail leads her into a conspiracy that could topple the monarchy. This is expected to be the first in an early Victorian series featuring Liberty Lane. Peacock is the pseudonym of Gillian Linscott, who previously wrote historical crime novels featuring Nell Bray, early twentieth-century suffragette. (UK title: *Death at Dawn.*) **Amateur detective/Traditional.**

Keywords: Duels

Perry, Anne.

Thomas & Charlotte Pitt Mysteries. ★ 📖

Perry's vision of Victorian London is a study in contrasts: its elegant houses, drawing rooms, and high society parties exist alongside all the social ills of the day. Police Inspector Thomas Pitt, who grew up as the son of servants, forms an unlikely romantic and professional partnership with Charlotte Ellison, a gently bred young woman. A romantic relationship between a socialite and a policeman is hardly acceptable in Britain's class-conscious society, but Charlotte is never one to follow the rules. Through his marriage to Charlotte, Pitt gains entrance to the world of London's elite. Set in the 1880s and 1890s. **Public detective/Traditional.**

Keywords: Pitt, Thomas; Policemen

The Cater Street Hangman. St. Martin's Press, 1979. 247pp. Hardbound, 031212385X.

Callander Square. St. Martin's Press, 1980. 221pp. Hardbound, 0312114303.

Paragon Walk. St. Martin's Press, 1981. 204pp. Hardbound, 0312595980.

Resurrection Row. St. Martin's Press, 1981. 204pp. Hardbound, 0312677979.

Rutland Place. St. Martin's Press, 1983. 235pp. Hardbound, 0312696213.

Bluegate Fields. St. Martin's Press, 1984. 308pp. Hardbound, 0312087187.

Death in the Devil's Acre. St. Martin's Press, 1985. 248pp. Hardbound, 0312188692.

Cardington Crescent. St. Martin's Press, 1987. 314pp. Hardbound, 0312001134.

Silence in Hanover Close. St. Martin's Press, 1988. 341pp. Hardbound, 031201824X.

Bethlehem Road. St. Martin's Press, 1990. Hardbound, 031204266.

Highgate Rise. Fawcett Columbine, 1991. 330pp. Hardbound, 0449905675.

Belgrave Square. Fawcett Columbine, 1992. 361pp. Hardbound, 0449906787.

Farriers' Lane. Fawcett Columbine, 1993. 374pp. Hardbound, 0449905691.

The Hyde Park Headsman. Fawcett Columbine, 1994. 392pp. Hardbound, 0449906361.

Traitor's Gate. Fawcett Columbine, 1995. 411pp. Hardbound, 0449906345.

Pentecost Alley. Fawcett Columbine, 1996. 405pp. Hardbound, 0449906353.

Ashworth Hall. Fawcett Columbine, 1997. 373pp. Hardbound, 0449908445.

Brunswick Gardens. Fawcett Columbine, 1998. 389pp. Hardbound, 0449908453.

Bedford Square. Ballantine, 1999. 330pp. Hardbound, 0449006964.

Half Moon Street. Ballantine, 2000. 312pp. Hardbound, 0345433270.

The Whitechapel Conspiracy. Ballantine, 2001. 341pp. Hardbound, 0345433289.

Southampton Row. Ballantine, 2002. 326pp. Hardbound, 034544003X.

Seven Dials. Ballantine, 2003. 345pp. Hardbound, 0345440072.

Long Spoon Lane. Ballantine, 2005. 323pp. Hardbound, 0345469275.

> After anarchists blow up a building, Thomas Pitt tracks the perpetrators to Long Spoon Lane, and a young nobleman is killed in the gunfire that ensues.
>
> **Keywords:** Anarchists

Buckingham Palace Gardens. Ballantine, 2008. 230pp. Hardbound, 9780755320608.

> After a high-powered meeting at Buckingham Palace, ostensibly to plan a railroad that would bisect Africa from north to south, one of the prostitutes brought in to entertain the participants is found murdered. Pitt is brought in to solve the case, in as hush-hush a manner as possible. Gracie Phipps, the Pittses' longtime maid, proves invaluable when she goes undercover at the palace.
>
> **Keywords:** Maids; Prostitutes; Spies

William Monk Novels. ★ 📖

William Monk, a London police detective circa 1856, turns to private investigation after disputing some of the force's official methods. Affected with amnesia, he occasionally gets glimpses of the man he used to be and doesn't like what he sees: a hard man, shrewd and intelligent, but disliked by many. Hester Latterly, a no-nonsense nurse who served with Florence Nightingale in the Crimean War, has an uncanny sense of people's true character. As Hester assists in Monk's investigations, she frequently steals the show. Perry's novels all contain excellent depictions of Victorian society—cobblestone streets, gas-lit alleys, and elegant drawing rooms—that never intrude on the suspense. Most end with dramatic courtroom scenes, with brilliant barrister Oliver Rathbone for the defense. **Private detective/Traditional.**

Keywords: Amnesia; Monk, William

The Face of a Stranger. Fawcett Columbine, 1990. 328pp. Hardbound, 0449905306.

A Dangerous Mourning. Fawcett Columbine, 1991. 330pp. Hardbound, 0449905543.

Defend and Betray. Fawcett Columbine, 1992. 385pp. Hardbound, 0449907554.

A Sudden, Fearful Death. Fawcett Columbine, 1993. 383pp. Hardbound, 044990637X.

The Sins of the Wolf. Fawcett Columbine, 1994. 374pp. Hardbound, 0449906388.

Cain His Brother. Fawcett Columbine, 1995. 390pp. Hardbound, 044990847X.

Weighed in the Balance. Fawcett Columbine, 1996. 355pp. Hardbound, 0449910784.

The Silent Cry. Fawcett Columbine, 1997. 361pp. Hardbound, 0449908488.

A Breach of Promise. Fawcett Columbine, 1998. 374pp. Hardbound, 0449908496. (Original title: *White Sepulchres.*)

The Twisted Root. Ballantine, 1999. 346pp. Hardbound, 0345433254.

Slaves of Obsession. Ballantine, 2001. 344pp. Hardbound. (Original title: *Slaves and Obsession.*)

Funeral in Blue. Ballantine, 2002. 344pp. Hardbound, 0345440013.

Death of a Stranger. Ballantine, 2003. 337pp. Hardbound, 0345440056.

The Shifting Tide. Ballantine, 2004. 352pp. Hardbound, 0345440099.

Dark Assassin. Ballantine, 2006. 320pp. Hardbound, 0345469291.

> As the new superintendent of the Thames River Police, while on patrol with his men Monk sees two young lovers plummet to their deaths from a bridge. The woman's background (she was looking into her father's mysterious demise) makes it unlikely she committed suicide.

Raybourn, Deanna.

Julia Grey Series. 📖

Raybourn balances historical detail, suspense, and the darker aspects of Victorian society with humor and whimsy in her ongoing series featuring Lady Julia Grey, a Victorian aristocrat, new widow, and very unlikely amateur detective. She solves crimes while attempting to cope with her very eccentric English family and trying to deny her attraction to the debonair and mysterious Nicholas Brisbane, her late husband's private enquiry agent. **Amateur detective/Traditional.**

Keywords: Grey, Lady Julia; Nobility; Widows

🦅 *Silent in the Grave.* Mira, 2007. 519pp. Hardbound, 9780778324102.

It is 1886, and Sir Edward Grey has just collapsed and died during a dinner party at his London townhouse. The family doctor blames Edward's heart condition, and his wife, Julia, believes him—despite suggestions by Edward's private enquiry agent, Nicholas Brisbane, that it was murder. Over a year later Julia comes across compelling evidence that proves Brisbane was right. As the pair follow a trail that should have gone cold long ago, Julia uncovers unpleasant and sordid facts about her late husband's behavior, as well as surprising truths about herself. RITA Award.

Silent in the Sanctuary. Mira, 2008. 553pp. Paper, 9780778324928.

After six months in sunny Italy, Lady Julia comes home to her family's Sussex estate, and she and Nicholas Brisbane tease and annoy one another with their new admirers. Then one of her family's many houseguests is murdered in their chapel, and her cousin, oddly enough, confesses to the crime.

Rowland, Laura Joh.

The Secret Adventures of Charlotte Brontë. **Overlook, 2008. 378pp. Hardbound, 9781590200339.** ✍

In 1848 Charlotte Brontë, a parson's daughter and pseudonymously successful author from the small village of Haworth in Yorkshire, travels to London with her sister Anne after her publisher accuses her of breaching her contract. On the train trip there they encounter a young governess, Isabel White, whose personal story moves them. When Isabel is subsequently murdered, Charlotte vows to find out who killed her. Sisters Anne and Emily come along for the ride, which becomes dangerous and breathtakingly romantic in turns. Rowland, best known for her mysteries of seventeenth-century Japan (see end of this chapter), chose to write about Charlotte Brontë as a way of honoring an author she had long admired and to give her a way to experience the adventurous life she secretly wanted to lead. **Amateur detective/Traditional.**

Keywords: Authors, women; Brontë, Charlotte (historical character); Brontë family (historical characters)

Thomas, Will.

Barker & Llewelyn Novels.

Scottish private enquiry agent Cyrus Barker and his intrepid young Welsh apprentice, Thomas Llewelyn, make a delightful team as they investigate cases throughout the British Isles in the 1880s. Barker is a rather smug and enigmatic fellow whose secret past is gradually revealed throughout the series; Llewelyn narrates their adventures. Authentic settings and explorations of social issues not often seen in Victorian mysteries are two of this series' hallmarks. **Private detective/Traditional.**

Keywords: Barker, Cyrus; Llewelyn, Thomas

Some Danger Involved. Touchstone, 2004. 304pp. Hardbound, 0743256182.

> In Victorian London, Barker and Llewelyn look into the crucifixion death of a young Jewish student; the perpetrators may be anti-Semites looking to begin a pogrom against the city's Jews.

> **Keywords:** Jews; Prejudice

To Kingdom Come. Touchstone, 2005. 277pp. Hardbound, 0743256220.

> Irish dissidents are being blamed for bombing the new Special Irish Branch of Scotland Yard, so Barker and Llewelyn pose as German explosives experts and infiltrate the group known as the Irish Republican Brotherhood. Preventing the group's ultimate mission—to destroy the monarchy once and for all—takes them to Wales, Liverpool, and Paris.

> **Keywords:** France; Revolutions and revolutionaries; Terrorists; Wales

The Limehouse Text. Touchstone, 2006. 337pp. Hardbound, 0743273346.

> In Limehouse, London's Chinatown, the pair discovers connections between a text stolen from a Nanking monastery and secret martial arts techniques a killer may want to obtain.

> **Keywords:** Martial arts

The Hellfire Conspiracy. Touchstone, 2007. 336pp. Hardbound, 9781416548058.

> Barker and Llewelyn search for a twelve-year-old girl who went missing from Bethnal Green, a squalid London district where her mother did charity work. Was she kidnapped by white slavers, or was she the victim of a serial killer preying on poor young girls?

> **Keywords:** Kidnapping; Serial killers

The Black Hand. Touchstone, 2008. 304pp. Paper, 9781416558958.

> It is 1885, and the intrepid pair become entangled with the Mafia after the bullet-riddled bodies of an Italian assassin and his wife turn up in a hogshead barrel.

> **Keywords:** Assassins; Mafia

Twentieth Century

In Edwardian times (1901–1910) and slightly thereafter, England saw a period of relative prosperity, and the lighthearted atmosphere is reflected in many of these novels. Mysteries set during or after World War I are darker and more suspenseful, not surprisingly, while those set in the 1920s and 1930s, when women were out in the workforce, have a strong social conscience.

Albert, Susan Wittig.

The Cottage Tales of Beatrix Potter. ✍ YA

Albert (one-half of the team who write as Robin Paige) begins her own series starring noted children's author Beatrix Potter, who moves from London to the Lake District village of Near Sawrey to recover from her fiancé's recent death. She frequently pays visits to her parents back home. In this lighthearted series, one of the coziest among cozy mysteries, there are no jaw-dropping dramatic moments or gruesome onstage deaths. Gossipy villagers provide entertainment, and the animal residents on Miss Beatrix's property interact with one another and proffer advice. **Amateur detective/Cozy**.

Keywords: Animals; Authors, women; Potter, Beatrix (historical character)

The Tale of Hill Top Farm. Berkley Prime Crime, 2004. 286pp. Hardbound, 0425196348.

Beatrix settles down in New Sawrey, having just purchased Hill Top Farm there, and discovers a few small mysteries to solve: the death of one villager and a few missing objects.

The Tale of Holly How. Berkley Prime Crime, 2005. 303pp. Hardbound, 0425202747.

While fixing up her farm Beatrix discovers the body of a local shepherd, Ben Hornby, and her pets and the village animals help her find out who killed him.

Keywords: Shepherds

The Tale of Cuckoo Brow Wood. Berkley Prime Crime, 2006. 329pp. Hardbound, 0425210049.

Beatrix returns from London to find her attic occupied by rats; the resident rat invited her family for a visit, and the rat population continues to multiply. The town vicar has a similar problem with unwanted visitors overstaying their welcome.

Keywords: Rats

The Tale of Hawthorn House. Berkley Prime Crime, 2007. 322pp. Hardbound, 9780425216552.

To her surprise, Beatrix discovers a foundling, Baby Flora, on her doorstep, and a ring left with the infant leads her to the residents of Hawthorn House.

Keywords: Abandoned children

The Tale of Briar Bank. Berkley Prime Crime, 2008. 320pp. Hardbound, 9780425223611.

Beatrix searches for the truth behind the mysterious death of antiquities collector Mr. Wickstead, killed by a falling tree at Briar Bank in Sawrey around Christmastime.

Allen, Conrad.

George Porter Dillman/Genevieve Masefield Series.

To escape people's notice, George Porter Dillman, shipboard detective for the Cunard Line in the early twentieth century, blends in with the well-to-do first class passengers. On the maiden voyage of the *Lusitania* in 1907 (detailed in the first book) he meets Genevieve Masefield, a spirited British lady who rejects his overtures of friendship at first. On subsequent voyages she joins him in his sleuthing. A cozy romantic series set aboard luxury liners as they sail from Britain or New York to ports around the world. (Conrad Allen is a pseudonym for Keith Miles, who also writes as Edward Marston.) **Public detective/Cozy-traditional.**

Keywords: Dillman, George Porter; Masefield, Genevieve; Shipboard adventure

Murder on the Lusitania. Minotaur, 1999. 266pp. Hardbound, 0312241143.

Murder on the Mauretania. Minotaur, 2000. 277pp. Hardbound, 031224116X.

Murder on the Minnesota. Minotaur, 2001. 295pp. Hardbound, 0312280920.

Murder on the Caronia. Minotaur, 2003. 290pp. Hardbound, 0312280912.

Murder on the Marmora. Minotaur, 2004. 295pp. Hardbound, 0312307918.

Murder on the Salsette. Minotaur, 2005. 263pp. Hardbound, 0312307934.

Murder on the Oceanic. Minotaur, 2006. 281pp. Hardbound, 0312342853.

Murder on the Celtic. Minotaur, 2007. 278pp. Hardbound, 9780312356194.

Benn, James R.

Billy Boyle World War II Mysteries.

Benn's detective hero, Lieutenant William (Billy) Boyle, is a young Boston Irish cop. He is not thrilled with the idea of being a soldier, and his family helps him escape a combat tour overseas by pulling strings. This gets him a job on General Eisenhower's staff, but all too soon he realizes he's in way over his head. He narrates his own adventures, in direct if occasionally brash style. **Public detective/ Traditional.**

Keywords: Boyle, Billy; Irish Americans; Policemen; Spies

Billy Boyle. Soho, 2006. 294pp. Hardbound, 1569474338.

> As Eisenhower's personal investigator in London in 1942, Billy Boyle determines the identity of a spy who may disrupt the Allied invasion of Norway.

The First Wave. Soho, 2007. 304pp. Hardbound, 9781569476.

> Lt. Billy Boyle, along with his boss, participates in the first wave of attacks to liberate Algeria from Vichy French forces. With the resulting confusion among the various factions, as well as a drug-smuggling operation to contend with, it's difficult for Billy to solve the multiple murders that occur.

> **Keywords:** Algeria—World War II

Blood Alone. Soho, 2008. 313pp. Hardbound, 9781569475164.

> Billy's new assignment for Ike: contacting the head of the Sicilian Mafia to ensure the Allies' safe entry into Sicily, a mission he gradually remembers after waking up in a field hospital with amnesia.
>
> **Keywords:** Amnesia; Italy—World War II; Mafia

Bowen, Rhys.

Bowen's latest sleuth has royal connections. Lady Victoria Georgiana Charlotte Eugenie Rannoch (better known as Georgie), a cousin of King George V and thirty-fourth in line for the English throne, comes from a less wealthy branch of the Windsors. Her feigning affluence even when she's dead broke results in hilarious situations. **Amateur detective/Cozy.**

Keywords: Maids; Royalty

Her Royal Spyness. Berkley Prime Crime, 2007. 324pp. Hardbound, 9780425215678.

> To make ends meet, Georgie, a thoroughly modern woman of the 1930s, leaves Scotland for London and secretly takes rather menial positions. When her brother is accused of murdering a man who turns up dead in her bathtub, Georgie steps up to clear his name.

A Royal Pain. Berkley Prime Crime, 2008. 320pp. Hardbound, 9780425221631.

> Georgie, who continues working as a maid in order to earn a little extra cash, is asked by Queen Mary to entertain Princess Hannelore of Bavaria in the hope that she'll distract the Prince of Wales away from Mrs. Simpson. Hanni proves to be quite a character, and she brings trouble to the fold when her communist acquaintance turns up dead in a local bookshop.
>
> **Keywords:** Communism; Princesses

Chesney, Marion.

Edwardian Murder Mysteries.

Chesney combined her interest in historical novels and mysteries with this lighthearted series set in the upper-class world of Edwardian London. She is a prolific author of Regency romances and, as M.C. Beaton, author of the Agatha Raisin and Hamish Macbeth mystery series. Lady Rose Summer, an outspoken London debutante, solves crimes with the help of Captain Harry Cathcart of Scotland Yard. **Amateur detective/Cozy.**

Keywords: Nobility; Summer, Rose

Snobbery with Violence. Minotaur, 2003. 226pp. Hardbound, 031230451X.

> Lady Rose Summer's wealthy father doesn't entirely trust the intentions of one of her suitors, so asks Captain Harry Cathcart to check him out. Then another aristocrat, the Marquess of Hedley, asks him to find out who killed one of his guests at a recent house party. Lady Rose, as it happens, was also one of the guests.

Hasty Death. Minotaur, 2004. 225pp. Hardbound, 0312304536.

> Rose, eager to escape her parents' clutches, moves out and joins the working world but finds that neither her new home nor her typist job is what she expected. Then she learns about the shooting death of a high society acquaintance, which encourages her to move back in with her parents.

Sick of Shadows. Minotaur, 2005. 215pp. Hardbound, 0312329644.

> To avoid Rose's parents' plan of sending her to India in search of a husband, Rose and Harry pretend they're engaged, but people grow suspicious when he spends too much time on detective work. Bored, Rose befriends a new debutante, Dolly Tremaine, and is crushed when her new friend is found floating in the river.

Our Lady of Pain. Minotaur, 2006. 224pp. Hardbound, 0312329687.

> Even though their engagement is a front, Rose exhibits signs of jealousy when Harry begins paying attention to coquette Dolores Duval. After Rose is seen warning her to stay away from Harry and later finds Dolores dead, she needs Harry's help in extricating herself from a murder charge.

Cleverly, Barbara.

Detective Joe Sandilands Series.

> Annotated under "India," at the end of this chapter; the later volumes of this series are set in twentieth-century England and Europe.

Dunn, Carola.

Daisy Dalrymple Series.

> In this cozy series Daisy Dalrymple, a viscount's daughter in 1920s England, takes a job as at a magazine after losing nearly everyone she loves in World War I. An emancipated woman with classic flapper style, Daisy hardly bats an eye over her developing relationship with Scotland Yard Inspector Alec Fletcher, though they come from social classes that wouldn't normally mix. Whether investigating crimes on English country estates or in the big city, Daisy makes a charming amateur sleuth. Dunn also writes Regency romances, and her graceful style spills over into her mysteries. **Amateur detective/Cozy.**

> **Keywords:** Dalrymple, Daisy; Nobility

Death at Wentwater Court. St. Martin's Press, 1994. 216pp. Hardbound, 0312110308.

The Winter Garden Mystery. St. Martin's Press, 1995. 226pp. Hardbound, 0312132174.

Requiem for a Mezzo. St. Martin's Press, 1996. 212pp. Hardbound, 0312140363.

Murder on the Flying Scotsman. St. Martin's Press, 1997. 213pp. Hardbound, 0312151756.

Damsel in Distress. St. Martin's Press, 1997. 234pp. Hardbound, 0312168063.

Dead in the Water. St. Martin's Press, 1998. 249pp. Hardbound, 0312191812.

Styx and Stones. St. Martin's Press, 1999. 231pp. Hardbound, 0312205929.

Rattle His Bones. Minotaur, 2000. 243pp. Hardbound, 0312205724.

To Davy Jones Below. Minotaur, 2001. 248pp. Hardbound, 0312266693.

The Case of the Murdered Muckraker. Minotaur, 2002. 262pp. Hardbound, 0312272847.

Mistletoe and Murder. Minotaur, 2002. 260pp. Hardbound, 0312287755.

Die Laughing. Minotaur, 2003. 276pp. Hardbound, 0312309139.

A Mourning Wedding. Minotaur, 2004. 288pp. Hardbound, 0312326270.

Fall of a Philanderer. Minotaur, 2005. 288pp. Hardbound, 031233589X.
> While Daisy, her husband Alec, and company are relaxing in the seaside village of Westcombe in 1924, they find the body of a local innkeeper, George Enderby, who had a way with the ladies.

Gunpowder Plot. Minotaur, 2006. 246pp. Hardbound, 0312349890.
> While Daisy and Alec await the birth of their first child, Daisy pays a visit to her old friend Gwen Tyndall, whose family regularly celebrates Guy Fawkes Day in grand style. Family squabbles among Gwen's relations quickly escalate into murder.

The Bloody Tower. Minotaur, 2007. 259pp. Hardbound, 9780312363062.
> Daisy and Alec investigate the death of a Yeoman Warder at the Tower of London.

Black Ship. Minotaur, 2008. 288pp. Hardbound, 9780312363079.
> The Fletchers, with their infant twins, relocate to a larger, more comfortable dwelling on the outskirts of London. A corpse turns up in the communal garden, and rumors of a local liquor smuggling operation reach the pair.

Eccles, Marjorie.

Shadows and Lies. **Minotaur, 2007. 336pp. Hardbound, 9780312368968.** 📖
> In 1910 a woman's bloodstained body is found on the grounds of the Shropshire estate of Sir Henry Chetwynd, and the gruesome discovery has a heavy impact on him, his wife, and their two children. Also, in London a woman named Hannah, who has lost all memory of the past dozen years, believes that the ongoing murder investigation in Shropshire holds the key. Set in Edwardian times and in South Africa at the end of the Victorian period. **Amateur detective/Traditional/Literary.**

> **Keywords:** Amnesia; Multi-period novels; Nobility; South Africa—19th century

The Shape of Sand. **Minotaur, 2005. 288pp. Hardbound, 0312352328.** 📖
> Eccles, best known for her modern police procedurals, delivers a more leisurely paced, eloquently written mystery evoking the Edwardian upper classes and life in Britain during the postwar period, with echoes of early twentieth-century Egypt. In 1946 the three Jardine sisters reunite when builders at their family home, Charnley, uncover a box of letters, photo-

graphs, and a diary dating from forty years earlier—just before their mother, Beatrice, mysteriously vanished (perhaps with her Egyptian archaeologist lover). Clues may be found in a trip to Egypt that Beatrice took a decade before she disappeared. **Amateur detective/Traditional/Literary.**

Keywords: Letters; Mansions; Mothers and daughters

Gordon-Smith, Dolores.

Jack Haldean Murder Mystery Series.

In a series of classic detective novels celebrating England during the boisterous Roaring Twenties, Jack Haldean, a daredevil pilot who proudly served his country in wartime, returns home to Sussex and nurtures his passion for writing by joining the staff of a magazine. His trustworthy nature serves him well in his investigations when crimes hit close to home. **Amateur detective/Cozy.**

Keywords: Authors; Haldean, Jack; Pilots

A Fete Worse Than Death. Carroll & Graf, 2007. 288pp. Hardbound, 9780786719853.

> During the summer of 1922 mystery novelist and ex-pilot Jack Haldean discovers that in order to find who killed a fellow officer at the Red Cross Fete, he has to look back to the Battle of the Somme.

> **Keywords:** Festivals

Mad About the Boy?. Soho Constable, 2008. 302pp. Hardbound, 9781569475119.

> A guest attending the silver anniversary bash held by a noted Sussex couple commits suicide—or was he murdered? Jack believes the latter.

> **Keywords:** Parties

King, Laurie R.

Mary Russell Series.

In Mary Russell, King created a feminine equal to Sherlock Holmes, a woman who can match him in both wit and cunning. Mary begins the series as Holmes's bookish and unconventional teenaged apprentice, but she soon proves that she can hold her own with the distinguished hero. Despite their vast age difference, the obvious chemistry between them proves difficult to ignore, and romance soon develops. Later, as Holmes's wife and partner in crime, Mary proves that she's as good a crime-solver as her famous husband. Set between 1915 and the 1920s, mostly in England. **Amateur detective/Traditional.**

Keywords: Russell, Mary; Sherlock Holmes retellings and themes

The Beekeeper's Apprentice. St. Martin's Press, 1994. 347pp. Hardbound, 0312104235.

A Monstrous Regiment of Women. St. Martin's Press, 1995. 368pp. Hardbound, 0312135653.

A Letter of Mary. St. Martin's Press, 1996. 276pp. Hardbound, 0312146701.

The Moor. St. Martin's Press, 1998. 307pp. Hardbound, 0312169345.

O Jerusalem. Bantam, 1999. 384pp. Hardbound, 0553110934.

Justice Hall. Bantam, 2002. 331pp. Hardbound, 0553111132.

The Game. Bantam, 2004. 368pp. Hardbound, 0553801945.

Locked Rooms. Bantam, 2005. 402pp. Hardbound, 055380197X.

> While en route from Bombay to San Francisco to settle her family's estate, Mary begins experiencing dreams related to the 1906 earthquake that devastated the latter city. Holmes and Mary, while looking into the reasons behind her memory loss, revisit the car accident that killed her family (and left her an orphan) years earlier. They also learn that many people closely involved with her family had died violently.

> **Keywords:** Amnesia; California—20th century; San Francisco earthquake

Langley-Hawthorne, Clare.

Ursula Marlow Series.

Ursula Marlow, an heiress, Oxford graduate, and would-be journalist, spends her spare time fighting for women's right to vote in London in 1910. This disappoints her father, a rich industrialist who'd like to get her married off. When murders occur close to home, she realizes how much she has yet to learn about the world. *The Serpent and the Scorpion* will be next. **Amateur detective/Traditional**.

Keywords: Marlow, Ursula; Suffragettes

Consequences of Sin. Viking, 2007. 262pp. Hardbound, 9780670038206.

> Ursula gets a late-night phone call from her good friend Winifred Stanford-Jones, who finds her lesbian lover murdered in their bed. Her father's legal advisor, Lord Oliver Wrotham, helps her clear Winifred's name.

> **Keywords:** Heirs and heiresses; Lesbians

Martin, Andrew.

Jim Stringer Series.

At the dawn of the Edwardian period there's money to be made in the railroad business, and no one knows this better than Jim Stringer, a young railway porter from Northeast England now living in London in 1903. This series vividly evokes the sights, smells, and sounds of a London fully in the grips of industry and progress. Additional volumes are in print in the UK. **Amateur detective/Traditional**.

Keywords: Railroads; Stringer, Jim

The Necropolis Railway. Harcourt, 2006. 246pp. Hardbound, 0156030683.

The Blackpool Highflyer. Harcourt, 2007. 350pp. Hardbound, 9780156030694.

The Lost Luggage Porter. Harcourt, 2008. 309pp. Paper, 9780156030748.

McPherson, Catriona.

Dandy Gilver Series.

Dandelion Dahlia "Dandy" Gilver, a middle-aged aristocrat in Perthshire, Scotland, in the 1920s, worked as a volunteer nurse during the Great War. Now that her inattentive husband is back home, her children are back in school, and the hubbub of wartime activity has died down, she needs a hobby, preferably one that's sufficiently diverting yet doesn't require too much thought: a little light sleuthing, for instance. She narrates tales of her own investigative adventures in honest, slightly snooty, and self-deprecatingly humorous fashion. **Amateur detective/Cozy.**

Keywords: Gilver, Dandy; Nobility; Scotland

After the Armistice Ball. Carroll & Graf, 2005. 302pp. Hardbound, 1845291301.

It's springtime in Perthshire in 1922, and Dandy decides to find out what happened to diamonds stolen from the Esslemonts' country house, the residence of the Duffy family, after the Armistice Ball. Then reports arrive of the death of Cara Duffy, the youngest Duffy daughter, during a fire in Galloway. Was it an accident or murder?

Keywords: Parties

The Burry Man's Day. Carroll & Graf, 2006. 336pp. Hardbound, 0786717408.

While visiting her friend Buttercup in her new castle in South Queensferry, Scotland, Dandy investigates the death of the local fellow portraying the Burry Man, a time-honored tradition, at the Ferry Fair.

Keywords: Festivals

Perry, Anne.

World War I Series.

A five-book series set against the backdrop of World War I. As Joseph, Judith, and Matthew Reavley each play different roles in the Great War, they solve murders along the way, always keeping in mind the larger mystery: Who is the mysterious Peacemaker, the power broker who tries to end the war through an Anglo–German alliance? When they discover this, they'll know who really killed their parents. The solutions are revealed in the last book. Joseph Reavley, the protagonist of *No Graves As Yet*, is based on the real-life Captain Joseph Reavley, Perry's grandfather, who served in France during the war. **Amateur detective/Traditional.**

Keywords: Brothers and sisters; Clergy; England—World War I

No Graves as Yet. Ballantine, 2003. 339pp. Hardbound, 0345456521.

Joseph Reavley, who teaches biblical languages at Cambridge, learns one day in 1914 that his parents were killed in a car crash—the same day that Archduke Ferdinand was assassinated in Sarajevo. Joseph's brother Matthew reveals that their father possessed a letter supposedly containing information that could destroy Western civilization. But the letter can't be found, and when Joseph learns of the murder of his favorite student, he knows his problems have only begun.

Shoulder the Sky. Ballantine, 2004. 352pp. Hardbound, 0345456548.

> It is 1915, and Joseph, Matthew, and Judith Reavley are all actively serving in World War I. Though they believe their parents' murder has been solved, they don't believe that the story's really over. In the midst of the chaos of war, Joseph discovers the dead body of a journalist.

Angels in the Gloom. Ballantine, 2005. 368pp. Hardbound, 0345456572.

> Joseph Reavley, badly wounded in Flanders, returns home to St. Giles only to discover the place, and its people, radically changed by the war. Then a scientist working for Britain's war effort on a torpedo guidance system is murdered, throwing the town further into disarray.

At Some Disputed Barricade. Ballantine, 2007. 306pp. Hardbound, 9780345456588.

> In 1917 the Reavleys and England as a whole have grown weary of the lengthy war. Joseph, a chaplain on the Western Front, tries to solve the murder of one of his fellow officers, believed killed by his own men, while Judith continues her valued work as an ambulance driver, and Matthew, in British intelligence, tries to unveil the Peacemaker's identity.

We Shall Not Sleep. Ballantine, 2007. 304pp. Hardbound, 9780345456601.

> In November 1918 World War I is drawing to a close, and the Reavleys hope to return at last to their home in the English countryside. Matthew travels to Ypres, following a lead that may reveal who the Peacemaker (and his parents' killer) really is, but is himself accused of killing a young nurse.

Roberts, David.

Lord Edward Corinth and Verity Browne Series.

A proper British mystery set among the aristocracy in the 1930s. Lord Edward Corinth, the jaded younger brother of the duke of Mersham, crosses societal lines to investigate crimes with crusading left-wing journalist Verity Browne. **Amateur detective/Traditional.**

Keywords: Browne, Verity; Corinth, Lord Edward; Journalists, women; Nobility

Sweet Poison. Carroll & Graf, 2000. 277pp. Hardbound, 0786708190.

Bones of the Buried. Carroll & Graf, 2001. 342pp. Hardbound, 0786709081.

Hollow Crown. Carroll & Graf, 2002. 309pp. Hardbound, 0786710527.

Dangerous Sea. Carroll & Graf, 2003. 248pp. Hardbound, 0786712155.

The More Deceived. Carroll & Graf, 2004. Hardbound, 0786718404.

A Grave Man. Carroll & Graf, 2005. Hardbound, 0786715960.

The Quality of Mercy. Carroll & Graf, 2006. Hardbound, 0786718404.

Something Wicked. Carroll & Graf, 2007. Hardbound, 9780786720484.

Todd, Charles.

Ian Rutledge Series.

Scotland Yard Inspector Ian Rutledge, shell-shocked after horrific experiences in France during World War I, returns to work in order to save his sanity. Banishing his personal demons proves just as difficult as solving cases, for the voice of Hamish MacLeod, a young soldier he was forced to execute for cowardice, taunts him constantly inside his head. Elegant prose and beautiful descriptions of English village life combine with haunting, psychologically intense drama. The novels are set a month apart, all in 1919. ("Charles Todd" is a pseudonym for mother and son writing team Carolyn Watjen and David Watjen.) **Public detective/Traditional.**

Keywords: Post-Traumatic Stress Disorder; Rutledge, Ian; Soldiers

A Test of Wills. St. Martin's Press, 1996. 282pp. Hardbound, 0312144318.

Wings of Fire. St. Martin's Press, 1998. 294pp. Hardbound, 0312170645.

Search the Dark. Thomas Dunne, 1999. 279pp. Hardbound, 0312200005.

Legacy of the Dead. Bantam, 2000. 308pp. Hardbound, 0553801686.

Watchers of Time. Bantam, 2001. 339pp. Hardbound, 0553801791.

A Fearsome Doubt. Bantam, 2002. 295pp. Hardbound, 0553801805.

A Cold Treachery. Bantam, 2005. 373pp. Hardbound, 0553803492.

> Sent out in a blizzard by Scotland Yard to investigate a crime, Rutledge encounters a horrific scene: the Elcott family has been murdered at their kitchen table, and their young son, Josh, is missing.

A Long Shadow. Morrow, 2006. 341pp. Hardbound, 006078671X.

> In early 1920, while investigating a crime in southern England, Rutledge discovers that he's being followed by a stalker who leaves engraved cartridge casings (which Rutledge last encountered on a French battlefield) as his calling card.

A False Mirror. Morrow, 2007. 371pp. Hardbound, 0060786736.

> Rutledge arrives in the small village of Hampton Regis to defuse a situation in which one of his former fellow officers, Stephen Mallory, is holding his ex-lover and several other people hostage.

> **Keywords:** Hostages

A Pale Horse. Morrow, 2008. 360pp. Hardbound, 9780061233562.

> The death of a man left in Yorkshire's Fountains Abbey, found wearing a gas mask, may somehow relate to another man whom Britain's War Office wants Rutledge to find—someone whose work was so covert that Rutledge isn't given his name. The investigation takes him to the Berkshire Downs, where a giant white horse was carved into the chalk hillside long ago.

Upton, Nicola.

An Expert in Murder. **Harper, 2008. 292pp. Paper, 9780061451539.**

Josephine Tey, a novelist from the golden age of mystery, stars in her own detective story. In 1934, after traveling by train from Scotland to London to attend the popular performance of her play *Richard of Bordeaux*, she meets up with murder. A young fan whom Tey had met on route is killed at King's Cross Station, a souvenir doll from the production in her possession. Naturally the police assume her killing relates directly to the play, or to Tey herself. Tey was one of the pseudonyms used by Scots novelist Elizabeth Mackintosh, and Upton acknowledges Mackintosh's discomfort with using historical figures in fiction by making the pseudonym her main character. **Amateur detective/Traditional.**

Keywords: Authors, women; Tey, Josephine (historical character)

Winspear, Jacqueline.

Maisie Dobbs Series. 📖 YA

When she was fourteen, Maisie Dobbs's mother died, and she went into service to help her father make ends meet. In 1929, thanks to a Cambridge education given to her by her employer's friend, thirty-three-year-old Maisie opens a detective agency in London. The scenarios she investigates regularly hearken back to the Great War, which forces Maisie to confront her personal memories of the time. **Private detective/Traditional.**

Keywords: Dobbs, Maisie; England—World War I

🎗 *Maisie Dobbs.* Soho, 2003. 294pp. Hardbound, 1569473307.
   Alex Award.

Birds of a Feather. Soho, 2004. 311pp. Hardbound, 1569473684.

Pardonable Lies. Henry Holt, 2005. 352pp. Hardbound, 0641840608.

Honoring the deathbed request of his late wife Agnes, who never believed their son Ralph was killed on a battlefield during World War I, Sir Cecil Lawton hires Maisie to find out what really happened to him. To solve this and other cases, Maisie returns to France, where she had served as a nurse during the war.

Keywords: France

Messenger of Truth. Henry Holt, 2006. 336pp. Hardbound, 0805078983.

In 1931 the twin sister of artist Nick Bassington-Hope, who died after falling from scaffolding, hires Maisie to prove his death was more than a tragic accident.

Keywords: Artists

An Incomplete Revenge. Henry Holt, 2008. 306pp. Hardbound, 9780805082159.

Maisie travels to Heronsdene in Kent to investigate a land deal for her benefactor, who is concerned about fires breaking out in the area. She finds the villagers consumed by prejudice against transient farm workers (who belong to the Roma people) and oddly preoccupied by a wartime tragedy that took place nearly two decades earlier.

Keywords: Gypsies; Prejudice

Europe

The Middle Ages

As in mysteries of medieval England (annotated previously this chapter), detectives must gather all their knowledge of religion and contemporary politics to solve crimes. These novels also have elements of adventure, as their protagonists often travel back and forth across Europe, either on pilgrimages or crusades.

Gordon, Alan.

Fools' Guild Mysteries. YA

Members of the Fools' Guild, trained as jesters to perform in the courts of Europe and the Middle East in the late twelfth and early thirteenth centuries, work behind the scenes to ensure peace and political stability. Theophilos, aka Feste the Fool, is the primary sleuth, though the mystery content isn't always primary. As fools, Theo and his wife Viola/Claudia/Aglaia can speak freely with their patrons, unlike most courtiers, and this gains them respect. The series juggles dry humor, mystery, history, and fast-paced adventure. The majority of the series should be read in order, but *Widow of Jerusalem* and *Antic Disposition* are retrospective tales and can stand alone. **Amateur detective/Traditional.**

Keywords: Jesters and fools; Theophilos

Thirteenth Night. Minotaur, 1999. 243pp. Hardbound, 0312200358.

Jester Leaps In. Minotaur, 2001. 276pp. Hardbound, 0312241178.

A Death in the Venetian Quarter. Minotaur, 2002. 288pp. Hardbound, 0312242670.

The Widow of Jerusalem. Minotaur, 2003. 288pp. Hardbound, 0312300891.

An Antic Disposition. Minotaur, 2004. 337pp. Hardbound, 0312300964.

The Lark's Lament. Minotaur, 2007. 272pp. Hardbound, 9780312354268.

In 1204 Theo and Claudia, along with young daughter Portia and apprentice Helga, pay a visit to a former member of the Fools' Guild, the Cistercian abbot named Folc. They hope he will help save the Fools' Guild from its enemies. Then one of Folc's monks is killed, and a mysterious riddle is found painted on the wall in his blood; this sends the group to Marseille in search of answers.

Keywords: Clergy; France; Monks

The Moneylender of Toulouse. Minotaur, 2008. 322pp. Hardbound, 9780312371098.

Later in 1204 it becomes clear that the Fools' Guild needs more allies among the Church, so Theo and company journey to Toulouse to "encourage" its current bishop, who is hostile to their work, to retire. When a moneylender with whom Bishop Raimon recently had a public argument is found dead in a tanner's pit, Theo hopes he can use this to his advantage . . . until another murder occurs, and a fellow fool is arrested.

Keywords: Clergy; France; Moneylenders

Gross, Claudia.

Scholarium. **Toby, 2004. 294pp. Hardbound, 1592640567.**

In 1413 in Cologne, Germany, scholars of religious texts vie with the church, who would prefer that detailed study of Christian documents be left to those they feel are qualified. When Frederico Casall, an admirer of Aquinas and Master of the Seven Liberal Arts at the scholarium of Cologne, is found murdered in the street, one of his fellow faculty members is charged with solving the crime. Gross, a German novelist, immerses readers in the world of medieval European scholarship and philosophy. **Amateur detective/Traditional.**

Keywords: Germany; Philosophers; Schools

Leoni, Giulio.

The Mosaic Crimes. **Harcourt, 2007. 317pp. Hardbound, 9780151012466.** ✍

Years before he is to write *The Inferno*, Dante Alighieri serves as prior of Florence. It is the year 1300, and the body of an artist, Ambrogio, has been found next to his recently completed mosaic. Amid the great struggle between the Guelphs and Ghibellines for control of the papacy, Dante becomes a very unlikely sleuth, meeting with a group of seven scholars known as the Third Heaven, who may know more than they're telling. (UK title: *The Third Heaven Conspiracy.*) **Amateur detective/Traditional.**

Keywords: Alighieri, Dante (historical character); Italy; Mosaicists

Newman, Sharan.

Catherine LeVendeur Mysteries. YA

Catherine LeVendeur begins the series as a novice/scholar at the Convent of the Paraclete in France in 1139, yet her curiosity and outspokenness make her unsuited to a contemplative life. The Jewish ancestry of her father, merchant Hubert LeVendeur, complicates matters for Catherine, as does her attraction to Edgar, a stonemaster's apprentice she encounters in the first book. Over the course of the series they marry and raise a family. Newman, a trained medievalist, creates sympathetic characters that belong to their time rather than to ours. Religious piety, romance, and political intrigue combine with lively storytelling. **Amateur detective/Traditional.**

Keywords: France; Jews; LeVendeur, Catherine

Death Comes as Epiphany. TOR, 1993. 319pp. Hardbound, 0312854196.

The Devil's Door. Forge, 1994. 384pp. Hardbound, 031285420X.

The Wandering Arm. Forge, 1995. 351pp. Hardbound, 0312858299.

7

Strong as Death. Forge, 1996. 384pp. Hardbound, 0312861796

🔖 *Cursed in the Blood.* Forge, 1998. 348pp. Hardbound, 0312865678. Herodotus Award.

The Difficult Saint. Forge, 1999. 350pp. Hardbound, 0312869665.

To Wear the White Cloak. Forge, 2001. 367pp. Hardbound, 0312869657.

Heresy. Forge, 2002. 352pp. Hardbound, 0765302462.

The Outcast Dove. Forge, 2003. 432pp. Hardbound, 0765303779.

The Witch in the Well. Forge, 2004. Hardbound, 0765308819.

> As legend has it, when the family well runs dry, their wealth will follow, and their descendants will die out. When Catherine's grandfather calls her home to the family castle of Boisvert in alarm, she refuses to believe in this and other pagan superstitions; then the murders begin.

> **Keywords:** Superstitions; Wells

The Renaissance and Reformation

In these mysteries the Renaissance isn't all glitter, romance, and entertainment; it also conceals lethal intent.

D'Almeida, Sarah.

Musketeers Mysteries. `YA`

All for one and one for all: in this swashbuckling mystery series, the four musketeers from Alexandre Dumas's novels (Porthos, Aramis, Athos, and D'Artagnan) become heroes and detectives, solving crimes in the court of King Louis XIII in early seventeenth-century France. D'Almeida, a native of Portugal, also writes historical fantasy under her married name, Sarah A. Hoyt. **Amateur detective/Traditional.**

Keywords: France; Musketeers

Death of a Musketeer. Berkley Prime Crime, 2006. Paper, 0425212920.

The Musketeer's Seamstress. Berkley Prime Crime, 2007. Paper, 9780425214893.

The Musketeer's Apprentice. Berkley Prime Crime, 2007. Paper, 9780425217696.

A Death in Gascony. Berkley Prime Crime, 2008. Paper, 9780425221013.

Early Modern Europe

Europe in the eighteenth and nineteenth centuries experienced (and foreshadowed) a number of political revolutions. Just like everyone else, the protagonists of these mysteries are forced to take sides, like it or not. Some are adventure stories as well, with the detectives crossing back and forth across country borders in pursuit of justice.

Akunin, Boris.

Erast Fandorin Series.

Erast Fandorin, the newest recruit to the Moscow Police in late nineteenth-century Russia, is a wide-eyed innocent who is eager to please. But Fandorin gets the job done, which is all that matters in the end. His bumbling detective skills are comic, and the bad guys are truly evil, which can make the series seem like a parody at times. Each novel follows a slightly different style in the mystery genre; *Winter Queen* was a traditional police procedural, *Leviathan* an homage to the golden age of mystery, *Turkish Gambit* a chatty crime novel with a touch of wartime romance, and *Death of Achilles* a fast-paced thriller. All appeared first in Russia, where Akunin's novels are best sellers. (Boris Akunin is a pseudonym of Grigory Chkhartishvili.) **Public detective/Traditional.**

Keywords: Fandorin, Erast; Policemen; Russia

The Winter Queen. Random House, 2003. 244pp. Hardbound, 1400060494.

Murder on the Leviathan. Random House, 2004. 224pp. Hardbound, 1400060516.

The Turkish Gambit. Random House, 2005. 240pp. Paper, 0812968786.

It is 1878, and Russia is at war with Turkey. Fandorin, a member of the diplomatic corps, meets telegraphist Varya Suvorova, on the Balkan front. Varya's intended, a Russian cryptographer, has been accused of spying for Turkey, and she is seeking the real culprit.

Keywords: Diplomats; Ottoman Empire; Spies; Telegraph operators

The Death of Achilles. Random House, 2006. 320pp. Paper, 0812968808.

In 1882 Fandorin comes home to Moscow after six years abroad, only to find his old war-hero friend General Sobolev, aka "Achilles," apparently dead of a heart attack after a night of passion with a German courtesan. He uncovers Sobolev's plan to finance a coup with a suitcase full of rubles, now missing. The scene then switches to the viewpoint of Klonov, a mysterious assassin trailing Fandorin.

Keywords: Assassins

Special Assignments. Random House, 2008. 352pp. Paper, 9780812978605.

Akunin's fifth English-language entry in the series contains two short novels. In the lighthearted and humorous *The Jack of Spades*, Fandorin and his new assistant/protégé, Anisii Tulipov, face off against a cunning swindler. *The Decorator*, a much darker tale, has Fandorin chasing a serial killer who targets prostitutes.

Sister Pelagia Series.

Sister Pelagia, a clumsy, bespectacled nun called a "walking disaster with freckles," is a surprisingly astute detective who dutifully solves crimes on behalf of Monsignore Mitrofanii, Bishop of Zavolzhsk, a village in a remote Russian province on the Volga River, during the mid-nineteenth century. With Akunin's dry sense of humor and many digressions, which give sly, amusing insights into religion, Russian capitalism, and his characters' eccentricities, solving the crime really isn't the point to these delightfully witty quasi-mysteries. **Amateur detective/Traditional.**

Keywords: Clergy; Nuns; Russia

Sister Pelagia and the White Bulldog. Random House, 2007. 266pp. Paper, 9780812975130.

Bishop Mitrofanii, sighing at his great-aunt's excessive grief over her recently deceased white bulldog, sends Sister Pelagia to her estate to discover who poisoned the dog and why.

Keywords: Aunts; Dogs

Sister Pelagia and the Black Monk. Random House, 2008. 368pp. Paper, 9780812975147.

A frightened monk arrives at Bishop Mitrofanii's door to let him know that a terrifying spirit of a black monk has been haunting the monastery at New Ararat. All of the men Mitrofanii sends to investigate end up murdered, so Sister Pelagia volunteers to check things out herself.

Keywords: Ghosts; Monks

Alleyn, Susanne.

Aristide Ravel Series.

In the politically unstable years just following the Terror, Aristide Ravel works undercover for the Parisian police force. His conscience troubles him, as he worries he might have sent innocent people to the guillotine. As one might expect, the atmosphere is at once culturally decadent and politically charged. Alleyn, a scholar of the French Revolution, has also written *A Far Better Rest*, a sequel to Dickens's *A Tale of Two Cities*. **Public detective/traditional.**

Keywords: France; French Revolution; Policemen; Ravel, Aristide

Game of Patience. Thomas Dunne, 2006. 285pp. Hardbound, 0312343639.

This police procedural opens in Paris in 1796, as Aristide Ravel and his superior, Commissaire Brasseur, look into the double murder of Louis Saint-Ange and a wealthy young woman, Célie Montereau, whom he had been blackmailing.

Keywords: Blackmail

A Treasury of Regrets. Thomas Dunne, 2007. 288pp. Hardbound, 9780312343712.

Jeannette Moineau, a young servant employed by the wealthy Duponts, is accused of poisoning the family patriarch, although she had no motive. Monsieur Dupont's daughter-in-law knows the charges are ridiculous and hires Ravel and Brasseur to find the real killer.

Keywords: Maids

Gregorio, Michael.

Hanno Stiffeniis Series.

Hanno Stiffeniis, a magistrate in French-occupied rural Prussia in the early nineteenth century, uses his innate intelligence and the lessons taught by his former mentor, Immanuel Kant, to solve mysteries. A dark series with plenty of twists, turns, and detail on Enlightenment-era philosophy. "Michael Gregorio" is the pseudonym of the husband and wife writing team of Michael Jacob and Daniela de Gregorio. **Public detective/Traditional.**

Keywords: Germany; Kant, Immanuel (historical character); Philosophers

Critique of Criminal Reason. Minotaur, 2006. 400pp. Hardbound, 0312349947.

In 1803 Hanno Stiffeniis is summoned by the kaiser to Königsberg to unmask a serial killer who has been terrorizing the city. Fortunately one of Stiffeniis's mentors and former professors is famed philosopher Immanuel Kant, who, though elderly and unable to do much physical investigating himself, persuades Hanno to use his logical, well-reasoned methodology to determine whodunit.

Keywords: Serial killers

Days of Atonement. Minotaur, 2008. 368pp. Hardbound, 9780312376444.

Hanno's investigation into the vicious killing of a mother and her three children in 1807, whose bodies are found together on a bed, forces him into competition with a French colonel who is one of the many officers overseeing Prussia's recent occupation by Napoleon's forces. Colonel Lavedrine, a fellow admirer of Kant (who had passed away a year earlier), becomes a thorn in Stiffeniis's side as he proceeds with a politically touchy investigation.

Keywords: Napoleonic Wars; Soldiers

Morris, R. N.

Porfiry Petrovich Series.

Roger (R. N.) Morris resurrects police investigator Porfiry Petrovich, the magistrate intent on solving the murders of a pawnbroker and her sister in Dostoevsky's *Crime and Punishment*, and challenges him to solve additional crimes. **Public detective/Traditional**.

Keywords: Petrovich, Porfiry; Russia; Serial killers

The Gentle Axe. Penguin Press, 2006. 305pp. Hardbound, 9781594201127.

It is 1867 in St. Petersburg, Russia, when Porfiry learns about the horrific deaths of two men in snow-covered Petrovsky Park. As in his earlier case involving Raskolnikov, the crazed perpetrator of the crimes in Dostoevsky's novel, Porfiry knows the situation is more complex than it seems. He pursues answers throughout the dark side of St. Petersburg: its drinking establishments, brothels, and pornography shops.

A Vengeful Longing. Penguin Press, 2008. 336pp. Hardbound, 9781594201806.

> After a doctor's wife and son die after consuming chocolates he brought home as a gift, the doctor is quickly accused of poisoning them. Porfiry Petrovich comes to learn that the solution is hardly that simple. As the heat bears down on St. Petersburg during the summer of 1868, Porfiry traces a possible killer's path to the city's filthy and corrupt underworld.

Myers, Beverle Graves.

Tito Amato Series (alternate series title: Baroque Mysteries).

In the 1730s the enchanting city of Venice is undergoing a cultural renaissance, and opera is a prime source of entertainment for the populace. Tito Amato has retained his beautiful soprano voice after being castrated as a child. In addition to being a successful opera singer, Tito discovers an exceptional talent for sleuthing. Celebrated on stage but often shunned in the private sphere, Tito feels quite conflicted about the reasons for his fame. And despite his affliction, Tito is nowhere near immune to matters of the heart. Readers of this lushly written series will learn plenty about eighteenth-century opera and theater. **Amateur detective/Traditional.**

Keywords: Amato, Tito; Castrati; Italy; Opera singers

Interrupted Aria. Poisoned Pen, 2004. 282pp. Hardbound, 1590581113.

> In 1731 Tito and his friend (and fellow castrato) Fenice Ravello leave Naples for Venice to sing at the San Stefano opera house. On opening night one of the prima donnas is found poisoned, and Fenice becomes the chief suspect.

Painted Veil. Poisoned Pen, 2005. 320pp. Hardbound, 1590581407.

> Tito's ego is crushed after being replaced by another castrato as lead at the Teatro San Marco. While he works on getting his voice back up to speed, he's distracted by the disappearance of set designer Luca Cavalieri, who later turns up dead in a canal.

Cruel Music. Poisoned Pen, 2006. 312pp. Hardbound, 1590582306.

> Tito travels to Rome in 1740 to sing for Cardinal Lorenzo Fabiani at his home and gets mixed up in the politics surrounding the election of the next pope.

The Iron Tongue of Midnight. Poisoned Pen, 2008. 303pp. Hardbound, 9781590582329.

> Tito travels to an isolated villa in the hills of Venice to take the lead in a private production of a new opera. He accepts the job despite the secrecy, both for the money and because his brother-in-law is part of the crew. The peaceful atmosphere of the country estate is shattered by murders that occur at midnight.

O'Brien, Charles.

Anne Cartier Series.

Murder and mystery in pre-revolutionary Paris, with co-detectives Anne Cartier, a vaudeville actress and teacher of the deaf, and Colonel Paul de Saint-Martin of the French highway patrol. They marry over the course of the series. **Amateur detective/Traditional.**

Keywords: Deafness; France; French Revolution; Teachers

Mute Witness. Poisoned Pen, 2001. 325pp. Hardbound, 1890208752.

Black Gold. Poisoned Pen, 2002. 396pp. Hardbound, 1590580109.

Noble Blood. Severn House, 2004. 320pp. Hardbound, 0727861042.

Lethal Beauty. Severn House, 2005. 239pp. Hardbound, 0727861840.

> In August 1787, at the opening of the Salon exhibition of paintings at the Louvre in Paris, Anne and Paul are shocked, along with other visitors, to see how Albert Bouchard's portrait of the late Comtesse Virginie de Serre has been defaced. Then Bouchard himself is murdered.
>
> **Keywords:** Portraits

Fatal Carnival. Severn House, 2006. 213pp. Hardbound, 0727864033.

> Anne and Paul travel to Nice for the winter of 1788, hoping that Paul's health will improve. They discover that a twenty-year-old murder and the recent escape of the artisan arrested for the crime are somehow linked to the more recent killing of a local army captain.

Cruel Choices. Severn House, 2007. 213pp. Hardbound, 9780727864635.

> In winter 1788 the French Revolution is on the horizon as Anne travels to Paris to investigate the disappearance of Lucie Gigot, a girl from the country who may have become involved with the Marquis de Sade's licentious nephew.

Assassins' Rage. Severn House, 2008. 244pp, Hardbound, 9780727866073.

> As mobs storm the Bastille on July 14, 1789, Paris erupts in chaos. While Paul investigates the murders of two of men working for the Duc d'Orléans, Anne examines why a local baker was lynched by angry residents.

Pope, Barbara Corrado.

Cézanne's Quarry. **Pegasus, 2008. 384pp. Hardbound, 9781933648835.**

> During the summer of 1885 painter Paul Cézanne enjoys considerable success in his home city of Aix en Provence, France. When beautiful, red-haired Solange Vernet turns up dead in a quarry outside Aix, Cézanne becomes a prime suspect because she spurned his affections, and because some of his earlier paintings depict strangled women that closely resemble her. Despite his suspicions, the local magistrate, Bernard Martin, treads carefully, for his future career depends on his crime-solving abilities. **Public detective/Traditional/Literary.**
>
> **Keywords:** Artists; Cézanne, Paul (historical character); France

Temple, Lou Jane.

Death du Jour. **Berkley Prime Crime, 2006. 264pp. Hardbound, 0425208060.**

> Fanny Delarue works as chef to the Monnards, a well-off Parisian bourgeois family, during the summer of 1790. When her neighbor and fellow culinary expert, Etienne de la Porte, is murdered, Fanny is distraught and

determines to solve the crime herself, but revolutionary activities are picking up. The Monnards flee to England after a mob invades their home, leaving Fanny vulnerable, especially when she discovers valuables in the spice box left to her by her parents. Second in the Spice Box Mystery series, volumes of which include recipes at the end; see "United States: Early United States" for the first volume, *The Spice Box*. **Amateur detective/Traditional.**

Keywords: Chefs; France; French Revolution

Twentieth Century

Mysteries set in early twentieth-century United States reflect the freewheeling atmosphere of the Roaring Twenties, and this is true for Europe to some degree. However, the majority of these novels mirror the confusion facing the populace during or after World Wars I and II. Amid the death and destruction of wartime, simple cases of murder can easily be overlooked—or so the perpetrators hope.

Cleverly, Barbara.

Laetitia Talbot Mysteries.

Cleverly, best known as the author of the Joe Sandilands series set in British India, begins a new series set in 1920s Crete. Strong-willed Laetitia (Letty) Talbot has the ambition to match her illustrious British pedigree. **Amateur detective/Traditional.**

Keywords: Archaeology; Talbot, Laetitia

The Tomb of Zeus. Delta, 2007. 384pp. Paper, 9780385339902.

In 1928, in her first job as director of an archaeological dig on the exotic isle of Crete, where ancient myth mingles with modern adventure, Letty is puzzled by the hanging death of a young woman.

Keywords: Crete

Bright Hair About the Bone. Delta, 2008. 352pp. Paper, 9780385339896.

After her Uncle Daniel's murder during a botched robbery, Letty receives a posthumous postcard from him. This sends her off to Burgundy, in France, where she discovers his death may be related to the ongoing search for Templar treasure.

Keywords: France; Knights Templar; Treasure

Kerr, Philip.

Bernie Gunther Series.

Bernhard (Bernie) Gunther, a sardonic private investigator in the 1930s and 1940s, uncovers political intrigue and corruption in Nazi Germany and in the war-ravaged land it becomes after 1945. Until publication of *The One from the Other* fifteen years after Gunther's last appearance, Kerr's series was known as the Berlin Noir trilogy; those novels were published in a single volume as *Berlin Noir* in 1993. **Private detective/Hard-boiled.**

Keywords: Germany—World War II; Gunther, Bernie

March Violets. Viking, 1989. 245pp. Hardbound, 0670824313.

The Pale Criminal. Viking, 1990. 272pp. Hardbound, 067082433X.

A German Requiem. Viking, 1991. 306pp. Hardbound, 0670835161

The One from the Other. Putnam, 2006. 372pp. Hardbound, 0399152997.

Pawel, Rebecca.

Carlos Tejada Alonso y León Series.

For those who lived through it, the Spanish Civil War (1936–1939) was more than just a precursor to World War II; it was a social revolution and fervent fight against fascism. Carlos Tejada, a young man moving up in the ranks of the Guardia Civil, has always supported the Nationalist cause. In late 1939, when these mysteries take place, the war has ended with a Nationalist victory over the Republican government, but its legacy remains. **Public detective/Traditional-Hard Boiled.**

Keywords: Spain; Spanish Civil War; Tejada, Carlos

🏵 *Death of a Nationalist.* Soho, 2003. 262pp. Hardbound, 1569473048.
      Edgar Award.

Law of Return. Soho, 2004. 274pp. Hardbound, 1569473439.

The Watcher in the Pine. Soho, 2005. 308pp. Hardbound, 156947379X.

In 1940 Carlos arrives with his pregnant wife, Elena, at Potes, a small mountain village in northern Spain, to take his first independent command. But the bucolic setting belies a history of violence; Carlos learns that guerrillas had killed his predecessor.

The Summer Snow. Soho, 2006. 328pp. Hardbound, 1569474087.

In Granada in 1945 Carlos's great-aunt Rosalia, who feared the spread of communism, is found dead, and her latest will has gone missing. This prompts authorities to temporarily transfer him from Potes to discover who killed her.

Pearce, Michael.

Seymour of Special Branch Series.

Pearce's second historical mystery series (after his Mamur Zapt mysteries, annotated under "The Middle East") stars Seymour of Special Branch, a multilingual British investigator sent to various European locales to solve crimes during the twentieth century's first decade. **Public detective/Traditional.**

Keywords: Greece; Italy; Morocco; Policemen; Seymour of Special Branch; Spain; Turkey

A Dead Man in Trieste. Carroll & Graf, 2004. 192pp. Paper, 0786714654.

A Dead Man in Istanbul. Carroll & Graf, 2005. 208pp. Paper, 0786715979.

A Dead Man in Athens. Carroll & Graf, 2006. 221pp. Paper, 0786718285.

A Dead Man in Tangier. Carroll & Graf, 2007. 223pp. Hardbound, 9780786720453.

A Dead Man in Barcelona. Soho Constable, 2008. 256pp. Hardbound, 9781569475379.

Tallis, Frank.

The Liebermann Papers.

Dr. Frank Tallis, a practicing clinical psychologist, uses his education and training to write a series of mysteries about Max Liebermann, a follower of Sigmund Freud at a time when psychoanalysis as a discipline was still fairly new. Liebermann applies his skills to solving police investigations at the suggestion of his good friend Oskar Rheinhardt, a police detective. Set in 1902 and shortly thereafter. **Amateur detective/Traditional.**

Keywords: Austria; Liebermann, Max; Psychologists

A Death in Vienna. Grove, 2005. 458pp. Hardbound, 0802118151. (UK title: *Mortal Mischief.*)

Vienna Blood. Random House, 2007. 485pp. Paper, 9780812977769.

United States

Colonial America

In the close-knit settlements in early America, tensions can run high, and this frequently leads to murder. The formal tone and dialogue evoke colonial times.

Lambdin, Dewey.

What Lies Buried: A Novel of Old Cape Fear. McBooks, 2005. 282pp. **Hardbound, 1590131169.**

In Wilmington, North Carolina, in 1762, the body of political leader Harry Tresmayne is found alongside a deserted stretch of road on Cape Fear. His friend, chandler Matthew Livesey, determines to find the killer, but his investigations turn up secrets from Harry's private life that many would prefer to keep hidden. Lambdin is best known for his nautical adventure stories (Chapter 8). **Amateur detective/Traditional.**

Keywords: Chandlers; North Carolina; Politicians

Pattison, Eliot.

Bone Rattler. Counterpoint, 2008. 456pp. Hardbound, 9781593761851. 📖

Pattison, best known for his series of contemporary Inspector Shan mysteries set in Tibet, brings to vivid life a clash of multiple cultures that occurred further back in history but much closer to home. Duncan McCallum, an exiled Scottish clan chief, witnesses an odd series of murders on the English convict ship transporting him and his fellow prisoners to the American colonies in 1759. As an indentured servant to Lord Ramsey on his estate in the woodlands of the Hudson River Valley, Duncan's quest for the truth entangles him deeply in the politics and beliefs of both sides in the French and Indian War. Longer than most mysteries, *Bone Rattler* also delves into the philosophical underpinnings of the war and the meaning of freedom for all parties involved: the English, French, Scots, and Iroquois. **Amateur detective/Traditional.**

Keywords: French and Indian War; Immigrants, Scottish; Indentured servants; New York

Early United States

In mysteries set between the end of the Revolution and the beginning of the Civil War, the emphasis is on America's social history: race relations, women's suffrage, and the growth of cities. These works are entertaining, although serious and occasionally grim.

Biddle, Cordelia Frances.

Martha Beale Mysteries.

Author Biddle counts notable men and women from Philadelphia's history among her ancestors, and she sets her latest series in that city in 1842. The novels are told in the present tense, using a formal, ornate writing style meant to evoke the period. Biddle also co-writes the Nero Blanc crossword puzzle mystery series with her husband. **Amateur detective/ Traditional.**

Keywords: Beale, Martha; Pennsylvania; Spinsters

The Conjurer. Minotaur, 2007. 306pp. Hardbound, 9780312352462.

Martha Beale, the spinster daughter of wealthy financier Lemuel Beale, is devastated when her father is presumed drowned, though his death would make her very wealthy. Thomas Kelman, an assistant to the mayor, joins the investigation; the crime is quite possibly related to the odd behavior of a clairvoyant.

Deception's Daughter. Thomas Dunne, 2008. 288pp. Hardbound, 9780312352479.

Martha and Thomas, a man she has come to admire, team up again when a prominent heiress, the daughter of one of Philadelphia's wealthiest families, goes missing.

MacLean, Anna.

Louisa May Alcott Mysteries. ✍

From the viewpoint of old age, Louisa May Alcott narrates tales of her own adventures as a "lady detective" while writing sensational romance novels under a pen name. The novels are set in Boston and environs in the 1850s, when "Louy" was in her early twenties and not yet a well-known author. A gentle, leisurely paced series that, in addition to enlightening readers about Alcott and her family, provides insight into social issues in pre–Civil War New England. MacLean, whose novels have been praised by the heir to the Alcott estate, is the pseudonym for Jeanne Mackin, author of many traditional historical novels. **Amateur detective/Cozy.**

Keywords: Alcott, Louisa May (historical character); Authors, women; Massachusetts

Louisa and the Missing Heiress. Signet, 2004. 304pp. Paper, 0451211790.

> The day after a tea party during which she seems unnaturally agitated, Louisa's childhood friend Dorothy Wortham, a Boston heiress, is found murdered.

> **Keywords:** Heirs and heiresses

Louisa and the Country Bachelor. Signet, 2005. 269pp. Paper, 0451214714.

> In 1855, while Louisa and her family are paying a visit to cousins in Walpole, New Hampshire, they learn about the mysterious death of a townsman, Ernst Nooteboom, who supposedly tumbled into a ravine while hiking.

> **Keywords:** New Hampshire

Louisa and the Crystal Gazer. Signet, 2006. 288pp. Paper, 0451218329.

> Louisa reluctantly accompanies her good friend Sylvia Shattuck to a séance in the heart of Boston and unexpectedly finds material for a future story during their first visit. On their second trip, the friends discover the medium has been murdered.

> **Keywords:** Séances

Schechter, Harold.

Edgar Allan Poe Series. ✑

> Edgar Allan Poe, the early nineteenth-century author who wrote creepy Gothic tales such as "The Tell-Tale Heart" and "The Murders in the Rue Morgue," stars in two historical mystery series. Schechter teams him up with historical figures who are his polar opposites, men who are both colorful and larger than life. The narrative switches back and forth between their points of view. If one is to believe Schechter, Poe may have gotten the ideas for his stories from the gruesome murders he investigates. **Amateur detective/Traditional.**

> **Keywords:** Authors; Poe, Edgar Allan (historical character)

Nevermore. Pocket, 2000. 322pp. Hardbound, 0671798553.

The Hum Bug. Atria, 2001. 400pp. Hardbound, 0671041150.

The Mask of Red Death. Ballantine, 2004. 308pp. Hardbound, 0345448413.

The Tell-Tale Corpse. Ballantine, 2006. 336pp. Hardbound, 0345448421.

> In 1845 Poe travels to Massachusetts with his child-wife, Virginia, to find a cure for her lingering illness, and gets caught up in solving a series of murders (with the help of a young Louisa May Alcott).

> **Keywords:** Alcott, Louisa May (historical character); Massachusetts

Temple, Lou Jane.

The Spice Box. **Berkley Prime Crime, 2005. 312pp. Hardbound, 0425200434.**

In 1860s New York City, Irish immigrant and orphan Bridget Heaney has always dreamed of working as head chef for one of the city's large households, and she gets her wish when Isaac Gold, a Jewish merchant, hires her. Then she discovers the body of her employer's youngest son, Seth, in the dough box on her first day on the job. For a short time Bridget must put aside her culinary tasks and find a killer. First in the Spice Box Mystery series, volumes of which include recipes at the end; see "Europe: Early Modern Era" for the second, *Death du Jour*; Temple also writes the Heaven Lee series of modern culinary mysteries. **Amateur detective/Cozy.**

Keywords: Chefs; Immigrants, Irish; New York

The Civil War

During the tumult of the Civil War (1861–1865), as thousands of men give their lives for the Union and the Confederacy, political lines are drawn, and tempers run high. Even in this chaotic time, murderers will be caught, and justice served.

Kilian, Michael.

Harrison Raines Civil War Mysteries.

Though he has always abhorred slavery, native Virginian Harrison "Harry" Raines always did his best to avoid politics. But during the Civil War not even he can remain neutral forever. In most circles Harry is known as a gambler and wastrel, which is why nobody suspects him of being a Union secret agent. Kilian, a Washington journalist, takes readers through the Civil War one key battle at a time. He died in 2005. **Amateur detective/Traditional.**

Keywords: Raines, Harry; Spies; Virginia

Murder at Manassas. Berkley Prime Crime, 2000. 306pp. Hardbound, 0425172333.

A Killing at Ball's Bluff. Berkley Prime Crime, 2001. 374pp. Hardbound, 0425178048.

The Ironclad Alibi. Berkley Prime Crime, 2002. 308pp. Hardbound, 0425183254.

A Grave at Glorieta. Berkley Prime Crime, 2003. 292pp. Hardbound, 0425188299.

The Shiloh Sisters. Berkley Prime Crime, 2004. 384pp. Hardbound, 0425194035.

Antietam Assassins. Severn House, 2005. 352pp. Hardbound, 0727862723.

In 1862 Harry Raines retreats to his home in western Virginia, eager to be away from the fighting. Then his boss, Allan Pinkerton (the future spymaster), asks him to investigate the hanging of a local minister, a Union sympathizer.

Parry, Owen.

Abel Jones Series. 📖

Major Abel Jones, a mild-mannered Union officer working as a clerk in Washington, D.C., in 1861, thought he had left the soldier's life behind. When General George McClellan recruits him to spy for the Union, little does McClellan know that the Welsh immigrant had already seen bloodier battles than he'd likely ever see in America—while fighting with the British Army in India in the 1850s. An elegantly written series that explores the changes the Civil War wrought throughout America. (Owen Parry is a pseudonym of Ralph Peters.) **Amateur detective/Traditional.**

Keywords: Jones, Abel; Louisiana; Spies

Faded Coat of Blue. William Morrow, 1999. 338pp. Hardbound, 0380976420. Herodotus Award.

Shadows of Glory. William Morrow, 2000. 311pp. Hardbound, 0380976439.

Call Each River Jordan. William Morrow, 2001. 321pp. Hardbound, 0060186380.

Honor's Kingdom. William Morrow, 2002. 328pp. Hardbound, 0060186348.

Bold Sons of Erin. William Morrow, 2003. 352pp. Hardbound, 006051390X.

Rebels of Babylon. Morrow, 2006. 309pp. Hardbound, 0060513926.

Abel Jones arrives in New Orleans during the winter of 1863 to investigate the killing of Susan Peabody, a Yankee heiress.

Santangelo, Elena.

Pat Montella Series.

Annotated in Chapter 12.

Reconstruction and the Gilded Age

The expansion of the Western frontier and the high-society atmosphere of America's eastern cities hide corruption and social injustice. It's up to the protagonists of these mysteries to make sense of it all.

Blaine, Michael.

The Midnight Band of Mercy. Soho, 2004. 372pp. Hardbound, 1569473714.

Max Greengrass, a freelance reporter for the *New York Herald* in 1893, determines why four cats were killed on the streets of Greenwich Village in ritualistic fashion. He pursues the story through all levels of society, but begins to fear for his safety when several of his best leads also turn up dead. Based on true events. **Amateur detective/Traditional**.

Keywords: Cats; New York

Emerson, Kathy Lynn.

Diana Spaulding Series.

In 1888 in New York City, a time and place when yellow journalism flourished, recent widow Diana Spaulding is one of the few women working as a newspaper reporter; she writes a regular gossip column for a scandal sheet. Romantic intrigue enters the picture when Diana meets Ben Northcote, who becomes her sleuthing partner (and fiancé) as the series continues. **Amateur detective/Traditional.**

Keywords: Journalists, women; New York; Spaulding, Diana

Deadlier Than the Pen. Pemberley, 2004. 266pp. Paper, 0970272766.

Fatal as a Fallen Woman. Pemberley, 2005. 274pp. Paper, 0970272790.

No Mortal Reason. Pemberley, 2007. 275pp. Paper, 9780977191345.

Lethal Legend. Pemberley, 2008. 239pp. Paper, 9780977191352.

Hall, Oakley M.

Ambrose Bierce Mystery Series. ✍

In these mysteries Tom Redmond, fledgling journalist, divulges his crime-solving adventures with Ambrose Bierce, infamous reporter in 1880s San Francisco. No social evil is left unexplored, either in Bierce's cynical journalism or in Hall's novels: prostitution, the plight of the Chinese, the dangers of mining, local politics, greedy railroad barons, and murder. **Amateur detective/Traditional.**

Keywords: Bierce, Ambrose (historical character); California; Journalists and reporters

Ambrose Bierce and the Queen of Spades. University of California Press, 1998. 272pp. Hardbound, 0520215559.

Ambrose Bierce and the Death of Kings. Viking, 2001. 288pp. Hardbound, 0670030074.

Ambrose Bierce & the One-Eyed Jacks. Viking, 2003. 216pp. Hardbound, 0670031801.

Ambrose Bierce and the Trey of Pearls. Viking, 2004. 224pp. Hardbound, 0670032700.

Ambrose Bierce and the Ace of Shoots. Viking, 2005. 182pp. Hardbound, 0670033901.

Haviland, Diana.

Death on the Ladies Mile. **Five Star, 2007. 364pp. Hardbound, 159414351X.**

In 1880 in New York City, society reporter Amanda Whitney insists on helping private detective Ross Buchanan solve the murder of a bride-to-be, a wealthy socialite whose father hires Ross to find out whodunit. He reluctantly accepts her assistance, only because she has connections to high society that he needs to solve the case. Then two more young women in bridal garb are killed in the same fashion. Meant to be first in the Gaslight and Shadows series, though further volumes never appeared. **Amateur detective/Traditional.**

Keywords: Journalists, women; New York; Serial killers; Socialites

Hockensmith, Steve.

Amlingmeyer Series.

For Otto and Gustav Amlingmeyer, brothers and cowpokes in Montana in 1893, reading Sherlock Holmes stories is one of their greatest passions. Or, rather, Otto reads the stories aloud to his brother, for Gustav is illiterate. When the pair (better known as Big Red and Old Red) come upon murderous happenings, they go about investigating the crimes just as they believe Holmes and Watson would. The novels are narrated by Big Red, who fancies himself a comedian, and does a pretty good job at it. A rollicking, tongue-in-cheek Conan Doyle pastiche. **Amateur detective/Traditional**.

Keywords: Amlingmeyer brothers; Sherlock Holmes retellings and themes

Holmes on the Range. Minotaur, 2006. 294pp. Hardbound, 0312347804.

> The Amlingmeyer brothers find the dead body of the ranch's general manager, who appears to have been the victim of a cattle stampede.
>
> **Keywords:** Cowboys; Montana; Stampedes

On the Wrong Track. Minotaur, 2007. 304pp. Hardbound, 0312347812.

> When the brothers are hired as agents for the Southern Pacific Railroad, the long-standing enemy of cattle drivers and free-range land everywhere, they quickly learn they've gotten more than they bargained for when a baggage handler loses his head—literally.
>
> **Keywords:** Railroads

The Black Dove. Minotaur, 2008. 296pp. Hardbound, 9780312347826.

> Old Red and Big Red transfer their detecting skills to San Francisco's China-town in the summer of 1893. Dr. Chan, a Chinese herbalist they knew from their railroad days, turns up dead, and the brothers are sure he was murdered. The solution may lie in a mysterious clue called the "black dove," but nobody's very willing to serve as their guide through the Chinese underworld.
>
> **Keywords:** California; Chinese Americans; Herbalists

Joyce, Brenda.

Francesca Cahill Novels.

Annotated in Chapter 4.

Newman, Sharan.

The Shanghai Tunnel. Forge, 2008. 334pp. Hardbound, 9780765313003.

Newman, whose background as a medievalist enlivened her Catherine LeVendeur Mysteries set in twelfth-century France, jumps ahead in time with her first mystery set in Portland, Oregon, which in 1868 is a frontier town bustling with growth and activity. Emily Stratton, a new widow, arrives in Portland with her teenaged son, hoping to make a new start there. Soon she learns that her late husband's shady business dealings didn't die with him.

Keywords: Oregon; Widows

Parker, Ann.

Silver Rush Mysteries.

Inez Stannert, the gun-toting, poker-playing part-owner of the Silver Queen saloon in 1870s and 1880s Leadville, Colorado, doesn't hesitate to stand up for herself when things get dicey, though her tough attitude masks the sorrows she has suffered. Her husband has been missing for several years, and her young son is staying with relatives back east. Not surprisingly, frequent motives for crimes in this silver mining boomtown include greed, jealousy, and the settling of old scores left over from the Civil War, barely ten years past. **Amateur detective/Traditional.**

Keywords: Colorado; Silver mining; Stannert, Inez

🏵 *Silver Lies.* Poisoned Pen, 2003. 410pp. Hardbound, 1590580842. WILLA Award.

Iron Ties. Poisoned Pen, 2006. 368pp. Hardbound, 1590582624.

> While taking photographs on a mountainside during the summer of 1880, Inez's photographer friend Susan Carothers witnesses what she believes is a killing along the railroad line, but when authorities come to investigate, the evidence and bodies have disappeared.

> **Keywords:** Photographers; Railroads

Ryan, P. B.

Nell Sweeney Series (also called Gilded Age Mysteries).

A series set in Gilded Age Boston, circa 1868. Young Irish immigrant Nell Sweeney, sharper than most Boston Brahmins give her credit for, is comfortable among all social classes, but she conceals an unsavory past. In the first book she takes a job as governess with the Hewitt family, and despite her better nature finds herself attracted to Will, a son of the family. Authentic and suspenseful. The author writes romances under her full name, Patricia Ryan. **Amateur detective/Traditional.**

Keywords: Governesses; Immigrants, Irish; Massachusetts; Sweeney, Nell

Still Life with Murder. Berkley Prime Crime, 2003. 309pp. Paper, 0425191060.

Murder in a Mill Town. Berkley Prime Crime, 2004. 272pp. Paper, 0425197158.

Death on Beacon Hill. Berkley Prime Crime, 2005. 259pp. Paper, 0425201570.

> The double killing of actress Virginia Kimball and her maid, Fiona, shocks Boston society; did Fiona shoot her mistress after Mrs. Kimball caught her stealing jewelry? Fiona's uncle asks Nell to help him clear her name.

> **Keywords:** Actresses; Maids

Murder on Black Friday. Berkley Prime Crime, 2005. 240pp. Paper, 0425206882.

> After losing their fortunes after the gold market crash on "black Friday" in 1869, two wealthy men turn up dead, and many assume it was suicide. Will Hewitt doesn't believe it, and asks Nell for help in investigating their deaths.

Murder in the North End. Berkley Prime Crime, 2006. 278pp. Paper, 0425212955.

> Colin Cook, an officer with Boston's detective bureau, is on the run after being accused of killing a man in Boston's North End. He turns to Nell, a fellow Irish immigrant, to help clear his name.

> **Keywords:** Policemen

A Bucket of Ashes. Berkley Prime Crime, 2007. 278pp. Paper, 9780425218730.

> This final series volume brings Nell back to Cape Cod, where the Hewitts have their summer cottage, and where secrets from her past threaten to reappear in the present. While contending with a possible pregnancy, Nell is devastated to discover that her only remaining brother has been murdered.

Tallman, Shirley.

Sarah Woolson Series.

Enterprising young attorney Sarah Woolson makes her own way in the world in 1880s San Francisco, but finds that few doors automatically open for a woman in a traditionally male profession. Still she perseveres, especially with her initial success in solving cases. Feisty and unconventional, Sarah narrates these lively mysteries. **Amateur detective/Traditional.**

Keywords: California; Lawyers, women; Woolson, Sarah

Murder on Nob Hill. Minotaur, 2004. 280pp. Hardbound, 0312328559.

> Having succeeded in obtaining a job at her judge father's law office, Sarah willingly takes the case of her first client, a young woman accused of her husband's murder.

The Russian Hill Murders. Minotaur, 2005. 280pp. Hardbound, 0312328575.

> Sarah continues to fight the contempt and sexism of her boss and colleagues while solving her latest cases: finding out who killed several people, including a local society matron, involved with a hospital charity project. Her investigations take her into the heart of Chinatown and the city's dark underworld.

The Cliff House Strangler. Minotaur, 2007. 320pp. Hardbound, 9780312357566.

> Sarah decides to open up her own law office. While waiting for her first clients, she unintentionally takes on a new case: discovering who strangled a reporter participating in a séance with Madame Karpova, a Russian clairvoyant, at San Francisco's famed Cliff House. Additional victims follow.

> **Keywords:** Séances

Thompson, Victoria.

Gaslight Mystery Series.

In turn-of-the-twentieth-century New York City, midwife Sarah Brandt teams up with Sergeant Detective Frank Malloy to solve a series of murders taking place amid Manhattan's world of high society and, on the opposite spectrum, its abject poverty. Sarah, a woman born to wealth and privilege, fights her attraction to the gruff Irish policeman, who continues to involve her in his investigations against his better judgment. **Amateur detective/Traditional.**

Keywords: Brandt, Sarah; Irish Americans; Midwives; New York; Policemen

Murder on Astor Place. Berkley Prime Crime, 1999. 278pp. Paper, 0425168964.

Murder on St. Mark's Place. Berkley Prime Crime, 2000. 277pp. Paper, 0425173615,

Murder on Gramercy Park. Berkley Prime Crime, 2001. 329pp. Paper, 0425178862.

Murder on Washington Square. Berkley Prime Crime, 2002. 326pp. Paper, 0425184307.

Murder on Mulberry Bend. Berkley Prime Crime, 2003. 346pp. Paper, 0425189104.

Murder on Marble Row. Berkley Prime Crime, 2004. 313pp. Hardbound, 0425196100.

Murder on Lenox Hill. Berkley Prime Crime, 2005. 291pp. Hardbound,

> The family of Grace Linton, a mentally slow teenaged girl from Lenox Hill, discovers that she's pregnant, and Sarah Brandt's search for her seducer leads her to investigate the family's church.

> **Keywords:** Mental illness; Pregnancy

Murder in Little Italy. Berkley Prime Crime, 2006. 304pp. Hardbound, 042520989X.

> Shortly after giving birth, a young woman of Irish heritage dies from complications, and her family accuses her Italian in-laws of killing her; her "premature" baby was obviously conceived before she and her husband met.

> **Keywords:** Immigrants, Irish; Immigrants, Italian; Pregnancy

Murder in Chinatown. Berkley Prime Crime, 2007. 320pp. Hardbound, 9780425215319.

> In a small Irish enclave in New York's Chinatown—the result of many Irish immigrant women marrying Chinese men, for Chinese women were not allowed to immigrate—the half-Irish, half-Chinese niece of one of Sarah's patients goes missing.

> **Keywords:** Immigrants, Chinese; Immigrants, Irish

Murder on Bank Street. Berkley Prime Crime, 2008. 324pp. Hardbound, 9780425221518.

> Frank Malloy, Sarah's longtime partner in crime solving, agrees to look further into the murder of Sarah's husband, Tom Brandt, which happened four years earlier. In looking into Dr. Brandt's treatment of delusional female patients, which proved unsuccessful, Malloy discovers their families may have taken revenge against him.

> **Keywords:** Physicians

Zellnik, M. J.

Libby Seale Series.

Libby Seale, a Jewish seamstress in Portland, Oregon, in 1894, has escaped an arranged marriage in New York City and now works at a vaudeville theater in the city. Peter Eberle, a reporter for the *Portland Gazette*, provides assistance (and a possible love interest). M. J. Zellnik is the pseudonym for the brother and sister writing team of Miriam and Joe Zellnik. **Amateur detective/Traditional.**

Keywords: Oregon; Seamstresses; Seale, Libby

Murder at the Portland Variety. Midnight Ink, 2005. 336pp. Paper, 0738707864.

While working as a costumer for the Portland Variety Theater, Libby's good friend Vera, a magician's assistant, is murdered.

Keywords: Costumers; Theater

A Death at the Rose Paperworks. Midnight Ink, 2006. 301pp. Paper, 0738708976.

Libby, now employed as a seamstress for the wealthy Rose family, helps solve the murder of the Rose family patriarch, who was mangled in the machinery at his own paperwork mill.

Keywords: Mill workers

Twentieth Century

Immigrant life, 1920s flappers, the Great Depression, and gangsters are the topics of historical mystery fiction of early twentieth-century America. Though a nostalgic atmosphere prevails overall, these mysteries demonstrate that solving murders back then was anything but simple.

Bowen, Rhys.

Molly Murphy Mysteries. YA

In this colorful, multi-award-winning series, Molly Murphy, a young, red-haired Irishwoman, takes another woman's place on a ship to America after killing a landowner's son in self-defense. Molly's first-person narration brings her spunky personality to the forefront and gives readers a prime view of turn-of-the-century New York City through an immigrant's eyes. Over the course of the series she takes over her boss Paddy Riley's detective agency. Handsome police detective Daniel Sullivan, who catches Molly's eye immediately, helps her out (and provides a love interest). **Amateur detective/Traditional** at the start; after the first book it becomes **Private detective/Traditional.**

Keywords: Immigrants, Irish; Ireland; Murphy, Molly; New York; Policemen

🎗 *Murphy's Law.* Minotaur, 2001. 226pp. Hardbound, 0312282060. Agatha Award; Herodotus Award.

Death of Riley. Minotaur, 2002. 275pp. Hardbound, 0312282117.

🎗 *For the Love of Mike.* Minotaur, 2003. 322pp. Hardbound, 0312313004. Bruce Alexander Historical Award; Anthony Award.

In Like Flynn. Minotaur, 2005. 321pp. Hardbound, 031232815X.

> Despite her continued anger over his engagement to a socialite, Molly gladly accepts Daniel's offer of employment. He engages her to go undercover at the home of Senator Flynn in Peekskill, New York, to prove that two spiritualists "helping" his wife find their kidnapped infant son, missing for five years, are frauds.

> **Keywords:** Mediums

Oh Danny Boy. Minotaur, 2006. 336pp. Hardbound, 0312997019.

> Molly comes to the aid of Daniel when he is imprisoned for supposedly taking a bribe. Molly suspects it's part of a conspiracy to remove Irishmen from New York City's police force. She also deals with an unexpected pregnancy, the result of one night she spent with her erstwhile beau.

In Dublin's Fair City. Minotaur, 2007. 272pp. Hardbound, 0312328192.

> In 1902 Molly sails back to Ireland to find the whereabouts of a would-be heiress, the sister a theater impresario was forced to leave behind in Ireland during the famine fifty years earlier. Yet trouble strikes even aboard ship, when an actress offers to trade staterooms with Molly and a dead young woman turns up in Molly's borrowed bed.

Tell Me, Pretty Maiden. Minotaur, 2008. 304pp. Hardbound, 978-0312349431.

> While walking through Central Park in December 1902, Molly and her longtime beau, Daniel Sullivan, come upon an unconscious, nearly frozen young woman clad only in a light gown. This is not the only case she's charged with solving, and juggling her multiple responsibilities proves challenging.

Casey, Donis.

Alafair Tucker Series.

Alafair Tucker, Oklahoma farm wife and mother of ten children in the early twentieth century, tries to keep her brood out of trouble. When one of her children is threatened (which has happened in each book in the series thus far), she helps solve the associated crime. A nicely paced series with glimpses of daily life on a busy farm and in the small towns of rural Oklahoma; many of the incidents are based on the author's stories about her pioneer ancestors. **Amateur detective/Traditional.**

Keywords: Farmers; Oklahoma; Tucker, Alafair

The Old Buzzard Had It Coming. Poisoned Pen, 2005. 226pp. Hardbound, 1590581490.

> In 1912 nasty drunkard Harley Day is found dead in a snowbank. His son John Lee and John's girlfriend Phoebe Tucker (Alafair's seventeen-year-old daughter), are accused of killing him.

Hornswoggled. Poisoned Pen, 2006. 242pp. Hardbound, 1590583094.

Alafair's daughter Alice has fallen in love with Walter Kelley, a widowed barber much older than her, and Alafair wants to reassure herself that he didn't kill his first wife.

The Drop Edge of Yonder. Poisoned Pen, 2007. 228pp. Hardbound, 9781590584460.

While out riding in the Oklahoma countryside, Alafair's brother-in-law Bill McBride and his party are attacked by mysterious gunmen, his fiancée, Laura, is raped and badly beaten, and Alafair's daughter Mary is injured by a stray bullet. Alafair continues to worry about Mary's safety, and for good reason: the killers are looking to strike again.

Churchill, Jill.

Grace and Favor Mysteries.

Like all too many Americans, siblings Lily and Robert Brewster lost their family fortune in the 1929 stock market crash. After their great-uncle Horatio's death they move from Manhattan to Westchester County to take up residence in his mansion, the Grace and Favor Cottage. Because they must live there for a decade before it becomes theirs, Lily and Robert take in boarders to make ends meet. Set during the Depression. (Jill Churchill is a pseudonym for Janice Young Brooks.) **Amateur detective/Cozy.**

Keywords: Brewster, Lily and Robert; Great Depression; Immigrants, German; New York

Anything Goes. William Morrow, 1999. 264pp. Paper, 0380802449.

In the Still of the Night. William Morrow, 2000. 267pp. Paper, 0380802457.

Someone to Watch over Me. William Morrow, 2001. 230pp. Hardbound, 0060199415.

Love for Sale. William Morrow, 2003. 214pp. Hardbound, 0060199423.

It Had to Be You. William Morrow, 2004. 224pp. Hardbound, 0060528435.

Who's Sorry Now? Morrow, 2005. 244pp. Hardbound, 0060734590.

A recent German immigrant to the Brewsters' town receives racial threats, and the local railroad porter is found brutally murdered.

Keywords: Racial conflict; Immigrants, German

Dams, Jeanne M.

Hilda Johansson Mystery Series.

Hilda Johansson, the Swedish maid for the wealthy Studebaker family of South Bend, Indiana, circa 1900, sniffs out clues to murder mysteries right under her employers' noses. While she fights her attraction to Patrick Cavanaugh, a local Irish Catholic policeman, she deals with anti-immigrant prejudice and the realities of servant life. **Amateur detective/Cozy.**

Keywords: Immigrants, Swedish; Indiana; Johansson, Hilda; Maids; Prejudice

Death in Lacquer Red. Walker, 1999. 225pp. Hardbound, 0802733298.

Red, White, and Blue Murder. Walker, 2000. 189pp. Hardbound, 0802733417.

Green Grow the Victims. Walker, 2001. 209pp. Hardbound, 0802733557.

Silence Is Golden. Walker, 2002. 226pp. Hardbound, 0802733735.

Crimson Snow. Perseverance, 2005. 246pp. Paper, 1880284790.

> While solving the murder of a popular local schoolteacher, Hilda discovers connections between the crime and the disappearances of other young women of South Bend. Dams based her novel on real-life murders that occurred in South Bend at the time.

Indigo Christmas. Perseverance, 2008. 252pp. Paper, 9781880284957.

> It's 1904, and Hilda and longtime beau Patrick are married, which means her life has changed considerably; as a former maid, she finds it difficult to adjust to having her own house servants. She and her husband (and in-laws) don't share the same religion, which poses problems. When her good friend Norah's husband is accused of several horrific crimes, Hilda can't help but be drawn into the investigation.

Duncan, Alice.

Lost Among the Angels. **Five Star, 2006. 280pp. Hardbound, 1594143633.**

> Mercy Allcutt, a proper Boston Brahmin, moves to Hollywood in 1926 in search of excitement and takes a job as secretary to private investigator Ernie Templeton, who only hires her for her looks. But plucky, enthusiastic Mercy proves to be an asset to his agency, accompanying him on a variety of cases, though her upper-class upbringing makes her a bit of a prude compared to typical Hollywood residents. **Private detective/Traditional**.
>
> **Keywords:** California; Secretaries

Fulmer, David.

The Dying Crapshooter's Blues. **Harcourt, 2007. 305pp. Hardbound, 9780151011759.**

> Atlanta in 1923 is a city rampant with racial conflict, corruption, and tension between the upper and lower classes. Joe Rose, a thief with a criminal record in many cities, arrives on the scene just as Little Jesse Williams, a local pimp who cheats at craps, is gunned down by a white police officer. On the same night, jewels are stolen from a wealthy mansion. For once Rose didn't commit the crime, but he's being framed for it nonetheless. He promises Jesse, as he lies dying, that he'll find the cop who killed him. **Amateur detective/Hard-boiled**.
>
> **Keywords:** Georgia; Racial conflict; Thieves

Valentin St. Cyr Series.

Fulmer's best-known series is set firmly during the birth of the jazz age, and in the place where it all started: Storyville, the red-light district of New Orleans, circa 1907. With his Creole heritage, Valentin St. Cyr, a former police investigator, mixes readily in both black and white society, which gives him a natural advantage as a private detective. **Private detective/Hard-boiled.**

Keywords: Creoles; Louisiana; St. Cyr, Valentin

Chasing the Devil's Tail. Poisoned Pen, 2001. 320pp. Hardbound, 1890208841.

Jass. Harcourt, 2005. 334pp. Hardbound, 0151010250.

Rampart Street. Harcourt, 2006. 336pp. Hardbound, 0151010242.

Glatzer, Hal.

Katy Green Series.

Katy Green, a classical violinist and sax player in pre–World War II California, goes on the road with the all-girl swing band The Ultra-Belles, but murder keeps them company on the tour. A series full of the sights and sounds of the Big Band era, as the setting makes the rounds from California to New York City to Hawaii as the band plays at different venues. **Amateur detective/Traditional.**

Keywords: California; Hawaii; Musicians; New York; Swing

Too Dead to Swing. Perseverance, 2002. 234pp. Paper, 1880284537.

A Fugue in Hell's Kitchen. Perseverance, 2004. 236pp. Paper, 1880284707.

The Last Full Measure. Perseverance, 2006. 289pp. Paper, 1880284847.

Haines, Kathryn Miller.

Rosie Winter Series.

In 1943 in New York City, would-be actress Rosie Winter hasn't had any luck with auditions for months. To pay her rent, rather than sign up for wartime factory work she takes a job at a small-time Manhattan detective agency. **Private detective/traditional**; becomes **Amateur detective/Traditional** in the second book.

Keywords: Actresses; New York-World War II

The War Against Miss Winter. Harper, 2007. 317pp. Paper, 9780061139789.

> Rosie finds herself in charge of the detective agency when her boss is found hanging in his closet. The police claim it's suicide, even though his hands were tied (literally). Rosie has no time to brood, for there are other cases to be solved, including a missing play.

The Winter of Her Discontent. Harper, 2008. 336pp. Paper, 9780061139802.

> Rosie, who broke up with her soldier boyfriend just before he shipped out, feels even more distraught when he's reported missing. Then her good friend Al confesses to murdering his actress girlfriend, even though Rosie knows he's not guilty. She and her roommate/sidekick, Jayne, go the distance by helping him, though they face their own struggles with money and keeping their spirits up.

Holmes, Rupert.

Swing. **Random House, 2005. 372pp. Hardbound, 140006158X.**
Award-winning playwright, lyricist, and novelist Holmes (who may never shake off his initial claim to fame as singer of the "Piña Colada Song") sets his second mystery at the Golden Gate International Exposition, held in San Francisco in 1940, just as America prepares for war. Ray Sherwood, a saxophonist in town with his band, meets up with composer Gail Prentiss and agrees to arrange her piano piece, called *Swing*, for a full orchestra. Then a woman he'd spoken to earlier plunges to her death from one of the exposition's towers. Holmes's novel comes complete with a CD of original music containing clues to the story line. **Amateur detective/ Traditional.**

Keywords: California; Musicians; Swing

King, Laurie R.

Locked Rooms. **Bantam, 2005. 402pp. Hardbound, 055380197X.**
Set in San Francisco, this volume of King's Mary Russell series is annotated under "British Isles: Twentieth Century."

Liesche, Margit.

Lipstick and Lies. **Poisoned Pen, 2007. 270pp. Hardbound, 9781590583203.**
Pucci Lewis, a WASP (Women's Airforce Service Pilot) and undercover spy during World War II, transports military planes to the destinations where they're needed. When she flies a B-24 to Willow Run Airport near Detroit, she encounters the corpse of a Nazi spy. As a result, the FBI recruits her to infiltrate a German spy ring. **Public detective/Traditional.**

Keywords: Michigan; Nazis; Pilots, women; Spies

Meade, Amy Patricia.

Marjorie McClelland Series.
Marjorie McClelland, a successful and attractive young mystery writer, lives a comfortable lifestyle in the quiet suburban Connecticut town of Ridgebury in the 1930s. While solving crimes in her own backyard, she becomes romantically involved with a charming British expatriate, Creighton Ashcroft, who has time and money to burn. With her sassy, wealthy heroine, flirty banter, and small town Depression-era setting, Meade's old fashioned mysteries re-create the classic atmosphere of vintage crime novels, such as those by Dorothy Sayers and Mignon Eberhart. **Amateur detective/Traditional.**

Keywords: Authors, women; Connecticut; Great Depression; Socialites

Million Dollar Baby. Midnight Ink, 2006. 351pp. Paper, 0738708607.
While taking a romantic stroll on the grounds of Creighton's newly purchased estate, Creighton and Marjorie find a corpse buried in the garden.

Ghost of a Chance. Midnight Ink, 2007. Paper, 9780738710921.

In 1935, to the disgruntlement of her police detective fiancé, Marjorie investigates the murder of a man killed by a dart while riding the Ferris wheel at the local church fair.

Keywords: Festivals

Shadow Waltz. Midnight Ink, 2008. 237pp. Paper, 9780738712493.

Not long after a seemingly happily married young husband and father inexplicably disappears, his wife asks Marjorie and Creighton to find him; instead, however, they find the dismembered body of his mistress.

Keywords: Mistresses

Richards, Linda L.

Death Was the Other Woman. **Minotaur, 2008. 272pp. Hardbound, 9780312377700.**

Richards (the editor of *January Magazine*) takes a hard-boiled look at LA during the early years of the Depression, as exemplified by the suitably pulpy cover art. However, it's not private detective Dex Theroux but his secretary, Kitty Pangborn, who steals the show. Kitty, forced to turn Girl Friday after her father's suicide derailed the family finances, narrates her adventures, which begin when Dex agrees to trail a beautiful woman's married boyfriend—who turns up dead soon afterward. **Private detective/Hard-boiled.**

Keywords: California; Detective agencies; Great Depression; Secretaries

Scoppettone, Sandra.

Faye Quick Series.

Faye Quick, who narrates with a quirky, wisecracking voice full of period slang, makes a name and career for herself as a private investigator in 1940s New York City. Many of the characters Faye associates with bear the names, coincidentally, of popular movie stars of the era. **Private detective/Hard-Boiled.**

Keywords: Detective agencies; New York—World War II; Quick, Faye; Secretaries

This Dame for Hire. Ballantine, 2005. 272pp. Hardbound, 034547810X.

In 1943, when her boss is drafted into the army, secretary Faye Quick steps up to take charge of the detective agency he was forced to abandon. She finds the body of a missing young woman on the streets of snowy Manhattan, leading her father to hire her to find the killer.

Too Darn Hot. Ballantine, 2006. 288pp. Hardbound, 0345478126.

During the red hot summer of 1943, Claire Turner hires Faye to find her boyfriend Charlie, who has gone missing. Then Faye finds the body of a man in Charlie's hotel room.

Latin America and the Caribbean

If detective novels can ever be considered "traditional" when they take place in as exotic a locale as this, Levack's series fits the bill.

Levack, Simon.

Aztec Mysteries. [YA]

Yaotl, an ex-priest and slave to the chief minister in Montezuma's Aztec empire circa AD 1517, eagerly solves crimes on behalf of the emperor. In this bloodthirsty, ritualistic culture, he'll likely be put to death if he doesn't. Levack's series takes place a mere two years before Cortes and his conquistadors arrive at the Aztec capital and shows a fully functional, complex Mesoamerican society in its heyday. In his fast-paced, humorous novels, the author has his characters speak in modern idiom to convey immediacy. **Public detective/Traditional.**

Keywords: Aztecs—16th century; Mexico; Sacrifices; Slaves and slavery

Demon of the Air. Minotaur, 2005. 296pp. Hardbound, 0312348347.

Yaotl must uncover the connections between two seemingly unrelated events: Emperor Montezuma's bizarre visions and dreams, and the odd prophecies made by a would-be sacrificial victim to the Great Pyramid just before he committed suicide.

Shadow of the Lords. Minotaur, 2006. 392pp. Hardbound, 031234841X.

While trying to protect his son, Yaotl flees from his master, Aztec chief minister Lord Feathered-in-Black, and pursues the truth behind sightings of Quetzalcoatl on the streets of the capital city.

City of Spies. Simon & Schuster UK, 2006. 331pp. Paper, 0743268393.

Yaotl has fled to the city of Tetzcoco, a land of political unrest, in the hopes that his former master won't hunt him down there. Meanwhile his former lover, Lily, turns up in the same city; she gets arrested for murder when her mission goes badly wrong.

Tribute of Death. Lulu, 2007. 448pp. Paper, 9781847997449.

In the year 1518, Yaotl guards the body of an old friend's wife, who recently died in childbirth, from sorcerers who would use her remains for nefarious purposes. When the corpse disappears Yaotl is blamed, which motivates him to investigate further. Levack self-published this novel after poor English-language sales resulted in the cancellation of the series.

The Middle East

Detectives, mostly with a Western mindset, confront the mysteries of the ever-fascinating Middle East. (Mysteries of ancient Egypt are annotated at the beginning of this chapter.)

Baron, Aileen.

Lily Sampson Series.

Baron's detective heroine is Lily Sampson, an American archaeologist and graduate student working on digs in the Middle East during a precarious time in history: the pre–World War II period, when the British are losing their hold on Palestine. Baron, who wrote her first novel at age seventy-six, is a retired professor of archaeology. **Amateur detective/Traditional.**

Keywords: Archaeology; Sampson, Lily; Spies

A Fly Has a Hundred Eyes. Academy Chicago, 2002. 272pp. Hardbound, 0897335090.

In 1938 Lily participates in an excavation in Jerusalem that's overseen by an eminent British archaeologist. When he is murdered and artifacts go missing, including an *amphoriskos* (vial) that Lily uncovered herself, she takes on the investigation herself after encountering resistance from the British police.

Keywords: Israel—20th century

The Torch of Tangier. Poisoned Pen, 2006. 236pp. Hardbound, 1590582217.

While completing her dissertation in 1942, Lily accepts the invitation of noted professor Hammond Drury to accompany him on a dig in Tangier, Morocco. However, their real mission involves working for the Allies, as they plan their offense against Rommel in North Africa.

Keywords: Morocco—World War II

Goodwin, Jason.

Yashim the Eunuch series.

Yashim Togalu, a eunuch in the opulent Topkapi Palace of the Ottoman sultan in 1836 Istanbul, uses his outsider status to his (and the people's) advantage as he solves crimes. These fast-paced mysteries combine delightful humor with literary sensibility. Goodwin, who studied Byzantine history at Cambridge University, has also written two critically acclaimed nonfiction accounts of Byzantium, including a travel memoir (*On Foot to the Golden Horn*) and a comprehensive history of the Ottoman Empire (*Lords of the Horizons*). **Amateur detective/Traditional.**

Keywords: Eunuchs; Ottoman Empire—19th century; Yashim the Eunuch

The Janissary Tree. Farrar Straus & Giroux, 2006. 299pp. Hardbound, 0374178607.

In 1836 the Ottoman Empire's influence is on the wane, and its sultan decides that modernizing the royal court is in order. Before he can do so, a series of murders disturbs the once-peaceful atmosphere. He asks Yashim to investigate, and Yashim turns up connections between the crimes and the Janissaries, an elite group of soldiers who were banned from the empire ten years earlier for disloyalty. Edgar Award.

Keywords: Janissaries

The Snake Stone. Farrar, Straus & Giroux, 2007. 290pp. Hardbound, 9780374299354.

Maximilian Lefèvre, a French archaeologist in search of lost treasure from Byzantium, has been acting suspiciously, so the sultan orders Yashim to check him out. Then Lefèvre is brutally murdered, and Yashim himself becomes a suspect. Sue Feder Memorial Historical Mystery Award.

Keywords: Archaeology; Treasure

Gordon, Alan.

Fools' Guild Mysteries.

Annotated under "Europe," previously in this chapter.

Harper, Tom.

Demetrios Askiates Series (also called Byzantine Mysteries).

A great battle between East and West is taking place in late eleventh-century Byzantium, as the armies of the First Crusade descend upon the land. These mercenaries have responded to Emperor Alexios's pleas to the pope, for Asia Minor needs help defending its lands against an incursion of Turks. Harper's detective, Demetrios Askiates, is a former soldier calling himself the "unveiler of mysteries." These novels are action-packed and colorful, and while crimes continue to occur (and be solved), the mystery content declines throughout the series. Harper also writes Napoleonic-era adventure novels as Edwin Thomas (Chapter 8). **Public detective/Traditional.**

Keywords: Askiates, Demetrios; Crusades and Crusaders

The Mosaic of Shadows. Thomas Dunne, 2005. 275pp. Hardbound, 0312338678.

In 1096 in Byzantium the emperor hires Demetrios to find a would-be assassin who launched an arrow that nearly killed him.

Keywords: Byzantium—11th century

Knights of the Cross. Thomas Dunne, 2006. 370pp. Hardbound, 0312338708.

By the winter of 1098 the Crusaders find themselves at the gates of Antioch, barely surviving a harsh siege of the fortress. Demetrios, accompanying the Crusade as a guide of sorts, tracks down the killer of a Norman knight.

Keywords: Knights; Syria—11th century

Siege of Heaven. Thomas Dunne, 2007. 518pp. Hardbound, 9780312338725.

This conclusion to the trilogy, more a straight historical adventure novel than a mystery, begins in 1098, where *Knights of the Cross* left off. The Crusaders are closing in on Jerusalem. Demetrios has grown weary of the mind-numbing slaughter and associated political and religious intrigue. When he's sent across the Egyptian desert on a diplomatic mission, his goal is mere survival.

Keywords: Egypt—11th century

Highland, Frederick,

Night Falls on Damascus. Thomas Dunne, 2006. 295pp. Hardbound, 0312337892.

Intrigue swirls around French-occupied Syria in 1933 in this twisting, occasionally convoluted historical mystery. Vera Tamiri, a beautiful woman of affluent background whose modern, feminist outlook bemuses the old-fashioned residents of Damascus, has been murdered. Police Inspector Nikolai Faroun is asked to solve the crime, amid pressures from various venues. At first he assumes a jealous lover did her in, but her philanthropic work with the city's downtrodden women may have been the real cause. **Public detective/ Traditional-Hard boiled.**

Keywords: Feminists; Policemen; Syria—20th century

Pearce, Michael.

Mamur Zapt Series.

Welshman Gareth Cadwallader Owen, formerly a member of the British Army, is better known as the Mamur Zapt, the British chief of Cairo's secret police during Edwardian times. He's intimately familiar with local geography and politics, unlike many of his fellow officers, which gives him a definite advantage in rooting out criminals and corruption; the murders he tackles are often politically motivated. With dry humor, he delicately navigates the uneasy political ground between Cairo's indirect British rulers and the Egyptian populace. Many of the earlier novels have been reissued by Poisoned Pen, with the titles slightly altered. **Public detective/Traditional.**

Keywords: Egypt—20th century; Mamur Zapt; Policemen

The Mamur Zapt and the Return of the Carpet. Doubleday, 1990. 176pp. Hardbound, 0385415206.

The Mamur Zapt and the Night of the Dog. Doubleday, 1991. 184pp. Hardbound, 0385415214

The Mamur Zapt and the Donkey-Vous. Mysterious, 1992. 265pp. Hardbound, 0892964863.

The Mamur Zapt and the Men Behind. Warner, 1993. 246pp. Hardbound, 0892964871.

The Mamur Zapt and the Girl in the Nile. Mysterious, 1994. 234pp. Hardbound, 0892965096.

The Mamur Zapt and the Spoils of Egypt. Mysterious, 1995. 186pp. Hardbound, 0892965606.

The Camel of Destruction. Poisoned Pen, 2002. 196pp. Hardbound, 1590580249.

The Snake Catcher's Daughter. Poisoned Pen, 2003. 194pp. Hardbound, 1590580516.

The Mingrelian Conspiracy. Poisoned Pen, 2003. 201pp. Hardbound, 1590580699.

The Fig Tree Murder. Poisoned Pen, 2003. 185pp. Hardbound, 1590580680.

The Last Cut. Poisoned Pen, 2004. 204pp. Hardbound, 1590580672.

Death of an Effendi. Poisoned Pen, 2004. 178pp. Hardbound, 1590580664.

A Cold Touch of Ice. Poisoned Pen, 2004. 226pp. Hardbound, 1590580656.

The Face in the Cemetery. Poisoned Pen, 2004. 217pp. Hardbound, 1590580702.

The Point in the Market. Poisoned Pen, 2005. 205pp. Hardbound, 1590581377.

Peters, Elizabeth.

Amelia Peabody Series. ★ YA

In the 1880s Amelia Peabody, a plain Victorian spinster, indulges her out-landish passion for Egyptology by traveling to Egypt and working as an amateur archaeologist. Radcliff Emerson, an Egyptologist she finds arro-gant and stuffy (at least at first), serves as Amelia's guide in both archaeo-logical excavations and crime solving. Under the bright desert sun, the two fall in love and marry; their precocious son Ramses (real name Wal-ter) solves his own mysteries in later books. Entertaining and smoothly told, with strong character development and vivid historical detail. Amelia's delightful sense of humor appears throughout. Peters is a pseud-onym for Barbara Mertz, a PhD in Egyptology who has written a number of nonfiction books on the subject. Peters's *Amelia Peabody's Egypt* (Mor-row, 2003, co-written with Kristen Whitbread) is a companion to the se-ries. **Amateur detective/Traditional.**

Keywords: Archaeology; Egypt—19th and 20th centuries; Mummies; Peabody, Amelia

Crocodile on the Sandbank. Dodd, Mead, 1975. 273pp. Hardbound, 0922890366.

The Curse of the Pharaohs. Dodd, Mead, 1981. 357pp. Hardbound, 0396079636.

The Mummy Case. Congdon & Weed, 1985. 313pp. Hardbound, 0865531404.

Lion in the Valley. Atheneum, 1986. 291pp. Hardbound, 0689116195.

The Deeds of the Disturber. Atheneum, 1988. 289pp. Hardbound, 0689119070.

The Last Camel Died at Noon. Warner, 1991. 352pp. Hardbound, 0446514837.

The Snake, the Crocodile and the Dog. Warner, 1992. 340pp. Hardbound, 044651585X.

The Hippopotamus Pool. Warner, 1996. 384pp. Hardbound, 0446518336.
Seeing a Large Cat. Warner, 1997. 386pp. Hardbound, 0446518344.

The Ape Who Guards the Balance. Avon Twilight, 1998. 376pp. Hard-bound, 0380976579.

The Falcon at the Portal. Avon Twilight, 1999. 366pp. Hardbound, 0380976587.

He Shall Thunder in the Sky. William Morrow, 2000. 400pp. Hardbound, 0380976595.

Lord of the Silent. William Morrow, 2001. 404pp. Hardbound, 0380978849.

The Golden One. William Morrow, 2002. 429pp. Hardbound, 0380978857.

Children of the Storm. William Morrow, 2003. 400pp. Hardbound, 0066214769.

Guardian of the Horizon. William Morrow, 2004. 399pp. Hardbound, 0066214718.

The Serpent on the Crown. Morrow, 2005. 350pp. Hardbound, 0060591781.

Magda Petherick, widow of a noted collector of Egyptian artifacts, asks the Emersons to remove the curse from a golden statuette formerly belonging to her husband.

Tomb of the Golden Bird. Morrow, 2006. 381pp. Hardbound, 9780060591809.

It is 1922, and the Emersons hope to claim digging rights in the Valley of the Kings, for Emerson feels that King Tutankhamen's tomb is located there. Unfortunately their rivals, Howard Carter and Lord Carnavon, refuse to cooperate with them. Then the Emersons are accused of hiding a man others seem to be looking for.

Reed, Mary, and Eric Mayer.

John the Eunuch Mysteries.

Sixth-century Byzantium. Though Emperor Justinian follows the new Christian religion, his Lord Chamberlain, John the Eunuch, quietly worships the bull-god Mithras. Wise and respected for his position, John still has trouble dealing with his forced emasculation by barbarian captors years before. A unique protagonist in a singular setting, where paganism rivals Christianity, and survival depends on striking a balance between political factions. **Public detective/Traditional.**

Keywords: Byzantium—6th century; Eunuchs; John the Eunuch; Paganism

One for Sorrow. Poisoned Pen, 1999. 292pp. Hardbound, 1890208191.

Two for Joy. Poisoned Pen, 2000. 345pp. Hardbound, 189020837X.

Three for a Letter. Poisoned Pen, 2001. 268pp. Hardbound, 1890208825.

Four for a Boy. Poisoned Pen, 2002. 292pp. Hardbound, 1590580311.

Five for Silver. Poisoned Pen, 2004. 276pp. Hardbound, 1590581121.

Six for Gold. Poisoned Pen, 2005. 218pp. Hardbound, 1590581458.

Empress Theodora accuses John of murdering Senator Symacchus in the Hippodrome. Emperor Justinian, wanting to give John time to prove himself innocent, sends him to a remote village in Egypt where sheep are supposedly committing suicide.

Keywords: Sheep

Seven for a Secret. Poisoned Pen, 2008. 296pp. Hardbound, 9781590584897.

> John is taken aback at the brutal death of a young woman who had claimed to be the model for a girl in a mosaic John keeps on the wall of his study, and to which he had been confiding his thoughts about the imperial court.

> **Keywords:** Mosaics

White, Jenny.

Kamil Pasha Series.

Kamil Pasha, a magistrate in the secular courts of the late nineteenth-century Ottoman Empire, finds his unwavering beliefs in modernity challenged as he solves crimes that place him in the world of the land's traditional, socially rigid, and patriarchal past. White, a social anthropologist and professor, seems perfectly at home in her setting—the waning of the Ottoman Empire—and has also authored multiple nonfiction works on Turkish culture and society. **Public detective/Traditional/Literary.**

Keywords: Ottoman Empire—19th century; Pasha, Kamil; Policemen

The Sultan's Seal. Norton, 2006. 351pp. Hardbound, 0393060993.

> In 1886, when the body of an English governess at the imperial harem washes up on the shore of Istanbul, magistrate Kamil Pasha finds that the case calls to mind another unsolved murder of a past governess from years earlier.

> **Keywords:** Governesses

The Abyssinian Proof. Norton, 2008. 396pp. Hardbound, 9780393062052.

> Valuable, sacred artifacts from the Ottoman past are being smuggled from Istanbul's religious houses and sold on the black markets of Europe. Kamil Pasha, in charge of foiling the thefts, takes particular interest in helping out a friend whose mosque has lost an ancient reliquary that has been kept as a secret safely hidden over the past few centuries.

> **Keywords:** Reliquaries

Asia, Africa, and the Antipodes

Africa

Arruda, Suzanne.

Jade del Cameron Series.

Jade del Cameron, a native of Cimarron, New Mexico, developed a tough skin while attached to the French Army as an ambulance driver during the First World War. In 1919 her lover's dying words send her to Africa in search of the brother she didn't know he had, an act that turns her life around. An adventurous series that puts readers right into the action and drama of East Africa, a land where ancient traditions vie with the unyielding proprieties of British rule. **Amateur detective/Traditional.**

Keywords: del Cameron, Jade; Journalists, women; Photographers

Mark of the Lion. NAL, 2006. 340pp. Hardbound, 0451217489.

In 1919 Jade obeys the last request of her soldier fiancé, David, to find his illegitimate half-brother in Nairobi. While there on assignment as a journalist, Jade also learns that David's father was likely killed while searching for his other son, though the official reports say that he was mauled to death by a hyena in his hotel room. During her investigations she attracts the unwelcome attention of a witch doctor.

Keywords: Kenya—20th century

Stalking Ivory. NAL, 2007. 339pp. Hardbound, 9780451220264.

While on photography assignment near Mounta Marsabit in the remote northern territories of British East Africa, Jade and friends stumble across the remains of several elephants and one man. Abyssinian poachers are the clear culprit, or are they?

Keywords: Elephants

The Serpent's Daughter. Obsidian, 2008. 340pp. Hardbound, 9780451222947.

Jade joins her mother on holiday in Tangier, Morocco, in 1920, but is astonished when her mother is kidnapped. Then Jade herself is arrested for a murder she didn't commit.

Keywords: Kidnapping; Morocco—20th century; Mothers and daughters

Australia and New Zealand

Druett, Joan.

Wiki Coffin Series.

William "Wiki" Coffin, son of a Maori woman and a New England sea captain, is a "linguister" (translator) who joins the U.S. South Seas Exploring Expedition at its point of embarkation in Virginia in 1838; the group's mission is to chart and explore the Pacific. The physical attributes of Druett's heavily built hero, and those of other Polynesians in the novels, are based on the Hurricanes, New Zealand's famous rugby team. The novels take place at sea, aboard a fictional seventh vessel (the *Swallow*) of the expedition, at various points throughout the world. Maritime historian Joan Druett, who has written nonfiction accounts of men, women, and shipwrecks on the high seas, is a New Zealander who has done research in the United States as well. **Amateur detective/Traditional.**

Keywords: Argentina—19th century; Brazil—19th century; Coffin, Wiki; Explorers; Maori; Shipboard adventure; South Seas Exploring Expedition; Translators

A Watery Grave. Minotaur, 2004. 292pp. Hardbound, 0312334419.

In 1838 Virginia, after being cleared of a murder charge in the death of Mrs. Tristram T. Stanton, wife of the ship's astronomer, Wiki determines that the real killer is a member of the expedition.

Shark Island. Minotaur, 2005. 292pp. Hardbound, 0312334567.

> While exploring a disabled vessel found beached on the shore of Shark Island, off the Brazilian coast, Wiki and company discover the body of its captain.

Run Afoul. Minotaur, 2006. 280pp. Hardbound, 0312353367.

> At the port of Rio, the *Swallow* literally runs into a ship captained by William Coffin, Wiki's father. Wiki finds his detective skills tested when Coffin is arrested for murder.

Deadly Shoals. Minotaur, 2007. 290pp. Hardbound, 9780312353377.

> In 1839, while aboard the *Swallow* off the coast of Patagonia, Wiki, acting as sheriff's representative, agrees to help a New England whaling ship's captain locate a trader who's been cheating him. While searching for him on the mainland, he finds the man's body.

Greenwood, Kerry.

Phryne Fisher Series.

The Honorable Phryne (rhymes with "briny") Fisher is an independently wealthy, fun-loving, and fashionable young woman living in 1920s Melbourne, though her freewheeling adventures often take her elsewhere. Phryne is passionate about drinking champagne, dancing until dawn with handsome men, and helping those in need, as she always remembers her working-class background and childhood poverty (her life changed when her father inherited millions from a distant relative). She runs her own private detective agency in Melbourne. Though her glamour and stylishness never fade, the intelligent Phryne never lets either get in the way of solving mysteries, and despite the light tone, the novels delve into serious issues. The books, first published in Australia beginning in 1989, appeared in almost random order in the United States; the correct chronological order is below. **Private detective/Traditional.**

Keywords: Australia—20th century; Fisher, Phryne; Socialites

Cocaine Blues. Poisoned Pen, 2006. 175pp. Hardbound, 1590582365. (Alternate title: *Death by Misadventure.*)

Flying Too High. Poisoned Pen, 2006. Hardbound, 1590582373.

Murder on the Ballarat Train. Poisoned Pen, 2006. Hardbound, 1590582411.

Death at Victoria Dock. Poisoned Pen, 2006. 164pp. Hardbound, 1590582381.

The Green Mill Murder. Poisoned Pen, 2007. 173pp. Hardbound, 1590582403.

Blood and Circuses. Poisoned Pen, 2006. 204pp. Hardbound, 1590582357.

Ruddy Gore. Poisoned Pen, 2005. 207pp. Hardbound, 1590581180.

Urn Burial. Poisoned Pen, 2005. 187pp. Hardbound, 1590581695.

Raisins and Almonds. Poisoned Pen, 2007. Hardbound, 9781590581681.

Death Before Wicket. Poisoned Pen, 2008. 240pp. Hardbound, 9781590585573.

Away with the Fairies. Poisoned Pen, 2005. Hardbound, 1590580222.

Murder in Montparnasse. Poisoned Pen, 2004. Hardbound, 1590580427.

The Castlemaine Murders. Poisoned Pen, 2004. 240pp. Hardbound, 1590581172.

Queen of the Flowers. Poisoned Pen, 2008. 249pp. Hardbound, 9781590581711.

Death by Water. Poisoned Pen, 2008. 270pp. Hardbound, 9781590582398.

A Question of Death. Poisoned Pen, 2008. 258pp. Hardbound, 9781590585344.

> A collection of Phryne short stories and other miscellany, with full-color illustrations.

India

Cleverly, Barbara.

Detective Joe Sandilands Series.

During the last days of the British Raj in the 1920s, Scotland Yard detective Joe Sandilands, ready to return home after a six-month stint with the Bengal Police, gets caught up in political intrigue and murder. Action-packed mysteries in an exotic setting; the locale changes to England (and France) after book four, as Sandilands is finally allowed to return home after an extended posting to India. **Public detective/Traditional.**

Keywords: Policemen; Sandilands, Joe

The Last Kashmiri Rose. Carroll & Graf, 2002. 287pp. Hardbound, 0786710594.

Ragtime in Simla. Carroll & Graf, 2003. 288pp. Hardbound, 0786712465.

The Damascened Blade. Carroll & Graf, 2004. 285pp. Hardbound, 078671333X.

The Palace Tiger. Delta, 2006. 320pp. Paper, 0385340095.

> Sandilands determines that the plane crash death of an Indian prince, the Maharajah of Ranipur, was no accident.
>
> **Keywords:** India—20th century; Princes

The Bee's Kiss. Delta, 2007. 230pp. Paper, 9780385340410.

> In 1926 in London Sandilands is assigned to find the killer of beautiful society matron Beatrice Joliffe, a former wartime nurse, who was killed in her hotel room.
>
> **Keywords:** England—20th century; Socialites

Tug of War. Carroll & Graf, 2007. 255pp. Hardbound, 0786719575

> While in Reims, Sandilands tries to determine the identity of a shell-shocked veteran. With a lucrative pension forthcoming, there are many who'd like to claim he's part of their family.
>
> **Keywords:** France—20th century

Folly du Jour. Soho Constable, 2008. 288pp. Hardbound, 9781569475133.

> In 1927 in Paris Sandilands' old friend Sir George Jardine has been arrested for killing a former military colleague during a performance at the Folies Bergère.

> **Keywords:** France—20th century; Theater

Japan

Parker, I. J.

Sugarawa Akitada Mysteries.

Lord Sugawara Akitada, a minor government official in the eleventh-century city of Heian Kyo (early Kyoto), jumps at the chance to get out of his boring job by solving crimes. The volumes were accepted for publication out of chronological order; the correct sequence is below. **Amateur detective/Traditional.**

Keywords: Akitada, Sugawara; Japan—11th century

The Dragon Scroll. Penguin, 2005. 432pp. Paper, 0143035320.

> In his first outing Akitada, a junior clerk in the Ministry of Justice, is assigned to track down missing tax convoys traveling from Kazusa Province, where his job becomes bogged down by political intrigue.

Rashomon Gate. Minotaur, 2002. 336pp. Hardbound, 0312287984.

Black Arrow. Penguin, 2006. 356pp. Paper, 0143035614.

> In the year 1015 Akitada and family travel to the remote northern province of Echigo so that he can serve as provisional governor. They encounter hostility from locals, but when multiple murders occur, Akitada struggles to find a way to assert his authority.

Island of Exiles. Penguin, 2007. 416pp. Paper, 9780143112594.

> Akitada disguises himself as a prisoner on remote Sado Island to find out who killed the exiled Prince Okisada. Then Akitada himself goes missing, forcing his assistant, Tora, to discover what happened to him.

The Hell Screen. Minotaur, 2003. 338pp. Hardbound, 031228795X.

Rowland, Laura Joh.

Sano Ichirō Samurai Mysteries.

Due to family obligations, Sano Ichirō reluctantly abandons his career as a history tutor to become a *yoriki*, a senior member of the Edo police force, in 1689. Despite his samurai status, he's an outsider in the police ranks, and his crime-solving successes make him many enemies. Always inquisitive, Sano looks behind people's masks of politeness to discover the truth behind many murders—and finds political intrigue that could topple the Tokugawa regime. Rowland depicts late seventeenth-century Edo (the city that will eventually become Tokyo) with scenes that contrast its delicate beauty, the excesses of its pleasure quarters, and the ugliness of its prisons and morgues. The first book is **Amateur detective/Traditional,** while the rest are **Public detective/Traditional.**

Keywords: Ichirō, Sano; Japan—17th century; Shoguns

Shinjū. Random House, 1994. 367pp. Hardbound, 0679434224.

Bundori. Villard, 1996. 339pp. Hardbound, 0679434232.

The Way of the Traitor. Villard, 1997. 307pp. Hardbound, 0679449000.

The Concubine's Tattoo. Minotaur, 1998. 326pp. Hardbound, 0312192525.

The Samurai's Wife. Minotaur, 2000. 293pp. Hardbound, 031220325X.

Black Lotus. Minotaur, 2001. 341pp. Hardbound, 0312268726.

The Pillow Book of Lady Wisteria. Minotaur, 2002. 292pp. Hardbound, 0312282621.

The Dragon King's Palace. Minotaur, 2003. 340pp. Hardbound, 0312282664.

The Perfumed Sleeve. Minotaur, 2004. 326pp. Hardbound, 0312318898.

The Assassin's Touch. Minotaur, 2005. 320pp. Hardbound, 0312319002.

>   Sano, now promoted to be second-in-command and lord chamberlain to the shogun, hunts down the killer of the chief of the shogun's intelligence service.

>   **Keywords:** Spies

Red Chrysanthemum. Minotaur, 2006. 304pp. Hardbound, 0312355327.

>   Sano's investigations become ever more personal. When his pregnant, well-meaning wife Reiko decides to investigate the case of a missing child on her own, she puts his career (and her own life) at risk; she is discovered, unconscious and covered in blood, next to the body of a nobleman turned traitor.

The Snow Empress. Minotaur, 2007. 293pp, Hardbound, 9780312365424.

>   In 1699 Sano and Reiko, in desperation, travel to the remote northern island of Ezogashima (Hokkaido) to rescue their eight-year-old son, who has been kidnapped by Sano's political enemy. While there they become embroiled in solving the murder of a woman of the native Ainu people who was the mistress of a local samurai warlord.

>   **Keywords:** Ainu; Kidnapping

Chapter 8

Adventures in History

Historical adventure novels are known for their heroic protagonists, fast pace, and well-realized settings. Daring heroes (and, less occasionally, heroines) travel far and wide in their quest to find treasure, capture pirates, discover new lands, seek justice, fight the enemy on land and sea, or face off against nature. In some novels the simple thrill of seeking danger in foreign lands becomes a quest in itself.

Physical setting is important to historical adventure novels. The word "adventure" implies a journey of some sort, and the protagonists spend a good part of the story traveling from one place to another. This allows readers to become armchair travelers, learning about new civilizations and different ways of life as they follow the hero on his or her mission. In the case of military novels, the setting incorporates not only the physical location, but also the culture of men forced to work closely together in pursuit of victory. Many historical adventure novels feature protagonists from the Western world who survive in settings far away from home, such as Jerusalem during the Crusades, the icy Arctic in the nineteenth century, or aboard ship during the Napoleonic Wars. In other novels, such as some of those written by Gary Jennings, the exotic narrator belongs to the culture described. This makes the unusual setting even more of a culture shock to readers.

Because the plot involves physical movement, the pace is usually brisk. In this respect, historical adventure novels have much in common with historical thrillers, but in the former, the protagonist's opponent is generally a known commodity. The hero realizes in general who or what the enemy will be—such as a military foe, a warring culture, or simply survival on a lengthy sea voyage—though he may not always know how to combat it. Victory is not always assured, but it is the ultimate aim. There may be romantic subplots, but the romance always remains secondary to the hero's mission.

Characters in historical adventure novels have strong moral codes, which give them mental strength in fighting military rivals and facing off against the natural dangers found in wild, primitive settings. This moral code may or may not be obvious to readers at the outset. Dorothy Dunnett's Renaissance hero, Francis Crawford of Lymond, has reasons for his seemingly traitorous acts, though these aren't made clear to readers until the end of the series. Even pirates, normally thought to be the most immoral of rascals, live and die by rules that define their ruthless profession.

The adventure genre as a whole isn't known for strong characterization, though this stereotype doesn't always hold for historical adventure. Some heroes, such as the eunuch slave Taita in Wilbur Smith's <u>Egyptian</u> series, are unbelievably wise and all-powerful, which adds to the exaggerated, larger-than-life setting. Likewise, some villains are one-dimensionally evil. On the other hand, many historical adventure novels emphasize character development. Military novels in series, for example, can also be read as coming of age tales. Their protagonists, typically young midshipmen or soldiers as the series begins, grow in courage and stature throughout their long military careers. Also, although characters are forced to choose one side or the other in wartime settings, their choices, just like in real life, aren't always black and white.

Men are the primary characters in historical adventure novels; they are also the primary readers of these novels. This shouldn't be surprising, because in history participation in military action and world exploration has traditionally been a man's role. There are exceptions, of course. Dorothy Dunnett's series of novels, with their swashbuckling action, political intrigue, and romantic heroes, attract more female than male readers. Adventure novels with female protagonists do exist, but they are the minority (see "Women Adventurers," last section).

The themes and types of historical adventure novels, as annotated below, are defined by the nature of the hero's mission and the physical setting—and in most cases, these are related.

Medieval Adventure

Medieval men leave their homes to head out to parts unknown in search of treasure, revenge, or salvation, or to conquer new territory. The Crusades, a series of religious expeditions in medieval times in which men and women from the British Isles and Western Europe headed to the Holy Land to recapture Jerusalem from Muslim "infidels," are an ideal subject for historical adventure. Within the last few years Viking adventure tales have rivaled Crusade settings in popularity. In both cases, much of the action and excitement lies not in fighting the enemy, but in the journey itself.

Cornwell, Bernard.

The Saxon Chronicles. `YA`

During the late ninth century Uhtred of Bebbanburg, a Saxon boy from Northumbria, becomes an unlikely Viking warrior after marauding Danes kill his family. Adopted by Ragnar the Fearless—a Dane whose daring ways, bloodlust, and pagan beliefs hold much appeal—Uhtred comes of age in a most unlikely fashion. His most fervent hopes are to fight in a shield-wall alongside his fellow warriors and reclaim his lost inheritance, stolen by his treacherous uncle. Uhtred, his loyalties torn, eventually sides with Alfred, King of Wessex, who alone of his fellow English monarchs has the courage and manpower to fend off a pending Viking invasion. As is his forte, Cornwell writes exciting battle scenes with well-realized male characters.

Keywords: Alfred "the Great," King of England (historical character); England—early Middle Ages; Uhtred; Vikings

The Last Kingdom. HarperCollins, 2005. 333pp. Hardbound, 0060530510.

The Pale Horseman. HarperCollins, 2006. 349pp. Hardbound, 0060787120.

Lords of the North. HarperCollins, 2007. 317pp. Hardbound, 9780060888626.

Sword Song: The Battle for London. HarperCollins, 2008. 314pp. Hardbound, 9780060888640.

Galland, Nicole.

Crossed: A Tale of the Fourth Crusade. **Harper, 2008. 640pp. Paper, 9780060841805.**
Annotated in Chapter 2.

Harper, Tom.

Demetrios Askiates Series.
Annotated in Chapter 7; the first two novels in this series are mysteries.

Holland, Cecelia.

Corbin Loosestrife Series.
Annotated in Chapter 2.

Low, Robert.

Oathsworn Trilogy. YA
A century after the events of Cornwell's <u>Saxon Chronicles</u>, Viking warriors take to their ships, traveling the "whale road" (the sea) in search of legendary treasure once owned by Attila the Hun. Orm Rurikkson, a teenager from Norway, joins the band of brothers known as the Oathsworn, a group of Viking raiders and mercenaries sworn to be loyal only to one another. Set during the mid- to late tenth century, when Norse paganism was ceding power to Christianity, Low's series evokes the heroism, brutal fighting, and solemn clarity of the ancient Norse poems. The action sweeps from the Baltic Sea to Scotland to lands as far south as Istanbul.

Keywords: Coming of age; Explorers; Europe—Middle Ages; Shipboard adventure; Treasure; Vikings

The Whale Road. Thomas Dunne, 2007. 340pp. Hardbound, 9780312361945.

The Wolf Sea. Thomas Dunne, 2008. 339pp. Hardbound, 9780312361952.

Whyte, Jack.

The Templar Trilogy.
Annotated in Chapter 2.

Young, Robyn.

Brethren Trilogy.

At the time of the ninth and last Crusade, circa AD 1260, Christianity is losing its hold and influence on the Holy Land. The two protagonists, whose stories unfold in alternating sections, are Will Campbell, a young Scotsman newly initiated as a Knight Templar, and Baybars Bundukdari, Sultan of Egypt, who wants to rid his land of Western invaders. Not surprisingly, a *Da Vinci Code*–like subplot looms large. Page-turning action and religious fervor in Europe and the Middle East in London, Paris, Egypt, and Syria during medieval times; *The Fall of the Templars* will complete the series.

Keywords: Crusades and Crusaders; Jerusalem—Middle Ages; Knights Templar; Muslims

Brethren. Dutton, 2006. 483pp. Hardbound, 0525949755.

In a novel spanning twelve years, new and idealistic recruit Will Campbell trains to be a Knight Templar to follow in the footsteps of his father, James—who has gone off to fight Muslim warrior Baybars Bundukdari, a former slave who has risen in power. Will searches for the whereabouts of a stolen book that reveals a secret society, the Brethren, within the Templar organization. He also develops a romantic interest in his mentor's niece, Elwen, which challenges his vows of celibacy.

Crusade. Dutton, 2007. 493pp. Hardbound, 9780525950165.

Peace has been established in Acre by AD 1274, yet the situation is precarious. Western merchants, seeking to turn a profit, ignite hostilities between Christians and Mamelukes once again, in collaboration with the Templar grand master. Will Campbell, a member of the Brethren, a clandestine group dedicated to maintaining peace, is caught in the middle.

Swashbuckling Adventure

These are larger-than-life stories of reckless adventure, swordplay, and derring-do set in Europe between the Renaissance and the eighteenth century. The clever, romantic heroes of swashbuckling adventure fight duels with both weapons and their wits in pursuit of honor or to defend their good name. The historical novels of French writer Alexandre Dumas, set in the eighteenth-century royal court, are early examples of the swashbuckling tradition; the most famous of these include *The Three Musketeers* and *The Count of Monte Cristo*. Baroness Orczy's *The Scarlet Pimpernel*, about a dashing rogue who rescues French aristocrats from the guillotine, is another prime example. Pirate novels with dashing heroes, such as Rafael Sabatini's *Captain Blood* (annotated later this chapter), may also be considered works of swashbuckling adventure. Though this is a declining subgenre, many of the novels mentioned here are classics.

Allende, Isabel.

Zorro. HarperCollins, 2005. 390pp. Hardbound, 0060778970.

Annotated in Chapter 10.

Dumas, Alexandre.

The Last Cavalier. **Pegasus, 2007. 751pp. Hardbound, 9781933648316.**

In the early nineteenth century Hector de Sainte Hermine, a royalist nobleman, is called away from his wedding to fight for the Bourbon cause, as his father and two brothers did before him. Captured and imprisoned by Napoleon for three years, Hector is released on condition he become a common sailor. He rises in the seamen's ranks, fighting for France against England, doing his best to die an honorable death but never succeeding. Throughout he never forgets his original plan: taking revenge against the man, and regime, that killed his family. This heroic, unfinished novel of self-discovery and retribution by a renowned storyteller, found in a Parisian archive after 125 years, comes complete with numerous flashbacks, asides, and historical tidbits that give readers a sweeping picture of the Napoleonic era.

Keywords: France—early modern era; Napoleonic Wars; Nobility; Shipboard adventure

Dunnett, Dorothy.

The novels of the late Scottish novelist Dorothy Dunnett are difficult to categorize. Swashbuckling adventures at heart, they are also highly praised in literary circles and beloved by readers in general. Many find Dunnett's novels hard to get into, due to the challenging language and the fact that she drops readers directly into the action without any introduction. Her novels take place on a wide scale, with fictional characters intermingling with historical personalities as they journey through the courts of Europe. Her characters, like the novels themselves, are multifaceted, erudite, and complex. Dunnett's knowledge of Renaissance Europe—politics, art, and personalities included—was encyclopedic, so much so that reading her novels is a true learning experience. Her characters are as apt to speak in Latin or in French (of the sixteenth-century variety) as they are to converse in English. The novels are so full of literary references that two companion volumes (*The Dorothy Dunnett Companion*, volumes 1 and 2, ed. Elspeth Morrison) have been published.

The Chronicles of Lymond. ★

This six-book series is set over a ten-year period, from the 1540s through the 1550s, and plays out over a wide stage that includes Europe, Malta, and the Ottoman Empire during the Renaissance. At the beginning of *The Game of Kings*, Francis Crawford of Lymond, the younger son of a sixteenth-century Scottish nobleman, has just returned to Scotland. Edward VI, the child king who was Henry VIII's only legitimate son, is on the English throne. His cousin Mary, Queen of Scots, is still a child. Lymond had betrayed his country to England five years earlier, only to turn around and betray the English in turn. Nobody knows what his next move will be.

Handsome, brilliant, charismatic, and dangerous, Lymond is the ultimate romantic hero. As swift with a sword as he is with his wits, he is an acknowledged rogue who has the uncanny ability to know which way things will tip in the political arena. Yet he is also an antihero, for some of his actions seem cruel and inexplicable, and he is only seen through the eyes of other characters. The truth behind the enigma, along with a certain mystery about his birth, is finally revealed at the end. **Literary.**

Keywords: Crawford, Francis; Europe—Renaissance/Reformation; Families; Nobility; Scotland—16th century; Swordsmen

The Game of Kings. Putnam. 1961. 543pp. Hardbound.

Queens' Play. Putnam, 1964. 432pp. Hardbound.

The Disorderly Knights. Putnam, 1966. 503pp. Hardbound.

Pawn in Frankincense. Putnam, 1969. 486pp. Hardbound.

The Ringed Castle. Putnam, 1972. 521pp. Hardbound.

Checkmate. Putnam, 1975. 581pp. Hardbound.

The House of Niccolò.

Dunnett's second major series is set firmly in the realm of European commerce in the mid-fifteenth century. Claes vander Poele, also called Nicholas and Niccolò, begins the series as an apprentice dyer in the House of Charetty, a trading house in Bruges. Although at first he seems to be a good-natured, unsophisticated lad, behind his buffoonish guise lies one of the sharpest mercantile minds of his era—one he will use to his advantage in taking revenge on the family members who failed him and his mother. As Claes changes before readers' eyes from a simple artisan to courier, master merchant, and engineer in his travels across Europe, the city of Bruges develops into the very center of European trade, with routes open to Scotland, Germany, and Venice, as well as lands as far away as Africa and China. Like the Lymond series, these novels are full of adventure, romance, intrigue, and plenty of mystery, not the least of which is the relationship between Dunnett's two series. **Literary.**

Keywords: Europe—Renaissance/Reformation; Nobility; van der Poele, Nicholas

Niccolò Rising. Knopf, 1986. 470pp. Hardbound, 0394531078.

The Spring of the Ram. Knopf ,1988. 469pp. Hardbound, 0394564375.

Race of Scorpions. Knopf, 1990. 534pp. Hardbound, 039457107X.

Scales of Gold. Knopf, 1992. 519pp. Hardbound, 0394586271.

The Unicorn Hunt. Knopf, 1994. 656pp. Hardbound, 039458628X.

To Lie with Lions. Knopf, 1996. 626pp. Hardbound, 0394586298.

Caprice and Rondo. . Knopf, 1998. 539pp. Hardbound, 0679454772.

Gemini. Knopf, 2000. 672pp. Hardbound, 0679454780.

Fraser, George MacDonald.

The Reavers. **Knopf, 2008. 267pp. Hardbound, 9780307268105.**
With the same rollicking humor that typified his Flashman tales, Fraser (this novel was released posthumously) delivers a swashbuckling tale set on the Scottish border during Elizabethan times. Four over-the-top characters—a roguish

highwayman, a gallant Englishman, a buxom heroine named Lady Godiva, and her companion—stumble onto a Spanish plot to replace King James VI of Scotland with an impostor. Fraser's final novel is chock-full of deliberate anachronisms, horrible puns, and other gleeful wordplay.

Keywords: Imposters; Scotland—16th century

Gentle, Mary.

A Sundial in a Grave: 1610. **Perennial, 2005. 672pp. Paper, 0380820412.**

Written as the recovered memoirs of Valentin Raoul Rochefort, a fictional spymaster and swordsman in the pay of France's finance minister, this lengthy epic (printed in minuscule type) begins in 1610, a relatively peaceful period during the reign of France's Henri IV. Soon enough, Rochefort becomes embroiled in Marie de Medici's treacherous scheme against her royal husband, in which he participates in order to expose it. While fleeing France to save himself, an encounter with his nemesis, Dariole, involves him in a separate assassination plot against England's James I. Cinematic action scenes (Gentle excels at depicting swordplay) join realistic, tangible descriptions of the royal courts and back streets of early seventeenth- century Paris and London.

Keywords: England—Stuart era; France—Renaissance/Reformation; Spies; Swordsmen

Humphreys, C. C.

Jack Absolute Series.

Humphreys, a British/Canadian stage actor, bases his roguish lead character on the romantic hero from Richard Brinsley Sheridan's Georgian-era play *The Rivals.* However, his Jack Absolute—the real one, as Jack willfully points out—is none too pleased to learn that Sheridan has appropriated his name and identity, for his newfound fame in London interferes with his work as a British spy. Rollicking action and humor during the late eighteenth century, in Britain, Canada, and America.

Keywords: Absolute, Jack; Canada—18th century; French and Indian War; Mohawk Indians; Quebec, Battle of; Saratoga, Battle of; Spies; United States—American Revolution

The Blooding of Jack Absolute. Thomas Dunne, 2007. 311pp. Hardbound, 9780312358235.

As the title suggests, this entry presents Jack's coming of age as a soldier and spy. Humphreys steps back to Jack's childhood and teenaged years, recounting his youth spent with his abusive Uncle Duncan. After reuniting with his parents and spending time at an aristocratic boarding school, a run-in with his lover's jealous patron results in his joining the Light Dragoons and fighting at the Battle of Quebec with General Wolfe, during which Mohawk Indians siding with the French capture him.

8

Absolute Honor. Thomas Dunne, 2008. 312pp. Hardbound, 9780312358242.

> Returning to England, Jack helps take a French privateer, falls in love with the wrong woman, and gets unwittingly embroiled in the Jacobite cause.

Jack Absolute. Thomas Dunne, 2006. 310pp. Hardbound, 0312358229.

> In 1777 Jack's victory in a duel over an actress forces him to flee London for his life, back to his old haunts in the American colonies, and into his former job as a spy. He works alongside his old commander and chum John Burgoyne during the Battle of Saratoga. Later, using his contacts within the Mohawk, his adopted people, he convinces the Indians to join the Revolution on the British side.

Pérez-Reverte, Arturo.

Captain Alatriste Series. YA

Novelist Pérez-Reverte may be best known in the United States for his intellectual thrillers, but he made his name in his native Spain with this best-selling swash-buckling series about a legendary seventeenth-century Spanish swordsman. During Spain's Golden Age, Captain Diego Alatriste y Tenorio, a veteran of fighting the Thirty Years' War in Flanders, becomes a hired assassin, but one with a noble streak. Alatriste's loyal teenaged squire Íñigo Balboa narrates the pair's adventures, as they become involved in high-stakes political schemes, Spain's military quest to dominate the rebellious Netherlands, and other notable affairs of honor and derring-do.

Keywords: Alatriste, Diego; Assassins; Mercenaries; Spain—Renaissance/Reformation; Swordsmen; Thirty Years' War

Captain Alatriste. Putnam, 2005. 253pp. Hardbound, 039915275X.

Purity of Blood. Putnam, 2006. 267pp. Hardbound, 0399153209.

The Sun Over Breda. Putnam, 2007. 273pp. Hardbound, 9780399153839.

The King's Gold. Putnam, 2008. 289pp. Hardbound, 9780399155109.

Sabatini, Rafael.

Scaramouche. **Houghton Mifflin, 1921. 392pp. Hardbound.** ★

Sabatini's masterpiece of a moral adventure tale is set in the years leading up to the French Revolution. To avenge the death of his best friend, killed in an unjust duel against the evil Marquis de La Tour d'Azyr, Andre-Louis Moreau goes underground, feigning to believe in a cause he had previously laughed at. In disguise as "Scaramouche," he hides amid a group of traveling actors and discovers an unexpected talent for rallying crowds against the injustices of the nobility.

Keywords: Disguise; France—early modern era; French Revolution; Nobility; Swordsmen

Willig, Lauren.

Pink Carnation Series.

Annotated in Chapter 4.

Military Adventure

These are fast-paced adventure novels that present men's experiences in military encounters throughout history. Here the hero's goals are twofold: to vanquish the enemy, and, of more immediate concern, simply to stay alive. Among historical adventure fiction, this is the most popular and fastest growing subgenre. Most occur in series. This section does not include general novels of war (found in Chapter 2), because they concentrate less on the heroes' quest or mission and more on the overall wartime experience, though some readers may enjoy fiction of both types.

Ancient Greece and Rome

These novels re-create ancient battles and portray the military life of long ago. Readers who enjoy them may also want to read Steven Pressfield's novels, particularly *Gates of Fire* (Chapter 2).

Dietrich, William.

The Scourge of God. HarperCollins, 2005. 334pp. Hardbound, 006073499X.
Annotated in Chapter 2.

Duffy, James.

Gladiators of the Empire Series. **YA**

Quintus Honorius Romanus, son of one of ancient Rome's wealthiest men in AD 63, finds himself the victim of identity theft after a deadly storm kills his parents. With a detestable slave named Lucius cannily switching places with him, Quintus joins a gladiatorial school rather than face a life of slavery. As Taurus the Gladiator, and from Britannia to Rome itself, Quintus—determined to take revenge on the impostor—establishes a reputation for himself in the arena, along with his new friends and fellow gladiators: Lindani, an African beast hunter, and Amazonia, a female gladiator. In the second novel the trio get caught up in the Roman civil war during the Year of the Four Emperors, AD 69. Exciting fight scenes combine with historical detail on gladiatorial combat; Duffy, a screenwriter, put himself through "gladiator camp" (via historical reenactment) to add authenticity to his writing.

Keywords: Gladiators; Romanus, Quintus Honorius; Rome

Sand of the Arena. McBooks, 2005. 415pp. Hardbound, 1590131118.

The Fight for Rome. McBooks, 2007. 408pp. Hardbound, 9781590131121.

Ford, Michael Curtis.

Ford's blood-soaked, testosterone-laden battle scenes and solid research will satisfy fans of heroic men's adventure fiction. *The Fall of Rome* begins directly after *The Sword of Attila*, though both read well independently.

The Fall of Rome. **Thomas Dunne, 2007. 306pp. Hardbound, 9780312333621.** ✍

Attila, ruler of the Huns, dies unexpectedly in AD 453, leaving his empire in chaos. The Western Roman Empire, already weakened by decades of attack by barbarian tribes, seeks to reestablish itself, but corruption among its leaders undermines it further. Odoacter, son of a Hun leader, flees with his brother into exile after their father's murder. After seeking refuge temporarily with his mother's people, he emerges as a strong Roman leader, but switches sides to avenge his father's killing. Odoacter is a historical figure, known today as the first barbarian king of Italy.

Keywords: Huns; Italy; Odoacter (historical character)

The Sword of Attila. **Thomas Dunne, 2005. 338pp. Hardbound, 0312333609.** ✍

In the early fifth century AD, two future leaders are brought up in each other's environment to enforce a peace treaty. Young Attila grows up in the Ravenna court, while Flavius Aetius, the future supreme general of Rome's armies, is sent to live among the nomadic Huns. When they return to their own people, the hope is that their knowledge of the other's ways will help them forge a lasting peace, but alas, it doesn't happen. This massive clash of cultures comes to a head at the bloody Battle of Chalons.

Keywords: Attila the Hun (historical character); Chalons, Battle of; Flavius Aetius (historical character); France; Huns

Gemmell, David, and Stella Gemmell.

Troy Series.

This version of the Trojan War may challenge those who know the original story. Some characters follow their roles in Homer's *Iliad*, while others are Gemmell creations. The obvious protagonist is Helikaon, known as the Lord of the Silver Bow (or Aeneas, Prince of Dardania), a warrior and trader along the Great Green (the Mediterranean). The inevitable war at Troy, begun by King Agamemnon of Mykene, is fought over control of these same trade routes. (Helen of Troy is a very minor character.) Gemmell, best known for his brawny fantasy novels, develops his female characters equally well here, notably Andromache, the strong-willed Priestess of Thera, reluctantly betrothed to Hektor, Prince of Troy. Gemmell's taut writing style, ferocious battle scenes, and excellent characterizations add new depth to the familiar legend. After his death in 2006, his widow, Stella—an editor who was his longtime researcher—completed his final book seamlessly.

Keywords: Greece; Helikaon; Mythology; Trojan War

Troy: Lord of the Silver Bow. Del Rey, 2005. 476pp. Hardbound, 0345458354.

Troy: Shield of Thunder. Del Rey, 2006. 490pp. Hardbound, 0345477014.

Troy: Fall of Kings. Del Rey, 2008. 447pp. Hardbound, 9780345477033.

Iggulden, Conn.

Emperor Series. ✍ YA

A four-part series set in ancient Rome in the first century BC. Iggulden is at his best when it comes to plotting, and his action scenes are swift and powerful. He's weaker at characterization, though, and acknowledges playing with history. In reality, his two protagonists, Caesar and Brutus, were fifteen years apart in age.

Keywords: Caesar, Julius (historical character); Emperors; Rome

Emperor: The Gates of Rome. Delacorte, 2003. 357pp. Hardbound, 0385336608.

> At the end of the Roman Republic, two boys grow up amid the brutality, violence, and intrigue that pervades the city. They are Gaius, the son of a powerful senator and nephew of one of Rome's greatest leaders, and Marcus, the bastard son of a prostitute. They train for combat together. Later, Gaius learns the craft of statehood in the Senate, and Marcus becomes a soldier on the battlefields of Greece. Gaius, otherwise known as Gaius Julius Caesar, will grow up to become the most powerful emperor that Rome has ever known; Marcus's identity is hidden until the end. When they meet again as men, their friendship is put to the test.

Emperor: The Death of Kings. Delacorte, 2004. 469pp. Hardbound, 0385336624.

> Off the coast of North Africa, pirates kidnap Caesar and hold him captive. After he ransoms himself, he is left to make his own way back to Rome. Meanwhile, back in the heart of the Empire, Brutus rises in political power.

Emperor: The Field of Swords. Delacorte, 2005. 466pp. Hardbound, 0385336632.

> Julius Caesar's military campaigns form the heart of this third volume. Having been elected consul Caesar, conqueror of an ever-broadening sweep of territories, crushes a rebellion against Rome, then casts his gaze westward, toward Gaul and Britain.

Emperor: The Gods of War. Delacorte, 2006. 383pp. Hardbound, 0385337671.

> Fresh from victories in the west, Caesar and his legions cross the Rubicon to face treachery in Rome. This last volume spans five years, encompassing the civil war with Pompey, Caesar's canny political exploits (including his being proclaimed dictator for life and his liaison with Cleopatra), and betrayal by his former best friend, Brutus, which leads to the fateful Ides of March in 44 BC.

Oden, Scott.

Men of Bronze. **Medallion, 2004. 473pp. Hardbound, 193281518X.**

The kingdom of Egypt, an empire in decline in 526 BC, is under attack by forces of the king of Persia. Hasdrubal Barca, a Phoenician mercenary in the pay of the pharaoh, remains loyal to his Egyptian master. The defection of Phanes (a high-ranking Greek general) from Egypt's ranks tests Barca's mettle to the utmost, and the political becomes personal as the two enemies engage in battle throughout Egypt and Palestine.

Keywords: Egypt; Mercenaries

Memnon. **Medallion, 2006. 503pp. Hardbound, 1932815392.** ✍

Memnon, a native Greek born on the island of Rhodes in the fourth century BC, flees his homeland after his father's beheading. He continues to rise in strength and power, eventually becoming a mercenary in the pay of Darius, King of Persia. When Alexander of Macedon musters his forces and invades Asia Minor, Memnon is there to meet them. His story unfolds from the viewpoint of a mysterious woman lying on her deathbed.

Keywords: Greece; Memnon of Rhodes (historical character); Mercenaries; Persia

Scarrow, Simon.

Cato Series.

This series follows the Roman invasion of Britain in AD 43 from the point of view of the invaders. In Germany, Centurion Lucius Cornelius Macro commands the Second Legion, the most powerful fighting force in the Empire. The soldiers are less than thrilled at being sent to the barbaric British Isles to subdue the native tribes and conquer the lands for Rome. They are also disturbed by the arrival of a new recruit, Quintus Licinus Cato, who is made second in command because of personal connections. As Cato grows from a beardless boy into a hardened soldier, he and Macro fight their way west toward Britain, uncovering not only enemies but also conspiracies against the Emperor Claudius. Scarrow's characters fight and swear like a bunch of Roman soldiers, which, of course, they are. The series continues in Great Britain, with additional volumes *The Eagle in the Sand* and *Centurion.*

Keywords: Cato, Quintus Licinus; England; Soldiers

Under the Eagle. Thomas Dunne, 2001. 246pp. Hardbound, 0312278705.

The Eagle's Conquest. Thomas Dunne, 2002. 310pp. Hardbound, 0312305338.

When the Eagle Hunts. Thomas Dunne, 2004. 272pp. Hardbound, 0312305354.

The Eagle and the Wolves. Thomas Dunne, 2004. 306pp. Hardbound, 0312324480.

The Eagle's Prey. Thomas Dunne, 2005. 306pp. Hardbound, 0312324510.

The Eagle's Prophecy. Thomas Dunne, 2006. 310pp. Hardbound, 0312324545.

The Age of Fighting Sail

These novels take place between 1775 and 1815, a forty-year period that saw Great Britain engage in a number of maritime battles. At its beginning was the American Revolution; at the end was Napoleon's final defeat at Waterloo. The high point for the era—and in many of the novels—was the Battle of Trafalgar in 1805, when Britain's Royal Navy, under Lord Horatio Nelson, succeeded in destroying a combined French-Spanish fleet. Due to its victory at Trafalgar, Britain effectively gained control of the world's oceans for the next 100 years.

Not only do these novels contain pulse-pounding battle scenes aboard ship, but they also provide good doses of character development, scenes of politics and treason, fast-paced action, and enough authentically described nautical detail to make landlubbing readers feel at home on the high seas. The originator of naval fiction set in the Napoleonic era was Captain Frederick Marryat (1792—1848), himself a British naval hero who survived more than fifty shipboard battles. His *Mr. Midshipman Easy* (1808), a humorous yet realistic take on life aboard a British man-of-war, served as a model for works by C. S. Forester, Alexander Kent, and others. The majority of the authors presented here are veteran sailors themselves, which lends a sense of realism to their heroic tales.

Forester, C. S.

Horatio Hornblower Series. ★

Horatio Hornblower is one of the most engaging and beloved heroes in all of naval literature. With strict technical accuracy, Forester brought to life the Age of Sail with a protagonist based partially on Lord Horatio Nelson, the hero of Trafalgar. In 1793, at the height of the French Revolution, the seventeen-year-old Hornblower joins the British Navy as a midshipman aboard the *Justinian*. He serves British interests in Europe, the Mediterranean, and the West Indies during the Napoleonic Wars, all the while rising in his career until he reaches the rank of admiral. C. Northcote Parkinson, author of the Richard Delancey series, was a devoted Forester fan. His fictional biography of Forester's hero, *The Life and Times of Horatio Hornblower* (Little, Brown, 1970) holds up well alongside Forester's own *Hornblower Companion* and does a good job of convincing the reader that Hornblower really lived. They are best enjoyed in historical order, below.

Keywords: Hornblower, Horatio; Napoleonic Wars; Navy; Shipboard adventure

Mr. Midshipman Hornblower. Little, Brown, 1950. 310pp. Hardbound.

Lieutenant Hornblower. Little, Brown, 1952. 306pp. Hardbound.

Hornblower and the Hotspur. Little, Brown, 1962. 344pp. Hardbound.

Hornblower and the Atropos. Little, Brown, 1953. 325pp. Hardbound.

Beat to Quarters. Little, Brown, 1937. 324pp. Hardbound. (Alternate title: *The Happy Return.*)

Ship of the Line. Little, Brown, 1938. 323pp. Hardbound. (Alternate title: *A Ship of the Line.*)

Flying Colours. Little, Brown, 1939. 294pp. Hardbound.

Commodore Hornblower. Little, Brown, 1945. 384pp. Hardbound. (Alternate title: *The Commodore.*)

Lord Hornblower. Little, Brown, 1946. 322pp. Hardbound.

Admiral Hornblower in the West Indies. Little, Brown, 1958. 329pp. Hardbound. (Alternate title: *Hornblower in the West Indies.*)

Hornblower During the Crisis. Little, Brown, 1967. 174pp. Hardbound. This novel, a compilation of two short stories taking place in 1805 (fourth chronologically), remained unfinished at Forester's death.

Kent, Alexander.

Richard Bolitho Novels.

Kent's lengthy series features conspiracy on the high seas, piracy, honor, loyalty, and treason, all seen through the eyes of Richard Bolitho, a young man who starts out as a midshipman in His Majesty's Navy in 1772. As he matures and gets promoted in rank, he sees action in New York, the Caribbean, India, New South Wales, the Mediterranean, and also back home in Portsmouth, England. The later volumes, beginning with *Second to None*, feature the exploits of Bolitho's nephew, Adam, captain of the frigate *Unrivalled*, in the aftermath of Waterloo in 1815. Alexander Kent is the pseudonym for Douglas Reeman, who writes contemporary and historical adventure novels under his own name. The novels, all in print from McBooks, are presented in historical order; the first three form what Kent calls the Midshipman Trilogy.

Keywords: Bolitho, Adam; Bolitho, Richard; Napoleonic Wars; Navy; Shipboard adventure

Richard Bolitho, Midshipman. Putnam, 1976. 158pp. Hardbound, 0399205144.

Midshipman Bolitho and the **Avenger.** Putnam, 1978. 143pp. Hardbound, 0399206523. (First two novels also published in one volume as *Midshipman Bolitho.*)

Band of Brothers. McBooks, 2005. 144pp. Hardbound, 1590131061.

Stand into Danger. Putnam, 1981. 296pp. Hardbound, 0399125396.

In Gallant Company. Putnam, 1977. 287pp. Hardbound, 0399119876.

Sloop of War. Putnam, 1972. 319pp. Hardbound.

To Glory We Steer. Putnam, 1968. 328pp. Hardbound.

Command a King's Ship. Putnam, 1974. 320pp. Hardbound.

Passage to Mutiny. Putnam, 1976. 319pp. Hardbound,

With All Despatch. Putnam, 1989. 289pp. Hardbound,

Form Line of Battle! Putnam, 1969. 320pp. Hardbound,

Enemy in Sight! Putnam, 1970. 350pp. Hardbound.

The Flag Captain. Putnam, 1971. 384pp. Hardbound.

Signal—Close Action! Putnam, 1974. 320pp. Hardbound, 0399114483.

The Inshore Squadron. Putnam, 1979. 256pp. Hardbound, 0399123032.

A Tradition of Victory. Putnam, 1982. 296pp. Hardbound, 0399127062.

Success to the Brave. Putnam, 1983. 284pp. Hardbound, 0399128786.

Colors Aloft! Putnam, 1986. 300pp. Hardbound, 039912988X.

Honour This Day. Putnam, 1988. 287pp. Hardbound.

The Only Victor. McBooks, 2000. 384pp. Hardbound, 0935526749.

Beyond the Reef. McBooks, 2000. 349pp. Hardbound, 093552682X.

The Darkening Sea. McBooks, 2000. 351pp. Hardbound, 0935526838.

For My Country's Freedom. McBooks, 2000. 300pp. Hardbound, 0935526846.

Cross of St. George. McBooks, 2001. 320pp. Hardbound, 0935526927.

Sword of Honour. McBooks, 2001. 320pp. Hardbound, 0935526935.

Second to None. McBooks, 2001. 350pp. Hardbound, 0935526943.

Relentless Pursuit. McBooks, 2001. 336pp. Hardbound, 1590130006.

Man of War. McBooks, 2003. 319pp. Hardbound, 159013091X.

Heart of Oak. McBooks, 2007. 270pp. Hardbound, 9781590131374.

Lambdin, Dewey.

Alan Lewrie Naval Adventure Series.

The bastard son of a snobbish London aristocrat, seventeen-year-old Alan Lewrie finds himself banished to the Royal Navy in 1780 by his own father after his latest amorous adventure lands him in hot water. Aboard the *Ariadne*, Lewrie—the bad boy of the high seas—discovers an unexpected liking for seamanship. He acquits himself well in naval battles, though his growth as a sailor does little to tame his scandalous ways on land.

Keywords: Lewrie, Alan; Napoleonic Wars; Navy; Shipboard adventure

The King's Coat. Fine, 1989. 397pp. Hardbound, 1556111428.

The French Admiral. Fine, 1990. 414pp. Hardbound, 1556112084.

The King's Commission. Fine, 1991. 400pp. Hardbound, 1556111878.

The King's Privateer. Fine, 1992. 360pp. Hardbound, 1556113242.

The Gun Ketch. Fine, 1993. 312pp. Hardbound, 1556113560.

H.M.S. Cockerel. Fine, 1995. 360pp. Hardbound, 155611446X.

A King's Commander. Fine, 1997. 374pp. Hardbound, 1556115040.

Jester's Fortune. Dutton, 1999. 373pp. Hardbound, 0525944826.

King's Captain. St. Martin's Press, 2000. 358pp. Hardbound, 0312268858.

Sea of Grey. Thomas Dunne, 2002. 391pp. Hardbound, 0312286856.

Havoc's Sword. Thomas Dunne, 2003. 384pp. Hardbound, 0312286880.

The Captain's Vengeance. Thomas Dunne, 2004. 352pp. Hardbound, 0312315473.

A King's Trade. Thomas Dunne, 2006. 339pp. Hardbound, 031231549X.

Troubled Waters. Thomas Dunne, 2008. 307pp. Hardbound, 9780312348052.

O'Brian, Patrick.

Aubrey/Maturin Series. ★

O'Brian's twenty <u>Aubrey/Maturin</u> novels form the best known, and easily the most admired, historical naval fiction series in existence. Against the backdrop of the Napoleonic Wars, Captain Jack Aubrey of His Majesty's Navy and his friend Stephen Maturin, ship's surgeon and occasional spy, engage the French and Spanish in a series of fierce sea battles. Though these novels offer as much authentic naval detail as readers can hope for, they provide much more. O'Brian's eloquent dialogue and literary writing style reflect that of the late eighteenth century. He also explores human relationships, using the friendship between Aubrey and Maturin—and the camaraderie that forms among all the men aboard a single vessel—as prime examples. The plots move more slowly than those of most naval adventure novels, but O'Brian's emphasis on thorough research and character development more than compensates. His detailed portraits of these brave men bring the Napoleonic era to life and, at the same time, demonstrate that human nature has not changed over the years. With O'Brian's death in 2000 came the end of the series, or so readers thought. An unfinished final volume, *21,* includes three chapters found on O'Brian's desk after his death.

Keywords: Aubrey, Jack; Maturin, Stephen; Napoleonic Wars; Navy; Shipboard adventure; Surgeons

Master and Commander. Lippincott, 1969. 384pp. Hardbound. 📖

Post Captain. Lippincott, 1972. 413pp. Hardbound, 039700804X.

H.M.S. Surprise. Lippincott, 1973. 318pp. Hardbound, 0397009984.

The Mauritius Command. Stein & Day, 1978. 268pp. Hardbound, 0812824768.

Desolation Island. Stein & Day, 1979. 276pp. Hardbound, 081282590X.

Fortune of War. W.W. Norton, 1991. 329pp. Hardbound, 0393308138.

The Surgeon's Mate. W. W. Norton, 1992. 382pp. Hardbound, 0393308200.

The Ionian Mission. W. W. Norton, 1992. 367pp. Hardbound, 0393308219.

Treason's Harbour. W. W. Norton, 1992. 334pp. Hardbound, 0393308634.

The Far Side of the World. W. W. Norton, 1992. 366pp. Hardbound, 0393308626.

The Reverse of the Medal. W. W. Norton, 1992. 287pp. Hardbound, 0393309606.

The Letter of Marque. W. W. Norton, 1990. 284pp. Hardbound, 0393028747.

The Thirteen-Gun Salute. W. W. Norton, 1991. 319pp. Hardbound, 0393029743.

The Nutmeg of Consolation. W. W. Norton, 1991. 315pp. Hardbound, 0393030326.

The Truelove. W. W. Norton, 1992. 256pp. Hardbound, 0393031098. (Original title: *Clarissa Oakes.*)

The Wine-Dark Sea. W. W. Norton, 1993. 261pp. Hardbound, 0393035581.

The Commodore. W. W. Norton, 1995. 281pp. Hardbound, 0393037606.

The Yellow Admiral. W. W. Norton, 1996. 261pp. Hardbound, 0393040445.

The Hundred Days. W. W. Norton, 1998. 280pp. Hardbound, 0393046745.

Blue at the Mizzen. W. W. Norton, 1999. 261pp. Hardbound, 0393048446.

21: The Unfinished Twenty-First Volume in the Aubrey-Maturin Series. W.W. Norton, 2004. 144pp. Hardbound, 039306025X.

Russell, S. Thomas.

Under Enemy Colors. **Putnam, 2007. 486pp. Hardbound, 9780399154430.**
The year is 1793. While Britain fights revolutionary-era France on the high seas, Royal Navy Lt. Charles Hayden, half French and half British, finds his loyalties torn. He serves with honor aboard the frigate HMS *Themis* in spite of his ambivalence about engaging French ships in battle. Good thing, too, because his cowardly superior, Capt. Josiah Hart, tyrannizes the ship's crew, and Hayden's resourcefulness and levelheadedness are sorely needed.

Keywords: Mixed heritage; Napoleonic Wars; Navy; Shipboard adventure

Stockwin, Julian.

Kydd Sea Adventures Series.
At the end of the eighteenth century Britain is at war with France, but it lacks sufficient personnel to man its ships. As a result of this shortage, Stockwin's hero, Thomas Kydd, a young wig-maker from the landlocked town of Guildford, is pressed into the Royal Navy. The conditions aboard ship are horrible, but Kydd has no choice but to accustom himself to his fate. He befriends fellow novice sailor Thomas Renzi, and to their surprise, the two find themselves relishing the cutthroat battles and dangerous excitement of the Age of Sail. By the seventh volume, *Command*, Kydd has finally become captain of his own ship, the brig-sloop *Teazer*. The action ranges from Britain and France to Malta and also to Australia, where Kydd transports convicts in order to keep his ship afloat monetarily. Stockwin is a retired Lt. Commander in the Royal Navy. His series is expected to last at least eleven volumes. *Privateer's Revenge* will be next.

Keywords: Kydd, Thomas; Napoleonic Wars; Navy; Shipboard adventure

Kydd. Scribner, 2001. 254pp. Hardbound, 0743214587.

Artemis. Scribner, 2002. 334pp. Hardbound, 0743214609.

Seaflower. Scribner, 2003. 320pp. Hardbound, 0743214625.

Mutiny. Scribner, 2004. 336pp. Hardbound, 0743258002.

Quarterdeck. McBooks, 2005. 320pp. Hardbound, 1590131150.

Tenacious. McBooks, 2006. 335pp. Hardbound, 1590131193.

Command. McBooks, 2007. 319pp. Hardbound, 9781590131206.

The Admiral's Daughter. McBooks, 2007. 323pp. Hardbound, 9781590131435.

Thomas, Edwin.

The Reluctant Adventures of Martin Jerrold.

Lt. Martin Jerrold, Thomas's charming but hapless hero, slept through the Battle of Trafalgar; he was trapped below decks with a horrible hangover. His adventures begin in 1806, as he is forced to redeem his ne'er-do-well reputation. Whether he's investigating a murder or fending for himself aboard ship, he strives to avoid falling into trouble, but he has an uncanny habit of attracting bad luck. Edwin Thomas also writes as Tom Harper.

Keywords: Jerrold, Martin; Napoleonic Wars; Navy; Shipboard adventure

The Blighted Cliffs. Thomas Dunne, 2004. 298pp. Hardbound, 0312325118.

After his embarrassing behavior at Trafalgar, Jerrold is banished by his uncle the admiral to the city of Dover, where he's assigned to a shipboard smuggler-catching operation. When he finds a body on the beach, he is immediately suspected of murder and must quickly clear his name. Unfortunately only Isobel, a girl from the Dover wharves, sympathizes with him.

Keywords: Detective stories; England—Georgian era; Smugglers

The Chains of Albion. Thomas Dunne, 2005. 302pp. Hardbound, 0312325134.

Jerrold, now captain of a vessel transporting French prisoners, loses his command when one of the prisoners escapes. The First Lord of the Admiralty insists that Jerrold find him, sending him on a manhunt throughout all of southern England.

Keywords: Prisoners

Treason's River. Thomas Dunne, 2007. 357pp. Hardbound, 9780312325169.

As Jerrold is in the process of fleeing to New York, British spies catch up with him and request he deliver a letter to a man in Pittsburgh, in the hopes of stopping another Anglo–American war.

Worrall, Jay.

Charles Edgemont Series.

Unlike many heroes of Napoleonic-era naval fiction, Charles Edgemont of His Britannic Majesty's Navy is an experienced sailor at the series beginning, yet he's relatively untested in battle conditions. He achieves independent command of a vessel when he's still young, which gives Worrall a chance to show how Charles reacts to this surprising change of fortune.

Keywords: Edgemont, Charles; Napoleonic Wars; Navy; Shipboard adventure

Sails on the Horizon. Random House, 2005. 284pp. Hardbound, 1400063051.

Charles, aged twenty-five in 1797, serves as second lieutenant aboard the *Argonaut*, a small ship of the line assigned to engage the Spanish—who have changed sides, and now fight against England—off Portugal's coast. But despite his quick promotion up the ranks to commander, when he returns home from war he faces his hardest battle: convincing Penny Brown, a beautiful (and pacifist) Quaker, to marry him.

Keywords: Portugal—early modern era; Quakers

Any Approaching Enemy. Random House, 2006. 276pp. Hardbound, 140006306X.

> As captain of the frigate *Louisa,* Charles joins Admiral Horatio Nelson's fleet patrolling the Mediterranean, where they search for a missing French squadron. He loses track of Nelson's ship after a horrific storm, but the British fleet regroups in Egypt, culminating in the Battle of the Nile in 1798.

> **Keywords:** Egypt—18th century; Nile, Battle of the

American Naval Warfare

Historical naval adventure novels told from the American point of view were rare until relatively recently, but readers now have several growing series to choose from.

Campbell, Broos.

Matty Graves Series. YA

Matty Graves, a young officer, narrates his own adventures during the first years of the U.S. Navy. His career begins aboard the USS *Rattle-Snake,* a small schooner sent to Caribbean waters in 1799. Matty has more problems to worry about than sea battles against France, however, such as his fellow shipmates—including his drunk of a cousin, Billy, who happens to be the captain. He also deals with politics and warfare on land, such as the Haitian Revolution. Matty's running commentary on the situations he finds himself in is wryly funny.

Keywords: Caribbean—18th century; Graves, Matty; Haitian slave revolt; Navy; Shipboard adventure

No Quarter. McBooks, 2006. 261pp. Hardbound, 1590131037.

The War of Knives. McBooks, 2007. 309pp. Hardbound, 9781590131046.

Peter Wicked. McBooks, 2008. 320pp. Hardbound, 9781590131527.

Fender, J. E.

Geoffrey Frost Series.

Captain Geoffrey Frost of Portsmouth, New Hampshire, a young but well-trained mariner, becomes a privateer recruited by the American cause during the revolution against Britain. His friend and aide is Ming Tsun, whom he had rescued, and been rescued by in turn, during their previous naval adventures in China. A ten-volume series is planned. The author is legal counsel for the Portsmouth Naval Shipyard.

Keywords: Frost, Geoffrey; Privateers; Shipboard adventure; United States—American Revolution

The Private Revolution of Geoffrey Frost. University Press of New England, 2002. 297pp. Hardbound, 1584652128.

8

Audacity, *Privateer out of Portsmouth.* University Press of New England, 2003. 298pp. Hardbound, 1584653167.

Our Lives, Our Fortunes. University Press of New England, 2004. 309pp. Hardbound, 1584653752.

On the Spur of Speed. University Press of New England, 2005. 313pp. Hardbound, 1584654759.

The Lucifer Cypher. Broadsides, 2006. 262pp. Paper, 0972630392.

Hammond, William C.

Richard Cutler Series.

Richard Cutler, a patriotic teenager from the coastal town of Hingham, Massachusetts, comes of age during the years of the American Revolution. Cutler's family still has strong ties with England, which allows readers to see the war from both sides. More volumes are expected.

Keywords: Cutler, Richard; Navy; Shipboard adventure; United States—American Revolution

A Matter of Honor. Cumberland House, 2007. 416pp. Hardbound, 9781581526098.

> To avenge his brother Will, who was flogged to death by the Royal Navy, Richard signs on with the American navy as a midshipman, serving under John Paul Jones. Hammond follows his life through the end of the war at Yorktown. In the interim, Richard sees considerable action aboard ship, and through his travels from England to France to the West Indies he encounters many of the Revolutionary War's major players.

Macomber, Robert N.

Lt. Peter Wake Series.

Naval historian Macomber carves out unique fictional territory with his ongoing series set along the coast of Florida, the Carolinas, and the Caribbean during the Civil War. By 1863 native New Englander Peter Wake has been following in his father's and grandfather's footsteps as a sailor, and he joins the U.S. Navy when conscription is imminent. Naval warfare in these tropical climes is both less glorious and less organized than he expects, but he rises in rank, obtaining larger commands and getting involved in pro-Union espionage. After war's end (and beginning with book four, *A Dishonorable Few*), his orders take him to Central America, the West Indies, and the west coast of South America.

Keywords: Caribbean—19th century; Florida—Civil War; Navy; Shipboard adventure; Spies; Wake, Peter

At the Edge of Honor. Pineapple, 2002. 278pp. Hardbound, 1561642525.

Point of Honor. Pineapple, 2003. 327pp. Hardbound, 1561642703.

Honorable Mention. Pineapple, 2004. 327pp. Hardbound, 1561643114.

A Dishonorable Few. Pineapple, 2005. 358pp. Hardbound, 1561643394.

An Affair of Honor. Pineapple, 2006. 366pp. Hardbound, 1561643688.

A Different Kind of Honor. Pineapple, 2007. 382pp. Hardbound, 9781561643981.

Nelson, James L.

Bowater Series.

Like Ker Clairborne in David Poyer's *A Country of Our Own*, Samuel Bowater is a reluctant recruit to the Confederate Navy—at least at first. A native of Charleston, South Carolina, on leave from the U.S. Navy, Bowater makes the hard decision to join his state against the Union.

Keywords: Bowater, Samuel; Navy; Shipboard adventure; United States—Civil War

Glory in the Name. Morrow, 2003. 420pp. Hardbound, 0060199695.

Though used to serving on larger vessels, Bowater is pleased enough to receive command of the tug C.S.S. *Cape Fear*, and he and his men use it to defend the Mississippi River against Yankees.

Thieves of Mercy. Morrow, 2005. 463pp. Hardbound, 0060199709.

In 1862 Captain Bowater travels to Memphis, Tennessee, on a vessel manned by colorful riverboat captain Mike Sullivan, to wait for his new ironclad to be built. Frustrated by construction delays, he passes the time ghostwriting Sullivan's dime novel. Meanwhile Bowater's lover, Wendy Atkins, leaves her home in Norfolk, Virginia, before Yankees invade, to go search for him.

Keywords: Ships; Tennessee—Civil War

Poyer, David.

Civil War at Sea Series.

Poyer's novels portray a side of the Civil War rarely seen in fiction: its naval battles.

Keywords: Clairborne, Ker; Confederacy; Eaker, Eli; Navy; Shipboard adventure

Fire on the Waters. Simon & Schuster, 2001. 445pp. Hardbound, 0684871335.

In 1861 Eli Eaker, son of a wealthy New York shipping magnate, abandons his father's hopes for him, as well as an arranged marriage to his cousin, by joining the fight for the Union. He signs up as a member of the crew of the U.S.S. *Owanee*, a ship assigned to defend Fort Sumter. There he meets Lt. Ker Clairborne, an Annapolis graduate who must choose between his career in the U.S. Navy and loyalty to his home state of Virginia.

Keywords: South Carolina—Civil War; Virginia—Civil War

A Country of Our Own. Simon & Schuster, 2003. 429pp. Hardbound, 0684871343.

Ker Clairborne, formerly a lieutenant in the Union Navy, has reluctantly resigned his commission to join his fellow Virginians on the side of the Confederacy. Aboard first the C.S.S. *Montgomery* and later the *Maryland*, he and his compatriots fight, raid, and sink Union vessels in the attempt to block trade goods from reaching their destinations.

That Anvil of Our Souls. Simon & Schuster, 2005. 448pp. Hardbound, 0684871351.

Poyer depicts the build-up to the *Monitor–Merrimack* confrontation, the famous encounter between Union and Confederate ironclad warships, from both sides, from the ships' construction to the inevitable battle. Historical characters include John Ericsson, designer/builder of the *Monitor*, while readers will have met many of the fictional characters in the earlier two books: Eli Eaker, Ker and Catherine Clairborne, and Theo Hubbard, who becomes Ericsson's assistant engineer.

Keywords: Hampton Roads, Battle of; Ships

Nineteenth-Century Land Warfare

Like novels of the Age of Fighting Sail, these land-based military adventures come in series. They follow a single hero through a series of major army campaigns in Europe, India, and the United States during the nineteenth century.

Cornwell, Bernard.

Richard Sharpe Series.

During the Peninsular Wars Richard Sharpe, a soldier among the ranks in the British army, saves the life of Sir Arthur Wellesley (later known as the Duke of Wellington) and is rewarded with a field commission. An unusual lieutenant, Sharpe is an outsider: never fully accepted by fellow officers due to his humble background, he nonetheless proves himself time after time on the battlefields of Europe in the Napoleonic era. Sharpe's earliest adventures, however, began in India. In the first three novels of the series Private Sharpe fights the evil Tippoo Sultan during the siege of Seringapatam in 1799 and ends up a hero. From India to Spain to Portugal, the series is filled with rip-roaring action, evil villains, fierce battles, and reckless heroism. *Sharpe's Trafalgar*, fourth chronologically, is the only novel to take place aboard ship rather than on land. The novels in this continuing series, most of which are based on real military campaigns, are listed in historical order.

Keywords: Napoleonic Wars; Sharpe, Richard; Soldiers

Sharpe's Tiger. HarperCollins, 1997. 385pp. Hardbound, 0002250101.

Sharpe's Triumph. HarperCollins, 1998. 291pp. Hardbound, 006101270X.

Sharpe's Fortress. HarperCollins, 1999. 294pp. Hardbound, 0060194243.

Sharpe's Trafalgar. HarperCollins, 2001. 288pp. Hardbound, 0060194251.

Sharpe's Prey. HarperCollins, 2001. 262pp. Hardbound, 0060002522.

Sharpe's Rifles. Viking, 1988. 304pp. Hardbound, 0670822221.

Sharpe's Havoc. HarperCollins, 2003. 320pp. Hardbound, 0060530464.

Sharpe's Eagle. Viking, 1981. 270pp. Hardbound, 0670639443.

Sharpe's Gold. Viking, 1981. 250pp. Hardbound, 0670639435.

Sharpe's Escape. HarperCollins, 2004. 368pp. Hardbound, 0060530472.

Sharpe's Fury. HarperCollins, 2006. 337pp. Hardbound, 000712015X.

Sharpe's Battle. HarperCollins, 1995. 304pp. Hardbound, 0060176776.

Sharpe's Company. Viking, 1982. 280pp. Hardbound, 0670639427.

Sharpe's Sword. Viking, 1983. 319pp. Hardbound, 0670639419.

Sharpe's Enemy. Viking, 1984. 351pp. Hardbound, 0670639400.

Sharpe's Honour. Viking, 1985. 320pp. Hardbound, 0670803898.

Sharpe's Regiment. Viking, 1986. 301pp. Hardbound, 0670811483.

Sharpe's Siege. Viking, 1987. 319pp. Hardbound, 0670808660.

Sharpe's Revenge. Viking, 1989. 348pp. Hardbound, 0670808679.

Waterloo. Viking, 1990. 378pp. Hardbound, 0670808687. (Alternate title: *Sharpe's Waterloo.*)

Sharpe's Devil. HarperCollins, 1992. 280pp. Hardbound, 0060179775.

Garland, David.

Jamie Skoyles Series.

A continuing series about the men who won America's freedom during the Revolutionary War, with a greater emphasis on military maneuvers than on character development. Garland is one of the lesser-known pseudonyms of Keith Miles, who writes historical mysteries as Edward Marston and Conrad Allen.

Keywords: New York—American Revolution; Pennsylvania—American Revolution; Saratoga, Battle of; Skoyles, Jamie; Valley Forge, Battle of

Saratoga. St. Martin's Press, 2005. 308pp. Hardbound, 0312327196.

Jamie Skoyles, a captain in the British army under General Johnny Burgoyne, arrives with his unit in New York's Hudson Valley in May 1777 to stamp out the colonists' stubborn rebellion against British rule.

Valley Forge. St. Martin's Press, 2006. 312pp. Hardbound, 0312327226.

After surrendering to the rebels at Saratoga, Skoyles becomes a prisoner of war, but he escapes quickly enough, with the aid of his comrade Sergeant Tom Caffrey. Ordered by his superior, General Howe, to spy on General Washington at Valley Forge, Jamie makes his way south. Surprisingly, he finds he has conflicting loyalties after observing the noble Washington in action.

Hackman, Gene, and Daniel Lenihan.

Escape from Andersonville. St. Martin's, 2008. 342pp. Hardbound, 9780312363734.

The third collaboration between actor Hackman and archaeologist Lenihan dramatizes an escape from Andersonville, a Confederate prison notorious for its wretched conditions. Nathan Parker, a Union captain, flees captivity after two months in 1864, determined to return and help his fellow soldiers get out as well. When higher-ups fail to act on his recommendation, he leads an audacious mission to rescue them himself.

Keywords: Confederacy; Georgia—Civil War; Prisoners

World Wars I and II

These novels feature fast-paced military maneuvers made by Allied forces against Germany during the two world wars. (The Prohaska novels by Biggins, told from the Austro-Hungarian viewpoint during World War I, are the exceptions.) Classic World War II adventure novels that readers might also enjoy, though not historical fiction by definition, include Nicholas Montsarrat's *The Cruel Sea* (1951) and Alistair MacLean's *The Guns of Navarone* (1957). Readers who enjoy these novels may want to consider reading war thrillers (Chapter 9) set during the same period.

Biggins, John.

Otto Prohaska Novels.

Otto Prohaska, submarine captain for the land-locked Austro-Hungarian Empire during the First World War, serves his country loyally and enthusiastically despite inept rulers, inadequate supplies, and an overabundance of red tape. Like his hero, Biggins displays plenty of wit and good humor. The final volume, a prequel to the series, has Prohaska narrating his youthful adventures from the viewpoint of old age. Originally published by St. Martin's Press in the mid-1990s.

Keywords: Austria-World War I; Prohaska, Otto; Shipboard adventure; Submarines; Navy

A Sailor of Austria. McBooks, 2005. 375pp. Paper, 159013107X.

The Emperor's Coloured Coat. McBooks, 2006. 359pp. Paper, 1590131088.

The Two-Headed Eagle. McBooks, 2006. 359pp. Paper, 1590131096.

Tomorrow the World. McBooks, 2007. 374pp. Paper, 9781590131107.

Fullerton, Alexander.

Nicholas Everard Naval Series.

Fullerton, a former submarine officer in the British Navy, brings his background to this series of novels set around naval action during the First and Second World Wars. Nick Everard begins his career as a lowly midshipman on a battleship, but his transfer to the destroyer H.M.S. *Lanyard* means he'll have a chance to use his abilities firsthand. The action, brutal at times, follows Britain's engagement with the German Navy through the eyes of not only Nick but also his brother and uncle. All the volumes were originally published in the UK between 1976 and 1984; the American editions are listed.

Keywords: England—World War I and World War II; Everard, Nicholas; Navy; Shipboard adventure

The Blooding of the Guns. Soho, 2002. 286pp. Hardbound, 1569472599.

Sixty Minutes for St. George. Soho, 2002. 308pp. Hardbound, 1569472939.

Patrol to the Golden Horn. Soho, 2002. 229pp. Hardbound, 1569473129.

Storm Force to Narvik. McBooks, 2004. 268pp. Paper, 1590130928.

Last Lift from Crete. McBooks, 2005. 270pp. Paper, 1590130936.

All the Drowning Seas. McBooks, 2005. 314pp. Paper, 1590130944.

A Share of Honour. McBooks, 2005. 315pp. Paper, 1590130952.

The Torch Bearers. McBooks, 2006. 379pp. Paper, 1590130987.

The Gatecrashers. McBooks, 2006. 347pp. Paper, 1590131002.

Hickam, Homer.

Josh Thurlow Novels.

The adventures of intrepid, rough-edged Coast Guard officer Josh Thurlow and his men during the Second World War, from the North Carolina coast to the tropical South Seas. Hickam's nonfiction work *Torpedo Junction*, about the first six months of naval action on America's east coast during World War II, serves as an unofficial companion to the series.

Keywords: Coast Guard; Shipboard adventure—World War II; Thurlow, Josh

The Keeper's Son. St. Martin's Press, 2003. 352pp. Hardbound, 0312301898.

Coast Guard Lt. Josh Thurlow patrols the waters around Killakeet Island, home to a lighthouse off the Outer Banks of North Carolina, during 1941–1942. For seventeen years he and his father, the lighthouse keeper, have been haunted by the disappearance of Josh's baby brother at sea. When German U-boats arrive, the Thurlows find the German commanders to be basically fair men—most of them, anyway—and one of them may even be able to assuage the guilt that torments Josh.

Keywords: Brothers; North Carolina—World War II

The Ambassador's Son. Thomas Dunne, 2005. 337pp. Hardbound, 0312301928.

In 1943 Josh heads to the Solomon Islands, in the South Pacific, to track down a missing Marine Corps hero, David Armistead, who may have deserted his post after coming face-to-face with the enemy. Among the men recruited to help Josh in his task is a future American president, PT boat skipper John Kennedy, who's awaiting court-martial.

Keywords: Marines; Solomon Islands—World War II

The Far Reaches. Thomas Dunne, 2007. 314pp. Hardbound, 9780312334758.

Later in 1943 Josh knows the Marines' incipient attack on the island of Tarawa is sure to fail, but he heroically steps into the carnage to rally the battle's survivors until reinforcements arrive. Wounded and nearly delirious, Josh awakens to find himself and several other survivors shanghaied by a beautiful Irish nun, Sister Mary Kathleen, who wants their help taking revenge on her former captors.

Keywords: Nuns; Tarawa, Battle of

Pearce, Donn.

Nobody Comes Back. **Forge, 2004. 255pp. Hardbound, 0765310848.**

This latest novel by Pearce, whose novel *Cool Hand Luke* was written thirty years earlier, is at once an action-packed novel of World War II's European theater and a brutal coming of age story. Sixteen-year-old Toby Parker, brainy child in a family of eccentric outcasts, enters his army career relatively unprepared, as is the case with many new recruits. He arrives at the front in the Ardennes right before the Germans attack on December 16, 1944; the pace never flags from that point onward.

Keywords: Belgium—World War II; Bulge, Battle of the; Coming of age; Soldiers

Pressfield, Steven.

Killing Rommel. **Doubleday, 2008. 295pp. Hardbound, 9780385519700.**

In 1942 young British tank officer Lt. R. Lawrence "Chap" Chapman arrives in North Africa as second-in-command of the Long Range Desert Group, an elite group of commandos secretly assigned to assassinate German Field Marshal Erwin Rommel. The "Desert Fox" and the Afrika Korps are bearing down on the Middle East's productive oil fields, fuel necessary for Hitler and the Axis armies to lead a successful march on Russia. Pressfield's first military novel not set in ancient times is packed with details on the movements and emotions of front-line troops in the midst of brutal desert warfare.

Keywords: Africa, North-—World War II; Afrika Korps; Rommel, Erwin (historical character); Soldiers

Reeman, Douglas.

Reeman, who served on destroyers with the British Navy during World War II, is a prolific author of twentieth-century naval adventure fiction. Following is a selection of his World War I and World War II novels. The author also writes as Alexander Kent.

For Valour. **McBooks, 2005. 320pp. Paper, 1590130499.**

In 1942 Graham Martineau, commander of the British destroyer *Hakka*, must overcome self-defeating thoughts of the ship and crew he once lost as he and the *Hakka* escort a supply convoy traveling to Soviet Russia through dangerous, German-controlled Arctic waters.

Keywords: Arctic—World War II; Navy; Shipboard adventure

A Prayer for the Ship. **McBooks, 2005. 281pp. Paper, 1590130979.**

Clive Royce, a young sublieutenant in the Royal Navy, assumes command of a motor torpedo boat patrolling the waters of the North Sea during World War II.

Keywords: Navy; Shipboard adventure—World War II; Soldiers

The White Guns. **McBooks, 2004. 365pp. Paper, 1590130839.**

It's 1945, and World War II has ended in Europe, but rancor still lingers among the men of the Royal Navy. Lt. Vere Marriott, stationed in Kiel Harbor, calms tensions among those who try to profit from Germany's reconstruction.

Keywords: Germany—World War II; Navy; Soldiers

Robbins, David L.

Liberation Road. Bantam, 2005. 445pp. Hardbound, 0553801759.

In the months following D-Day in mid- to late 1944, the Red Ball Express, a huge convoy of thousands of trucks and tens of thousands of men, kept Allied troops fortified with needed supplies—food, fuel, and ammunition—from the Normandy coast to the German border. Most of the soldiers driving these routes were African Americans. In this dangerous time, two men struggle to prove their worth to the Allies and themselves. Joe Amos Biggs, a black driver, takes progressively more dangerous assignments to prove he's the equal of any soldier despite his race. At the same time Ben Kahn, a middle-aged Jewish rabbi who swore an oath not to bear arms, urges men in his unit not to give up the fight.

Keywords: African Americans; France—World War II; Jews; Rabbis; Red Ball Express; Soldiers; Truck drivers

Shaara, Jeff.

Shaara's political/military novels set during World Wars I and II are annotated in Chapter 2.

A Miscellany

A mixture of additional novels featuring military battles in the nineteenth and twentieth centuries.

Reeman, Douglas.

Royal Marines Series.

Whereas most works of naval fiction feature officers of the British Royal Navy, Reeman's series have members of the Royal Marines as protagonists. Over ninety years of British history, from the Crimean War in the 1850s through World War II in 1944, four generations of the Blackwood family serve their country with distinction. Their service takes them to the far-flung reaches of the Empire: Africa, China, Gallipoli, and Southeast Asia. All reissued by McBooks. Reeman also writes as Alexander Kent.

Keywords: Blackwood family; Marines; Shipboard adventure—19th and 20th centuries

Badge of Glory. Morrow, 1984. 357pp. Hardbound, 0688021328.

First to Land. Morrow, 1984. 294pp. Hardbound, 068804509X.

The Horizon. McBooks, 2002. 367pp. Paper, 1590130278.

Dust on the Sea. McBooks, 2002. 368pp. Paper, 1590130286.

Knife Edge. McBooks, 2005. 300pp. Paper, 1590130995.

8

Voyages of Exploration and Trade

When men (and occasionally women) set out aboard ship to discover new lands or trade in merchandise, they frequently find the journey to be a struggle for survival. In keeping with historical accuracy, the stories don't always end happily. Here the sea, ferocious and all-powerful, becomes almost a character in itself.

Máté, Ferenc.

Ghost Sea. **Norton, 2006. 263pp. Hardbound, 092025649X.**

In the years after World War II, ketch operator and coastal trader S. V. Dugger is hired by an artifacts collector, George Hay, to recover sacred tribal masks stolen by two Kwakiutl Indians—who have also kidnapped Kate, Hay's wife and Dugger's secret lover. Dugger and his crew, which includes Hay himself, frantically track the Indians through the islands' deserted waterways. The Pacific Northwest may not seem like an appropriately exotic setting, yet few readers will be familiar with the coastal geography and Kwakiutl culture of British Columbia's northern islands. This fast-paced tale, thoroughly grounded in local history, is based on a true story.

Keywords: British Columbia—20th century; Kwakiutl Indians; Masks; Traders

Turteltaub, H. N.

Menedemos and Sostratos Series.

The lighthearted, diverting adventures faced by two merchants, the scholarly Sostratos and his wilder cousin Menedemos, on their trading journeys across the Aegean Sea and elsewhere during the third century BC. H. N. Turteltaub is the pseudonym for science fiction/alternate history novelist Harry Turtledove.

Keywords: Cousins; Greece—ancient/prehistoric; Merchants; Shipboard adventure—ancient/prehistoric; Traders

Over the Wine-Dark Sea. Forge, 2001. 381pp. Hardbound, 0312876602.

The Gryphon's Skull. Forge, 2002. 384pp. Hardbound, 0312872224.

The Sacred Land. Forge, 2003. 384pp. Hardbound, 0765300370.

Owls to Athens. Forge, 2004. 382pp. Hardbound, 0765300389.

At last the Rhodian cousins arrive in Athens, where they hope to trade their recent acquisitions of olive oil, perfume, and wine for better loot. While in the city Sostratos looks forward to intellectual diversion, whereas Menedemos, as usual, gets in trouble by seducing a married woman, this time the wife of their host.

Simmons, Dan.

The Terror. **Little, Brown, 2007. 769pp. Hardbound, 9780316017442.**

Annotated in Chapter 9.

Thompson, Harry.

To the Edge of the World. **MacAdam/Cage, 2006. 800pp. Hardbound, 1596921900.** ✍ 🖉

In 1831 Lt. Robert Fitzroy, youthful commander on the H.M.S. *Beagle*, takes Charles Darwin, a twenty-two-year-old naturalist, on the ship's second voyage of discovery along the South American coast. The two men are a study in contrasts. Fitzroy is a Scots nobleman and staunch Christian fundamentalist, while Darwin is an easygoing would-be clergyman. Over the next five years, as the *Beagle*'s crew observes and documents the wonders they encounter, Darwin's research into local flora and fauna leads him to doubt his religious convictions, damaging their friendship irrevocably. This philosophical nautical adventure, in which the men discover as much about themselves and each other as about local fauna, flora, and geography, was long-listed for the Man Booker Prize. (UK title: *This Thing of Darkness*.)

Keywords: Darwin, Charles (historical character); Explorers; Fitzroy, Robert (historical character); Friendship; Naturalists; Shipboard adventure—19th century; South America—19th century

Pirate Novels

A number of naval adventure novels feature battles against pirates, but novels in this section are told from the pirate's point of view.

Sabatini, Rafael.

The Sea-Hawk. **Houghton Mifflin, 1923. 366pp. Hardbound.** ★

In Elizabethan times, Cornish gentleman Oliver Tressilian is sold into slavery in Arabia by his half-brother, who covets his wealth for himself. Oliver turns the tables by becoming a Barbary pirate and espousing Islam. Though successful in his new life, Oliver—a classic antihero—is prepared to give up all he has gained to wreak vengeance on those who have wronged him.

Keywords: England—Tudor era; Pirates; Slaves and slavery

Captain Blood Series. ★

In 1680s England, Irish physician Peter Blood does well by saving the life of a man involved in Monmouth's Rebellion, but this noble act is his downfall. Mistakenly declared a traitor by the English government, he is sentenced to ten years of indentured servitude on a Barbados plantation, where he falls in love with the daughter of the man who owns him. He manages to escape on board a stolen Spanish ship and begins a new life as a ruthless pirate on the high seas.

Keywords: Barbados—17th century; Blood, Peter; Pirates

Captain Blood, His Odyssey. Houghton Mifflin, 1922. 356pp. Hardbound. (Alternate title: *Captain Blood*.)

Captain Blood Returns. Houghton Mifflin, 1931. 296pp. Hardbound.

The Fortunes of Captain Blood. Houghton Mifflin, 1936. 240pp. Hardbound.

Parody

These humorous novels poke fun at the genre through the picaresque adventures of an incorrigible antihero.

Fraser, George MacDonald.

Flashman Papers.

Scotsman George MacDonald Fraser is the so-called editor of the <u>Flashman Papers</u>, a series of bawdy adventure novels that at once belong to and spoof the historical adventure genre. Their hero, British army colonel Sir Harry Flashman, is a completely disreputable and endearing Victorian rogue who somehow manages to turn up at, and participate in, nearly every major event in Victorian-era history. Nothing whatsoever is held sacred. From John Brown's messy raid on Harper's Ferry in 1859, through bumbling Englishmen's squabbles over India, you can be sure that Flashman was there to smooth-talk his way through it all.

Keywords: England—Victorian era; Flashman, Harry; India—19th century

Flashman. Knopf, 1969. 256pp. Hardbound.

Royal Flash. Knopf, 1970. 257pp. Hardbound, 0394443357.

Flash for Freedom! Knopf, 1971. 287pp. Hardbound, 0394479475.

Flashman at the Charge. Knopf, 1973. 288pp. Hardbound, 0394487567.

Flashman in the Great Game. Knopf, 1975. 340pp. Hardbound, 0394498933.

Flashman's Lady. Knopf, 1978. 330pp. Hardbound, 0394501357.

Flashman and the Redskins. Knopf, 1982. 479pp. Hardbound, 0394528522.

Flashman and the Dragon. Knopf, 1986. 320pp. Hardbound, 0394553578.

Flashman and the Mountain of Light. Knopf, 1990. 365pp. Hardbound, 0679400710.

Flashman and the Angel of the Lord. Knopf, 1994. 394pp. Hardbound, 0679441727.

Flashman and the Tiger. Knopf, 1999. 336pp. Hardbound, 0375410244.

Flashman on the March. Knopf, 2005. 335pp. Hardbound, 1400044758.

Exotic Adventure

These novels pit the protagonist, nearly always male, against the unknown dangers found in exotic lands, such as ancient Egypt, the wilds of Africa, Mexico, and Asia. Because these novels' excitement appeals to men just as romances do to women, they are also called "male romances." Classic novels of exotic adventure, though not historical fiction in the usual definition, include Rudyard Kipling's *Lord Jim*, Joseph Conrad's *Heart of Darkness*, and H. Rider Haggard's *King Solomon's Mines* and *She*. Literary novels of exotic adventure are listed in Chapter 10.

Brando, Marlon, and Donald Cammell.

Fan-Tan. Knopf, 2005. 249pp. Hardbound, 1400044715.

This posthumous novel, the result of a 1970s-era collaboration between actor Brando and film director Cammell (with editing and further writing by David Thomson after the lost manuscript turned up) is a rollicking sea story set on the China Sea in 1927. While languishing in a Hong Kong prison, Anatole "Annie" Doultry saves the life of a fellow prisoner, earning him the gratitude of pirate queen Madame Lai Choi San. After his release Madame Lai persuades Annie to join her in a heist of a wealthy British merchant ship.

Keywords: China—20th century; Pirates; Pirates, women

Bull, Bartle.

Shanghai Station series.

The action spans three continents—Asia, Europe, and Africa—in this steamy adventure series set in the early twentieth century.

Shanghai Station. Carroll & Graf, 2004. 320pp. Hardbound, 0786713143.

The exotic port city of Shanghai is on the brink of revolution in 1918. Mao Tse-tung incites the peasants to embrace communism and revolt against their leaders. Alexander Karlov, in Shanghai with his father, plots revenge against the Bolsheviks who killed his mother and kidnapped his twin sister, Katerina, when they were escaping from Russia.

Keywords: China—20th century; Communism

China Star. Carroll & Graf, 2006. 442pp. Hardbound, 0786716770.

It's now 1922, four years after the events in *Shanghai Station*. Alexander Korlov is in Paris looking for Katerina while hunting—and being hunted by—Bolshevik agent Viktor Polyak, the man who engineered her kidnapping, brainwashed her, trained her as an assassin, and turned her into his sex slave. After the pair reunite they board the *China Star* en route to Shanghai, with Polyak in hot pursuit.

Keywords: China—20th century; France—20th century; Kidnapping; Shipboard adventure

Chabon, Michael.

Gentlemen of the Road. Del Rey, 2007. 204pp. Hardbound, 9780345501745. **YA**

This short novel features two unlikely friends who wander the Silk Road during the mid-tenth century as thieves-for-hire and general swindlers. As Zelikman, a scrawny German Jewish physician, and Amram, an oversized African ex-soldier, make their way through the

Caucasus Mountains, living by their wits, they run into a deposed Khazar prince who asks for their help in reclaiming his throne. First serialized in the *New York Times* Sunday magazine, each chapter of this rollicking tale (which includes illustrations) ends with a cliffhanger.

Keywords: Jews; Khazar Empire—10th century; Physicians; Picaresque novels; Princes; Silk Road; Thieves

Clavell, James.

Asian Saga. ★

Epic in scope, the novels in Clavell's <u>Asian Saga</u>, lengthy tales of English adventurers who dare to penetrate exotic foreign markets, are classics of the genre. These sprawling novels incorporate dozens of characters and just as many subplots. In scenes of bloody violence and intense beauty, they portray the experiences of Westerners as strangers in a strange land. The novels are listed in historical order. The saga continues with *King Rat* (©1962, set in World War II Singapore); *Noble House* (©1981, set in 1963 Hong Kong), and *Whirlwind* (©1986, set in 1979 Iran).

Shōgun. Atheneum, 1975. 802pp. Hardbound.

In 1600 Elizabethan adventurer John Blackthorne arrives in Japan after a shipwreck. He seeks to turn this misadventure into an advantage for himself and England, as he envisions a way to wrest control of the Japanese trade from the Portuguese. In Japan he encounters a completely alien culture, one torn by political strife. His captor and mentor is Lord Toranaga, a powerful feudal lord who seeks to use Blackthorne to consolidate power under himself as Shōgun. As Blackthorne learns samurai ways under Toranada's guidance, Lady Mariko, a Catholic woman who dares to fall in love with the barbarian Englishman, is torn between the different ways of life each man represents.

Keywords: Japan—17th century; Samurai

Tai-Pan. Atheneum, 1966. 590pp. Hardbound.

This novel does for China and Hong Kong what *Shōgun* did for Japan. In 1840s Hong Kong, the land has just come under British rule, but its customs and people are still a mystery to most Westerners. Englishman Dirk Struan is Tai-Pan (supreme ruler) of the Noble House Trading Company, whose mission is to supply the hot commodity of tea to hungry English markets. Despite the length and incredible number of characters, this is a fast-moving novel that combines politics, treachery, romance, and adventure to portray the attitudes of the Chinese and English toward each other.

Keywords: China—19th century; Tea; Traders

Gai-Jin. Delacorte, 1993. 1038pp. Hardbound, 0440218098.

Clavell returns to Japan with this novel, set in 1862. Noble House, the giant British shipping empire from *Tai-Pan*, has established a base at Yokohama, and Malcolm Struan is its up-and-coming leader. However, the Japanese are less than thrilled at the incursion of yet more greedy foreigners ("gai-jin") into their country, and those who adhere to the old samurai traditions will do anything to see them gone.

Keywords: Japan—19th century; Samurai; Traders

Dietrich, William.

Ethan Gage Series. **YA**

At the end of the eighteenth century, expatriate American adventurer Ethan Gage leaves revolutionary Paris to follow Napoleon's ill-fated expeditions to the Middle East, where he becomes embroiled in mysteries surrounding ancient artifacts. Exciting, high-concept, intellectual novels told on an epic scale, and narrated in lively style by Gage himself.

Keywords: Gage, Ethan; Napoleonic Wars

Napoleon's Pyramids. HarperCollins, 2007. 384pp. Hardbound, 9780060848323.

> While in Paris in 1798, Ethan wins an ancient Egyptian medallion in a dice game, whereupon he begins attracting unwanted attention from police, thieves, and members of a Masonic cult. Managing to escape, he joins Napoleon's army on its campaign into Egypt, where he embarks upon a quest to decipher the medallion's odd symbolism—which may involve the secrets of the Great Pyramids.
>
> **Keywords:** Egypt—18th century; Medallions; Pyramids

The Rosetta Key. HarperCollins, 2008. 339pp. Hardbound, 9780061239557.

> After his unsuccessful Egyptian venture, by 1799 Napoleon has moved on to invading Palestine. Ethan also makes for the Holy Land, in pursuit of the Book of Thoth, an ancient Egyptian scroll whose writings may unleash magical powers.
>
> **Keywords:** Palestine—18th century; Scrolls

Iggulden, Conn.

Genghis Khan Series (also called Conqueror Series). ✍ **YA**

An action-packed series about fearsome Mongol warrior Genghis Khan, ruler of the Asian steppe in the thirteenth century.

Keywords: Genghis Khan (historical character); Mongolia—13th century; Warriors

🏹 *Genghis: Birth of an Empire.* Delacorte, 2007. 383pp. Hardbound, 9780385339513. (UK title: *Wolf of the Plains.*)

> Temujin grows up as the second son of the Wolf clan leader, but he and his family are banished from the tribe and left to starve after his father's assassination. The harsh conditions bolster his spirit, and after many successful raids on Tartar camps, he gradually attracts other exiles to his cause: to unite all of the warring Mongol tribes under one strong leader. Alex Award.

Genghis: Lords of the Bow. Delacorte, 2008. 400pp. Hardbound, 9780385339520.

> Genghis, conqueror and new leader of the Mongol tribes, sets his sights on conquering the wealthy cities of the Chin (modern-day China) while contending with the rivalry between his two eldest sons.

Jennings, Gary.

The late Gary Jennings wrote colorful, blood-soaked adventures that emphasize the strange, barbarous customs of cultures largely unknown to Western readers.

Aztec Series.

Mixtli, an Aztec scribe and warrior during the magnificent prime of the Aztec Empire in the sixteenth century, narrates the tale of his rise from commoner to noble. At the same time, he witnesses the arrival of the Spaniards, whose greed for gold and empire-building causes the downfall of Montezuma's people. The shocking descriptions of the Aztecs' religion, sexual habits, and other customs are not for the squeamish, but Jennings also uses them as social commentary. For example, the Spaniards' practice of burning heretics ironically contrasts with the supposed barbarity of the Aztecs' human sacrifices. *Aztec Autumn* and *Aztec Blood* continue the story with later generations of Aztecs, now slaves in the land now called New Spain. The final two volumes were completed based on outlines and detailed notes left by Jennings after his death in 1999; Robert Gleason was Jennings's longtime editor, and Podrug writes both novels and nonfiction.

Keywords: Aztecs; Mexico—16th century; Mixtli

Aztec. Atheneum, 1980. 754pp. Hardbound, 0689110456. ★

Aztec Autumn. Forge, 1997. 380pp. Hardbound, 0312862504.

Aztec Blood. Forge, 2001. 525pp. Hardbound, 0312862512.

Aztec Rage. Forge, 2006. 428pp. Hardbound, 0765310147.

   Credited coauthors on *Aztec Rage* are Junius Podrug and Robert Gleason.

Matsuoka, Takashi.

Cloud of Sparrows Series. `YA`

Eloquently written, mystical adventure in the tradition of James Clavell. The novels begin in 1861, as Japan has reluctantly reopened its borders to Westerners after two centuries of isolation.

Keywords: Japan—18th century; Missionaries

Cloud of Sparrows. Delacorte, 2002. 405pp. Hardbound, 0385336403.

   In the city of Edo, Lord Genji of the Okumichi clan, the last of his line, has the gift of prophecy, though few believe his gifts are real. He foresees the end of the traditional samurai way of life, so he welcomes the presence of several American missionaries who have come to preach the word of God to the Japanese. When henchmen of the Shogunate seek to overthrow Lord Genji and erase his message, he, his missionary guests, and his geisha lover flee over dangerous terrain to Cloud of Sparrows Castle. Here the hidden motives of everyone in the group are revealed.

Autumn Bridge. Delacorte, 2004. 415pp. Hardbound, 0385336411.

   Emily Gibson came to Japan as a missionary in 1861. Six years later she finds herself romantically drawn to Lord Genji, her Japanese host, and he finds it difficult to deny his feelings for her. In the process of tracing Genji's ancestry, Emily discovers a series of scrolls about the Okumichi clan's secret history written by an early fourteenth-century noblewoman who lived at Cloud of Sparrows Castle. Emily, while reading Lady Shizuka's centuries-old writings, can't help but see parallels to her own life.

Keywords: Japan—14th century; Scrolls

Smith, Wilbur.

Most exotic adventure novels take a Western man and place him in an alien locale, but the protagonists of Wilbur Smith's fast-paced African and Egyptian novels belong to the unusual culture the author depicts—and are themselves part of the attraction.

Ballantyne Novels. ★

Smith's Ballantyne family saga follows members of the Ballantyne family of southern Africa from the 1860s until the present day. Their progenitors are a sister and brother, Robyn and Zouga Ballantyne, whose lives are intertwined with the violent history of Rhodesia (now Zimbabwe). The action revolves around the slave trade, piracy, exploration of the African interior, ivory hunts, diamond mining, and clashes with the native tribes. See also Smith's *The Triumph of the Sun*, listed with the Courtney series.

Keywords: Ballantyne family; Diamond mining; Rhodesia—19th century

Flight of the Falcon. Doubleday, 1982 . 545pp. Hardbound, 0385178336. (Original title: *A Falcon Flies.*)

Men of Men. Doubleday, 1983. 518pp. Hardbound, 0385178344.

The Angels Weep. Doubleday, 1983. 468pp. Hardbound, 038518736X

The Leopard Hunts in Darkness. Doubleday, 1984. 423pp. Hardbound, 0385187378.

The Courtneys.

The extended Courtney series comprises twelve novels, organized into three self-contained sub-series. Like Smith's other African novels, including the Ballantyne saga, they are full of rollicking, steamy romance, dangerous elephant hunts, and breathtaking descriptions of the African wilderness.

The first three volumes, beginning with *Birds of Prey*, were written after the original sequence and continue the saga with earlier generations of Courtneys. Set between the late seventeenth and early eighteenth centuries, at the beginning of South Africa's development as a Dutch colony, they are exotic, swashbuckling adventures complete with piracy and privateering on the high seas.

The Triumph of the Sun, the latest novel, takes place not in South Africa but in the Sudan, during the 1884 siege of Khartoum. Arab forces commanded by the fanatical Muslim leader known as the Mahdi overtake the city, trapping British citizens within. Ryder Courtney, along with British Hussar Captain Penrod Ballantyne (see Smith's novels about this family), band together to rescue the woman they both desire, the British consul's daughter, Rebecca Benbrook.

When the Lion Feeds, *The Sound of Thunder*, and *A Sparrow Falls* form the second Courtney sequence. Between the 1870s and the beginning of World War I, South Africa saw a number of tumultuous events, such as the Zulu Wars, the gold rush, and the Boer War, fought between the British and Dutch over the colony. Two brothers living in the Natal region of South Africa, Sean and Garrick Courtney, become estranged after both a tragic accident and a woman come between them.

The Burning Shore begins the next Courtney sequence with the story of Michael Courtney, Sean's son, and his adventures in World War I. After Michael is killed, his French wife, Centaine, returns to her late husband's South African homeland. Her two children—one by Michael, one by an Afrikaner—grow up separately, unaware of their blood relationship. Their personal and political rivalry, and that of their descendants, provides considerable action and suspense throughout the series.

Keywords: Colonialism; Courtney family; South Africa—17th through 20th centuries

Birds of Prey. St. Martin's Press, 1997. 554pp. Hardbound, 0312157916.

Monsoon. St. Martin's Press, 1999. 613pp. Hardbound, 031220339X.

Blue Horizon. St. Martin's Press, 2003. 624pp. Hardbound, 0312278241.

The Triumph of the Sun. St. Martin's, 2005. 500pp. Hardbound, 0312318405.

When the Lion Feeds. Viking, 1964. 403pp. Hardbound.

The Sound of Thunder. London: Heinemann, 1966. 437pp. Hardbound.

A Sparrow Falls. Doubleday, 1978. 587pp. Hardbound, 038513603X.

The Burning Shore. Doubleday, 1985. 420pp. Hardbound, 0385187386.

Power of the Sword. Little, Brown, 1986. 618pp. Hardbound, 0316801712.

Rage. Little, Brown, 1987. 627pp. Hardbound, 0316801798.

A Time to Die. Random House, 1990. 448pp. Hardbound, 0394584759.

Golden Fox. Random House, 1990. 433pp. Hardbound, 0394589718.

Egyptian Novels.

In his Egyptian adventures, Smith doesn't stint on unpleasantries, such as castrations, bloody murders, and gruesome descriptions of ancient Egyptian surgeries. There is plenty of local color and action, but these books require strong stomachs.

Keywords: Egypt—ancient/prehistoric; Eunuchs; Magic and magicians; Pharaohs; Physicians; Slaves and slavery

River God. St. Martin's Press, 1993. 530pp. Hardbound, 0312106122.

Circa 1780 BC, when the Hyksos tribes were beginning to overrun Egypt, Taita, the eunuch slave of the evil Lord Intef, helps his protégée Lady Lostris—Lord Intef's daughter—carry on a love affair with General Tanus, an army officer. Though Lostris goes ahead with an unwanted marriage to the weak pharaoh, she manages to pass off Tanus's children as the royal heirs. The entire royal court is forced to move to Ethiopia to save themselves from the barbarian invaders. Taita more than makes up for his physical deficiency with extraordinary abilities in art, medicine, and politics, so much so that he seems almost superhuman.

Warlock. Thomas Dunne/St. Martin's Press, 2001. 549pp. Hardbound, 0312278233.

Long after the death of Queen Lostris, the Hyksos still rule in Lower Egypt. Taita, an ancient warlock living in the Egyptian desert, returns to help Lostris's grandson, Prince Nefer, the true royal heir, regain his inheritance amid war, treachery, and deceit. With the aid of Taita's undiminished mystical powers, he and Nefer take on Lord Naja, the false pharaoh, who will stop at nothing to see Nefer dead.

Keywords: Heirs and heiresses

The Quest. Thomas Dunne, 2007. 504pp. Hardbound, 9780312314820.

Egypt is suffering through numerous calamities: a series of plagues has hit its crops and people, and the Nile has dried up. Pharaoh sends Taita to the source of the Nile in southern Africa to find out what's up, but once there he and his loyal companion, Meren Cambyses, face numerous dangers—including evil sorcery. This latest installment of Smith's colorful, blood-soaked series includes liberal doses of fantasy.

Keywords: Plague

The Seventh Scroll. St. Martin's Press, 1995. 486pp. Hardbound, 0312119992.

Listed here for the sake of completeness, this present-day novel was written as a sequel to *River God.* In ancient Ethiopia the eunuch slave Taita had carefully hidden the pharaoh's wealth, setting traps so that it would never be found. When modern adventurers find an ancient papyrus written by Taita, it sets off a race against time to find the pharaoh's treasure.

Keywords: Treasure

Willocks, Tim.

🎗 *The Religion.* Farrar, Straus & Giroux, 2007. 618pp. Hardbound, 9780374248659.

Willocks portrays the 1565 Siege of Malta as a formidable showdown between East and West. Suleiman the Magnificent, Ottoman emperor, calls for *jihad* against the Knights of St. John, the rulers of Malta, a small island that is one of the last Christian strongholds in the Mediterranean. The Knights, who call themselves "the Religion," prepare to defend Malta to the death. Carla la Penautier, a noblewoman exiled to Italy twelve years earlier for bearing an illegitimate child, asks Mattias Tannhauser, German soldier-of-fortune and former janissary, to accompany her home to Malta to find her son. Meanwhile, the Knights plan to use Tannhauser's presence on Malta to lure him to their cause. Squeamish readers who can get past the gore—which is considerable—will also discover a poignant, surprising love story in these pages. Promoted as the first of the <u>Tannhauser Trilogy</u>. The Reading List (award).

Keywords: Knights of St. John; Malta—16th century; Malta, Siege of; Mercenaries; Nobility

Women Adventurers

While most historical adventure fiction is geared toward men, with limited female involvement, these novels feature strong women who make dangerous journeys through unknown lands. They also incorporate a strong romantic element, which increases their appeal to female readers. Novels of women on the American frontier are presented in Chapter 6.

Arruda, Suzanne.

Jade del Cameron Series.

These mysteries set in early twentieth-century Africa are annotated in Chapter 7.

Asensi, Matilde.

Everything Under the Sky. **HarperCollins, 2008. 387pp. Hardbound, 9780061458415.** `YA`

In 1923, when the husband from whom she has long been separated, Rémy de Poulain, dies in Shanghai, Spanish artist Elvira Aranda travels there with her teenaged niece to settle his affairs and claim his body. Elvira, horrified to learn about Rémy's outstanding debts, sees a chance at repaying them after discovering a mysterious chest that purports to lead to the long-lost, treasure-laden tomb of China's first emperor. Along with several companions well-versed in Chinese history and culture, Elvira makes the grueling journey into China's interior, meeting with numerous puzzles and riddles, all based on the country's ancient lore, which—little by little—unlock the secret of the tomb's locale. Members of the Green Gang, Shanghai's notorious mafia, pursue them throughout.

Keywords: China—20th century; Treasure; Widows

Mercury, Karen.

Mercury's romantic adventures set in colonial Africa are listed in Chapter 4.

Chapter 9

Historical Thrillers

The diverse subgenre of historical thrillers includes novels set in a wide range of locales and eras. What they all share is a common plot pattern and type of protagonist. Historical thrillers are suspenseful stories set in the past that feature intelligent protagonists (typically male, but not always) who find themselves in perilous situations. Readers of this subgenre enjoy watching how the heroes or heroines use all of their resources, intellectual and emotional as well as physical, to extricate themselves from danger. Because the exact form that the enemy will take is almost always unknown, the protagonists never know what or whom to guard against. This heightens tension considerably. The complex and multifaceted plots of historical thrillers keep readers alert and intent on the story.

When the protagonists are thrust into a dangerous situation, they do not always realize at first how to proceed. Even one wrong move could mean failure, betrayal, or even death. Throughout these novels, protagonists must make big decisions, often with little warning. As they become more familiar with the situation, they grow more confident. Because of the moral judgments that the heroes are compelled to make, historical thrillers tend to be serious books. Although they may be fast-paced, they are not light, easy reads.

In historical thrillers, the dilemmas in which protagonists find themselves often have political ramifications. On their shoulders may rest the fate of one or more nations. Many historical thrillers are set around pivotal times in political history, such as the French Revolution or World War II. The exception to this rule is psychological suspense novels. In these works the motives of the protagonists and villains tend to be personal rather than political.

The pacing of historical thrillers depends on the category they fall into, though they all have an engrossing, page-turning quality. Literary thrillers combine an elegant writing style with an abundance of historical detail, and this slows down their pace somewhat. Although there is less physical action in these novels, the numerous plot twists force readers to pay close attention.

On the opposite side of the spectrum, war thrillers are considerably more action-oriented, and readers will cheer and fear for the protagonists as they struggle to stay out of the enemy's clutches. Some novels, like Caleb Carr's literary psychological suspense thrillers, may fall into more than one category.

Though not a large category when compared with other subgenres, the popularity of historical thrillers is on the rise. Several best-selling contemporary thriller writers (e.g., Tess Gerritsen, M. J. Rose) have recently authored thrillers with historical subplots. Many readers who love contemporary thrillers, but who wouldn't ordinarily touch historical fiction, readily pick up historical thrillers; witness the widespread and continuing popularity of novels such as Kate Mosse's *Labyrinth*, Katherine Neville's *The Eight*, and Iain Pears's *An Instance of the Fingerpost*. The popularity of Dan Brown's *The Da Vinci Code*, though not set in the past, trained many eyes on a burgeoning sub-subgenre: the historical religious thriller.

Historical thrillers share some elements with the mystery and adventure genres. As in historical mysteries, there may be a crime committed and a detective determined to solve it, but this isn't a requirement. David Liss's Edgar Award–winning novel *A Conspiracy of Paper* is an example of this type, and novels of psychological suspense may also fit this description. Readers who enjoy the frenetic pace and twentieth century settings of war thrillers may also enjoy adventure novels set during World Wars I and II (Chapter 8).

Literary Thrillers

Ever since publication of Umberto Eco's benchmark novel *The Name of the Rose* in 1983, this category has burgeoned. Historical literary thrillers don't necessarily deal with literature and books, although many do. These novels involve intellectual puzzles wrapped inside mysteries and topped off with investigative action, as the protagonists sift through multiple clues to uncover secrets or find a killer. They are set against a detailed, well-researched historical backdrop, one unfamiliar enough for readers to find fascinating. Exciting yet thoughtful books, they allow readers to follow protagonists' internal thought processes as they race to solve a mystery or expose a conspiracy. Most literary thrillers are quite lengthy, and though the pace may not be as fast as others in this subgenre, they are compelling reads nonetheless. The quality of the writing is important, and the language used by the authors is erudite, complex, and appropriate to the period. Literary thrillers have great appeal outside the thriller genre: the labyrinthine, intelligent plots will appeal to readers of literary fiction, and the suspense and detection will please mystery fans as well.

Bayard, Louis.

The Pale Blue Eye. HarperCollins, 2006. 411pp. Hardbound, 0060733977. 📖

Gus Landor writes his last testament on April 19, 1831, stating that he'll surely be dead in two or three hours, maybe four. In his narrative we read how his calm life of retirement in the Hudson Valley, after years as a NYC police detective, was disrupted when West Point authorities asked him to investigate the murders of several cadets. He requests that another cadet, a poet named Edgar Allan Poe, join him in his investigations as a spy. Elegant, spare language joins a twisting, suspenseful plot with a shocking final revelation.

Keywords: New York—early United States; Poe, Edgar Allan (historical character); Policemen; West Point

Cox, Michael.

The Meaning of Night. **Norton, 2006. 701pp. Hardbound, 0393062031.** 📖

Cox, the English author of several anthologies of ghost stories, spent thirty years writing his first novel, a suspenseful literary epic set in Victorian London, written in the style and language of novels from that era. It takes the form of a confession of Edward Glyver, a bibliophile and murderer (and very unreliable narrator) who admits to his cold-blooded action on the first page. Glyver believes that his longtime rival, Phoebus Daunt, has robbed him of his rightful inheritance and will do anything to thwart him, including killing a stranger on London's streets purely as practice. Cox sets Glyver's obsessive pursuit of his supposed wealth against a backdrop of a London teeming with squalor and vice.

Keywords: England—Victorian era; Murderers

Eco, Umberto.

The Name of the Rose. **Harcourt Brace, 1983. 502pp. Hardbound, 0151446474.** ★ 📖

Lengthy, dense, and erudite, filled with Latin and Italian phrases and references to historical figures, Eco's classic work will please readers looking for an intellectual challenge. At its heart is a mystery. In 1327 William of Baskerville, a fifty-year-old monk, becomes involved with investigating a series of bizarre deaths at an Italian monastery. At the same time, the novel also explores philosophical issues, such as complex theological arguments and the nature of art and literature in the Middle Ages. This novel inspired America's fascination with the literary thriller.

Keywords: Italy—Middle Ages; Monks

Gleeson, Janet.

British novelist Gleeson has experience with the London auction scene, which comes through in her literary thrillers about eighteenth-century artisans and their creations.

The Serpent in the Garden. **Simon & Schuster, 2005. 341pp. Paper, 0743260058.**

In 1763 noted portraitist Joshua Pope is commissioned to paint the likeness of a soon-to-be-wed couple, the female half of whom insists on wearing an accursed emerald necklace during the sittings. When the body of a stranger is found among the pineapple plants in the conservatory on the groom's estate, and the necklace vanishes, Pope is accused of the theft—and forced to investigate who the victim and killer really were.

Keywords: Artists; England—Georgian era; Portraits

The Thief Taker. **Simon & Schuster, 2006. 305pp. Paper, 0743290186.**

Agnes Meadowes, a widow, works as a cook for the wealthy Blanchards, a family of silversmiths in 1750s London. When a recently commissioned wine cooler is stolen, and an apprentice is murdered, patriarch Richard Blanchard asks Agnes to investigate. To keep the wine cooler's theft under wraps, Agnes serves as liaison to the local thief-taker, but matters grow dangerous when the kitchen maid, Rose, is found murdered.

Keywords: Cooks; England—Georgian era; Silversmiths

Kostova, Elizabeth.

🏹 *The Historian.* **Little Brown, 2005. 647pp. Hardbound, 0316011770.** ★ 📖

Playing on readers' continual interest in vampires, debut novelist Kostova tells the story of a young, unnamed American teenager living in 1972 Amsterdam, and her quest to unravel a mystery about an ancient book and pile of letters left to her by her historian father. The letters, all addressed to "my dear and unfortunate successor," date from 1930; they reveal the obsession of her father's mentor, Professor Rossi, with discovering the truth about Vlad the Impaler, the fifteenth-century Wallachian nobleman who inspired the Dracula legend. The story jumps from place to place across Europe and switches among the young woman's narration; that of her father, Paul, in flashback; and letters written by Rossi before he disappears. Book Sense Book of the Year.

Keywords: Dracula; Historians; Multi-period novels; Netherlands—20th century; Vampires; Vlad the Impaler (historical character)

Liss, David.

Benjamin Weaver Series. 📖

Literary thrillers set amid the world of commerce in eighteenth-century London.

Keywords: England—Georgian era; Stock market; Weaver, Benjamin

🏹 *A Conspiracy of Paper.* Random House, 2000. 442pp. Hardbound, 0375502920.

London in 1719 is a burgeoning commercial center, and the stock market is the scene for much of the action. Benjamin Weaver, a thief-taker, former boxer, and all-around person-for-hire, turns to investigation once he receives word that his estranged father has been run down in a carriage accident. Suspecting that the death was hardly accidental, Benjamin becomes caught up in the schemes and plots surrounding eighteenth-century London's version of Wall Street, complete with crooks, clandestine meetings, and fortunes to be won and lost. The author evokes the somewhat formal language of two centuries past while maintaining the fast-paced nature of a modern thriller. Edgar Award.

A Spectacle of Corruption. Random House, 2004. 381pp. Hardbound, 0375508554.

Benjamin Weaver returns in this sequel to *A Conspiracy of Paper*, set in mid-eighteenth-century London. Imprisoned for a murder he didn't commit, Benjamin engineers his escape with the help of a mysterious benefactor. To clear his name, he goes into disguise as a rich merchant with an interest in politics. His investigations uncover a conspiracy with grave implications for the future of the monarchy.

Keywords: Disguise; Merchants

The Whiskey Rebels. **Random House, 2008. 519pp. Hardbound, 9781400064205.**

Liss sets his latest literary suspense novel in an underused historical period: the Whiskey Rebellion of the 1790s. Revolutionary War veterans living in the wilds of western Pennsylvania, angry at the new federal government's taxation of their valuable cash crop—distilled whiskey—take their frustrations out on local excise agents, prompting President Washington to call out the militia. Joan and Andrew Maycott, a young couple from Philadelphia, gamble on whiskey to make a new life for themselves, which draws Alexander Hamilton's ire. They and Ethan Saunders, a disgraced ex-spy recruited by Hamilton to find his former fiancée's missing husband, find themselves on opposite sides of the conflict.

Keywords: Pennsylvania—colonial period; Whiskey Rebellion

Pearl, Matthew.

The Poe Shadow. **Random House, 2006. 370pp. Hardbound, 1400061032.**

Edgar Allan Poe's death in October 1849 remains shrouded in mystery to this day. While on a lecture tour he left Richmond, Virginia, en route to Philadelphia. After several days he reappeared in a drunken state in a Baltimore tavern, and he died several days later. Quentin Clark, a Baltimore attorney and avid Poe admirer, seeks to rehabilitate his idol's reputation by determining the true cause of his death. To do so, he travels to Paris to look up the real-life model for Poe's master detective, Auguste Dupin.

Keywords: France—early modern era; Lawyers; Maryland—early United States; Poe, Edgar Allan (historical character)

Pears, Iain.

An Instance of the Fingerpost. **Riverhead, 1998. 691pp. Hardbound, 1573220825. ★ 📖**

In 1660s Oxford, England, a fellow of New College is found murdered. Four different people recount the story behind the crime, and each gives a vastly different version of events. Only one of them is telling the real truth, but which one? A young woman stands accused of the crime, and though she would seem to have a motive, she may or may not be the killer. Interspersed throughout the text are some wry observations on English life and politics. Full of plot twists, and written with an authentic feel for seventeenth-century language, Pears's novel was hailed as the long-awaited successor to Eco's *The Name of the Rose.*

Keywords: England—Stuart era

Penney, Stef.

🏶 *The Tenderness of Wolves.* **Simon & Schuster, 2007. 371pp. Hardbound, 9781416540748. 📖**

In the small, remote settlement of Dove River in Canada's Northern Territory in 1867, fur trader Laurent Jammet is brutally murdered in his cabin. Mrs. Ross, his neighbor, discovers the body. Because her seventeen-year-old son, Francis, disappeared on the same day, he quickly becomes the prime and, indeed, only suspect. As winter closes in, various people begin to converge on the town, including Hudson Bay Company representative Donald Moody. Mrs. Ross, determined to clear her son's name, begins following tracks leading north through desolate wilderness before the coming snow obscures any traces of evidence. Remarkably,

Scottish novelist Penney, who suffered from agoraphobia, never set foot in Canada during the research or writing. Costa Book of the Year.

Keywords: Canada—19th century; Mothers and sons; Wilderness

Sansom, C. J.

Matthew Shardlake Series. 📖

These lengthy, detailed novels, which blur the line between literary thrillers and historical mysteries, unveil the darker side of Tudor England. They are set in the 1530s and 1540s, a time of religious unrest as Henry VIII takes it upon himself to break with the Catholic Church and become its leader in England; conspiracies abound. With his curmudgeonly attitude, Matthew Shardlake, a middle-aged, hunchbacked attorney, is hard to warm to at first, but his sharp intelligence and wit should quickly win readers over. *Revelation* will be the next entry.

Keywords: England—Tudor era; Hunchbacks; Lawyers; Shardlake, Matthew

Dissolution. Viking, 2003. 336pp. Hardbound, 0670032034.

The dissolution of the title refers to the dismantling of the monasteries in Tudor England. In 1537 Henry VIII reigns, and Anne Boleyn has recently been beheaded. Controversies rage between the Catholics and those loyal to the king and his newly created Church of England. Thomas Cromwell leads the reformers, and when a man loyal to him is murdered at the monastery at Scarnea, Cromwell sends Matthew Shardlake to investigate. Once there Matthew uncovers more than he bargained for, including sexual scandals, murder, and treason.

Keywords: Monks

Dark Fire. Viking, 2004. 400pp. Hardbound, 0670033723.

In 1540 Matthew Shardlake's defense of a friend's niece, who has been accused of murder, seems doomed to fail, for the young woman won't speak up in court to defend herself. Lord Cromwell, needing Matthew's services for a job of his own, agrees to postpone her death sentence for two weeks so that Matthew can hunt down "Greek fire," a weapon of mass destruction required by the king. His search leads him into the dark world of Tudor alchemy.

Keywords: Alchemy; Greek fire

Sovereign. Viking, 2007. 592pp. Hardbound, 9780670038312.

It is the autumn of 1541, and Archbishop Thomas Cranmer sends Matthew north to York to prepare the city for the king's progress, a journey he'll undertake in the hopes of quelling a rebellion. But he was also given a more secret and dangerous mission: to ensure the safety of a political prisoner in York so that he can be transported back to London for "questioning" (in other words, torture). Matthew also investigates the murder of a Papist glazier who may have ties to the rebellion.

Schatzing, Frank.

Death and the Devil. Morrow, 2007. 400pp. Hardbound, 9780061349485.

In 1260 the great cathedral of Cologne is being constructed, under the able direction of architect Gerhard Morart. When a mysterious man clad in black pushes

Morart to his death from the cathedral's scaffolding, the only witness is Jacob the Fox, a petty thief. Though naïve about the political conspiracy currently rocking Cologne—the result of a fierce rivalry between the local archbishopric and the townspeople—Jacob is forced to form alliances to outrun and unmask the plotters.

Keywords: Cathedrals; Germany—Middle Ages; Morart, Gerhard (historical character); Thieves

Welsh, Louise.

Tamburlaine Must Die. **Canongate, 2005. 149pp. Hardbound, 1841955329.**

Aficionados of Elizabethan-era literature know that Christopher Marlowe, gifted playwright and spy, met his end in a tavern in Deptford, stabbed through the eye with a dagger during a fight with another man over the bill. In this slim novel, Welsh reimagines the last, frantic week of Marlowe's all-too-short life through his own fictional remembrances of his final days. Charged with heresy, libel, and atheism by the queen's Privy Council, Marlowe is given a few days to discover who has gotten him in trouble by posing as the blasphemous title character of his play *Tamburlaine.*

Keywords: England—Tudor era; Marlowe, Christopher (historical character); Playwrights

Psychological Suspense

Psychological suspense is a difficult subcategory to define. These novels combine elements of the thriller, horror, mystery, and literary fiction genres to form a category of their own. In a nutshell, they are dark, chilling books whose intense psychological impact causes excitement to build in the reader as the story draws closer to its conclusion. The suspense is usually internal, rather than action-oriented, and mind games are a common plot device. More often than not the novels conclude with a major plot twist. In historical novels of psychological suspense, the historical background, eerie and atmospheric, plays into the novel's intensity. A typical setting may include the gas-lit streets of Victorian London or a city in nineteenth- or early twentieth-century America. The gloomy, threatening tone enhances the dark atmosphere, and, as in most thrillers, the protagonists find themselves in danger from an unknown source. Although a crime may be committed, as is the case in mystery novels, here the identity of the murderer may or may not be a secret. Instead, this fact may be revealed to the reader early on, so that the novel's suspense lies in the protagonist's desperate hope of unmasking the culprit before he or she strikes again. As in horror novels, ghosts from the past—imagined or real—may be present. Finally, as is the case in literary historicals, the subjects are serious or bleak. The language used by the authors is elegant, but not inaccessibly so, and although pacing may be slower than in most thriller novels, these are compulsive page-turners.

Airth, Rennie.

John Madden Series.

Scotland Yard Detective John Madden, a battle-scarred veteran with horrible memories of his experiences in the First World War, takes on challenging cases that involve not only identifying a deadly killer, but hunting him down and catching him.

Keywords: England—20th century; Madden, John; Post-Traumatic Stress Disorder; Serial killers; Veterans

River of Darkness. Viking, 1999. 386pp. Hardbound, 0670885959.

Just after the end of World War I, Madden is called in to help solve a set of murders in the Surrey countryside. A young couple well beloved by their community have been gruesomely stabbed to death in their manor house, along with their servants. After the identity of the killer is revealed, the real mystery becomes a question of whether Madden and his compatriots can stop him in time.

The Blood-Dimmed Tide. Viking, 2005. 340pp. Hardbound, 0670899968.

In 1932, over a decade since his first chronicled investigation, Madden has retired from Scotland Yard and lives peacefully on a farm in the English countryside with his wife and children. The brutal murder of a young girl calls him out of retirement and forces him to rejoin his former colleagues in finding a serial killer with connections to international espionage in up-and-coming Nazi Germany.

Barron, Stephanie.

A Flaw in the Blood. **Bantam, 2008. 289pp. Hardbound, 9780553805246.**

Barron's first stand-alone novel under that name (she's best known for her Jane Austen mysteries, and also writes under her real name, Francine Mathews) centers on the death of Britain's Prince Albert in 1861 at the young age of forty-two. Patrick Fitzgerald, an Irish barrister who foiled an assassination attempt against Queen Victoria twenty years earlier, obeys the royal widow's request to come to Windsor Castle, but a murder attempt against him and his ward, physician Georgiana Armistead, forces them to flee to France for their safety. The answer to the puzzle may relate to the blood disease borne by Victoria's son Prince Leopold. Victoria herself is one of Barron's many narrators.

Keywords: England—Victorian era; Hemophilia; Lawyers; Physicians, women; Victoria, Queen of England (historical character)

Benson, Ann.

Plague Trilogy.

A series of psychological suspense novels/medical thrillers set in the fourteenth century and in the twenty-first century.

Keywords: Canches, Alejandro; Crowe, Janie; England—high Middle Ages; Multi-period novels; Physicians; Physicians, women; Plague; Spain—Middle Ages

The Plague Tales. Delacorte, 1997. 474pp. Hardbound, 0385316518.

In England in the year 2005, former surgeon Janie Crowe, in the course of research on virulent disease, unwittingly releases the virus causing the Black Death into the London populace. In a parallel story set in 1348, Spanish physician Alejandro Canches becomes a papal envoy to the court of England's Edward III and finds himself fighting the bubonic plague in the year of its greatest outbreak. There are some gruesome moments, naturally, but also plenty of plot twists as the pair race to dispel the deadly disease. Suspense rises toward the end, for there is no guarantee the pair can stop the plague's progress in time.

The Burning Road. Delacorte, 1999. 467pp. Hardbound, 0385332890.

This sequel to *The Plague Tales* picks up with Janie Crowe in 2007, as she pursues her fight against the plague and her discoveries in genetics, helped along by suggestions from Alejandro's journal. Alejandro, back in the fourteenth century, becomes involved with the Hundred Years' War while in France. Both tales portray the triumph against evil and the difficulties of coping in a repressive society.

Keywords: Hundred Years' War

The Physician's Tale. Delacorte, 2006. 514pp. Hardbound, 0385335059.

In the final volume of her trilogy, Benson continues her parallel themes of physicians in the fourteenth and twenty-first centuries fighting virulent outbreaks of disease. While Alejandro tries to rescue his foster daughter, Kate, from the nefarious marriage plans her real father, Edward III, has for her, Janie Crowe and her husband take refuge in a Massachusetts compound with other survivors, using Alejandro's journal to aid in finding a cure for a nasty bacteriological attack.

Brightwell, Gerri.

The Dark Lantern. **Crown, 2008. 319pp. Hardbound, 9780307395344.** 📖 **YA**

In Victorian London circa 1893, a young woman named Jane arrives from the country to become the new housemaid for the wealthy Bentley family. Robert Bentley, a scientist set on proving the effectiveness of anthropometry (identifying criminals by physical measurements), becomes the new head of household while his elderly mother lies dying upstairs. Robert's wife believes Jane is an impostor, but what is Jane hiding? Brightwell's debut draws many disparate plotlines together to create an eerie, Gothic-style suspense novel, with a classic *Upstairs/Downstairs* setting, which proves to be more than the sum of its parts.

Keywords: Anthropometry; England—Victorian era; Gothic novels; Impostors; Maids

Boyne, John.

Crippen: A Novel of Murder. **Thomas Dunne, 2006. 352pp. Hardbound, 0312343582.**

In 1910 would-be doctor Hawley Crippen brutally hacked to death his wife, Cora, and nearly got away with it. Boyne re-creates this historical incident, concentrating on Crippen's attempted escape across the Atlantic to Canada with his mistress, Ethel LeNeve, as Scotland Yard inspector Walter Dew boards a cruise ship in hot pursuit.

Keywords: Crippen, Hawley (historical character); England—20th century; Murderers; Shipboard adventure

Carr, Caleb.

Laszlo Kreizler Series. ★

Serial killers roam the streets of late nineteenth-century New York. Literary, suspenseful, and occasionally gruesome.

Keywords: Kreizler, Laszlo; New York—Reconstruction/Gilded Age; Serial killers

The Alienist. Random House, 1994. 496pp. Hardbound, 0679417796.

Before he became president, Theodore Roosevelt was, among other things, the police commissioner for New York. In 1896 a serial killer preying on young male prostitutes stalks the city. Not willing to turn the case over to the corrupt officials who report to him, "T.R." assembles his own group of crime solvers, including Laszlo Kreizler, a psychologist and the "alienist" of the title. His investigations take him from the crime-ridden underworld of New York to the highest of high society—members of which try to prevent him from continuing, as they fear seeing their names dragged through the mud. All the while, danger is about to strike from another direction. Anthony Award.

The Angel of Darkness. Random House, 1997. 629pp. Hardbound, 0679435328.

Stevie Taggart, a young urchin saved by Laszlo Kreizler from a life of crime in *The Alienist*, returns to narrate this sequel of sorts. When a young woman appeals to Kreizler and his friends to help her find her kidnapped daughter, they can hardly refuse, but the more they find out about the case and the woman's past, the more they suspect that she may be more involved than she admits. Once again we are thrust into the shadowy atmosphere of late nineteenth-century New York City in this fast-paced, suspenseful thriller.

Chance, Megan.

The Spiritualist. Three Rivers, 2008. 418pp. Paper, 9780307406118. 📖

Peter Atherton, a prominent attorney, belonged to the upper-class New York elite. When he is murdered in 1856, his body found stabbed and floating in the East River, his wife Evelyn is accused of killing him. It's thought that Evie, who came from a middle-class background, would have benefited the most from his death, especially as their relationship had grown strained. To clear her name, Evie reluctantly enters the shadowy world of the spiritualist movement. The medium Peter had contacted prior to his death, the enigmatic Michel Jourdain, intrigues and discomfits her.

Keywords: Mediums; New York—early United States; Spiritualism

Flacco, Anthony.

Nightingale Series.

Sergeant Randall Blackburn and Shane Nightingale, a young orphan he adopts after events in the first book, form an investigative team that combines the former's formal skills in detection with the latter's youthful ingenuity and knowledge of the San Francisco streets. Flacco is an actor, screenwriter, and editor.

Keywords: Adopted children; California—20th century; Orphans; Policemen

The Last Nightingale. Ballantine, 2007. 258pp. Paper, 9780812977578.

In the aftermath of the great San Francisco earthquake of 1906, the city reels under the immense devastation, and a serial killer nicknamed "the Surgeon" sees the perfect opportunity to strike with minimal chance of capture. Three women of the Nightingale family number among his victims, and the adopted son of one of them, twelve-year-old Shane Nightingale, was an unwitting witness to his mother's ghastly death. Shane, who has an uncanny sense of intuition, joins with city cop Randall Blackburn to catch the murderer.

Keywords: San Francisco earthquake; Serial killers

The Hidden Man. Ballantine, 2008. 285pp. Paper, 9780812977585.

It's now 1915, and Shane Nightingale and his father have grown older and wiser. They continue their partnership when the World's Fair comes to San Francisco. A serial killer tracking the fair's starring attraction, mesmerist James "J. D." Duncan, will surely succeed unless the pair—or the intended victim—can predict his actions quickly enough to stop him.

Keywords: Hypnotists; World's Fair

Fleming, James.

White Blood. **Atria, 2007. 368pp. Hardbound, 9780743299381.**

Fleming, the nephew of Ian Fleming, sets his debut thriller in remote Smolensk, Russia, in 1914. Naturalist Charlie Doig, a man of Scots Russian heritage and with an overactive libido, returns from an expedition in Burma to woo his beautiful cousin Elisaveta at his family's mansion, which is called Pink House. Then two Russian soldiers are billeted at his home, annoying everyone with their barbed remarks; one may be a Bolshevik with deadly intentions.

Keywords: Bolshevik Revolution; Naturalists; Russia—20th century; Soldiers

Ford, Jeffrey.

🎗 *The Girl in the Glass.* **Dark Alley, 2005. 286pp. Paper, 0060936193.**

Diego, an illegal seventeen-year-old Mexican immigrant, disguises himself as an Indian mystic and accompanies his mentor, Thomas Schell, in his schemes to bilk the last remaining wealth from the residents of Long

Island's Gold Coast in 1932. Along with burly Antony, who acts as henchman, the trio conduct fake séances without compunction, until Schell sees an apparition of a young girl in a glass who, he believes, connects with the disappearance of shipping heiress Charlotte Barnes. Edgar Award.

Keywords: Great Depression; Immigrants, Mexican; Ku Klux Klan; New York—20th century; Séances; Thieves

Franklin, Ariana.

Adelia Aguilar Series. 📖 YA

Adelia Aguilar, the twelfth-century version of a coroner, trained as a physician in Salerno, Italy, where women were allowed to practice medicine. These are chilling forensic thrillers with occasionally graphic violence and fascinating detail of medieval England, a specialty of the author—historical novelist Diana Norman writing under a pseudonym.

Keywords: Aguilar, Adelia; Coroners; England—high Middle Ages; Physicians, women

🎗 *Mistress of the Art of Death.* Putnam, 2007. 384pp. Hardbound, 9780399154140.

Due to her expertise, Adelia's help is requested in solving crimes in England on behalf of its king, Henry II. Four children of Cambridge have been murdered; the city's Jews are being blamed, but the king believes them innocent. Or perhaps he simply wants them free to pay taxes, because the realm desperately needs the funds. Because of Adelia's sex and unorthodox methodology (doing autopsies of the dead, for instance), she risks being accused of witchcraft, and there are those who would kill to prevent her from learning the truth. Ellis Peters Historical Award; The Reading List.

Keywords: Children; Jews

The Serpent's Tale. Putnam, 2008. 371pp. Hardbound, 9780399154645.

Adelia is called away from her considerably more peaceful (and less dangerous) life in East Anglia, where she delivers babies and cares for her own young daughter. King Henry wants her to look into the poisoning death of his beloved mistress, Rosamund Clifford. Naturally Henry's queen, Eleanor of Aquitaine, is the prime suspect.

Keywords: Clifford, Rosamund (historical character); Mistresses

City of Shadows. **Morrow, 2005. 422pp. Hardbound, 9780060817268.**

Berlin in 1922 is undergoing tremendous upheaval: inflation is high, as is anti-Semitism, and the Nazis are beginning to rise in power. Esther Solomonova, a secretary and one of the city's many émigrés from Russia, becomes involved with her boss's scheme to prove that a local insane asylum patient calling herself Anna Anderson is the heir to the Russian imperial throne. People close to Anna are being murdered, and Esther's own life may be in danger.

Keywords: Anderson, Anna (historical character); Germany—20th century; Nazis; Secretaries

Gerritsen, Tess.

The Bone Garden. **Bantam, 2007. 307pp. Hardbound, 9780345497604.**

In modern Boston, Julia Hamill discovers a skeleton in the garden of the quaint old house she just purchased. When forensic investigation by perennial Gerritsen heroine Maura Isles reveals that the long-deceased woman was murdered, Julia searches through local archives for more information. Flashbacks to 1830 tell the story of Norris Marshall, a medical student turned "resurrectionist" (grave robber) for the sake of his studies. To prove he isn't the notorious serial killer known as the West End Reaper, Norris teams up with Rose Connelly, an Irish seamstress who caught a glimpse of the perpetrator.

Keywords: Grave robbers; Massachusetts—early United States; Medical students; Multi-period novels; Seamstresses

Gray, John MacLachlan.

Not Quite Dead. **Minotaur, 2007. 304pp. Hardbound, 9780312374716.**

After the notorious author/critic Edgar Allan Poe collapses in Baltimore in 1849—the event that led to his real-life death—he asks the attending physician, his childhood friend Dr. William Chivers, to help him hide from members of the Irish mob who are out to get him. His path crosses that of novelist Charles Dickens while the latter is on tour in the United States. Dickens, already uncomfortable with the reception he's been receiving, is hardly pleased to be sharing lodgings with the disreputable Poe. The viewpoint switches between the first-person narration of Chivers and the third-person account of Finn Devlin, an Irish scalawag who murdered Dickens's American publisher. Their paths all collide in a spectacular finale.

Keywords: Authors; Dickens, Charles (historical character); Mafia; Murderers; Physicians; Poe, Edgar Allan (historical character)

Hayder, Mo.

The Devil of Nanking. **Grove, 2005. 363pp. Hardbound, 0802117945.**

Hayder's multi-period thriller stretches from the 1937 massacre of hundreds of thousands of Nanking residents by Japanese invaders to 1990, when fragile Englishwoman Grey Hutchins, herself the survivor of rape and other traumas, tracks down a snippet of 16mm film that preserves images of the earlier atrocities. In Tokyo Grey locates an elderly Chinese professor who was a Nanking survivor, but she gains his help only after she takes a job at a hostess club and meets an old mobster who takes drugs to extend his lifespan—drugs the professor also claims to need. Scenes shift between the modern story and the professor's 1937 diary.

Keywords: China—20th century; Diaries and journals; Japan—20th century; Multi-period novels; Nanking, Massacre of

Kellerman, Faye.

Straight into Darkness. **Warner, 2005. 432pp. Hardbound, 0446530409.**

In Munich in 1929, Hitler and the Nazi party are gaining both power and prestige. Axel Berg, an inspector in the city's homicide unit, risks his own livelihood as he pursues the truth behind a serial killer's rampage through the city. As Berg strikes out on his own, avoiding political pressure to blame the murders on the Jewish husband of one of the victims, anti-Semitic sentiment rises along with the body count.

Keywords: Germany—20th century; Nazis; Policemen; Prejudice; Serial killers

Jakeman, Jane.

Claude Monet Series. ✍

A duo of thrillers combining art history, crime, and psychological suspense, and featuring famed Impressionist painter Claude Monet.

Keywords: Artists; Monet, Claude (historical character)

In the Kingdom of Mists. Berkley, 2004. 355pp. Hardbound, 0425195120.

In the City of Dark Waters. Berkley, 2006. 313pp. Hardbound, 0425209814.

Monet and his wife, Alice, arrive in Venice in 1908, fleeing the scandal of his brother-in-law's murder, which had dogged them in Paris, and so that Monet can get some painting done. Revel Callender, an English lawyer on a year's excursion in Venice, is hired by an Italian count to go through the papers of a recently deceased female relative. Soon after, the count himself is murdered, and Monet hires Callender to investigate the death of his brother-in-law back in Paris. Callender begins to see unusual parallels between the two cases.

Keywords: Italy—20th century; Lawyers

Meyers, Annette.

Repentances. **Five Star, 2004. 304pp. Hardbound, 1410401871.**

Artists frequently reuse canvases, and "repentances" are the ghostly images of original paintings that reappear as the oil on the newer painting ages. This theme of hidden truth from the past resonates in Meyers's novel, beginning in 1936 Greenwich Village as Jewish immigrant Nathan Ebanholz hires an agent to bring his wife and child from Eastern Europe to America. After learning the truth, that they were killed back in Poland, Ebanholz kills the agent's wife, Stella—a woman with whom he was having an affair. This action, and Ebanholz's subsequent crime, haunts all of the characters to the present day.

Keywords: Immigrants, Polish; Jews; Murderers; New York—20th century

Michod, Alec.

The White City. **St. Martin's, 2004. 232pp. Hardbound, 0312313977.**

Someone has been killing young boys in Chicago in 1893, leaving their bodies on the grounds of the Columbian Exposition, otherwise known as the World's Fair. When Billy Rockland, the child of one of the city's notable architects, goes missing at the fair, Dr. Elizabeth Handley, an early forensic psychologist, is called in to find him.

Keywords: Illinois—Reconstruction/Gilded Age; Psychologists; Serial killers; World's Fair

Mosse, Kate.

Sepulchre. **Putnam, 2008. 544pp. Hardbound, 9780399154676.** 📖

In 1891 at their widowed aunt's invitation, Léonie Vernier and her brother Anatole travel from Paris to Rennes-les-Bains, a small village in the Pyrenees in southern France. Mystery surrounds their Aunt Isolde's late husband, who delved into the occult. In a parallel tale, while ostensibly writing a biography of Debussy at Rennes-les-Bains, Meredith Martin, a present-day researcher, quietly researches her ancestors. A sepulchre from Visigothic times and a deck of tarot cards rumored to possess strange powers reveal eerie ties between the two young women.

Keywords: Biographers; France—early modern era; Gothic novels; Multi-period novels; Tarot

Phillips, Arthur.

Angelica. **Random House, 2007. 331pp. Hardbound, 9781400062515.**

In 1880s London Joseph Barton insists to his wife, Constance, that their daughter, four-year-old Angelica, be given her own bedroom. Constance fears that resumption of marital relations may prove dangerous for her, with her history of miscarriage; she is also convinced that a blue specter with sexual motives is preying on the child. Is the ghost real, or is it a product of her imagination? When Constance brings a medium into the household to exorcise the ghost, the atmosphere turns truly menacing.

Keywords: Daughters; England—Victorian era; Ghosts; Mediums

Rose, M. J.

Reincarnationist Series.

Annotated in Chapter 12.

Rubenfeld, Jed.

The Interpretation of Murder. **Henry Holt, 2006. 367pp. Hardbound, 0805080988.**

Something dreadful must have happened on Sigmund Freud's first and only visit to the United States, because after he returned to Vienna, he referred to Americans as "savages." Rubenfeld, a professor of law at Yale, spins a tale around this true-life incident, imagining that Freud and his protégé, Carl Jung, arrive in Manhattan during the summer of 1909 for a lecture tour, only to be confronted by a potential serial killer who preys on beautiful young debutantes. The second attack victim managed to escape, but has amnesia, so it's up to Freud and his psychoanalytic techniques to revive her memory.

Keywords: Freud, Sigmund (historical character); New York—20th century; Psychologists; Serial killers; Socialites

Simmons, Dan.

The Terror. **Little, Brown, 2007. 769pp. Hardbound, 9780316017442.** 📖

By 1847 the vessel called *The Terror*, under Captain Francis Crozier, has been trapped in Arctic ice for two years. Back in 1845 Sir John Franklin led a two-ship expedition to Canada's frozen wasteland in search of the Northwest Passage. Through the eyes of Crozier, Franklin's second-in-command, and Harry Goodsir, surgeon on the *Erebus*, we see the men from both vessels succumb to starvation, madness, hypothermia, infection, and other dreaded mishaps. Meanwhile, a supernatural "Thing" made of ice, a bearlike creature, terrorizes the crew. Simmons has made a career out of crafting award-winning speculative fiction, and while some of his earlier works used historical events as a springboard (the far-future settings of *Ilium and Olympos* deliberately resembled ancient Greece), this is his first true historical novel. It, too, has its share of horror and suspense.

Keywords: Canada—19th century; Crozier, Francis (historical character); Franklin, Sir John (historical character); Northwest Passage; Shipboard adventure

Wheeler, Thomas.

The Arcanum. **Bantam, 2004. 325pp. Hardbound, 055380314X.** ✍

This action-packed occult thriller, set in New York City in 1919, presupposes that a mysterious manuscript called the *Book of Enoch* has been lost—stolen from the founder of the secret society known as the Arcanum before his death in Hyde Park. His fellow society members, including Arthur Conan Doyle and Harry Houdini, trace its path to New York's infamous Bowery district, where a serial killer is on the loose.

Keywords: Conan Doyle, Arthur (historical character); New York—20th century; Secret societies; Serial killers

Crime Thrillers

Novels in this subgenre center on crime, although they aren't mysteries. Unlike the works in Chapter 7, which describe and exemplify the art of detection, crime thrillers incorporate heart-thumping chase scenes, gritty settings, and graphic violence in their explorations of the criminal mind from the outside and inside. Gangsters, organized crime, bank heists, and men on the run in search of vengeance or their own form of justice often appear in these novels, which regularly take place on the stark Western plains or in the dark underworld of Western American cities. Crime thrillers share elements in common with traditional Westerns (Chapter 6) and historical mysteries of the noir variety, although here the sense of menace and quick pacing come to the forefront. A subcategory new to this edition.

Abbott, Megan.

Abbott writes noir in the style of Raymond Chandler, but with a definite feminist slant.

Die a Little. **Simon & Schuster, 2005. 256pp. Hardbound, 0743261704.**

In 1954, when Pasadena schoolteacher Lora King begins investigating the background of Alice Steele, the gorgeous femme fatale who married her beloved brother, Bill, she gets drawn into a world of drug deals, sex, and corruption—and finds she likes it more than she'll ever admit.

Keywords: California—20th century; Teachers

The Song Is You. **Simon & Schuster, 2007. 242pp. Hardbound, 9780743291912.**

Abbott bases her smart second novel on the real-life disappearance of star-let Jean Spangler from a Hollywood studio in 1949. Now it's 1951, and Gil "Hop" Hopkins, a smooth-talking publicist who's being blackmailed for withholding information about her disappearance, decides to solve the missing-person case himself. The bold pulp fiction–style cover, with its bold portrait of a busty brunette, perfectly complements his journey through the glamorous yet very dark Hollywood underworld.

Keywords: California—20th century; Spangler, Jean (historical character)

Blake, James Carlos.

Blake's specialty is novels about real-life historical criminals, punks, and other men on the edges of society, who exhibit all the ruthlessness, violence, and tough-guy attitude you'd expect of them.

Handsome Harry. **Morrow, 2004. 304pp. Hardbound, 0060554789.** ✍

Notorious Depression-era bank robber John Dillinger is well-known to-day, but "Handsome" Harry Pierpont, Dillinger's partner and semi-offi-cial leader of the Dillinger Gang, is less so. On the night before his 1934 execution for murdering a sheriff, Pierpont narrates—with an appropriate level of bravado—his own adventures in crime, beginning with his forma-tive teenaged years, through small-time heists, to his education (by the residents of an Indiana prison) in the art of bank robbery.

Keywords: Bank robbers; Great Depression; Indiana—20th century; Pierpont, Harry (historical character)

Culhane, Patrick.

Black Hats: A Novel of Wyatt Earp and Al Capone. **Morrow, 2007. 304pp. Hardbound, 9780060892531.** ✍

Writing as Patrick Culhane, prolific mystery/crime novelist Max Allan Collins pens a tale of an imaginary encounter between legendary Western lawman Wyatt Earp and notorious gangster Al Capone in his younger years. In 1920 Earp runs a detective agency in Los Angeles. He is hired by Doc Holliday's widow, Kate Elder, to rescue her son, speakeasy owner Johnny, from the clutches of Capone in New York City.

Keywords: California—20th century; Capone, Al (historical character); Earp, Wyatt (historical character); Gangsters; Lawmen; New York—20th century

Hackman, Gene, and Daniel Lenihan.

Justice for None. St. Martin's Press, 2004. 307pp. Hardbound, 0312324251.

In 1929 in Vermilion, Illinois, a small town in the state's rural eastern corn belt, Boyd Calvin—railroad man, war veteran, and former resident of the local soldiers' home—comes upon a man sitting calmly by the body of his recently deceased ex-wife and immediately flees the scene. Captured and thrown in jail for her murder, Boyd escapes to inner-city Chicago with a black man falsely accused of rape, which leads to some gruesome scenes suggestive of *The Jungle*. After Boyd returns to Vermilion to face the music, the remainder of the book turns into a tense courtroom drama.

Keywords: Illinois—20th century; Veterans

Leonard, Elmore.

Carl Webster Series.

Carl Webster, born Carlos—the son of a half-Cheyenne man and a Cuban woman—is the best-looking, most sharply dressed lawman in 1930s and 1940s Oklahoma. His adventures as a deputy U.S. marshal are firmly set against a backdrop of speakeasies, bank robberies, gangsters, and gun molls.

Keywords: Great Depression; Lawmen; Mixed heritage; Oklahoma—20th century; Webster, Carl

The Hot Kid. Morrow, 2005. 315pp. Hardbound, 0060724226.

> Seven years after notorious bank robber Emmet Long took an ice-cream cone from fifteen-year-old Carlos Webster, Carl gets his revenge, gunning him down in a shootout. Now it's Dust Bowl Oklahoma, circa the early 1930s, and Carl's hot on the trail of Jack Belmont, an oilman's son with a deadly reputation for crime.

Up in Honey's Room. Morrow, 2007. 292pp. Hardbound, 9780060724245.

> At the height of World War II, Carl Webster searches for two German POWs who escaped from an Oklahoma detention camp. He follows the trail to Detroit, where he believes they've been hidden by Walter Schoen, a butcher with German connections who bears a striking resemblance to Heinrich Himmler. Carl gets to know Honey Deal, Walter's bombshell of an ex-wife, in the hopes she'll lead him to Walter.
>
> **Keywords:** Ex-wives; Oklahoma—World War II; Prisoners of war

Strick, Wesley.

Out There in the Dark. Thomas Dunne, 2006. 323pp. Hardbound, 0312343817.

In Tinseltown during the World War II years, film studio exec Arthur Lustig hires a private investigator, Mike Roarke, to look into the background of B-movie actor Harley Hayden, who's been sleeping with Arthur's daughter. Lustig finds nothing on him, but Hayden turns the tables by hiring Roarke to investigate Derek Sykes, a German director with a secret who's been giving Hayden trouble. Screenwriter and author Strick portrays 1940s Hollywood as a hotbed of corruption and vice, which should come as no surprise.

Keywords: Actors; California—World War II; Film industry

Woods, Stuart.

Rick Barron Series.

The hard-boiled adventures of former Beverly Hills cop Rick Barron, who, after a stroke of luck, becomes a security officer at a movie studio and gets caught up in the drunken and crime-ridden antics of Hollywood starlets and their associates.

Keywords: Barron, Rick; California—World War II; Film industry

The Prince of Beverly Hills. Putnam, 2004. 321pp. Hardbound, 0399152202.

In Los Angeles in 1939 Rick Barron leaves the police force for a position as security chief at Centurion Studio after he saves big-name star Clete Barrow from bad publicity after a deadly car accident he caused. He continues to come to the rescue of Clete and other Hollywood stars, hobnobs with Greta Garbo and Clark Cable, and discovers incriminating X-rated pictures in the safe of his recently deceased predecessor—which attracts the attention of the local mob.

Keywords: Organized crime

Beverly Hills Dead. Putnam, 2008. 304pp. Hardbound, 9780399154690.

In this less-than-suspenseful, episodic sequel to *Prince of Beverly Hills*, set firmly in the McCarthy era, Rick, now Chief of Production at Centurion, begins casting a blockbuster Western flick. Meanwhile, hearings organized by the House Un-American Activities Committee begin sniffing out Hollywood communists.

Keywords: Communism

Religious Thrillers

This subcategory, new to this edition, owes much to the popularity of *The Da Vinci Code*. Although not historical fiction, Dan Brown's best-selling novel sparked enormous interest in religious conspiracies that hark back to the early days of the Christian church. Secrets hidden in biblical documents, paintings, or other artifacts threaten to reemerge into the world, forcing those who would prefer they be kept hidden to take drastic action. Secret societies, cryptic symbols hidden in paintings, and biblical relics are common elements. Controversial because they incorporate unorthodox theories—Mary Magdalene as Jesus's wife, for instance—religious thrillers provoke discussion and occasional outcry among readers who disagree with their ideas. All of the titles below not only focus on historical events, but are set in the past themselves.

Bergren, Lisa T.

The Gifted Series.

Annotated in Chapter 11.

Khoury, Raymond.

The Last Templar. **Dutton, 2006. 404pp. Hardbound, 0525949410.**

In an explosive opening scene, four horsemen disguised as Knights Templar burst in upon a gallery opening at the Metropolitan Museum of Art, an exposition of Vatican artifacts, and steal an encoding device—destroying art and killing people in their path. Archaeologist Tess Chaykin, recognizing their disguise, bands together with FBI agent Sean Reilly to learn their motivation. Scenes shift between the present day and the last days of the Templars in the late thirteenth and early fourteenth centuries.

Keywords: Archaeology; Christian themes; Knights Templar; Middle East—13th century; Multi-period novels; New York—20th century

Malarkey, Tucker.

Resurrection. **Dutton, 2006. 384pp. Hardbound, 159448919X.** 📖

This leisurely paced religious thriller takes place in a unique locale (Cairo just after World War II) and centers on the recent discovery of the Gnostic Gospels in the desert near Nag Hammadi. After her archaeologist father's untimely death, former wartime nurse Gemma Bastian travels from London to Cairo to settle his affairs. While staying with his father's good friend David Lazar and his family, Gemma attracts the romantic interest of David's two sons. Revelations about her father's recent finds, including a possible gospel written by Mary Magdalene, lead her to believe that someone was willing to kill to preserve their secrets. **Literary.**

Keywords: Christian themes; Egypt—20th century; Gnostic Gospels

McGowan, Kathleen.

The Expected One. **Simon & Schuster, 2006. 449pp. Hardbound, 0743299426.** ✍ 📖

In the novel's first part, American feminist author Maureen Paschal, who has been plagued with biblical visions for years, travels to France's Languedoc region at the behest of a mysterious aristocrat in hopes of finding Mary Magdalene's lost gospel. The second part is straight historical fiction, in which events leading up to the crucifixion are seen from the viewpoint of Mary herself. Two-thirds contemporary religious thriller and one-third biblical fiction, *The Expected One* is frequently mentioned in the same breath as Dan Brown's *The Da Vinci Code*. Both contain fast-paced story lines centered on Jesus Christ, Mary Magdalene, and a millennia-old effort by the Catholic Church to hide the truth about their relationship. However, McGowan insists that her story is not only historically true, but autobiographical. The first novel in a projected trilogy called <u>The Magdalene Line</u>; *The Book of Love* will be the next volume.

Keywords: Autobiographical novels; Biblical themes; Catholicism; Feminists; Mary Magdalene (biblical figure); Multi-period novels; Palestine—ancient/prehistoric

Mosse, Kate.

Labyrinth. **Putnam, 2006. 515pp. Hardbound, 0399153446.** 📖

While on an archaeological dig in the mountains outside Carcassonne in southern France, Alice Tanner discovers two skeletons, as well as an odd pattern of a labyrinth inscribed on the cave's walls and on a ring. This discovery not only causes

Alice to experience strange visions, it also begins an epic race to uncover the secret that the ring unlocks. In a parallel story, Alaïs, a Cathar teenager in thirteenth-century Carcassonne, is asked by her father to guard a book that reveals part of the secret of the Holy Grail.

Keywords: Cathars; Christian themes; France—Middle Ages; Holy Grail; Labyrinths; Multi-period novels

Navarro, Julia.

The Brotherhood of the Holy Shroud. **Bantam, 2007. 399pp. Hardbound, 9780385339629.**

The Shroud of Turin, which is believed by many to bear the image of Jesus Christ, has fascinated people ever since its appearance in fourteenth-century Europe. In the aftermath of a fire in Turin Cathedral in the present day, the body of a tongueless man is found. As members of the Italian Art Crimes Department investigate this odd occurrence, connections to two groups of secret societies related to the shroud are revealed. A modern story alternates with episodes detailing the shroud's history over the past 2,000 years.

Keywords: Christian themes; Italy—multi-period; Multi-period novels; Secret societies; Shroud of Turin

Sierra, Javier.

The Secret Supper. **Atria, 2006. 329pp. Hardbound, 0743287649.**

In the year 1497 the pope sends Father Agostino Leyre, a Dominican inquisitor, to Milan to investigate whether Leonardo da Vinci is incorporating heretical symbolism into his masterwork *The Last Supper*. Leyre, who narrates, observes the painting in progress and grows ever more uncomfortable with what he finds: the apostles have been painted without haloes, one of them holds a knife, and Leonardo has painted himself into his work, with his back turned away from Jesus. A thriller about Christian symbology and the mysteries and omissions in Leonardo's painting.

Keywords: Christian themes; da Vinci, Leonardo (historical character); Inquisition; Italy—Renaissance/Reformation; Paintings

International Intrigue

In these novels world history forms a backdrop against which one or more protagonists must race against the clock to solve a puzzle or unmask a killer before danger strikes. The action takes place on one or more continents, typically Europe or Asia, during a time of political unrest. Secrets from the past come back to haunt the protagonists, and the conspiracies they uncover often follow upon one or more political events from the recent past, such as a revolution or war. To investigate, many protagonists enter the hidden arena of the political underworld, going into disguise to uncover a conspiracy, solve a crime, or expose wide-scale corruption. This is not a large category, but these fast-paced novels are popular with a large variety of readers, including fans of mysteries, traditional historical novels, and modern political thrillers. In these stories events are set against a grand and global backdrop, often in exotic locales, and the protagonists are sophisticated and cosmopolitan. They may include elements of espionage (covered later this chapter), but this isn't usually the main focus.

Bennett, Ronan.

Zugzwang. **Bloomsbury USA, 2007. 277pp. Hardbound, 978073934209.**

British novelist Bennett's fifth novel, written in weekly installments and published in the *Observer* beginning in January 2006, centers on an international chess tournament being held in St. Petersburg, Russia, in April 1914. Several people have been murdered in the city, including a noted journalist. The police believe Dr. Otto Spethmann, a renowned psychoanalyst, to be a suspect, to his great surprise and worry. Meanwhile Dr. Spethmann becomes increasingly involved with the lives of two patients, one a chess master, the other a beautiful young woman. The plotline is itself reminiscent of a chess game, with illustrations of a chess match accompanying the story.

Keywords: Chess; Psychologists; Russia—20th century

Hoyt, Richard.

Sonja's Run. **Forge, 2005. 352pp. Hardbound, 0765306158.**

This breathtaking, adventurous suspense novel begins in 1852, as half-Russian, half-Chinese poet Sonja Sankova slugs Peter "Colonel Cut" Koslov at Tsar Nicholas I's Christmas Eve party after Koslov makes offensive comments. In London on the same night, photographer Jack Sandt convinces journalist Karl Marx to find a way to let him take daguerreotype images inside Russia. Sonja and Jack meet and fall in love but are forced to flee Koslov across the wide reaches of the Russian empire.

Keywords: Mixed heritage; Photographers; Poets; Russia—early modern era

Neville, Katherine.

The Eight. **Ballantine, 1989. 550pp. Hardbound, 0345351371. ★**

After the French Revolution, former religious novice Mireille narrowly escapes the guillotine, only to find herself caught up in international intrigue. She is given the task of scattering pieces of the legendary Montglane Service, a chess set once owned by Charlemagne, around the globe because its power can be dangerous in the wrong hands. Her adventures bring her in contact with some of the greatest political powers of the day, including Robespierre and Talleyrand. In a present-day story line, computer whiz Catherine Velis teams up with a chess master to reassemble the pieces of the set herself before someone else does. The travels of both women take them across the European continent, from France to Algeria and back again. Chess symbolism, secret codes, numeric patterns, and danger abound. *The Fire* will be the sequel.

Keywords: Algeria—20th century; Chess; France—early modern era; French Revolution; Multi-period novels

Petit, Caroline.

The Fat Man's Daughter. **Soho, 2005. 276pp. Hardbound, 1569473870.**

In 1937 nineteen-year-old Leah Kolbe, daughter of an American dealer in Chinese antiquities, travels from Hong Kong to Japanese-occupied Manchuria after her father's untimely death, at the behest of a mysterious tall Chinaman, Mr. Chang, who works for the Chinese resistance. Chang, preying on Leah's desire to recoup some of her inheritance, lost by her father in offshore investments, convinces her to smuggle imperial Chinese treasure out of Manchuria under Japan's nose. *Deep Night* will be the sequel.

Keywords: China—20th century; Fathers and daughters; Smugglers; Treasure

Terrell, Heather.

The Chrysalis. **Ballantine, 2007. 225pp. Hardbound, 9780345494665.**

Mara Coyne hopes she'll make partner in her upscale Manhattan law firm by defending Beazley's, a big-name auction house that wants her to confirm the provenance of a lost masterpiece, Johannes Miereveld's *The Chrysalis*, which is about to go on the market again. Then a Dutch woman turns up, claiming that the painting was stolen by the Nazis after World War II and that it properly belongs to her family. As Mara becomes romantically involved with Beazley's current client, an old college friend, she discovers their case isn't as airtight as it appears. This multi-period novel switches among the modern day, the World War II period, and seventeenth-century Holland.

Keywords: Lawyers; Multi-period novels; Netherlands—17th century and World War II; Paintings

War Thrillers

Nowhere is the battle between good and evil so clearly drawn as in war thrillers. Larger-than-life heroes battle against dark forces. In wartime the enemy may be lurking behind every corner, and sometimes it's impossible to tell who the enemy is. A few minutes may mean the difference between success and failure, and in war thrillers, it's a race against time to strike against your enemies before they strike against you. This intensifies the suspense of these fast-paced novels. World War II in particular presents ripe opportunities for authors of historical thrillers, for members of the Nazi party make dastardly villains. Many of these authors also write contemporary war thrillers.

Follett, Ken.

Follett's novels have nonstop thrills and fast-paced action, with larger-than-life heroes and heroines who face danger at every turn. His spy thrillers are listed later in this chapter.

Jackdaws. **Dutton, 2001. 451pp. Hardbound, 0525946284.** ★

Felicity "Flick" Clairet is a British agent in France during World War II. When her plan to foil the German communication system goes awry and her husband disappears, she takes it upon herself to form an all-female team—the Jackdaws—whose job it will be to gain access to German lines of communication. However, the Germans know of their existence, so their mission won't be easy.

Keywords: France—World War II; Spies, women

Night over Water. **Morrow, 1991. 400pp. Hardbound, 0688046606.** ★

A group of European jet-setters—which include a murderer, a thief, an aristocrat, and a scientist—board the Pan American Clipper, a luxurious jumbo jet bound for New York, for one heart-stopping night flight across the Atlantic in 1939.

Keywords: Airplanes; Europe—World War II

Frei, Pierre.

Berlin. **Atlantic, 2006. 425pp. Hardbound, 0802118321.**

In the American sector of occupied Berlin in 1945, a month after the war has ended, an investigator for the U.S. Military Police and a German police inspector join forces to solve the murder of a beautiful young woman who was raped and strangled, her body left in a subway station. When it becomes clear that she's not the only such victim, the men realize they're dealing with a problem much more serious and widespread than originally believed.

Keywords: Germany—World War II; Policemen

Frost, Mark.

🌳 *The Second Objective.* **Hyperion, 2007. 319pp. Hardbound, 9781401302221.**

During the winter of 1944, just before the Battle of the Bulge, Hitler sends a large number of English-speaking German troops behind enemy lines in the hopes of disrupting the Allies' plans to invade Germany. But a small group of twenty commandos have a second objective: to assassinate Eisenhower. This is historical fact. Frost tells the story from the viewpoints of the last two commandos remaining: Bernie Oster, an American of German parentage who dislikes the idea of fighting people he once lived alongside, and Erich Von Reinsdorf, a cruel and single-minded Nazi. We also see the action from the other side, as Earl Grannit, a cop formerly with the NYPD, and his fellow soldiers try to prevent the Nazis from succeeding. The Reading List (Award).

Keywords: Assassinations; German Americans; Germany—World War II; Nazis; Policemen

Gabbay, Tom.

Jack Teller Series.

Fast-paced, high-stakes thrillers centering on European political intrigue during times of war. Gabbay, a screenwriter, tells the backstory of his hero, Jack Teller, in his second novel.

Keywords: Teller, Jack

The Berlin Conspiracy. **Morrow, 2006. 294pp. Hardbound, 0060787856.**

Former CIA agent Jack Teller had hoped to retire in peace, but in 1963 he's called to fly to Berlin, where his contact tells him about an assassination attempt against JFK that will take place during his upcoming visit to East Germany.

Keywords: Assassinations; East Germany—20th century; Spies

The Lisbon Crossing. Morrow, 2007. 310pp. Hardbound, 9780061188435.

It's 1940, and stuntman Jack Teller leaves Hollywood in a hurry after a disgruntled husband puts a hit out on him. He arrives in neutral Lisbon, Portugal, with German film star Lili Sterne. She is in search of her childhood friend, Eva, who's in hiding from the Nazis. While there Jack stumbles on a conspiracy to deliver Britain into Nazi hands, and the duke of Windsor may be at the helm of it.

Keywords: Nazis; Portugal—World War II; Stuntmen

Gobbell, John J.

Gobbell sets his military thrillers in the South Pacific theater of World War II: Japan, the Philippines, and southern China. He is best known for his four-volume Todd Ingram series, about a navy lieutenant who sees action in the Philippines during the war.

A Call to Colors. **Presidio, 2007. 487pp. Paper, 0891418903.**

The Battle of Leyte Gulf, the largest naval battle in history, took place in late October 1944 around the Philippine island of Leyte. Gobbell, himself a veteran of the encounter, recounts a rousing story of General MacArthur's offensive against the Imperial Japanese Navy from the viewpoint of Commander Mike Donovan, skipper of the destroyer USS *Matthew*, who gets caught in the middle between MacArthur's fleet and the Japanese ships sent to destroy it.

Keywords: Leyte Gulf, Battle of; Philippines—World War II

Griffin, W. E. B., and William E. Butterworth IV.

Men at War Series.

A six-book (at present) series of military spy thrillers, following the spies of Colonel William "Wild Bill" Donovan's Office of Strategic Services (OSS), a precursor of the CIA, during the Second World War. Wild Bill, an old law school chum of Franklin Delano Roosevelt, has an innate sense of leadership and confidence that makes men want to work for him. The series takes place between 1941 and 1943. The first four novels were published as paperback originals in the 1980s and released later in hardcover; the latest two novels, written nearly twenty years later, were coauthored by Griffin and his son.

Keywords: Donovan, Wild Bill; Spies; United States—World War II

The Last Heroes. Putnam, 1997 (©1985). 342pp. Hardbound, 0399142894.

The Secret Warriors. Putnam, 1998 (©1985). 321pp. Hardbound, 0399143815.

The Soldier Spies. Putnam, 1999 (©1986). 340pp. Hardbound, 0399144943.

The Fighting Agents. Putnam, 2000 (©1987). 311pp. Hardbound, 0399146121.

The Saboteurs. Putnam, 2006. 305pp. Hardbound, 0399153489.

The Double Agents. Putnam, 2007. 333pp. Hardbound, 9780399154201.

Kanon, Joseph.

Alibi. Henry Holt, 2005. 405pp. Hardbound, 080507886X.

Adam Miller, an American soldier assigned to investigate German war crimes, arrives in Venice in 1945 on a visit to his mother, Grace, a rich expatriate. While Grace resumes her romance with an old flame, Gianni Maglione, a doctor who may or may not have Nazi connections, Adam falls in love with a Jewish woman. Things heat up when Adam's new love recognizes Maglione and accuses him of having betrayed her own father to the Nazis.

Keywords: Italy—World War II; Jews; Nazis

Lawton, John.

Frederick Troy Series.

Inspector Frederick Troy of Scotland Yard, occasionally viewed with suspicion by his comrades thanks to his Russian birth and aristocratic background, takes on assignments that help him ferret out conspiracies for the British government. The settings range from 1941 in the first novel, when Troy was a youthful sergeant, to the Cold War circa 1963 in the fifth; the next title will be *Second Violin.*

Keywords: Blitz; Cold War; England—World War II; Policemen; Troy, Frederick

Bluffing Mr. Churchill. Atlantic Monthly, 2004. 322pp. Hardbound, 0871139073. (Original title: *Riptide.*)

In 1941 SS officer Wolfgang Stahl flees Berlin, with Hitler's plans to invade Russia, after his cover as an American spy is blown. MI5 officer Walter Stilton teams up with Stahl's American partner to find him, but when tragedy strikes, Troy is called in to ferret out the truth.

Black Out. Viking, 1995. 342pp. Hardbound, 067085767X.

As London suffers through the Blitz in 1944, Scotland Yard detective Frederick Troy is asked to look into the possible connection between body parts found a at a bomb site and the disappearance of a scientist studying German atomic rocketry. Conspiracies abound.

Old Flames. Atlantic Monthly, 2003. 416pp. Hardbound, 0871138646.

In this Cold War thriller set in 1956, Troy uses his knowledge of all things Russian to his advantage, posing as one of Khrushchev's bodyguards on his visit to London.

Flesh Wounds. Atlantic Monthly, 2005. 343pp. Hardbound, 0871136988. (Original title: *Blue Rondo.*)

In London in the late 1950s, Troy solves murders back in his old haunts, the city's East End, and a former girlfriend who married an American presidential candidate comes back into his life.

A Little White Death. Atlantic Monthly, 2006. 440pp. Hardbound, 0871139324.

> Troy, ill with tuberculosis and sidelined during 1963, returns to active duty to look into a mysterious double suicide.

Mrazek, Robert J.

The Deadly Embrace. **Viking, 2006. 274pp. Hardbound, 0670034789.**

In London in 1944 plans for Operation Overlord, better known as the D-Day invasion, are in motion. Lt. Liza Marantz, a Jewish American trained as a forensic pathologist, is assigned to work for Major Sam Taggart, a former NYC homicide detective, at SHAEF, the Allied high command. She's responsible for censoring outgoing correspondence to ensure that nobody leaks any information about the Allies' plan. Then several young women turn up murdered, making Liza and Sam wonder if the women had compromised the upcoming invasion through their relationships with high-ranking Allied officers.

Keywords: D-Day; England—World War II; Forensic pathologists; Jews

Quinn, Peter.

Hour of the Cat. **Soho, 2005. 400pp. Hardbound, 1585675970.**

In 1938 gumshoe and former NYC cop Fintan Dunne haunts the city's streets while attempting to exonerate a man who is on death row for a murder he didn't commit. The more he investigates, the more the case reveals connections to Nazi Germany and Hitler's burgeoning belief in eugenics. Over in Berlin at the same time, Admiral Canaris, head of military intelligence, tries to reconcile his faith in Germany with his hatred of Hitler's policies and megalomania. The two story lines coalesce as the novel progresses.

Keywords: Detective stories; Eugenics; Germany—World War II; New York—World War II

Rabb, Jonathan.

Rosa. **Crown, 2005. 416pp. Hardbound, 1400049210.**

Rosa Luxemburg, a Marxist revolutionary who helped form the German Communist Party, was murdered by authorities in January 1919 after an unsuccessful attempt at fomenting a revolution in Berlin. Her body wasn't discovered until months later, which is where Rabb's imaginative interpretation comes in. *Rosa* begins a month prior, in December 1918, as Berlin detective Nikolai Hoffner and his assistant investigate the odd designs carved into the backs of the corpses of several middle-aged women found in the city's slums. Then Luxemburg's body turns up in mid-January in a morgue, with similar markings. As Hoffner tries to understand the connection between Luxemburg's death and the serial killer's signature mark, it leads him to suspect a conspiracy of anti-Semitism—which will later give rise to the Nazi party.

Keywords: Communism; Detective stories; Germany—World War I; Luxemburg, Rosa (historical character); Revolutions and revolutionaries

Robbins, David L.

The Assassins Gallery. **Bantam, 2006. 411pp. Hardbound, 0553804413.**

In 1945, as World War II draws to a close, Professor Mikhal Lammeck, an expert in historical killings, is brought in to solve the murders of two civilians in Newburyport, Massachusetts. His detection leads him to pinpoint the killer as a Persian-born woman named Judith, a trained assassin, who has Franklin Roosevelt in her sights.

Keywords: Assassins; Detective stories; Massachusetts—World War II

Wallner, Michael.

April in Paris. **Nan A. Talese, 2007. 248pp. Hardbound, 9780385519144.**

In Paris in 1943 twenty-two-year-old Corporal Roth is asked to serve as translator in the Gestapo's interrogation room—a job he detests—after his superiors learn he can speak accentless French. While taking a stroll down Parisian streets in disguise as a French civilian, he meets and falls in love with Chantal, daughter of an antiquarian bookseller, not realizing she works for the Resistance. When their involvement becomes known, Roth is accused of being a traitor.

Keywords: Disguise; France—World War II; Nazis; Soldiers

Spy Thrillers

Spy thrillers take place during or just before wartime, when military intelligence is operating at its highest level. The difference between these and war thrillers is that the protagonists, rather than being men on the front lines of the fighting, are secret agents working undercover for one or both sides. During the Cold War espionage thrillers were all the rage, for they closely reflected historical reality: spies working covertly amid sinister political intrigue. After the fall of the Soviet Union in 1991 espionage fiction declined in popularity, but novelists soon found other appealing settings in earlier political conflicts of the twentieth century: World Wars I and II. Common locales include one or more European cities during World War II, such as Paris at the time of the German Occupation. The heroes of espionage thrillers (they are almost always men) work alone, because in these times of changing political loyalties, there's no one for them to trust. The atmosphere is dark and threatening, with the enemy all around, and they could be betrayed or caught at a moment's notice. The protagonists are as likely to be antiheroes as heroes, for many are ordinary men forced to become spies due to circumstances beyond their control.

Boyd, William.

🌳 *Restless*. **Bloomsbury USA, 2006. 304pp. Hardbound, 1596912367.**

Ruth Gilmartin, an ESL instructor and single mother living in Oxford in 1976, is understandably shocked when her aging mother, Sally, reveals that her real name was Eva Delectorskaya, a Russian émigré recruited by British intelligence in Paris during World War II. Sally believes someone is out to kill her and asks Ruth to help her by locating Lucas Romer, her boss during the war. Eva's story, recounted through her memoirs, intertwines with that of Ruth, puzzling out her mother's true identity over thirty years later. Costa Book Award.

Keywords: Disguise; England—World War II; Manuscripts; Multi-period novels; Spies, women

Broadbent, Tony.

Jethro Novels.

Cat burglar (or "creeper") Jethro navigates the fog-engulfed streets of London, known as "the Smoke" in underworld slang, in the years just after World War II.

Keywords: Blackmail; England—20th century; Fascism; Jethro; Spies; Thieves

The Smoke. Thomas Dunne, 2002. 302pp. Hardbound, 0312290276.

> In 1947 in London food and wealth are hard to come by, so Jethro takes full advantage of his cleverness and ability to sneak into secure places. His success in stealing jewels from the Soviet embassy attracts the attention of His Majesty's Secret Service, which recruits him to return to the embassy to steal a codebook.

🏵 *Spectres in the Smoke.* Thomas Dunne, 2005. 322pp. Hardbound, 0312290268.

> It's now 1948, and MI5 still needs Jethro's assistance; they have enough blackmail-worthy material on him to be persuasive. This time they ask him to break into the headquarters of a Fascist group to steal some records that might implicate a member of the royal family. Bruce Alexander Historical Award.

Downing, David.

John Russell Series.

John Russell, a British expatriate earning a living as a freelance journalist in Berlin in 1939, would prefer to dissociate himself from matters political. However, that proves to be all but impossible. Like Alan Furst, Downing writes about a reluctant hero caught up in a tangled web of international espionage.

Keywords: Germany—World War II; Journalists and reporters; Russell, John; Spies

Zoo Station. Soho, 2007. 293pp. Hardbound, 9781569474532.

> When a Soviet agent persuades John Russell to write a pro-German piece for *Pravda* in order to make some extra money, he keeps the British government fully informed. As a result, he gets drawn far deeper into a dangerous web of espionage.

Silesian Station. Soho, 2008. 336pp. Hardbound, 9781569474945.

> Russell finds himself in the predicament of spying for three major superpowers in order to secure his own safety—or so he thinks—and to free his German actress girlfriend, recently arrested by the Gestapo.

When a young Jewish woman expected to arrive in Berlin goes missing, things get really complicated.

Follett, Ken.

Eye of the Needle. Arbor House, 1978. 313pp. Hardbound, 006074815X. ★

When German intelligence discovers that the Allies will be landing in Normandy rather than Calais, British agents must find a way of preventing Die Nadel, a crack German agent, from reaching Hitler before the D-Day invasion can commence.

Keywords: D-Day; France—World War II; Spies

The Key to Rebecca. Morrow, 1980. 381pp. Hardbound, 0688037348. ★

Daphne du Maurier's classic novel of romantic suspense holds the key to a code used by one of Rommel's German spies in North Africa during World War II—and it's up to British intelligence to decipher it.

Keywords: Egypt—World War II; Spies

Furst, Alan.

Furst's novels are set in Europe prior to or during World War II. His heroes are ordinary people who, in the confusion and political intrigue surrounding the war, become involved in history-changing events—frequently against their better judgment. They can't fully believe in the actions they are forced to take, but they do so because there's no other choice for survival. Furst's scenes call to mind scenes from *Casablanca*: smoke-filled bars, shabby hotels, star-crossed lovers scheduling rendezvous in darkened alleyways, and the complexity of military intelligence. Although he is a literate writer, his novels are accessible to general readers. All of his novels can stand alone.

Dark Voyage. Random House, 2004. 256pp. Hardbound, 1400060184.

In 1941, when too many British ships have been lost to attacks and maritime disasters, the British navy asks Eric DeHaan, captain of the Dutch freighter *Noordendam*, to undertake a secret espionage mission along the Swedish coast with his ship disguised as a Spanish freighter. Like the ship itself, which has no true home, all among the merchant marine crew are fugitives of one sort or another.

Keywords: Shipboard adventure—World War II; Ships; Spies

The Foreign Correspondent. Random House, 2006. 273pp. Hardbound, 1400060192.

Carlo Weisz is a foreign correspondent for Reuters and the new editor of an underground Paris-based newspaper that opposes Mussolini in 1939. As he gets drawn deeper into the Italian resistance, his activities attract the attention of the OVRA, the Italian secret police, which murdered both his predecessor and his lover.

Keywords: France—World War II; Journalists and reporters; Spies

The Spies of Warsaw. Random House, 2008. 266pp. Hardbound, 9781400066025.

Jean-François Mercier, a distinguished veteran of the Great War, serves as a military attaché at the French embassy in Warsaw in 1937, as war with Germany looms on the horizon. The covert part of Mercier's job is working with a network of spies to round up as much prewar intelligence as he can. One of his agents, an engineer at a German arms manufacturer, suspects the Gestapo are on to him—and he's right.

Keywords: Poland—World War II; Spies

Higgins, Jack.

Eagle Series. ★

After *The Eagle Has Landed* stood the test of time as a classic World War II thriller, Higgins wrote a sequel—over a decade later.

Keywords: Devlin, Liam; England—World War II; Nazis; Spies

The Eagle Has Landed. Holt, 1975. 382pp. Hardbound, 0030137462.

In 1943 German paratroopers land in the English countryside. Their objective is to kidnap or kill Prime Minister Winston Churchill at his country house in Norfolk. What makes this novel different from most World War II thrillers is that it's told from the Nazi point of view, and a surprisingly human and almost sympathetic one at that. Kurt Steiner, their commander, is on this suicide mission only reluctantly. His efforts are helped on the ground by IRA gunman Liam Devlin, who has been preparing the way for the Germans' arrival. One wrong move, and their cover is blown.

The Eagle Has Flown. Simon & Schuster, 1991. 335pp. Hardbound, 0671724584.

This sequel to *The Eagle Has Landed* picks up at the end of World War II with Liam Devlin, formerly of the IRA. Heinrich Himmler, the head of the German SS, asks Devlin to rescue Kurt Steiner, a POW held by the British in London. What Devlin doesn't know is that Himmler's real plan is to divert attention while he moves in to assassinate Hitler and take over Germany himself.

Hyde, Christopher.

The House of Special Purpose. Onyx, 2004. 385pp. Paper, 0451411080.

The titular "house of special purpose" was the dwelling in Ekaterinburg, Russia, where the Russian imperial family—Nicholas, Alexandra, and their children—where brutally murdered during the Bolshevik Revolution of 1918. Over two decades later, in 1941, American news photographer Jane Todd and Scotland Yard detective Morris Black are recruited as spies for the OSS. Their mission is to investigate the existence of a reel of film rumored to show the execution of the Russian royals. Their enemies are close on their trail.

Keywords: Assassinations; Bolshevik Revolution; Romanov family; Russia—World War II; Spies

Mathews, Francine.

The Alibi Club. Bantam, 2006. 309pp. Hardbound, 055380331X.

On the eve of the German invasion of Paris in May 1940, four women who frequent the Alibi Club, one of the city's most infamous after-hours haunts, get drawn into a web of passion and espionage that begins with the murder of Philip Stilwell. His lover, model Sally King, wants the truth behind his death; nightclub singer Memphis Jones, a character modeled on Josephine Baker, refuses to go home to Tennessee; British aristocrat Nell Bracecourt yearns for excitement, and finds it; and Irène Curie, daughter of Marie and Pierre, holds a secret that could change the course of the war.

Keywords: Curie, Irène (historical character); France—World War II; Nightclubs; Nobility; Singers; Spies

Ross, Joel N.

Double Cross Blind. **Doubleday, 2005. 372pp. Hardbound, 0385513887.**

Disguised as his brother Earl, an OSS agent who betrayed his unit in Crete to the Nazis, American soldier Tom Wall matches wits with a captured Nazi agent who may know about an upcoming Japanese attack on Pearl Harbor. Set in London in 1941.

Keywords: England—World War II; Spies

White Flag Down. **Doubleday, 2007. 370pp. Hardbound, 9780385513890.**

Ross bases his second historical thriller on the pretext that Russia and Germany were using Switzerland as a meeting point to sign a treaty of nonaggression. In September 1942 Lieutenant Grant, an American pilot, catches a glimpse of an enemy weapon, a prototype for a jet aircraft, before crashing his photo reconnaissance plane in Switzerland—a supposedly neutral country. After being captured by and then escaping from Swiss authorities, Grant returns to the crash site to retrieve his camera. En route he gets caught up in an international search for a powerful secret document.

Keywords: Pilots; Spies; Switzerland—World War II

Sansom, C. J.

Winter in Madrid. **Viking, 2008. 537pp. Hardbound, 9780670018482.**

In autumn 1940, in a city recently devastated by the Spanish Civil War, World War I vet and reluctant British secret service agent Harry Brett arrives to work as an interpreter. His true mission, however, is to spy on a former classmate from his public school days, Sandy Forsyth, a businessman involved in shady deals that could convince Franco to enter World War II on the side of the Nazis. Meanwhile Sandy's live-in girlfriend, ex-Red Cross nurse Barbara Clare, secretly pulls strings in the hope of discovering that her Communist lover, Harry's old friend Bernie Piper, is still alive.

Keywords: Communism; Friendship; Spain—World War II; Spies

Silbert, Leslie.

The Intelligencer. **Atria, 2004. 338pp. Hardbound, 0743432924.** ✍

Was Elizabethan playwright Christopher Marlowe killed defending himself in a bar fight, or was his death associated with his role as "intelligencer" for the queen? His story intertwines with that of Kate Morgan, a young private investigator from New York who moonlights as a spy. Her latest assignment is to fly to London to determine the significance of a mysterious sixteenth-century manuscript written in code.

Keywords: England—Tudor era; Manuscripts; Marlowe, Christopher (historical character); Multi-period novels; Spies; Spies, women

Silver, Mitch.

In Secret Service. **Touchstone, 2007. Hardbound, 1416537945.**

This multi-period spy novel alternates chapters between Yale historian Dr. Amy Greenberg, who travels to Dublin to retrieve a decades-old manuscript from her grandfather's safe deposit box, and the manuscript itself, an unpublished document written by Ian Fleming, author of the James Bond novels. Fleming's manuscript details the secret friendship between Edward, Duke of Windsor, and Adolf Hitler, a relationship that has implications for the modern-day monarchy and the world.

Keywords: England—World War II; Fleming, Ian (historical character); Historians; Manuscripts; Multi-period novels; Spies

Walters, Guy.

The Traitor. **Simon & Schuster, 2005. 512pp. Hardbound, 0743270150.**

Tortured by the Nazis while imprisoned on Crete in 1943, Captain John Lockhart, a British spy, agrees to turn traitor and spy on the Greeks in order to save the life of his wife, Anna, who's being held in a Belgian concentration camp. His conscience is nowhere near clear, however, especially when he is asked to assume command of the British Free Corps, a pro-Hitler band of British officers.

Keywords: Crete—World War II; Nazis; Spies; Traitors

Chapter **10**

Literary Historical Novels

Literary historical novels use historical settings, eloquent language, and multi-layered plotlines to convey contemporary themes. Librarians and readers may not think of literary fiction as a type of genre fiction, but for readers' advisory purposes, it helps to group them together in this way. Together these novels form one of the fastest-growing and most popular subgenres of historical fiction. These days, more and more literary novelists are looking to the past for inspiration, and with great success.

The use of language is important to readers of literary historicals, and the writing style used in these novels can be described as elegant, poetic, or lyrical. Although some literary novelists choose to tell their stories in a straightforward fashion, others use a more experimental style, making use of flashbacks, stories-within-stories, and multiple narrative viewpoints. Dialogue can be equally creative. Some authors choose not to enclose their characters' words in quotation marks so that they flow more fully into the story.

These critically acclaimed works are reviewed in major newspapers, and they often win literary prizes. Because they address serious issues, their focus may be darker than most, and they may not have an optimistic ending. Their authors tend to incorporate unique settings, ones not often used by traditional historical novels. The novels themselves are character-driven rather than plot-driven, and although they tend not to be quick reads, the intriguing, complex characters and multi-layered plots have a way of drawing readers into the story.

In addition to providing a detailed portrait of life during earlier times, authors of literary historical fiction use the past as a vehicle to express a universal or modern theme. Their characters somehow manage to transcend time and speak to us from their own perspective in a way that we, today, can understand. However, despite the assiduous historical research that the authors conduct, their novels are as apt to be labeled "contemporary fiction" as they are "historical fiction." This apparent paradox is due to their emphasis on seemingly timeless subjects. Similarly, with a few notable exceptions (e.g., Tracy Chevalier, Sarah Waters, Jude Morgan, Susan Vreeland), many authors in this chapter are not thought of as historical novelists. Not only are they not tied to a particular historical period, but few of their novels occur in series, and many also write works of fiction set in the present day. Not only will literary historicals appeal to historical fiction fans, but they also have the ability to reach a wide, mainstream audience.

The word "literary" tends to scare off genre fiction readers, but people shouldn't assume that these novels are inaccessible. They can run the gamut from challenging tomes (e.g., Salman Rushdie's *The Enchantress of Florence*) to uncomplicated yet poetic reads (e.g., Shan Sa's *Alexander and Alestria*). Most fall somewhere in between. Readers' advisors should also be aware that "literary" refers to a writing style rather than any indication of quality, and that a book's placement in this chapter doesn't necessarily denote a higher quality novel than those found in other chapters. Because literary historicals are thought-provoking works whose ideas can be explored on many levels, they make good choices for reading groups.

Due to the number of literary historical novels currently being published, this is a fairly long chapter. Besides the novels annotated below, readers of literary historicals may appreciate literary thrillers (Chapter 9). Some books found in other chapters, especially Chapter 5 (sagas) and Chapter 7 (Western historical novels), qualify as literary and are tagged with the word **Literary** in boldface at the end of the annotation.

Readers who enjoy literary historicals may appreciate some titles from other subgenres that are tagged as appropriate for reading groups 📖, as they provide thoughtful explorations of historical times. Finally, as described in this book's introduction, many classic or benchmark novels in other chapters, denoted by ★, have cross-genre appeal and may interest readers of literary historical fiction as well.

Biblical

Literary novels with biblical themes tend to be controversial, because they often interpret the lives of characters from the Bible in new and frequently unorthodox ways. Readers interested in biblical fiction from an evangelical Christian point of view should consult Chapter 11; biblical settings also appear in traditional historical novels (Chapter 2).

Diamant, Anita.

🌸 *The Red Tent.* **St. Martin's Press, 1997. 321pp. Hardbound, 0312169787.** ✍ ★ 📖

The red tent is the haven where women must seclude themselves during menstruation and childbirth. In this novel about Dinah from the Bible, the tent also symbolizes the feminine spirit. The only daughter of Jacob, Dinah grows up with four mothers: Leah, her natural mother, plus Jacob's other wives: Rachel, Zilpah, and Bilhah. Dinah's life story takes a female spin on well-known biblical events, such as Jacob's lengthy courtship of Rachel and the rise to glory of Dinah's half-brother Joseph. Dinah is mentioned in the Bible primarily in the context of her rape and subsequent rescue by her brothers. Here, her relationship with a Canaanite man is a forbidden romance that her brothers destroy with one vengeful act. Other novels of women's lives in biblical times appear in Chapters 2 and 11. Book Sense Book of the Year.

Keywords: Biblical themes; Dinah (biblical figure); Mothers and daughters; Polygamy

Williams, Niall.

John. Bloomsbury USA. 2008. 288pp. Hardbound, 9781596914674. ✑

The elderly Apostle John, the loyal disciple of Jesus known for writing the Book of Revelation, spends his last days on the Isle of Patmos, the place where he experienced his original, terrifying visions. Many of John's fellow exiles, anxious for the return of the Messiah, grow impatient and restless and begin doubting Christ's divinity. While John reminisces about Jesus and his ministry, he fears for the future of Christianity, for his followers' return to the mainland may result in disunity.

Keywords: Apostles; Biblical themes; Exile; John the Apostle (historical character); Patmos—ancient/prehistoric

The Roman Empire

Browner, Jesse.

The Uncertain Hour. Bloomsbury USA, 2007. 224pp. Paper, 9781596913394. ✑

Sentenced to die by Nero because of presumed treasonous activities, which the emperor falsified against him, Roman senator and aristocrat Titus Petronius chooses to commit suicide rather than live with the dishonor. On the final evening of his life in the year AD 66, Petronius holds a sumptuous party at his home for his closest friends, reflecting on his past and on the meaning of life. A philosophical, somber novel with rich descriptions of a Roman banquet's décor and delicacies.

Keywords: Banquets; Petronius Arbiter (historical character); Rome; Senators, Roman

Other Ancient Civilizations

These novels present characters from ages long past in new and unique ways; they tell ancient tales with a modern sensibility.

Divakaruni, Chitra Banerjee.

The Palace of Illusions. Doubleday, 2008. 277pp. Hardbound, 9780385515995. 📖

Divakaruni, who grew up listening to the tales of the *Mahabharat*, writes her own, feminist interpretation of the great Indian epic, this time from the viewpoint of Panchaali, the king's daughter who married the five Pandava brothers. Panchaali and her twin brother are equally well-educated as children, though she grows up knowing her marriage will change the course of history by starting a great war. Not only does she juggle her relationships with all five men simultaneously, but she joins them in their quest to regain their birthright from their cousins, all the while contending with a bitter mother-in-law. A novel about a long-distant era (the author's estimate is the fifth millennium BC), a time when gods walked the earth and history mingled with myth.

Keywords: Brothers; Families; Heirs and heiresses; India; *Mahabharat*; Mythology; Princesses; Royalty

Essex, Karen.

Stealing Athena. **Doubleday, 2008. 452pp. Hardbound, 9780385519717.**
A multi-period story; annotated under "Europe: Early Modern Europe" in this chapter.

Shan, Sa.

Alexander and Alestria. **HarperCollins, 2008. 245pp. Hardbound, 9780061543548.** ✍
Shan Sa (in the Chinese tradition, the surname is listed first) imagines a love affair between two legendary world rulers: Alexander the Great, King of Macedon, and a warrior woman he first meets on the battlefield, Alestria, Queen of the Amazons. Alestria, an orphan who grew up among horses on the Siberian steppes, was adopted by and made the heir of the previous Amazonian queen. The pair fall in love, despite a prophecy stating that Alestria's affair will bring down the Amazon nation. Alexander, Alestria, and her Amazon serving girl, Ania, all speak in the first person, using bold language that celebrates the glories of life.

Keywords: Alexander the Great (historical character); Amazons; Greece; Persia

The British Isles

The setting for all novels in this section is England, unless otherwise indicated in the keywords.

The Middle Ages

Novels set in Britain's medieval period, from the fifth through fifteenth centuries AD. Not a common category, despite the many traditional historical novels (Chapter 2) set in this period; see the first volume of *Historical Fiction* for additional novels in this category.

Guill, Jane.

Nectar from a Stone. **Touchstone, 2005. 436pp. Paper, 0743264797.**
In 1351, having killed her abusive husband Maelgwyn in self-defense, Elise dumps his body in the river and flees her small Welsh village with her maid, Annora, to a distant town, in the hopes of starting a new life there. En route they are drawn into the path of Gwydion, a Welshman planning revenge on his family's killers. Elise and Gwydion fall in love, but elements from their past reach out to touch and claim them both.

Keywords: Abusive relationships; Murderers; Wales

The Tudor Era

The Elizabethan period (1558–1603) takes center stage here, and the plots revolve around the theatrical world and the royal court.

Garrett, George.

Elizabethan Trilogy. ✍ ★

The late former poet laureate of Virginia, Garrett's best known works are those comprising his loose trilogy of Elizabethan England, thought by some to be the most imaginative historical re-creations in literature. They are challenging reads to the newcomer, because their plotlines aren't linear, but Garrett's research is impeccable and his prose wonderfully descriptive. The books can be read in any order.

Death of the Fox. Doubleday, 1971. 739pp. Hardbound, no ISBN.

There's political intrigue aplenty as Sir Walter Raleigh, explorer and courtier in Tudor England, meditates on the adventurous life he led as Queen Elizabeth's captain before his downfall and execution by Elizabeth's successor, King James I.

Keywords: Explorers; Raleigh, Sir Walter (historical character)

Entered from the Sun. Doubleday, 1990. 349pp. Hardbound, 0385190956.

The murder of Christopher Marlowe—playwright, actor, and contemporary of Shakespeare—in a tavern brawl in Deptford is presented from the point of view of several witnesses who may also be participants.

Keywords: Actors; Marlowe, Christopher (historical character); Playwrights

The Succession. Doubleday, 1983. 583pp. Hardbound, 0385024215.

In 1603, as Elizabeth I reign comes to an end, the succession is still uncertain. Will she choose her distant cousin, James VI of Scotland, son of one of her greatest enemies, to follow her? The story of both personalities is told through their own thoughts as well as those of other political leaders of the time, from James's birth in 1566 until Elizabeth's own death in 1603.

Keywords: Elizabeth I, Queen of England (historical character); James I, King of England (historical character)

The Stuart Era

Novels dealing with the reality of day-to-day life in Stuart England (1603–1714), both at the royal court in London and in outlying areas. Not currently a popular category.

Bennett, Ronan.

Havoc, in Its Third Year. Simon & Schuster, 2004. 256pp. Hardbound, 0743258568.

John Brigge, governor of a small town in rural northern England during that country's Civil War, holds tight to his Catholic beliefs despite growing Puritan sentiments around him. After being asked to investigate the death of an Irish Catholic mother's newborn child, he becomes convinced that the mother is innocent, though he feels increasing personal and political pressure from his fellow townspeople to convict her.

Keywords: Catholicism; English Civil War; Governors; Infanticide

The Georgian Era

A grim, often shocking undercurrent appears beneath the surface of Georgian society (1714–1837). Some of these authors offer new interpretations of well-known literary figures and stories about the era.

Ackroyd, Peter.

The Lambs of London. Doubleday/Talese, 2006. 224pp. Hardbound, 0385514611. ✍

In the early nineteenth century, the paths of Charles Lamb, clerk for the East India Company, and his reclusive his sister Mary cross that of William Ireland, the seventeen-year-old son of an antiquarian bookseller. When William acquires a trove of papers related to Shakespeare, a subject about which both Lamb siblings are passionate, he discovers what he claims is the text of a previously undiscovered play.

Keywords: Booksellers; Brothers and sisters; Forgeries; Lamb, Charles (historical character); Lamb, Mary (historical character); Plays

Chevalier, Tracy.

Burning Bright. Dutton, 2007. 311pp. Hardbound, 9780525949787. 📖 **YA**

The title of Chevalier's fourth novel derives from the work of William Blake, late eighteenth-century poet and visionary, yet he doesn't figure as prominently in the story as readers might expect. Rather, the focus is on two children of London's Lambeth district: Maggie Butterfield, the street-smart daughter of a local con artist, and Jem Kellaway, a young man newly arrived from the English countryside. Both are drawn into the circle of Blake, Kellaway's neighbor, as the people of London navigate uneasily through a new world created in the aftermath of the French Revolution.

Keywords: Blake, William (historical character); Children; Coming of age; Neighbors; Poets

Clark, Clare.

The Nature of Monsters. Harcourt, 2007. 382pp. Hardbound, 9780151012060

British novelist Clark's second work of fiction (after the Victorian literary suspense novel *The Great Stink*) is an atmospheric literary Gothic at heart. In 1718 London Eliza Tally, a pregnant teenager, is forced into service at a chemist's laboratory, little knowing that her sadistic employer wishes to perform experiments on her unborn child. With the help of a friendly local bookseller, Eliza attempts to extricate herself and her fellow maid, Mary, from his clutches.

Keywords: Gothic novels; Pregnancy

Darwin, Emma.

The Mathematics of Love. **Morrow, 2006. 406pp. Hardbound, 0061140260.** 📖

This multi-period novel of love and war, written by Charles Darwin's great-great-granddaughter, introduces two stories that gradually intersect. In 1819, at his estate of Kersey Hall in Lancashire, Stephen Fairhurst adjusts to life with a missing leg, courtesy of the Battle of Waterloo. His correspondence with artist Lucy Durward, sister of a widow who rejected his marriage proposal, becomes romantic as they discuss his wartime experiences. About 150 years later, in 1976, teenaged Anna Ware is sent to Kersey, now a dilapidated rural school owned by her uncle. She grows infatuated with a local war photographer, Theo, and learns about Stephen's life by reading his old letters.

Keywords: Artists, women; Coming of age; Families; Letters; Multi-period novels; Photographers; Veterans

Davies, Martin.

The Conjurer's Bird. **Shaye Areheart, 2005. 384pp. Hardbound, 1400097339.** ✎ 📖

A rare specimen of the "bird of Ulieta," brought back by Captain Cook after his second voyage to the South Seas in 1774 and ensconced in the collection of eighteenth-century naturalist Joseph Banks, has disappeared from the historical record. Fitz, a present-day conservationist in London, is drawn into the mystery of the bird by his ex-wife. As Fitz becomes engrossed in the mystery, he draws connections between the bird and Banks's mistress, a woman whose name remains unknown today.

Keywords: Banks, Joseph (historical character); Birds; Multi-period novels; Naturalists

Elphinstone, Margaret.

Light. **Canongate, 2006. 421pp. Paper, 1841958808.**

On Ellan Bride, a remote island off the Isle of Man, in 1831, sisters-in-law Lucy and Diya Geddes keep the lamp in the lighthouse burning at night. When builder Archibald Buchanan arrives on Ellan Bride with his assistant, with the goal of constructing a replacement lighthouse, the women worry about the change it will mean for them and their families.

Keywords: Families; Islands; Isle of Man; Lighthouses

Markovits, Benjamin.

Imposture. **Norton, 2007. 200pp. Hardbound, 9780393329735.** ✎ 📖

When Eliza Esmond meets Lord Byron's look-alike former doctor, John Polidori, outside a London publishing office, she mistakes him for Byron himself. The bookish young woman is instantly smitten, particularly when he suggests a private meeting. Polidori goes to great lengths to maintain the deception, both to pursue his wooing of Eliza and to continue his obsession with Byron, who had previously severed the relationship.

Keywords: Byron, Lord (historical character); Impostors; Physicians; Poets; Polidori, John (historical character)

McMahon, Katherine.

The Alchemist's Daughter. **Crown, 2006. 338pp. Hardbound, 0307238512.** 📖

In 1727 in Buckinghamshire nineteen-year-old Emilie Selden, a true child of the Enlightenment, has been raised in seclusion by her brilliant and overbearing scientist father, who instructs her in chemistry, alchemy, and physics. When Robert Aislabie, an adventurer from London, arrives on the doorstep of Selden Manor, Emilie falls in love, beginning a passionate affair with him that leaves her pregnant. They marry, but Emilie soon discovers her husband isn't what he seems.

Keywords: Alchemy; Fathers and daughters; Scientists, women

Morgan, Jude.

Indiscretion. **St. Martin's, 2006. 378pp. Hardbound, 0312362064.** YA

The heroine of this literary Regency romance is Miss Caroline Fortune, a clever young woman who becomes a companion to the very wealthy Mrs. Catling when her father's gambling debts force her to seek employment. Settled in Brighton, Caroline is introduced to polite society, and when one ardent male admirer seeks to make her his mistress, she keeps his dishonest proposal to herself. Caroline later finds herself in a difficult position when her would-be lover turns up as the fiancé of a good friend.

Keywords: Companions; Regency romances

Passion. **St. Martin's, 2005. 536pp. Hardbound, 031234368X.** ✍ 📖 YA

From the time of the French Revolution through the 1830s, Morgan imagines the inner lives of four women closely linked with renowned romantic poets Byron, Shelley, and Keats: Mary Shelley, daughter of philosopher William Godwin and the author of *Frankenstein*; Lady Caroline Lamb, whose obsession with Byron causes her to risk everything; Fanny Brawne, the middle-class girl devoted to Keats, her brilliant lover; and Augusta Leigh, Byron's sensible half-sister, whose affair with him creates a huge scandal.

Keywords: Authors, women; Brawne, Fanny (historical character); Incest; Lamb, Lady Caroline (historical character); Leigh, Augusta (historical character); Mistresses; Poets; Shelley, Mary (historical character)

The Victorian Era

These novels of life in Victorian times (1837–1901) recount events and ways of life kept hidden from proper Victorian society: poverty, abuse, homosexuality, and secret love affairs. In this sense they are very modern novels, despite being well researched and written in language appropriate to the time.

Barlow, John.

Intoxicated. **Morrow, 2006. 353pp. Hardbound, 0060591765.**

In his hilarious spoof of the soft-drink industry, Barlow introduces Rhubarilla, an irresistible concoction made of rhubarb and coca leaf developed by Rodrigo Vermilion, a midget, and Isaac Brookes, a businessman and investor who rescues Rodrigo from falling from a train. The popularity of Rhubarilla spreads through Victorian England, though its success brings the Brookes family to the brink of ruin.

Keywords: Businessmen; Soft drinks

Barnes, Julian.

Arthur and George. **Knopf, 2006. 385pp. Hardbound, 030726310X.** ✍ 📖 **YA**

Barnes focuses his attention on two historical personalities whose paths crossed later on in life: Arthur Conan Doyle, famous for his Sherlock Holmes historical mysteries, and George Edalji, a half-Indian, half-Scottish lawyer. In 1906, as the legal record states, Conan Doyle successfully defended Edalji against a false charge of animal mutilation, drummed up because of Edalji's race. Alternating between their stories from childhood forward, Barnes fills in the background about both men as he illuminates the social structure, beliefs, and prejudices of late Victorian and early Edwardian England

Keywords: Authors; Conan Doyle, Arthur (historical character); Edalji, Goerge (historical character); Lawyers; Prejudice

Behrens, Peter.

🌱 *The Law of Dreams.* **Steerforth, 2006. 394pp. Hardbound, 1586421174.** ✍ 📖

In this coming of age novel beginning in 1847 in Ireland, fifteen-year-old Fergus O'Brien is sent to a workhouse after the potato crops fail, his siblings die of typhus, and his family's cabin is set ablaze, his ill parents lying inside. After he escapes he makes his way to Dublin, then Liverpool, then Wales, suffering numerous hardships and growing up the hard way. He finally makes his way to Montreal with Molly, his red-haired lover, learning that the "law of dreams" is to keep moving. Based on the author's family history. Governor General's Literary Award.

Keywords: Coming of age; Immigrants, Irish; Ireland—19th century; Potato famine; Poverty; Quebec—19th century

Byatt, A. S.

🌱 *Possession: A Romance.* **Random House, 1990. 555pp.** ★ 📖

Roland Michell and Maud Bailey are two modern British academics, scholars of Victorian literature. Their interests intersect in the discovery of correspondence between one of Maud's distant relatives, nineteenth-century feminist Victorian poetess Christabel LaMotte, and Randolph Henry Ash, a much more famous author of the same era. Were they conducting a secret affair? As Maud and Roland sift through hundred-year-old letters and stumble upon literary clues, they draw continually closer to the truth—and to each other as well. Booker Prize.

Keywords: Authors; Extramarital affairs; Historians; Letters; Multi-period novels; Poets, women

Clark, Clare.

The Great Stink. **Harcourt, 2005. 356pp. Hardbound, 0151011613.**

In 1855 William May, an engineer and Crimean War veteran suffering from post-traumatic stress disorder, takes a job revamping London's overflowing sewer system, in horrible shape after that year's cholera epidemic. Deep in the malodorous underground tunnels, corruption of many sorts runs rampant. On one trip down, the already psychologically fragile May witnesses a brutal murder, which turns out to be politically motivated. When he finds himself accused of the crime, only sewer rat Long Arm Tom can help him clear his name.

Keywords: Detective stories; Post-Traumatic Stress Disorder; Sewers

Dietz, Laura.

In the Tenth House. **Crown, 2007. 356pp. Paper, 9780307352842.** 📖

Dr. Ambrose Gennett is a forward-thinking physician of the mind in 1896 in London. When he runs into a troubled young woman at a train station, Lily Embly, who utters an uncanny prophecy about his home life, he becomes convinced she is disturbed and that only he can help her. Lily earns her living by conducting fake séances, though she has real clairvoyant ability. Both their worlds come crashing down when Lily presides over a séance at the home of some very wealthy patrons.

Keywords: Physicians; Psychics; Séances

Faber, Michel.

The Crimson Petal and the White. **Harcourt, 2002. 848pp. Hardbound, 015100692X.** ★ 📖

Sugar, an intellectual prostitute, survives an impoverished childhood to become the mistress of a wealthy nobleman and the confidant of his daughter. It was only after British author Faber found success with a modern psychological novel (*Under the Skin*) and some other shorter pieces that he unveiled his masterpiece, which had languished in a bottom drawer for twenty years. It's an epic, literary page-turner, complete with lush, evocative descriptions of nineteenth-century London. Faber's choice of such a protagonist for his re-creation of a Victorian epic makes it the kind of novel that never would have existed at that time.

Keywords: Mistresses; Prostitutes

Hagen, George.

Tom Bedlam. **Random House, 2007. 464pp. Hardbound, 9781400062225.**

Hagen's epic, picaresque, Dickensian-style saga starring the title character spans a generation, with settings ranging from the tenements of Victorian London to a medical school in Scotland and then to South Africa during World War I. Tom, raised in poverty by a sickly mother who continually preaches Christian platitudes, is abandoned by his father as a child and grows up striving to escape the shadows of the porcelain factory where she works. His other main missions in life are to locate the older brother he previously didn't know existed and become an ideal husband and father, a job his own father failed at miserably.

Keywords: Brothers; South Africa—World War I

Hickey, Elizabeth.

The Wayward Muse. **Atria, 2007. 304pp. Hardbound, 9780743273145.** ✍
In her second novel about the complex relationship between artists and their muses (the first being *The Painted Kiss*, about Gustav Klimt and Emilie Flöge; see "Europe: Early Modern Europe"), Hickey focuses on the love triangle among painter Dante Gabriel Rossetti; Jane Burden, a Oxford lass from impoverished circumstances whose beauteous looks came to symbolize the pre-Raphaelite movement; and William Morris, Rossetti's good friend. Rossetti chooses his fiancée, Lizzie, over Jane despite their passionate love affair, prompting Jane's marriage to Morris, who adores her. When Lizzie dies, the remaining parties form an unusual ménage à trois.

Keywords: Artists; Artists' models; Burden, Jane (historical character); Love triangles; Muses; Rossetti, Dante Gabriel (historical character)

Hobbs, Peter.

🏵 *The Short Day Dying.* **Harcourt, 2005. 195pp. Paper, 0156032414.** 📖
Charles Wenmoth, a Methodist lay preacher and apprentice blacksmith in Cornwall, writes a journal spanning four seasons in the year 1870. In it, he reflects on his strong faith (which his parishioners often fail to heed); the breathtaking beauty of the region; its abject poverty; and his loneliness, which is partly wrapped up in his unrequited love for Harriet French, a young blind woman consumed by a fatal illness. The poetic style of his narrative, in which punctuation-free sentences flow into one another, reflects his feelings of melancholy and the quiet rhythms of the land. Betty Trask Award.

Keywords: Christian themes; Loneliness; Preachers

Starling, Belinda.

The Journal of Dora Damage. **Bloomsbury USA, 2007. 464pp. Hardbound, 9781596913363.**
To prevent her family from falling deeper into poverty, Dora Damage takes over her crippled husband's book-binding business, which introduces her to a sordid world she never suspected existed. Peter Damage's aristocratic clients have a taste for expensive pornographic tomes, so Dora dutifully and secretly binds them. The arrival of a runaway American slave—whom a nobleman's wife asks her to hide—complicates her life further.

Keywords: Bookbinders; Pornography; Slaves, runaway

Waters, Sarah.

🏅 *Fingersmith.* **Riverhead, 2002. 511pp. Hardbound, 1573222038. ★ 📖**

Waters takes a third turn at lesbian Victoriana (after *Tipping the Velvet* and *Affinity*) in this novel about Sue Trinder, an orphan in London in 1862 who is raised in a house of pickpockets, or "fingersmiths." When Sue schemes to steal Maud Lilly's inheritance by posing as her maid, planning her marriage to a gentleman, then having her declared insane, she doesn't count on her own unexpected attraction to Maud. The story isn't as straightforward as this appears. Ellis Peters Historical Dagger.

Keywords: Heirs and heiresses; Impostors; Lesbians; Orphans; Pickpockets; Thieves

Twentieth Century

General

A mélange of literary novels set in twentieth-century Britain and Ireland. The two world wars form part of the background of these novels, but they aren't the focus.

James, Reina.

This Time of Dying. **St. Martin's, 2007. 296pp. Hardbound, 9780312364441.**

In October 1918, as England struggles to survive the loss of many young men in World War I, the Spanish influenza epidemic strikes. Henry Speake, a local undertaker, knows that a quarantine will be the country's main hope of survival, but the government believes he's being unnecessarily alarmist. He and Allen Thompson, a schoolteacher and widow above his station, grow closer to one another, doing what they can to survive as London's social order crumbles around them.

Keywords: Influenza; Teachers; Undertakers; Widows

Leavitt, David.

The Indian Clerk. **Bloomsbury USA, 2007. 485pp. Hardbound, 9781596910409. ✍ 📖**

In 1913 renowned mathematician G. H. Hardy, a professor at Cambridge University, receives a letter from a twenty-three-year-old clerk from Madras, Srinivasa Ramanujan, which suggests the younger man is an undiscovered math genius. Hardy works tirelessly to bring Ramanujan to Cambridge. Upon his arrival, Hardy becomes the unofficial mentor to the solitary, very religious man, who has difficulty adjusting to English society, as it's considerably more broad-minded than his own.

Keywords: Hardy, G. H. (historical character); Immigrants, Indian; Mathematicians; Ramanujan, Srinivasa (historical character)

Levy, Andrea.

🏅 *Small Island.* **Picador, 2005. 441pp. Paper, 0312424671. 📖**

In 1948 England is still recovering from the war. With her husband, Bernard, still away, Queenie Bligh of London is forced to take in lodgers to make ends meet. Gilbert Joseph, a Royal Air Force veteran from Jamaica, takes up residence at her house at 21 Nevern Street with his wife, Hortense. They're shocked and displeased by their neighbors' racist attitudes, and when Bernard finally returns home, he is less than thrilled to find black immigrants occupying his house. Commonwealth Writers' Prize; Orange Prize; Whitbread Book of the Year.

Keywords: Boardinghouses; Immigrants, Jamaican; Neighbors; Racial conflict; Veterans

O'Brien, Edna.

The Light of Evening. **Houghton Mifflin, 2006. 294pp. Hardbound, 0618718672.** 📖

From her hospital bed in Dublin, seventy-eight-year-old Dilly recollects the events of her life while waiting for her daughter Eleanora, a famous novelist, to arrive at her bedside. She remembers, in stream-of-consciousness style, her childhood in rural Ireland, her emigration to America in the 1920s, and her return home after a failed romance, after which she marries and raises a family at her husband's estate, Rusheen. The novel then shifts in its second half to Eleanora, detailing the complicated mother–daughter relationship from her viewpoint.

Keywords: Authors, women; Immigrants, Irish; Ireland; Mothers and daughters

O'Farrell, Maggie.

The Vanishing Act of Esme Lennox. **Harcourt, 2007. 256pp. Hardbound, 9780151014118.** 📖

Iris Lockhart, a young woman in modern-day Edinburgh, receives an unexpected and shocking letter: a great-aunt she never knew existed, Esme Lennox, is being released from the psychiatric hospital where she was a patient for sixty years. Granted power of attorney for Esme over her grandmother, Kitty, who has Alzheimer's, Iris—with Esme's help—pieces together a painful story from her family's history. Earlier sections detail Esme's life in 1930s Edinburgh, through her forced institutionalization at age sixteen for reasons Iris gradually discovers.

Keywords: Alzheimer's disease; Families; Hospitals; Institutionalization; Multi-period novels; Scotland; Sisters

Pears, Iain.

The Portrait. **Riverhead, 2005. 211pp. Hardbound, 1573222984.**

Henry McAlpine, a Scottish portrait painter living in self-exile on an island of Brittany's coast in the early twentieth century, accepts a commission to capture an old friend, an influential art critic, William Nasmyth, on canvas. The novel's core is a dramatic monologue, as McAlpine addresses Nasmyth, reminiscing about their careers in London and elsewhere. As McAlpine's tone becomes darker and more ironic, the reader learns about the critic's harsh treatment of several artists and McAlpine's plot for revenge.

Keywords: Art critics; Artists; France; Revenge

World War I

Barker, Pat.

Life Class. **Doubleday, 2008. 249pp. Hardbound, 9780385524353.** 📖

As did her famed <u>Regeneration</u> trilogy, Booker winner Barker's twelfth novel centers on the Great War, this time from the viewpoints of young London art students whose views on life, love, and art are irrevocably changed. An unexpected love triangle develops among Paul Tarrant, his fellow student Elinor Brooke, and a well-known painter, Kit Neville, who admires Eleanor. Later, as a Red Cross volunteer close to the front in Ypres, Paul finds it increasingly difficult to reconcile his past life with his wartime experiences. Neville also joins up, while Eleanor pursues her art studies at home, refusing to engage with the war either through her art or in life.

Keywords: Artists; Belgium; Love triangles; Soldiers

Barry, Sebastian.

A Long Long Way. **Viking, 2005. 292pp. Hardbound, 0670033804.** 📖 **YA**

Eighteen-year-old Willie Dunne, older brother of Annie from Irish poet Barry's previous novel (*Annie Dunne*, 2002), ships out to Belgium with other Allied forces, leaving behind his sweetheart, Gretta. After enduring horrific circumstances while fighting along the Western Front, Willie returns home to Dublin on furlough in 1916—only to encounter the Easter Rising, which he and his fellow soldiers are obliged to put down despite his fervent nationalist sentiments.

Keywords: Coming of age; Easter Rising; Ireland; Soldiers

Shields, Jody.

The Crimson Portrait. **Little, Brown, 2006. 304pp. Hardbound, 0316785288.**

Catherine, a despondent, haughty war widow in England in 1915, reluctantly honors her husband Charles's final wish: that their home be turned into an army hospital in the case of his death. Initially puzzled by the head surgeon's request that all mirrors be removed, Catherine understands this when she sees the wounded soldiers, all of whom have facial disfigurements. She becomes close to Julian, a patient whose face is encased by bandages, and attempts to re-create his damaged face in her late husband's image.

Keywords: Disfigurement; Hospitals; Soldiers; Widows

World War II

Men and women from all walks of life become involved in the Second World War, taking on major responsibilities both on the front and at home. In these somber tales, the atmosphere is overlaid with both tragedy and hope.

Davies, Peter Ho.

The Welsh Girl. **Houghton Mifflin, 2007. 256pp. Hardbound, 9780618007004.** 📖

Seventeen-year-old Esther Evans, a barmaid in northern Wales in mid-1944, longs to escape her provincial village and her shepherd father's nationalistic attitude by eloping to London with her English soldier boyfriend. Then he rapes her, dashing her hopes, while at the same time a German POW camp is set up at the foot of the nearby hills. Karsten Simmering, an English-speaking POW ashamed of having surrendered, escapes with Esther's help. They enjoy a brief romance that forces them to make tough decisions.

Keywords: Barmaids; Prisoners of war; Wales

Kennedy, A. L.

🌱 *Day.* **Knopf, 2008. 373pp. Hardbound, 9780307266835.** 📖

It is 1949, and Alfie Day, formerly a tail gunner for Britain's Royal Air Force, reevaluates his life in the aftermath of World War II. He becomes an extra in a war-related documentary in an attempt to regain a lost sense of purpose and the camaraderie he shared with his fellow soldiers, but instead it draws his thoughts inward, forcing him to relive his experiences as a POW in a German prison camp as well as his traumatic childhood. His few optimistic thoughts center on his memories of Joyce, a married woman with whom he shared a fleeting wartime romance. Costa Book Award.

Keywords: Prisoners of war; Soldiers

McEwan, Ian.

🌱 *Atonement.* **Doubleday, 2002. 351pp. Hardbound, 0385503954 .** ★ 📖 **YA**

A girl's childhood mistake has immense repercussions for all around her in this astute psychological novel. When Bryony Tallis, thirteen years old in 1935, thoughtlessly accuses the housemaid's son Robbie of raping her cousin, Robbie is sent to prison and later serves in the Second World War. Only later does Bryony, serving as a nurse in the war herself, realize that she may have been mistaken. She meditates on how her action may have ruined three lives. National Book Critics' Circle Award; ALA Notable Book.

Keywords: Children; Nurses; Sisters

Shaffer, Mary Ann, and Annie Barrows.

The Guernsey Literary and Potato Peel Pie Society. **Dial, 2008. 274pp. Hardbound, 9780385340991.** 📖 **YA**

In London in 1946, Juliet Ashton, an author in search of a new topic to write about, finds it when Dawsey Adams spies her name on the flyleaf of a book of essays she once owned and decides to write her. She and Dawsey, who lives on Guernsey, begin a correspondence in which they discuss literary matters, their respective childhoods, his island's previous Nazi occupation, and the eponymous book club begun by Guernsey residents to keep their plans secret from the Germans. When other Guernsey residents share their stories as well, Juliet travels there to meet these delightful storytellers in person. This charming novel's many lighthearted moments counterbalance a considerably more somber subplot involving one brave and beloved Guernsey resident.

Keywords: Epistolary novels; Guernsey

Waters, Sarah.

🔖 *The Night Watch*. **Riverhead, 2006. 464pp. Hardbound, 159448905X.** 📖

Best known for her Victorian-era fiction, Waters jumps ahead to World War II in this novel about ordinary people living and surviving both in wartime and afterward. The plot jumps backward in time in three episodes: the first set in a London boardinghouse during the war's aftermath in 1947; the second in 1944, as London suffered under heavy bombing raids; and the third in 1941. As Kay Langrish, a night-shift ambulance driver during the war, struggles to find her lost lover and readjust to peacetime life, the other characters carry just as much baggage, most of it having been gained since the novel's beginning. Lambda Literary Award.

Keywords: Ambulance drivers; Blitz; Friendship; Multi-period novels

Europe

The Middle Ages

Novels of medieval Europe show a world on the brink of change. Superstition gives way to reason, clergymen occupy themselves with intellectual pursuits, and adventurers take picaresque journeys throughout the continent.

Ali, Tariq.

A Sultan in Palermo. **Verso, 2005. 246pp. Hardbound, 1844670252.** ✍

The "sultan in Palermo" in the year 1153 is King Roger of Sicily, otherwise known as Sultan Rujari of Siqillya to his Muslim subjects, whose language and culture dominate his court. His steady friendship with Muhammad al-Idrisi, the royal cartographer, is based on their mutual exploration of intellectual topics. But the aging Rujari knows his reign will soon come to an end, and to secure his throne, he feels it necessary to forge stronger ties with Palermo's bishops. Idrisi, caught in the middle, must decide where his conscience lies. Fourth in Ali's Islam Quintet (which includes *Shadows of the Pomegranate Tree, The Book of Saladin*, and *The Stone Woman*), a series that presents Islamic culture over the past 1,400 years.

Keywords: Cartographers; Friendship; Italy; Muslims; Roger II, King of Sicily (historical character)

Haasse, Hella.

In a Dark Wood Wandering. **Academy Chicago, 1989. 574pp. Hardbound, 0897333365.** ✍ ★

Haasse's first novel to be translated into English is her best known and most accessible. Her hero is Charles d'Orléans—scholar, poet, courtier, nephew of the mad King Charles VI of France, and prisoner in England for twenty-five years after the Battle of Agincourt during the Hundred Years' War. The real story begins at his birth in 1394, as his mother Valentine Visconti, the Italian-born Duchess of Orléans, lies in childbed. Haasse's vision encompasses all of French and English society during the fifteenth century: the feuds with each other and with neighboring lands, the coming of Joan of Arc, and the journey of the long-wandering soul to its home, as reflected in Charles's poetry and in the book's title. First published in the Netherlands in 1949.

Keywords: Charles d'Orléans (historical character); France; Hundred Years' War; Royalty

9

Unsworth, Barry.

The Ruby in Her Navel. **Doubleday/Talese, 2006. 399pp. Hardbound, 0385509634.** 📖

In twelfth-century Palermo, a land known for its tolerance of the many cultures and religions (particularly the Muslim majority) within its borders, Thurstan Beauchamp, son of a Norman knight, works in the accounting office of King Roger. Dispatched on a variety of journeys to uncover conspiracies against his king, naïve Thurstan meets up with his childhood sweetheart, encounters an intriguing belly dancer, and gets caught up in deadly intrigue without even realizing it. Unsworth's historical novels regularly use historical events as a way of expressing modern themes, and so he does here, in a novel that demonstrates the danger of blind loyalty to one's ruler and country.

Keywords: Belly dancers; Italy; Muslims; Nobility

10

11

The Renaissance and Reformation

12

New developments in art, science, and religion transform the European world. These novels show how these cultural revolutions impacted people's lives. In general, they are set during the years 1450 to 1650, a period especially popular with literary novelists.

13

Belli, Gioconda.

The Scroll of Seduction. **Rayo, 2006. 323pp. Hardbound, 0060833394.** ✍

Manuel, a professor of Spanish obsessed with the tragic romance of Queen Juana of Castile, tells her story to Lucia, a seventeen-year-old student at a Catholic boarding school in Madrid, in the hopes of seducing her with the tale. As Lucia gets drawn deeper into Juana's story, Manuel tries to manipulate her psyche to answer one question: Did Juana truly go mad after her husband's death, or was she simply a victim of power-hungry relatives? A multi-period story of love, history, obsession, and madness in both the sixteenth century and the present.

14

Keywords: Juana, Queen of Castile (historical character); Mental illness; Multi-period novels; Spain; Students

15

Brooks, Geraldine.

People of the Book. **Viking, 2008. 372pp. Hardbound, 9780670018215.** 📖 YA

Brooks fictionalizes the mostly unknown history of the Sarajevo Haggadah, an illuminated Hebrew manuscript, going backward in time from Sarajevo during the Bosnian War and World War II, to Vienna in 1894, then to seventeenth-century Venice, and finally to its creation in fifteenth-century Seville. In depicting the lives of the individuals through whose hands it passed, and who saved it from destruction multiple times, she traces the intermingled history of three races (Jews, Christians, Muslims) in the Mediterranean region. The historical vignettes connect through the modern tale of Hanna Heath, an irascible Australian rare book conservator hired to restore the Haggadah.

Keywords: Austria—early modern era; Book conservators; Italy; Jews; Manuscripts; Multi-period novels; Muslims; Sarajevo Haggadah; Spain

Chevalier, Tracy.

Girl with a Pearl Earring. Dutton, 1999. 233pp. Hardbound, 052594527X. ★ 📖

In seventeenth-century Delft, young Griet supports her family by becoming a maidservant in the household of the well-known painter Vermeer. Due to her innate sense of rightness in art, she develops a bond with Vermeer that encourages him to make her the subject of a painting. This not only arouses his wife's jealousy, it causes scandal among his household and throughout the city. A big hit with female readers and reading groups.

Keywords: Artists; Maids; Netherlands; Paintings; Vermeer, Johannes (historical character)

Delibes, Miguel.

The Heretic. Overlook, 2006. 350pp. Hardbound, 1585675709.

Cipriano Salcedo is born in Valladolid, Spain, on the very day in 1517 that Martin Luther nails his ninety-five theses to a church door in Wittenberg. Raised by his distant father after his mother's death in childbirth, Cipriano grows up to be a wealthy merchant whose religious leanings drift toward Lutheranism. But the Inquisition has feelers out everywhere, as he and his fellow reformers learn firsthand after he returns from a trip to Germany on their behalf.

Keywords: Inquisition; Religious reformers; Spain

Dunant, Sarah.

The Birth of Venus. Random House, 2003. 397pp. Hardbound, 1400060737. ★ 📖

Fourteen-year-old Alexandra Cecchi, a cloth merchant's daughter, comes of age in fifteenth-century Florence. She dreams of a career as an artist, encouraged by a young painter in her household, but her dreams are dashed when her parents arrange her marriage to a much older man. At the same time, the fanatical monk Savonarola comes to power, loudly preaching that love of art and "pagan" books leads only to damnation. Despite an unhappy married life, Alessandra pursues her attraction to both art and the painter.

Keywords: Artists, women; Italy

In the Company of the Courtesan. Random House, 2006. 371pp. Hardbound, 1400063817. 📖

Bucino Teodoldo, a cunning dwarf, relates his adventures with courtesan Fiammetta Bianchini, beginning in 1527, when they escape the sack of Rome with little more than the clothes on their backs (and swallowed jewels in their stomachs). Arriving in Venice, the fabled island city known for its opulence and vice, Bucino helps Fiammetta gradually reclaim her proper place in society. Also aiding the intrepid pair is La Draga, a blind healer whose salves restore Fiammetta's beauty, but she may be hiding secrets of her own.

Keywords: Courtesans; Dwarfs; Italy

Essex, Karen.

Leonardo's Swans. **Doubleday, 2006. 344pp. Hardbound, 0385517068.** ✍ 📖

In the late fifteenth century, two brilliant, noble sisters compete for the attentions of two men in Renaissance Italy. Isabella d'Este, the beautiful, cultured eldest daughter of the Duke of Ferrara, never envies her plain, fun-loving sister, Beatrice, until Beatrice is wed to Ludovico Sforza, Duke of Milan, a power-hungry man more than twice her age who already has an acknowledged mistress. As Beatrice's fortunes rise, Isabella settles into domesticity with her childhood sweetheart, the marquis of Mantua, but she can't deny her attraction to Ludovico. The Este sisters' sexual rivalry is compounded by their joint desire to be immortalized in oils by the great artistic genius, Leonardo da Vinci, Ludovico's court painter.

Keywords: Artists; da Vinci, Leonardo (historical character); d'Este, Beatrice (historical character); d'Este, Isabella (historical figure); Italy; Nobility; Sisters

Holdstock, Pauline.

A Rare and Curious Gift. **Norton, 2005. 355pp. Hardbound, 0393059685.**

Sofonisba Fabroni, a character strongly based on Renaissance woman artist Artemisia Gentileschi, is the daughter of a well-known painter who wants to create a name for herself in Florence's art world, though her sex works against her. She develops a tumultuous relationship with rakish sculptor Matteo Tassi, which leads to an accusation of rape (also taken from Artemisia's life story). The "curious gift" of the title is a slave with unusual piebald skin, a young woman whose presence sets off a chain of calamitous events. An earthy, brutally realistic portrait of Medici-era Florence, geared to readers with strong stomachs.

Keywords: Artists, women; Italy; Rape

Mujica, Bárbara.

Sister Teresa. **Overlook, 2007. 384pp. Hardbound, 9781585678341.** ✍ **YA**

Novelist and Spanish professor Mujica portrays St. Teresa of Ávila, born in Spain in 1515, as a beautiful, feisty young woman who is sent to a convent to avoid romantic scandal but, while there, develops an intense spiritual fervor. Sister Angelica, a seamstress's daughter who becomes one of her fellow Carmelite nuns, narrates her story, showing both her religiosity as well as her very human qualities. Teresa endures numerous illnesses and questioning by the Inquisition—her ideas for spiritual reform were considered suspect—with an inner strength grounded in her mystical belief in God.

Keywords: Inquisition; Nuns; Saints; Spain; St. Teresa of Ávila (historical character)

Rushdie, Salman.

The Enchantress of Florence. **Random House, 2008. 355pp. Hardbound, 9780375504334.** 📖

Rushdie connects his stories of two mid-sixteenth-century worlds—the Mughal Empire of Akbar the Great and Renaissance Florence, home to Machiavelli—by means of a yellow-haired stranger who travels to Akbar's court. While there he relates the story of Qara Köz, a beautiful and mysterious Mughal princess who commanded her own destiny by making the journey to Florence decades earlier. Both challenging and rewarding—thanks to its poetic, convoluted sentences and the multiplicity of characters both real and imaginary—it incorporates many themes, such as the clash between East and West, the relationship between love and ambition, the nature of the feminine, and the power of storytelling.

Keywords: Italy; Mughal Empire; Muslims; Princesses; Storytellers

Early Modern Europe

Political changes sweep throughout Europe, affecting both royalty and average people. Other novels in this section show changes on a smaller scale, such as how art and music influence people's lives. Set roughly between the late seventeenth and the early twentieth centuries.

Abidi, Azhar.

Passarola Rising. **Viking, 2006. 244pp. Hardbound, 0670034657.** ✍ 📖 **YA**

Abidi whimsically fictionalizes the aeronautical escapades of real-life Brazilian brothers Bartolomeu and Alexandre Lourenço throughout Europe during the 1730s. Their airship *Passarola* captures the attention of King João of Portugal, who has them fly from country to country on political and scientific missions, though the Inquisition, which deems their voyages heretical, seeks to stop them at every opportunity. A lighthearted, adventurous fable that also expresses a serious message.

Keywords: Airships; Explorers; Inquisition; Lourenço, Bartolomeu (historical character); Portugal

Balint, Christine.

Ophelia's Fan. **Norton, 2004. 348pp. Hardbound, 0393059251.** ✍ 📖 **YA**

Harriet Smithson, born in Ireland in 1900 to poverty-stricken actor parents, grows up to become an accomplished actress: the toast of London's Drury Lane, and the woman who introduces Shakespeare to Parisian society in the late 1820s. As Ophelia in Charles Kemble's English Theatre's production of *Hamlet*, she captivates composer Hector Berlioz and becomes his muse, the inspiration for his *Symphonie Fantastique*. She writes her life story in letters to her son that resemble scenes from a play.

Keywords: Actresses; France; Muses; Smithson, Harriet (historical character); Theater

Cunningham, M. Allen.

Lost Son. **Unbridled, 2007. 470pp. Hardbound, 9781932961348.** ✍

Using a variety of different writing styles and jumping back and forth in time, Cunningham evokes the imagined life of Rainer Maria Rilke. He looks back on his troubled past after his arrival in Paris, in the year 1902, to write a biography of sculptor Auguste Rodin. Having left his family behind in Germany, Rilke feels alone and strange in an unfamiliar city. He tries to come to terms with his unhappy childhood, also reminiscing from time to time about his relationship with Lou Salomé—writer, lover, and muse.

Keywords: Authors; France; Muses; Rilke, Rainer Maria (historical character)

Dudman, Clare.

98 Reasons for Being. **Viking, 2005. 342pp. Hardbound, 067003424X.** ✍

In 1852 German physician Heinrich Hoffman, superintendent of an insane asylum in Frankfurt, uses "talk therapy" to cure one of his mute and unresponsive patients, Hannah Meyer, a resident of the city's Jewish ghetto. Labeled a nymphomaniac, Hannah is in reality anything but. In hearing her tale of thwarted romance and prejudice, Hoffman begins to open up in return, finding inspiration for his own life in ridding her of mental illness.

Keywords: Germany; Jews; Mental illness; Prejudice; Psychiatrists

Dunlap, Susanne.

Émilie's Voice. **Touchstone, 2006. 304pp. Paper, 0743265068.** 📖

When noted composer Marc-Antoine Charpentier hears the pure, angelic voice of Émilie Jolicoeur, daughter of a humble instrument maker in Paris in 1676, he is enchanted. Charpentier offers to give her lessons in voice and deportment, with the eventual goal of presenting her at Versailles. Schemes both romantic and political surround the court of Louis XIV, and many rich and powerful aristocrats wish to control her. In order to survive, Émilie may pay the price of her innocence.

Keywords: France; Nobility; Singers

Liszt's Kiss. **Touchstone, 2007. 333pp. Paper, 9780743289404.** 📖

In 1832 in Paris Anne de Barbier-Chouant loses her mother to cholera, and her father, the marquis, forbids her to play her mother's beloved piano. Marie D'Agoult, her mother's friend and a patron of the arts, introduces Anne to artistic society and expands her musical horizons by arranging piano lessons with celebrated Hungarian composer Franz Liszt. Captivated by Liszt, Anne doesn't realize he's using her infatuation to get closer to Marie. Marie, for her part, helps her young charge discover the secret her father has been keeping from her.

Keywords: Composers; D'Agoult, Marie (historical character); France; Liszt, Franz (historical character); Musicians

Edge, Arabella.

The God of Spring. Simon & Schuster, 2007. 340pp. Hardbound, 9780743294843. (Original title: *The Raft.*)

> One of French artist Théodore Géricault's best known paintings was *The Raft of the Medusa*, depicting the wreck of a frigate off the coast of Africa in 1818, a traumatic event in which only 15 of the 150 original survivors set adrift on a raft made it back alive. By 1818 Géricault has returned home to France and is looking for a way out of his inappropriate relationship with Alexandrine, his uncle's wife. The wreck of the *Medusa* takes his mind off their affair and serves as his artistic inspiration, as he obsessively hunts down survivors to hear their firsthand accounts.
>
> **Keywords:** Artists; France; Géricault, Théodore (historical character); Paintings; Shipwrecks

Essex, Karen.

Stealing Athena. Doubleday, 2008. 452pp. Hardbound, 9780385519717. ✍ 📖

> The Elgin marbles, magnificent stone sculptures removed from the Parthenon in 1801 by the seventh earl of Elgin, the British ambassador to Turkey, still inspire controversy. Did preservation or greed motivate Elgin? Did his transportation of the statues to England constitute vandalism? Should the statues be returned to Athens? Using the dual viewpoints of Mary Nisbet, Countess of Elgin during Napoleonic times, and Aspasia, courtesan and mistress of ancient Greek politician Perikles, Essex weaves a novel about passion, determination, sexual improprieties, and the prices women pay for their attachments to ambitious men.
>
> **Keywords:** Aspasia (historical character); Courtesans; Elgin Marbles; Ferguson, Mary Nisbet (historical character); Greece—ancient/prehistoric; Multi-period novels; Ottoman Empire; Sculptures

Faulks, Sebastian.

Human Traces. Random House, 2006. 557pp. Hardbound, 0375502262.

> At a resort in Deauville, France, in 1880, a Breton medical student named Jacques Rebière meets Thomas Midwinter, an Englishman equally passionate about the study of the mind. They form a friendship that leads to a professional partnership. Training separately as physicians, eventually they realize their dreams by opening a sanitarium to cure the mentally ill in the Austrian Alps, along with the help of Thomas's sister, Sonia, who marries Jacques. Their relationship nearly implodes when Jacques, a burgeoning Freudian, clashes with the more Darwinian-minded Thomas over one patient's care.
>
> **Keywords:** Austria; France; Friendship; Mental illness; Psychiatrists

Hassinger, Amy.

The Priest's Madonna. Putnam, 2006. 316pp. Hardbound, 0399153179. ✍ 📖

> Marie Denarnaud develops a close relationship with her parish priest, Bérenger Saunière, in the small French village of Rennes-le-Chateau when he is assigned there in the late nineteenth century. When she grows older she takes a job as his housekeeper, causing rumors to fly that they are lovers. Strongly attracted to him,

Marie struggles to understand his strong devotion to the Catholic Church, an institution that has been responsible for great evil. Then Marie and Bérenger discover ancient artifacts beneath the church floor, treasure that may deal with a long-held secret in Church history.

Keywords: Catholicism; Christian themes; Denarnaud, Marie (historical character); France; Housekeepers; Priests; Saunière, Bérenger (historical character); Treasure

Hickey, Elizabeth.

The Painted Kiss. **Atria, 2005. 270pp. Hardbound, 0743492609.** ✍ 📖

In 1944 Emilie Flöge lives with her niece in their family's country house at Kammer am Attersee after escaping the Nazis. Gustav Klimt's drawings were all Emilie was able to save of her former life, and they release memories of her past in 1870s Vienna. After she and a much older Klimt become friends, young Emilie is introduced to his sensual world of nude models, discarded mistresses, and decadent high society. A few years later they briefly become lovers, but their passion is not to last. Later, as proprietor of a Viennese fashion salon, which Gustav finances, Emilie obtains success on her own terms.

Keywords: Artists; Artists' models; Austria; Flöge, Emilie (historical character); Klimt, Gustav (historical character)

Jacobson, Dan.

All for Love. **Metropolitan, 2006. 260pp. Hardbound, 0241142733.** ✍

This historical work, an unusual amalgam of fiction and nonfiction (it has footnotes), recounts the passionate, destructive love affair between Louise of Belgium, the married Archduchess of Austria, and Lieutenant Géza Mattachich, an ambitious Croatian soldier in the Hungarian army who is ten years her junior. Heedless of the consequences, which are many—poverty, loss of status, accusations of insanity—they flit from place to place across Europe, risking all for love.

Keywords: Austria; Extramarital affairs; Louise, Princess of Belgium (historical character); Mattachich, Géza (historical character); Royalty

Japin, Arthur.

In Lucia's Eyes. **Knopf, 2005. 235pp. Hardbound, 1400044642.** ✍ 📖

In his memoirs, notorious libertine Giacomo Casanova recorded his first love affair with Lucia, a servant girl whom he met when he was a sixteen-year-old seminary student in Pasiano, Italy. She fled from him, for reasons unknown, breaking his heart. Japin reimagines this episode from Lucia's viewpoint, making the dreaded smallpox the reason for Lucia's flight. Disfigured and ashamed, Lucia flits from place to place across Europe. Sixteen years later, in Amsterdam, she has settled into a life as the masked courtesan Galathee de Pompignac, when she encounters him once more.

Keywords: Casanova, Giacomo (historical character); Courtesans; Disfigurement; Italy; Madams

Kehlmann, Daniel.

Measuring the World. **Pantheon, 2006. 259pp. Hardbound, 0375424466.** ✍

Mathematician Carl Gauss, a notable curmudgeon, is urged by his wife to accompany explorer Alexander von Humboldt on his trek across the Russian Urals. They meet at a conference in Berlin in 1828. The novel then switches gears to recap their lives from youth forward; Gauss's brilliant mind makes his daily life pale in comparison, while Humboldt's wanderlust makes him intensely restless for new sites to explore. Despite its serious subject matter—two Enlightenment-era luminaries and their professional partnership—Kehlmann's quirky, wry, and surprisingly light tone carries the story.

Keywords: Explorers; Gauss, Carl (historical character); Germany; Humboldt, Alexander von (historical character); Mathematicians

Kohler, Sheila.

Bluebird, Or the Invention of Happiness. **Other, 2007. 424pp. Hardbound, 9781590512629.** ✍ 📖 **YA**

Lucy Dillon is a descendant of Irish Catholics who found refuge in France in the mid-eighteenth century. As a young woman she joins the retinue of Marie Antoinette, and her soldier father arranges her marriage to one of his protégés, Frederic, the future Marquis de la Tour du Pin. A practical woman determined to make the best of everything, Lucy shepherds her husband and growing family onto a creaky ship bound for America as mobs rage outside Versailles. The family eventually settles on a farm just north of Albany, New York, where Lucy happily becomes a dairy farmer, marking her family's homemade butter molds with her family crest.

Keywords: Dillon, Henriette-Lucy (historical character); France; French Revolution; New York

Löhr, Robert.

The Chess Machine. **Penguin Press, 2007. 344pp. Hardbound, 9781594201264.**

In 1770 Baron Wolfgang von Kempelen, a minor Austro-Hungarian nobleman, invents a chess-playing machine, the "Mechanical Turk," to curry favor with Empress Maria Theresa, who is impressed by scientific inventions. The baron's real secret weapon lies concealed inside the machine: an Italian dwarf (and chess master) controls the machine's moves from within. Although its debut performance is a great success, people begin to suspect subterfuge, particularly as the machine gains popularity outside of Vienna.

Keywords: Austria; Chess; Dwarfs; Inventors; Nobility

Lovric, Michelle.

The Remedy. **ReganBooks, 2005. 440pp. Hardbound, 0060837039.**

In this heady Gothic adventure, a young Venetian woman in the late eighteenth century, having done something to offend her family, is thrust into a convent against her will. After an affair gone wrong, she attempts escape and lands in the lap of the Venetian underworld. Members of this group train her as an actress, rename her Mimosina Dolcezza, and introduce her to political scheming.

She pursues her new career, working the stages of Europe, until she meets and falls in love with roguish Englishman Valentine Greatrakes, leader of London's medical underworld.

Keywords: Actresses; Gothic novels; Italy; Theater

Maguire, Elizabeth.

The Open Door. **Other, 2008. 236pp. Hardbound, 9781590512838.** ✍ 📖

Through these fictionalized memoirs, Maguire brings to life an unfairly dismissed nineteenth-century American writer, Constance Fenimore Woolson, who formed an epistolary friendship with Henry James, an author she greatly admired. The two meet in person in Europe in 1879 during one of Constance's lengthy sojourns abroad. Although close, their connection was marked by jealousy (she was more commercially successful than he) and betrayal (her unexpected discovery of his homosexuality; his refusal to acknowledge her great talent).

Keywords: Authors, women; Friendship; Italy; James, Henry (historical character); Woolson, Constance Fenimore (historical character)

Morgan, Jude.

Symphony. **St. Martin's Press, 2007. 373pp. Hardbound, 9780312369514.** ✍ 📖

The marriage between Romantic composer Hector Berlioz and Anglo-Irish actress Harriet Smithson, known as La Belle Irlandaise to her French audiences, was a turbulent one that led to his composition of the *Symphonie Fantastique,* but also to tragedy, infidelity, alcoholism, and madness. Morgan begins by introducing them separately, so that readers can observe the genius of both in their own right. His style is more idiosyncratic, literary, and impressionistic than that of Christine Balint in *Ophelia's Fan* (annotated previously in this section).

Keywords: Actresses; Berlioz, Hector (historical character); Composers; France; Smithson, Harriet (historical character)

Naslund, Sena Jeter.

Abundance. **Morrow, 2006. 530pp. Hardbound, 0060825391.** ✍ 📖 **YA**

In this sympathetic account, Marie Antoinette narrates her life story from her pampered childhood as an Austrian archduchess to her tragic and demeaning end at the guillotine at the height of the French Revolution. Throughout her life she remains a continual outsider at the French court, even as she grows to symbolize what it represents. A spirited, caring young woman who never would have dreamed of saying "let them eat cake" to hungry peasants, Marie Antoinette is nonetheless kept sheltered, in the bosom of her growing family, from their hatred of the royal family's excesses.

Keywords: France; French Revolution; Marie Antoinette, Queen of France (historical character); Royalty

Quick, Barbara.

Vivaldi's Virgins. **HarperCollins, 2007. 284pp. Hardbound, 0060890525.** ✍ 📖 **YA**

By 1737 Anna Maria dal Violin, formerly an orphaned child prodigy, has risen to become concert mistress at the Ospedale della Pietà, a convent home for foundlings whose music school is directed by renowned maestro Antonio Vivaldi. The novel alternates between Anna Maria's adult narration and letters to her absent mother, a woman about whom she knows nothing. Anna will risk much—including roaming the dangerous streets of Venice—to find out about her. Based on the life story of one of Vivaldi's star pupils, the "woman musician of Venice" known as Anna Maria della Pietà.

Keywords: della Pietà, Anna Maria (historical character); Italy; Musicians; Vivaldi, Antonio (historical character)

Riera, Carme.

In the Last Blue. **Overlook, 2007. 384pp. Hardbound, 9781585678532.**

A prize-winning author in her native Spain (she writes in Catalan), Riera writes about a little-known aspect of history: the attempted, and failed, escape of a small group of Majorcan Jews from the Spanish Inquisition in the 1680s. Eventually thirty-seven of them are captured after attempting to flee by boat overseas and are later burned at the stake. The novel tells of their daily lives within their communities and the fierce and often confusing struggles between Jews and Christians, in a land where many Jews had forcibly converted to Catholicism.

Keywords: Inquisition; Jews; Majorca; Spain

Smith, Dominic.

The Mercury Visions of Louis Daguerre. **Atria, 2006. 306pp. Hardbound, 0743271149.** ✍

In 1846, in a mercury-induced haze caused by too much exposure to the deadly chemical in his fledgling daguerreotype business, inventor Louis Daguerre decides to compile a list of ten items he must photograph before the world ends. He and his good friend Charles Baudelaire, the bohemian French poet, search throughout Paris for the perfect subjects for these images. Among them is Daguerre's lost love, Isobel Le Fournier, whom he hasn't seen in forty-four years and about whom he constantly reminisces.

Keywords: Daguerre, Louis (historical character); France; Photographers

Tipton, James.

Annette Vallon. **HarperCollins, 2007. 481pp. Hardbound, 9780060822217.** ✍

Little is known of the real Annette Vallon, but Tipton takes the available facts about the year William Wordsworth spent in pre-revolutionary France to craft a novel about the woman who inspired his work, became his mistress, and gave birth to his illegitimate daughter, Caroline. Born to a family of the minor aristocracy, Annette meets and falls in love with William when both are still young, and before he became famous for his poetry. Although the lovers are separated early on, Annette remains strong when revolutionary fervor sweeps the country, becoming a Scarlet Pimpernel of sorts for residents of the Loire Valley.

Keywords: France; French Revolution; Mistresses; Muses; Nobility; Poets; Vallon, Annette (historical character); Wordsworth, William (historical character)

Von der Lippe, Angela.

The Truth About Lou. **Counterpoint, 2007. 282pp. Hardbound, 9781582433585.** ✍

What was it about Lou Andreas-Salomé that managed to compel three brilliant but very different men—Freud, Rilke, and Nietzsche—into her circle? A Russian émigré poet, intellectual, and muse who defines herself by the men she associates with, Lou tells her own story in stream-of-consciousness fashion as she makes her way across late nineteenth-century Europe.

Keywords: Andreas-Salomé, Lou (historical character); Authors, women; Europe; Muses

Vreeland, Susan.

Life Studies. **Viking, 2005. 292pp. Hardbound, 0670031771.**

Vreeland's fiction has always been inspired by art, artists, and the creative process. The historical short stories in this collection, unlike her novels, take ordinary people as the main characters, while focusing outwardly on more well-known historical figures. Characters include the wet nurse who cares for Berthe Morisot's baby daughter, Monet's gardener, Manet's widow, and more. An equal number of contemporary stories about the meaning of art balance the volume.

Keywords: Artists; Short stories

Luncheon of the Boating Party. **Viking, 2007. 434pp. Hardbound, 9780670038541.** ✍ 📖

Impressionist painter Pierre-Auguste Renoir, living in Paris during the city's recovery from the Franco-Prussian War in 1880, longs to reinvent his career by creating a masterwork—one that embodies the exuberance of *la vie moderne.* This becomes his famed painting titled *Luncheon of the Boating Party*, in which Renoir and his friends relax on the terrace of the Maison Fournaise, a café along the Seine. With expressive prose, Vreeland tells the story of the painting's origins from the viewpoint of Renoir and seven of his friends/models, detailing both the hedonism of the era and the process by which great art is created.

Keywords: Artists; Artists' models; France; Friendship; Paintings; Renoir, Pierre-Auguste (historical character)

Twentieth Century

General

A selection of novels taking place in Europe during the first half of the twentieth century. Modern wars and revolutions influence the background of these novels to some degree. Those dealing exclusively with World Wars I or II are listed later.

Amis, Martin.

House of Meetings. Knopf, 2007. 241pp. Hardbound, 9781400044559. 📖

In 2004 a wealthy Russian expatriate returns as a tourist to the Siberian gulag where he was imprisoned over fifty years before. In a memoir written for his pampered stepdaughter in America, he records incidents dating back to 1946 involving his pacifist brother, Lev, and Lev's beautiful Jewish wife, Zoya. At the Norlag concentration camp, where both men are sent after World War II, their relationship becomes strained; not only is the narrator a man inured to violence, but he's jealous of Lev's relationship with Zoya. Everything changes for all three after a night Lev spends with Zoya at the "house of meetings," a place for conjugal visits.

Keywords: Brothers; Gulags; Jews; Love triangles; Siberia

Diliberto, Gioia.

The Collection. Scribner, 2007. 288pp. Hardbound, 9780743280655. 📖 **YA**

A sort of *The Devil Wears Prada* set during the Jazz Age, this novel of haute couture in the City of Lights features Isabelle Varlet, who develops her seamstress talents in a small French village. Encouraged by her employer, she moves to Paris in 1919 to develop them further. Isabelle takes a position in the studio of Gabrielle "Coco" Chanel, called "Mademoiselle" by her assistants, and is introduced to the highly competitive world of high fashion.

Keywords: Chanel, Coco (historical character); France; Seamstresses

Enquist, Per Olov.

The Book About Blanche and Marie. Overlook, 2006. 218pp. Hardbound, 1585676683. ✍ 📖

Blanche Wittman was a famous patient at the Hotel Salpetrière in Paris, the subject of numerous experiments to cure her of "hysteria" in the late nineteenth century. Later she became an assistant in physicist Marie Curie's laboratory, through which job Blanche lost three limbs to radiation poisoning. In her notebooks Blanche often ruminates about the nature of love, though it continually eludes her, as it does Marie.

Keywords: Amputees; Curie, Marie (historical character); France; Friendship; Scientists, women; Wittman, Blanche (historical character)

Holland, Travis.

The Archivist's Story. Dial, 2007. 239pp. Hardbound, 9780385339957.

In Moscow in 1939 Pavel Dubrov, a former literature professor mourning the death of his wife, now works—reluctantly—as an archivist in Lubyanka prison, where his job is to censor books written by political prisoners. After coming across an unsigned manuscript, he believes that its author is Isaac Babel, a writer incarcerated at Lubyanka, and is ordered to authenticate it. Instead, Pavel makes the fateful decision to try to rescue it, at risk of his own life and liberty.

Keywords: Archivists; Censorship; Manuscripts; Russia

Mailer, Norman.

The Castle in the Forest. **Random House, 2007. 477pp. Hardbound, 9780394536491.** ✎ 📖

> Mailer, always a provocative writer, takes on a project to interpret via fiction how Adolf Hitler came to personify pure malevolence. To do so, he looks back into Hitler's childhood and family history, moving from the 1830s to the early twentieth century in Austria and finding multiple instances of incest and sexual deviance. The person recounting his tale is an SS officer named Dieter who reveals he's really one of many devils working for Satan, charged with guiding young Adolf on a path of evil.
>
> **Keywords:** Austria; Devil; Hitler, Adolf (historical character); Hitler family; Incest

McCann, Colum.

Zoli. **Random House, 2006. 333pp. Hardbound, 1400063728.** 📖

> Zoli Novotna, a member of the Roma people from Slovakia, becomes a symbol for her marginalized culture. Zoli narrates her life story beginning in the 1930s, when she and her grandfather flee the Fascist guards who drowned the rest of their family. The point of view shifts throughout the novel, but always focuses on Zoli. She achieves fame as a singer during World War II and, having been taught to read (against the wishes of her people), she begins writing poetry which, to her horror, is used as Communist propaganda. Based loosely on the life of Papusza, a Polish poet whose life spanned most of the twentieth century.
>
> **Keywords:** Communism; Europe; Gypsies; Poets; Holocaust; Singers

Meek, James.

🎋 *The People's Act of Love.* **Canongate, 2005. 391pp. Hardbound, 1841957305.** 📖

> In 1919, during the final years of the Russian Revolution, a number of people live in close quarters in a remote Siberian village: Anna Petrovna, a young, attractive mother; members of an odd Christian sect whose religion requires self-mutilation; and soldiers of the Czech Legion, the nominal rulers of the area. Into this strange and unforgiving landscape comes Samarin, a convict from a prison camp, recounting a horrifying story of his escape. His tale mesmerizes the villagers, but when the local shaman is killed, the town erupts in violence and betrayal. ALA Notable Book.
>
> **Keywords:** Bolshevik Revolution; Prisoners; Siberia; Soldiers

Mosby, Katherine.

Twilight. **HarperCollins, 2005. 291pp. Hardbound, 0066212715.** 📖

> Lavinia Gibbs (a character first introduced in the author's earlier *The Season of Lillian Dawes*), a thirtyish woman of a socially prominent New York family, scandalizes her parents by spurning her boring fiancé and heading to Europe in search of personal fulfillment on the eve of World War II. In

Paris she begins an affair with a married Frenchman, Gaston Lesseur, and their relationship changes her irrevocably.

Keywords: Extramarital affairs; France; Love triangles

Reuss, Frederick.

Mohr. Unbridled, 2006. 309pp. Hardbound, 1932961178.

Annotated later in this chapter, under "China and Hong Kong."

Romano-Lax, Andromeda.

The Spanish Bow. Harcourt, 2007. 554pp. Hardbound, 9780151015429. 📖 **YA**

When Feliu Delargo is given a cello bow as a bequest, his life transforms, propelling him from his small Catalan village to Barcelona, where anarchist sentiments are in full swing, and later to Madrid, where he becomes a favored musician and confidant to Queen Ena. He forms a friendship and rivalry with piano prodigy Justo Al-Cerraz. As they go on tour throughout Europe, their fame brings them to the attention of numerous famous people, Picasso, Franco, and Hitler among them. Their lives become intertwined with Aviva, a Jewish violinist, whose presence eventually forces Feliu to make a heartbreaking decision.

Keywords: Cellists; Love triangles; Musicians; Spain

Sington, Philip.

Zoia's Gold. Scribner, 2006. 385pp. Hardbound, 0743291107. ✎

Marcus Elliot, a British-born art connoisseur, travels to Sweden to compile a catalog of works by Madam Zoia, the famed Russian émigré artist who painted on gold leaf, who recently passed away in her Swedish home. The more he learns about Zoia's unconventional life, the more intrigued he grows, especially as he learns that the approaching art sale may violate the terms of her will. He imagines her life in flashback: her youth in the Romanov court in the early twentieth century; her imprisonment by the Bolsheviks in the 1920s; and her time spent in bohemian Paris, as toast of the city and the lover of many attractive men.

Keywords: Artists, women; France; Korvin-Krukovsky, Zoia (historical character); Russia

World War I

These novels evoke not only the futility and tragedy, but also the bustle of activity, of the First World War (1914–1918). They also recount stories of fleeting wartime romances.

Arslan, Antonia.

Skylark Farm. Knopf, 2006. 275pp. Hardbound, 1400044359. ✎ 📖 **YA**

In fictionalizing her own family's story of survival, Arslan, of Armenian heritage, brings to light a comparatively little-known aspect of World War II: the Armenian genocide, in which hundreds of thousands of Armenians were methodically exterminated by the Turks in 1915. The Arslanian family lives in harmony with their Greek and Turkish neighbors on their country retreat, Skylark Farm, in a small Anatolian village. Yerwant, the author's grandfather, tries to return home from his studies in Venice, but discovers that he's too late: the remaining members of his family—those who haven't been killed—were previously forced south, on foot, toward Syria.

Keywords: Armenian genocide; Arslan family (historical characters); Families; Turkey

Boyden, Joseph.

Three Day Road. **Viking, 2005. 354pp. Hardbound, 0670034312.** 📖

Xavier Bird and Elijah Whiskeyjack, Cree Indians and best friends, enlist in the Canadian Expeditionary Forces during World War I, expecting to be sent to France to fight the German army. Ostracized by their fellow soldiers because of their ethnicity, they train as snipers even more diligently, though the brutality of war transforms them both: one goes mad with guilt over his all-too-successful role as a killing machine, while the other takes pride in the number of men he can destroy. In a parallel story line set in Canada, Xavier's aunt Niska, a Cree healer, waits for her nephew to return.

Keywords: Canada; Cree Indians; Friendship; Prejudice; Soldiers

De Bernières, Louis.

🏵 *Birds Without Wings.* **Knopf, 2005. 554pp. Hardbound, 1400043417.** 📖

In his epic about the rise of the modern Turkish state, told through multiple narrators, De Bernières intertwines the story of Mustafa Kemal (later better known as Atatürk), military leader and Turkey's first president, with that of the small southwestern Anatolian village of Eskibahce during the Great War. During the final years of the Ottoman Empire, Christian and Muslim residents of Eskibahce live together in ethnic and religious harmony. When outside events intervene, the village is completely torn apart, its young men sent off to Gallipoli, its remaining residents separated by religion, its peaceful atmosphere destroyed. ALA Notable Book.

Keywords: Ataturk, Kemal (historical character); Exile; Ottoman Empire; Turkey

Mitchell, Emily.

The Last Summer of the World. **Norton, 2007. 390pp. Hardbound, 9780393064872.** ✎ 📖

Debut novelist Mitchell looks beyond the obvious in the life of Edward Steichen—a pioneering portrait photographer—in her examination of his interpersonal relationships, particularly with his wife, Clara, as well as his military service in France during World War I. While on aerial reconnaissance missions over the French countryside, Steichen witnesses the devastation wrought by war; later, in a series of flashbacks, he thinks about his deteriorating relationship with Clara and the love triangle he created when he became too close to Marion Beckett, her best friend.

Keywords: France; Love triangles; Married life; Photographers; Steichen, Edward (historical character)

9

10

11

12

13

14

15

Murphy, Yannick.

Signed, Mata Hari. **Little Brown, 2007. 288pp. Hardbound, 9780316112642.** ✍

Was Mata Hari truly a German spy during World War I, or was she framed? From her prison cell in Paris in 1919, where she faces execution, the Dutchwoman born as Margaretha Zelle reimagines her life up to that point. She reminisces about her childhood in the Netherlands in the late nineteenth century, her years spent as wife (to a brutal army officer) and young mother on the island of Java, and her time spent earning money as a burlesque dancer and performer in Paris during the early years of the war.

Keywords: Java; Mata Hari (historical character); Netherlands; Spies, women

Seebohm, Caroline.

The Innocents. **Algonquin, 2007. 288pp. Hardbound, 9781565125001.**

Annotated in the "United States" section.

World War II

These novels of World War II in Europe (1939–1945) are serious in tone; some of their scenes can be disturbing, even though few battle scenes are evoked. They emphasize humanity's propensity for survival, love, and hope even under the harshest of conditions.

Arvin, Nick.

Articles of War. **Doubleday, 2005. 179pp. Hardbound, 0385512775.** 📖

Eighteen-year-old George Tilson, a farm boy from rural Iowa known as "Heck" for his refusal to swear, gets sent straight into action in the European theater in World War II and comes face to face with his own fear of combat. He briefly becomes involved with a French girl, though his fear, again, prevents him from following through with the affair. A harrowing tale of a young man's personal experiences during war, a time when traditional morals no longer make sense.

Keywords: Coming of age; France; Soldiers

Bielski, Nella.

The Year Is '42. **Pantheon, 2004. 207pp. Hardbound, 0375422862.**

Until 1942, life for Wehrmacht officer Karl Bazinger had been fairly pleasant; stationed in occupied Paris, he enjoyed all the culinary and cultural opportunities the city had to offer. But when the SS accuses him of collaborating with a member of the French Resistance, he initiates a transfer to Kiev, where he forms a bond with a Russian woman doctor.

Keywords: France; Physicians, women; Soldiers; Ukraine

Charlesworth, Monique.

The Children's War. **Knopf, 2004. 367pp. Hardbound, 1400040094.** 📖

Charlesworth observes World War II through the eyes of two children whose lives barely intersect. In 1939 Ilse Blumenthal's mother, Lore, sends her from Germany to Morocco to live with her uncle as a way of keeping her safe from the Nazis, because Ilse's father is Jewish. Meanwhile, back home, Lore takes a job as nursemaid to a wealthy German family whose son, Nicolai, is the same age as Ilse.

Keywords: Children; Germany; Jews; Morocco; Nazis

Dean, Debra.

🌸 *The Madonnas of Leningrad.* **Morrow, 2006. 231pp. Hardbound, 0060825308.** 📖 **YA**

In modern-day Seattle Marina Buriakov, a Russian émigré gradually losing her mind to Alzheimer's, can barely remember her granddaughter's upcoming wedding, though she can still piece together memories of the lengthy siege of Leningrad. As a docent at the Hermitage Museum back in 1941, Marina—after helping her fellow employees save its precious art collections—commits their former locations and characteristics to memory. ALA Notable Book.

Keywords: Alzheimer's disease; Leningrad, siege of; Hermitage Museum; Immigrants, Russian; Multi-period novels; Russia

Drucker, Eugene.

The Savior. **Simon & Schuster, 2007. 204pp. Hardbound, 9781416543299.**

Gottfried Keller, a young German violinist, is ordered to perform concerts for prisoners near death in concentration camps during the last days of Nazi Germany. His German commanders want him to perform an experiment, which makes Gottfried feel guilty: Is giving the prisoners unfounded hope a kind of cruel and unusual punishment?

Keywords: Germany; Holocaust; Nazis; Prisoners; Violinists

Grant, Richard.

Another Green World. **Knopf, 2006. 384pp. Hardbound, 0307263592.**

Four Americans who first meet and become friends in 1929 in Weimar Germany, at a summer festival for the German Youth Movement, find their lives entwining fifteen years later, when one uncovers the existence of documents detailing Hitler's Final Solution. By then the four of them—a young German American man dealing with his homosexuality, a woman in FDR's administration, an American journalist working for the Red Army, and an expatriate Pole who is part of the Jewish Resistance—each have different parts to play.

Keywords: Friendship; Gay men; German Americans; Germany; Jews; Journalists and reporters

Gutcheon, Beth.

Leeway Cottage. **Morrow, 2005. 416pp. Hardbound, 0060539054.** 📖

Annabelle Sydney Brant, a child of privilege, has always enjoyed summers at her family's cottage in Dundee, Maine, but when her father dies, she leaves her overbearing mother behind for a new life in Manhattan. There she meets and marries Laurus Moss, a pianist from Copenhagen. When he travels to England to help the Danish Resistance in their struggle against the Nazis, she remains home, holding on to their marriage despite their separation.

Keywords: Denmark; Maine; Married life

Slouka, Mark.

The Visible World. **Houghton Mifflin, 2007. 242pp. Hardbound, 0618756434.** 📖

An unnamed American man of Czech parentage grows up hearing only snippets of stories about his parents' lives during World War II and his despondent mother's possible love affair with a member of the Resistance—a man she never forgot. He travels through their homeland as an adult in search of answers, but unable to find them, he imagines what may have happened. In a novel-within-a-novel, he pictures his mother as a young woman in love with a young Czech soldier directly involved in the plot to assassinate SS leader Reinhard Heydrich.

Keywords: Assassins; Czechoslovakia; Immigrants, Czech; Mothers and sons; Multi-period novels; Revolutions and revolutionaries

Thorpe, Adam.

The Rules of Perspective. **Henry Holt, 2006. 338pp. Hardbound, 0805080422.**

Heinrich Hoffer, director of the Kaiser Wilhelm Museum in the small German town of Lohenfelde during the final days of World War II, takes refuge with his colleagues in the building's basement as Allied bombs begin to land. He also hides one of his favorite Van Gogh paintings in the museum's vault in the hopes of keeping it safe from theft by the SS. After the bombing ceases American corporal Neal Parry, a former artist, discovers the masterpiece amid the rubble and ponders what to do with it.

Keywords: Germany; Museums; Paintings

The United States

Colonial America

These are tales of survival, as settlers in pre-revolutionary America make homes for themselves in a new and often harsh land. Their interactions with the land's native inhabitants often turn out differently than expected.

Noyes, Deborah.

Angel and Apostle. **Unbridled, 2005. 289pp. Hardbound, 1932961100.** 📖 **YA**

Noyes's reimagining of characters from Nathaniel Hawthorne's *The Scarlet Letter* focuses on Hester Prynne's elfin child, Pearl, the fruit of her adultery. In 1649 in Boston, Pearl grows up puzzled by their status as outcasts but finds a steadfast friend in Simon Milton, the blind son of a local shipping family. As Pearl becomes a woman, she slowly comes to understand her mother's mistake and how it affected both their lives. She and Hester move to England and settle in the countryside. Pearl chooses to marry not Simon but his older brother, Nehemiah—setting in motion a dangerous love triangle that mirrors her mother's own experience.

Keywords: Coming of age; England—Stuart era; Illegitimate children; Love triangles; Massachusetts

Sharratt, Mary.

The Vanishing Point. **Mariner, 2006. 369pp. Paper, 0618462333.** 📖

Hannah Powers, trained in the arts of medicine by her physician father, leaves her home in Gloucestershire, England, after her father's death to make her home with May, her older sister. Because her marriage prospects were ruined after one too many sexual escapades, May had agreed to marry a distant cousin from Maryland, Gabriel Washbrook. When Hannah arrives in colonial Maryland, she finds Gabriel living alone in the untamed wilderness, claiming that May had died in childbirth. But even as Hannah falls in love with Gabriel, she doesn't fully trust him, and vows to discover the truth about her lost sister.

Keywords: Frontier and pioneer life; Maryland; Sisters; Wilderness

The American Revolution

These novels of America's founding (circa 1775–1783) look at the Revolutionary War, and its major participants, in a new light. The portraits are not always flattering.

Barton, Emily.

Brookland. **Farrar, Straus & Giroux, 2006. 478pp. Hardbound, 0374116903.** 📖

In letters to her married daughter, who's expecting her first child, Prudence Winship Horsfield speaks of her past obsession to build a suspension bridge spanning the East River so that residents of colonial "Brookland" (Brooklyn) could more easily reach Manhattan. The eldest daughter of a gin distiller in the early 1780s, ambitious Prue Winship, trained in the family business, becomes an early feminist visionary and marries a man as gifted as she. However, her preoccupation with her bridge-building dream proves costly to her long-suffering, middle sister Pearl.

Keywords: Bridges; Businesswomen; Feminists; New York; Sisters

Hill, Lawrence.

🐾 *Someone Knows My Name.* **Norton, 2007. 486pp. Hardbound, 9780393065787.** 📖 **YA**

In 1745 eleven-year-old Aminata Diallo is stolen from her West African village and forced aboard a slave ship bound for South Carolina. Little by little she uses her innate intelligence to rise in the world, as far as a young

African woman of her time is able. Taught to read by an indigo plantation's overseer, she later becomes the property of a Jewish trade inspector in Manhattan. After escaping, she works for the British documenting Black Loyalists in the Book of Negroes before they can be granted passage to Nova Scotia as a reward for their service. In later life she joins the British colony of Freetown, Sierra Leone, from where she is brought to London to tell her story in support of abolition. (Original title: *The Book of Negroes*.) Commonwealth Writers' Prize.

Keywords: Abolitionists; New York; Plantations; Sierra Leone—18th century; Slaves and slavery; South Carolina; West Africa—18th century

Early United States

Set roughly in the period after the American Revolution and before the Civil War (1783–1861), these are novels of a new and growing country, with riches yet to be discovered. Race relations is a common topic, and many novels show the psychological impact of slavery on people both black and white.

Allende, Isabel.

Daughter of Fortune Series. ★ 📖 YA

A two-volume series about Chilean women's coming of age and their experiences with early American culture.

Keywords: California; Chile—19th century; Chinese Americans; Families; Gold Rush; Immigrants, Chilean; Mixed heritage

🌲 *Daughter of Fortune.* HarperCollins, 1999. 399pp. Hardbound, 006019491X.

Rich in characterization and the spirit of adventure, this is the story of Eliza Sommers, a young woman of Chilean birth who comes to California with her lover, Joaquín, at the time of the 1849 Gold Rush. Upon arrival Eliza finds this supposed land of opportunity teeming with prostitutes, ruthless prospectors, and other newly arrived immigrants, including many Chinese, all crazed with gold fever. WILLA Award; Oprah's Book Club.

Portrait in Sepia. HarperCollins, 2001. 300pp. Hardbound, 0066211611.

In this sequel to *Daughter of Fortune*, Aurora del Valle, the granddaughter of Eliza Sommers, is brought up in her forebear's homeland of Chile but remains tormented by childhood memories of San Francisco's Chinatown. As she grows up, she decides to uncover her hidden family heritage.

Zorro. HarperCollins, 2005. 390pp. Hardbound, 0060778970. 📖 YA

Diego de la Vega, a half-Spanish, half-Shoshone young man born in southern California in 1795, learns both cultures' traditions, but grows up knowing his destiny will be to defend the land's underdogs—its native peoples—from European brutality. Sent to Barcelona with his "milk brother," Bernardo, for his formal education at sixteen, Diego trains as a swordsman and joins an underground movement, La Justicia, dedicated to fighting oppression and helping the poor. He carries these sound principles with him upon his return home, where he vows to continue his fight for social justice.

Keywords: California; Fencers; Mixed heritage; Shoshone Indians

Andersen, Kurt.

🏵 *Heyday*. **Random House, 2007. 622pp. Hardbound, 9780375504730.**

Crammed with the author's prodigious research into life throughout America circa 1848—a year that saw the discovery of gold in California, the end of the Mexican War, and a new wave of revolutionary social change engulfing Europe—*Heyday* is written as an epic, old-fashioned novel of ideas. Ben Knowles leaves England for New York in the hopes of observing progressive American society firsthand and quickly encounters a plethora of eccentric characters. As he and his companions pursue the westward trail left by Polly Lucking, the actress and part-time prostitute he loves, Ben is himself pursued by a crazed French official set on revenge. Langum Prize.

Keywords: Gold Rush; New York; Picaresque novels; Prostitutes

Clinch, Jon.

🏵 *Finn*. **Random House, 2007. 287pp. Hardbound, 9781400065912.** 📖 **YA**

In Mark Twain's classic novel, the body of Huckleberry Finn's father—obnoxious, racist, alcoholic, and brutal—was found drifting down the Mississippi in a house cluttered with strange objects. Clinch takes this scene and creates an entire backstory for Pap Finn, though his novel is more literary (and more harrowing) in tone than the original and can be read completely independently. His Finn, son of a widely respected, bigoted judge, is a man utterly without a conscience. Possessed of an uncontrollable lust for black women, he takes an ex-slave named Mary for a mistress and is immensely relieved that their son, Huck, can pass for white. ALA Notable Book.

Keywords: Fathers and sons; Missouri; Mixed heritage; Racial conflict; Slaves, runaway

Diamant, Anita.

The Last Days of Dogtown. **Scribner, 2005. 261pp. Hardbound, 0743225732.** 📖

By 1814 Dogtown, a small village on Cape Ann in eastern Massachusetts, was a declining settlement, inhabited mainly by an eclectic community of societal outcasts too lazy or too stubborn to move away. Diamant takes readers into the stories of this community's final days, including those of Judy Rhines, an unmarried, middle-aged white woman who's having an affair with a freed slave, and Black Ruth, an African woman who works as a stonemason and wears men's clothes.

Keywords: African Americans; Massachusetts; Racial conflict; Slaves, former

Frazier, Charles.

Thirteen Moons. **Random House, 2006. 422pp. Hardbound, 0375509321.** 📖

In the 1830s orphaned twelve-year-old Will Cooper is sent to run a remote trading post on the edge of Cherokee land in North Carolina. Adopted by Bear, a Cherokee chief, Will develops an undying affection for him and his people, one that remains when they are forced westward along the Trail of Tears. From the viewpoint of extreme old age, Will tells his own story in folksy, humorous, self-deprecating style, speaking of his longing for home, his love of the land, and his lifelong yearning for Claire Featherstone, an enigmatic young woman he wins and then loses. A lyrical novel of the American frontier, its people, and how both were transformed.

Keywords: Cherokee Indians; Frontier and pioneer life; North Carolina; Orphans

Jones, Edward P.

🏵 *The Known World.* **Amistad/HarperCollins, 2003. 400pp. Hardbound, 0060557540.** ★ 📖

In Manchester County, Virginia, Henry Townsend, a former slave turned powerful slave owner, dies in 1840. He leaves behind a widow, Caldonia, who doesn't follow Henry's example of keeping a safe distance between her slaves and herself. When Caldonia becomes personally involved with one of her slaves, but fails to free him, it upsets the social order on the plantation; their known world begins to disintegrate. Jones also details Henry Townsend's history and the social conditions that led him to enslave other African Americans. A powerful, subtle testimonial against slavery. Pulitzer Prize; National Book Critics' Circle Award; ALA Notable Book.

Keywords: African Americans; Plantations; Slaves, former; Slaves and slavery; Virginia

McBride, James.

Song Yet Sung. **Riverhead, 2008. 359pp. Hardbound, 9781594489723.** 📖 **YA**

Lying injured in a slave-catcher's attic in March 1850, Liz Spocott experiences visions of a disturbing future. Her precognitive dreams persuade the old woman shackled to her to reveal "the code," a secret language used by runaway slaves. When Liz escapes again and fumbles her way through the Chesapeake Bay region en route to possible freedom, she encounters a mix of people, both black and white, who help her, while two notorious slave-catchers follow her trail. McBride (author of the memoir *The Color of Water*) deliberately connects the present to the past, posing questions on whether contemporary black culture honors the freedom that was so hard earned.

Keywords: Maryland; Psychics; Slaves, runaway

Pritchett, Michael.

The Melancholy Fate of Capt. Lewis. **Unbridled, 2007. 392pp. Hardbound, 9781932961416.** ✍ 📖

Why did Meriwether Lewis, three years after his successful journey to the Pacific with fellow explorer William Clark and their company, choose to die by his own hand? High school history teacher Bill Lewis, his namesake and present-day biographer, seeks to understand the doubts and loss of confidence that surrounded Capt. Lewis both during and after the famous expedition west. Pritchett recounts the stories of the two men, who despite the 200-year gap between them and their very different backgrounds, endure similar situations: both are middle-aged, struggle with depression, and search for answers.

Keywords: Explorers; Lewis, Meriwether (historical character); Multi-period novels; Teachers

Rawles, Nancy.

🌲 *My Jim.* **Crown, 2005. 176pp. Hardbound, 1400054001.** 📖 🅈🅰

Rawles writes her homage/sequel to Mark Twain's *Huckleberry Finn* using the style of a slave narrative. Her protagonist is Sadie, wife of Jim, the runaway slave who accompanied Huck on his adventures down the Mississippi. Sadie Watson has been part of Jim's life from childhood on; they grew up together on a Missouri plantation and "jumped the broom" once they were old enough, always dreaming of one day becoming free. But when their master dies, Sadie and their children are sold off, prompting Jim to run away. Alex Award.

Keywords: African Americans; Married life; Missouri; Plantations; Slaves, runaway

Straight, Susan.

A Million Nightingales. **Pantheon, 2006. 340pp. Hardbound, 0375423648.** 📖

Moinette, a beautiful "mulatress" (mixed-race slave girl), serves as personal maid to a plantation owner's daughter in early nineteenth-century Louisiana. But when her young mistress dies, Moinette is sold away to another plantation without the chance to see her mother once more. She survives abuse and degradation at the hands of her new owner, never giving up hoping she'll obtain her freedom one day. Moinette narrates her own story in stream-of-consciousness style, illuminating not only her personal experiences but antebellum Louisiana as a whole.

Keywords: African Americans; Louisiana; Mixed heritage; Plantations; Slaves and slavery

White, Michael.

Soul Catcher. **Morrow, 2007. 432pp. Hardbound, 9780061340727.** 📖

Augustus Cain, a Mexican War veteran and inveterate gambler down on his luck (and short on cash), is forced to return to the one task he is, unfortunately, gifted at: tracking down runaway slaves and returning them to their rightful owners for profit. When Mr. Eberly, a rich Virginia plantation owner, hires him to find two slaves, Henry and Rosetta, Cain cannot refuse. The journey proves transformative for both Rosetta, who will do anything not to return, and Cain, who begins to wonder if redemption is possible for men such as he.

Keywords: Slave catchers; Slaves, runaway; Veterans; Virginia

The Civil War

These novels show the emotional impact of the Civil War (1861–1865) on all Americans: loyal Union followers, Confederate sympathizers, and those simply caught in the middle. Extended battle scenes aren't necessary to show the immense devastation that war can bring.

Bahr, Howard.

🏅 *The Judas Field.* **Holt, 2006. 292pp. Hardbound, 0805067396.** 📖

Bahr has chronicled the Civil War in fiction twice before (*The Black Flower*, *The Year of Jubilo*), and here he revisits Franklin, Tennessee, from the perspective of two decades later. In 1885 Cass Wakefield travels from Mississippi to Franklin in the company of his childhood friend, Alison, who is dying of cancer and wishes to bring home her father's and brother's remains. As they walk over the land where so many Confederate soldiers died, Cass's memories—which he had long suppressed—begin to reemerge. Michael Shaara Award.

Keywords: Confederacy; Franklin, Battle of; Soldiers; Tennessee

Brooks, Geraldine.

🏅 *March.* **Viking, 2005. 280pp. Hardbound, 0670033359.** ✍ 📖 **YA**

Brooks takes another look at Mr. March, Jo's absent father in *Little Women*, telling the half of the story that Louisa May Alcott left out. A cleric and staunch abolitionist from Concord, Massachusetts, John March leaves behind his family to aid the Union cause during the Civil War. In letters home to his daughters and his beloved Marmee, his voice is calm and reassuring, but as he adjusts to life as a teacher on a ruined Virginia estate, and later on a plantation along the Mississippi, March loses much of his idealistic outlook, realizing that both the South and North were equally capable of brutality and racism. Pulitzer Prize.

Keywords: Abolitionists; Families; Married life; Plantations; Racial conflict; Virginia

Doctorow, E. L.

🏅 *The March.* **Random House, 2006. 384pp. Hardbound, 0375506713.** ✍ **YA**

As General William Tecumseh Sherman and his army march through Georgia and the Carolinas, pillaging and destroying everything in their wake, they attract numerous followers, including a ragtag band of freed slaves and assorted refugees. Rather than focus on a single person's perspective, Doctorow switches among the points of view of numerous people, both Union and Confederate, either part of, or affected by, this "march to freedom" that lasts until Appomattox. His Sherman is at once cruel, egotistical, and charismatic, but Doctorow's true ability is his characterizations of so-called common people, such as Pearl, a half-Negro plantation daughter who could pass for white; judge's daughter Emily Thompson, who becomes a battlefield nurse; and Colonel Wrede Sartorius, a renowned Union surgeon who briefly becomes Emily's lover. Michael Shaara Award; National Book Critics' Circle Award.

Keywords: Confederacy; Generals; Georgia; Sherman, William Tecumseh (historical character); South Carolina

Frazier, Charles.

🏆 *Cold Mountain*. **Algonquin Books of Chapel Hill, 1997. 356pp. Hardbound, 0871136791.** ★ 📖 **YA**

> In 1864 Inman, a wounded Confederate deserter, slowly makes his way home from the Civil War and into the arms of Ada, the woman he loves. In his absence she ekes out a living on her late father's farm at Cold Mountain in the Blue Ridge Mountains of North Carolina. Ada's life is no less difficult, and she manages to keep the derelict farm going with the help of a drifter named Ruby. Inman's arduous journey, described similarly to *The Odyssey*, is rendered with clarity and lyricism. This novel is the standard to which all Civil War novels, literary and not, have been compared since its publication. National Book Award; Book Sense Book of the Year; ALA Notable Book.
>
> **Keywords:** Confederacy; Farmers; North Carolina; Soldiers

Hicks, Robert.

The Widow of the South. **Warner, 2005. 414pp. Hardbound, 0446500127.** ✍ 📖 **YA**

> In 1894 an elderly, dying soldier approaches Carrie McGavock at the cemetery she and her husband created for over 1,000 Confederate dead after the battle of Franklin, Tennessee, and asks if she has room for one more. The scene then shifts to November 30, 1864. Carrie, a despondent farm wife, is mourning her three lost children. She finds newfound purpose when her plantation, Carnton, is turned into a makeshift hospital for Confederate soldiers after the devastating battle, and when Zachariah Cashwell, a soldier from Arkansas, steals her heart.
>
> **Keywords:** Cemeteries; Confederacy; Franklin, Battle of; Hospitals; McGavock, Carrie (historical character); Plantations; Soldiers; Veterans

Melman, Peter Charles.

Landsman. **Counterpoint, 2007. 323pp. Hardbound, 9781582433677.**

> In 1861 twenty-year-old Elias Abrams, illegitimate son of a Jewish indentured servant, flees his New Orleans home because of a murder charge and enlists in the Third Louisiana Infantry. He grows up quickly as a member of the Confederate Army, and the battle scenes are rendered in brutal clarity. When Elias's correspondence with Nora Bloom, a young Jewish woman from his hometown, turns romantic, he decides that in order to meet her, he must return to face the music back home.
>
> **Keywords:** Confederacy; Jews; Letters; Louisiana; Soldiers

Olmstead, Robert.

Coal Black Horse. **Algonquin, 2007. 224pp. Hardbound, 9781565125216.** 📖

> Robey Childs's mother, fearing that her husband is in danger while fighting for the Confederacy, sends the fourteen-year-old off to retrieve him from battle, his only protectors on the journey a reversible coat—one side

9

10

11

12

13

14

15

blue, the other gray—and a beautiful coal-black horse. While en route to Gettysburg, where a scene of carnage awaits, Robey's horse is stolen from him, and he witnesses numerous brutal acts that cause him to face moral decisions like a man.

Keywords: Coming of age; Confederacy; Gettysburg, Battle of; Horses; Pennsylvania; Soldiers

Robinson, Marilynne.

🌶 *Gilead.* **Farrar, Straus & Giroux, 2004. 247pp. Hardbound, 0374153892.** 📖

This evocative, philosophical novel of the relationships between fathers and sons, and how people determine what they leave behind as a legacy, begins in 1956 as Reverend John Ames of Gilead, Iowa, the septuagenarian father of a young son, composes a letter about his forebears, because he may not be alive to see his son grow up. He writes about the fraught relationship between his grandfather, a fiery abolitionist from Kansas during the Civil War years, and his father, a pacifist. In depicting the daily life among generations in Middle America, Robinson reflects the heart and soul of a nation. ALA Notable Book; National Book Critics' Circle Award; Pulitzer Prize.

Keywords: Abolitionists; Epistolary novels; Fathers and sons; Iowa; Multi-period novels

Scott, Joanna Catherine.

The Road from Chapel Hill. **Berkley, 2006. 340pp. Paper, 0425212521.** 📖

It is 1860, and Eugenia Mae Spotswood, once a pampered Southern belle from Wilmington, now spends her days in destitution, tending to a ramshackle cabin while her father toils at a gold mine in Charlotte. Her story intertwines gradually —and tragically—with that of Tom, a crippled young black man who becomes her only remaining slave, and Clyde, a farm boy who had captured Tom into slavery, and who gets drawn into the Civil War on the Union side.

Keywords: Farmers; North Carolina; Poverty; Slaves, runaway; Slaves and slavery

Wray, John.

Canaan's Tongue. **Knopf, 2005. 341pp. Hardbound, 1400040868.**

Thaddeus Morelle, leader of the "Island 37 Gang" on Geburah Plantation in southern Mississippi in 1863, is known as the "redeemer"; he and his fellow criminals persuade slaves to run away, but afterward, the group murders them and redeems their bodies for cash from their original masters. Virgil Ball, Morelle's half-blind right-hand man, has become conflicted about his participation in such atrocities, but finds escaping his role may be harder than continuing with it. Based on the true story of John Murrell, a notorious Civil War–era criminal.

Keywords: Gangs; Mississippi; Murderers; Outlaws; Plantations

Wright, Stephen.

The Amalgamation Polka. **Knopf, 2006. 323pp. Hardbound, 067945117X.**

Liberty Fish was born in upstate New York in 1844, the son of fervent abolitionists who run a stop on the Underground Railroad, though his mother, Roxana, was born on a slave-owning plantation in South Carolina. Naturally, when war breaks out Liberty dutifully fights for the Union, but when the true horror of battle proves more than he can stomach, he deserts his post and makes his way to his grandparents' Southern plantation—where he finds his racist grandfather performing cruel experiments on his slaves. Part picaresque epic, part dark comedy.

Keywords: Abolitionists; Picaresque novels; Plantations; Racial conflict; Slaves and slavery; Soldiers; South Carolina

Reconstruction and the Gilded Age

These novels are set between 1865 and 1900. Although the Civil War is over, its legacy remains. Cities reinvigorate themselves in its wake, immigrants flood America's borders, and settlers head out West in search of open land. Though slavery has been abolished, racial problems haven't disappeared, not by a long shot.

Bauman, Natasha.

The Disorder of Longing. **Putnam, 2008. 422pp. Hardbound, 9780399154959.** 📖

Ada Pryce is hardly a proper society wife in 1890s Boston: she engages in inappropriate intellectual pursuits, treats her social inferiors as equals, and longs for the personal freedom she experienced back in her university days. Her husband, Edward, attempts to curb her wild ways by carefully watching her behavior and restricting her pleasure in the sexual act by adopting tantric practices. Edward's other preoccupation, collecting exotic orchids, becomes Ada's surprising key to escaping her gilded cage. She doesn't hesitate to use it, either, fleeing her repressed Victorian life to the jungles of Brazil.

Keywords: Brazil; Feminists; Massachusetts; Orchids

Cokal, Susann.

Breath and Bones. **Unbridled, 2005. 407pp. Hardbound, 1932961062.** 📖

Famke Summerfugl, a beautiful, red-haired consumptive well aware of her own sensuality, adores the idea of being an artist's muse. When her lover, English pre-Raphaelite painter Albert Castle, leaves Copenhagen in 1884 with his portrait of her in hand, Famke decides to follow him. Her journey takes her to America, where she marries a Mormon as his third wife in order to enter the country. On her steamy trip through the Old West, from Colorado to California, she follows Castle's trail from whorehouse to whorehouse in this offbeat swashbuckling adventure.

Keywords: Mormons; Muses; Painters; Picaresque novels; West, the

Cunningham, M. Allen.

The Green Age of Asher Witherow. Unbridled, 2004. 275pp. Hardbound, 1932961003.

Asher Witherow, the child of Welsh immigrant parents, grows up in the harsh coal mining community of Nortonville, California, in the 1860s and 1870s. Nortonville is a town replete with superstition and mystical belief in Welsh legends, thanks to the strong religious convictions of its inhabitants. As Asher comes of age, his own beliefs are shaped by his experience in the mines—where he begins working as a child—as well as the influence of an odd local preacher and a tragedy he endured at age eight: witnessing the burning death of his best friend, Thomas, in a mining accident.

Keywords: California; Coal mining; Coming of age; Immigrants, Welsh

Gaffney, Elizabeth.

Metropolis. Random House, 2005. 461pp. Hardbound, 1400061504. 📖

In 1868, after P.T. Barnum's American Museum catches fire, a German American immigrant, fingered as the culprit, finds himself the target of an arson investigation that spans all of Manhattan. He initially finds refuge among the Whyos, an Irish street gang who rename him "Frank Harris," and falls in love with one of their members, pickpocket Beatrice O'Gamhna. As Harris's luck continues to change, Gaffney's sweeping, Dickensian epic of post–Civil War New York encompasses the building of the Brooklyn Bridge, its filthy streets and their inhabitants, and the frenetic atmosphere of a quickly growing city that emerges as perhaps the most important character of all.

Keywords: Bridges; Gangs; Immigrants, German; Immigrants, Irish; New York

Maltman, Thomas.

🌟 *The Night Birds.* Soho, 2007. 370pp. Hardbound, 9781569474624. 📖 **YA**

Natives and settlers coexist uneasily in rural Minnesota in 1876, the present home of the Sengers, a German American family. Swarms of locusts have devastated the land, leaving the settlers hungry and impoverished. When his enigmatic aunt Hazel comes to live with them, fourteen-year-old Asa Senger listens to her stories about American plains folklore, their German immigrant ancestors, and the Sengers' involvement in the Great Sioux Uprising, an 1862 rebellion by Dakota Indians that resulted in the hanging of thirty-eight Dakota men. Alex Award; Spur Award.

Keywords: Coming of age; Dakota Indians; Frontier and pioneer life; Great Sioux Uprising; Minnesota

McCaig, Donald.

Canaan. Norton, 2007. 428pp. Hardbound, 9780393062465. 📖

This partial sequel to *Jacob's Ladder* (1998) covers the troubled years between Appomattox and the Little Bighorn. Its scope is considerably wider than McCaig's earlier novel, however, as it surveys the devastation wrought throughout America by the Civil War. The novel continues the story of the Gatewood family, barely making a living on their Virginia plantation during Reconstruction. Meanwhile, out on the Great Plains Edward Ratcliff, a former Gatewood slave who fought for the Union, initially finds acceptance among the Lakota. He marries a Santee woman, She-Goes-Before, who narrates her own tale of heartbreak and survival.

Keywords: Families; Plantations; Santee Indians; Slaves, former; Virginia; West, the

Morrison, Toni.

🏶 *Beloved.* **Knopf, 1987. 275pp. Hardbound, 0394535979.** ★ 📖
Sethe, a former slave in post–Civil War rural Ohio, is tormented by memories of her previous life on Sweet Home Farm, from which she had run away. Her most painful memory, revealed gradually in flashbacks, is that she murdered her infant daughter rather than see her be recaptured. Her daughter later reappears, fully grown, as a ghostly young woman whom Sethe calls Beloved. The ghost's presence causes difficulties with Sethe's remaining family members, not least of all with Sethe herself. Pulitzer Prize.

Keywords: Ghosts; Infanticide; Ohio; Slaves, former

O'Connor, Joseph.

Redemption Falls. **Free Press, 2007. 457pp. Hardbound, 9781416553168.** 📖
O'Connor's third novel (a sequel of sorts to his previous book, *Star of the Sea*, set nearly two decades later) forms a scrapbook of literary and historical memorabilia, centering on the Irish American experience during the Civil War, Reconstruction, and the westward expansion. As teenaged Eliza Mooney travels, on foot, from Baton Rouge, Louisiana, toward Redemption Falls in "Mountain Territory" in search of her lost brother Jeddo, James Con O'Keefe, the land's unofficial governor, argues with his wife, Lucia, about whether to adopt the mute boy—one of the Civil War's youngest veterans. O'Connor intersperses the main narratives with newspaper articles, songs, posters, and letters, all written as if authentic to the time.

Keywords: Irish Americans; West, the

Oliver, Julia.

Devotion. **University of Georgia, 2006. 214pp. Hardbound, 082032874X.** ✍ **YA**
By virtue of her birth as the youngest daughter of former Confederate president Jefferson Davis, Varina Anne "Winnie" Davis grows up in late nineteenth-century Georgia as a living symbol of the Old South, due to her work to educate the masses about her father's true character. Her reputation is that of a gentle, old-fashioned Southern belle, though Winnie earns her living as a journalist, and her love affair with an attorney and abolitionist from Boston doesn't meet with favorable reactions back home. Oliver tells her story through fictionalized journals, letters, and observations by those close to her.

Keywords: Confederacy; Davis, Varina (historical character); Diaries and journals; Georgia; Journalists, women

Rushforth, Peter.

A Dead Language. MacAdam/Cage, 2006. 750pp. Hardbound, 1596921927.

Benjamin Franklin Pinkerton, an American naval lieutenant, is known to opera fans as the man who abandoned Madame Butterfly, the Japanese woman who loved him, prompting her to commit suicide. Using a similar stream-of-consciousness style to that used in *Pinkerton's Sister* (a sequel of sorts; see the following section), Rushforth imagines Pinkerton's childhood and family life in 1880s and 1890s New York, which caused young Ben to develop such an emotionless, reserved personality.

Keywords: Brothers and sisters; New York; Socialites

Siegel, Robert Anthony.

All Will Be Revealed. MacAdam/Cage, 2007. 282pp. Hardbound, 9781596922051.

At a séance in 1896 in New York, crippled photographer Augustus Auerbach (he uses a wheelchair) first encounters a beautiful medium, Verena Swann, who claims to channel his mother's spirit. Verena, a widow, once had clairvoyant abilities, but now longs to escape a career that feels empty and false. As their mutual affection grows, Verena's greedy brother-in-law, Leopold, decides to exploit Augustus for his own gain. With a pornographer for a main character, one might expect this to be a tawdry story of salacious behavior in Gilded Age America, but Siegel's second novel manages to be lyrical, evocative, and emotionally involving.

Keywords: Mediums; New York; Photographers; Pornographers; Widows

Smith, Lee.

On Agate Hill. Algonquin, 2006. 367pp. Hardbound, 1565124529. 📖

Smith, a frequent chronicler of the Southern way of life, re-creates the life of a young orphan from North Carolina, Molly Petree, imagining her diary, letters, court records, poems, and other documents dating from the post–Civil War period. She begins her journal in 1872, at age thirteen, a "ghost girl" forced to leave her home at Agate Hill by Yankees and shuffled around to relatives after that. As Molly comes of age, she strives not only to take on whatever hardships life throws at her, but to triumph.

Keywords: Coming of age; Diaries and journals; North Carolina; Orphans; Plantations

Thompson, Pamela.

Every Past Thing. Unbridled, 2007. 328pp. Hardbound, 9781932961393. ✍ 📖

By November 1899 Mary Jane Elmer, long-suffering wife to the moody artist Edwin Romanzo Elmer, has been mourning the death of their daughter Effie for the past ten years. In an attempt to make a new start, they leave their home in rural western Massachusetts for the hubbub of New York City, a place where feminist and anarchist sentiments run high. While Edwin re-establishes himself at an art academy, Mary Jane attempts to reconnect with her former lover, whose last known address is at an anarchists' enclave in the East Village.

Keywords: Anarchists; Artists; Elmer, Edwin Romanzo (historical character); Elmer, Mary Jane (historical character); Married life; Massachusetts; New York

Vinton, Victoria.

The Jungle Law. MacAdam/Cage, 2005. 306pp. Hardbound, 1596921498. ✍
📖 **YA**

9

Rudyard Kipling moves with his pregnant wife, Caroline, to rural Vermont in 1892 in search of a peaceful atmosphere in which to raise a family and to find inspiration for the literary creation that will become *The Jungle Books*. Eleven-year-old Joe Connolly, a neighbor's son, finds Kipling an amiable companion, and Kipling discusses his work-in-progress with the child, most notably the formation of the character Mowgli, a feral child raised by animals. Joe's father, Jack, a recent Irish immigrant, sees Kipling's influence and storytelling as harmful to Joe's development.

10

Keywords: Authors; Immigrants, Irish; Kipling, Rudyard (historical character); Neighbors; Vermont

Wiggins, Marianne.

11

The Shadow Catcher. Simon & Schuster, 2007. 318pp. Hardbound, 9780743265201. 📖

A fictional character named Marianne Wiggins, obviously based on the author, brings her novel about renowned Western photographer Edward Curtis (1868–1952) to a Hollywood producer, who wants to transform it into a screenplay. Based on her research, Wiggins rejects the producer's romanticized concept of Curtis as an adventurous risk-taker—his gorgeous portraits of Native Americans were staged, and he abandoned his wife, Clara, and their four children to pursue his career. As Marianne searches for clues to Curtis's enigmatic personality, the scene shifts to her novel, which is recounted from Clara's viewpoint. Using the technique of novelist W. G. Sebald, Wiggins intersperses photographs by Curtis throughout the story.

12

13

Keywords: Curtis, Edward (historical character); Married life; Photographers; West, the

Twentieth Century

14

General

A mélange of fictional portraits set in the United States between 1900 and 1950—a time of nostalgia for many people, but an unfamiliar world to younger readers. This is a large, diverse category showing the wide range of people's experiences in early twentieth-century America. Novels about World War II are listed separately.

15

Banks, Russell.

The Reserve. HarperCollins, 2008. 287pp. Hardbound, 9780061430251. 📖

Twice-divorced heiress Vanessa Cole's life changes irrevocably when Jordan Groves lands his biplane on the lake of her adoptive parents' remote Adirondack estate during their annual Fourth of July celebration. Although the year is 1936, the hardships of the Depression barely penetrate this microcosm of wealth and privilege. Jordan, an internationally famous artist, is beguiled by Vanessa's beauty and forceful personality, although her father's illness unhinges her already unbalanced mind. Her instability proves destructive for everyone in her path.

Keywords: Artists; Great Depression; Heirs and heiresses; Mental illness; New York

Bigsby, Christopher.

🏵 *Beautiful Dreamer*. Thomas Dunne, 2006. 192pp. Hardbound, 0312355831. 📖 **YA**

Jake Benchley, a middle-aged white widower in rural turn-of-the-century Tennessee, comes to the aid of a black man who did nothing wrong other than use the whites-only front entrance to a local store. This heroic act nearly costs Jake his life. After the black man is lynched for supposedly raping the store proprietor's wife (a false accusation), his traumatized son James tends to the severely beaten Benchley. The pair flees the scene together after James takes his own revenge against the lynchers' brothers, who had stopped by Jake's home to cause more trouble. While on the run, Jake and James form a strong bond that feels almost like that of family. ALA Notable Book.

Keywords: African Americans; Racial conflict; Tennessee—20th century

Blackwell, Elise.

The Unnatural History of Cypress Parish. Unbridled, 2007. 210pp. Hardbound, 9781932961317.

Sitting in his New Orleans apartment as he waits for Hurricane Katrina, ninety-year-old Louis Proby remembers the great flood that destroyed his home, Cypress Parish, back in 1927. Back then, teenaged Louis, the son of a well-off logging superintendent, fell in love with the beautiful daughter of a French immigrant family. When he takes a job driving a lumber official back and forth to New Orleans, he learns of the decadent city's temptations, as well as the government's plans to flood his hometown in order to save New Orleans.

Keywords: Floods; Hurricanes; Louisiana; Lumber industry

Bloom, Amy.

🏵 *Away*. Random House, 2007. 240pp. Hardbound, 9781400063567. 📖

Her parents dead in a Russian pogrom and her daughter Sophie taken from her during the same event, twenty-two-year-old Lillian Leyb arrives in New York City in 1922 with nothing to lose. Desperately eager to learn English, find a job, and forget her past, she takes a position as seamstress to the Goldfadn Yiddish Theatre, where she becomes involved with the Bursteins, both father and son. When she hears that Sophie may be alive and in Siberia, Lillian races across the continent from city to city, braving countless hardships and making desperate bargains in the hope of reuniting with her daughter. ALA Notable Book.

Keywords: Immigrants, Russian; Jews; Mothers and daughters; New York; Picaresque novels

Cooney, Ellen.

A Private Hotel for Gentle Ladies. **Pantheon, 2005. 303pp. Hardbound, 0375423400.**

> When she spies her husband kissing another woman, Charlotte Heath, a woman recovering from an extended illness who never felt at home among her snobbish in-laws, flees her small Massachusetts town for Boston. She takes up residence at the Beechmont hotel, which turns out to be a male brothel. This lyrical novel about a young married woman's sexual awakening isn't as titillating as the premise suggests, but it provides sufficient amounts of historical detail about Boston in the early twentieth century.
>
> **Keywords:** Brothels; Extramarital affairs; Hotels; Massachusetts

Domingue, Ronlyn.

The Mercy of Thin Air. **Atria, 2005. 310pp. Hardbound, 0743278801.** 📖

> Just after graduating from Tulane's medical school in 1929, Raziela "Razi" Nolan drowns in her lover Andrew's swimming pool. Ever since then she has existed "between," in a state between life and the afterlife. She tells the story of her grand passion with Andrew, her life in New Orleans as an early advocate for birth control, and the troubled relationship between a modern-day young couple, Amy and Scott, whose house she haunts seventy years later.
>
> **Keywords:** Feminists; Ghosts; Louisiana; Physicians, women

Ephron, Amy.

One Sunday Morning. **Morrow, 2005. 213pp. Hardbound, 0060585528.** 📖 **YA**

> Don't judge the depth and impact of Amy Ephron's novels by their length; despite their brevity, they carry a powerful message. One Sunday morning in 1920s New York City, four women playing bridge spy an acquaintance, Lizzie Carswell, leaving a hotel with a man other than her husband. Instantly suspecting impropriety, the women agree to keep Lizzie's "secret" (which isn't what any of them thinks), though rumors have a way of escaping. The false gossip changes all of their lives.
>
> **Keywords:** Friendship; Gossip; New York

Gallagher, Nora.

Changing Light. **Pantheon, 2007. 222pp. Hardbound, 9780805242072.**

> In 1945 painter Eleanor Garrigue flees New York and her marriage to a man who never appreciated her talents for the desert landscape around Los Alamos, New Mexico. When she encounters a semiconscious man in the desert, she rescues him and nurses him at her home, not knowing his identity. He is Leo Kavan, a Czechoslovakian scientist who deserted the Manhattan Project after his good friend and colleague died of radiation poisoning.
>
> **Keywords:** Manhattan Project; New Mexico; Painters, women

Goldberg, Myla.

Wickett's Remedy. **Doubleday, 2005. 326pp. Hardbound, 0385513240. [RG]**

"Wickett's Remedy" is a concoction developed by medical student Henry Wickett, son of a notable Boston family, and the reason he drops out of medical school—shocking his new bride, Irish American shopgirl Lydia Kilkenny. Then the Spanish influenza of 1918 arrives in America, changing their lives forever. Lydia, feeling obligated to help, becomes a nurse's assistant for a research experiment employing human subjects. Quirky and revealing comments from the deceased appear in the novel's margins.

Keywords: Influenza; Massachusetts; Medical students; Nurses

Gruen, Sara.

🏵 *Water for Elephants.* **Algonquin, 2006. 335pp. Hardbound, 1565124995. ★ 📖 YA**

Jacob Jankowski, ninety-some years old and in a nursing home, reminisces about his youth during the Great Depression, when his parents' unexpected deaths forced him to join the circus to make a living. As a member of the Benzini Brothers' Most Spectacular Show on Earth, Jacob uses his veterinary training to care for the show's animals. He can't deny his attraction to Marlena, half of the equestrian act, despite his fear of August, the circus owner's cruel second-in-command (and Marlena's husband). And then there's Rosie, the star of the show—a large gray elephant he and Marlena both care for. Much more than a circus story, Sara Gruen's third novel, a huge book club favorite, takes a nostalgic, romantic trip into the past with its realistic portrayals of circus performers, the bonds between humans and animals, and its touching love story. Alex Award; Book Sense Book of the Year.

Keywords: Circus; Elephants; Friendship; Great Depression

Horan, Nancy.

Loving Frank. **Ballantine, 2007. 377pp. Hardbound, 9780345494993. ✍ 📖**

In 1904 charismatic architect Frank Lloyd Wright first meets Mamah Borthwick Cheney, the wife of one of his clients. They begin a passionate affair, and their elopement to Europe five years later causes a scandal that rocks polite society in Cheney's hometown of Oak Park, Illinois. How could they abandon their spouses and children? While Mamah, an intellectual with feminist sympathies, feels guilty for leaving her children, she had never been content in her marriage, and in Europe she finds others who share her ideas. She and Wright eventually return to Wisconsin, where Frank builds a retreat called Taliesin for them both, though their story is destined to end in tragedy.

Keywords: Architects; Cheney, Mamah (historical character); Extramarital affairs; Illinois; Wright, Frank Lloyd (historical character)

Hunt, Samantha.

The Invention of Everything Else. **Houghton Mifflin, 2008. 272pp. Hardbound, 9780618801121. ✍ 📖**

Nikola Tesla, scientist and inventor, quietly lives out his last days in the Hotel New Yorker in 1943, preferring his pigeons over human companionship. He forms an unlikely bond with Louisa, a young chambermaid with a penchant for snooping through hotel guests' personal belongings. Her decision to read some of his papers, and their shared interest in pigeons, enable both of them to open up about their personal histories.

Keywords: Engineers; Friendship; Inventors; Maids; New York; Tesla, Nikola (historical character)

James, Caryn.

What Caroline Knew. **St. Martin's, 2006. 230pp. Hardbound, 0312343124.** 📖

Caroline Stephens, a socialite in 1920s New York City who is bored with her conventional life, gets involved in the local art scene. She becomes the patron of Nicholas Leone, a handsome young painter, but when he unveils a scandalous nude portrait of her during his first exhibition, it horrifies the audience and destroys her reputation. Were she and Nicholas lovers, and did she actually pose for him in such a compromising position?

Keywords: Artists; New York; Portraits; Socialites

Jordan, Hillary.

Mudbound. **Algonquin, 2008. 320pp. Hardbound, 9781565125698.** 📖

"Mudbound" is the name Laura McAllan gives the farm on the Mississippi Delta that she and husband Henry purchase in 1946. Laura, a professor's daughter and schoolteacher from Memphis, has difficulties adjusting to rural farm life—there's no electricity or running water—and her racist father-in-law, who moves in with the couple. As their marriage slowly disintegrates, Henry's brother Jamie faces nightmares from his stint as a wartime bomber pilot, and the McAllans' black sharecroppers contend with the local community's racial prejudices.

Keywords: Families; Farmers; Married life; Mississippi; Prejudice; Racial conflict; Veterans

Lawrence, Starling.

The Lightning Keeper. **HarperCollins, 2006. 416pp. Hardbound, 0060825243.**

This sequel to Lawrence's 1997 novel *Montenegro*, about an English botanist/spy sent to Montenegro at the turn of the century, has Toma Pekoceviæ (who appeared as a precocious young man in the earlier book) as its protagonist. Toma, son of a Serbian hero, has fulfilled his mother's dream by coming to America—by way of Naples, where he had met ironworks heiress Harriet Bigelow six years earlier. They reconnect in New York City in 1914, when Harriet's family has fallen on hard times. Toma, a gifted engineer, designs a water turbine that may help save her family dynasty.

Keywords: Engineers; Heirs and heiresses; Immigrants, Serbian; Inventors; New York

Mills, Mark.

Amagansett. **Putnam, 2004. 398pp. Hardbound, 0399151842.** 📖

Mills combines the suspense and lyricism of the literary thriller with a gentle love story in this tale of love and death in a Long Island fishing community in 1947. Conrad Labarde, a first-generation Basque fisherman, is shocked to find the body of a beautiful young woman tangled in his nets. He immediately recognizes her as socialite Lillian Wallace, his lover, and when police turn up a connection between the two, he becomes a suspect. Yet the novel is far more than a simple murder mystery, as Mills details the complicated history of Amagansett, a working-class town whose summer and winter residents have little in common, and the way the changes of postwar America affect them all.

Keywords: Basque Americans; Detective stories; Fishermen; New York; Prejudice; Veterans

Morris, Mary McGarry.

The Lost Mother. **Viking, 2005. 274pp. Hardbound, 0670033898.** 📖 **YA**

In rural Vermont during the Great Depression, poverty-stricken Henry Talcott and his two children, Thomas and Margaret, are reduced to living in a tent in the woods, their beautiful mother having abandoned them for reasons and location unknown. Henry, a butcher, must continually be on the move in search of work, which forces him to leave the children alone, aside from the help of neighbors, for lengthy periods of time. Meanwhile, Thomas and Margaret never give up hoping for their mother's return.

Keywords: Abandoned children; Great Depression; Poverty; Vermont

Mosher, Howard Frank.

On Kingdom Mountain. **Houghton Mifflin, 2007. 288pp. Hardbound, 9780618197231.**

Jane Hubbell Kinneson, an eccentric, independent-minded, fifty-year-old librarian, is the sole resident of Kingdom Mountain, Vermont, a town in the wilderness along the American–Canadian border. Her cousin Eben wants to build a highway and ski resort on her beloved mountainside, and Miss Jane refuses to give in. Then a stunt pilot named Henry Satterfield crashes his biplane in her yard, prompting a gentle romance and a hunt for secret treasure.

Keywords: Librarians; Mountains; Pilots; Spinsters; Treasure; Vermont

Mullen, Thomas.

🌱 *The Last Town on Earth.* **Random House, 2006. 394pp. Hardbound, 1400065208.** 📖

During the influenza epidemic of 1918, the small mill town of Commonwealth, Washington, decides to quarantine itself against further contagion in order to keep its residents safe. When a cold and ill soldier approaches the two guards posted along the road leading to Commonwealth, begging to be let in, he is too disoriented to pay attention to their warnings. His death precipitates a string of tragic events at odds with the town's peaceful principles. James Fenimore Cooper Prize.

Keywords: Influenza; Quarantine; Soldiers; Washington State

Olds, Bruce.

The Moments Lost: A Midwest Pilgrim's Progress. **Farrar, Straus & Giroux, 2007. 468pp. Hardbound, 9780374118211.**

Franklyn Shivs (a character based on a historical figure named Frank Shavs), a farm boy from Wisconsin, travels to Chicago and becomes a beat reporter for that city's *Tribune*, where he gets his big break covering the Iroquois Theater fire of 1903 and becomes involved with Chicago's bohemian lifestyle. Ten years later, while working for a socialist weekly, he is sent to Michigan's Upper Peninsula to cover a Wobblie-led copper mine strike; he risks losing his professional detachment when he falls in love with one of the union leaders.

Keywords: Illinois; Journalists and reporters; Michigan; Strikes

Ozick, Cynthia.

Heir to the Glimmering World. **Houghton Mifflin, 2004. 310pp. Hardbound, 0618470492.** 📖

In 1935 eighteen-year-old Rose Meadows takes a position as research assistant to Professor Rudolph Mitwisser, a recent German Jewish refugee living with his large family in the Bronx during the Great Depression. The Mitwissers are living there at the whim of James A'bair, wealthy son of a famous author of children's books, who has become intrigued by Rudolph's studies in Karaism, an ancient Jewish sect. Rose, already having trouble adjusting to the chaos of his unruly household, finds her life disrupted further when James himself comes into their lives. Ozick modeled the James A'bair character on the real-life Christopher Robin, son of A. A. Milne.

Keywords: Authors; Great Depression; Jews; New York; Orphans

Phillips, Caryl.

Dancing in the Dark. **Knopf, 2005. 209pp. Hardbound, 1400043964.** ✑ 📖

Bert Williams, born in the Caribbean in 1874, rises to become the most famous black vaudeville performer in early twentieth-century America, often donning blackface to the delight of his New York audiences. But in private Bert, a sensitive man inclined to brooding, must deal with the humiliation his success brings him, for "playing the coon" for white audiences causes rancor among black society.

Keywords: Actors; African Americans; Blackface; New York; Racial conflict; Vaudeville; Williams, Bert (historical character)

Prasad, Chandra.

On Borrowed Wings. **Atria, 2007. 311pp. Hardbound, 9780743297820.** 📖 YA

When Adele Pietra's father and brother are killed in a quarry accident in the 1930s, she leaves her small Connecticut town and heads to Yale, disguised as her brother, Charles, who had planned to attend on a scholarship. On campus, working-class Adele (who goes by "Charlie") befriends wealthy students from Manhattan and elsewhere, fighting her attraction to one of them and praying her impersonation won't be discovered.

Keywords: Coming of age; Connecticut; Disguise; Students; Universities

Pynchon, Thomas.

Against the Day. **Penguin Press, 2006. 1085pp. Hardbound, 159420120X.**

The author's mammoth exploration of technological genius, early twentieth-century history, and civilization as a whole begins in 1893, when a club of balloonists takes flight in a large-scale skyship, en route to the Columbian Exposition in Chicago. Over the next thirty years, using a multiplicity of plots and styles—from satirical to metaphysical, from humorous to lyrical and serious—numerous characters weave their way in and out of the narrative as they become involved with the Mexican Revolution, labor disputes in Colorado, World War I, and scientific inventions galore.

Keywords: Balloonists; Mexican Revolution; World's Fair

Rushforth, Peter.

Pinkerton's Sister. **MacAdam/Cage, 2005. 729pp. Hardbound, 1931561990.**

In a turn-of-the-century New York townhouse, Alice Pinkerton, a thirty-five-year-old spinster thought by her neighbors to be the classic "madwoman in the attic" (an appellation she abhors), creates a rich inner life for herself through books. The characters found in classic works of fiction become closer to her than the people she encounters in her own life. In stream-of-consciousness style, Alice revisits her childhood memories and views them through the window of literature. Rushforth's *A New Language*, in the previous section, is a prequel of sorts.

Keywords: Books; New York; Spinsters

Sharratt, Mary.

🌶 *The Real Minerva.* **Houghton Mifflin, 2004. 259pp. Hardbound, 0618462325.** 📖

In 1923 Minerva, Minnesota, is a small town where conservative sentiment prevails. Fifteen-year-old Penny Niebeck, embarrassed by her mother, Barbara's, affair with her married boss, runs away from home to become the "hired girl" of Cora Viney. Cora, a former Chicago socialite who lives on a farm, scandalizes the town by wearing men's clothes and raising her baby daughter alone. Penny, Cora, and Barbara all rise up from their confining circumstances, struggling to reinvent themselves whatever the cost. WILLA Award.

Keywords: Farmers; Minnesota; Mothers and daughters

Steinke, René.

Holy Skirts. **Morrow, 2005. 360pp. Hardbound, 0688176941.** ✍

Baroness Elsa von Freytag-Loringhoven was an iconoclast at a time and place already known for its flamboyance, Greenwich Village circa 1917. Uninhibited from a young age, Elsa leaves her staid German home for Berlin in 1904, becoming the star in a burlesque show. Over the next decade and more she flaunts herself across

Europe, becoming involved with numerous men, including her third husband, a German baron. But her flame burns brightest in prewar New York City, where she becomes a performance artist and Dadaist poet, a bohemian among bohemians.

Keywords: Artists, women; Freytag-Loringhoven, Elsa von (historical character); Germany; New York; Poets

Zimpel, Lloyd.

A Season of Fire and Ice. **Unbridled, 2006. 225pp. Hardbound, 1932961194.**
Farmer Gerhardt Praeger bravely endures the harsh conditions of homesteading the Dakota Territory in the 1880s, believing that he, his wife, and their seven sons will survive the natural disasters and bad weather that have forced so many of their fellow settlers back east. He records events from their day-to-day life in his personal journal. However, he can't help feeling envious of his bachelor neighbor, Leo Beiderman, who seems to suffer little or no misfortune. Tensions rise between them, leading their small community toward an inevitable showdown.

Keywords: Diaries and journals; Farmers; Frontier and pioneer life; Neighbors; North Dakota

World War I

Barrett, Andrea.

The Air We Breathe. **Norton, 2007. 296pp. Hardbound, 9780393061086.**
In the fall of 1916, as Americans debate whether or not to enter World War I, wartime sentiments haven't yet penetrated Tamarack Lake, a remote town in the Adirondacks where tubercular patients travel to be healed—in the public sanatorium, or, if they have money, in private "cure cottages." Gossip is the local pastime, but when rich patient Miles Fairchild initiates a discussion group among the residents, emotions run high, and anti-immigrant sentiments make themselves felt.

Keywords: Gossip; New York; Prejudice; Sanitariums

Lowenthal, Michael.

Charity Girl. **Houghton Mifflin, 2007. 323pp. Hardbound, 9780618546299.**
It's a comparatively little known fact that during World War I, young women who contracted STDs were rounded up and imprisoned in detention camps in the hopes of keeping America's soldiers safe. Frieda Mintz, a seventeen-year-old Boston department store clerk in 1918, has a brief romance with an army private, who names her as the source for his syphilitic infection. When her own condition flares up, Frieda is fired and sent to a detention camp, where she befriends her fellow "inmates" and undergoes harsh medical treatments.

Keywords: Detention camps; Massachusetts; Syphilis

Seebohm, Caroline.

The Innocents. **Algonquin, 2007. 288pp. Hardbound, 9781565125001.** 🟥

Dorothea and Iris Crosby, beautiful, nineteen-year-old, identical twins, enjoy a privileged lifestyle in New York City in 1911. The suffering of one of their maids, who loses friends and family in the horrific Triangle Shirtwaist Factory fire, motivates the girls to leave their social pursuits and help the victims. When America enters World War I they sign up immediately as Red Cross nurses, gaining a new perspective on life and loss while tending to wounded and dying French soldiers.

Keywords: Coming of age; France; New York; Nurses; Twins

World War II

Baker, Kevin.

Strivers Row. **HarperCollins, 2006. 547pp. Hardbound, 0060195835.** ✍ 📖 🟥

In the final novel of his loose trilogy about the multicultural history of New York City's streets (also including *Dreamland* and *Paradise Alley*), Baker fictionalizes the early years of civil rights leader Malcolm X. In 1943, while the war rages overseas, a mood of restlessness and despair occupies Harlem's black citizens, and the region threatens to erupt in violence. When Jonah Dove, a resident of the upper-class black neighborhood of Strivers Row who can easily pass for white, is rescued from a brawl by Malcolm Little, a street hustler originally from Michigan, it changes both men's lives.

Keywords: African Americans; Harlem; Malcolm X (historical character); New York

McNamer, Deirdre.

Red Rover. **Viking, 2007. 224pp. Hardbound, 9780670063505.** 📖

As boys, Neil and Aidan Tierney enjoyed riding across the plains of Montana on horseback together. When World War II breaks out, they separate, Aidan joining the FBI and serving in Argentina, while Neil signs on as a bomber pilot alongside his friend, Roland Taliaferro. By 1946 Aidan is back home, suffering from a mysterious disease; Neil suspects a government cover-up when Aidan dies, an apparent suicide. When an elderly Roland meets up with Neil in 2003, he tells Aidan's brother the truth about what happened.

Keywords: Brothers; Montana; Pilots

Paul, Caroline.

East Wind, Rain. **Morrow, 2006. 260pp. Hardbound, 0060780754.** 📖 🟥

"East wind, rain": to Japanese listeners, mention of these code words in a weather-related radio broadcast meant war with the United States. In December 1941 the residents on the Hawaiian island of Niihau enjoy an isolated, peaceful existence thanks to the island's religious owner, Mr. Robinson. When a Japanese plane crash-lands there in December 1941, Irene and Yoshio Harada, Niihau's only Japanese American residents, face a difficult dilemma. Only they know that the presence of the plane's injured pilot, fresh from the attack on Pearl Harbor, indicates the world is now at war.

Keywords: Hawaii; Japanese Americans; Pearl Harbor

Redel, Victoria.

The Border of Truth. **Counterpoint, 2007. 336pp. Hardbound, 9781582433660.**
During the summer of 2003 Manhattan academic Sara Leader fills out paperwork to complete an international adoption and realizes she knows little about her elderly father's past. As Sara progresses with her research, a parallel narrative reveals the Holocaust story of her father, Richard, who was born Itzak Lejdel, and who arrived in America on a refugee ship from Brussels in 1940. When the *Quanza* is refused permission to dock in Virginia, Itzak writes pleading letters to First Lady Eleanor Roosevelt, speaking in humorous tones of his love for American culture and, more movingly, of his fears of being sent back to Nazi Europe.

Keywords: Fathers and daughters; Holocaust; Jews; Letters; Multi-period novels

Canada, Greenland, and the Arctic

Although Canada and other northern settings don't figure prominently in other subgenres of historical fiction, they proliferate in the literary arena. Many of these books evoke the adventurous spirit of early explorers and the haunting atmosphere of the Canadian Arctic.

Adamson, Gil.

The Outlander. **Ecco, 2008. 400pp. Hardbound, 9780061491252.**
Mary Boulton, a nineteen-year-old widow, flees into the unfamiliar territory of the Canadian high plains and Rocky Mountains in 1903 after shooting her husband to death. Distraught after the loss of her child, frightened of her husband's two brothers—who she knows are close behind—Mary takes refuge in the recesses of her mind, reflecting on her unhappy marriage and her current state as she charts a path through the wilderness. Mary encounters a multitude of eccentric characters en route, and tension builds throughout, for she and readers both know that a final showdown is inevitable.

Keywords: Canadian West—20th century; Mountains; Murderers; Runaways; Widows; Wilderness

Boyden, Joseph.

Three Day Road. **Viking, 2005. 354pp. Hardbound, 0670034312.**
Annotated under "Europe: Twentieth Century: World War I."

Brown, Peter.

The Fugitive Wife. **Norton, 2006. 412pp. Hardbound, 0393061108.**
In 1900 Esther Crummey, a farm girl from the Midwest, escapes her volatile husband and the recent death of their son by signing on as a horse-handler for the Cape Nome Company, a group of prospectors heading to Alaska with the image of gold in their eyes. Nate Deacon, the

company's East Coast–trained visionary of a foreman, attracts her, but she knows well that her possessive husband, Leonard, will soon be on their trail.

Keywords: Abusive relationships; Alaska—20th century; Gold mining; Gold Rush

Harding, Georgina.

The Solitude of Thomas Cave. **Bloomsbury USA, 2007. 256pp. Hardbound, 9781596912724.** 📖

From the beginning, readers know whaler Thomas Cave will survive the brutal winter he spends alone on the barren island of Greenland in 1616, the result of a bet with his fellow shipmates. As Cave establishes himself in this inhospitable environment, he writes in his journal, reflecting on people and moments from his past, particularly his Danish wife, Johanne, who died in childbirth. As he comes to terms with his grief, he becomes a more spiritually aware person.

Keywords: Diaries and journals; Greenland—17th century; Sailors

Heighton, Steven.

Afterlands. **Houghton Mifflin, 2006. 406pp. Hardbound, 0618139346.** ✍ 📖 **YA**

While on an expedition to the North Pole in 1871, the twenty-five-member crew of the U.S. tugboat *Polaris* found themselves trapped in ice off the Greenland coast for months. Even worse, the group was separated, with six aboard ship and the remaining nineteen (a multinational group including Germans, Inuits, Americans, and Danes) on an ice floe. In detailing their survival experience and the aftermath, Heighton bases his moving story partly on the memoirs of Lt. George Tyson, one of the survivors.

Keywords: Arctic—19th century; Explorers; Shipwrecks; Tyson, George (historical character)

Johnston, Wayne.

The Custodian of Paradise. **Norton, 2007. 510pp. Hardbound, 9780393064919.** 📖

In this novel, more of a companion than a sequel or prequel to Johnston's earlier *The Colony of Unrequited Dreams* (2000), Sheilagh Fielding, the fictional muse and soul mate of Joey Smallwood, takes center stage. In fact, Joey is merely a side note in the life of this strong, gifted, Amazon of a woman (she stands six foot three) who, after a lonely childhood in early twentieth-century Newfoundland, gives birth to twins at age sixteen, leaves them to be raised by her mother in New York City, and returns home to become an eccentric journalist. Late in life a mysterious man called "the Provider" reveals to her the secrets hidden in her family.

Keywords: Newfoundland—20th century

Lindbergh, Judith.

The Thrall's Tale. **Viking, 2006. 450pp. Hardbound, 0670034649.** 📖

The lives of three women intertwine in bleak, pagan Greenland beginning in AD 985. Katla, the beautiful Christian slave of an Icelander named Einar, attracts the unwanted attention of Einar's son, Torvald, and gives birth to his daughter after a brutal rape. Katla despises her daughter, Bibrau, but Thorbjorg, a seeress who cares for both of them, takes Bibrau as an apprentice, teaching her about Norse mysticism. When Christianity plants a firmer foot in Greenland, it changes the women's relationships with their faith and one another irrevocably.

Keywords: Greenland—10th century; Rape; Slaves and slavery

McKay, Ami.

The Birth House. **Morrow, 2006. 385pp. Hardbound, 0061135852.** 📖 **YA**

Dora Rare, the only daughter in a long line of Rares inhabiting Nova Scotia's Scots Bay community, becomes the apprentice of Miss Babineau, an outspoken Acadian midwife, during the World War I years. When Dr. Gilbert Thomas, a self-proclaimed expert in painless childbirth, comes to town set on exposing the dangers of midwifery, Dora and her mentor strive to protect the sanctity of women's long-held birthing traditions.

Keywords: Midwives; Nova Scotia—World War I

Redhill, Michael.

Consolation. **Little, Brown, 2006. 340pp. Hardbound, 0316734985.** 📖 **YA**

Before his death Toronto historian David Hollis discovered potential evidence of the earliest known photographs of the city, dating from 150 years earlier. Research led him to believe the negatives were aboard a ship that sank in Toronto's harbor, with the wreck currently buried beneath a local landfill. In an attempt to vindicate her late husband, his widow, Marianne, searches for more information on the photographer, Jem Hallam. In a twin narrative set in the 1850s, Hallam, a British apothecary, immigrates to Canada. Having left his family behind, he copes with his loneliness and the prospect of starting over in a new, frontier city. The two stories connect in an unexpected fashion.

Keywords: Apothecaries; Cities; Historians; Immigrants, British; Multi-period novels; Ontario—19th century; Photographers; Widows

Simonds, Merilyn.

The Holding. **Norton, 2004. 312pp. Hardbound, 0393060616.**

In 1859 Margaret MacBayne emigrates from Scotland with her family to northern Canada in search of a better life but discovers that the harsh lifestyle, eking out a living in the wilderness, is hardly an improvement on what she left. Through illness and death, Margaret and her three elder brothers are left to themselves, and Margaret takes pride in self-sufficiency and growing her herb garden when her brothers leave for logging jobs. A century later Alyson Thomson, a young woman living on the MacBayne farm with her fiancé, Walker, discovers Margaret's diary, which recounts a cryptic story of abandonment, grief, and revenge.

Keywords: Diaries and journals; Frontier and pioneer life; Immigrants, Scottish; Multi-period novels; Ontario—19th century; Wilderness

Urquhart, Jane.

A Map of Glass. MacAdam/Cage, 2006. 371pp. Hardbound, 1596921706. 📖

In the present day Sylvia Bradley, a reclusive fiftyish woman, travels to Toronto to meet Jerome McNaughton, the artist who had discovered the body of her lover, Andrew Woodman, frozen in ice on Timber Island in Lake Ontario a year earlier. Andrew had suffered from early onset of Alzheimer's. As Sylvia makes peace with the past, Urquhart also details, in a separate section, the story of Andrew's colorful ancestors, lumber barons on Timber Island a hundred years earlier.

Keywords: Alzheimer's disease; Artists; Families; Multi-period novels; Ontario—19th century

Latin America and the Caribbean

These novels analyze the turbulent political environments of Latin American and South American countries, primarily in the nineteenth century, and how leaders' policies affected the native populace. Many of the authors relate these historical events to today's political situation.

Allende, Isabel.

Inés of My Soul. HarperCollins, 2006. 321pp. Hardbound, 0061161535. ✍ 📖

With considerable pride and spirit, Inés Suárez recounts her life story from the viewpoint of old age in the year 1580. Her story begins in 1526, in Spain, where she meets her first husband, an adventurer named Juan who leaves her behind while he journeys to South America. After following him to Peru, she learns of his recent death and subsequently meets the love of her life, conquistador Pedro de Valdivia, who left his fragile wife behind in Spain. Together Pedro and Inés, his official mistress, endure considerable hardship—the hot South American climate, the hostility of the native Indian tribes—to build Chile's capital city, Santiago.

Keywords: Chile—16th century; de Valdivia, Pedro (historical character); Explorers, women; Extramarital affairs; Peru—16th century; Suárez, Inés (historical character)

Portrait in Sepia. HarperCollins, 2001. 300pp. Hardbound, 0066211611.

Annotated this chapter, under "The United States: Early United States."

Alvarez, Julia.

Saving the World. Algonquin, 2007. 368pp. Hardbound, 156512510X. ✍ 📖

In narratives separated by two centuries, Alvarez explores the theme of the self-lessness and politicization of humanitarian efforts past and present. Alma Huebner, a best-selling Latina novelist suffering from writers' block, languishes in Vermont while her husband, Richard, travels to the Dominican Republic on a mission to help cure AIDS. As she explores the history surrounding one of her characters, Isabel Sendales y Gómez—a woman who traveled from Spain to the New World on a mission to eradicate smallpox—Alma discovers new purpose in living.

Keywords: AIDS; Dominican Republic—19th century; Physicians; Sendales y Gómez, Isabel (historical character); Multi-period novels; Smallpox; Vermont

Anderson, Paul.

Hunger's Brides. Carroll & Graf, 2004. 1358pp. Hardbound, 0786715413. ✍

Born in 1648, Juana was a child prodigy and brilliant scholar who became a favorite at the royal court of Mexico City. At age nineteen she withdrew to a convent, continuing her compositions and theological arguments there, but puzzling her contemporaries by signing a vow of silence in her own blood at age forty. Her story is framed by a modern tale of a college professor who leaves the apartment of his dying lover, a former student who was obsessed with Sor Juana's story. It takes a strong person to pick up Anderson's epic novel about Baroque-era Mexican nun Sor Juana de la Cruz, simply because it weighs nearly five pounds. An abbreviated version of Anderson's debut, *Sor Juana or the Breath of Heaven*, distills the original down to a mere 752 pages.

Keywords: de la Cruz, Sor Juana (historical character); Mexico—17th century; Multi-period novels; Nuns; Poets, women

Arana, Marie.

Cellophane. Dial, 2006. 367pp. Hardbound, 0385336640. 📖

Don Victor Sobrevilla Paniagua, an engineer, moves his wife and large family from Lima to the heart of the Peruvian rainforest in the 1940s to found a paper factory. Things move along swimmingly there and at the family hacienda, named Floralinda, until Victor discovers the formula for cellophane. This act of creation functions as a sort of truth serum, forcing him and all of his family members to confess past sins and reveal their most private, intimate thoughts aloud.

Keywords: Cellophane; Engineers; Families; Magical realism; Peru—20th century

Cezair-Thompson, Margaret.

🌿 *The Pirate's Daughter.* Unbridled, 2007. 392pp. Hardbound, 9781932961409. 📖

In 1946 a boat carrying Hollywood film star Errol Flynn is almost shipwrecked off the Jamaican coast. Life changes for many on this West Indian island after that, including for Ida Joseph, who has an affair with the swashbuckling screen legend when she's a senior in high school. Flynn never takes responsibility for his and Ida's daughter, May, a mixed-race child who never really feels at home in her seaside village and spends a fair amount of time trying to find herself. Essence Magazine Literary Award.

Keywords: Flynn, Errol (historical character); Illegitimate children; Jamaica—20th century; Mixed heritage

Esquivel, Laura.

Malinche. Atria, 2006. 191pp. Hardbound, 074329033X. ✍ 📖 **YA**

Esquivel casts a sympathetic light on Malinalli, mistress and interpreter to Cortés, describing her as a linguistically gifted young woman with deep knowledge of her culture's traditions and spirituality. She honestly believes that Cortés is the reincarnation of the Aztec god Quetzalcoatl and falls in love with him despite herself. Soon enough, however, she realizes that Cortés doesn't have her people's interests at heart at all.

Keywords: Aztec Indians; Conquistadors; Cortés, Hernán (historical character); Explorers; Malinali (historical character); Mexico—16th century

Farley, Christopher John.

Kingston by Starlight. **Three Rivers, 2005. 330pp. Paper, 1400082455.** ✍

Farley (a senior editor at *Time* magazine) chooses cross-dressing, eighteenth-century pirate Anne Bonny as the subject for his poetic historical adventure. Anne narrates her story beginning with her comfortable childhood in rural Ireland. Her father's gambling debts push the family on to South Carolina, where her mother dies. Anne, abandoned by her father, sets sail for the Bahamas, where she disguises herself as a young man named Bonn. Calico Jack Rackham, pirate ship captain, and an intriguing swordfighter named Read add excitement to her life.

Keywords: Bonny, Anne (historical character); Caribbean—18th century; Ireland—18th century; Pirates, women

Gonzalez, Béa.

The Mapmaker's Opera. **Thomas Dunne, 2007. 288pp. Hardbound, 9780312364663.**

Diego Clemente, a young man obsessed with maps and ornithology, moves from Seville to the Yucatán in 1910 to help compile a guide to Mexican birds. Against the backdrop of the Mexican Revolution, Diego falls in love with Sophia Duarte, an exuberant artist and bird enthusiast, and together they strive to save the last two passenger pigeons in captivity. Gonzalez's novel itself takes the form of an opera, with characters and their singing roles listed as "dramatis personae" and the chapters fitting neatly into scenes and acts.

Keywords: Artists; Birds; Cartographers; Mexico—20th century

King, Rachael.

The Sound of Butterflies. **Morrow, 2007. 352pp. Hardbound, 9780061357640.** 📖

Thomas Edgar, an amateur butterfly collector, leaves his wife, Sophie, behind in England when he travels to the Brazilian rainforest in search of specimens in 1904. Months later he returns home a broken man, unable to speak of what happened. As Sophie searches for answers to her husband's condition, she reads his diaries, which reveal information on unspeakable acts that he witnessed, as well as hidden truths about their marriage.

Keywords: Brazil—20th century; Butterflies; Diaries and journals; England—20th century; Married life

Sherwood, Frances.

Night of Sorrows. **Norton, 2006. 425pp. Hardbound, 0393058255.** ✍ 📖

> Sherwood lets readers see the Spanish conquest of Mexico from the viewpoint of both sides, portraying both invader and native as savage, violent, and exotic. Hernán Cortés, an ambitious, bloodthirsty adventurer, arrives in Mexico in 1519 with a group of conquistadors hungry for gold and glory. While he plays the native Aztecs and Mayans against one another in his attempt to conquer them and their lands for Spain, the Aztec princess named Malintzin, his translator and mistress, grows strangely attached to him.
>
> **Keywords:** Aztec Indians; Conquistadors; Cortés, Hernán (historical character); Explorers; Malinali (historical character); Mayan Indians; Mexico—16th century

Urrea, Luis Alberto.

❦ *The Hummingbird's Daughter.* **Little, Brown, 2005. 499pp. Hardbound, 0316745464.** ✍ 📖

> Urrea bases his novel on historical fact and family legend surrounding a distant cousin, Teresita Urrea, known as the "patron saint of Cabora," born the illegitimate daughter of a wealthy Mexican rancher and a Yaqui woman in 1873. Though raised in poverty, Teresita is educated well and develops a strong affinity for folk healing. Proclaimed as a local saint, particularly after she comes back from near death after a horrible beating, Teresita attracts both spiritual pilgrims and political revolutionaries wanting to use her to further their cause. ALA Notable Book.
>
> **Keywords:** Healers; Mexico—19th century; Magical realism; Mixed heritage; Urrea, Teresa (historical character); Yaqui Indians

The Middle East

Literary novels with Middle Eastern settings incorporate the themes of religious conflict, colonialism, and women's personal and sexual liberation.

Mossanen, Dora Levy.

Courtesan. **Touchstone, 2005. 290pp. Paper, 0743246780.** 📖

> Simone, a young woman in late nineteenth-century Paris, decides to marry for love rather than follow in the footsteps of her grandmother, Madame Gabrielle, and her mother, Françoise, both of whom were renowned courtesans. She falls in love with Cyrus, the Shah's Persian jeweler, and moves with him to his homeland, plunging her into the world of Persian Jews and the mysterious diamond trade. Flashbacks to earlier eras provide additional insight into the lives of Simone's forebears.
>
> **Keywords:** Courtesans; Jews; Multi-period novels; Persia—19th century

9

10

11

12

13

14

15

Phillips, Arthur.

The Egyptologist. **Random House, 2004. 394pp. Hardbound, 1400062500.**

It is 1922, and Oxford-educated Egyptologist Ralph Trilipush is obsessed with locating the tomb of a purported (but likely fake) pharaoh, Atum-hadu, whose pornographic verses he has managed to translate from the original hieroglyphics. He convinces his rich fiancée's father to fund his venture, for Howard Carter has recently discovered Tutankhamen's tomb, and Trilipush is jealous of his rival's success. His story is told through journal entries, cablegrams, and the like. Three decades later an Australian private detective, Harold Ferrell, tracks Trilipush's movements around the world, hoping to prove that he's a murderer. A multi-layered, complex story with numerous twists and turns and at least one unreliable narrator.

Keywords: Egypt—20th century; Egyptologists; Pharaohs

Roiphe, Anne.

An Imperfect Lens. **Shaye Areheart, 2006. 296pp. Hardbound, 1400082110.**

Cholera arrives in Alexandria, Egypt, in the 1880s, decimating the multicultural population. Louis Thullier, a protégé of Pasteur, arrives there as part of a mission to eradicate the deadly disease and bring glory to France in the process. He falls in love with Este Malina, the daughter of a Jewish family long resident in the city, who becomes a lab assistant for his research team. Although their mutual search for a cure draws them closer to one another, political intrigue and religious differences threaten to divide them.

Keywords: Cholera; Egypt—19th century; Jews

Asia, Africa, and the Antipodes

Many literary writers choose to set their novels in historical Asia, Africa, Australia, or the Pacific Islands. British, Dutch, and French imperialism was in full force during the nineteenth century, and common topics include colonialism's effects on distant countries' native peoples. Modernization in general is another theme. When Western visitors pay visits to faraway locales with the goal of exploration or settlement, change inevitably follows. Readers of exotic adventure (Chapter 8) may enjoy these novels.

Africa

Christianse, Yvette.

Unconfessed. **Other, 2006. 347pp. Hardbound, 1590512405.** ✍ 📖

Based on a historical figure the author discovered in South African court records dating from the 1820s, Sila van den Kaap is a slave who tells her story from Robben Island off Cape Town, where she's been imprisoned and sentenced to hard labor for killing her son, Baro. She writes her confession to Baro using stream-of-consciousness style, from her childhood in Mozambique through her time as a slave to Dutch settlers, where one owner's promise to free her in his will was contradicted by his son after his death.

Keywords: Murderers; Prisoners; Slaves and slavery; South Africa—19th century; van den Kaap, Sila (historical character)

Gurnah, Abdulrazak.

Desertion. **Pantheon, 2005. 262pp. Hardbound, 0375423540.**

In 1899 in Mombasa (in what is now Kenya) an English Orientalist, Martin Pearce, falls in love with Rehana, the beautiful sister of the Muslim man who rescues him from the dry East African desert. Five decades later, during Zanzibar's fight for independence from Britain, Jamila, Rehana's granddaughter, has a forbidden affair with a young man named Amin. Amin's brother Rashid, who travels to England for an education, narrates their story as he pieces together the history of Rehana and Martin.

Keywords: Families; Interracial romance; Kenya—19th century; Multi-period novels; Muslims; Zanzibar—20th century

Sleigh, Dan.

Islands. **Harcourt, 2004. 758pp. Hardbound, 015101115X.**

In this epic novel Sleigh captures the context and spirit of Dutch colonialism in South Africa during the second half of the seventeenth century. Over a fifty-year period, seven different men recount their experiences, speaking of the hardships they faced during settlement and their uneasy (and often cruel and violent) relationships with the native tribes, showing how South Africa's history of apartheid began with the country's founders. All of their tales center on Pieternella, the half-Dutch daughter of a Hottentot woman, who comes to symbolize the country's complex social and racial heritage.

Keywords: Colonialism; Racial conflict; South Africa—17th century

Australia, New Zealand, and the Pacific Islands

Ciment, Jill.

The Tattoo Artist. **Pantheon, 2005. 207pp. Hardbound, 0375423257.**

Sara and Philip Ehrenreich, a surrealist artist and an anarchist, are the ultimate bohemian power couple of the 1920s Greenwich Village art scene. In search of adventure in the wake of World War II, they voyage to the South Pacific to collect native masks. On the South Seas island of Ta'un'uu they are blamed for a local disaster and have their faces forcibly tattooed as punishment. Stranded on the island for thirty years, Sara becomes a noted tattoo artist, a fact only discovered by the outside world when *Life* magazines comes calling.

Keywords: Artists; Castaways; Islands; Oceania—20th century; Tattoos

Grenville, Kate.

🏵 *The Secret River.* **Canongate, 2005. 334pp. Hardbound, 1841957976.** 📖

William Thornhill suffers the punishment experienced by many other minor criminals in London in 1806: rather than being sentenced to death, his sentence is commuted to transportation to New South Wales. He, his pregnant wife, and their many children survive the arduous journey, and over time William gains his freedom, becoming a landowner along the Hawkesbury River, where Australia's native Aborigines have already settled. The violent culture clash that ensues should surprise no one. Based on the history of Grenville's ancestors, pioneers in New South Wales. ALA Notable Book; Commonwealth Writers' Prize.

Keywords: Aborigines; Australia—19th century; Colonialism; Frontier and pioneer life; Prisoners; Racial conflict

Restrepo, Laura.

Isle of Passion. **Ecco, 2005. 294pp. Hardbound, 0060088982.** ✍

In 1908 Clipperton Island, a remote South Pacific atoll called the "isle of passion" by Magellan centuries earlier, belonged to Mexico. Ramón Arnaud, a Mexican army captain, arrives there with his bride, Alicia, and other soldiers and their families, with a mission of securing the island's sovereignty against France. The group thrives for a time, but before long political events back home—the Mexican Revolution and World War I—leave them stranded and forgotten, leading to a classic *Lord of the Flies*–type scenario.

Keywords: Arnaud, Ramón (historical character); Clipperton Island; Oceania—20th century

Tiffany, Carrie.

Everyman's Rules for Scientific Living. **Scribner, 2006. 224pp. Hardbound, 0743286375.** 📖 **YA**

In the countryside of 1930s Australia, the Better Farming Train travels from town to town, bringing along experts to educate rural citizens in agricultural and domestic improvement. Jean Finnegan, the convoy's seamstress, falls in love with the agricultural expert/soil scientist, Robert Pettergree. They settle down on a farm, hoping to test their theories with the scientific method, but Jean soon finds that Robert's unfailing methodology, the Rules for Scientific Living, extends to their marriage as well.

Keywords: Australia—20th century; Farmers; Married life; Seamstresses

China and Hong Kong

Bock, Dennis.

The Communist's Daughter. **Knopf, 2007. 287pp. Hardbound, 9781400044627.** ✍ 📖

Bock reimagines the life and motivations of Norman Bethune, a historical battlefield surgeon from Canada. He writes his memoirs, an apology of sorts, for the illegitimate (and fictional) daughter he never met. Rebelling against religion and capitalism, he becomes a Communist as an adult. During the 1930s he selflessly dedicates himself to saving lives on the battlefield during the Spanish Civil War and in China, in the service of Chairman Mao.

Keywords: Bethune, Norman (historical character); Communism; Illegitimate children; Physicians; Spanish Civil War; Sino–Japanese War

Epstein, Jennifer Cody.

The Painter from Shanghai. **Norton, 2008. 414pp. Hardbound, 9780393065282.**

Pan Yuliang (1899–1977), a daring post-Impressionist painter from Shanghai, comes to life in Epstein's debut. Pan overcomes childhood misfortune: born in 1895 with the name Xiuqing, her uncle sells her to a brothel to pay for his opium addiction. She reinvents herself as an artist in prewar Shanghai, with the help of her lover (later her husband), a Republican official. She pursues her passion for painting wherever it takes her: to 1920s Paris, with its heady bohemian atmosphere, and later back to Shanghai, where her nude self-portraits create controversy.

Keywords: Artists, women; China; France; Pan, Yuliang (historical character)

McCunn, Ruthanne Lum.

God of Luck. **Soho, 2007. 239pp. Hardbound, 9781569474662.**

McCunn illuminates a little-known episode of Chinese history: its participation in the cruel slave trade of the nineteenth century, in which Chinese men were kidnapped from their homes and shipped to Peru as slaves in that country's guano mines. Ah Lung is one of these unfortunate laborers, forced to toil in an industry whose victims survive no more than a few years. Back home in China his much-loved wife, Bo See, remains faithful, stopping at nothing to get her husband back.

Keywords: Immigrants, Chinese; Kidnapping; Mines and mining; Peru—19th century; Slaves and slavery

Min, Anchee.

Empress Orchid Series. **YA**

A two-volume series of biographical novels about the last empress of China, recounted in the first person. As in her earlier *Becoming Madame Mao*, Min depicts her subject, a much-reviled woman from early twentieth-century Chinese history, sympathetically and convincingly.

Keywords: China—19th century; Concubines; Empresses; Tzu Hsi, Empress of China (historical character)

Empress Orchid. **Houghton Mifflin, 2004. 336pp. Hardbound, 0618068872.**

Tzu Hsi, better known as Orchid, enters China's Forbidden City as a minor concubine to the emperor in 1852. In this insular environment ritual is everything, and thousands of hopeful women vie for his attention. She sets out to seduce him and succeeds, falling in love and bearing him a much-needed heir. Orchid becomes empress at her husband's death, fighting off calls for her ouster and holding the troubled country together almost single-handedly.

The Last Empress. **Houghton Mifflin, 2007. 308pp. Hardbound, 9780618531462.**

Min continues Orchid's story over the next fifty years, through her death in 1908. She narrates the tale of her raising her son, Tung Chih, to be a good ruler, a project that fails when he dies of syphilis at a young age. Her hopes in her nephew aren't any more successful, forcing her to assume a primary role in political decision making for her country. She emerges as a strong, indomitable woman, capable of leading China through a tumultuous era that saw the Boxer Rebellion and conflicts with numerous European countries as well as Japan.

Reuss, Frederick.

Mohr. **Unbridled, 2006. 309pp. Hardbound, 1932961178.** ✍

In his effort to understand why German Jewish playwright and physician Max Mohr left behind his beloved wife, Käthe, and daughter, Eva, in 1930s Germany when he immigrated to Shanghai, Reuss has created a documentary novel that mixes fact (in the form of sepia-toned photographs and actual letters between the couple) and fiction. While Mohr uses his medical training to tend to the victims of China's war with Japan, Käthe copes without him back home, taking comfort in their love for one another.

Keywords: China—20th century; Germany—20th century; Married life; Mohr, Max (historical character); Physicians

See, Lisa,

Peony in Love. **Random House, 2007. 284pp. Hardbound, 9781400064663.** 📖 **YA**

The Peony Pavilion, an epic opera dating from 1598, captures the hearts of three unmarried, romantic-minded women of the seventeenth century. While watching the opera from behind a screen on her birthday, sixteen-year-old Peony defies her family by falling in love with an irresistibly handsome young man invited there by her parents. Knowing that she's already promised in marriage and cannot marry him, she dies of longing without realizing that the one she loves is Wu Ren, her own betrothed. Peony then becomes a "hungry ghost," unable to reach the afterlife, and remains ever-present in the lives of Ren and his new wife, Tan Ze,

Keywords: China—17th century; Ghosts; Opera

Snow Flower and the Secret Fan. **Random House, 2005. 258pp. Hardbound, 1400060281.** ★ 📖 **YA**

See's novel, a surprise best seller and a book club favorite, evokes the strong bonds of friendship between women in nineteenth-century rural China. In an era when women endured painful foot-binding rituals, they also developed a secret written language, *nu shu*, to communicate with one another. Aged eighty, Lily reminisces about her youth, or "daughter days," when in the 1830s she formed an intimate friendship (a *laotong*, or sworn sisterhood) with Snow Flower, a girl from a larger town. Over time, as they marry and grow apart through distance, a misunderstanding threatens to break their lifelong bond.

Keywords: China—19th century; Friendship

Shan, Sa.

Empress. **HarperCollins, 2006. 319pp. Hardbound, 0060817585.** ✍ 📖 **YA**

Shan Sa, a native of Beijing who moved to France at the age of nineteen, takes on the persona of Empress Wu, China's first and only female emperor, who ruled during the Tang Dynasty in the seventh century. Given the name Heavenlight, she at first disappoints her family by being a girl, but they are thrilled when, at age twelve, she becomes one of the emperor's 10,000 concubines. Through her intelligence, wit, and political acumen, she attracts the attention of the imperial heir; after his death she rules in his stead. Known as a ruthless monarch, although she achieves all she once desired, she becomes a prisoner of her own power.

Keywords: China—7th century; Concubines; Empresses; Wu Hou, Empress of China (historical character)

Wagenstein, Angel.

Farewell, Shanghai. **Handsel, 2007. 382pp. Hardbound, 9781590512548.** 📖

By the late 1930s Jews were fleeing Nazi Germany in droves, but countries had difficulty coping with the sudden influx of refugees. For Elisabeth and Theodore Weissberg, two famous musicians, their only hope for escape is to leave their homeland for the Hongku ghetto of Shanghai, where they and thousands of other European Jews were forced to live. Hilda Braun, a German Jewish actress formerly of Paris, also calls Shanghai her new home, determined to continue her previously opulent lifestyle. Based on true events, Bulgarian novelist Wagenstein's tale moves from the personal to the epic as he illustrates the plight of refugees living under a Nazi regime not often heard about.

Keywords: China—World War II; Jews; Musicians; Refugees

Japan

Avery, Ellis.

The Teahouse Fire. **Riverhead, 2007. 391pp. Hardbound, 1594489300.** 📖

Nine-year-old orphan Aurelia Bernard arrives in Kyoto in 1866 with her uncle, a priest, on an unofficial Christian mission to the country. Fleeing when he becomes abusive, she takes refuge in the Baishian teahouse, and the tea master's adolescent daughter, Yukako, unofficially adopts her. Given a new name and obliged to learn a new language, Aurelia observes how the traditional Japanese tea ceremony, with Yukako's help, is forced to adapt to the ways of a newly modernized Japan. She also develops a crush on Yukako that persists through their years together. A literary family saga that spans thirty years of the early Meiji period.

Keywords: Families; Japan—19th century; Lesbians; Tea

Golden, Arthur.

Memoirs of a Geisha. **Knopf, 1997. 434pp. Hardbound, 0375400117.** ★ 📖

In 1929 nine-year-old Chiyo is taken from her home and sold into slavery at a geisha house. Her hair dressed, her make-up perfect, she is given a new name—Sayuri—and trained in the elegant arts of pleasing men. Her virginity is sold to the highest bidder, and her popularity and skill grow steadily, but she never gives up the image of a man who was kind to her as a child. After World War II begins and industry wins out over tradition, Sayuri must find a new path to forge in the world. What amazed critics and readers alike is how the author, a young male American from Boston, could have authentically captured the life of a Japanese woman.

Keywords: Geisha; Japan—20th century

Jedamus, Julith.

The Book of Loss. **St. Martin's, 2005. 295pp. Hardbound, 0297847732.**

In late tenth-century Kyoto, an unnamed lady in waiting to the Japanese empress vies with Izumi, a noted poetess and her fellow lady in waiting, for the affections of her lover, Kanesuke, who was exiled for seducing the emperor's favorite daughter. In her diary she recounts detailed court rituals, her feelings of jealousy, and her intense rivalry with Izumi, which becomes a political force that threatens the emperor's rule.

Keywords: Diaries and journals; Japan—10th century; Ladies in waiting; Love triangles; Poets, women

Schuyler, Nina.

The Painting. **Algonquin, 2004. 299pp. Hardbound, 1565124413.**

In Japan in 1869 Ayoshi, a beautiful young woman unhappy in her arranged marriage to a crippled man, pours out her passion for a former lover into a dreamy, romantic painting. Fearful that her husband will find it, Ayoshi wraps it around one of his ceramic vases before he ships it to a customer in Paris. Jorgen, a disabled Danish soldier working at a Parisian import shop, discovers the painting, and its haunting imagery distracts him from the injury he sustained in the Franco–Prussian War; it also prompts him to explore his feelings for the shop owner's sister, Natalia.

Keywords: Arranged marriages; France—early modern era; Japan—19th century; Paintings; Veterans

Korea

Drabble, Margaret.

The Red Queen. **Harcourt, 2004. 334pp. Hardbound, 0151011060.** ✍

This novel's first half comprises the memoirs of Hyegyong, Crown Princess of Korea in the eighteenth century, a time when women had little power of their own. Nonetheless, Hyegyong not only survives numerous political intrigues at the royal court but also her mad, possessed husband. Barbara Halliwell, a modern-day academic from Oxford, is given a copy of the centuries-old memoir just before her plane trip to Seoul. After her arrival, her adventures parallel those of the outspoken, intrepid crown princess.

Keywords: Hyegyong, Princess of Korea (historical figure); Korea—18th century; Multi-period novels; Princesses; Scholars

South Asia

Literary novels set in Ceylon (modern Sri Lanka), India, Pakistan, and Tibet.

Divakaruni, Chitra Banerjee.

The Palace of Illusions. **Doubleday, 2008. 277pp. Hardbound, 9780385515995**
Annotated previously in this chapter, under "Other Ancient Civilizations."

Kingman, Peg.

Not Yet Drown'd. **Norton, 2007. 428pp. Hardbound, 9780393065466.** YA
When Catherine MacDonald, a young Scottish widow, receives a mysterious parcel one afternoon in 1822, it sends her on an irresistible quest to the far side of the world. Sandy, her twin, was reportedly killed a year earlier in a monsoon flood, but a sheaf of traditional bagpipe music sent to Catherine, curiously retitled "Not Yet Drown'd," appears to be in his own handwriting. Accompanied by her engineer brother Hector, her stepdaughter Grace, a runaway American slave, and an enigmatic Hindu maid, Catherine leaves Edinburgh aboard a ship transporting Hector's revolutionary new steamship engine to India. Along the way she finds adventure aplenty, begins a new romance, and learns much about the company she keeps.

Keywords: Bagpipes; India—19th century; Scotland—Victorian era; Shipboard adventure; Tea; Twins; Widows

Mukherjee, Bharati.

The Tree Bride. **Theia, 2004. 293pp. Hardbound, 1401300588.**
Mukherjee, a chronicler of India's history from colonialism to the present, picks up the story of her narrator in *Desirable Daughters*, Tara Chatterjee, a Calcutta-born woman living in modern San Francisco and struggling to put her life back together after a bomb blast nearly ended it. She continues researching the life of her great-great-aunt, Tara Lata, who was married symbolically to a tree in 1879 Calcutta after her child-fiancé died. Tara Lata grows up to fight for Bengal's independence from Britain.

Keywords: Colonialism; Families; Immigrants, Indian; India—19th century; Multi-period novels; Revolutions and revolutionaries

Slaughter, Carolyn.

A Black Englishman. **Farrar, Straus & Giroux, 2004. 335pp. Hardbound, 0374113998.**
In 1920 Welsh-born Isabel Herbert arrives in India with her British army officer husband, Neville, a rather distant and uncaring fellow, and becomes enraptured by the country's beauty and customs. She also falls in

love with Samresh "Sam" Singh, a native Indian who is an Oxford-trained doctor. Their passionate love affair is thwarted at all turns—by society's disapproval, religious terrorist attacks, and Isabel's vengeful husband.

Keywords: Extramarital affairs; India—20th century; Interracial romance; Physicians

Shanghvi, Siddharth Dhanvant.

The Last Song of Dusk. **Arcade, 2004. 298pp. Hardbound, 1559707348.**

Magical realism meets postcolonial India in Shanghvi's debut, which centers on the marriage of two beautiful people who seem destined to lead a charmed life. In the 1920s Anuradha Patwardhan leaves Udaipur for Bombay to marry Vardhamaan Gandharva, a handsome physician. Their son, Mohan, grows up to be equally attractive, but the family's happiness soon turns to melancholy, a sentiment that not even the arrival of a mysterious orphan girl can lift.

Keywords: Arranged marriages; Families; India—20th century; Magical realism; Physicians

Southeast Asia

Includes historical novels set in Burma (modern Myanmar), Cambodia, Indonesia, Laos, Malaysia, the Philippines, Singapore, Thailand, and Vietnam. For additional novels, see the first volume of *Historical Fiction.*

Aw, Tash.

🏶 *The Harmony Silk Factory.* **Riverhead, 2005. 384pp. Hardbound, 157322300X.** 📖

The life of Johnny Lim, a Chinese peasant who became a successful silk merchant in 1940s British-ruled Malaya (modern Malaysia), unfolds from the very different viewpoints of three who knew him: his grown son, Jasper; his aristocratic wife, Snow, who reveals her thoughts through her diary; and his British friend, Peter Wormwood. Is Johnny a hero who saved his people during the Japanese invasion, or a crook who uses his textile store as a front for illegal activities? As each person reveals his or her take on Johnny's personality and actions, readers can gradually put together the greater picture, although much about his character remains hidden. Costa Book Award.

Keywords: Businessmen; Fathers and sons; Malaysia—20th century

Nguyen, Kien.

Le Colonial. **Little, Brown, 2004. 322pp. Hardbound, 0316285013.**

In 1773 three French missionaries—a bishop, a painter, and a teenaged runaway—travel to Annam (modern Vietnam) on an expedition financed by France's government. They expect to easily convert its people to Christianity, but in this land of heathen religion, famine, and civil war, they begin to feel their own faith tested, almost as if their God has failed them. Despite the violence prevalent throughout the land, Nguyen's prose is quite poetic, particularly when describing the picturesque Vietnamese landscape.

Keywords: Colonialism; Missionaries; Vietnam—18th century

Chapter 11

Christian Historical Fiction

Novels in the very popular subgenre of Christian historical fiction, as the name suggests, place historical or fictional characters in conflicts that reflect the Christian worldview of the authors. It's not too tongue-in-cheek to say that these authors preach to the converted, for their main audience is their fellow Christians—more often than not, Christian women. The authors share their own deeply held Christian beliefs via thoughtful stories about characters who strive to live a godly life in an imperfect world. As John Mort discusses in his thorough analysis, *Christian Fiction: A Guide to the Genre* (Libraries Unlimited, 2002), the major conflict in the novels must deal somehow with Christian principles. The characters struggle to understand God's message for them, since knowing this will guide them in major life decisions.

Christian historicals have the potential to offer readers one advantage over other historical fiction subgenres: they don't flinch from portraying the religious facets of life in earlier times—eras when, one might suggest, religion played a larger role in the average person's life than it does now. Although biblical novels form the foundation of Christian historical fiction, some authors choose settings in which Christianity was in crisis, such as the Roman Empire right after the Crucifixion. Other authors choose periods of general strife and hardship, such as rural America during the Great Depression, the frontier West in the mid-nineteenth century, or any period of wartime. The struggles the characters face during rough times draw them closer to God, and their faith helps pull them through.

Although many Christian novels are "gentle reads"—novels with no sexual content, and very little else of shock value—they don't necessarily stint on realism in the historical setting. Of course this depends on the era and type of novel. Within the last five years, more authors (such as Deeanne Gist, Ruth Axtell Morren, and Julie Klassen) have been pushing the boundaries of the genre with sexually experienced heroes and heroines; secondary characters who fall prey to temptation; and edgier, more sensual situations (though they draw the line at explicitness). This has contributed to the gradual mainstreaming of the subgenre.

Though Catholic historical novels exist, dealing mostly with saints' lives, this chapter emphasizes the Protestant experience, at least as far as the two branches of Christianity diverge. Christian fiction (which may be called inspirational fiction, especially on bookstore shelves) generally does the same. Frequent characters in Christian historicals include members of those cultural/religious groups persecuted throughout history: early Israelites forced to serve as slaves in Egypt, early Christians in ancient

Rome, Protestant believers during the European Reformation, slaves and abolitionists during the American Civil War, and finally the Jews during the Holocaust—as well as those Christians sympathetic to their plight.

Christian fiction is considered separately in the publishing world from "secular" trade fiction. Not only does it have its own trade associations, the CBA (Christian Booksellers' Association) and ECPA (Evangelical Christian Publishers Association), but the publishers also differ. Although some are book publishers first and foremost (e.g., Bethany House), others are only one part of a larger ministry organization. Some are imprints of a larger publishing firm (HarperCollins' Zondervan, Random House's WaterBrook). For the most part, Christian authors stay within the subgenre, though some started out as secular romance writers (e.g., Francine Rivers, Robin Lee Hatcher) before finding their current home in Christian fiction. The personal Christian journeys of many authors mentioned in this chapter are told in Diane Eble's biographical compendium *Behind the Stories* (Bethany House, 2002).

The subgenres of Christian historical fiction form a microcosm of the larger historical fiction genre. There are traditional historical novels, sagas, Western historical novels, romances, and even multi-period epics—each given its own chapter in this volume—written from a Christian viewpoint. Although no "literary" subgenre is provided here, readers looking for lyrical prose would do well to seek out some of Christian historical fiction's most elegant stylists, such as Lynn Austin, Tracy Groot, Jan Watson, Jane Kirkpatrick, and Liz Curtis Higgs. Because of the Christian fiction label, mainstream readers may give these and other such authors a pass, which would be their loss. As in the rest of this book, only those novels with significant historical content are included.

Likewise, trends currently popular with secular readers are reflected in this subgenre: strong women protagonists; drama at European royal courts; multi-period stories; and biographical novels about people familiar to a mainstream, not just religious, audience. For example, Nancy Moser's novels about Martha Washington (*Washington's Lady*), Jane Austen (*Just Jane*), and Nannerl Mozart (*Mozart's Sister*) are avidly read by many who don't normally seek out Christian fiction; Linda Chaikin's Silk House trilogy plays into current interest in sixteenth-century European royalty.

This chapter equates Christian fiction with evangelical fiction, as this is what most readers mean when they ask for "Christian fiction." However, others define the genre more broadly; for example, John Mort's guide surveys all types of fiction with Christian themes. Readers' advisors must determine the parameters of taste for readers who request Christian historical fiction. Within this book, nonevangelical novels on Christian topics appear in other chapters, such as the "Biblical" section of Chapter 2 (Traditional Historical Novels) as well as in Chapter 10. Readers interested in these works can find them in the subject index under "Biblical themes" and "Christian themes."

Christian Historical Novels

9

Biblical

Both the Old and New Testaments are natural subjects for Christian novelists, as the Bible is the basis for all Christian faith. Through reading these works readers get the chance to reacquaint themselves with well-known biblical stories and explore the motivations of major figures in depth. The historical background plays a strong role in these novels. This section includes novels set anywhere from the age of the Patriarchs—Abraham, Jacob, and Joseph—through the time of the Crucifixion. Traditional (Chapter 2) and literary (Chapter 10) historical novelists also set their novels in biblical times.

10

Austin, Lynn N.

11

Chronicles of the King. YA ✍

Lynn Austin based her Old Testament novels on a character rarely touched upon in fiction. Hezekiah, King of Judah, is a religious reformer who abolishes idol worship and brings the Jewish people back to God during the eighth and seventh centuries BC. To do so, he survives the schemes of his weak-willed father, King Ahaz, and prevents an Assyrian takeover of the land. *The Strength of His Hand* takes readers to the end of Hezekiah's reign, in which his unfruitful wife's deceit threatens to destroy his faith. The last two books cover the reign of Hezekiah's son, King Manesseh, who nearly ruins everything his father worked for. Originally published by Beacon Hill from 1995 to 1999, the novels have been rewritten and were later re-released by Bethany House.

12

Keywords: Hezekiah, King of Judah (biblical figure); Judah, Kingdom of; Kings; Manesseh, King of Judah (biblical figure)

Gods & Kings. Bethany House, 2005. 316pp. Paper, 0764229893. (Original title: *The Lord Is My Strength.*)

13

Song of Redemption. Bethany House, 2005. 348pp. Paper, 0764229907 . (Original title: *The Lord Is My Song.*)

The Strength of His Hand. Bethany House, 2005. 300pp. Paper, 0764229915. (Original title: *The Lord Is My Salvation.*)

14

Faith of My Fathers. Bethany House, 2006. 311pp. Paper, 0764229923. (Original title: *My Father's God.*)

15

Among the Gods. Bethany House, 2006. 347pp. Paper, 0764229931.

Barnett-Gramckow, Kacy.

Genesis Trilogy. 📖 YA

A trilogy about pivotal moments from Genesis not often retold as novels, and especially not from a female perspective. Barnett-Gramckow paints vivid word pictures with her concise, carefully chosen language and authentically biblical-sounding character names. Her female protagonists keep their faith amid trying circumstances.

Keywords: Floods; Muteness; Noah's Ark; Tower of Babel

The Heavens Before. Moody, 2004. 383pp. Paper, 0802413633.

> Annah, mute ever since she saw her cruel brother kill their father, decides to end her life because her fellow villagers believe her to be mad. Down by the river she meets a young man named Shem whose father, Noakh, is the follower of the Most High—and who has been constructing an ark to save his fellow believers once the world's wickedness is wiped out by a huge flood.

He Who Lifts the Skies. Moody, 2004. 396pp. Paper, 0802413684.

> Barnett-Gramckow sticks closely to Scripture in her retelling of the building of the Tower of Babel. Years after the Great Flood Keren, a great-granddaughter of Annah and Shem, refuses to join her sister Sharah as a fellow wife of Nimr-Rada, a tyrant who proclaims himself king and who has turned his back on God by building a tower high enough to reach the heavens.

A Crown in the Stars. Moody, 2005. 420pp. Paper, 0802413692.

> Shoshannah, daughter of Keren, grows up in her family's faith in the Most High but knowing little of her mother's involvement in the fall of Nimr-Rada. While away visiting relatives, she visits the Great City for the first time and observes that the former tyrant has become a martyr. Mistaken for her look-alike mother, Shoshannah is captured and brought before her aunt Sharah, the queen—after which she unwittingly becomes part of a plot for revenge.

Berg, Elizabeth.

The Handmaid and the Carpenter. **Random House, 2006. 153pp. Hardbound, 1400065380.** ✍ 📖 **YA**

> Berg normally writes contemporary fiction about women's lives and relationships, but here she turns her hand to the Nativity story, told simply and in spare language. Mary is nearly thirteen and Joseph sixteen when they meet and fall in love at a wedding in ancient Nazareth. Their betrothal is arranged for a year hence, although when the angel Gabriel informs Mary that she is to bear a divine child, Joseph has trouble accepting it.

> **Keywords:** Mary (biblical figure); Nativity; Palestine—ancient/prehistoric

Burton, Ann.
Women of the Bible Series.

Annotated in Chapter 2.

Douglas, Lloyd C.

The Robe. Houghton Mifflin, 1942. 695pp. Hardbound. ★ 📖

> Marcellus Gallio, a young Roman soldier sent to Judea as punishment, is ordered to carry out the crucifixion of a Jewish upstart. In a dice game he wins the robe worn by Christ on the cross. Though he's bewildered at first by his new acquisition, it inspires him to find out more about Christ and his teachings. This leads him on adventures throughout the Roman Empire. After learning about Christ

and his growing influence in the Roman world, Marcellus finally converts to Christianity. Widely reprinted.

Keywords: Crucifixion; Judea—Roman period

Garrett, Ginger.

Chosen: The Lost Diaries of Queen Esther. **NavPress, 2005. 298pp. Paper, 1576836517.** ✍ 📖 **YA**

Garrett presents this clearly written, fictionalized version of Queen Esther's life as a series of journal entries written beginning in 480 BC. Forced to leave her cousin Mordecai and Cyrus, the man she loves, when King Xerxes of Persia chooses her for his harem, Hadassah, a Jewish girl, spends a year learning how to make herself attractive to the king. Given the new name Esther, meaning "star," she intrigues Xerxes with her intelligence and purity, which convince him to make her his queen. She discovers her true strength once she learns about a palace conspiracy to kill all of Persia's Jews.

Keywords: Diaries and journals; Esther, Queen of Persia (biblical figure); Jews; Persia—ancient/prehistoric; Queens

Dark Hour. **NavPress, 2006. 283pp. Paper, 1576838692.** ✍ 📖 **YA**

When Athaliah, daughter of Jezebel, came to Judah to marry Prince Jehorah, heir to the throne, she meant to undermine Judaism, restore the worship of Baal and other idols, and destroy the royal line of David. In a brutal murder spree she eliminates her rivals, leaving herself as the sole ruler of Judah for seven years. During this dark time only Jehoshebeth, daughter of one of Athaliah's fellow wives, dares to stand against her. Based on a little-known episode in Chronicles 21–23; this was projected to be the first volume in Garrett's Serpent Moon trilogy; however, future volumes are on hold.

Keywords: Jehosheba (biblical figure); Judah, Kingdom of—ancient/prehistoric; Princesses; Queens

Groot, Tracy.

🎋 *Madman.* **Moody, 2006. 314pp. Paper, 9780802463623.** **YA**

During the time of Jesus's ministry, Tallis, a servant of an Athenian philosopher, travels to Hippos in Palestine to discover what happened to the Greek academy that his master had founded. He learns that not only has the school dissolved, but its former professors have committed suicide, been murdered, or gone mad. As Tallis gets closer to solving the mystery, he unravels a tale of darkness and horror. An affecting, appropriately paced historical novel about the Gerasene demoniac from the gospels. Christy Award.

Keywords: Demons; Gerasene demoniac; Palestine—ancient/prehistoric

Hunt, Angela.

Magdalene. **Tyndale House, 2006. 425pp. Paper, 1414310285.** ✍ **YA**

In her straightforward retelling of Mary Magdalene's life, Hunt counters the *Da Vinci Code*–fueled controversy that she may have been Jesus's wife and the mother of his posthumous child. Her Mary Magdalene (called Miryam of Magdalan) is his devoted friend and disciple, though she's a strong woman in her own right and certainly not a prostitute. After her son unwittingly calls the wrath of Rome down upon her family, Miryam is left alone in the world. Yeshua the Messiah restores her faith in God, but her desire for revenge prevents her from seeing his mission clearly.

Keywords: Apostles; Mary Magdalene (biblical figure); Palestine—ancient/prehistoric

LaHaye, Tim, and Jerry B. Jenkins.

The Jesus Chronicles. ✍ **YA**

A projected four-book series about the creation of the Gospels, the lives of the men who wrote them, and the very early history of the Christian church. The authors' approach reflects modern Christian fundamentalist beliefs. Dialogue and characters are both fairly wooden, and much of the narrative comes directly from the New Testament. LaHaye and Jenkins co-wrote the popular Left Behind series of apocalyptic thrillers.

Keywords: Apostles

John's Story: The Last Eyewitness. Putnam Praise, 2006. 310pp. Hardbound, 0399154124.

At ninety years of age John, the last living apostle (the others having been martyred), is eager to begin spreading the word about Jesus's message. After narrowly avoiding being boiled in oil for heresy, John is exiled to the island of Patmos. In conversations with his scribe, Polycarp, he recalls his first meetings with Jesus and his debates with Gnostic believers.

Keywords: Greece—ancient/prehistoric; John the Apostle (historical character)

Mark's Story: The Gospel According to Peter. Putnam Praise, 2007. 320pp. Hardbound, 9780399154478.

Mark, a young man present at the Last Supper, hears Jesus's final message for his followers. Over the years he learns much from his friend and mentor, Simon Peter, and spreads the word about Jesus and his beliefs far and wide.

Keywords: Palestine—ancient/prehistoric; Saints; St. Mark (historical character); St. Peter (historical character)

Lliteras, D. S.

In his short works of biblical fiction, Lliteras manages to develop flesh and blood characters and emotionally compelling situations.

The Master of Secrets. **Hampton Roads, 2007. 268pp. Hardbound, 9781571745385.** ✍ 📖

In Golgotha just after the Crucifixion, a young boy named Addas seeks to find his father, one of Jesus's disciples. He meets Jeshua, an entertaining and crafty rogue—a first-century version of a snake-oil salesman—who protects him while teaching him how to swindle others. A picaresque novel of faith.

Keywords: Crucifixion; Palestine—ancient/prehistoric

The Silence of John. **Hampton Roads, 2005. 236pp. Hardbound, 157174410X.** ✍

The Apostle John remains silent at Jesus's Crucifixion, leading Jesus's female followers to look to themselves for comfort and understanding. In evoking their emotional pain in the immediate aftermath of the Crucifixion, Lliteras explores the importance of the women—Mary Magdalene, Mary, and others—in Jesus's circle.

Keywords: Apostles; Crucifixion; John the Apostle (historical character); Palestine—ancient/prehistoric

Morris, Gilbert.

Lions of Judah. ✍ **YA**

Morris, evangelical fiction's most prolific author, turns to biblical fiction with this series about Christ's Jewish ancestors.

Heart of a Lion. Bethany House, 2002. 352pp. Paper, 0764226819.

No Woman So Fair. Bethany House, 2003. 351pp. Paper, 0764226827.

The Gate of Heaven. Bethany House, 2004. 317pp. Paper, 0764226835.

Till Shiloh Comes. Bethany House, 2005. 318pp. Paper, 0764229192.

Joseph has always been the favorite of his father, Jacob. His brothers, believing that he will be chosen as Jacob's successor, sell him into slavery in Egypt—where he struggles for years in captivity but gradually rises in power.

Keywords: Brothers; Egypt—ancient/prehistoric; Joseph (biblical figure); Slaves and slavery

By Way of the Wilderness. Bethany House, 2005. 384pp. Paper, 0764229206.

This straightforward retelling of the life of Moses begins with his infancy, when Pharaoh's daughter rescues him from a basket floating in the Nile, through his forty years in exile, and eventually his return to Egypt to deliver the Hebrew people out of slavery.

Keywords: Egypt—ancient/prehistoric; Exile; Moses (biblical figure)

Daughter of Deliverance. Bethany House, 2006. 316pp. Paper, 0764229214.

In the city of Jericho, Rahab's father forces her into prostitution to pay his gambling debts, an act that causes her great shame. Her life changes when two spies with the invading Israeli army ask her to hide them in exchange for her and her family's safety.

Keywords: Palestine—ancient/prehistoric; Prostitutes; Rahab (biblical figure)

Rice, Anne.

Christ the Lord Series.
Annotated in Chapter 2.

Rivers, Francine.
Sons of Encouragement Series. ✍ 📖 YA
Following upon the Lineages of Grace series, which were novellas about five strong biblical women in the lineage of Christ, Francine Rivers began a new series of novellas about biblical men. Each includes a discussion guide with questions based on Scripture. In order, they cover the lives of Aaron, younger brother of Moses; Caleb, contemporary of Joshua who led his people to the Promised Land; Jonathan, good friend of King David; Amos, biblical prophet; and Silas, scribe for the Apostle Paul.

Keywords: Israel—ancient/prehistoric; Priests; Prophets; Scribes

The Priest. Tyndale House, 2004. 228pp. Hardbound, 0842382658.

The Warrior. Tyndale House, 2005. 230pp. Hardbound, 0842382666

The Prince. Tyndale House, 2005. 242pp. Hardbound, 0842382674.

The Prophet. Tyndale House, 2006. 231pp. Hardbound, 0842382682.

The Scribe. Tyndale House, 2007. 231pp. Hardbound, 9780842382694.

Rourke, Mary.

Two Women of Galilee. **MIRA, 2006. 244pp. Hardbound, 0778323749.**
Annotated in Chapter 2.

Thoene, Bodie, and Brock Thoene.

A.D. Chronicles. 📖 YA
In modern-day Israel, Moshe Sachar shows his son a collection of ancient scrolls that tell the stories presented in these novels. Many familiar characters from the Thoenes' Zion Legacy series (annotated later this chapter), which went backward in time from twentieth-century Israel to the first century, reappear here. Everyone seems to be searching for the Messiah who can lead them to the light of God. The fourth through sixth novels form a subseries with the traditional Nativity story as a backdrop. Historical characters mingle with fictional ones.

Keywords: Israel—ancient/prehistoric; Jesus Christ (historical character); Jews; Mary (biblical figure); Nativity

First Light. Tyndale House, 2003. 395pp. 395pp. Hardbound, 0842375066.

Second Touch. Tyndale House, 2004. 359pp. Hardbound, 0842375090.

Third Watch. Tyndale House, 2004. 441pp. Hardbound, 0842375120.
A number of the followers of Yeshua of Nazareth wait patiently for him to declare himself the Messiah. These include Zahav, a Jewish woman secretly

in love with Alexander, a Greek man, and a newly married couple struggling with the husband's sudden blindness.

Keywords: Blindness

9

Fourth Dawn. Tyndale House, 2005. 342pp. Hardbound, 0842375155. ✍

This and the next two volumes begin thirty years earlier than *Third Watch* and focus on events surrounding Jesus's birth. In Judea King Herod, nervous about rumors of the coming Messiah, is losing his grip on reality. At the same time in Nazareth, an angel visits a teenager named Mary and tells her she will give birth to the Messiah, causing her to worry about her relationship with her fiancé, Yosef. Zachariah, a priest, and his elderly wife Elizabeth, barren for many years, also prepare for the birth of their child, who will be known as John the Baptist.

10

Fifth Seal. Tyndale House, 2006. 342pp. Hardbound, 084237518X. ✍

As newlyweds Yosef and Mary prepare for the birth of their child, trying to staunch gossip about the timing of her pregnancy, a prophetess named Hannah predicts the Messiah's imminent arrival, as do Magi observing the night sky.

11

Sixth Covenant. Tyndale House, 2007. 326pp. Hardbound, 9780842375214. ✍

Mary has given birth to baby Yeshua in the rural village of Bethlehem, prompting crowds to travel there and leading mad, paranoid King Herod to commit a desperate, violent act.

12

Seventh Day. Tyndale House, 2007. 300pp. Hardbound, 9780842375245. ✍

The Thoenes' seventh entry covers Jesus's early ministry and the resurrection of Lazarus (here called El'azar).

13

Eighth Shepherd. Tyndale House, 2008. 300pp. Hardbound, 9780842375283. ✍

Word about Yeshua's abilities to heal and raise people from the dead travels quickly throughout Judea. Zachai, a bitter tax collector, hopes that Yeshua can restore his faith in God.

14

The Roman Empire

This section lists novels set after the Crucifixion that deal with Roman citizens other than Christ or his apostles. Christianity was a fledgling religion during the early years of the Roman Empire up until Emperor Constantine's formal conversion, circa AD 312. These novels portray the deeply held faith of early Christians in ancient Rome, forced to practice their religion in secret under threat of death.

15

Hanegraaff, Hank, and Sigmund Brouwer.

Last Disciple Trilogy. 📖 **YA**

This ongoing series based in Preterism—the belief that biblical prophecies about the "last days" referred to events occurring in the first century, culminating with the fall of Jerusalem in AD 70—offers a different interpretation of the Book of Revelation. It serves as a counterpoint to the popular

Left Behind series of futuristic thrillers by Tim LaHaye and Jerry B. Jenkins, which presume that the Rapture is still forthcoming. The action is violent, the narrative simply written and episodic, and the message didactic. Brouwer is a prolific Christian novelist; Hanegraaff is an evangelical Christian speaker, author, and radio talk-show host. *The Last Temple* will be the final volume.

Keywords: Apocalypse; Rome—ancient/prehistoric; Scrolls

The Last Disciple. Tyndale House, 2004. 394pp. Hardbound, 0842384375.

As Nero continues his persecution of Christians in the first century AD, Gallus Sergius Vitas, a Roman aristocrat and military hero who serves as Nero's advisor, does his best to protect Christians who are the immediate target of the emperor's wrath. When Vitas falls in love with a Christian woman, his enemies use his marriage as an excuse to bring him down.

The Last Sacrifice. Tyndale House, 2005. 344pp. Hardbound, 0842384413.

Vitas has been sentenced to die a horrible death in the arena. The key to his salvation lies in his decoding a scroll written by John the Evangelist, the last disciple, before Nero's right-hand man does.

Rivers, Francine.

Mark of the Lion Trilogy. ★ 📖

Political intrigue, adventure, romance, and faith all come together in Rome in AD 70. The violence displayed in the novels evokes these troubled times. These long-time reader favorites have been reprinted frequently.

Keywords: Gladiators; Rome—ancient/prehistoric; Slaves and slavery

A Voice in the Wind. Tyndale, 1993. 442pp. Paper, 0842377506.

After the fall of Jerusalem Hadassah, a virtuous young Christian woman, is sold into slavery in Rome and forced to serve the Valerian family. Although they turn out to be kind masters, the decadent behavior of their children, Marcus and Julia, worries Hadassah, who longs to share her new faith with them.

🌺 *An Echo in the Darkness.* Tyndale, 1994. 442pp. Paper, 0842313079.

Hadassah, believed to be dead, works secretly as a physician's assistant on the outskirts of Rome. The Valerians, humbled by Hadassah's faith, realize how empty their lives are without her. For Marcus, a chance encounter with Hadassah leads to his own conversion. Gold Medallion.

🌺 *As Sure as the Dawn.* Tyndale, 1995. 448pp. Paper, 0842339760.

Atretes, an ex-gladiator who appeared briefly in *A Voice in the Wind*, decides to return home to Germany with his infant son. His son's nurse, Rizpah, a widowed Christian woman, accompanies them. Initial animosity between Rizpah and Atretes turns to attraction. Gold Medallion.

Vidal, César.

The Fisherman's Testament. **Zondervan, 2008 173pp. Paper, 9780310281047.** ✑ 📖

Vidal's Spanish-language best seller takes a look at Christianity's early days. In the year AD 62 Emperor Nero, paranoid about this new religious sect's threat to the Roman Empire, sends General Marco Junio Vitalis to interrogate an elderly fisherman named Peter, who was once an apostle of Jesus. Peter's testament proves to be unexpectedly moving.

Keywords: Apostles; Rome—ancient/prehistoric; Saints; St. Peter (historical character)

The British Isles

The Early and High Middle Ages

In these novels of medieval times Christianity is the accepted religion, but believers face challenges in making it accessible to the common people.

Rose, David.

Godiva. **Whitaker House, 2004. 357pp. Paper, 0883680289.** ✍

Young Godiva watches invading Danes, under the leadership of Canute, destroy her beloved town in AD 1016. Ten years later, after she has married the earl of Mercia, beautiful Godiva bravely donates her own jewels to help Coventry pay King Canute's harsh taxes. When her act only angers him, she accepts his challenge to save her people by riding naked through the town. The story has potential, but readers must put up with the author's simplistic prose and anachronistic language. First in the proposed Viking Sagas series.

Keywords: England—early Middle Ages; Godiva, Lady of Mercia (historical character); Nobility

Pella, Judith.

Mark of the Cross. **Bethany House, 2006. 448pp. Paper, 0764201328.**

This stand-alone novel (a rarity for Pella) set in thirteenth-century England is a tale of family drama in which two half-brothers, one legitimate and one not, vie for the love of the same woman. Philip de Tollard has always wanted his father, Ralph Aubernon, Lord of Hawken, to acknowledge him. When Hawken dies, Philip's half-brother Gareth accuses him of murder and schemes to steal his sweetheart, Lady Beatrice.

Keywords: Brothers; England—high Middle Ages; Heirs and heiresses

Thomson, Cindy.

Brigid of Ireland. **Monarch, 2006. 320pp. Paper, 1854247476.** ✍ **YA**

A novel about Ireland's patron saint, a woman who lived at the same time as St. Patrick. Brigid, born a slave in fifth-century Ireland, grows up in her pagan father's household but finds comfort in her mother's religion, Christianity. After Brigid formally converts she begins performing miracles, but her actions make her a subject of fear and hatred among the Irish, who cling to superstition. As she avoids the wrath of a renegade druid, she travels throughout Ireland sharing God's message with the country's people, never losing hope that she will find her mother again.

Keywords: Ireland—early Middle Ages; Paganism; Saints; St. Brigid (historical character)

The Tudor Era

In 1533 King Henry VIII broke with the Catholic Church to divorce Catherine of Aragon and marry Anne Boleyn. With this defiant act, the head of the English church was changed, but religious practice in England was essentially same as before. Most novels set during this era (except the Hardy entry, below) clearly take the side of the Protestant cause, considered heresy by many at that time.

Hardy, LeAnne.

Glastonbury Tor. **Kregel, 2006. 239pp. Paper, 0825427894.** 📖 **YA**

During the English Reformation, when Henry VIII began seizing the Catholic Church's treasures for the crown, Colin Hay escapes from his brutish father by becoming a novice monk, fulfilling his late mother's wishes. He finds sanctuary at Glastonbury Abbey but feels conflicted between monastery doctrine and the prayers of a local family who own an English Bible. Among the abbey treasures Colin finds an ancient drinking bowl that may be the Holy Grail. A novel of faith, its loss, and its rediscovery, that is remarkable for its refusal to take sides.

Keywords: Abbeys; Arthurian themes; Catholicism; England; Holy Grail; Monks

Parshall, Craig, and Janet Parshall.

The Thistle and the Cross Series.

This series spans more than two centuries, from the Protestant Reformation to the American Revolution. Subsequent volumes move the original characters' descendants (and their message of faith) from Scotland to the New World. Fictional characters interact with historical ones, including preacher and reformer John Knox. Unlike LeAnne Hardy's take on the Reformation (above), the Parshalls' version is quite polemic, presenting Protestantism as an enlightened alternative to the unyielding intolerance of Catholicism. The books can be read independently.

Keywords: Mackenzie family; Patriots; Religious reformers

Crown of Fire. Harvest House, 2005. 415pp. Paper, 0736912789.

In St. Andrews, Scotland, in 1546, when burnings of heretic Protestants have become commonplace, Ransom Mackenzie chooses to follow reformer John Knox. He falls in love with a young woman, Margaret, while in hiding in the Scottish Highlands, but is forced to leave her behind when Knox asks for his help in London.

Keywords: Scotland

Captives and Kings. Harvest House, 2007. 341pp. Paper, 9780736913256.

Andrew and Philip Mackenzie, brothers in early seventeenth-century Scotland, have always been rivals. Philip and his son, Peter, flee after their involvement in a plot against King James is uncovered. As they struggle with their new life in the Jamestown colony, Andrew, an advisor to the king, gets caught up in political intrigue himself.

Keywords: Brothers; Scotland; Virginia—colonial period

Sons of Glory. Harvest House, 2008. 405pp. Paper, 9780736913263.

> The Mackenzie family's religious struggles continue in the American colonies, as Nathan Mackenzie, despite his patriot sympathies, is forced to defend British soldiers after the Boston Massacre. His beliefs put him in conflict with his brother Edward, a minister who feels that he serves God's purpose best by siding with Britain.
>
> **Keywords:** Brothers; Clergy; Massachusetts—American Revolution

The Georgian Era

The growth of Britain as a world power. British imperialism vies with individual citizens' religious beliefs.

Bunn, T. Davis, and Isabella Bunn.

Heirs of Acadia.

These books feature descendants of the characters written about in the <u>Song of Acadia</u> series (set in Canada and Louisiana), which Bunn cowrote with Janette Oke. Bunn's coauthor this time is his wife, Isabella.

Keywords: Abolitionists; Nobility

The Solitary Envoy. Bethany House, 2004. 319pp. Paper, 0764228579.

> During the War of 1812 in Washington, D.C., Erica Langston's father is killed and their family business is destroyed. Afterward Erica travels alone to England to deal with her father's creditors. There she confronts Gareth Powers, a British major she had first encountered in the streets of Washington during the war.
>
> **Keywords:** War of 1812; Washington, D.C.—early United States

The Innocent Libertine. Bethany House, 2004. 318pp. Paper, 076422929X.

> Abigail Aldridge causes a family scandal in 1824 in London by tending to the poor in a dangerous section of Soho. Sent back to America in disgrace, Abbie begins again with the help of her patron, a wealthy countess.

The Noble Fugitive. Bethany House, 2005. 313pp. Paper, 0764200933.

> Serafina Gavi, daughter of a noble Venetian family, intends to reunite with Luca, the artist she loves, even if it means jumping ship in England while her parents sail on to America. Once in London she realizes her dream is hopeless, and with no other options, she takes a job as a chambermaid at Harrow Hall. There she meets John Falconer, a former Caribbean slave trader who has turned to Christianity.

The Night Angel. Bethany House, 2006. 315pp. Paper, 0764201263.

> Serafina reunites with her parents, and they relocate to Washington, D.C., where John Falconer and her father begin a new business venture: prospecting for gold in the Carolina mountains. But Falconer keeps his humanitarian, antislavery sentiments in mind throughout, which makes his journey dangerous.
>
> **Keywords:** Washington, D.C.—early United States

Falconer's Quest. Bethany House, 2007. 317pp. Paper, 9780764203589.

Falconer continues spreading the word against slavery wherever he travels. He settles down with the woman he loves, a widow and her son from a Moravian community in North Carolina, but after tragedy strikes, events take him across the Atlantic to France, where he continues his abolitionist mission.

Keywords: North Carolina—early United States

Higgs, Liz Curtis.

Grace in Thine Eyes. **WaterBrook, 2006. 447pp. Paper, 1578562597.** 📖

This sequel to the <u>Thorn in My Heart Series</u> picks up some twenty years later with the daughter of Leana and Jamie, Davina McKie, a beautiful girl of seventeen. It is 1808 in the Scottish lowlands, and Davina, a talented fiddler who has been mute since childhood, goes to visit her parents' distant cousins on the Isle of Arran. She agrees to provide entertainment for the duke of Hamilton one evening, but when one of his guests dishonors her, Davina's protective brothers take revenge. Based on the biblical story of the rape of Dinah.

Keywords: Biblical themes; Muteness; Rape; Scotland—19th century; Violinists

<u>Thorn in My Heart Series.</u> 📖

Higgs does a masterful job of transporting the biblical story of Leah, Rachel, Jacob, and Esau to late eighteenth-century Galloway, in the Scottish Lowlands. Because polygamy was illegal in 1780s Scotland, Higgs uses an old Scottish custom to get around the problem. She also sprinkles elements of traditional folklore and dialect into the story, giving it an authentic feel. Even mainstream romance readers will appreciate the poignant romance, but have some tissues handy.

Keywords: Biblical themes; Love triangles; Scotland—18th century; Sisters

Thorn in My Heart. WaterBrook, 2003. 484pp. Paper, 157856512X.

Rowena McKie goads her favorite son, Jamie, into claiming his father's birthright over his twin brother. For his protection she sends Jamie on a journey to visit her brother, Lachlan McBride, with directions to take one of Lachlan's daughters to wife. Plain Leana falls in love with Jamie, but Jamie is determined to choose her carefree younger sister, Rose, as his bride.

Fair Is the Rose. WaterBrook, 2004. 464pp. Paper, 1578561272.

With Leana's help Jamie has finally discovered the true meaning of love and marriage. Leana's greedy father Lachlan still refuses to let the couple return to Jamie's home at Glentrool to make a life for themselves, but Lachlan is not their biggest problem. Rose's selfishness, borne of a legal loophole, ultimately causes her sister and Jamie more pain than they can bear.

🌺 *Whence Came a Prince.* WaterBrook, 2005. 551pp. Paper, 1578561280.

In 1790 in Galloway, Scotland, the Kirk has declared Leana's marriage to Jamie McKie invalid. Jamie and Rose are finally, lawfully wed and charged with raising Leana's son. Jamie struggles with his love for two very different women, only one of whom he is allowed to have. His father-in-law's greed makes him long to return home, but he worries that his brother will kill him for stealing his birthright. Christy Award.

Moser, Nancy.

Just Jane. Bethany House, 2007. 367pp. Paper, 9780764203565. ✍ 📖 **YA**

Jane Austen speaks about her writing and family life, beginning in her early twenties as she tries to write the perfect opening line for the novel that will become *Pride and Prejudice*. Her relationships with family members, particularly her sister Cassandra, are warm and supportive. Although Jane enjoys brief flirtations with men, most notably neighbor Tom Lefroy, she never marries, preferring to devote her attention to her writing and live life on her own terms.

Keywords: Austen, Jane (historical character); Authors, women

Schaub, Christine.

The Longing Season. Bethany House, 2006. 248pp. Paper, 9780764200601. ✍ 📖

Schaub uses John Newton's transformation from slave trader to fervent abolitionist as inspiration for her second novel, which recounts the story behind his writing of the hymn "Amazing Grace." England in the 1740s had much to gain from the slave trade, and John Newton, son of a merchant ship captain, became an active participant, despite having been a slave at one point himself. While John sails from Africa to Newfoundland and back again, cursing his lot in life, waiting for him back home is Mary Catlett, the woman who has never given up hope of his returning. Book Two in the <u>Music of the Heart</u> series, after *Finding Anna* (see under "The United States: Reconstruction and the Gilded Age").

Keywords: Abolitionists; Hymns; Newton, John (historical character); Slaves and slavery

The Victorian Era

Christian novels set during the Victorian period (1837–1901) include a mix of social classes—the wealth of the rich versus the deplorable plight of the poor, especially the Irish.

Lang, Maureen.

<u>Oak Leaves Series.</u>

Lang incorporates her own experience with Fragile X Syndrome, a mental disability her son was born with, into her new series about family heritage, coming to terms with a serious medical diagnosis, and God's unconditional love.

Keywords: Diaries and journals; Fragile X Syndrome; Ireland—19th century; Multi-period novels

The Oak Leaves. Tyndale, 2007. 401pp. Paper, 9781414313450.

Talie Ingram, a young mother in contemporary Chicago, discovers the journals of an ancestor, Cosima Escott, in her mother's attic. In her writings Cosima, who lived during the Victorian era and moved from Ireland to England after marrying, expresses her concerns about a "curse" of feeblemindedness that affected male children in her family and may be the cause of her infant son Ben's affliction. The journals force Talie to face, reluctantly, her own son's developmental delays.

On Sparrow Hill. Tyndale, 2008. 403p. Paper, 9781414313467.

Lang continues her theme of adjusting to God's plan for one's life in this sequel to *The Oak Leaves,* which tells the contemporary tale of Rebecca Seabrooke, manager of Hollinworth Hall. A distant cousin of the Hollinworths pays a visit to the family manor, asking questions about a Victorian-era ancestor, a correspondent of Cosima Escott Hamilton, who opened a school for the mentally disabled.

Twentieth Century

McCusker, Paul.

A Season of Shadows. **Zondervan, 2005. 332pp. Paper, 0310254329.**

Julie Harris, a socialite from Washington, D.C., uncovers her husband Stewart's secret past after his death. She risks much by traveling to London during wartime, posing as an aide at the American embassy and infiltrating a fascist group that may have the answers she seeks.

Keywords: England—World War II; Socialites; Spies; Widows

Europe

The Middle Ages

Classic stories of good and evil set in medieval Europe. In these dark times, when the innocent and the faithful suffer terrible fates, people's faith is challenged as they begin to question whose side God is on.

Baker, C. D.

Journey of Souls Series.

As tradition holds, and as Baker recounts, in the year 1212 two children, one in France and one in Germany, experienced visions of Jesus, who directed them to call for a crusade, an army of children, to free Palestine from the Infidel. Despite assurances they were under God's protection, the children suffered extreme hardship, and many were sold into slavery en route. Baker focuses on a small group of young pilgrims, siblings Wil, Karl, and Maria, first as they cross the treacherous Alps, and later as members of their party struggle home, having lost many of the original group to starvation, disease, or slavery. The second book steps back slightly by telling the story of Heinrich, the siblings' father, beginning with his childhood in late twelfth-century Germany.

Keywords: Children's Crusade; Crusades and Crusaders; Germany; Palestine—13th century

Crusade of Tears. RiverOak, 2004. 550pp. Paper, 1589190092.

Quest of Hope. RiverOak, 2005. 496pp. Paper, 1589190114.

Pilgrims of Promise. RiverOak, 2005. 500pp. Paper, 9781589190146.

Bergren, Lisa T.

The Gifted. 📖 YA

In fourteenth-century Italy, a group of spiritually talented individuals known as the Gifted (whose existence was predicted in a first-century letter from St. Paul to the Corinthians) begin making themselves known. Their goal is to fight Satan, in the form of the Inquisition, by deciphering the letter's secret. A fast-paced historical novel with some fantasy elements. *The Blessed* will be the final volume.

Keywords: Inquisition; Italy; Letters; Priests; Sorcerers

The Begotten. Berkley Praise, 2006. 367pp. Hardbound, 0425210162.

In the year 1339 Father Piero, a Dominican priest in possession of fragments of a letter written by the Apostle Paul, locates the first of the people known as the Gifted: Daria D'Angelo, a young proto-feminist who can heal the dead. Their path intertwines with that of Captain Gianni de Capezzana, who is out to fight Abramo Amidei, a minion of Satan who is known as the Sorcerer. While members of the church hierarchy try to keep St. Paul's letter a secret, the Gifted band together in Siena, Italy, to find others like them and to challenge the dark forces opposing the true faith.

The Betrayed. Berkley Praise, 2007. 394pp. Hardbound, 9780425217085.

Daria, Father Piero, Gianni, and other members of the Gifted try to figure out God's plan for them, traveling from church to church in Venice to find the scattered pieces of a mysterious map that may reveal their destiny. But their enemies are closing in: the group is betrayed by a former friend, and Lord Amidei wishes to use Daria's gift for evil.

The Renaissance and Reformation

Heroes and heroines of the Protestant Reformation, when citizens throughout Europe rejected papal authority in pursuit of individual faith, take center stage here.

Chaikin, Linda Lee.

The Silk House Trilogy.

Political, religious, and romantic intrigue in the court of Catherine de Medici in the late sixteenth century, centering on the infamous St. Bartholomew's Day Massacre, when France's most wealthy Protestants (Huguenots) were killed by a violent Catholic mob at the instigation—as tradition holds—of King Charles IX, the Queen Mother, and her allies from the Guise family. This was originally meant to be a four-book series; the final volume of the trilogy ends with unresolved plotlines.

Keywords: Catherine de Medici, Queen of France (historical character); France; Huguenots; Queens; Seamstresses; Silk weavers; St. Bartholomew's Day Massacre

Daughter of Silk. Zondervan, 2006. 315pp. Paper, 031026300X.

Rachelle Dushane-Macquinet, a Huguenot from a family of silk weavers in Lyon, follows her grandmother and sister to the royal court in Paris, where they are invited to design a trousseau for Princess Marguerite de Valois. The Queen Mother and de facto ruler of France, Catherine de Medici, plots revenge against the country's Protestant Huguenots, though Rachelle keeps her origins hidden. When Rachelle and her Catholic suitor, Marquis Fabien de Vendôme, uncover the queen's deadly plot, it puts them both in grave danger.

Written on Silk. Zondervan, 2007. 351pp. Paper, 9780310263012.

Marguerite de Valois, Queen Catherine's daughter, will shortly be marrying Henri of Bourbon, a distant cousin who is a Huguenot. While creating the wedding gown for the new royal bride, Rachelle takes pains to hide her own Protestant beliefs and the queen draws her further into her web.

Threads of Silk. Zondervan, 2008. 327pp. Paper, 9780310273103.

The Queen Mother plots to use Rachelle and Fabien in her schemes to assassinate her biggest enemy, the Duc de Guise.

Early Modern Europe

Inspirational rather than preachy, these novels set in eighteenth- and nineteenth-century Europe feature women of the time who struggle with their faith and God's plans for their future.

Dennis, Jeanne Gowen, and Sheila Seifert.

Marta's Promise. Kregel, 2006. 316pp. Paper, 0825424895.

Marta Ebel, a young Lutheran Reformer, leaves Germany for Russia in 1766 to escape the religious wars at home. She, a mysterious man named Carl Mueller, and a five-year-old boy named Hans enter Russia by posing as a family unit. Although Carl reveals little of his background, that doesn't prevent Marta from falling in love with him. The authors write in a formal style in an attempt to evoke the tone of the era.

Keywords: Exile; Religious reformers; Russia

Moser, Nancy.

Mozart's Sister. Bethany House, 2006. 332pp. Paper, 9780764201233. ✍ 📖 **YA**

Nannerl Mozart and her brother Wolfgang, five years younger, begin performing music together in 1762, when both are children. Accompanied by their overprotective father, Leopold, they grace the stages of Salzburg and Vienna, performing before royalty and earning accolades everywhere. But Leopold has ambitious plans for his son, which don't include Nannerl. Although she feels frustrated at the lack of options available to women in her time, Nannerl gradually learns that God's plan for her life is different than what she had hoped.

Keywords: Austria; Brothers and sisters; Mozart, Maria Anna (historical character); Musicians, women

O'Neill, Caroline Coleman.

Loving Søren. **Broadman & Holman, 2005. 294pp. Paper, 080543089X.** ✍

This elegantly written first novel about Regina Olsen, the young woman jilted but never forgotten by Danish philosopher Søren Kierkegaard, begins in Copenhagen in 1837. Regina grows intrigued by the lanky young man's sense of irony, his earnestness, and his refusal to conform to polite society. Although Regina forms an understanding with Fritz Schlegel, her former history teacher, Søren rarely escapes her thoughts. When he breaks off their romance to serve God through his writing, the heartbreak overshadows their lives from that point forward.

Keywords: Denmark; Engagements; Kierkegaard, Søren (historical character); Olsen, Regina (historical character); Philosophers

Twentieth Century

International and political intrigue during the Bolshevik Revolution and World War II, primarily, as well as later periods in Russian history. The authors interweave the protagonists' religious dilemmas with the politics of the time. The novels of the Second World War in Europe are grittier than many other novels in this subgenre; they don't downplay the hardships and tragedies suffered by the characters. It isn't going too far to imply that the Nazis, with their unredeemable policies of evil, represent the devil himself.

Beazely, Jan, and Thom Lemmons.

🌺 *King's Ransom.* **WaterBrook, 2004. 371pp. Paper, 1578567785.** ✍

During the dark days of World War II, Tsar Boris III of Bulgaria knows he is walking a fine line, trying to keep Germany as an ally while avoiding invasion by neighboring Russia. His strong Christian beliefs, however, prevent him from sending Bulgaria's 50,000 Jews to concentration camps. He works tirelessly alongside Orthodox and Jewish leaders to save the Jews from certain death at the hands of the Third Reich, earning him his country's eternal gratitude. The authors intertwine the story of Tsar Boris's heroic actions with a romance between Daria, the Bulgarian royal family's Jewish attendant, and Dobri, one of the tsar's bodyguards. Christy Award.

Keywords: Boris III, Tsar of Bulgaria (historical character); Bulgaria—World War II; Holocaust; Jews; Kings

Chaikin, Linda Lee.

The Midwife of St. Petersburg. **WaterBrook, 2007. 335pp. Paper, 9781400070831.**

Karena Peshkev, daughter of a Jewish midwife living in the Russian countryside in 1914, dreams of attending medical school but settles for working alongside her mother. At her wealthy cousin Tatiana's mansion she meets and falls in love with Colonel Alexsandr Kronstadt, though he is promised to Tatiana. In an attempt to connect with someone associated with the Imperial College of Medicine, Karena attends a Bolshevik meeting. After she is accused by the Russian police of being a traitor, she and her mother flee to St. Petersburg, where their only hope lies in Alex saving them.

Keywords: Bolshevik Revolution; Jews; Midwives; Russia

Downs, Susan K, and Susan May Warren.

Heirs of Anton.

International intrigue and romance in twentieth-century Russia, as four courageous women survive difficult political times and slowly uncover their heritage. Everything leads back to Anton Klassen, a Mennonite merchant from South Russia during the last years of the tsars. The novels are meant to be read in reverse chronological order; the story about Anton, ancestor of three of the women, is not revealed completely until the final volume.

Keywords: Bolshevik Revolution; Disguise; Families; Russia; Spies, women

Ekaterina. Barbour, 2003. 280pp. Paper, 1593101619.

When Ekaterina "Kat" Moore receives a package in the mail containing a mysterious brass key, she boards a plane to Russia, her family's homeland, in search of answers. Once there she runs into FSB agent Captain Vadeem Spasonov, who believes she may be part of a smuggling ring. Set in the present day.

Nadia. Barbour, 2004. 288pp. Paper, 1593101635.

Nadia "Hope" Moore, a former spy for the CIA, secretly travels behind the Iron Curtain in 1970 to save her estranged husband, Mickey, from certain death in a Russian gulag.

Marina. Barbour, 2005. 287pp. Paper, 1593103506.

Marina Shubina, widowed and pregnant when the Third Reich invades Russia, has no choice but to fight for her country. Her only hope lies in the leader of her group of freedom fighters, American OSS agent Edward Neumann.

Oksana. Barbour, 2006. 286pp. Paper, 1593103492. ✍

In 1917, before the imperial family is confined to house arrest, Tsar Nicholas II entrusts Anton Klassen, a Ukrainian merchant, with the well-being of a chambermaid named Oksana. Anton agrees, not realizing that the real Oksana has exchanged places with Grand Duchess Olga. In Petrograd Anton and "Oksana" hide from the revolutionaries, agreeing to a marriage of convenience for her protection. Republished as *The Sovereign's Daughter* by Barbour in 2008.

Keywords: Olga, Grand Duchess of Russia (historical character)

Goyer, Tricia.

Montana-based novelist Goyer writes about ordinary people who discover their inner strength while caught up in the tides of war. Her novels set in World War II (including *Dawn of a Thousand Nights*, annotated under "The United States") are skillfully researched, based on interviews with those who survived the conflict.

Arms of Deliverance. **Moody, 2006. 316pp. Paper, 0802415563.** 📖

In Europe during 1944 three women see their personal and professional priorities drastically change. Lee O'Donnelly grew up in a privileged home environment and uses her family's connections to get a job reporting from the front lines. She finds herself paired with a rival reporter, Mary Kelley, her equal in ambition though of lesser social status. Katrine, a Czech Jew who saved her life by passing as an Aryan, risks everything when she becomes pregnant with the child of a Nazi officer obsessed with racial purity.

Keywords: Europe—World War II; Jews; Journalists, women; Nazis

Chronicles of the Spanish Civil War.

Drama and romantic intrigue during the Spanish Civil War (1936–1939), when left-wing supporters of the newly formed Spanish Republic battled the fascist, Nazi-supported Nationalist regime, led by Franco. A young American woman, Sophie Grace, gets pulled into the conflict when she travels to Madrid to meet her fiancé, Michael, a news reporter. Caught up in a war she doesn't fully understand, Sophie finds her life's purpose in sharing the story of the beleaguered Spanish people with the outside world.

Keywords: Journalists, women; Spain; Spanish Civil War

A Valley of Betrayal. Moody, 2007. 319pp. Paper, 0802467679.

A Shadow of Treason. Moody, 2007. 288pp. Paper, 9780802467683.

A Whisper of Freedom. Moody, 2008. 314pp. Paper, 9780802467690.

Night Song. Moody, 2004. 528pp. Paper, 0802415555. 📖 **YA**

During the darkest days of World War II, the prisoners held at Hitler's Mauthausen death camp in Austria formed an orchestra to keep hope alive. Jakub Hanauer, a young Jewish prisoner weak with starvation, joins the orchestra in a desperate attempt to stay alive. At the same time Evie, an Austrian socialite and member of the Resistance, is sent back to Vienna from her home in America; as war breaks out, she finds herself separated from the man she loves, an American army medic.

Keywords: Austria—World War II; Holocaust; Jews; Orchestras

Thoene, Bodie.

Zion Covenant. ★

Elisa Lindheim, a violinist in Vienna hiding under an Aryan name, joins with her friend Leah Feldstein to rescue their fellow Jews from pre–World War II Austria regardless of the personal cost. John Murphy, a *New York Times* reporter, aids their efforts. Some of the lucky ones escape to the Holy Land or America, but other Jews find that there's nowhere for them to go. Continued by the Thoenes' Zion Chronicles series (listed under "The Middle East") . The final three volumes, considered "director's cuts," include scenes from *The Twilight of Courage* (annotated under "The Middle East") and previously unpublished scenes from this series, the

Thoenes' <u>Zion Legacy</u> series, and their <u>Zion Chronicles</u> series. The 2005 reissues of the novels credit both Bodie Thoene and Brock Thoene as authors.

Keywords: Europe—World War II; Holocaust; Israel—World War II; Jews; Journalists and reporters; Violinists

Vienna Prelude. Bethany House, 1989. 410pp. Hardbound, 1556610661.

Prague Counterpoint. Bethany House, 1989. 380pp. Hardbound, 1556610785.

Munich Signature. Bethany House, 1990. 396pp. Hardbound, 155661079.

Jerusalem Interlude. Bethany House, 1990. 400pp. Hardbound, 1556610807.

Danzig Passage. Bethany House, 1991. 413pp. Hardbound, 1556610815.

Warsaw Requiem. Bethany House, 1991. 510pp. Hardbound, 1556611889.

London Refrain. Tyndale House, 2005. 282pp. Paper, 1414303580.

Paris Encore. Tyndale House, 2005. 293pp. Paper, 1414305443.

Dunkirk Crescendo. Tyndale House, 2005. 322pp. Paper, 1414305451.

The United States

Colonial America and the American Revolution

One of the founding principles of the United States was religious freedom, so it's not surprising that Christian novelists have been inspired by these periods in American history.

Bright, Bill, and Jack Cavanaugh.

Fire. **Howard, 2005. 384pp. Paper, 1582294593.**

Annotated with the rest of the <u>Great Awakenings</u> series, under "Early United States" (below).

Hochstetler, J. M.

American Patriot Series.

Romance, mystery, and espionage during the American Revolution, as patriotic Elizabeth Howard decides whether to side with the man she loves, a British officer, or with her conscience. A third volume, *Wind of the Spirit*, is expected in 2009.

Keywords: Massachusetts—American Revolution; Patriots; Spies, women

Daughter of Liberty. Zondervan, 2004. 368pp. Paper, 0310252563.

In 1775 Elizabeth Howard, a twenty-year-old woman from Boston, secretly goes against her parents, strong British sympathizers, to join the rebellion as a spy called Oriole. Then she meets Jonathan Carleton, a wealthy Virginia landowner and captain in the 17th Light Dragoons. Their attraction throws a wrench into her plans.

Native Son. Zondervan, 2005. 296pp. Paper, 0310252571.

> Carleton, now working alongside George Washington, is sent into Indian Territory as a mediator, while Elizabeth risks her life gathering intelligence for the patriot cause.

Moser, Nancy.

Washington's Lady. **Bethany House, 2008. 414pp. Paper, 9780764205002.** ✍ 📖 **YA**

> In 1757, when her husband Daniel dies in their seventh year of marriage, Martha Custis is only twenty-six. She wishes only to live simply and raise her two surviving children—that is, until she meets Colonel George Washington, hero of the French and Indian War. They marry and settle at his plantation at Mount Vernon, but when war looms on the horizon, she puts aside her dreams of domestic happiness and supports her husband's new military role. She endures many personal tragedies before becoming the nation's reluctant, and original, first lady.
>
> **Keywords:** First ladies; Virginia—colonial period; Washington, Martha (historical character)

Parshall, Craig, and Janet Parshall.

Sons of Glory. **Harvest House, 2008. 405pp. Paper, 9780736913263.**

> Annotated with the rest of <u>The Thistle and the Cross Series</u>, under "The British Isles: The Tudor Era."

The Early United States

Between the Revolution and the Civil War the United States grew into a powerful nation. These novels look at social issues and problems within America's borders: the development of the American Christian church, the exploitation of mill workers, and growing racial tensions in the South.

Bright, Bill, and Jack Cavanaugh.

<u>The Great Awakenings.</u>

> A four-book series about the religious revival in early American history. With Bill Bright's health failing as the series progressed, the authors decided to write and publish *Proof* first, despite its being chronologically last, because it was the story Bright (founder of Campus Crusade for Christ) wanted to write most. Each can be read independently, though the stories are connected; the protagonists are members of the same family.
>
> **Keywords:** Religious reformers

Fire. Howard, 2005. 384pp. Paper, 1582294593.

> During the Great Awakening of 1740, a time when preachers George Whitefield and Jonathan Edwards stirred the populace to embrace Christianity, Josiah Rush returns to Havenhill, Connecticut, from exile, having unintentionally caused a deadly fire seven years earlier.

Now a pastor, Josiah uses his spiritual gifts to drive what he terms a "soul sickness," an epidemic of anti-Christian beliefs, out of the town.

Keywords: Clergy; Connecticut—colonial period; Fires; Great Awakening

Storm. Howard, 2006. 352pp. Paper, 1582294933.

Asa Rush arrives at Yale College as a freshman in 1798, having been recruited by the school's president to rekindle the Christian spirit on campus. What's more, President Dwight wants Asa to bring his archrival, sophomore Eli Cooper, to Christ, a big challenge because Asa and Eli are competing for the same woman.

Keywords: Connecticut; Universities

Fury. Howard, 2006. 336pp. Paper, 1582295735.

It's 1825, and sixteen-year-old Daniel Cooper lives with his Uncle Asa and Aunt Camilla in upstate New York, his parents having drowned. When he witnesses a murder outside his employer's casket shop, he starts running for his life, because his uncle doesn't believe his story—and the killers are coming after him.

Keywords: New York

Proof. Howard, 2005. 366pp. Paper, 1582294372.

In 1857 young lawyer Harrison Shaw is thrilled to become an intern to J. K. Jarves, one of New York City's most powerful attorneys. He resigns in disgust when he discovers how corrupt his mentor's lifestyle is, but not before converting Jarves's daughter, Victoria, to Christianity. Jarves takes revenge by suing the church in which Victoria was saved, demanding proof that the Holy Spirit really exists.

Keywords: Lawyers; New York

Foster, Sharon Ewell.

Abraham's Well. Bethany House, 2006. 335pp. Paper, 9780764228872. 📖 **YA**

Young Armentia grows up in the Appalachians of North Carolina, watched over by her loving parents, her older brother Abraham, and a kindly married couple of white and Indian blood. But an act of childhood mischief, and the arrival of greedy white men, makes her realize that she and her family are slaves. In 1838 Armentia's family—along with thousands of other Black Cherokee, both slave and free—are forced westward on foot along the Trail of Tears to what is now Oklahoma. Foster writes in the honest, direct, occasionally folksy style of a slave narrative, recounting in the first person Armentia's lifelong journey from innocence to resigned wisdom.

Keywords: African Americans; Black Cherokee Indians; North Carolina; Oklahoma; Slaves and slavery; Trail of Tears

Gohlke, Cathy.

🏵 *William Henry Is a Fine Name.* Moody, 2006. 250pp. Paper, 0802499732. **YA**

Robert Leslie Glover and William Henry are best friends growing up together in Maryland, although Robert is white and William Henry a free black boy. In 1859, when Robert is thirteen, he learns that his abolitionist father is involved in the Underground Railroad, something William Henry knows all too much about. Robert's mother, daughter of a cruel Southern plantation owner, doesn't share her husband's thoughts about slavery. As Robert makes sense of his own beliefs, he knows he has some tough decisions ahead. Christy Award.

Keywords: Abolitionists; Friendship; Maryland; Slaves and slavery; Underground Railroad

Gouge, Louise M.

Ahab's Legacy.

This series takes Captain Ahab (from Melville's *Moby-Dick*) and creates a romantic partner for him, but it doesn't stop there. Gouge continues the story of Ahab's widow and son as they make new lives for themselves in pre–Civil War Boston and Nantucket.

Keywords: Abolitionists; Massachusetts; Ship captains; Widows

Ahab's Bride. RiverOak, 2004. 348pp. Paper, 1589190076.

Hannah Oldweiler, a gentle girl in early nineteenth-century Nantucket, falls in love with Captain Ahab, a sailor who never lets anything, especially the sea, get the best of him.

Hannah Rose. RiverOak, 2005. 319pp. Paper, 1589190408.

After Ahab's death at the hands (so to speak) of the great white whale, Hannah Rose is left to raise their son, Timothy, alone. She rekindles her faith in God, despite his taking her beloved Ahab from her. Friends introduce her to the abolitionist movement.

Son of Perdition. RiverOak, 2005. 318pp. Paper, 1589190416.

Timothy Jacobs (out of defiance, he doesn't use his father's surname) resents the burden of his father's legacy. Determined to face life on his own terms, he enters the U.S. Naval Academy alongside a man who blames Ahab for his father's death, and whose sister, Jemima, interests Timothy romantically.

Morris, Gilbert, and Lynn Morris.

The Creoles.

With this four-book series, centering on four female friends who met at the Ursuline Convent School, the father-daughter writing team chronicles religious, cultural, and racial differences in early- to mid-nineteenth-century Louisiana.

Keywords: Creoles; Friendship; Louisiana

The Exiles: Chantel. Thomas Nelson, 2003. 267pp. Paper, 0785270027.

The search for her baby sister, long thought to be dead, leads red-haired Chantel Fontaine from New Orleans through Louisiana's swampland in search of answers.

Keywords: Sisters

The Immortelles: Damita. Thomas Nelson, 2004. 255pp. Paper, 0785268065.

> While Damita De Salvedo's fortunes decline, those of her former slave girl Rissa, now a wealthy independent freedwoman, begin to rise.
>
> **Keywords:** Slaves, former

The Alchemy: Simone. Thomas Nelson, 2004. 272pp. Paper, 0785270043.

> Simone d'Or, a young woman from high society, becomes entranced by the beautiful singing voice of Colin Seymour, a man of much lower social standing.
>
> **Keywords:** Singers; Socialites

The Tapestry: Leonie. Thomas Nelson, 2005. 272pp. Paper, 0785270051.

> Leonie Vernay, who was left at the Ursuline school as a baby, is working as a seamstress in New Orleans when a stranger brings her news of her long-lost family.
>
> **Keywords:** Seamstresses

Parr, Delia.
Candlewood Trilogy.

Gentle, comforting reads centering on Emma Garrett, a fiftyish widow who opens a boardinghouse in Candlewood, New York, in 1841, during the time of the Erie Canal's construction. Emma mothers her paying guests, discussing their problems and tending to their spiritual needs. In the latter half of the series Zachary Breckenwith comes courting, but she fears her sons' reaction and isn't sure remarriage is the path God wants her to follow.

Keywords: Innkeepers; New York; Widows

A Hearth in Candlewood. Bethany House, 2006. 317pp. Paper, 0764200860.

Refining Emma. Bethany House, 2007. 319pp. Paper, 9780764200878.

Where Love Dwells. Bethany House, 2008. 320pp. Paper, 9780764200885.

Peterson, Tracie, and Judith Miller.

Lights of Lowell.

Romantic drama centering on the textile factory town of Lowell, Massachusetts, and on a slave-holding plantation in Mississippi in the mid-nineteenth century.

Keywords: Abolitionists; Abusive relationships; Massachusetts; Mill workers; Mississippi; Plantations; Slaves and slavery

A Tapestry of Hope. Bethany House, 2004. 351pp. Paper, 0764228943.

> Jasmine Wainwright, a Mississippi planter's daughter, barely tolerates her arranged marriage to an abusive mill owner from Lowell, Bradley Houston, a man who puts his business before everything.

A Love Woven True. Bethany House, 2005. 349pp. Paper, 0764228951.

> In 1849, after her husband's death, Jasmine Houston and her son, Spencer, settle in Lowell, where her relationship with Nolan, her former brother-in-law, heats up. Then her father calls her home to Mississippi, where she heeds her mammy's deathbed promise to find and free her son.

The Pattern of Her Heart. Bethany House, 2005. 381pp. Paper, 076422896X.

> By 1857 Jasmine and Nolan are married, with a growing family. Upon hearing of a deadly yellow fever epidemic down in Mississippi, it's up to Jasmine to decide what to do with the plantation's slaves.

The Civil War

Readers who believe Christian novelists can't write realistic battle scenes or craft compelling social dramas should consider these selections, set between 1861 and 1865.

Austin, Lynn N.

Refiner's Fire.

In this loose trilogy, Austin relates women's Civil War experiences from multiple perspectives.

Keywords: Abolitionists; Plantations; Slaves and slavery

🎗 *Candle in the Darkness.* Bethany House, 2002. 431pp. Paper, 1556614365. Christy Award.

Fire by Night. Bethany House, 2003. 429pp. Paper, 1556614438.

A Light to My Path. Bethany House, 2004. 432pp. Paper, 1556614446.

> This final volume looks at the Civil War from a slave's viewpoint. Kitty, a house slave on a South Carolina plantation, barely remembers her parents, runaway slaves who were hanged after trying to escape. When her young mistress, Claire, marries a Mr. Fuller, Kitty meets Grady, a former slave of Caroline Fletcher's (from *Candle in the Darkness*). As the Yankees approach the Fuller plantation, Kitty and Grady decide whether to make a run for it.
>
> **Keywords:** South Carolina

Phillips, Michael.

Shenandoah Sisters.

Reading as one very long novel, Phillips's series follows two young women of Shenandoah County, North Carolina, during and just after the Civil War. Katie Clairborne, orphaned daughter of a white plantation owner, bands together with Mayme Jukes, an escaped African American slave girl, to keep Katie's family plantation running smoothly. While the white characters and Mayme speak proper English without even a Southern accent, many former slaves use a strong African American dialect that is incomprehensible at times. Phillips's Carolina Cousins Series (see the next section) follows.

Keywords: Cousins; Friendship; Mixed heritage; North Carolina; Plantations; Slaves and slavery

Angels Watching Over Me. Bethany House, 2003. 316pp. Paper, 0764227009.

A Day to Pick Your Own Cotton. Bethany House, 2003. 318pp. Paper, 0764227017.

The Color of Your Skin Ain't the Color of Your Heart. Bethany House, 2004. 314pp. Paper, 0764227025.

Together Is All We Need. Bethany House, 2004. 317pp. Paper, 0764227033.

Reconstruction and the Gilded Age

Late nineteenth-century America has grown in popularity as a setting over the last five years, and these novels deal primarily with social rather than political change. Also see the later books of Michael Phillips's Shenandoah Sisters series, annotated above.

Austin, Lynn.

🏶 *A Proper Pursuit.* **Bethany House, 2007. 432pp. Paper, 9780764228919.** 📖
Twenty-year-old Violet Hayes, a recent graduate of finishing school in 1893, can't believe it when her father decides to remarry a woman she detests. Violet travels to Chicago to find her long-lost mother, whom she barely remembers, and to see the World's Fair. Her grandmother and three great-aunts introduce her to the suffrage movement, high society, and ministering to the inner city poor. Violet's small-town naïveté falls by the wayside as she chooses among several suitors and discovers who she really is. Christy Award.

Keywords: Aunts; Coming of age; Great aunts; Illinois; World's Fair

Gold, August, and Joel Fotinos.

The Prayer Chest. **Doubleday, 2007. 202pp. Hardbound, 9780385520232.**
All of the light goes out of Joseph Hutchinson's life when his beloved wife, Miriam, dies of pneumonia. A farmer living on Long Island in 1891, Joseph is left to raise their son and daughter on his own. In the attic of his home, where he often went to pray before Miriam died, he discovers a mysterious wooden box containing writings left by one of his ancestors more than a hundred years earlier. He and his family learn to apply the "secrets of the prayer chest" to enrich their own lives. Although the characters are Christians, this gentle, spiritual parable can also be appreciated by readers from other religious traditions.

Keywords: New York; Prayers; Widowers

Miller, Judith.

Postcards from Pullman. 🔲YA
Pullman, Illinois, on Chicago's South Side, was founded in 1880 by entrepreneur George Pullman as a model town designed to house the employees of his railway car company. Judith Miller uses Pullman as a setting for her trilogy about Olivia Mott, an Englishwoman who becomes a chef for the famed Florence Hotel and later, a spy along the rails.

Keywords: Chefs; Illinois; Railroads; Spies, women

In the Company of Secrets. Bethany House, 2006. 381pp. Paper, 9780764203527.

> In 1892 Olivia Mott and her wealthy employer's pregnant daughter, Lady Charlotte, leave London for America, hoping to make a fresh start. Olivia obtains a job at an elegant hotel by lying about her experience. While she and Charlotte strive to keep their pasts well hidden, Olivia grows attracted to Pullman employee Fred DeVault and learns that the town is harboring secrets.

Whispers Along the Rails. Bethany House, 2007. 377pp. Paper, 9780764202773.

> Olivia is torn between her jobs as an assistant hotel chef and a railroad spy, just as she is torn between the affections of two suitors. Lady Charlotte, who left her son with Olivia when she fled to Chicago, takes a job at Marshall Field's when her money runs out.

An Uncertain Dream. Bethany House, 2008. 376pp. Paper, 9780764202780.

> Workers at Pullman Car Works go on strike, putting Olivia in a bind, especially when her gentleman friend, Fred DeVault, begins stirring up union activity. And Charlotte, newly returned from England, aims to make a new start back home in Chicago.

Peterson, Tracie.

Ladies of Liberty.

Three women in late nineteenth-century Philadelphia defy the norms of their time by championing worthwhile social causes. Strong religious content.

Keywords: Pennsylvania

A Lady of High Regard. Bethany House, 2007. 336pp. Paper, 9780764227776.

> Because she comes from wealth, Mia Stanley's parents disapprove of her career writing articles for *Godey's Lady's Book* and focusing on local social issues. She also has a talent for matchmaking. In pursuing the person who's been preying on the wives of seamen along Philadelphia's docks, she risks her safety and may end up alienating the man she loves.
>
> **Keywords:** Detective stories; Journalists, women; Matchmakers

A Lady of Hidden Intent. Bethany House, 2008. 363pp. Paper, 9780764201462.

> Catherine Newbury leaves her home in Bath, England, in 1850 when her father is falsely imprisoned for slave trading. She creates a new life for herself as a fashionable seamstress in Philadelphia, but her past comes crashing back when she meets one of her new clients.
>
> **Keywords:** Disguise; Seamstresses

A Lady of Secret Devotion. Bethany House, 2008. 367pp. Paper, 9780764201479.

> In 1857, to earn money for her impoverished family, Cassie Stover accepts a position as companion to Mrs. Jameston, an elderly society matron. Cassie grows suspicious of Mrs. Jameston's spoiled, dissolute son Sebastian and suspects he's cheating his mother. She and Mark Langford, a Boston insurance agent who believes Sebastian killed his best friend, team up to investigate his alleged crimes.

> **Keywords:** Companions; Detective stories; Elder abuse

Phillips, Michael.

Carolina Cousins Series.

> Phillips continues the story of Katie Clairborne and Mayme Jukes of Rosewood Plantation in Shenandoah County, North Carolina (heroines of his <u>Shenandoah Sisters</u> series; see the previous section). The two young women, one white and one a former slave, have learned about their shared ancestry: Mayme is the illegitimate daughter of Katie's Uncle Templeton. As they come of age during the last years of the Civil War and Reconstruction, they and members of their extended family deal with the reality of race relations in the South. Although Rosewood remains a place where men and women of both races live together in harmony, in the outside world the Ku Klux Klan terrorizes anyone with dark skin.

> **Keywords:** Cousins; Ku Klux Klan; Mixed heritage; North Carolina; Plantations; Racial conflict; Slaves, former

A Perilous Proposal. Bethany House, 2005. 347pp. Paper, 0764200623.

The Soldier's Lady. Bethany House, 2006. 346pp. Paper, 0764200429.

Never Too Late. Bethany House, 2007. 318pp. Paper, 9780764200434.

Miss Katie's Rosewood. Bethany House, 2007. 343pp. Paper, 9780764203978.

Schalesky, Marlo.

Veil of Fire. **RiverOak, 2007. 317pp. Paper, 9781589190771.**

> A mysterious veiled figure appears in the hills on the outskirts of the small town of Hinckley in the aftermath of the greatest firestorm in Minnesota history. Residents don't know what to think: Is it a ghost, a monster, or a disfigured survivor? Schalesky recounts the true story of the blaze—which killed 418 residents of east central Minnesota on September 1, 1894—from the viewpoints of several fictional characters.

> **Keywords:** Disfigurement; Fires; Minnesota

Schaub, Christine.

Finding Anna. **Bethany House, 2005. 316pp. Paper, 0764200593.** ✎

> In 1873 Horatio Spafford penned the classic hymn "It Is Well with My Soul" as a courageously hopeful response to devastating loss. When his law office goes up in flames during the Great Chicago Fire of 1871, he is separated from his wife, Anna, and their four daughters. The family reunites, but as Horatio helps the city rebuild, Anna struggles with loneliness and despair. They decide to take a European

vacation as a family, but Spafford, occupied with business interests, sends Anna and their daughters across the ocean ahead of him—precipitating an even greater personal tragedy. First in the Music of the Heart series; the second is *The Longing Season*, annotated under "The British Isles: The Georgian Era."

Keywords: Great Chicago Fire; Hymns; Illinois; Lawyers; Spafford, Horatio (historical character)

Watson, Jan.

Troublesome Creek Series. 📖 **YA**

A gentle, nostalgic series in which Laura Grace "Copper" Brown, a teenager growing up in the Kentucky hills in the late nineteenth century, learns that life as an adult brings unexpected pleasures and hardships. Folksy dialogue and storytelling.

Keywords: Coming of age; Kentucky; Married life; Midwives

Troublesome Creek. Tyndale House, 2005. 369pp. Paper, 1414304471.

It is 1881, and sixteen-year-old Copper Brown—her temperament complements her fiery red hair—resists the changes coming to her beloved Troublesome Creek, Kentucky. As she comes of age, her stepmother desires to turn her from a free-spirited tomboy into a proper young lady. As a way of asserting her independence, Copper abandons her childhood love and, after a hasty courtship, marries city doctor Simon Corbett.

Willow Springs. Tyndale House, 2007. 385pp. Paper, 9781414314723.

Copper relocates to Lexington, Kentucky, where her husband's medical practice thrives, though she has difficulty adjusting to city life and society's expectations of a doctor's spouse.

Torrent Falls. Tyndale House, 2008. 393pp. Paper, 9781414314730.

A widow with a young daughter, Copper moves back to her home in the Kentucky mountains in 1888 and gingerly opens her heart to love again. She establishes a successful practice as a midwife but fears her new beau—John, her childhood love—is keeping secrets from her.

The Twentieth Century

These are thoughtful tales of pain, endurance, and hope during difficult times like the Depression and world wars.

Austin, Lynn.

A Woman's Place. **Bethany House, 2006. 446pp. Paper, 0764228900.** 📖

Four women from diverse backgrounds—Virginia, an insecure housewife; Helen, an elderly, lonely schoolteacher; Rosa, a newly married Italian American; and Jean, a young woman in search of fulfillment—meet and become unlikely friends in the aftermath of Pearl Harbor. All sign up, à la Rosie the Riveter, to do their part for the war effort, choosing to work at a local shipbuilding factory in small-town Michigan in 1941. The women ponder gender expectations (Is their work appropriate for their gender? What would their boyfriends/husbands think?) and react to the presence of a nearby German POW camp.

Keywords: Factories; Friendship; Michigan—World War II; Prisoners of war

Bell, James Scott.

Glimpses of Paradise. **Bethany House, 2005. 411pp. Paper, 0764226487.**

Bell focuses on two young people who come of age during the First World War and the Roaring Twenties. Doyle Lawrence and Zee Miller grew up childhood friends in Zenith, Nebraska, and though romance blooms between them, neither wishes to give up his or her dreams or ask the other to do the same. Zee escapes her Baptist father's strict lifestyle by becoming an actress in Los Angeles, while Doyle goes to Princeton per his rich father's wishes. When war breaks out Doyle drops out of school, enlists, and is shipped overseas. By the time the pair reconnect in postwar LA, they have become different people.

Keywords: Actresses; California; Coming of age; Friendship; Nebraska

Dickson, Athol.

🏵 *River Rising.* **Bethany House, 2006. 304pp. Paper, 076420162X.** 📖

Hale Poser, a poor African American man raised in an orphanage, comes to Pilotville, Louisiana, in 1927 to learn more about his family history. To his surprise, this bayou town along the Mississippi seems to be a utopia for black–white relations; there are few signs of racism on the surface. Hale's peacemaking and healing talents win him many followers, but when a black infant is kidnapped, he discovers a cover-up of similar events in Pilotville's past that rocks the town to its foundations. Christy Award.

Keywords: African Americans; Biblical themes; Kidnapping; Louisiana; Racial conflict

Goyer, Tricia.

Dawn of a Thousand Nights. **Moody, 2005. 382pp. Paper, 0802408559.**

In this novel, subtitled "a story of honor," Goyer celebrates the unsung heroes and heroines of World War II's Pacific theater. Daniel Lukens, a combat fighter pilot for the Army Air Corps, and the woman he loves, fellow pilot and flight instructor Libby Conner, leave Hawaii, the island where they fell in love, when war breaks out. Dan, captured by the Japanese in the Philippines, endures the Bataan Death March, while Libby, a member of the Women's Air Ferrying Squadron, transfers military planes to bases where they're needed most.

Keywords: Hawaii—World War II; Pilots, women; Prisoners of war

Hatcher, Robin Lee.

The Victory Club. **Tyndale House, 2005. 350pp. Paper, 0842376666.**

Hatcher writes about the World War II home front experience through the viewpoints of four women working together at an air field in Boise, Idaho. Margo, Dottie, Lucy and Penelope share their feelings about loved ones off fighting overseas, and they band together to start a "victory club" to help the less fortunate.

Most of them are Christians, but each struggles separately with her faith and against sin.

Keywords: Friendship; Idaho—World War II

Hickman, Patricia.

Millwood Hollow Series. YA

A four-book series about the three Welby siblings, who come of agecoming of age in poverty-ridden rural Arkansas during the Depression. They latch onto Jeb Nubey, an illiterate man hiding from the law, and all are forced into a life of deception when the townspeople of Nazareth, Arkansas, mistake them for a widowed preacher and his three children. After Jeb is unmasked, he finds his talents as a preacher are sorely needed. The author's humorous situations don't feel contrived, and they make for heartwarming tales of redemption.

Keywords: Arkansas; Children; Clergy; Great Depression

Fallen Angels. Warner Faith, 2003. 319pp. Paper, 044661484X.

Nazareth's Song. Warner Faith, 2004. 322pp. Paper, 0446616346.

Whisper Town. Warner Faith, 2005. 264pp. Paper, 0446692344.

Earthly Vows. Warner Faith, 2006. 320pp. Paper, 0446692352.

Sawyer, Kim Vogel.

My Heart Remembers. **Bethany House, 2008. 348pp. Paper, 9780764202629.** YA

Maelle Gallagher lost her Irish immigrant parents in a tenement fire in New York City in 1886, when she was eight. Although she attempts to follow her father's final words of advice—to "take care o' the wee ones"—Maelle and her younger brother, Mattie, and sister, Molly, are separated, shipped out West on an orphan train, and placed with different families. By 1902 Maelle is an adult, but she has never given up hope of finding her siblings again. She travels to Missouri, using the few facts she remembers about where they were taken. Separate plot threads follow Matt and Molly (who was renamed Isabelle) on their individual journeys back to one another.

Keywords: Adopted children; Immigrants, Irish; Missouri; Orphans

Wall, Wilma.

Forbidden. **Kregel, 2004. 320pp. Paper, 0825439477.** 📖

In California's Central Valley just before World War II, German Mennonite farm girl Annie Penner forms a romantic attachment to Donald Nakamura, a Japanese American Baptist and pre-med student. They lose touch during wartime, because Donald and his family are held in an internment camp, but they don't forget each other. They rekindle their love after war's end but face prejudice from their families, and American law at the time prohibits interracial marriage.

Keywords: California—World War II; Internment camps; Interracial romance; Japanese Americans; Mennonites

The Caribbean

Fast-paced romance and swashbuckling adventure on the high seas in the mid-seventeenth century, complete with—of course!—pirates and buried treasure.

Tyndall, M. L.

Legacy of the King's Pirates.

An inspirational version of the popular *Pirates of the Caribbean* movies. Edmund Merrick, the brave and handsome hero of the first two novels, is a born-again Christian.

Keywords: Caribbean—17th century; Pirates

The Redemption. Barbour, 2006. 317pp. Paper, 1597893595.

> Lady Charlisse Bristol, escaping an abusive uncle, voyages from London to the Caribbean in the 1660s in search of the merchant father she never knew. When her ship runs aground on a deserted island, Edmund Merrick, a former pirate turned privateer, rescues her from near starvation. Attracted to her valiant spirit, Edward agrees to help her in her quest.

The Reliance. Barbour, 2006. 334pp. Paper, 1597893609.

> Edmund, believing that his wife Charlisse has died in a fire, drowns his sorrows in rum. In reality Charlisse is being held captive (along with another woman, Lady Isabel Ashton) by Edmund's archenemy, pirate captain Kent Carlton, on his ship *The Vanquisher.*

The Restitution. Barbour, 2007. 334pp. Paper, 9781597893619.

> How much can God forgive? A former pirate makes good, as Kent Carlton seeks to capture the love of the woman he once ravished, Isabel Ashton, who was shunned by her family and local society after giving birth to Kent's illegitimate son. When the infant is kidnapped, Kent stops at nothing to find his child and earn Isabel's forgiveness.

The Middle East

Bodie Thoene and Brock Thoene dominate this category with their well-researched novels about the birth of modern Israel. For novels set in the ancient Middle East, see the "Biblical" section.

Thoene, Bodie.

Zion Chronicles. ★

Bodie Thoene set her first major series against the backdrop of the formation of the State of Israel in 1947–1948. When Jews who survived the Holocaust head to Jerusalem to found a new nation, they face Arab conspiracies as well as danger from the British forces occupying Palestine. Major characters include Ellie Warne, an American photojournalist, and Rachel Lebowitz, a Holocaust survivor who gets trapped in Jerusalem during the siege. The Thoenes' Zion Covenant series, set in World War II–era Germany, is a prequel to the Zion Chronicles, although the

Chronicles were written earlier. *Gates of Zion* and *Key to Zion* both won the Gold Medallion.

Keywords: Holocaust; Israel—20th century; Jews

🏆 *The Gates of Zion.* Bethany House, 1986. 368pp. Paper, 0871238705.

A Daughter of Zion. Bethany House, 1987. 330pp. Paper, 087123940X.

The Return to Zion. Bethany House, 1987. 343pp. Paper, 0871239396.

A Light in Zion. Bethany House, 1988. 352pp. Paper, 0871239906.

🏆 *The Key to Zion.* Bethany House, 1988. 351pp. Paper, 1556610343.

Thoene, Bodie, and Brock Thoene.

🏆 ***The Twilight of Courage.* Thomas Nelson, 1994. 614pp. Hardbound, 0785281967.**

In the spring of 1940 over 300,000 Allied troops were rescued from northern France in what was called the "miracle of Dunkirk." Amid the tumult, an American journalist who recently escaped from Warsaw rescues a Jewish baby. This stand-alone novel serves as a bridge between the Zion Covenant and Zion Chronicles series; a sequel was planned but never published. Gold Medallion.

Keywords: France—World War II; Jews; Journalists and reporters; Poland—World War II

Zion Legacy.

This series, the Thoenes' first attempt to reach a wider audience with a mainstream publisher, follows directly upon their Zion Chronicles. It begins on May 14, 1948, the day the British exit Jerusalem, leaving Jewish and Muslim forces to their own devices. A fictional cast of Jewish characters fights for control of the Old City while the Arabs slowly close in. The plot moves slowly; by the beginning of *Jerusalem Scrolls*, only two weeks have passed. The novels also introduce a subplot that gradually consumes the entire series. A scroll dating from the first century AD, found by one of the Israeli leaders, reveals a romance between a young Jewish widow and a Roman centurion. This earlier plotline begins the A.D. Chronicles series (listed under "Biblical") .

Keywords: Israel—ancient/prehistoric and 20th century; Jews; Scrolls

Jerusalem Vigil. Viking, 2000. 322pp. Hardbound, 0670889113.

Thunder from Jerusalem. Viking, 2000. 311pp. Hardbound, 0670892068.

Jerusalem's Heart. Viking, 2001. 328pp. Hardbound, 0670894877.

The Jerusalem Scrolls. Viking, 2001. 272pp. Hardbound, 0670030120.

Stones of Jerusalem. Viking, 2002. 263pp. Hardbound, 0670030511.

Jerusalem's Hope. Viking, 2002. 272pp. Hardbound, 0670030848.

Africa, Asia, and the Antipodes

These novels, set primarily between the seventeenth and nineteenth centuries, deal with colonization and missionary work in remote places. This is a growing category.

Chaikin, Linda Lee.

East of the Sun Trilogy.

Romantic and suspenseful historical adventure amid the gold and diamond mining industries of 1890s South Africa. Evy Varley leaves her aunt and uncle's English home to return to South Africa, where her parents were killed during the Zulu War of 1878. There she discovers unexpected mysteries about her past. Sir Rogan Chantry, son of a local aristocrat, is right in the thick of it.

Keywords: Diamond mining; Gold mining; South Africa—19th century

Tomorrow's Treasure. WaterBrook, 2003. 392pp. Paper, 1578565138.

Yesterday's Promise. WaterBrook, 2004. 364pp. Paper, 1578565146.

Today's Embrace. WaterBrook, 2005. 384pp. Paper, 1578565154.

Ewen, Pamela Binnings.

The Moon in the Mango Tree. B&H, 2008. 480pp. Paper, 9780805447330. ✍ **YA**

In a novel based on her grandmother's experiences, debut novelist Ewen chronicles the life of Barbara Perkins, a young woman enamored of singing opera, who chooses instead to accompany her missionary doctor husband to the Siam jungles in the 1920s. As Barbara adjusts to a very different lifestyle from what she knows, she grows to love the people and the local culture.

Keywords: Married life; Missionaries; Perkins, Barbara (historical character); Physicians' spouses; Opera singers; Thailand—20th century

Leon, Bonnie.

The Queensland Chronicles.

A romantic trilogy about a young, independent woman from proper Boston who readjusts her way of thinking when she marries a man whose family runs a cattle station in the Australian backcountry.

Keywords: Australia—19th century; Drought; Married life; Ranchers

The Heart of Thornton Creek. Revell, 2005. 344pp. Paper, 080075896X.

After her attorney father dies, Rebecca Williams, a young woman in Boston, in 1871, is left nearly penniless. To assure a future for herself, she agrees to marry one of his clients, Daniel Thornton, even though she doesn't love him. Rebecca accompanies him back to his native Queensland, though she is fearful of starting a new life in an unfamiliar land. Rebecca slowly reciprocates Daniel's feelings as the couple settle into their new home, but her overbearing father-in-law, Bertram, doesn't approve of her.

For the Love of the Land. Revell, 2005. 313pp. Paper, 0800758978.

> Daniel and Rebecca, blissfully happy, are expecting their first child, but Daniel feels the strain of running Douloo Station and supporting his family following his father's death. The couple's faith and resolve are tested as Douloo Station deals with a severe drought.

When the Storm Breaks. Revell, 2006. 306pp. Paper, 0800758986.

> The drought continues, leading to a devastating fire that leaves the Thorntons homeless and living in a tent on their property. Daniel visits a disreputable loan shark, while Rebecca converts a young Aboriginal girl to Christianity.

The Sydney Cove Series.

Two wounded souls begin new lives in mid-nineteenth-century Australia, enduring degrading conditions aboard ship and slowly regaining their trust in God. *Longings of the Heart* will be next in this projected trilogy.

Keywords: Australia—19th century; Frontier and pioneer life; Prisoners

To Love Anew. Revell, 2007. 297pp. Paper, 9780800731762.

> Hannah Talbot, accused of theft by her abusive employer, is transported to New South Wales aboard a prison ship. En route she encounters John Bradshaw, a former factory owner who lost his fortune and family after an accident resulted in a man's death.

Orcutt, Jane.

All the Tea in China. Revell, 2007. 349pp. Paper, 9780800731793.

> Twenty-five-year-old Isabella Goodrich, a spinster skilled in swordplay, leaves her home in Oxford, England, against her relatives' wishes to become a missionary after she meets missionary Phineas Snowe. When Snowe leaves England for China, she sneaks aboard the ship carrying him to the Far East. En route the independent Isabella learns considerably more about herself, the world, and her enigmatic companion. This was meant to be the first volume in Orcutt's Rollicking Regency series; the author died of leukemia in March 2007.
>
> **Keywords:** China—19th century; Coming of age; Missionaries; Shipboard adventure; Spinsters; Swordswomen

Christian Sagas

Sagas celebrate the strength of family over time, so their continued popularity in Christian fiction should be no surprise. Among novels published in the last five years, multi-volume series and American settings dominate.

American Sagas

Christian authors explore the great span of American history, from colonial days through World War II and after.

Bateman, Tracey.

The Penbrook Diaries.

These multi-period stories, switching between the 1940s and 1840s, demonstrate how love can transcend racial boundaries, despite the bigotry and intolerance of the times. They also explore how complex racial histories can be masked by the color of one's skin.

Keywords: Diaries and journals; Georgia—early United States; Ku Klux Klan; Mixed heritage; Multi-period novels; Slaves and slavery

The Color of the Soul. Barbour, 2005. 352pp. Paper, 1593104448.

When Andy Carmichael, a mixed-race reporter living in Chicago with his family, travels home to Georgia to interview an elderly woman writer for a proposed biography, he doesn't realize he'll be uncovering secrets that will unlock his own heritage. Miss Penbrook, who has lived through over a hundred years of Georgia's turbulent history, provides Andy with diaries dating from the 1840s. They are written by two women from her family: a white woman and a mixed-race slave.

Freedom of the Soul. Barbour, 2006. 284pp. Paper, 9781597892216.

In 1949 Shea Penbrook leaves Oregon for her forebears' homeland of Georgia after discovering the diaries of Jason "Mac" Penbrook, her great-great-grandfather, which reveal his relationship with a former slave, Celeste, who became Shea's great-great-grandmother. In her attempt to claim Penbrook Manor as her rightful inheritance, she runs up against Jonas Riley, its current owner. The 1840s story line is based on the author's family history.

Cote, Lyn.

Blessed Assurance. **Avon Inspire, 2007. 511pp. Paper, 9780736914598.**

Between 1871 and 1920 three generations of Wagstaffs survive politically and socially troubling times. The Great Chicago Fire tests the limits of Jessie Wagstaff and her young son, Linc; Linc fights his own battles against child labor in 1906 San Francisco; and his daughter Meg confronts racial violence in 1920s New Orleans. Each finds a romantic partner who proves an equal in strength. This is an omnibus edition of three short novels: *Whispers of Love, Lost in His Love,* and *Echoes of Mercy,* previously published in 1999 and 2000.

Keywords: California—20th century; Great Chicago Fire; Illinois—20th century; Louisiana—20th century; San Francisco earthquake

Women of Ivy Manor. 📖

Cote's saga about four generations of women forging their own paths in life spans the entire twentieth century, focusing on both political and social history. She lets readers view firsthand the shifts in fashion, dance, and music, and lets them observe how women were affected by the changing times. In these coming of age novels, her protagonists' relationships with their overprotective mothers and rebellious daughters are fraught with tension; the women don't learn from their mothers' mistakes, especially where men are concerned. Inspirational without being preachy, this series should also interest mainstream readers.

Keywords: Coming of age; Journalists and reporters; Maryland—20th century; Mothers and daughters; Soldiers, women; Spies, women

Chloe. Warner Faith, 2005. 290pp. Paper, 0446694347.

Chloe Kimball, born in 1900 on her rich parents' estate of Ivy Manor in Tidewater, Maryland, grows up surrounded by wealth but lacking love and attention. She escapes to New York City during the Jazz Age and marries a gorgeous man she barely knows, but neither marriage nor motherhood brings her happiness.

Bette. FaithWords, 2005. 304pp. Paper, 0446694355.

Elizabeth "Bette" Leigh Black grows up in the years prior to World War II and enjoys a happy home environment with her mother, Chloe, and stepfather. Her marriage to Curtis Sinclair seems happy at first, but when he's sent overseas, he falls in love with a French-woman, forcing Bette and her daughter to survive on their own. To make ends meet, and to support her country's wartime efforts, Bette returns to her prewar work in anti-Nazi espionage.

Leigh. FaithWords, 2006. 304pp. Paper, 0446694371.

Bette's daughter, Linda Leigh Sinclair, wants to explore more of life than her loving but sheltered home at Ivy Manor has shown her., She becomes a reporter and travels the country covering events of the civil rights movement. While in San Francisco at the height of the 1960s counterculture, Leigh falls for the wrong guy.

Carly. FaithWords, 2006. 304pp. Paper, 0446694363.

In an effort to prove her worthiness to her strong-willed mother, Leigh, Carly Lorraine Sinclair overcomes her shyness by joining the military and serving overseas in Kuwait during Operation Desert Storm. When she is wounded in action, the previous three generations of women of Ivy Manor are there to care for her.

Hoff, B. J.

American Anthem.

Hoff's Christian soap opera takes place in late nineteenth-century New York City and the nearby Hudson River Valley. She incorporates multiple plotlines and characters to illustrate a wide range of American immigrant experiences. Susanna Fallon grows intrigued by her brother-in-law Michael, a pianist, but worries about the role he may have played in her late sister's death. Andrew Carmichael, a Scottish physician, accepts a female doctor into his practice. Finally, the McGovern family adjusts to a new life in America.

Keywords: Immigrants, Irish; Immigrants, Scottish; New York—Reconstruction/ Gilded Age

Prelude. W Publishing Group, 2002. 281pp. Paper, 0849943892.

Cadence. W Publishing Group, 2003. 264pp. Paper, 0849943906.

Jubilee. W Publishing Group, 2004. 280pp. Paper, 0849943914.

Mountain Song Legacy.

Gentle romantic drama in the small coal mining town of Skingle Creek in north-eastern Kentucky between the late nineteenth and early twentieth centuries.

Keywords: Coal mining; Kentucky—Reconstruction/Gilded Age; Teachers

A Distant Music. Harvest House, 2006. 255pp. Paper, 0736914048.

Jonathan Stuart, who teaches the local children in a one-room schoolhouse, is loved by one and all for his kindness, storytelling abilities, and love of music. In 1892, when his prized flute goes missing, twelve-year-old Maggie MacAulay, one of his most devoted pupils, and her terminally ill best friend, Summer, stop at nothing to bring music back to his life. This is an expanded version of an early novella of Hoff's, *The Penny Whistle.*

The Wind Harp. Harvest House, 2006. 254pp. Paper, 0736914587.

It's now 1904, and Maggie MacAulay returns to Skingle Creek from Chicago, where she has been teaching at Hull House. She is distraught upon seeing her family struggling with poverty after her father's accident in the coal mines, so she decides to stay put, becoming a teacher just like her former mentor. No one is more surprised than she when her feelings for Mr. Stuart turn into something more.

The Song Weaver. Harvest House, 2007. 244pp. Paper, 9780736914598.

By the end of 1904 Jonathan and Maggie are married, but they are called home from their honeymoon in Lexington upon hearing devastating news about Maggie's pregnant sister, Eva Grace.

Kelly, Leisha.

Country Road Chronicles.

A continuation of the Wortham Family Series (see below) set in rural Illinois farm country, picking up the story of the Worthams and Hammonds, their good friends, and their neighbors, in 1938. In this series two Wortham children, Sarah and Frank, take their turns narrating alongside their parents. *Sarah's Promise* will be next.

Keywords: Great Depression; Illinois—20th century; Neighbors; Prayers; Wortham family

Rorey's Secret. Revell, 2005. 286pp. Paper, 0800759850.

The entire novel takes place over a period of several days, and very busy ones at that for the Wortham and Hammond families. When Thelma Hammond goes into labor, no doctor is available, forcing Julia Wortham to deliver the child herself. When the Hammonds' barn goes up in flames and Samuel Wortham is injured, his daughter Sarah realizes that thirteen-year-old Rorey may hold the key to who did it.

Rachel's Prayer. Revell, 2006. 312pp. Paper, 0800759869.

It's now 1942, and Julia Wortham worries about her son, Robert, who enlisted in the army after Pearl Harbor, along with three of the Hammond sons. Robert's girlfriend, Rachel Gray, writes a prayer that helps both families get through these difficult times.

Wortham Family Series.

During the Great Depression the Wortham family bottoms out financially, but they find the greatest rewards in helping their new neighbors. Elderly Emma Graham helps them out in turn when they need it most. Taken together, the books in this smoothly written series, centering on the importance of hope and faith during hard times, read like one long novel. All are written in the first person, with the narrator alternating (between Sam and Julia Wortham) in each chapter.

Keywords: Great Depression; Illinois—20th century; Neighbors; Wortham family

Julia's Hope. Revell, 2002. 318pp. Paper, 080075820X.

Samuel Wortham loses his job after the stock market crash of 1929, and he, his wife Julia, and their two children hitchhike from Harrisburg, Pennsylvania, to the small town of Vernon, Illinois. Their decision to seek shelter in an abandoned farmhouse leads them to its owner, elderly Emma Graham, and her great capacity for kindness.

Emma's Gift. Revell, 2003. 314pp. Paper, 0800758579.

In 1931 the Worthams' neighbor Wilametta Hammond dies, leaving behind ten children and a grieving husband. As Julia struggles to understand God's purpose in taking away a beloved and much-needed wife and mother, she and Samuel take on the difficult task of caring for the Hammond children in their father's absence.

Katie's Dream. Revell, 2004. 330pp. Paper, 0800759109.

When Samuel and Julia return from the Fourth of July celebrations in 1932, they find Samuel's brother, Edward, waiting for them. Not only are they surprised to see him out of prison, but Edward claims that the young girl accompanying him is Samuel's illegitimate daughter, Katie.

Till Morning Is Nigh: A Wortham Family Christmas. Revell, 2007. 160pp. Paper, 9780800718879.

This Christmas-themed novella, fitting chronologically after *Katie's Dream*, is set during the holiday season of 1932, not a particularly joyful time. It has been a year since Wilametta Hammond and Emma Graham passed away; Julia Wortham relies on her inner strength and her faith in God to pull the two families through.

Morris, Gilbert.

House of Winslow. ★

This very popular saga of the extended Winslow family begins with Gilbert Winslow, who in 1620 becomes a spy for the Church of England against the rabble-rousing Pilgrims. Later Gilbert has a change of heart, remaining with the Pilgrims after their journey to Massachusetts on the *Mayflower*. Subsequent Winslows participate in nearly every major event in American history. Morris jumps 200 years from colonial times to the Civil War over the first eight books, touching briefly on the American Revolution in between. After that the pace slows considerably, with the last few books set during the 1929 stock market crash and in the 1930s. The series concludes with its fortieth volume, as Winslows fight for freedom in the Spanish Civil War.

Keywords: Winslow family

The Honorable Imposter. Bethany House, 1987. 331pp. Paper, 0871239337.

The Captive Bride. Bethany House, 1987. 238pp. Paper, 0871239787.

The Indentured Heart. Bethany House, 1988. 288pp. Paper, 1556610033.

The Gentle Rebel. Bethany House, 1988. 285pp. Paper, 1556610068.

The Saintly Buccaneer. Bethany House, 1989. 299pp. Paper, 1556610483.

The Holy Warrior. Bethany House, 1989. 284pp. Paper, 1556610548.

The Reluctant Bridegroom. Bethany House, 1990. 303pp. Paper, 1556610696.

The Last Confederate. Bethany House, 1990. 333pp. Paper, 1556611099.

The Dixie Widow. Bethany House, 1991. 318pp. Paper, 1556611153.

The Wounded Yankee. Bethany House, 1991. 304pp. Paper, 1556611161.

The Union Belle. Bethany House, 1992. 334pp. Paper, 1556611862.

The Final Adversary. Bethany House, 1992. 301pp. Paper, 1556612613.

The Crossed Sabres. Bethany House, 1993. 317pp. Paper, 1556613091.

The Valiant Gunman. Bethany House, 1993. 320pp. Paper, 1556613105.

The Gallant Outlaw. Bethany House, 1994. 288pp. Paper, 1556613113.

The Jeweled Spur. Bethany House, 1994. 299pp. Paper, 155661392X.

The Yukon Queen. Bethany House, 1995. 285pp. Paper, 1556613938.

The Rough Rider. Bethany House, 1995. 303pp. Paper, 1556613946.

The Iron Lady. Bethany House, 1996. 320pp. Paper, 1556616872.

The Silver Star. Bethany House, 1997. 304pp. Paper, 1556616880.

The Shadow Portrait. Bethany House, 1998. 304pp. Paper, 1556616899.

The White Hunter. Bethany House, 1999. 304pp. Paper, 155661909X.

The Flying Cavalier. Bethany House, 1999. 318pp. Paper, 0764221159.

The Glorious Prodigal. Bethany House, 2000. 320pp. Paper, 0764221167.

The Amazon Quest. Bethany House, 2001. 320pp. Paper, 0764221175.

The Golden Angel. Bethany House, 2001. 316pp. Paper, 0764221183.

The Heavenly Fugitive. Bethany House, 2002. 320pp. Paper, 0764225995.

The Fiery Ring. Bethany House, 2002. 314pp. Paper, 0764226223.

The Pilgrim Song. Bethany House, 2003. 316pp. Paper, 076422638X.

The Beloved Enemy. Bethany House, 2003. 319pp. Paper, 0764227041.

The Shining Badge. Bethany House, 2004. 320pp. Paper, 0764227432.

The Royal Handmaid. Bethany House, 2004. 320pp. Paper, 0764228560.

The Silent Harp. Bethany House, 2004. 315pp. Paper, 0764227610.

The Virtuous Woman. Bethany House, 2005. 313pp. Paper, 0764226614.

The Gypsy Moon. Bethany House, 2005. 315pp. Paper, 0764226878.

The Unlikely Allies. Bethany House, 2005. 316pp. Paper, 0764227793.

The High Calling. Bethany House, 2006. 318pp. Paper, 0764228250.

The Hesitant Hero. Bethany House, 2006. 286pp. Paper, 0764229451.

The Widow's Choice. Bethany House, 2006. 316pp. Paper, 0764200275.

The White Knight. Bethany House, 2007. 316pp. Paper, 9780764200281.

Singing River Series.

Though not as popular or significant as the House of Winslow novels, Morris's new series uses the same light, flowing style. After her mother dies and her father goes to prison, Lanie Freeman is left to raise her four younger siblings in their hometown of Fairhope, Arkansas. This would be difficult enough for a teenager in any time, but during the Great Depression love and strength of will are the only things remaining to hold this family of orphans together.

Keywords: Arkansas—20th century; Freeman family; Great Depression; Orphans

The Homeplace. Zondervan, 2005. 327pp. Paper, 0310252326.

The Dream. Zondervan, 2006. 314pp. Paper, 0310252334.

The Miracle. Zondervan, 2007. 286pp. Paper, 9780310252344.

The Courtship. Zondervan, 2007. 293pp. Paper, 9780310252351.

Peterson, Tracie, and Judith Miller.

The Broadmoor Legacy.

Romance and family drama among the upper-class Broadmoor family in a beautiful, underused historical setting: the Thousand Islands resort area in upstate New York, with the St. Lawrence River as the scenic backdrop. Three cousins—Fanny, Amanda, and Sophie Broadmoor—continue their close friendship despite their parents' squabbles. Set in the late nineteenth century.

Keywords: Broadmoor family; Cousins; Heirs and heiresses; New York—Reconstruction/Gilded Age; Resorts; Thousand Islands

A Daughter's Inheritance. Bethany House, 2008. 383pp. Paper, 9780764203640.

> Fanny Broadmoor was always close to her grandparents, who lovingly raised her after her parents died. When her grandfather passes away in 1897, his will divides his estate in three: one part to Fanny's greedy Uncle Jonas, another to her Uncle Quincy, and the remaining third to Fanny, in lieu of her late father. Jonas, who becomes her guardian, schemes to control Fanny's inheritance, to the point of manipulating her burgeoning romance with the family's boat-keeper.

Price, Eugenia.

Price's sagas of the antebellum South are annotated in Chapter 5.

Snelling, Lauraine.

The Brushstroke Legacy. **WaterBrook, 2006. 392pp. Paper, 1578567890.**

> Ragni Clausen, a single thirtyish woman from Chicago worn down by caring for her Alzheimer's-affected father, sets out for North Dakota with her rebellious teenaged niece, Erika, to investigate her great-grandmother's ramshackle cabin. As the pair fixes it up, they find paintings left behind by Nilda, their ancestor, and rekindle their family bond. A parallel story speaks to Nilda's experiences traveling west in the early 1900s with her daughter to become a housekeeper.

> **Keywords:** Aunts; Housekeepers; Multi-period novels; North Dakota—20th century; Norwegian Americans

Daughters of Blessing Series.

> Blessing, a small farming town in North Dakota's Red River Valley, has been the fictional setting for Snelling's sagas about Norwegian Americans. This spin-off from her earlier <u>Red River of the North</u> and <u>Return to Red River</u> series centers on four women of the next generation. Genealogical tables are included. *Rebecca's Reward* will continue their story.

> **Keywords:** Farmers; North Dakota—20th century; Norwegian Americans

A Promise for Ellie. Bethany House, 2007. 314pp, Paper, 0764228099.

> It is May 1900, and Ellie Wold and Andrew Bjorklund have spoken of marriage for years. They set their wedding date for after harvest time, but when their new barn burns, it precipitates a tragedy that tests their commitment.

Sophie's Dilemma. Bethany House, 2007. 334pp. Paper, 9780764203992.

> Sophie Knutson, elated when Hamre Bjorklund comes home to Blessing, accepts his marriage proposal. Eager to escape her father's clutches, Sophie elopes with him to Ballard, Washington, near Seattle, but his job as a fisherman leaves her frequently alone and missing her family.

A Touch of Grace. Bethany House, 2008. 319pp. Paper, 9780764228117.

> Grace Knutson, Sophie's twin sister, has been deaf since birth. Her love for Toby Valders seems destined to go unrequited, but Jonathan Gould, a city boy sent west to experience farm life, helps her forget him. He invites her to New York, but his overbearing mother doubts Grace's suitability as a daughter-in-law.

> **Keywords:** Deafness

Africa, Asia, and the Antipodes

Wall, Wilma.

9

The Jade Bracelet. **Kregel, 2006. 304pp. Paper, 0825439485.**
Wall's saga about three American women living in China and America spans most of the twentieth century, from the Communist insurgency through the present day. Elsa Meier, born in China to missionary parents in the 1930s, has always felt at home among the Chinese people. When the Reds make it clear they want foreigners gone, the family returns to America, though Elsa resents her mother Rachel's overbearing nature and unrealistic expectations. Only when Elsa gives birth to her own daughter, Crystal, do she and Rachel begin to reconcile.

Keywords: China—20th century; Chinese Americans; Missionaries; Mothers and daughters

10

11

Christian Historical Romances

Most of these novels can be described as historical romances rather than romantic historicals (defined in Chapter 4), though all of them end on a hopeful note. It's a given that in order for the romance to work, both heroine and hero must follow the Christian faith. Romances with nonbelievers don't lead to marriage unless the non-Christian party discovers God.

12

The British Isles

With the exceptions of Carol Umberger's and Kathleen Morgan's novels, set during turbulent periods of Scottish history, British politics remain firmly in the background. This keeps the focus on the developing romance.

13

Klassen, Julie.

Lady of Milkweed Manor. **Bethany House, 2007. 411pp. Paper, 9780764204791.** 📖
Twenty-year-old Charlotte Lamb, a vicar's daughter in Regency England, is a fallen woman. So as not to disgrace her stern father and her community any further, she boards a train to London for an extended stay at a home for unwed mothers. Ashamed and desperate to keep her identity hidden, Charlotte is distraught to find a former suitor, Dr. Daniel Taylor, employed at the manor, but he agrees to keep her secret. An unusual coming of age story and gentle romance that examines love, sacrifice, and single motherhood during the Regency period.

14

15

Keywords: Coming of age; England—Regency era; Illegitimate children; Physicians; Pregnancy

Morgan, Kathleen.

As High as the Heavens. **Revell, 2008. 360pp. 9780800758165.**

In 1568 noblewoman Heather Gordon hopes to help Mary, Queen of Scots, escape Lochleven Castle, where she is being held prisoner. Heather journeys to a cottage in the Highlands to find the secret twin brother of a nobleman who has access to Lochleven, a man who has no idea of his real heritage.

Keywords: Nobility; Scotland—16th century

These Highland Hills.

Couples fall in love against the backdrop of clan wars in late sixteenth-century Scotland.

Keywords: Scotland—16th century

Child of the Mist. Revell, 2005. 332pp. Paper, 080075963X.

In 1563 Anne MacGregor is betrothed to Niall Campbell to settle a truce between their warring families. But Anne has the gift of healing, a dangerous thing to possess in an era when witches are being hunted, and Niall believes she may be involved with a traitorous plot against him.

Keywords: Healers

Wings of Morning. Revell, 2006. 286pp. Paper, 0800759648.

Regan MacLaren, widowed on her wedding night, is injured and loses her memory while seeking to avenge her husband's death. Iain Campbell rescues her from near death. During her recovery they fall in love; she doesn't discover until later that he may be her husband's killer.

Keywords: Amnesia

A Fire Within. Revell, 2007. 314pp. Paper, 9780800759650.

Caitlin Campbell, sister of Niall from *Child of the Mist*, meets Darach MacNaghten when he arrives to free his older brother, chief of the MacNaghtens, who is being held prisoner in the Campbell dungeon. When his plan fails, Darach takes Caitlin hostage.

Keywords: Hostages

Morren, Ruth Axtell.

Dawn in My Heart. **Steeple Hill, 2006. 352pp. Paper, 0373785674.**

In London in 1814, after his older brother's death Tertius Pembroke, Fourth Earl of Skylar, returns from the West Indies, knowing it's his duty to marry and produce an heir. Lady Gillian Edwards seems an ideal choice, but she's in love with another man. Morren pushes the boundaries of the inspirational fiction genre with this Regency romance about a nonvirginal heroine and a hero who fears he's been cursed by black magic; neither becomes a Christian until partway through the novel.

Keywords: England—Regency era; Nobility

The Healing Season. **Steeple Hill, 2007. 448pp. Paper, 9780373785889.**

Dr. Ian Russell, a former army surgeon, meets Eleanor Neville, an actress on the London stage, when he's called to administer to her best friend, who is very ill. Although attracted to the beautiful Eleanor, Ian, a godly man in search of a woman he can love, is disgusted by her sinful lifestyle. Eleanor is grateful for his help but hates his arrogant attitude.

9

Keywords: Actresses; England—Regency era; Physicians

The Rogue's Redemption. **Steeple Hill, 2008. 416pp. Paper, 97810373786008.**

Miss Hester Leighton, an outspoken American newly arrived in London, meets Major Gerrit Hawkes, a war-hardened veteran, at a masked ball. They begin keeping company, but his reputation isn't exactly pristine. Readers first saw Gerrit in *Dawn in My Heart*, as the lover whom Gillian Edwards couldn't forget.

10

Keywords: England—Regency era; Veterans

11

Palmer, Catherine.

Miss Pickworth Series.

Romance and adventure set during England's Regency period. Miss Pickworth, a writer for a London newspaper, hunts down material on unlikely couples for her gossip column. Palmer uses formal phrasing to try to evoke Jane Austen.

12

Keywords: England—Regency era; Gossip; Nobility; Widows

The Affectionate Adversary. Tyndale House, 2006. 337pp. Paper, 084237549X.

On the surface Charles Locke, an adventurous commoner, and Sarah Carlyle, a widowed aristocrat, seem like an ideal match: he seeks a fortune in the tea trade, while Sarah's wealth has brought her nothing but heartache. They fall in love as she nurses him back to health after a pirate attack at sea, but she doesn't completely trust him.

13

The Bachelor's Bargain. Tyndale House, 2006. 367pp. Paper, 0842319298.

Anne Webster, a housemaid, accepts the mock marriage proposal of roguish Ruel Chouteau, Marquess of Blackthorne, when she believes she is dying, because it will ensure her family won't starve. When she makes an unexpected recovery she is forced to deal with the reality of their marriage.

14

Umberger, Carol.

15

Scottish Crown Series.

A romantic series set during Scotland's Wars for Independence in the early fourteenth century.

Keywords: Nobility; Scotland—high Middle Ages

Circle of Honor. Integrity, 2002. 292pp. Paper, 1591450055.

The Price of Freedom. Integrity, 2003. 280pp. Paper, 1591450063.

The Mark of Salvation. Integrity, 2003. 262pp. Paper, 1591450071.

The Promise of Peace. Integrity, 2004. 260pp. Paper, 1591451663.

> Keifer McNab has been sent to foster with Adam Mackintosh, hero from *Circle of Honor*. There he trains as a knight and grows up with Adam's daughter, Nola, as a playmate. As Nola grows up, she develops romantic feelings for her foster brother. Keifer, though he's loyal to Robert Bruce, remains bitter over having lost his father as a boy and hesitates to trust anyone.

Americana Romances

Gentle romantic tales set in America's small towns in the nineteenth and early twentieth centuries. Politics rarely intrude, but Maureen Lang's novels, set during World War II, are an exception.

Clark, Dorothy.

Beauty for Ashes. Steeple Hill, 2004. 330pp. Paper, 0373785151.

> In 1820 in Philadelphia, Elizabeth Frazier, a young woman running away from an arranged marriage with a wealthy, abusive man, is mistaken for the woman who answered Justin Randolph's ad for a bride in name only. Justin, a widower, seeks nothing more than a mother for his two small daughters, a condition that Elizabeth, skittish around men, happily agrees to.

> **Keywords:** Marriages of convenience; Pennsylvania—early United States

Joy for Mourning. Steeple Hill, 2005. 296pp. Paper, 0373785429.

> Laina Brighton, a rich widow (and sister of Justin from *Beauty for Ashes*), transforms her newly purchased mansion into a home for orphans, something that Philadelphia desperately needs. This brings her into the circle of Thaddeous Allen, a handsome doctor, and their partnership becomes a subject of local gossip.

> **Keywords:** Pennsylvania—early United States; Widows

Cox, Carol.

A Fair to Remember Series.

> Romance, mystery, and intrigue when the World's Fair comes to Chicago in 1893.

> **Keywords:** Illinois—Reconstruction/Gilded Age; World's Fair

Ticket to Tomorrow. Barbour, 2006. 317pp. Paper, 1593109482.

> Annie Crockett arrives at the World's Fair with Silas Crockett, her late husband's business partner, with plans to exhibit their invention, a "horseless carriage." A scuffle with another man at the train station leads to a mix-up of bags, drawing the pair into danger. As Annie deals with her standoffish former in-laws, who have never approved of her, she finds herself attracted to Nick Rutherford, Silas's nephew.

Fair Game. Barbour, 2007. 315pp. Paper, 9781597894913.

> Dinah Mayhew moves to Chicago and secures a job at the World's Fair; she also hopes to find her father, whom she hasn't seen for years. She teams up with Seth Howell, a handsome pastor, to minister to inner-city children, but

when Dinah's annoying cousin Gladys disappears, the romantic pair abandon their plans in order to search for her.

A Bride So Fair. Barbour, 2008. 288pp. Paper, 9781597894920.

Emily Ralston, who works in the Children's Building during the World's Fair, teams up with Stephen Bridger to find the parents of a boy found wandering around the fairgrounds. They court danger when a woman believed to be the boy's mother turns up dead.

Gabhart, Ann H.

The Outsider. **Revell, 2008. 352pp. Paper, 9780800732394.**

Gabrielle Hope, a young woman living with her mother in a quiet Shaker community in Kentucky in 1812, has always feared the prophetic visions that came to her without warning. When her foresight predicts the illness of a young Shaker man, the physician brought from the outside to save him disturbs her world and challenges her loyalty to the group. A gentle, expressive romance set in a bygone world.

Keywords: Kentucky—early United States; Psychics; Shakers

Gist, Deeanne.

🏆 *A Bride Most Begrudging.* **Bethany House, 2005. 347pp. Paper, 0764200720.**

Lady Constance Morrow of Deptford, England, arrives in the Virginia colony in 1643 after an unpleasant voyage; she had intended only to say good-bye to her convict uncle, who was being transported to America, but the ship's captain threw her in the hold with other "tobacco brides." With no papers to prove her identity, she finds herself the wife of Drew O'Connor, a man who expects her to cook, clean house, and care for his younger sister. Christy Award.

Keywords: Nobility; Virginia—colonial period

Lang, Maureen.

Pieces of Silver Series.

Romances on the World War I home front, as men and women confront their own prejudices.

Keywords: German Americans; Prejudice; Virginia—World War I; Washington, D.C.—World War I

Pieces of Silver. Kregel, 2005. 301pp. Paper, 0825436680.

Liesel Bonner, an American of German ancestry working in Washington, D.C., in 1917, loses her government job when higher-ups begin suspecting anyone with a German surname of treason. Then FBI agent David de Serre begins nosing around, asking questions about Josef von Woerner, the man Liesel had hoped to marry.

Remember Me. Kregel, 2006. 336pp. Paper, 9780825436727.

Later in 1917 Josef Warner wakes with no memory of who or where he is, although Hank, the man who rescues him and brings him home to Culpepper, Virginia, says that he's Josef's biological father. Josef falls in love with Lissa Parker, a local nurse with patriotic fervor. If she knew about his wanted past, she might very well change her mind about him.

Lessman, Julie.

Daughters of Boston Trilogy.

In Boston in 1916 three women search for romance and their place in the world as the Great War rages overseas.

Keywords: Irish Americans; Massachusetts—World War I; Sisters

A Passion Most Pure. Revell, 2007. 477pp. Paper, 9780800732110.

Faith O'Connor, crippled after a bout of polio in childhood, fears she'll never find a man to love her for who she is. While trying to accept the fact that her father may be called up to fight in World War I in Europe, Faith grows puzzled by the flattering attention her beautiful sister Charity's suitor, Collin McGuire, has been paying her.

A Passion Redeemed. Revell, 2008. 480pp. Paper, 9780800732127.

Strong-willed Charity O'Connor, a beautiful yet selfish blonde, refuses to believe it when newspaper editor Mitch Dennehy claims not to be interested in her. He's already been burned once—after his engagement to her older sister, Faith, fell apart thanks to Charity's scheming.

MacLaren, Sharlene.

Little Hickman Creek Series.

Gentle, down-to-earth novels about women who find romance on the early American frontier.

Keywords: Frontier and pioneer life; Kentucky—Reconstruction/Gilded Age

Loving Liza Jane. Whitaker House, 2007. 351pp. Paper, 9780883688168.

In the late nineteenth century Liza Jane Merriwether answers an ad for a schoolteacher in the small town of Little Hickman, Kentucky. Widower Benjamin Broughton, a man whose daughters need a mother figure, offers her a place to stay, but he has already sent away for a mail-order bride.

Keywords: Mail-order brides; Teachers

Sarah, My Beloved. Whitaker House, 2007. 365pp. Paper, 9780883684252.

Sarah Woodward, running away from an arranged marriage, has traveled from Boston to Little Hickman Creek to be the mail-order bride of Ben Broughton, but his heart is already taken. Rocky Callahan, a friend of Ben's who needs help raising his niece and nephew, offers her a marriage of convenience.

Keywords: Marriages of convenience

Courting Emma. Whitaker House, 2008. 382pp. Paper, 9781603740203.

Emma Browning, a cynical twenty-eight-year-old spinster, doesn't believe in either love or God. Then Little Hickman's new pastor comes to stay at her boardinghouse, and her drunk, abusive father discovers Christianity and mends his ways.

Keywords: Innkeepers; Spinsters

Morren, Ruth Axtell.

Lilac Spring. **Steeple Hill, 2005. 294pp. Paper, 037378550X.**
Cherish Winslow, daughter of a shipbuilder in the small seacoast town of Haven's End, Maine, in 1875, has been in love for years with Silas van der Zee, her father's apprentice. He feels the same for her, though he fears she's out of his league, particularly with her family's recent financial hardships.

Keywords: Maine—Reconstruction/Gilded Age; Shipbuilders

Wild Rose. **Steeple Hill, 2004. 360pp. Paper, 0373785275.**
Geneva Patterson, an orphaned young woman in Haven's End in 1873, is known as "Salt Fish Ginny" because she makes ends meet by selling vegetables and catching fish; that and her habit of wearing men's clothes don't endear her to eligible bachelors. When Captain Caleb Phelps, a wealthy shipping magnate, comes to his summer home in Haven's End to escape from a financial scandal, the paths of these two outcasts cross.

Keywords: Businessmen; Maine—Reconstruction/Gilded Age

Wick, Lori.

Tucker Mills Trilogy.
The small mill town of Tucker Mills, Massachusetts, in the 1830s and 1840s is the setting for Wick's series of faith-filled romances. The novels should be read in order, as stories from the earlier volumes thread through the later ones. Fairly heavy Christian content.

Keywords: Housekeepers; Massachusetts—early United States; Mill workers; Physicians

Moonlight on the Millpond. Harvest House, 2005. 284pp. Paper, 0736911588.
Woody Randall offers his nephew Jace a position at his sawmill when his health fails. Jace develops a romantic interest in Maddie Shepard, the storekeeper's niece, but his controlling older sister fuels gossip about them that derails their relationship.

Just Above a Whisper. Harvest House, 2005. 300pp. Paper, 0736911596.
In 1839 Reese Thackery, a former indentured servant in Tucker Mills, takes a position as housekeeper at Conner Kingsley's manor. Although she feels attracted to him, her former master's cruel treatment of her makes her skittish.

Leave a Candle Burning. Harvest House, 2006. 316pp. Paper, 0736913734.
Dannan MacKay comes to town to take over his uncle's medical practice and falls in love with a woman who, as he learns later, is already spoken for. Scottie Peterson is happily married, but her husband is

bedridden. Dannan takes comfort in caring for his late cousin's three-year-old daughter.

Prairie Romances

In the traditional prairie romance, a young woman heads west as a schoolteacher, housekeeper, or mail-order bride, grows closer to God during difficult times, and discovers romance where she least expects it. The differences between these novels and romantic Christian Westerns (covered later this chapter) lie in prairie romances' gentle, heartwarming quality and their emphasis on the domesticity of pioneer life. Quiet rather than action-oriented, prairie romances are apt to be set in farming communities on the Midwestern or Canadian plains, rather than on ranches, in the mountains, or in the Southwestern desert.

Bittner, Rosanne.

Follow Your Heart. **Steeple Hill, 2005. 336pp. Paper, 037381125X.**

Railroad employee Jude Kingman arrives on the Nebraska plains in the 1870s with the directive of buying the land from the existing settlers. Surprisingly, farmer's daughter Ingrid Svensson doesn't hold his job against him.

Keywords: Nebraska—Reconstruction/Gilded Age; Railroads

Oke, Janette.

This prolific and highly esteemed author, born into a farming family in Alberta during the Depression, writes novels about settlers' experiences throughout North American history. She is best known for her portraits of love, marriage, and family life on the Canadian prairie. In her works she evokes strong Christian values and presents faith as the cornerstone of romantic love. *Love Comes Softly*, Oke's first novel, became an instant classic and pioneered the inspirational fiction genre. Although she has written other series (see volume 1 of *Historical Fiction*), these two are her best known and most popular.

Love Comes Softly Series. ★ YA

On the day of her husband's burial, nineteen-year-old Marty Claridge accepts a marriage proposal from Clark Davis, a stranger whose young daughter, Missie, needs a mother. Thrown together by tragedy, over time Marty and Clark fall in love, form a real marriage, and raise a family. Subsequent volumes deal with their children and grandchildren's lives. Neither the exact location nor the era is stated, but it is probably somewhere in the Canadian West in the mid-nineteenth century. Little details of pioneer life—making soap, killing chickens, sewing new clothes—add even more character to this gentle, romantic series. The series, originally published between 1980 and 1989, was revised and republished starting in 2003.

Keywords: Alberta—19th century; Davis family; Frontier and pioneer life; Marriages of convenience

Love Comes Softly. Bethany House, 2003. 237pp. Paper, 0764228323.

Love's Enduring Promise. Bethany House, 2003. 239pp. Paper, 0764228498

Love's Long Journey. Bethany House, 2003. 200pp. Paper, 0764228501.

Love's Abiding Joy. Bethany House, 2003. 240pp. Paper, 076422851X.

Love's Unending Legacy. Bethany House, 2004. 239pp. Paper, 0764228528.

Love's Unfolding Dream. Bethany House, 2004. 222pp. Paper, 0764228536.

Love Takes Wing. Bethany House, 2004. 240pp. Paper, 0764228544.

Love Finds a Home. Bethany House, 2004. 237pp. Paper, 0764228552.

Prairie Legacy. YA

This sequel to the <u>Love Comes Softly series</u> continues the Davis family saga beginning with Marty and Clark's confused teenaged granddaughter, Virginia Simpson. As in Oke's previous novels, details from the larger world rarely intrude, but the series begins during the Depression years.

Keywords: Alberta—20th century; Davis family; Great Depression

The Tender Years. Bethany House, 1997. 384pp. Paper, 1556619529.

A Searching Heart. Bethany House, 1999. 256pp. Paper, 076422140X.

A Quiet Strength. Bethany House, 1999. 256pp. Paper, 0764221566.

Like Gold Refined. Bethany House, 2000. 251pp. Paper, 0764221612.

Sawyer, Kim Vogel.

Waiting for Summer's Return. **Bethany House, 2006. 348pp. Paper, 9780764201820.**

While traveling with her family from Boston to Oklahoma in 1894, Summer Steadman experiences every wife and mother's worst nightmare: she loses her husband and four children to typhoid. She settles in the German-Mennonite community of Gaeddert, Kansas, where she can remain close to their graves. Summer takes a position as teacher to the young son of widower Peter Ollenberger, which causes rumors to fly.

Keywords: Mennonites; Oklahoma—Reconstruction/Gilded Age; Teachers; Widows

Where Willows Grow. **Bethany House, 2007. 348pp. Paper, 9780764201837.**

In 1936 Anna Mae Phipps is left alone to tend their farm and raise their two daughters when her husband, Harley, takes a WPA job on the other side of Kansas. She resents him for leaving them during a time of drought, especially when he doesn't stay in close touch. Jack Berkley, a neighbor and former boyfriend who runs a nearby dairy farm, hopes to win Anna Mae back by helping her out and planting seeds of doubt about her marriage.

Keywords: Farmers; Great Depression; Kansas—20th century

Christian Historical Westerns

Although Western historical novels have generally dropped in popularity, Westerns predominate in Christian fiction, which gives Western lovers plenty to choose from. The settings are not quite as varied as in traditional Western historicals (Chapter 6). Most of these novels take place during the latter half of the nineteenth century, as men and women make their way westward to settle the land after the Civil War. Traditional Westerns in this category have declined in popularity; most of these novels feature strong female protagonists and/or are aimed at a female audience. See also "Prairie Romances," above.

Frontier Novels

Brave nineteenth-century women and men confront the dangers and opportunities of America's Western frontier. Although the discomforts of pioneer life may cause them to question God's existence, they never truly give up hope. Christian frontier novels normally tell the story from a woman's viewpoint; Al Lacy's and JoAnna Lacy's novels are exceptions. Not surprisingly, women are the principal readers of frontier novels.

Kirkpatrick, Jane.

A Land of Sheltered Promise. **WaterBrook, 2005. 417pp. Paper, 1578567335.** ✍ 📖

Three novellas, entitled *Faith, Hope,* and *Charity,* span a century's worth of women's experiences on the same plot of land in eastern Oregon, the Big Muddy Ranch. In 1901 Eva Bruner, a sheepherder's wife, faces life without her husband, who has been accused of murder. In 1984 Cora Swenson tries to rescue her granddaughter from a New Age cult. Finally, in 1997 the land is donated to a nondenominational youth camp. All three segments are based on historical incidents, and the Big Muddy is a real place, close to the land on which the author herself lives.

Keywords: Cults; Oregon—20th century; Ranchers

Change and Cherish Historical Series. ✍ 📖

Kirkpatrick's latest trilogy about strong women pioneers traces the life of Emma Wagner Giesy, a German American woman who became one of Oregon's first settlers. Both the Wagners and the Giesys, Emma's parents and in-laws, belong to the Bethelite colony, a religious sect in Bethel, Missouri, whose members believe in simple and communal living. The series, replete with authentic dialogue that reflects the characters' ancestry, brings to life a woman who sought balance between her need for independence and her desire for community.

Keywords: Bethelites; Families; Frontier and pioneer life; German Americans; Giesy, Emma Wagner (historical character); Oregon—early United States; Utopian communities; Washington state—early United States

A Clearing in the Wild. **WaterBrook, 2006. Paper, 1578567343.**

In 1851 teenager Emma Wagner marries Christian Giesy, a kind man of her father's age who assists Wilhelm Keil, the Bethelites' founder, with the colony's leadership. Then Keil, believing that the outside world is encroaching too much on their lifestyle, decides to send Christian and other men on a mission to found a new settlement in the Pacific Northwest. Strong-willed Emma, who has always chafed against the restrictions placed on women, demands to accompany the group, keeping her pregnancy hidden.

A Tendering in the Storm. WaterBrook, 2007. 403pp. Paper, 9781578567355.

By 1856 the Giesys have settled along Willapa Bay in Washington State. Conflict arises when Wilhelm Keil arrives with a second contingent of Bethelites. While Keil's group moves south to Oregon Territory to found a new colony, called Aurora Mills, the Giesys informally break away from the Bethelites. Then tragedy strikes, leaving a pregnant Emma to raise her family alone—which makes her vulnerable to bad influences, including her husband's cousin Jack.

Keywords: Abusive relationships

A Mending at the Edge. WaterBrook, 2008. 397pp. Paper, 9781578569793.

Emma has rejoined the Bethelites at their Oregon settlement to escape from her abusive second husband, Jack, but by 1862 their restrictions on her life are beginning to chafe once more. She fights for the right to live independently and raise her four children on her own terms, although Wilhelm Keil pressures her to reconcile with her estranged, abusive husband.

Lacy, Al, and JoAnna Lacy.

Kane Legacy Series.

The Lacys, prolific chroniclers of the American Western experience, follow the men and women of the Kane family as Texas marches toward statehood. The series begins in 1835, a year before the Battle of the Alamo. Heavy religious content.

Keywords: Alamo, Battle of the; Kane family; Texas—early United States

A Line in the Sand. Multnomah, 2007. 320pp. Paper, 9781590529249.

Web of Destiny. Multnomah, 2008. 304pp. Paper, 9781590529256.

High Is the Eagle. Multnomah, 2008. 304pp. Paper, 9781590529263.

A Place to Call Home Series.

In 1838 thousands of Cherokee, Seminole, and other Native American tribes are forcibly moved from the Carolinas to Oklahoma Territory along the Trail of Tears. Love blossoms in the most unlikely of places, but these strong-willed men and women pray that their faith in God will help them survive the journey. The last two volumes continue their story through the Oklahoma Land Rush of 1889.

Keywords: Army; Cherokee Indians; Mixed heritage; Oklahoma—Reconstruction/Gilded Age; Oklahoma Land Rush of 1889; Policemen; Trail of Tears

Cherokee Rose. Multnomah, 2006. 304pp. Paper, 1590525620

Cherokee Rose, a mixed-race Indian, puts up with rude comments and cruel treatment by the soldiers shepherding her and her people along the Trail of Tears to Oklahoma. Lieutenant Britt Claiborne, a fellow Christian, discourages their bad behavior.

Bright Are the Stars. Multnomah, 2006. 272pp. Paper, 1590525639.

By 1839 Cherokee Rose and Britt are married and have made their home in Oklahoma, where they raise their two daughters, but Britt's job as a member of the Cherokee Police Force brings trouble into their life.

The Land of Promise. Multnomah, 2007. 288pp. Paper, 9781590525647.

The U.S. Army, despite its promises to the Cherokee over fifty years earlier, plan to relocate them to reservations and open up land in Oklahoma to white settlement. Britt, the United Cherokee Nation Chief of Police, gets caught in the middle. When white families begin to arrive, Britt and Cherokee Rose learn that they, too, are searching for a place to call home.

Miller, Judith.

Freedom's Path Series.

Through her stories about two families whose lives intersect, Miller personalizes the experiences of the earliest settlers of Nicodemus and Hill City, Kansas, beginning in 1877 and spanning the next five years. Nicodemus was founded by former black slaves fleeing the South after the Civil War, while its neighbor, Hill City, was settled almost wholly by Caucasians. The families of Ezekiel Harban, a sharecropper and ex-slave, and Samuel Boyle, a white doctor from Kentucky, arrive expecting a progressive settlement, but are shocked to find conditions very primitive. Although both families feel misled, they endure many hardships, trusting in God to get them through.

Keywords: African Americans; Frontier and pioneer life; Kansas—Reconstruction/Gilded Age; Slaves, former

First Dawn. Bethany House, 2005. 379pp. Paper, 0764229974.

Morning Sky. Bethany House, 2006. 384pp. Paper, 0764229990.

Daylight Comes. Bethany House, 2006. 384pp. Paper, 0764200003.

Morris, Gilbert.

Lone Star Legacy.

A preachy series about the tumultuous birth of Texas in the 1830s and 1840s as seen through the eyes of a courageous and virtuous woman. Famous names like Davy Crockett, Sam Houston, and Jim Bowie make appearances.

Keywords: Alamo, Battle of the; Frontier and pioneer life; Hardin family; Ranchers; Texas—early United States

Deep in the Heart. Integrity, 2003. 391pp. Paper, 1591451124.

Jerusalem Ann Hardin, used to raising her four children alone while her husband Jake is off somewhere, accepts Clay Taliferro's help when the bank threatens to foreclose on her Arkansas farm. Once she's back on her feet with Clay's help, Jerusalem Ann gathers up her family and heads to Austin, Texas, to reunite with Jake.

The Yellow Rose. Integrity, 2004. 400pp. Paper, 1591451124.

During Texas's struggle to gain independence from Mexico, Jerusalem Ann's husband dies at the Alamo. Having narrowly escaped death herself, she settles with her family on the Brazos River and looks forward to a possible romance with Clay. It's still a dangerous time and place, and Comanche raids menace her settlement.

The Eyes of Texas. Integrity, 2005. 400pp. Paper, 1591451140.

In 1841 Texas has become the newest state. On the Yellow Rose Ranch, Jerusalem Ann and Clay do their best to keep their property safe from Mexican bandits and marauding Indian tribes.

Pella, Judith.

The titles of the novels in Pella's trilogy, set in Maintown, Oregon, in the 1880s, refer to quilting patterns (which are included in the endpapers of each book).

Keywords: Clergy; Oregon—Reconstruction/Gilded Age; Quilters

Bachelor's Puzzle. Bethany House, 2007. 351pp. Paper, 9780764201332

Hearing that a new, single circuit-riding minister will be arriving in town shortly, the unmarried ladies of the church congregation decide to create a patchwork quilt showcasing their talents. But the newcomer, handsome Zack Hartley, seems more comfortable with housework than preaching.

Sister's Choice. Bethany House, 2008. 349pp. Paper, 9780764201349.

Maggie Newcomb has a crush on Colby Stoddard and tries to impress his irascible mother by becoming an expert quilter. Pretty Tamara Brennan arrives in town and upsets all Maggie's plans.

Peterson, Tracie.

Alaskan Quest.

In 1915 Jacob Barringer and Leah Barringer, brother and sister, have made their home on the rugged, icy Alaskan frontier, where they run a trading post and raise sled dogs. When Jacob leaves on an Arctic expedition, Leah finds the isolation difficult to tolerate. Then a man from her past, Jayce Kincaid, comes back into her life, stirring up unwelcome feelings. Meanwhile, Pinkerton agent Helaina Beecham travels north in search of Jayce. The lives of all four characters intertwine in this fast-paced series about survival, love, and forgiveness in an unforgiving land. Leah and Jacob were characters in Peterson's earlier Yukon Quest series.

Keywords: Alaska—20th century; Brothers and sisters; Explorers; Spies, women

Summer of the Midnight Sun. Bethany House, 2006. 378pp. Paper, 0764201433.

Under the Northern Lights. Bethany House, 2006. 384pp. Paper, 0764202197.

Whispers of Winter. Bethany House, 2006. 384pp. Paper, 0764227750.

Heirs of Montana.

In the final years of the Civil War the Chadwick family's journey westward to Montana symbolizes their journey closer to God. Conditions are rough, and not everyone survives. Too many annoying characters populate the series in the beginning, but once they reach Montana, the story comes together. In the later volumes Dianne Chadwick Selby strives to balance her need for independence with her role as a wife and mother.

Keywords: Chadwick family; Married life; Montana—Reconstruction/Gilded Age; Ranchers

Land of My Heart. Bethany House, 2004. 392pp. Paper, 0764227696.

The Coming Storm. Bethany House, 2004. 398pp. Paper, 076422770X.

To Dream Anew. Bethany House, 2004. 398pp. Paper, 0764227718.

The Hope Within. Bethany House, 2005. 398pp. Paper, 0764227726.

Snelling, Lauraine.

Dakotah Treasures Series.

How does one understand and forgive people who seem to deserve it the least? A series set in Snelling's trademark location of North Dakota during the 1880s.

Keywords: North Dakota—Reconstruction/Gilded Age; Sisters; Torvald family

Ruby. Bethany House, 2003. 320pp. Paper, 0764290762.

> Sisters Ruby and Opal Torvald leave the big city for the Black Hills of Dakotah Territory to claim their inheritance from their dying father. Their dubious legacy turns out to be Dove House, an establishment of ill repute, which comes pre-populated with a collection of soiled doves.
>
> **Keywords:** Brothels; Heirs and heiresses

Pearl. Bethany House, 2004. 349pp. Paper, 076422221X.

> Dove House has become respectable thanks to Ruby's efforts. Chicago native Pearl Hossfuss answers Ruby's ad for a schoolteacher for the town of Little Missouri, but her romance with a local carpenter gets derailed by her memories of a scarred childhood.
>
> **Keywords:** Teachers

Opal. Bethany House, 2005. 348pp. Paper, 0764222201.

> Fourteen-year-old Opal Torvald, Ruby's younger sister, refuses to outgrow her tomboy ways. After an incident in which a man is killed rescuing her from trouble, Opal feels horribly guilty and closes her heart off to love—but perhaps a minister newly arrived from back east, Jacob Chandler, will change that.
>
> **Keywords:** Clergy; Tomboys

Amethyst. Bethany House, 2005. 320pp. Paper, 0764200542.

> At her abusive father's request, Amethyst O'Shaunasy travels from Pennsylvania to Medora in Dakotah Territory to bring her nephew home. While there she falls in love with Jeremiah McHenry, a former military man. Meanwhile, as Opal Torvald grows up, Jacob Chandler tries to convince her to marry him.

Whitson, Stephanie Grace.

Pine Ridge Portraits.

A trilogy set on a U.S. Army post at Fort Robinson, Nebraska, beginning in the 1870s and continuing through World War II. Gritty and realistic, as authentic Westerns should be.

Keywords: Army; Nebraska–Reconstruction/Gilded Age, World War II

Secrets on the Wind. Bethany House, 2003. 319pp. Paper, 0764227858.

Watchers on the Hill. Bethany House, 2004. 320pp. Paper, 0764227866.

Footprints on the Horizon. Bethany House, 2005. 317pp. Paper, 0764227874.

> It seems at first like World War II won't ever reach Fort Robinson, but the POW camp constructed just outside town brings the war home. While some of the townspeople are harsh toward the German prisoners, others feel sorry for them, and one brave woman risks censure by hiring prisoners to work on her ranch.
>
> **Keywords:** Prisoners of war

Romantic Westerns

These novels are more action-oriented and set farther west than prairie romances (see section above). In the past, mail-order bride or frontier schoolmarm stories dominated this category, but today's romantic Westerns feature strong-willed female protagonists facing difficult situations who want to make a new start in life. Although they don't need men to survive, they discover that love with the right man can make their lives complete.

Alexander, Tamera.

Fountain Creek Chronicles.

Heart-wrenching romance centering on the Pikes Peak mining town of Willow Springs, Colorado Territory, in the late 1860s. These interconnected novels (characters from earlier novels make appearances in the later ones) can be read independently.

Keywords: Colorado—Reconstruction/Gilded Age

Rekindled. Bethany House, 2006. 334pp. Paper, 0764201085.

> Kathryn and Larson Jennings have been married for ten years, though their childless state and emotional scars from his childhood strain their relationship. When Larson fails to return home from a trip

north, Kathryn believes he's dead and has trouble keeping their ranch afloat. But Larson isn't dead—he was badly burned in a fire. When he sees her embrace another man and learns that she's pregnant, he figures she's better off without him.

Keywords: Disfigurement; Disguise; Married life; Ranchers

🎗 *Revealed.* Bethany House, 2006. 330pp. Paper, 0764201093.

Annabelle Grayson, a former prostitute, seeking a new start after she is widowed, decides to travel from Colorado to her late husband's lands in Idaho. She hires Matthew Taylor, his brother, to be her guide along the trail, although he clearly despises her because of her past and doesn't believe her unborn child is her husband's. Ironically, he has his own demons he'd prefer to keep hidden. RITA Award.

Keywords: Prostitutes; Trail guides; Widows

🎗 *Remembered.* Bethany House, 2007. 381pp. Paper, 9780764201103.

Véronique Girard's father, Pierre, had promised to send for her and her mother when he left France for Colorado twenty-five years earlier, but that never happened. In 1871 Véronique promises her dying mother to make the journey overseas to find her missing father. She hires Jack Brennan, a man whose wife and son were killed years earlier, to transport her between Colorado's dangerous mining towns as she searches for Pierre. Christy Award.

Keywords: Immigrants, French; Trail guides; Widowers

Timber Ridge Reflections.

Alexander's second Western romance series takes place in Timber Ridge, Colorado Territory, in post–Civil War times and showcases the breathtaking landscape of the Rocky Mountains.

Keywords: Colorado—Reconstruction/Gilded Age; Mountains; Photographers, women

From a Distance. Bethany House, 2008. 269pp. Paper, 9780764203893.

In 1875 Elizabeth Westbrook, determined to snag a position as a photojournalist, hires Daniel Ranslett, a former Confederate sharpshooter, to guide her through the Rockies. The Civil War still hangs heavy over both characters, and a photo taken by Elizabeth accidentally reveals secrets from Daniel's past.

Bateman, Tracey.

Westward Hearts Series.

Interconnected novels about women who find love as they make their way westward across the Great Plains.

Keywords: Orphans; Prostitutes; Wagon trains; West—early United States

Defiant Heart. Avon Inspire, 2007. 258pp. Paper, 9780061246333.

In 1847 Fannie Caldwell, an orphan sold into indentured servitude, seizes a long-awaited opportunity to escape from an abusive master with her younger brother and sister. She convinces Blake Tanner to take them as passengers on his wagon train heading westward to Oregon.

Distant Heart. Avon Inspire, 2007. 262pp. Paper, 9780061246340.

> Toni Rodden, a prostitute whom Fannie and her siblings have befriended en route, doesn't believe that Sam Two-Feathers, the half-Indian scout accompanying the wagons, will be able to forgive her scandalous past.

9

Bedford, Deborah.

Blessing. Steeple Hill, 2005. 312pp. Paper, 0373785461.

> Uley Kirkland came to the town that became Tin Cup, Colorado, in the 1880s to work in the mines, so she disguised herself as a young man. Aaron Brown discovers her gender when Uley tries to prevent him from committing a crime—or so she believes at first. He agrees to keep her secret if she helps him clear his name.
>
> **Keywords:** Colorado—Reconstruction/Gilded Age; Disguise; Mines and mining

10

11

Bittner, Rosanne.

Walk by Faith. **Steeple Hill, 2004. 304pp. Paper, 0373785321.**

> In the 1860s, after being abandoned by her husband, Clarissa Graham and her young daughter join a wagon train heading west from Missouri to Montana. Lieutenant Dawson Clements, an ex-soldier who becomes the group's leader, stays behind to care for them when her daughter becomes ill.
>
> **Keywords:** Montana—Reconstruction/Gilded Age; Wagon trains

12

Bull, Molly Noble.

The Winter Pearl. **Steeple Hill, 2004. 328pp. Paper, 0373785291.**

> Fleeing from her alcoholic Uncle Lucas, who wants to force her into marrying him after her aunt's death, Honor McCall takes refuge in a boarding house run by Reverend Jethro Peters and his mother. Set in Colorado in 1888.
>
> **Keywords:** Clergy; Colorado—Reconstruction/Gilded Age

13

14

Carie, Jamie.

Snow Angel. **B&H, 2007. 284pp. Paper, 9780805445336.**

> Noah Wesley finds a beautiful young woman collapsed outside the door of his cabin in Juneau, Alaska, in 1897, and cares for her until her condition improves. Elizabeth wishes desperately to travel to the Klondike's gold fields, though she refuses to tell him why. But even as she flees her enemies, who are getting closer, the private detective hired by her birth mother—who hasn't seen Elizabeth since she was a baby—is also on her trail.
>
> **Keywords:** Adopted children; Alaska—Reconstruction/Gilded Age; Gold Rush

15

Connealy, Mary.

Lassoed in Texas Series.

A series of humorous romantic romps set on the Texas frontier in the 1860s.

Keywords: Texas—Reconstruction/Gilded Age

Petticoat Ranch. Barbour, 2007. 285pp. Paper, 9781597896474.

> In 1867, when mountain man Clay McClellen learns his twin brother has been murdered, he rushes to the Texas frontier to take revenge on the killers and marry his late brother's widow, Sophie, who has been left to raise four daughters alone.
>
> **Keywords:** Widows

Calico Canyon. Barbour, 2008. 288pp. Paper, 9781597899383.

> Schoolteacher Grace Calhoun, on the run from her abusive stepfather, takes refuge in Daniel Reeve's canyon home. Daniel happens to be the father of five rowdy sons—one set of twins, another set of triplets—who caused endless trouble in Grace's classroom, and whose behavior led to Grace getting fired.
>
> **Keywords:** Children; Teachers; Widowers

Copeland, Lori.

Wildflower Series.

Gentle romances set in late nineteenth-century Texas.

Keywords: Texas—Reconstruction/Gilded Age

Yellow Rose Bride. Steeple Hill, 2006. 311pp. Paper, 0373785720.

> In Amarillo n 1898 Vonnie Taylor, a seamstress, is asked to sew the wedding dress for the new fiancée of her ex-husband, handsome rancher Adam Baldwin. A Christian-focused rewrite of Copeland's earlier novel *Bridal Lace and Buckskin.*
>
> **Keywords:** Seamstresses

Bluebonnet Belle. Steeple Hill, 2007. 377pp. Paper, 9780373785919 .

> When Dr. Gray Fuller comes to Dignity, Texas, from Dallas in 1876, hoping to bring modern medicine to the small community, he's challenged by April Truitt, a young woman peddling an herbal tonic.
>
> **Keywords:** Healers; Physicians

Gist, Deeanne.

Essie Spreckelmeyer Series.

Essie Spreckelmeyer, a blonde spinster in late nineteenth-century small-town Texas, has a forthright manner and independent mind that don't endear her to proper society, but she doesn't much care. Big-hearted tales of unexpected romance.

Keywords: Businessmen; Feminists; Spinsters; Texas—Reconstruction/Gilded Age; Tomboys

Courting Trouble. Bethany House, 2007. 332pp. Paper, 9780764202254.

> Essie Spreckelmeyer, a thirty-year-old woman in Corsicana, Texas, in the 1890s, is a tomboy with an eccentric streak. When it becomes apparent that no marriage proposals are forthcoming, she takes the initiative and sets out to attract a suitable man herself.

Deep in the Heart of Trouble. Bethany House, 2008. 394pp. Paper, 9780764202261.

> By 1898 Essie, having given up on catching a husband, has founded the Corsicana Velocipede Club, and she scandalizes the town by riding her bicycle in bloomers. Tony Morgan, an oil man from Beaumont who was disinherited by his wealthy father, runs into Essie after she takes a tumble while sliding down a banister at her father's home. Tony wants Judge Spreckelmeyer to give him a job and help him regain his inheritance. Essie proves to be a major distraction.

🏵 *The Measure of a Lady.* **Bethany House, 2006. 314pp. Paper, 0764200739.**

When Rachel Van Buren's father dies in Gold Rush–era San Francisco, it's left to her to create a godly home for her younger brother and sister—not an easy task in a city full of vice. She reluctantly accepts Johnnie Parker's offer to stay at his boardinghouse, though she fights her strong physical attraction to him and faces an even more difficult challenge when her sister, Lissa, falls prey to temptation. Christy Award.

Keywords: Brothers and sisters; California—early United States; Gold Rush

Hake, Cathy Marie.

Hake writes inspirational romantic Westerns featuring strong heroines and humorous situations.

Bittersweet. **Bethany House, 2006. 399pp. Paper, 9780764203336.**

Laney McCain, younger sister of Josh McCain from *Letter Perfect*, has always been in love with Josh's best friend, neighbor Galen O'Sullivan, and hopes he'll eventually see her as a potential wife. First she has to foil the schemes of Ivy Grubb, a squatter who's been helping out on Galen's farm.

Keywords: California—early United States; Farmers

Fancy Pants. **Bethany House, 2007. 378pp. Paper, 9780764203176.**

Lady Sydney Hathwell, stranded in New York after a broken engagement in 1889, writes to her Uncle Fuller and asks to visit him on his Texas ranch. Confused by her name, her uncle assumes she's male. When she arrives during her uncle's absence, disguised as a boy, "Big Tim" Creighton, the ranch foreman, takes it upon himself to turn foppish Sydney into a real man.

Keywords: Disguise; Ranchers; Texas—Reconstruction/Gilded Age

Forevermore. **Bethany House, 2008. 350pp. Paper, 9780764203183.**

Hope Ladley is a breath of fresh air in widower Jakob Stauffer's household. She's always cheerful as she helps him with housekeeping, farm work, and assisting his sister, Annie, with the care of his young daughter.

But Hope was hired as temporary help; she'll be moving along as soon as the job is done. But what if Jakob doesn't want her to leave? Annie's abusive husband decides he wants her back, complicating matters further. Humorous romance with a serious side, set in 1890s Texas.

Keywords: Farmers; Housekeepers; Texas—Reconstruction/Gilded Age

Letter Perfect. **Bethany House, 2006. 379pp. Paper, 0764201654.**

In 1859 Ruth Caldwell, an outspoken young woman whom nobody would ever call graceful, promises her dying mother that she'll travel out to California to reunite with her long-lost father. When her stagecoach arrives in Folsom, Josh McCain can't help being intrigued by her, even if it means his family may lose its claim on the Broken P Ranch. Then Ruth starts having accidents that can't be explained by her clumsiness.

Keywords: California—early United States; Ranchers

Hatcher, Robin Lee.

Loving Libby. **Zondervan, 2005. 304pp. Paper, 0310256909.**

Olivia Vanderhoff has made a new life for herself in the Idaho wilderness in the 1890s, after escaping from her cruel father six years earlier. She mistakenly shoots Remington Walker, a detective her father hired to find her, and tends to him as he recovers. A Christian-focused rewrite of Hatcher's 1995 novel *Liberty Blue*.

Keywords: Disguise; Idaho—Reconstruction/Gilded Age

Mills, DiAnn.

Awaken My Heart. **Avon Inspire, 2008. 261pp. Paper, 9780061376016.**

In Spanish-ruled Texas circa 1803, Mexican rebel Armando Garcia agrees to the kidnapping of Marianne Phillips, the Virginia-born daughter of a wealthy settler, to further his people's political cause. To his surprise, she empathizes with the Mexicans' plight. Their unlikely love runs into roadblocks from all over: her father's cruelty, her would-be fiancé, and the touchy political situation.

Keywords: Kidnapping; Revolution and revolutionaries; Texas—early United States

Texas Legacy Series.

Fast-paced romantic adventure in 1880s and 1890s Texas, with feisty heroines, strong heroes, and stereotypical Western dialogue. The final volume wraps up loose ends from the original trilogy.

Keywords: Texas—Reconstruction/Gilded Age and 20th century

Leather and Lace. Barbour, 2006. 318pp. Paper, 1597891274.

Casey O'Hare, a former outlaw, leaves Utah in 1884, hoping to start a new life in Kahlerville, Texas. The man who takes her prisoner claims he's protecting her from her former gang leader, but is he?

Lanterns and Lace. Barbour, 2006. 317pp. Paper, 1597893560.

In 1895 Jenny Martin arrives in Kahlerville, letting nothing stop her from finding her two-year-old niece, Rebecca, and raising her as her own. But before she died Jessica Martin, a resident of the local brothel, had already persuaded the town's doctor to adopt her daughter.

Lightning and Lace. Barbour, 2007. 317pp. Paper, 9781597893572.

Travis Whitworth, a preacher, arrives in Kahlervile in 1898, disguising his true identity because he's hiding from his past. Only he has the ability to help Bonnie Kahler recover from her husband's death two years earlier and to get Bonnie's unruly teenaged son, Zack, to shape up.

Keywords: Preachers

A Texas Legacy Christmas. Barbour, 2007. 286pp. Paper, 9781597898225.

Zack Kahler, all grown up in 1911, leaves New York City for Texas to celebrate Christmas. He brings along a young charge, a homeless boy named Curly, and both of them win the heart of boardinghouse owner Alice Hawkins.

Keywords: Christmas

Morris, Gilbert.

Wagon Wheel Series.

Strong-willed, unconventional heroines find romance while traveling the wagon trains out West in the 1850s.

Keywords: West—early United States; Trail guides; Wagon trains

Santa Fe Woman. B&H, 2006. 326pp. Paper, 0805432892.

When Jori Hayden's family lose their fortune, circumstances force them to make their way westward. The family hire Chad Rocklin, a former prisoner anxious to redeem himself, to guide them along the Santa Fe Trail.

A Man for Temperance. B&H, 2007. 331pp. Paper, 9780805432909.

At age thirty-two Temperance Peabody, a member of a religious colony in Oregon Territory in 1850, has given up hope of ever marrying. A cholera outbreak leaves many children in the region orphaned, and Temperance volunteers to return them to family members back east. She and her trail guide en route, Thaddeus Brennan, a man prone to hard drinking and occasional violence, are completely mismatched.

Keywords: Spinsters

Pittman, Allison.

Crossroads of Grace Series.

The three protagonists in Pittman's romantic Westerns have led tough lives. Gradually they learn that God has been with them throughout, if they only knew where to look.

Keywords: Frontier and pioneer life; Silver mines; Wyoming—Reconstruction/ Gilded Age

Ten Thousand Charms. Multnomah, 2006. 319pp. Paper, 1590525752.

> A prostitute with a child on the way in Wyoming Territory in the 1860s, Gloria feels undeserving of God's grace. At a mining camp she meets John William MacGregan, a Christian widower who needs a wet nurse for his infant daughter.

> **Keywords:** Prostitutes; Wet nurses; Widowers

Speak Through the Wind. Multnomah, 2007. 384pp. Paper, 9781590526255.

> Young Kassandra, rescued from the streets of New York's Five Points District in 1841 by a kindly minister, makes a series of bad decisions. She ends up as a prostitute in San Francisco. Then, when she and a friend head to Wyoming Territory to strike it rich in the silver mines, Kassandra meets Gloria, who teaches her about God's capacity for forgiveness.

> **Keywords:** California; Prostitutes

With Endless Sight. Multnomah, 2008. 384pp. Paper, 9781601420121.

> In 1861 fourteen-year-old Belinda heads west from Illinois to Wyoming Territory with her family. Tragedy strikes, leaving her wounded and alone. Forced to depend on the man who was the cause of her turmoil, Belinda relies on God to get her through difficult times. Hope emerges from an unexpected source: a house of ill repute.

Rivers, Francine.

Redeeming Love. **Multnomah, 1997. 464pp. Paper, 1576731863.** ★ 📖

> Angel, a prostitute in Gold Rush–era California, has felt worthless and ill-used ever since she was sold into a life of sin as a child. Her life is transformed when Michael Hosea, a devout farmer, marries her. Although she'll have none of him at first, Michael shows her the path to love and salvation. This beloved retelling of the classic biblical story of Gomer and Hosea was originally written for the secular market (Bantam, 1991, same title).

> **Keywords:** Biblical themes; California—Reconstruction/Gilded Age; Gold Rush; Prostitutes

Wick, Lori.

Big Sky Dreams Series.

> Prolific inspirational romance novelist Wick sets her latest series on the Montana plains—Big Sky Country—in 1880. Former prostitutes in the Old West seek to leave their pasts behind them. *Jessie* will conclude the series.

> **Keywords:** Frontier and pioneer life; Montana—Reconstruction/Gilded Age

Cassidy. Harvest House, 2007. 302pp. Paper, 9780736916189.

> Cassidy Norton, a successful seamstress in Token Creek, Montana Territory, in 1880, longs for a family but fears her past will deter any serious suitor.

> **Keywords:** Seamstresses

Sabrina. Harvest House, 2007. 302pp. Paper, 9780736920780.

Sabrina Matthews, a prostitute in Denver, befriends a police officer and his wife, who teach her about Christ. When life in this frontier city becomes too difficult, she heads to Token Creek, where she hopes to put her past behind her.

Keywords: Prostitutes

9

10

11

12

13

14

15

Chapter 12

Time-Slip Novels

A woman spies a painting of an eighteenth-century man hanging on the wall of an English castle and feels as if she might have known him before. A businessman in the present day undergoes hypnosis to help him deal with a psychological issue, and the sessions reveal his past life as a slave in nineteenth-century America. Scientific investigators from the future take a trip back to the fourteenth century to study medieval societies for themselves—but once there, they can't find a way to return home. These three plotlines are all common to the time-slip novel.

Although these novels may not normally be thought of as a subgenre of historical fiction, it can help librarians and readers to consider them as such. Not only do they have many readers in common, but they have a similar appeal. These creatively written novels allow readers to imagine, if only for a time, that slipping from one time period to another is indeed possible. Thus, they appeal to readers' sense of wishful thinking in a way that more straightforwardly written historical novels cannot do. Through them readers will experience the strong pull that the past exerts on characters living in later times.

Time-slip novels appeal to readers of a variety of genres, not only historical fiction, but also fantasy, romance, adventure, and occasionally mystery and even science fiction. They also bridge the gap between them. Because of this, publishers' labels for these books can vary. Works of fiction with a strong emphasis on time travel or the supernatural may be labeled as fantasy, whereas novels in which people from the future go back into the past are apt to be called science fiction. Time-slips recounting a love that transcends time will appeal strongly to romance readers, as will novels in which a modern-day man or woman returns to an earlier time to find a soul mate. Finally, suspenseful stories of a centuries-old curse carried down through the generations may fall into the category of mystery, thriller, or even horror.

The novels annotated in this chapter include classics of these diverse genres, all of which fit the time-slip definition, as well as recently published titles that explore the same themes. Although the subgenre as a whole is not nearly as popular in the United States as it is in Great Britain, time-travel romances continue to be popular among romance readers. A selected number of these novels are included below, in particular those that provide a significant amount of historical content.

Regardless of the various ways they may be categorized, their appeal to historical fiction readers lies in their ability to give additional insight into people who lived, and into events that occurred, at various times in the past. Through them readers will get the chance to view the past firsthand through a modern character's eyes, and the differences between "now" and "then" are often quite striking. Time-slips also often demonstrate that despite these differences, human nature is the same regardless of the era.

Time Travel

In time-travel novels, one or more characters travel back to an earlier time period, either deliberately or by accident. Little by little they must learn to conduct themselves according to the customs of their new setting, figuring out how best to survive in an era when present-day technology didn't exist. Most of all, they must take care not to appear too modern, for any inappropriate behavior may attract unwanted attention. Characters unlucky enough to be caught in the past without modern conveniences can make for some humorous scenes, though the characters themselves usually see their state of affairs as less than amusing. A common plot device features characters who arrive in the past at a time of particular unrest, such as a time of great war or disease, which makes their continued survival even more precarious. In the end, whether they return to their own era or not, most conclude that life in earlier times wasn't nearly as simple and romantic as they had originally believed.

General

The plotlines of these time-travel novels are fairly straightforward, but there's nothing ordinary about the stories themselves. After the novelty of living in an earlier time wears off, the protagonists must learn how to survive as best they can.

DuVall, Nell.

Train to Yesterday. **Five Star, 2008. 290pp. Hardbound, 1594146632.**
Penny Barton, a railroad heiress and marketing executive for an Ohio-based high-speed rail company, accidentally slips back in time to 1855 during a promotional photo shoot. Once firmly ensconced in the day-to-day concerns of pre–Civil War Coshocton, Ohio, Penny worries along with other residents about the railroad's impact on the local shipping business and finds romance with a dry-goods merchant and investor, Fletcher Dawe. She also gets the scoop on how her ancestors earned their fortune.

Keywords: Heirs and heiresses; Merchants; Ohio—early United States; Railroads

Edwards, Selden.

The Little Book. **Dutton, 2008. 401pp. Hardbound, 9780525950615.** 📖
Wheeler Burden, a forty-seven-year-old resident of San Francisco in 1988, inexplicably finds himself thrust back in time to Vienna in the year 1897. He finds the city very familiar thanks to his beloved mentor, who saw late imperial Vienna as the cradle of modern intellectual thought. Wheeler's story, as related by his mother, encompasses Freudian analysis, the philosophy of baseball, the history of rock

and roll, modern feminism, the growing waves of anti-Semitic sentiment in nineteenth-century Europe, the truth behind many Burden family legends, and much more. The distinct and wonderfully eccentric characters he meets gradually unlock the reasons for his presence in that time and place. A poignant and unusual love story, Edwards's debut (thirty years in the writing) is also a delightful tribute to the vanished world of fin de siècle Vienna.

Keywords: Austria—early modern era

Elyot, Amanda.

By a Lady. **Three Rivers, 2005. 372pp. Paper, 1400097991.**

Actress C. J. (Cassandra Jane) Welles almost lands her plum role, playing Jane Austen in a Broadway play, but when she walks through a door on the set during her audition, she finds herself in Bath, England, during Austen's own time (circa 1801). C. J. uses her dramatic skills and knowledge of the period to pretend she's a native of Georgian England but is continually surprised by the era's social strictures. Her fortune changes when Lady Euphoria Dalrymple, an eccentric aristocrat, mistakes her for her niece and introduces her to society—which includes the deliciously debonair earl of Darlington as well as Jane Austen herself. A frothy, entertaining adventure with plentiful period detail.

Keywords: Actresses; Austen themes; England—Georgian era

Finney, Jack.

Time and Again Series. ★ YA

In a government-sponsored time-travel project, Si Morley is sent back in time to 1882 New York City.

Keywords: New York—Reconstruction/Gilded Age

Time and Again. Simon & Schuster, 1970. 399pp. Hardbound, 0671204971.

> In Si's current mission, he must discover whether the past can coexist with the present. While back in 1880s New York he falls in love, but then has to make the big decision about whether or not to remain. This classic time-travel novel should appeal to readers interested in learning more about historical Manhattan.

From Time to Time. Simon & Schuster, 1995. 303pp. Hardbound, 0671898841.

> This sequel to *Time and Again* finds Si returning to the future (for him, the twentieth century), where his superiors have a new project for him: learning how to change history to prevent World War I.

Rigler, Laurie Viera.

Confessions of a Jane Austen Addict. **Dutton, 2007. 293pp. Hardbound, 9780525950400.**

Distraught about her broken engagement, Los Angeles native Courtney Stone takes refuge in her favorite pastime—reading Jane Austen novels—and wakes up the next morning in the body of Jane Mansfield, an Englishwoman in the year 1813. Forced by circumstances into living this strange woman's life, not only does she have to deal with an insufferable mother (who's determined to marry her off as quickly as possible) but also things like corsets, doctors with outdated practices, and Mr. Edgeworth, the real Jane's dashing suitor. More disturbingly, Courtney also begins recalling Jane's memories.

Keywords: Austen themes; England—Regency era

Romantic

People from the present day travel back in time and end up finding their soul mates. Problems arise when they are forced to make decisions about whether to return to the present, possibly leaving their loved ones behind, or remain in the earlier time period with the ones they love.

Brown, Laurie.

Hundreds of Years to Reform a Rake. **Sourcebooks, 2007. 391pp. Paper, 9781402210136.**

Josephine Drummond, a modern-day investigator of paranormal happenings, gets dragged back into the past by the ghost of Lord Deverell Thornton, Earl of Waite. A Regency-era rake, Dev is horrified at the thought that his longtime home, Waite Castle, may be turned into a tourist attraction. His family was swindled out of their fortune nearly two centuries earlier, and he needs Josie's help to change history. As Josie adjusts to Regency customs (quite a culture shock for a technology-savvy gal), she finds herself strongly attracted to two different but similar men: the ghostly version of Dev and the real one.

Keywords: England—Regency era; Ghosts

Deveraux, Jude.

A Knight in Shining Armor. **Pocket, 1989. 341pp. Hardbound, 0671678574. ★**

Abandoned on a trip to England by her callous boyfriend and his annoying teen-aged daughter, Dougless Montgomery happens upon the tomb of a knight from Elizabethan times. No one is more surprised than she when he appears in the flesh—except perhaps the knight himself, Nicholas Stafford, who is amusingly befuddled by his unexpected appearance. The two grow closer after Dougless hears Nicholas's story, and she travels back in time to 1560s England to help him clear his name. A slightly revised version was reissued by Pocket in 2002.

Keywords: England—Tudor era; Knights

Gabaldon, Diana.

Outlander Saga.

Annotated in Chapter 4.

Garcia y Robertson, R.

Knight Errant Series (also called War of the Roses Series). ✍

While hiking in present-day England, Californian Robyn Stafford encounters Edward, Earl of March, a knight from the fifteenth century. Thus begins their story. This time-travel romance never takes itself too seriously, as Robyn somehow manages to bring technological gadgets from the future back with her. A fourth volume is expected.

Keywords: Edward IV, King of England (historical character); England—high Middle Ages; Wars of the Roses

Knight Errant. Forge, 2001. 479pp. Hardbound, 0312869967.

Lady Robyn. Forge, 2003. 399pp. Hardbound, 0312869959.

White Rose. Forge, 2004. 384pp. Hardbound, 0312869940.

By this entry, Robyn has traveled from the present to the Middle Ages and back again several times. When she returns to the past once more, in the year 1461, Robyn is pregnant with Edward's child, and her scatterbrained assistant, Heidi, accompanies her. As part of Heidi's duties, she protects Robyn and her unborn child by distracting men's attention away from her (which results in some lusty scenes).

George, Linda.

Ask a Shadow to Dance. **Five Star, 2005. 298pp. Hardbound, 1594143676.**

While taking a river cruise along the Mississippi, Dr. David Stewart spies a mysterious woman in black lingering on the ballroom floor and sees her again, shortly thereafter, on the deck. He finds her very attractive, and Lisette's old-fashioned clothing and unfamiliarity with modern-day landmarks pique his curiosity. The next day David sees both of their names on a list of passengers who boarded the *Cajun Star* in 1885, a riverboat that vanished shortly thereafter. He determines to stop at nothing to save her life, as well as his own.

Keywords: Riverboats; Tennessee—Reconstruction/Gilded Age

Landry, Sandra.

The Last Bride. **Berkley Sensation, 2005. 307pp. Paper, 0425204448.**

Claire Peltier, a French translator in modern-day New Orleans, breaks off her engagement to her fiancé after having haunting dreams about another man. Following her instincts, she travels to France to find him. A trip to the labyrinth of Chartres Cathedral sends her back in time—to Normandy in the year 1202, where she meets Aiden Delacroix, a widowed nobleman who desperately needs a wife and an heir.

Keywords: France—Middle Ages; Labyrinths; Nobility; Translators

The Wishing Chalice. **Berkley, 2004. 327pp. Paper, 0425194582.**

After suffering a miscarriage and the subsequent breakup of her marriage, Isabel Herbert traveled from America to Cumbria, England, to recuperate at her late grandmother's cottage. While out walking one day she discovers an ancient chalice and sees a ghostly image of a man and woman who are clearly in love. She is then thrust back in time to the early fourteenth century and finds herself in the arms of Hunter of Windermere Castle, the man from her vision, who can't comprehend the odd new behavior of his formerly frigid wife, Detra.

Keywords: Chalices; England—high Middle Ages

Lee, Julianne.

Knight Tenebrae Series.

The adventures of British reporter Lindsay Pawlowski and American navy pilot Alex MacNeil both in twenty-first century and fourteenth-century Scotland, during the reign of Robert the Bruce. The unlikely pair's relationship turns romantic during the first book and develops further throughout. Some fantasy elements. Lee has written other time-travel fantasy novels as J. Ardian Lee and also wrote a Tudor-era novel as Laurien Gardner (see Chapter 2).

Keywords: Journalists, women; Pilots; Scotland—high Middle Ages; Warriors, women

Knight Tenebrae. Ace, 2006. 356pp. Paper, 0441014399.

Alex MacNeil meets Lindsay Pawlowski, a reporter for the London *Times,* when she interviews him about an odd find in Scotland's Firth of Forth: an F-18 fighter jet was unearthed from the silt of the firth after lying there for what was clearly centuries. When he flies her home to Great Britain, they pass through a vortex ringed with fire that casts them into Scotland in the year 1302. It quickly becomes clear that Robert Bruce's forces need warriors like Alex in their fight against England, though Lindsay is forced to pose as his (male) squire in order to survive.

Knight's Blood. Ace, 2007. 292pp. Paper, 9780441014859.

Alex and Lindsay MacNeil are married, with a son, and have returned home from the fourteenth century. When their child is kidnapped and taken back into the past, Lindsay follows closely behind, resuming her disguise as a squire in order to find and rescue him. She comes to enjoy the life of a medieval warrior and finds herself strongly attracted to the leader of her band.

Knight's Lady. Ace, 2008. 294pp. Paper, 9780441015733.

Alex and Lindsay are separated from each other while fighting for Robert Bruce in the Highlands. Alex struggles to recover from his battle injuries, while Lindsay is taken by her band's leader, the Knight An Reubair, to his home in Ireland—where she tries to resist his attempts at seduction.

Matheson, Richard.

Bid Time Return. **Viking, 1974. 278pp. Hardbound, 0670162329. (Alternate title:** *Somewhere in Time.***)** ★

Richard Collier, a writer dying of a brain tumor in the 1970s, pays a visit to a turn-of-the-century hotel in San Diego, California. There he spots the portrait of a beautiful actress, Elise McKenna, who performed at the hotel seventy-five years earlier. Having never been in love, Richard grows obsessed by his newfound feelings and literally wills himself back in time to fall in love with Elise in person.

Matheson's novel was made into a well-known film, *Somewhere in Time*, starring Christopher Reeve and Jane Seymour.

Keywords: Actresses; Authors; California—20th Century

Thompson, Dawn.

The Falcon's Bride. **LoveSpell, 2006. 326pp. Paper, 0505526794.**

Most time-travel romances bring the protagonist from the present to the past, but in Thompson's version, a Regency-era heroine is transported back to the year 1695. Thea Barrington travels to Ireland to marry wealthy Nigel Cosgrove to support her family, despite rumors of his cruel behavior (which turn out to be true). An old gypsy on his estate foretells her marriage to Ros Drumcondra, a seventeenth-century Irish chieftain and gypsy warlord who was an enemy of her fiancé's family. She can't fathom how this is possible until she enters a portal to the past.

Keywords: England—Stuart era; Gypsies

Wolff, Veronica.

Highlands Series. ✍

Modern-day women travel back into the past and meet historical Highland heroes.

Keywords: Scotland—17th century

Master of the Highlands. Berkley Sensation, 2008. 281pp. Paper, 9780425218990.

Lily Hamlin escapes temporarily from her high-pressure Silicon Valley job by renting a croft in the Scottish Highlands. While out exploring the countryside she discovers a mysterious map whose patterns send her back in time to 1654—just as Ewen, seventeenth chief of Clan Cameron, is trying to save his people from Oliver Cromwell's army.

Keywords: Cameron, Ewen (historical character)

Sword of the Highlands. Berkley Sensation, 2008. 320pp. Paper, 9780425222485.

Entranced by a portrait of the handsome James Graham, Marquis of Montrose, Magdalen Deacon, a curator at the Metropolitan Museum, gets drawn back in time to seventeenth-century Scotland. As she learns more about his support of the Royalists during the English Civil War, she and James become romantically entangled.

Keywords: English Civil War; Montrose, James Graham, Marquis of (historical character)

Thrillers

Once they are back in the past, protagonists race against time to complete their missions. These are fast-paced, action-oriented, time-travel stories. For other time-slip thrillers, see M. J. Rose's <u>Reincarnationist Series</u>, in the "Reincarnation" section of this chapter.

Baker, Virginia.

Jack Knife. Jove, 2007. 343pp. Paper, 9780515142525.

Sara Grant and David Elliot slip into London's past from 2007 to catch Jonathan Avery, a crazed scientist from the present who has the potential to change history and erase their own time line. Once back in the year 1888, they find a city terrorized by a serial killer who calls himself Jack the Ripper. Inspector Jonas Robb, bemused by the appearance of two strangers with knowledge of the man he's looking for, joins forces with the pair. As the carnage builds and the suspense rises, the trio find evidence that the paths of Avery and the Ripper are linked.

Keywords: England—Victorian era; Jack the Ripper; Serial killers

Science Fiction

One might think that science fiction and historical fiction are polar opposites that can't be combined, but Kage Baker and Connie Willis prove this idea wrong. They mingle the two genres with their very popular novels of protagonists from the future who make exploratory journeys into the past.

Baker, Kage.

The Company.

Baker's series mixes historical fiction, science fiction, and humor in the adventures of Mendoza, a girl originally born into sixteenth-century Spain. Mendoza is recruited by scientists from the twenty-fourth century to work for Dr. Zeus, Incorporated, a company that makes money preserving cultural artifacts from the past. Trained as a botanist, Mendoza—rendered nearly immortal through drugs and implants—is sent back in time to various eras to safeguard endangered plant species. Her occasionally bumbling colleagues create some very funny scenes. As the series progresses, Mendoza and her compatriots discover that the company's motives aren't nearly as altruistic as they would seem. Not all of the volumes have strong historical elements, but the entire series is included to provide a complete list.

Keywords: Botanists; California—Civil War; Cyborgs; England—Tudor era; Mexico—16th century

In the Garden of Iden. Harcourt, Brace, 1997. 329pp. Hardbound, 0151002991.

Sky Coyote. Harcourt Brace, 1999. 310pp. Hardbound, 0151003548.

Mendoza in Hollywood. Harcourt Brace, 2000. 326pp. Hardbound, 015100448X.

The Graveyard Game. Harcourt Brace, 2001. 298pp. Hardbound, 0151004498.

Black Projects, White Knights: The Company Dossiers. Golden Gryphon, 2002. 288pp. Hardbound, 1930846118.

The Life of the World to Come. Tor, 2004. 334pp. Hardbound, 0765311321.

Mendoza has been sent far back in time, to humankind's prehistoric past, as punishment for defending her late nineteenth-century (and, previously, sixteenth-century) lover. As she keeps herself busy growing vegetables for people back in the present day, Alec Checkerfield—a man who identically resembles her previous two lovers—arrives from the twenty-fourth century with news about Dr. Zeus's plans.

The Children of the Company. Tor, 2005. 300pp. Hardbound, 076531455X.

Baker reworks six previously published short stories into a single narrative about General Labienus, a corrupt big shot at Dr. Zeus who was once a god in ancient Sumeria; he wants to take over the world.

The Machine's Child. Tor, 2006. 351pp. Hardbound, 0765315513.

In this direct sequel to *The Life of the World to Come*, Mendoza's three lovers—Nicholas Harpole, Edward Bell-Fairfax, and Alec Checkerfield—band together uneasily within Checkerfield's body to save the woman all three of them love from a company prison cum torture chamber.

Gods and Pawns. Tor, 2007. 335pp. Hardbound, 9780765315526.

Seven short stories set in the Dr. Zeus company universe.

The Sons of Heaven. Tor, 2007. 430pp. Hardbound, 9780765317469.

This final volume of the series wraps up loose ends, leading up to the date of the Silence, in July 2355, after which the company and its cyborgs will have no knowledge of the future.

Levinson, Paul.

The Plot to Save Socrates. **Tor, 2006. 271pp. Hardbound, 0765305704.**

In this lighthearted science fiction adventure, Sierra Waters, PhD candidate in the year 2042, jumps at the opportunity to participate in an experiment. She has recently learned, via a fragment of an ancient manuscript, that Socrates may have escaped his purported demise in 399 BC (poison by hemlock at the behest of the Athenians) at the last minute via time travel. She and one of her faculty advisors, Dr. Thomas O'Leary, head back in time to ancient Greece, where they discover that the famed philosopher has no interest in their plans to save him.

Keywords: Greece—ancient/prehistoric; Philosophers; Socrates (historical character)

Willis, Connie.

🌳 *Doomsday Book.* **Bantam, 1992. 445pp. Paper, 0553351672.** ★ 📖

In this classic of both historical and science fiction, Kivrin, a young Oxford scientist in the twenty-first century, is sent back in time to study the Middle Ages firsthand. An accident in calculation places her not in 1320 but in 1348, right before the bubonic plague hit Oxford—and her colleagues can't reach her to bring her back home. Though Kivrin has been inoculated against the plague, she knows true helplessness as she watches the people she's befriended in medieval times succumb to the disease, one by one. Hugo Award; Nebula Award.

Keywords: England—high Middle Ages; Plague; Scientists

Reincarnation

These works presuppose that one or more modern-day characters are the reincarnations of people who had previously lived. Parallel stories, one set now and another in the past, allow readers to explore these characters' connections to an earlier place and time. In these novels modern-day individuals are given the opportunity to right wrongs that were set in motion long ago. Many novels about reincarnation center on a love story, in which people are finally given the opportunity to reunite with their soul mates from a previous existence. As the protagonists come to terms with the existence of their past lives, they unlock a psychological healing process.

Bass, Mary Beth.

Follow Me. **LoveSpell, 2005. 308pp. Paper, 9780505526342.**

Boston florist Claire Islington's relationship with her uptight doctor fiancé can't compare with her memory of the single passionate encounter she shared with a mysterious man in a Vermont country inn. That was seven years ago, and she's never seen Harcourt Abernathy again—which is not surprising, because he was a botanical illustrator who lived in Georgian England. Harcourt's late wife strongly resembled Kate, and he has longed for years to connect with her again. A suspenseful paranormal romance that succeeds despite occasional vague language.

Keywords: England—Georgian era; Illustrators; Widowers

Brallier, Kate.

The Boundless Deep. **Forge, 2008. 432pp. Paper, 9780765319722.**

Grad student Liza Donovan has been experiencing visions of nineteenth-century Nantucket, so she jumps at the chance to spend summer break there with her best friend, Jane, and Jane's aunt, Kitty, who lives on the island. Ship's captain Obadiah Young, who owned Kitty's house in the 1840s, figures strongly in Liza's dreams, which become progressively more erotic. As Liza and museum curator Adam Gallagher investigate the past (and become romantically involved), they learn more about Obadiah's relationship with his wife, Lucy, and her mysterious death. A romantic novel with likeable, modern protagonists and haunting evocations of the nineteenth-century whaling industry.

Keywords: Dreams; Graduate students; Massachusetts—early United States; Ship captains; Whaling industry

Cullars, Sharon.

Again. **Brava, 2006. 297pp. Paper, 0758213700.**

After their chance meeting at her sister's wedding, Tyne Jensen, an African American journalist in Chicago, feels a strange, unexpected connection to architect David Carvelli. Their attraction develops quickly into intimacy, but then she recognizes him as the man who's been appearing in the erotic dreams she's been having at night. Their present-day lives parallel those of an interracial couple living in New York in 1897, whose relationship may have led to murder.

Keywords: Architects; Interracial romance; Journalists, women; New York—Reconstruction/Gilded Age

Davidson, Andrew.

The Gargoyle. **Doubleday, 2008. 480pp. Hardbound, 9780385524940.** 📖

An unnamed man, victim of a car accident that left him horribly disfigured, lies recovering in a hospital burn ward, discouraged by multiple surgeries and despondent about his life. He and Marianne Engel, a mysterious, beautiful sculptress of gargoyles, form an unlikely bond when she pays him a visit from the psych ward and reveals their shared past: they were once lovers in fourteenth-century Germany. Is she a madwoman, or is she saner than anyone he's ever met? Either way, her compelling tales of love that transcends time draw him away from thoughts of suicide, but sins from his past aren't easily banished.

Keywords: Disfigurement; Germany—Middle Ages; Multi-period novels; Sculptresses

Dennis, Mary Ellen.

The Landlord's Black-Eyed Daughter. **Five Star, 2007. 407pp. Hardbound, 9781594145759.**

The daughter of an innkeeper in England in 1787, Elizabeth Wyndham pays off her father's debts by writing Gothic romances. She finds the personification of her ideal hero in highwayman Rand Remington, a recent veteran of the war with the American colonies. Both feel they have met previously, in past lives that date from the thirteenth century—when they were star-crossed lovers whose relationship ended in betrayal and tragedy. Romantic adventure based partially on Alfred Noyes's poem "The Highwayman."

Keywords: Authors, women; England—Georgian era; England—high Middle Ages; Highwaymen

Erskine, Barbara.

Erskine, the queen of the British time-slip novel, intertwines her historical works with strong threads of suspense and romance. She has additional novels in print in the UK.

Lady of Hay. **Delacorte Press, 1986. 545pp. Hardbound, 0385295391.** ✍ ★

During a hypnosis session British journalist Jo Clifford experiences a past life as Matilda de Braose, Lady of Hay, a noblewoman who lived at the time of King John. The beautiful, forthright Matilda was a woman truly ahead of her time, managing her estates as well as a man ever could. But she made the fatal mistake of taunting King John about the death of his nephew, Prince Arthur, whom John very likely had killed to secure his own succession to the throne. Matilda paid for her mistake most cruelly, and unless Jo can free herself from the memory of her past life, the danger may repeat itself in the present.

Keywords: De Braose, Matilda (historical character); England—high Middle Ages; Hypnotism; Nobility

Rose, M. J.

Reincarnationist Series.

Rose, a well-known thriller writer, centers her latest series on a private reincarnationist society, its investigations over time, and its members' quests to obtain memory tools that help people recall their past lives. These multi-period novels mix modern-day events, historical settings, and the paranormal with action-packed suspense.

The Reincarnationist. MIRA, 2007. 451pp. Hardbound, 9780778324201.

Ever since he survived a terrorist bombing, Josh Ryder has had flashbacks to a previous life as Julius, a pagan priest in fourth-century Rome who loved a vestal virgin. He now works for the Phoenix Foundation, a group that counsels children who experience past life regressions. In the presence of a Roman woman's remains, discovered in a secret underground tomb in Italy, Josh's visions of Julius and Sabina, the priestess he loved, overpower him. Soon it becomes clear that his group has competition for the "memory stones" they discover in a pouch next to the body, for they will purportedly restore people's past-life memories. Josh and a fellow researcher, Yale archaeologist Gabriella Chase, race to find them before their enemies do.

Keywords: Archaeology; Rome—ancient/prehistoric; Vestal virgins

The Memorist. MIRA, 2008. 531pp. Hardbound, 9780778325840.

In the present, Israeli journalist David Yalom plots an explosive finale to the Vienna Philharmonic's gala performance at an international security conference as revenge for a hired security company's failure to protect his family from a terrorist bomb. At the same time, Meer Logan arrives in Vienna to find the cause of haunting memories of music that have plagued her since childhood. A letter hidden in an antique gaming box sets Meer and her father on a path to find an ancient bone flute linked to Beethoven. As Meer gleans clues to its hiding place via flashbacks to a previous life in 1814 Vienna, a fast-paced quest begins, involving players from the Logans to FBI agents, security experts, and members of a centuries-old secret society. This ambitious thriller successfully links past and present on multiple levels.

Keywords: Austria—early modern era; Journalists and reporters; Musicians; Terrorism

Seton, Anya.

Green Darkness. **Houghton Mifflin, 1973. 591pp. Hardbound, 0395139376.** ★ **YA**

When Celia Marsdon and her husband Richard visit his family's hereditary manor of Medfield Place in Sussex, she begins to relive the experiences of an earlier Celia. In a parallel tale, Celia de Bohun has a love affair with Stephen Marsdon, a priest, in 1552 in England, which leads to heartbreak and tragedy.

Keywords: England—Tudor era; Lovers; Priests

Past in the Present

Like novels of reincarnation, novels in this category tell parallel stories: one in the modern day, the other in the past. Here characters from an earlier period of history manage to communicate with present-day individuals, through dreams and visions or in spirit form. Characters in one era may feel an inexplicable connection to someone living in another time, or ghosts may appear to alert a present-day character to a past event—something that created negative karma that only a living person can put right.

Grady, Erin.

🏵 *Echoes*. **Berkley, 2004. 355pp. Paper, 0425200736.**

Tess Carson leaves New York for a remote California mountain town to care for the daughter of her missing sister, Tori, and to prove Tori innocent of murdering her boss, Frank Weston. While fighting her attraction to Frank's son Grant, a former Hollywood star, Tess begins seeing visions dating back to the frontier West that may be connected to Tori's disappearance. WILLA Award.

Keywords: California—Reconstruction/Gilded Age; Sisters

Whispers. **Berkley, 2006. 343pp. Paper, 0425209636.**

Grady follows up her previous romantic suspense novel with another, set in present-day and 1890s-era Diablo Springs, Arizona, a small town reputed to be haunted. Gracie Beck, a thirtyish single mother, returns to Diablo Springs on the heels of her grandmother's death and her daughter's recent car accident. She runs into Reilly Alexander, an author she knew long ago, and learns she has inherited a century-old curse along with the hotel her late grandmother managed.

Keywords: Arizona—Reconstruction/Gilded Age; Authors; Hotels

Morrison, Toni.

Beloved. **Knopf, 1987. 275pp. Hardbound, 0394535979.**
Annotated in Chapter 10.

Murphy, Kim.

Whispers Series.

Ghosts of Civil War–era residents on a Virginia plantation get involved in the lives of the Cameron family, demonstrating that the past never dies.

Keywords: Ghosts; Virginia—Civil War and Reconstruction/Gilded Age

Whispers from the Grave. Coachlight, 2007. 273pp. Paper, 9780971679054.

When attorney Chris Olson goes to spend a relaxing vacation with her friend Judith Cameron at her Virginia Ranch, Poplar Ridge, she runs right into ghosts from the past. She falls hard for Judith's brother, Geoff, at the same time that she begins dreaming about a Confederate soldier who strongly resembles him. She also starts to experience visions of Civil War–era events through the eyes of Margaret, a woman from the past with a terrible secret.

Whispers Through Time. Coachlight, 2008. 276pp. Paper, 9780971679078.

In the opening scene, set several years in the future, Geoff Cameron is shot to death by his vengeful ex-wife. His seven-year-old daughter Sarah, who witnesses his murder, refuses to speak from that day forward, though Geoff's ghost communicates with her. In an attempt to prevent the tragedy and learn about its relationship to events long past, Geoff's wife Chris travels back in time to the Reconstruction years.

Santangelo, Elena.

Pat Montella Series.

A mystery time-slip series featuring sassy Italian American Pat Montella, an unlikely detective. She has a particular sensitivity to finding spirits from the past who linger in the present. This leads her into unusual situations—some rather zany, some chilling.

Keywords: Ghosts; Italian Americans

By Blood Possessed. St. Martin's Minotaur, 1999. 326pp.

Hang My Head and Cry. St. Martin's Minotaur, 2001. 322pp.

Poison to Purge Melancholy. Midnight Ink, 2006. 419pp. Paper, 0738708909.

Pat Montella, feeling brave, agrees to spend part of the Christmas holidays in Williamsburg, Virginia, with the family of her boyfriend, Hugh Lee (whom she met in the first book). Unfortunately his mother's house is haunted, and Pat sees clear evidence of this firsthand. A parallel story line presents an unsolved mystery dating from the house's early years, circa 1783.

Keywords: Christmas; Virginia—American Revolution

Chapter 13

Alternate History

What if the South won the Civil War? What if the Roman Empire never fell? What if the Spanish Armada succeeded in invading Queen Elizabeth's England? Novels of alternate history (also called "alternative history") examine other possible outcomes for past events. The plots hinge on one particular event—a single military maneuver during a major battle, or the early death of a world leader—and imagine that it turned out differently than in real life. They follow this train of thought in detail, exploring how history might have changed as a result.

Whether alternate history fits as a true subgenre of historical fiction is up for debate. After all, these novels don't just bend the rules of the genre, they break them outright. The plots run counter to accepted historical fact, and they do so deliberately. In addition, historical fiction is set in the past by definition, while some alternate history novels are set in the present—albeit a very different version of it. For these reasons, some historical fiction readers won't touch alternate histories with a ten-foot pole.

On the other hand, the "what if" game is one frequently played by historians as well as historical novelists. Historians often ponder the reasons behind events and the causal relationships between them. To write plausible scenarios of alternate history, novelists not only have to know what really happened, but they also have to know the reasons people acted as they did. They must have a good grasp of the major players and their personalities, enough to be able to speculate how these people might have reacted when faced with alternative situations.

Alternate history novels will appeal to philosophically minded historical novel readers who enjoy pondering the causes and effects of historical events. They give people the opportunity to explore the supposed turning points of history and ponder how inevitable the outcomes really were. Like time-slip novels, alternative histories appeal to people's imaginations and curiosity. It's only human to think about what might have happened if one had the chance to go back and change something in the past. Changing even a seemingly small event could have had enormous repercussions—or it could have made no difference at all.

These works may be fast paced and action oriented (those that predict a different outcome to a battle), or they may be leisurely and literary (those based around religious themes). Either way, they are creative and thought-provoking. Readers who like alternate history novels may also appreciate nonfiction works on the same topic. Good places to start are *What If?* (Berkley, 2000) and its sequel *What If? 2* (Berkley, 2001), two essay collections in which prominent historians imagine what might have been. Both are edited by Robert Cowley, the founding editor of *Military History Quarterly*.

In libraries and bookstores, alternate histories tend to be categorized as either general fiction or science fiction. The latter is more typical, but a better catchall term for them is "speculative fiction." Many appear under science fiction imprints (Baen, DAW, Del Rey) and are written by authors (Harry Turtledove, Stephen Baxter, Harry Harrison) from the science fiction field. A classic example is Philip K. Dick's *The Man in the High Castle*, a Hugo Award winner about an alternative World War II. Short story anthologies are common, though this isn't the case with historical fiction in general.

Following is a selection of alternate history titles, organized first by historical locale and then by era or theme. Because the focus here is on history and historical plausibility, novels with obvious science fiction plot devices (aliens, modern technology in our historical past, far-future settings, etc.) are excluded. Time-travel alternate histories and "what ifs" for present-day events are also omitted, for the most part, though some anthologies mix these types of stories in with the rest.

World History

The books in this category show how changing one major event in history could have had repercussions all over the world.

World Wars I and II

Like adventure novels (Chapter 8) and thrillers (Chapter 9) set during World Wars I and II, these are fast-paced page-turners, for the most part. How might the world have changed if events during either war had happened differently?

Conroy, Robert.

1945. Ballantine, 2007. 432pp. Paper, 9780345494795.

Extremists kidnap Emperor Hirohito following the bombings of Hiroshima and Nagasaki, preventing him from announcing Japan's surrender. This forces President Truman's hand. As the United States leads an invasion into the Japanese homeland under the leadership of General Douglas MacArthur, Japan firmly resists and makes one last stand to win the war. The result, presented convincingly, is a devastating bloodbath. Conroy tells the story from multiple perspectives.

Keywords: Japan—World War II

Deighton, Len.

SS-GB. Knopf, 1979. 343pp. Hardbound, 0394504097. ★

Many alternate history novels imagine a German victory in World War II, and this classic was one of the first to do so. It is 1941. Churchill is dead, Germany has won the Battle of Britain, and London is under Nazi occupation. America never comes into the picture at all. A simple murder investigation by Scotland Yard turns into something more sinister as police inspectors uncover a conspiracy involving the SS and the British monarchy.

Keywords: England—World War II

Dick, Philip K.

🏵 *The Man in the High Castle.* **Putnam, 1962. 239pp. Hardbound.** ★

It is 1962, and America lost World War II in 1947. The country is now divided in two by the Nazis in the East and Japanese in the West. Not only can't they agree with each other on boundaries, but they may be going to war with each other over them. The Americans, living in a bleak, occupied country, feel oppressed and despondent—especially the Jews, who live in hiding. Different parts of the picture are told in overlapping stories. The ending is vague yet thought-provoking. It may seem odd to see Philip K. Dick, a prolific author of speculative and science fiction, in a guide to historical fiction, but this well-known novel is a classic regardless of the genre label. Hugo Award.

Keywords: United States—World War II

Gingrich, Newt, and William R. Forstchen.

Pacific War Trilogy.

Gingrich and Forstchen's counterfactual scenario turns on an assumption that Japan's attack on Pearl Harbor was led by Admiral Isoroku Yamamoto himself (who doesn't withdraw the Japanese fleet after the first two strikes, as Admiral Nagumo did in real life). This results in a more devastating blow to the U.S. Navy, which alters the course of the war from that point forward. Photos included. Albert S. Hanser is credited as a contributing editor.

Keywords: Hawaii—World War II; Japan—World War II; Pearl Harbor

Pearl Harbor: A Novel of December 8th. St. Martin's, 2007. 366pp. Hardbound, 9780312363505.

Gingrich and Forstchen look at World War II's Pacific arena not only from the usual Allied viewpoint, but also from the less common perspective of the Japanese. Although the prologue begins at midnight, Tokyo time, on December 8, 1941, the majority of the novel looks back to significant incidents leading up to the Pacific War in Japan, China, England, Hawaii, and elsewhere.

Days of Infamy. St. Martin's, 2008. 369pp. Hardbound, 9780312363512.

The Japanese, under Commander Yamamoto, lead a third wave of attacks on Pearl Harbor, then proceed to hunt down the remaining American fleet, which is under the command of Admiral Bull Halsey, in the hopes of inflicting further damage. Halsey, for his part, looks for a means of taking vengeance on the Japanese. The action takes place over a four-day period, December 7 through 11, 1941.

Harris, Robert.

Fatherland. **Random House, 1992. 338pp. Hardbound, 0679412735.** ★

This alternate history thriller begins in 1964, as Hitler is about to celebrate his seventy-fifth birthday. The Third Reich won World War II twenty years earlier, and a state of cold war exists between the United States and

Germany, rather than the United States and Russia. Just as U,S. President Joseph Kennedy (father of John F.) heads to Germany to meet with Hitler, police investigator Xavier March investigates a drowning in suburban Berlin. The victim is a high-level Nazi, and his death is ruled a suicide. March suspects otherwise, and he and American journalist Charlotte Maguire uncover a conspiracy leading them back to the dark days of the war.

Keywords: Germany—World War II; Nazis

Kerr, Philip.

Hitler's Peace. **Putnam, 2005. 448pp. Hardbound, 0399152695.**

Kerr, best known for his <u>Berlin Noir</u> series of historical spy thrillers, turns his hand to alternate history but keeps to his usual tone of dark political intrigue. What if Hitler's Germany, realizing defeat was inevitable, had sought a peace agreement with the United States and Great Britain at the Tehran Conference of 1943, a gathering attended by Allied leaders Roosevelt, Churchill, and Stalin? The protagonist, Willard Mayer, a philosophy professor turned OSS operative sent from Washington to evaluate these secret goings-on, has a checkered past not even his employer knows about.

Keywords: Europe—World War II

Niles, Douglas, and Michael Dobson.

MacArthur's War: A Novel of the Invasion of Japan. **Forge, 2007. 492pp. Hardbound, 9780765312877.**

The U.S. Navy has been dealt severe blows both at Pearl Harbor and at the Battle of Midway, which in this version was a decisive victory for the Japanese. General Douglas MacArthur is sent to take command of American naval forces in the Pacific region, which eventually culminates in a full-scale invasion of Japan. His intense egotism proves troublesome, but an even greater setback proves to be the failure of the Manhattan Project in the desert of New Mexico. The coauthors, who previously collaborated on two other World War II–era alternate histories (*Fox on the Rhine* and *Fox at the Front*), tell their story from the viewpoints of numerous fictional characters.

Keywords: Japan—World War II; MacArthur, Douglas (historical character)

Sheers, Owen.

Resistance. **Talese/Doubleday, 2007. 506pp. Hardbound, 9780385522106.** 📖

Sheers, a Welsh poet, takes a smaller-scale approach to alternate history, focusing on the women living in the isolated, rural Olchon valley in the Black Mountains of Wales during the darkest days of the war, circa 1944. The Normandy invasion has failed, the Germans occupy southern England, and Sarah Lewis and other sheep farmers' wives wake one morning to find their husbands have disappeared. After two months of fending for themselves, with no word from their menfolk, a German patrol led by Captain Albrecht Wolfram arrives, with a specific mission to accomplish. The harsh winter that follows forces the two groups into a very uneasy collaboration. **Literary.**

Keywords: Sheep farmers; Wales—World War II

Turtledove, Harry.

Days of Infamy Series.

The Japanese launch an attack on Pearl Harbor on December 7, 1941, and then proceed to invade Hawaii—leaving the United States vulnerable to attack on the mainland as well. This duology stands alone from Turtledove's extended alternate history series about twentieth-century history, of which the <u>Settling Accounts</u> quartet of novels (below) is a part. Ferocious combat scenes combine with unstinting portrayals of day-to-day survival in a land occupied by the enemy.

Keywords: Hawaii—World War II; Japanese Americans; Prisoners of war

Days of Infamy. Roc, 2004. 440pp. Hardbound, 0451213076.

The Japanese occupation of Hawaii has dire consequences for its residents, such as a wife who toils on her assigned garden plot while her soldier husband survives near-starvation conditions at a POW camp. A Japanese Hawaiian family finds its loyalties split, with the immigrant father loyal to his homeland while his sons side with the Americans. Turtledove, as always, uses many characters' viewpoints—civilian and military, leaders and not, real and fictional—to present all sides of the conflict.

End of the Beginning. Roc, 2005. 440pp. Hardbound, 0451216687.

Times have become even tougher for those who live under Japanese occupation: the population endures an atmosphere of racial tensions, forced prostitution, and food shortages. The United States refuses to give up hope of retaking Hawaii and gears up for a final assault against Japan.

Settling Accounts Series.

Turtledove has created an alternate history empire of his own, with several sequential, interlocking series of novels. His latest series (following the stand-alone *How Few Remain,* then his <u>Great War</u> series, and finally his <u>American Empire</u> series) leads up to an alternative version of World War II—which replicates a Holocaust-like scenario in North America.

Keywords: Confederacy; Featherston, Jake; Genocide; Racial conflict; United States—World War II

Return Engagement. Del Rey, 2004. 623pp. Hardbound, 0345457234.

The Confederacy, under Jake Featherston, continues its policies of genocide against African Americans and begins launching attacks against Washington, D.C.. U.S. President Al Smith's best hope lies in an untried administrator named Franklin Roosevelt.

Drive to the East. Del Rey, 2005. 594pp. Hardbound, 0345464060.

Turtledove continues his displacement of historical World War II–era scenarios to the North American continent, which is in a state of civil war. The Confederacy has effectively split the United States in two, and its president, Jake Featherston, becomes more Hitler-like as he moves ever closer to a final solution to the country's Negro "problem."

The Grapple. Del Rey, 2006. 616pp. Hardbound, 0345457250.

> With the Confederate army faltering in the Midwest, circa 1943, the tide of war appears finally to be turning toward the United States. Although both sides try to win the race to develop nuclear weapons, the U.S. federal government confirms the existence of extermination camps authorized by Featherston out West.

In at the Death. Del Rey, 2007. 609pp. Hardbound, 9780345492470.

> The Confederacy, faced with certain defeat, ultimately surrenders to the United States and its German allies, bringing an end to this alternate version of World War II, but several questions still remain at the end. This volume concludes not only the Settling Accounts quartet but also Turtledove's extended alternate history series.

The Man with the Iron Heart. **Del Rey, 2008. 530pp. Hardbound, 9780345504340.** ✍

> One of Turtledove's rare stand-alone alternate histories, this entry examines the possibility that SS leader Reinhard Heydrich survived the assassination attempt that in real life killed him in Czechoslovakia in 1942. Instead, he formulates a devious plan for Nazi resistance: they launch a guerrilla war peppered with violent acts of terrorism, creating a powerful, invisible foe that the Allies find nearly impossible to fight. The eerie parallels between this scenario and the U.S. current war in Iraq should be blatant.

> **Keywords:** Europe—World War II; Heydrich, Reinhard (historical character); Nazis; Terrorism

Walton, Jo.

Small Change Series. 📖 **YA**

> Walton's chilling alternate history scenario presents an alternate world in which the United Kingdom negotiated peace with Nazi Germany over Churchill's objections in 1941. *Farthing*, the first novel, takes the form of an old-fashioned country house mystery, but one set in a counterfactual world in which Fascism subtly encroaches on British citizens' daily lives; the second, *Ha'penny*, reads as a psychological suspense thriller. The author, a World Fantasy Award winner, has wryly given her series the title "Still Life with Fascists."

> **Keywords:** England—World War II; Fascism; Nazis; Policemen

Farthing. Tor, 2006. 319pp. Hardbound, 0765314215.

> It is 1949, but in a world slightly askew from our own. Lucy Eversley, daughter of two members of the Farthing set—aristocratic Brits with Fascist sympathies who had overthrown Churchill eight years earlier—is surprised to be invited to their country retreat; she had been ostracized from the group after marrying a London Jew. Lucy realizes their motive after a leading politician from the Farthing set is murdered on the estate grounds, and her husband is framed for the crime. Only Inspector Peter Carmichael of Scotland Yard dares to look beyond the obvious for the true culprit. The novel alternates between the viewpoints of Lucy and Carmichael. Walton has said that *Farthing*, which garnered stellar reviews, was written in only seventeen days.

> **Keywords:** Detective stories; Jews; Politicians

Ha'penny. Tor, 2007. 319pp. Hardbound, 9780765318534.

> Inspector Carmichael, sent to investigate a bombing in a London suburb that killed popular actress Lauria Gilmore, becomes increasingly aware of a conspiracy to kill both the Fascist-leaning prime minister and Hitler. He doggedly pursues the truth through a twisted maze of political shenanigans, despite governmental pressure to blame the murder on Jews or homosexuals. The novel's alternate viewpoint comes from Viola Lark, a young actress who has been assigned a leading role in the assassination plot.
>
> **Keywords:** Actresses

Half a Crown. Tor, 2008. 320pp. Hardbound, 9780765316219.

> In 1960 Peter Carmichael—officially the head of the Watch, Britain's Fascist-leaning secret police—forms an unlikely, secret alliance to rid his country of Nazi influence once and for all.

Short Story Collections

Anthologies of short alternate history stories appear regularly. The following collections present fictional "what if" scenarios from a wide range of historical periods.

Czerneda, Julie E., and Isaac Szpindel, eds.

ReVisions. DAW, 2004. 312pp. Paper, 0756402409.

> These fifteen stories, though vastly different in terms of time period and locale, presuppose that a particular technological invention, scientific discovery, or social change happened at a different time in history, or perhaps never occurred at all. The authors, best known for their tales of fantasy or science fiction, include Kage Baker, Cory Doctorow, Laura Anne Gilman, Kay Kenyon, Geoffrey Landis, and Mike Resnick.

Markham, J. David, and Mike Resnick, eds.

History Revisited: The Great Battles: Eminent Historians Take on the Great Works of Alternative History. BenBella, 2008. 304pp. Paper, 1933771100.

> For this collection, the editors selected seven previously published (and highly regarded) stories of alternate history—all of which have a military fiction bent—and asked historians to discuss the probability of each counterfactual take. Authors include Kim Stanley Robinson, Mike Resnick, Michael Flynn, and Harry Turtledove. Their stories examine alternate takes on the atom bomb, Lincoln's assassination, the Napoleonic Wars, and more.

Turtledove, Harry.

Alternate Generals III. Baen, 2005. 306pp. Paper, 0743498976.

> Turtledove's third entry in this sporadic series offers up thirteen alternate military history scenarios, with settings ranging from Roman times to

medieval China to the Civil War to World War II to Roman times. Authors include Esther Friesner, Judith Tarr, Roland Green, Mike Resnick, and of course Turtledove himself. If these stories prove fascinating, two previous volumes in this series await.

Ancient Rome

The power and grandeur of ancient Rome has inspired many historical novelists. But what if Rome never fell, or what if it was conquered before the Roman Empire even began? Stephen Baxter's *Emperor* (annotated in the next section) may also be of interest.

Roberts, John Maddox.

Hannibal Series.

What if Hannibal succeeded in conquering Rome during the Second Punic War in the third century BC? For fans of military history.

Keywords: Carthage; Punic Wars

Hannibal's Children. Ace, 2002. 359pp. Hardbound, 0441009336.

As a condition of Rome's surrender to Carthage, Romans head into exile up north, where they form their own empire. A century later descendants of the exiled Romans launch a campaign against the victor's descendants—"Hannibal's children"—to get their country back.

The Seven Hills. Ace, 2005. 362pp. Hardbound, 0441012450.

Rome has finally gathered its strength and conquered Carthage, but a rift in the newly reunited Roman Republic quickly forms. Roman commander Marcus Scipio, who has allied with Egypt, and Titus Norbanus, a "New Man" from Rome's northern outpost, battle it out between themselves.

Europe and the British Isles

Major events in European history—the Viking invasions of the British Isles, the repulse of the Spanish Armada by England, and others—are given new interpretations.

Baxter, Stephen.

Time's Tapestry Series.

A four-volume series about a single family's influence on the history of Western civilization (or perhaps the other way around), sweeping from Roman Britain through the Second World War. Each narrative unfolds episodically, using chronological vignettes connected by a mysterious prophecy that people from each successive generation strive to interpret correctly. The first volume, *Emperor*, reads almost like a straight historical novel; the reason for the novels' classification as alternate history becomes clearer as the series progresses, as rival forces from the distant future (including a mysterious Weaver) gradually announce their presence—and their guiding influence on historical events.

Keywords: Multi-period novels; Prophecies

Emperor. Ace, 2007. 302pp. Hardbound, 9780441014668.

In the year 4 BC a young Britannic woman dying in childbirth begins muttering a prophecy in Latin, a language she doesn't speak. Her words predict Britain's invasion by Rome; they also promise freedom and happiness for her son, Nectovelin, and his descendants. Over the next four and a half centuries her son's family does their utmost to ensure that the prophecy comes true: siding with Rome against their fellow Celts and, later, arranging for the construction of Hadrian's Wall. As the Roman Empire's influence on Britain rises and ebbs and Christianity's popularity grows in its wake, the family's descendants gradually lose touch with one another and with the prophecy.

Keywords: England—Roman period; Hadrian's Wall

Conqueror. Ace, 2007. 302pp. Hardbound, 9780441014965.

Baxter's second volume spans the so-called Dark Ages in England, from the early seventh century through the Norman Conquest. The plot relates a series of conquests of one culture by another and their subsequent absorption into the fabric of the country; first the Saxons, then the Vikings' sack of the monastery at Lindisfarne circa AD 793, followed by Alfred the Great's victory over the Danes, then William the Conqueror's victory at Hastings in 1066. The prophecy here, an Old English poem called the Menologium of the Blessed Isolde, foretells the rise and fall of kings.

Keywords: England—early Middle Ages; Poems

Navigator. Ace, 2008. 323pp. Hardbound, 9780441015597.

In this entry the action picks up just after the Norman Conquest and continues to the voyages of Columbus in 1492, focusing primarily on Christian–Muslim relations.

Keywords: Muslims; Spain-Renaissance/Reformation

Weaver. Ace, 2008. 336pp. Hardbound, 9780441015924.

Baxter's series ends with a bang and with a true counterfactual history scenario: a German invasion of southern England in the 1940s. This prompts the characters to ponder whether this scenario had been meticulously planned from the very beginning.

Keywords: England—World War II

Gentle, Mary.

Ilario Series.

This duology set in Gentle's "secret history" universe (where her four-volume <u>Ash</u> series was likewise set) takes place in an alternate fifteenth-century Mediterranean world, one in which Carthage has become a powerful, Visigoth-ruled kingdom (thrown into perpetual darkness by an ancient curse), Christians are divided into two opposing factions, and the papal throne has been empty for centuries. The focus isn't on historical plausibility, but on a single protagonist, Ilario, an Iberian hermaphrodite whose quest to become a master painter is thwarted by his/her parents—who would lose their positions at court were it known that Ilario was their child. While running from their murderous intentions, Ilario lands in Carthage, Venice, and Rome, gaining new perspectives on art and on a world that insists on treating people according to their gender. The skewed historical time line is combined with convincing historical and geographical details, resulting in an atmosphere that feels authentically Mediterranean yet at the same time completely surreal. Some fantasy elements. Originally published as one long volume in the UK.

Keywords: Artists; Carthage–Renaissance/Reformation; Europe—Renaissance/Reformation; Hermaphrodites

Ilario: The Lion's Eye. Eos, 2006. 303pp. Paper, 0060821833.

Ilario: The Stone Golem. Eos, 2006. 361pp. Paper, 0061344982.

Turtledove, Harry.

Atlantis Series.

Turtledove's trilogy presupposes a divergent historical scenario that reaches further back in time than most alternate histories: What if, in the place of North America's East Coast, a separate continent formed in the midst of the Atlantic Ocean? Its discovery in the mid-fifteenth century leads quickly to colonization, and all of the consequences thereof.

Keywords: Atlantis; Colonialism

Opening Atlantis. Roc, 2007. 440pp. Hardbound, 9780451461742.

In the mid-fifteenth century, after a fisherman discovers a new island continent lying halfway between Europe and Terranova (present-day North America), it is given the logical name of Atlantis and promptly settled by enterprising Englishmen. The story of its founding family, the Radcliffes, is traced over several generations, as conflicts arise with the rival Kersauzon family (who are of Breton origin), and wars from the European mainland begin to affect their island paradise.

The Americas

These novels recount alternate scenarios for events in North American history, from major events such as the Civil War and the growth of the Western frontier, to religious and social changes sparked by a single individual.

The American Frontier

The U.S. poor treatment of Native Americans in the nineteenth-century West has inspired novelists to imagine alternative scenarios, ones with a more positive outcome.

Flint, Eric.

Trail of Glory Series.

Described as an alternate history of the American frontier. Speculative fiction writer Flint imagines a different version of the War of 1812. He demonstrates that making one seemingly minor change to one man's life story may have had ramifications for American history from that point forward. The capstone to the series is that the tragic Trail of Tears, one of the most shameful events in U.S. history, never happens.

Keywords: Cherokee Indians; Houston, Sam (historical character); Racial conflict; War of 1812

The Rivers of War. Del Rey, 2005. 489pp. Hardbound, 0345465679. (Alternate title: *1812: The Rivers of War.*)

According to history, Sam Houston received a severe arrow wound during the 1814 Battle of Horseshoe Bend, part of the campaign Andrew Jackson and his Cherokee allies waged against the Creek Indians. This thwarted Houston's active participation in the remainder of the war with Great Britain. In Flint's version, Houston's injury remains minor, and he and Napoleonic war veteran Patrick Driscol unite to save Washington from British forces. The Battle of Fort McHenry never happens, and the Battle of New Orleans unfolds slightly differently.

1824: The Arkansas War. Del Rey, 2006. 427pp. Hardbound, 0345465695.

Ten years after the events in *The Rivers of War*, freed slaves and Indian tribes driven out of the eastern states have formed an independent nation in the Arkansas territory, under the leadership of Patrick Driscol. Southern politician Henry Clay, who has wangled his way into the presidency, decides to invade this new country, the makeup of which offends his racial sensibilities. Andrew Jackson and John Quincy Adams form a political alliance to oppose him.

The Civil War

The U.S. Civil War (1861–1865) is the most common setting for alternate history novels, demonstrating how the impact of this long-ago war still resonates with both historians and the American public. What might have happened if a single commander had acted differently, or if the North had lost just one more battle? Might the Confederacy have won?

Conroy, Robert.

1862. Presidio, 2006. 420pp. Paper, 0345482379.

After diplomatic envoys from the Confederacy are seized by the Union while en route to Britain aboard a British vessel (a historical incident known as the Trent Affair), Great Britain is drawn into the Civil War on the side of the Confederacy. This forces the United States to fight a war not only against itself, but also against the greatest industrial power of the age.

Keywords: Confederacy; United States—Civil War

Fleming, Thomas J.

The Secret Trial of Robert E. Lee. **Forge, 2006. 336pp. Hardbound, 0765313529.**

What if Robert E. Lee, defeated Confederate general, was tried for treason after the end of the Civil War in 1865? The secret military tribunal convenes in Lee's hometown of Arlington, Virginia. Charles Dana, newspaper journalist and former assistant secretary of war, leads the group of radical Republicans who want to see Lee punished even more severely. Jeremiah O'Brien, a *New York Tribune* reporter and one of Dana's former protégés, finds his respect for Lee growing the longer he observes the trial.

Keywords: Generals; Journalists and reporters; Lee, Robert E. (historical character); Traitors; Virginia—Reconstruction/Gilded Age

Gingrich, Newt, and William Forstchen.

Gettysburg Series. ✍

An alternate history of the Civil War, which imagines a Confederate victory at the Battle of Gettysburg.

Keywords: Confederacy; Gettysburg, Battle of; Grant, Ulysses (historical character); Lee, Robert E. (historical character); Pennsylvania—Civil War; Washington, D.C.—Civil War

Gettysburg. St. Martin's Press, 2003. 463pp. Hardbound, 031230935X.

More successful and more widely praised than the authors' previous effort (*1945*, annotated previously in this chapter), *Gettysburg* follows the traditional Civil War history up to July 1863. In this alternative scenario, General Lee succeeds in rebuffing Union forces at the Battle of Gettysburg, which leads to a battle victory for the South. The military strategies are well-researched, logical, and believable.

Grant Comes East. St. Martin's Press, 2004. 404pp. Hardbound, 0312309376.

After victory at Gettysburg Lee decides to march on Washington, D.C., and finish off the Union once and for all—even if it means weakening his armies beyond repair. It also means ultimately defeating President Abraham Lincoln, who is determined to preserve the Union whatever the cost. Lincoln orders his best general, Ulysses S. Grant, to come east to confront Lee.

Never Call Retreat: Lee and Grant, the Final Victory. St. Martin's, 2005. 496pp. Hardbound, 0312342985.

Despite a Confederate victory at Gettysburg and subsequent advance on Washington, D.C., General Lee realizes that the military might of the Union and the strength of the federal government cannot be overcome, culminating in his surrender in August 1863—a year and a half earlier than in historical reality.

Chapter 14

Historical Fantasy

This chapter includes historical novels that contain elements of the fantastic: magic, supernatural powers, mythical creatures, and more. Because historical novels depend so much on accurate renderings of past events, it may seem strange to include historical fantasy as a subgenre. Obviously, accuracy isn't an absolute requirement here. Like many examples of genre-blending, these novels bend the rules a little. Historical novelists always combine their research with a good amount of creativity, and in historical fantasy they explore their imaginations in greater depth.

The historical fiction and fantasy genres have much in common. Both make use of detailed and vividly rendered settings that offer readers the opportunity to slip into another world. Like traditional historical novels, fantasy novels tend to be long books, and they frequently occur in series. Pacing is leisurely, at least in the beginning, but readers quickly become engrossed in the story lines. There is also considerable crossover in terms of both authors and readers, and novels in this chapter bridge the gap. A recent survey of subscribers to _Locus_, a major trade magazine for the fantasy/science fiction field, revealed that 43 percent of its respondents frequently read historical fiction (September 2007; 32), a figure that steadily increases each year. A number of popular authors (e.g., Judith Tarr, Ann Chamberlin, Roberta Gellis) write in both genres.

Novels in this chapter are set firmly in a historical period and reflect the customs of the time. Historical events are included in the story either as a major part of the plot or as a backdrop. On the fantasy side, both the protagonists and villains make use of magic to achieve their ends. The characters may have the ability to speak with gods and goddesses, or they may be partly divine themselves.

As in most fantasy novels, the plots of historical fantasy revolve around a battle between good and evil—or, put another way, light and dark. As in most heroic tales, the good guys usually win in the end. The roles of light and dark tend to be based on the cultures or religions of the historical period in question, but which one is "good" and which is "evil" can vary. In Sara Douglass's <u>The Crucible</u> trilogy, the Church is the force of light, but in Marion Zimmer Bradley's classic _The Mists of Avalon_, the protagonists struggle against the encroaching influence of Christianity on a mystical, Goddess-ruled Celtic world.

Much historical fantasy centers on characters from myth and legend, such as heroes from Greek mythology, King Arthur and his entourage, ancient Norse or Irish warriors, and mystical figures from medieval times such as Joan of Arc and the Knights Templar. Other authors use the conventions of myth and legend and build original stories around them. Nearly all historical fantasy novels are set in a preindustrial period in the British Isles or Europe. Modern settings exist but aren't common, because they can't always convey the otherworldly atmosphere required by fantasy.

Sometimes the line between historical fiction and fantasy is difficult to define. Jack Whyte's pre-Arthurian novels (see Chapter 2) contain no magical elements, but readers and librarians often classify them as fantasy because they are based on Arthurian legend and feature characters that may or may not have been historical figures. On the other hand, Elizabeth Cunningham's fantastical trilogy about a Celtic Mary Magdalene (annotated this chapter), which has scenes of enchantment and Celtic ritual, is just as often called historical fiction. Jules Watson's Dalriada trilogy, set in Roman-era Scotland (see Chapter 2), although marketed as fantasy, has only minor supernatural elements. Cross-references between these chapters are provided in some cases.

Although fantasy as a genre has burgeoned in the last five years, the number of historical fantasy titles published has slowed. Many of those listed below are new volumes in existing series. For example, new entries in the Avalon series, begun by Marion Zimmer Bradley and continued by her collaborator, Diana Paxson, appear at regular intervals. On the other hand, novels of historical paranormal romance—set in historical times, with supernatural happenings driving the plot—have exploded in popularity. A small number of these are included here, specifically those incorporating considerable historical detail, and they are noted as such in the annotations.

This chapter is organized by subcategories based around cultures (Celtic, Norse) or historical periods (medieval, Renaissance) that have similar characteristics. In general, books that use "alternate" versions of historical settings, such as Lian Hearn's popular Otori series, set in an alternate feudal Japan, aren't included here. Readers who enjoy these novels, as well as fantasy in general, will want to explore the subject in more depth in Diana Tixier Herald's and Bonnie Kunzel's *Fluent in Fantasy: The Next Generation* (Libraries Unlimited, 2007). Time-slip novels (see Chapter 12), which include supernatural plot devices, are also worth investigating.

Fantasy of the Ancient World

Many fantasies set in the ancient world—Greece, Rome, Egypt, and Mesopotamia —take classical myths about powerful heroes from long ago and retell them for a modern audience, with a bit of creative license thrown in. Gods and goddesses become involved in characters' personal lives, affecting history along the way.

Allen, Justin.

Slaves of the Shinar. **Overlook, 2007. 429pp. Hardbound, 9781585679164.**

This novel about a large-scale culture clash in ancient Mesopotamia (the land that is now Iraq) begins as Uruk, a thief from the jungles of sub-Saharan Africa, makes his way from the fabled city of Ur, where he acquires several companions on the road, to the even bigger city of Kan-Puram. In a parallel story Ander, an escaped slave of the brutal warrior race called Niphilim, reaches Kan-Puram just ahead of the Niphilim army. Together with an all-volunteer army of their own, Ur and Ander prepare for war. Described as an epic fantasy, Allen's debut reads almost like mainstream historical fiction about the ancient world; the Niphilim, who are mentioned in the Bible as a race of giants, are the only element that could be considered fantastic.

Keywords: Giants; Mesopotamia; Thieves

Douglass, Sara.

The first two novels of her <u>Troy Game</u> series fit this category; they are annotated under "Multi-Period Historical Fantasy Series."

Gemmell, David, and Stella Gemmell.

Troy Series.

Annotated in Chapter 8.

Graham, Jo.

Black Ships. Orbit, 2008. 411pp. Paper, 9780316068000. 📖 **YA**

Using deliberate prose that echoes the ancient legends, first novelist Graham tells an alternative, feminine version of the *Aeneid* in her tale of Gull, daughter of a slave from fallen Troy, who was dedicated as a child to serve the oracle at Delphi. When nine black ships carrying Prince Aeneas and his fellow Trojan exiles appear on the horizon, Gull chooses to leave Pylos and serve as Aeneas's guide on his adventures through the Mediterranean world. They sail from Greece to Egypt and on toward Italy, where they both find their destinies.

Keywords: Greece; Mythology; Oracles

Le Guin, Ursula K.

Lavinia. Harcourt, 2008. 279pp. Hardbound, 9780151014248. 📖 **YA**

In the *Aeneid*, Lavinia was the king's daughter, fated to marry Aeneas of Troy, with whom she would begin a dynasty that would, centuries later, found the Roman Empire. Le Guin's austerely beautiful and contemplative novel, set in the half-wild, ethereal world of ancient Italy, looks beyond the epic poem to give Lavinia the life and voice Virgil never granted her. In heeding the prophecy that she will marry a foreigner rather than her mother's chosen suitor, Lavinia sets in motion a chain of events that leads to civil war among the people of Latium. The novel loops back and forth from Lavinia's old age to her youthful meetings in a sacred grove with the ghostly poet himself. She learns from Virgil about the future he created for her, including her regrettably brief marriage to Aeneas, a man destined to die young, and the unavoidable, tragic consequences her choice of partner has on her people.

Keywords: Italy; Mythology; Virgil (historical character)

Lennox, Mary.

The Moon Runners. **Five Star, 2004. 392pp. Hardbound, 159414107X.**

Lennox based her debut novel on the story of Atalanta, a fleet-footed huntress from Greek mythology. In 1350 BC Princess Atalante of Thessaly, marked by the goddess Artemis from birth, prepares to defend her lands against the greedy armies of Macedonia. However, Prince Melanion of Macedonia, his royal father's war leader, had promised to protect Thessaly, his mother's homeland. When Atalante and Melanion meet, they fall in love, disrupting the plans of their parents and of the fickle war goddess Artemis.

Keywords: Greece; Mythology; Princesses

Tarr, Judith.

Alexander the Great Series. ✍

A fantastical duology set in the world of Alexander the Great, and slightly beforehand.

Keywords: Greece; Mythology; Persia; Queens

Queen of the Amazons. Tor, 2004. 320pp. Hardbound, 0765303957.

Hippolyta, Queen of the Amazon clan living in eastern Persia, has given birth to a talented but unusual daughter. Her tribes claim that the girl, named Etta, has no soul. Selene, the niece of the Amazons' seer, becomes her guardian, but not even Selene can stop Etta from running away to see Alexander, the valiant Macedonian conqueror who strives to rule the known world.

Keywords: Alexander the Great (historical character); Amazons; Warriors, women

Bring Down the Sun. Tor, 2008. 224pp. Hardbound, 9780765303974.

Tarr creates a gritty romantic fantasy centering on Olympias, legendary mother of Alexander the Great, beginning in her youth, before she married Philip of Macedon. Here she is Polyxena, a free-spirited and flirtatious priestess of the Great Goddess, who entices Philip into a promise of marriage. Philip renames her Myrtale, "crowned one." After they wed she uses her connections to the goddess to further his and her son's ambitions.

Keywords: Olympias, Queen of Macedonia (historical character); Priestesses

Wolfe, Gene.

Latro Series.

Ever since he was injured in battle, Latro, a "barbarian" soldier in Xerxes's army in ancient Greece, has woken up every morning with no memory of his past. He records everything in a daily journal to keep track of what he experiences. His travels and adventures throughout the ancient world make up the plots of the trilogy. To make up for his constant amnesia Latro is given the ability to speak with gods, and their observations are amusing and astute. Latro's accounts are rambling but also fascinating, particularly in his portrayal of Greece as seen by someone discovering it anew each day. The first two volumes were republished as the single-volume *Latro in the Mist. Soldier of Sidon,* which takes Latro to ancient Egypt, won the World Fantasy Award in 2007.

Keywords: Amnesia; Egypt; Greece; Soldiers

Soldier of the Mist. Tom Doherty Associates, 1986. 335pp. Hardbound, 0312937342.

Soldier of Arete. Tom Doherty Associates, 1989. 354pp. Hardbound, 0312931859.

🎗 *Soldier of Sidon.* Tor, 2006. 319pp. Hardbound, 0765316641. Hardbound, 0765316641.

Arthurian Fantasy

Arthurian fantasies are magical tales set in the mists of Britain's so-called Dark Ages, circa the fifth or sixth centuries AD, after the Romans have abandoned the island and before the Saxons have taken control. In most versions King Arthur appears as the hero of legend, a great king who manages to unite the warring Celtic tribes for a brief time against Saxon invaders. Included as part of the overall legend are the quest for the Holy Grail, a moral tale marked with Christian symbolism, and the tragic love story of Tristan and Iseult, whose romance began with the drinking of a magical love potion. Authors incorporate fantastical elements in the powers of the great sorcerer Merlin, Arthur's mentor, and the evil necromancy of Morgause and Morgan le Fay, alternately described as Arthur's sisters or aunts. Arthurian fantasies will appeal to readers who enjoy magical, heroic tales of love, honor, and chivalry. Many have romantic elements that appeal to readers, especially women. Because of this, fans may wish to investigate traditional historical novels (Chapter 2) and romantic novels (Chapter 4) set during the Middle Ages.

Bradley, Marion Zimmer.

The Mists of Avalon. **Knopf, 1982. 876pp. Hardbound, 0394524063.** ★ **YA**
Bradley's heroine is Morgaine ("le Fay"), daughter of Igraine of Avalon and her first husband, Gorlois of Cornwall. Trained by her aunt Viviane in the art of being a priestess, Morgaine learns how to lift the mists separating the otherworldly land of Avalon from the Isle of Glastonbury, the site of a Christian monastery. Morgaine's rival throughout her life is Gwynhwyfar, a beautiful Christian woman fostered at Glastonbury as a child. While Morgaine struggles between her love for men and her love for Avalon, Gwynhwyfar's ever-deepening religiosity leads Arthur to abandon his belief in the Goddess in favor of his wife's religion, to his and Avalon's downfall. The late Marion Zimmer Bradley's decision to retell Arthurian legend from a feminine viewpoint was ingenious and, at the time, wholly original. Not only did it shed a new light on the religious and gender implications of the traditionally male-dominated story, but her

complex, beautifully characterized novel became one of the best-selling fantasy novels of all time.

Keywords: Arthurian themes; Priestesses

Clegg, Douglas.

Mordred, Bastard Son. **Alyson, 2006. 260pp. Paper, 1555838995.**

Horror novelist Clegg puts a new spin on Mordred, King Arthur's nemesis (and illegitimate son by his half-sister, Morgan le Fay) as well as the Arthurian legend as a whole. Mordred narrates his life story to a monk in exchange for assistance in hiding from his father's men, who are determined to try him for treason. Brought up by his sorceress mother and trained in the druidic arts, Mordred grows up conflicted about his father, a tyrant king determined to sacrifice his family in favor of the Camelot ideal. He's also troubled by his attraction to other young men.

Keywords: Arthurian themes; Gay men; Illegitimate children

Massie, Allan.

Arthur the King. **Carroll & Graf, 2004. 292pp. Hardbound, 0786713844.**

Presented as a fictional tale told by medieval astrologer Michael Scott to his pupil, the Holy Roman Emperor Frederick II, Massie's version of the King Arthur legend begins in post-Roman Britain, as various petty kings skirmish for power and position. Arthur himself is a servant boy whom Merlin schools in language, leadership, and the ways of the world. The story line is bawdy, direct, and occasionally poetic, with numerous asides on the part of the narrator.

Keywords: Arthurian themes; Astrologers

Stewart, Mary.

<u>Arthurian Saga.</u> ★ `YA`

Set in fifth-century Britain, this classic series was based on two medieval sources of Arthurian lore, Geoffrey of Monmouth's *History of the Kings of Britain* and Malory's *Morte d'Arthur*. The novels are tightly written, with multifaceted characters and authentic dialogue that give a realistic feel for the period. The first three volumes are told from the viewpoint of legendary sorcerer Merlin.

Keywords: Arthurian themes; Witchcraft

The Crystal Cave. William Morrow, 1970. 529pp. Hardbound.

The illegitimate daughter of a Welsh princess, Merlin grows up with the gift of prophecy, which leads him to High King Vortigern and sets him on the path to becoming a royal advisor.

The Hollow Hills. William Morrow, 1973. 402pp. Hardbound, 0688001793.

During the reign of Uther Pendragon, prophet Merlin Ambrosius guards the future King Arthur, preparing for the day that Arthur can take up the sword Caliburn and the rule of a kingdom.

The Last Enchantment. William Morrow, 1979. 439pp. Hardbound, 0688034810.

> Arthur has become king, but foul sorceries—which result in an incestuous liaison with his scheming half-sister, Morgause—threaten the future of Camelot. Merlin falls in love with the sorceress Nimue, which leads to his own downfall.

The Wicked Day. William Morrow, 1983. 314pp. Hardbound, 0688025072.

> Mordred, son of King Arthur and his half-sister, the witch Morgause, never intends to be Arthur's doom, but fate turns against him. A sympathetic portrait of this often maligned character.

Zettel, Sarah.

Paths to Camelot Series. YA

Three stand-alone novels about the women of Camelot: lyrical, romantic historical fantasy about four knights of the Round Table, King Arthur's nephews, and the women they come to love. *Camelot's Blood*, the fourth novel in the quartet, has not been published in the United States.

Keywords: Arthurian themes; Knights; Sorcerers

In Camelot's Shadow. Luna, 2004. 507pp. Paper, 0373811128.

> Risa of the Morelands learns that her father has promised her in marriage to an evil sorcerer, Euberacon, to save her mother's life. In fleeing Euberacon's clutches, she is rescued by Sir Gawain, who is en route to Camelot to warn King Arthur of treachery in his kingdom. An adaptation of two traditional Arthurian poems, "Gawain and the Green Knight" and "Sir Gawain and the Loathly Lady."

For Camelot's Honor. Luna, 2005. 506pp. Paper, 037380218.

> Elen, a Welsh chieftain's daughter, seeks to take revenge against Urien, the man who murdered her family for siding with King Arthur, and his sorceress lover, Morgaine, Arthur's evil half-sister. Transformed into a hawk, Elen alerts Merlin about her predicament, and he sends Sir Geraint to rescue her. Loosely based on the legend of Geraint and Enid.

Under Camelot's Banner. Luna, 2006. 553pp. Paper, 0373802315.

> Lynet Carnbrea, daughter of the steward of Castle Cambryn in Cornwall, travels to Camelot to ask Queen Guinevere to aid her troubled lands. Gareth, Lancelot's squire and Gawain's youngest brother, sees the chance to redeem himself in his master's eyes and achieve knighthood by helping Lynet with her quest.

Celtic Fantasy

Celtic fantasy novels feature myths and traditions of the Celtic peoples, tribal cultures that lived in the British Isles, all of Western Europe, and lands as far south as Galatia (modern Turkey) from the first millennium BC through the eighth or ninth centuries AD. Frequent topics include the heroic adventures of ancient Celtic warriors, who had the ability to speak with the gods; protagonists' use of magic to prevent invasion by Rome; and the turbulent relationship between earth-based religions and Christianity. Fantasy authors tend to play up the matriarchal aspects of Celtic society, which makes the novels appealing to women. However, the religious rituals frequently owe more to modern paganism than to any ancient tradition. Because some Celtic fantasies are set in post-Roman Britain (fifth or sixth centuries AD), and because many novelists imagine King Arthur as a great Celtic king, there will be some crossover between this and the previous section. In addition, readers will want to investigate traditional historical novels set in prehistoric Europe and Asia (Chapter 2).

Bradley, Marion Zimmer.

Avalon Series. ★ YA

The novels of Bradley's series, completed by novelist Diana Paxson after Bradley's death, are mystical works that juxtapose the male-dominated world of ancient Rome with the matriarchal Celts of her imaginary world of Avalon. They can all stand alone, but most readers will want to read *Mists of Avalon* first. *Sword of Avalon*, about the origins of Excalibur, will be the next volume.

Keywords: Celts; Druids; England—Roman period; Priestesses

Marion Zimmer Bradley's Ancestors of Avalon. Viking, 2004. 363pp. Hardbound, 0670033146. Written by Diana Paxson.

This prequel to the Avalon series begins in the sea kingdoms of Atlantis just before its destruction. Tiriki, high priestess on an Atlantean island, realizes that it's time for her people to begin a new life in the British Isles. She and her lover, Micail, establish separate settlements and try to keep their spiritual beliefs alive, but Damisa, one of Tiriki's acolytes, proves to be a dangerous rival.

Keywords: Atlantis

Marion Zimmer Bradley's Ravens of Avalon. Viking, 2007. 394pp. Hardbound, 9780670038701. Written by Diana Paxson. ✍

This latest entry retells the story of Boudica (a historical figure who has been firmly ensconced by now in ancient legend), seen here as a Celtic priestess circa AD 60. Her mentor is Lhiannon, a druid priestess who trains her in the mystical arts. Boudica helps her people by agreeing to marry Prasutagos, High King of the Iceni and a Roman ally. When he dies the Romans refuse to acknowledge her queenship and take brutal revenge against Boudica and her daughters. Lhiannon's story continues in *The Forest House*.

Keywords: Boudica (historical character); Queens

The Forest House. Viking, 1994. 416pp. Hardbound, 0670844543.

Eilan, the clairvoyant daughter of a goddess-worshipping Druid in first-century Britain, is chosen to become a priestess of the Forest House. Though she falls in love with half-Celtic, half-Roman soldier Gaius Marcellius, their romance is forbidden. By the time Eilan is selected to be High Priestess, she has another big secret to keep.

Lady of Avalon. Viking, 1997. 460pp. Hardbound, 0670857831.

> In Roman Britain the efforts of three heroic women pave the way for Goddess worship in the mystical land of Avalon as well as the coming of King Arthur. The first, Caillean, seals the land of Avalon away from the mortal (Christian) world and fosters the boy-child Gawen, son of Eilan and Gaius from *The Forest House.* Dierna, one of her successors as lady of Avalon, falls in love with a man she cannot have. Two centuries later the lady Ana gives birth to five daughters—including Viviane, Igraine, and Morgause—destined to play great roles in Avalon and in *The Mists of Avalon.*

The Mists of Avalon. Knopf, 1982. 876pp. Hardbound, 0394524063.

> Listed under "Arthurian Fantasy."

Priestess of Avalon. Viking, 2001. 394pp. Hardbound, 0670910236. Completed by Diana L. Paxson. ✍

> In AD 259 Helena, a ten-year-old British princess, returns to her birthplace of Avalon and reassumes her birth name, Eilan. She becomes a powerful priestess, foreseeing the man she will eventually marry—the Roman Constantius—and the son they will have together, who will be known as Constantine the Great. A fantastical biographical novel of St. Helena, whose own history is largely unknown.

> **Keywords:** St. Helena (historical character); Princesses; Saints

Cunningham, Elizabeth.

The Maeve Chronicles. ✍

> Cunningham's Mary Magdalene, called Maeve, is no mere follower of Jesus but an uninhibited, strong-willed Celtic warrior woman who's destined to be his mate and equal in every way. At once deeply spiritual and unabashedly irreverent, as far as traditional interpretations of Scripture are concerned, Cunningham's novel takes a feminist, earthy, very witty, and modern (contemporary slang is used throughout) look at the traditional Bible story, incorporating elements of Celtic, Egyptian, and Christian mythology.

> **Keywords:** Biblical themes; Celts; Druids; Isle of Mona; Mary Magdalene (biblical figure); Palestine—Roman period

Magdalen Rising: The Beginning. Monkfish, 2007. 404pp. Hardbound, 0976684322.

> Maeve, called Little Bright One as a child, is raised by eight warrior witches on Tir nam Ban, the Isle of Women. Having experienced visions from a young age, she undergoes spiritual training with a wise woman and druids on the Isle of Mona. It's here that she finally meets Esus of Nazareth, the young man she's been seeing in dreams, and she knows he's destined to be her soul mate. When a hostile druid selects Esus to be the victim in the Great Sacrifice, Maeve risks her life to save him. Previously published as *Daughter of the Shining Isles* by Barrytown in 2000.

The Passion of Mary Magdalen. Monkfish, 2006. 620pp. Hardbound, 0976684306.

> Maeve travels across the Iberian Peninsula and the Roman Empire during the first century, becoming a whore, slave, and healer. Eventually she lands in Palestine, where she settles and opens her own brothel in Magdala—where she at last encounters Yeshua, the man she once knew as Esus, again.

Guler, Kathleen Cunningham.

Macsen's Treasure series.

Romantic historical fantasy adventure set in the pre-Arthurian period, about a Welsh spy named Marcus ap Iowerth and his clairvoyant lover, Claerwen.

Keywords: Arthurian themes; Celts; England—early Middle Ages; Spies

Into the Path of Gods. Bardsong, 1998. 413pp. Hardbound, 0966037103.

In the Shadow of Dragons. Bardsong, 2001. 379pp. Hardbound, 096603712X.

The Anvil Stone. Bardsong, 2006. 400pp. Hardbound, 0966037154.

> While Marcus ap Iowerth continues his quest to unite all of Britain against encroaching Saxon invaders, the land's people search frantically for an ancient, sacred sword of prophecy, one destined to belong to a future king called Arthur.

Marillier, Juliet.

The Bridei Chronicles. YA

Smoothly written historical fantasy, with a glimmer of romance, centering on the Picts of northern Britain (modern-day Scotland) in the sixth century AD. The Picts defend their territory against incursions by Gaels, a Celtic people, who begin establishing settlements in lands just to the south. Marillier bases her series on the life of Bridei, a historical Pictish king who ruled for three decades during the mid-sixth century. Along with carefully researched elements of Pictish culture (including an imaginative re-creation of their pagan religion, about which little is known), Marillier dramatizes the coming of Christianity to early Scotland. A fourth volume is planned.

Keywords: Bridei I, King of the Picts (historical character); Druids; Paganism; Picts; Scotland—early Middle Ages

The Dark Mirror. Tor, 2005. 510pp. Hardbound, 0765309955.

> Young Bridei, a child of the royal line, becomes the foster son of Broichan, one of the most powerful druids in the Kingdom of Fortriu. When the Fair Folk abandon a baby on Broichan's doorstep, a girl he names Tuala, Bridei braves his people's enmity by taking her in and caring for her.

Blade of Fortriu. Tor, 2006. 496pp. Hardbound, 0765309963.

> Bridei, who has ruled peacefully as king of the Priteni for the past five years, looks forward to the day when the Gaels will leave his land for good. To consolidate his alliance with Alpin, a local chieftain, Bridei sends Ana, a hostage from the Light Isles who was raised at the court of Fortriu, northward to marry him. Faolan, Bridei's chief spy and assassin, accompanies her. Once

there Ana uncovers a conspiracy surrounding a man Alpin has been keeping as a prisoner.

The Well of Shades. Tor, 2007. 496pp. Hardbound, 9780765309976.

To root out possible threats to his kingdom, Bridei sends Faolan on a secret mission to Ireland, his homeland, where Faolan also hopes to uncover the truth about his past.

Keywords: Ireland—early Middle Ages

Osborne-McKnight, Juilene.

Song of Ireland. **Forge, 2006. 336pp. Hardbound, 0765312433.**

Osborne-McKnight, a college professor and professional folklorist/story-teller, writes her version of an ancient legend: how the Celtic people, led by the bard Amergin, crossed the waters to found a new civilization on the emerald isle called Eire. When they arrive they discover, to their surprise, that they are not alone. Already inhabiting the isle are the "little people" called the Danu (Tuatha de Danann, in legend), faerie folk who have guarded the land since the dawn of time. These mystical people, despite having foreseen the coming of the Celts, cannot prevent the fierce culture clash that results.

Keywords: Bards; Celts; Fairies; Ireland—early Middle Ages

Watson, Jules.

Dalriada Trilogy.

Annotated in Chapter 2.

Medieval Fantasy

These novels are set amid the courts of medieval Europe, but not quite as we know them. Their heroes are men and women with supernatural abilities who manipulate politics from behind the scenes. Settings can vary and may include the British Isles, Europe, and the Middle East (including Byzantium) between the fifth and fifteenth centuries. In keeping with an age in which life was short and difficult, the tone is serious and sometimes dark. Many aspects of medieval times—such as people's belief in miracles, witchcraft, and sorcery—can seem mystical to modern readers. In medieval fantasy novels, these elements truly do become magical.

Avery, Fiona.

The Crown Rose. **Pyr, 2005. 454pp. Hardbound, 1591023122.** ✍

Growing up in mid-thirteenth-century France, Princess Isabelle, the younger sister of King Louis IX and daughter of the formidable queen dowager Blanche of Castile, knows that she is destined to become a leader in the Church. When a mysterious young man saves her from certain death as a child, she feels an uncanny connection to him, though she knows he isn't what he appears to be. Is there a tie between him and the trio of sisters that has protected the French royal family from harm for years? Avery's crystalline prose places readers in a mystical version of medieval France, one that hides many secrets.

Keywords: Christian themes; France; Holy Grail; Isabelle, Princess of France (historical character); Royalty

Bergren, Lisa Tawn.

The Gifted.

Annotated in Chapter 11.

Chamberlin, Ann.

Joan of Arc Tapestries. ✍

Fifteenth-century France, torn apart by warring Burgundians, Frenchmen, and the English, is the scene for this magical tapestry based on the story of Joan of Arc. The mysterious voices Joan (Jehanne/Jehannette) hears, however, come not from the God of Christianity but from the gods of an ancient pagan religion. Chamberlin's Merlin isn't the famed magician from King Arthur's court, but someone else entirely. *Gloria* is actually the fourth book in the series; the third was published only in German (*Der Erbe des Ermiten*).

Keywords: France; Gilles de Rais (historical character); St. Joan of Arc (historical character); Paganism; Peasants; Saints; Witchcraft

The Merlin of St. Gilles' Well. Tor, 1999. 320pp. Hardbound, 0312865511.

A young Breton peasant boy named Yann, crippled by an arrow struck by Guy de Rais, begins seeing visions of a young girl who will lead the French to victory. Guy's son Gilles—one day to be known as Bluebeard—is raised alongside Yann in the Old Religion.

The Merlin of the Oak Wood. Tor, 2001. 333pp. Hardbound, 0312872844.

In 1425, France is suffering under years of war and English occupation. Gilles de Rais waits patiently for La Pucelle ("the virgin") to appear, but time is running out. In the novel's second half Jehannette d'Arc doesn't understand the voices she hears. Yann—now Merlin—knows that she will emerge as La Pucelle, the savior of her people.

Gloria: The Merlin and the Saint. High Country, 2005. 448pp. Hardbound, 1932158618.

Yann, the Merlin, continues the story of Jehanne of Lorraine. It's now 1428, and Yann, disguised as an Augustinian monk named Jean Pasquerel, realizes that Jehanne of Lorraine, a mere peasant girl, will be the one to lift the curse laid upon France by Templar knights. Gilles de Rais, a devotee of Jehanne's who believes he is her soul mate in the Old Religion, follows her into battle as she lifts the siege of Orléans.

Douglass, Sara.

The Crucible Trilogy.

In this fantastical version of medieval English and European history, as written by Australian fantasy novelist Douglass, the fourteenth century isn't merely grim, replete with plague, and full of spiritual fervor, it's also a world in which demons (and angels) walk the earth alongside mortal men and women. The calamities that plague England's populace are a direct result of these battles fought between the Church and the devil in both the mortal and otherworldly realms. Readers will recognize names from the Lancaster and York family trees during the Hundred Years' War (genealogies are provided) in these novels, though they often behave far differently than their historical selves did. The protagonist is Brother Thomas Neville, nobleman and Dominican friar, charged by the archangel Michael to rid the world of evil.

Keywords: Angels; Christian themes; England; Hundred Years' War; Nobility

The Nameless Day. Tor, 2004. 448pp. Hardbound, 0765305410.

The Wounded Hawk. Tor, 2005. 494pp. Hardbound, 0765303639.

The Crippled Angel. Tor, 2006. 368pp. Hardbound, 0765303647.

Holland, Cecelia.

Corban Loosestrife Series.

Annotated in Chapter 2.

Tarr, Judith.

William the Conqueror Series. ✍ YA

If you can imagine William of Conqueror, who established Norman rule in England after the 1066 Battle of Hastings, as the heir to Druidic earth magic, you'll understand the premise of this highly imaginative duology. His goal in conquering England is to bring the land back to the ancient, pagan religion that was temporarily vanquished during the centuries of Saxon rule.

Keywords: England; Magic and magicians; Paganism

Rite of Conquest. Roc, 2004. 300pp. Paper, 0451460022.

> William of Normandy, bastard son of a Norman duke and a Druidic wisewoman, resists tapping into his innate magical powers. Mathilda of Flanders, his witch consort, helps him to master and harness them, so that he may break the stranglehold that Christianity has long had on England.
>
> **Keywords:** Druids; Illegitimate children; William I "the Conqueror," King of England (historical character); Witchcraft

King's Blood. Roc, 2005. 376pp. Paper, 0451460456.

> This sequel to *Rite of Conquest* picks up the story with the next generation of Norman rulers. William the Conqueror's heir, Red William (better known in history as William Rufus), seeks to undo everything his father has accomplished magic-wise. England's best hopes in restoring the realm, once again, to the Old Religion are Henry, William's younger brother, and Edith, a convent-bound Scottish princess.

> **Keywords:** William II, King of England (historical character)

Tudor and Renaissance Fantasy

Like those set in medieval times, fantasies of the Tudor era (England) and the Renaissance (rest of Europe) feature characters who work their magic around a royal court. Some use a lighthearted and whimsical tone; others are far darker.

Carroll, Susan.

Daughters of the Earth Novels.

Annotated in Chapter 4.

Brennan, Marie.

Midnight Never Come. Orbit, 2008. 379pp. Paper, 9780316020299. **YA**

> While Queen Elizabeth I rules all of England, a secret, shadow world below London is ruled by Invidiana, Queen of the Fae. By 1588 the faerie have established firm strongholds in the politics of Elizabethan England, though their existence is known only to a few. Two courtiers and spies—Lady Lune of the Fae and her mortal counterpart, Michael Deven, spymaster Francis Walsingham's agent—discover each other's worlds and form an unlikely, secret alliance to rid the queen of Invidiana's influence. A dark, fantastic novel of political intrigue in an authentically detailed setting.

> **Keywords:** England—Tudor era; Fairies; Magic and magicians; Royalty; Spies

Duncan, Dave.

Alchemist Series. ✑ **YA**

> Mystery and black magic in a fantastical version of Renaissance Venice. Maestro Filippo Nostradamus—renowned physician, clairvoyant, astrologer, and alchemist —asks his teenaged apprentice, swordsman Alfeo Zeno, to look into strange occurrences on his behalf. Alfeo is allowed to use his fledgling magical talents in his investigations.

> **Keywords:** Alchemy; Detective stories; Italy—Renaissance/Reformation; Magic and magicians; Nobility; Nostradamus (historical character); Psychics; Zeno, Alfeo

The Alchemist's Apprentice. Ace, 2007. 313pp. Paper, 0441014798.

> A high-ranking Venetian nobleman has dropped dead of poison during a dinner party, fulfilling Nostradamus's prediction that he wasn't long for this

world. Accused of engineering the crime to demonstrate his clairvoyant abilities, Nostradamus depends on Alfeo to solve it.

The Alchemist's Code. Ace, 2008. 308pp. Paper, 9780441015627.

Using his psychic skills, Nostradamus realizes that a nobleman's missing daughter has eloped with a young man, and he charges Alfeo with finding the runaway couple. Their skill in resolving this interpersonal matter attracts the notice of Venice's Council of Ten, who give them a more dangerous mission.

Lackey, Mercedes, and Roberta Gellis.

Scepter'd Isle Series. ✍ YA

Alongside the world of Henry VIII's England in the mid-sixteenth century, two factions of the otherworldly Sidhe vie for control over the mortal realm. Elves from the bright and dark courts (the Seleighe and Unseleighe Sidhe) attempt to influence the royal succession and wield power themselves. Boisterous, magical, and entertaining.

Keywords: Elizabeth I, Queen of England (historical character); Elves; England —Tudor era; Magic and magicians; Queens

This Scepter'd Isle. Baen, 2004. 480pp. Hardbound, 0743471563.

Denoriel, one of the Sidhe from the Bright Court, attaches himself to Harry Fitzroy, Henry VIII's young bastard son. Meanwhile, their dark rivals do all they can to ensure that Princess Mary will succeed to the throne, which will bring the Inquisition to England.

Ill Met by Moonlight. Baen, 2005. 522pp. Hardbound, 0743498909.

Visions of the future have revealed that Princess Elizabeth will one day reign, which prompts the Unseleighe Sidhe, under the leadership of dark lord Vidal Dhu, to prevent her succession.

By Slanderous Tongues. Baen, 2007. 533pp. Hardbound, 9781416521075.

Henry VIII is dead, and Princess Elizabeth, fourteen years old, contends with enemies both mortal and otherworldly. This time her Sidhe guardians, Denoriel and his twin sister, are also in danger.

And Less Than Kind. Baen, 2008. 610pp. Hardbound, 9781416555339.

The evil elf-lord Vidal Dhu convinces Queen Mary, a devout Catholic, to wed and produce an heir so that her sister, Princess Elizabeth, will never come to the throne.

Miscellaneous British and European Fantasy

A miscellany of fantasy novels set in other periods of British or European history, the seventeenth through the early twentieth centuries.

Abé, Shana.

The Drákon Series.

A trilogy of sensual romantic fantasy novels set in eighteenth-century England and central Europe. The novels center on members of the drákon, a mysterious clan of shape-shifters from Darkfrith, in the hills of northern England, who can turn from human form into smoke and then, finally, into dragon form. Historical paranormal romance.

Keywords: Dragons; England—Georgian era; Shape-shifters; Thieves

The Smoke Thief. Bantam, 2005. 292pp. Hardbound, 0553804480.

> In 1737, it's the responsibility of the Alpha drákon, Kit, Marquess of Langford, to capture the "smoke thief," a fugitive drákon that has been stealing the jewels of London's upper class. He doesn't realize that his prey is a woman, Rue Hawthorne, the strongest female drákon for generations.

The Dream Thief. Bantam, 2006. 279pp. Hardbound, 0553804936.

> Lady Amalia "Lia" Langford, daughter of Kit and Rue from the first book, joins forces with Zane, a thief from London's streets, to find the legendary Draumr, a diamond buried somewhere in the Carpathian Mountains of Transylvania with the power to control the drákon.

Queen of Dragons. Bantam, 2008. 288pp. Hardbound, 9780553805284.

> It's now 1774, and Kimber Langford, Earl of Chasen, is shocked to discover the existence of another group of drákon living in the Carpathian Mountains. Young Princess Maricara, of this distant branch, warns him about a killer preying on the drákon.

Barnes, Jonathan.

The Somnambulist. **Morrow, 2008. 353pp. Hardbound, 9780061375385.** 📖

Edward Moon, a quirky stage magician by profession, has a second, more invigorating career. He sidelines as a freelance detective in early twentieth-century London alongside his sidekick/assistant/partner, a mute, milk-chugging giant known as the Somnambulist. To relieve his constant feeling of ennui, Moon jumps at the chance to help a police detective solve yet another unsolvable crime (his specialty). The initial murder case leads to another that's even more bizarre and gruesome, and also to an odd religious cult determined to overtake London. A twisted, phantasmagorical tale that—even it really does have "no literary merit," as the admittedly unreliable narrator states up front—is ridiculously diverting and utterly uncategorizable.

Keywords: Detective stories; England—20th century; Magic and magicians

Clarke, Susanna.

🏵 *Jonathan Strange and Mr. Norrell.* **Bloomsbury, 2004. 782pp. Hardbound, 1582344167.** ★ 📖 **YA**

Mr. Norrell, a reclusive scholar in England in 1806, has regained the lost art of working magic, becoming the first new magician in hundreds of years. He uses his abilities for England's gain during the Napoleonic Wars. Then out of nowhere comes Jonathan Strange, an arrogant nobleman whose magical abilities rival Norrell's. Mr. Norrell takes Strange as a pupil, but Strange finds Norrell's approach to magic far too restrictive and sedate for his taste. A widely praised, best-selling novel. Hugo Award; World Fantasy Award. **Literary.**

Keywords: England—Georgian era; Magic and magicians; Napoleonic Wars; Teachers

Hand, Elizabeth.

Mortal Love. **Morrow, 2004. 367pp. Hardbound, 0061051705.**
This dense, challenging dark fantasy explores the complex relationship between artists and their muses, and between creative genius and madness. Hand juxtaposes late Victorian England (circa 1883) with contemporary London in her tale of two men, a nineteenth-century American painter in London and a modern-day writer, who are both drawn to mysterious, auburn-haired women who beguile them and trigger obsessive feelings. The parallels between the two men's experiences are obvious, and the women who capture their attention are remarkably similar—almost impossibly similar. **Literary.**

Keywords: Artists' models; England—Victorian era; Painters

Lackey, Mercedes.

The Elemental Masters. YA
Young women in the early twentieth century discover their innate magical powers in this series of reimagined fairy tales. *Fire Rose*, although not technically part of this series from the publisher's standpoint, is set in the same world and follows the same conventions.

Keywords: Fairy tales; Magic and magicians

Fire Rose. Baen, 2001. 448pp. Hardbound, 0671876872.

The Gates of Sleep. DAW, 2002. 389pp. Hardbound, 0756400600.

The Serpent's Shadow. DAW, 2001. 343pp. Hardbound, 0886779154.

Phoenix and Ashes. DAW, 2004. 405pp. Hardbound, 0756401615.

The Wizard of London. DAW, 2005. 342pp. Hardbound, 0756401747.
This historical fantasy based on Hans Christian Anderson's "The Snow Queen" is set in Victorian England. Isabelle Harton, who runs a school for mage-born students in London with her husband, takes young Sarah, child of African missionaries, as a pupil. When a rogue mage threatens the lives of Sarah and one of her friends, it forces Isabelle to confront her past.

Keywords: England—Victorian era; Students

Reserved for the Cat. DAW, 2007. 328pp. Hardbound, 9780756403621.
Ninette Dupond, an aspiring dancer from Paris now living in London in 1910, follows the advice of her animal companion, a telepathic cat, to impersonate a famous Russian ballerina. Although two mages take

her in hand and guide her career, the real ballerina, a powerful mage, takes offense and comes after her.

Keywords: Dancers; England—20th century

Novik, Naomi.

Temeraire Series. `YA`

During the Napoleonic Wars, battles between England and France rage ferociously on land, on sea . . . and in the air. Britain's Royal Aerial Corps, composed of fire-breathing dragons and their airborne riders, may prove to be the edge that country needs in staving off Napoleon. Their secret weapon is Temeraire, a Chinese dragon who "imprints on" (forms a bond with) Captain William Laurence of the Royal Navy. Because the egg containing the as-yet-unhatched Temeraire was originally meant for Napoleon, diplomatic problems ensue. A wildly inventive, highly acclaimed series that mixes the seafaring adventure of Patrick O'Brian's Aubrey/Maturin novels with the sapient dragons of the type found in Anne McCaffrey's Dragonriders of Pern series. Based on this series, Novik was awarded the John W. Campbell Award for Best New Writer (a science fiction award) in 2007.

Keywords: Dragons; England—Georgian era; Napoleonic Wars

His Majesty's Dragon. Del Rey, 2006. Paper, 0345481283. (Alternate title: *Temeraire.*)

Throne of Jade. Del Rey, 2006. 398pp. Paper, 345481291.

Black Powder War. Del Rey, 2006. 365pp. Paper, 0345481305.

Empire of Ivory. Del Rey, 2007. 404pp. Paper, 9780345496874.

Victory of Eagles. Del Rey, 2008. 332pp. Hardbound, 9780345496881.

Putney, Mary Jo.

The Guardians Series.

A loose trilogy about members of the Guardians, men and women with empathic abilities and the power to magically affect the forces of nature. The novels play out against a backdrop of Jacobite-era England and Scotland and, in the final volume, mid-eighteenth-century Europe. Historical paranormal romance.

Keywords: England—Georgian era; Magic and magicians; Nobility; Weather

A Kiss of Fate. Ballantine, 2004. 340pp. Hardbound, 0345449169.

> Gwynne Owens, a wealthy widow and the daughter of a Guardian, doesn't come into her full mage abilities until she marries Duncan Macrae, a powerful Scottish mage. Together they determine how much advantage they should give to Bonnie Prince Charlie.

Stolen Magic. Ballantine, 2005. 337pp. Hardbound, 0345476891. (As M. J. Putney.)

> Only Meg, a virginal serving maid believed to be mad, can save Simon Malmain, the Earl of Falconer (and head of the Guardian Council), when his enemy transforms him into a unicorn.

A Distant Magic. Ballantine, 2007. 333pp. Hardbound, 9780345476913.

> In 1753 Nikolai Gregorio, a magically gifted pirate captain dedicated to abolishing slavery, kidnaps Jean Macrae, daughter of a Scottish Guardian. A freed slave from the future convinces them they must time-travel forward to ensure that the abolitionist movement succeeds.

> **Keywords:** Abolitionists; Pirates; Time travel

The Marriage Spell. **Ballantine, 2006. 322pp. Hardbound, 0345449185.**

> Jack Langford, a nobleman and naval officer in Napoleonic-era England, has always scorned the supernatural talents he was born with. When Abigail Barton, a talented wizard healer, casts a spell powerful enough to save his life after a grievous injury, he agrees to her condition that he marry her and give her his name. As the pair grows closer romantically, Jack becomes more interested in exploring his magical heritage. Historical paranormal romance.

> **Keywords:** Healers; Magic and magicians; Napoleonic Wars; Nobility

The Americas

A miscellany of fantasy novels set in North America; not a heavily used setting.

Bull, Emma.

Territory. **Tor, 2007. 318pp. Hardbound, 9780312857356.**

> This fantastical retelling of the lead-up to the legendary shoot-out at the O.K. Corral—which took place in Tombstone, Arizona, in 1881—features the usual cast of characters, including Doc Holliday, Wyatt Earp, his brothers, and of course the Clantons and McLaurys, notorious cattle rustlers with a criminal streak. Enter, also, widow Mildred Benjamin, employee of the local paper, who, along with drifter/horse-tamer Jesse Fox, discovers that dark magic is afoot in Tombstone.

> **Keywords:** Arizona—Reconstruction/Gilded Age; Magic and magicians

Clark, Francis.

Waking Brigid. **Tor, 2008. 366pp. Hardbound, 9780765318107.**

> Savannah, Georgia, in 1874 becomes the setting for a classic showdown between good and evil. When Satan worshippers begin sacrificing women of the city to the demon Belial, the Catholic church invites a select group of white magicians to Savannah to fight them. When their powers prove insufficient, Brigid Rourke, an Irish nun who has long suppressed the secret pagan magic she can wield, steps up to the plate. Savannah native Clark passed away before this dark fantasy novel was published.

> **Keywords:** Demons; Georgia—Reconstruction/Gilded Age; Immigrants, Irish; Magic and magicians; Nuns; Paganism

9

10

11

12

13

14

15

Irvine, Alexander C.

The Narrows. **Del Rey, 2005. 341pp. Paper, 0345466985.**

Jared Cleaves, an assembly-line worker in Henry Ford's Detroit-based factory during the World War II years, is assigned to work on the company's secret production of golems: creatures manufactured from clay, which will be sent overseas to fight Nazi forces on the front lines. Jared wants to contribute more to the war effort than participating in this rather dull job, and his curiosity gets him dangerously involved in supernatural military espionage.

Keywords: Factories; Golems; Michigan—World War II; Spies

The Middle East

Lindskold, Jane.

The Buried Pyramid. **Tor, 2004. 399pp. Hardbound, 0765302608.**

Jenny Benet, a young American woman, accompanies her uncle, British archaeologist Neville Hawthorne, on his mission to find the legendary Buried Pyramid, the lost tomb of a pharaoh who may also have been Moses the Lawgiver. They contend with a rival party of archaeologists and also discover that supernatural forces are hell-bent on thwarting their mission. A brainy, leisurely paced Indiana Jones–type adventure story set in the Victorian period.

Keywords: Archaeology; Egypt—19th century; Pyramids

Multi-Period Historical Fantasy Series

Novels in these fantasy series span centuries and continents but focus on the same themes throughout.

Douglass, Sara.

The Troy Game.

This complex series, complete in four volumes, traces connections among the Trojan War in ancient times, the founding of Britain by Brutus, the warrior king of Troy, and Britain's role during World War II.

Keywords: Labyrinths; Mythology; Reincarnation

Hades' Daughter. Tor, 2003. 592pp. Hardbound, 0765305402.

Ariadne, Princess of Crete and Mistress of the Labyrinth, takes revenge on her lover Theseus for abandoning her after giving birth to a daughter. When she undoes the Labyrinth in her grief, it throws the world into chaos. A hundred years later Brutus, great-grandson of Aeneas, heads to Albion (Britain) to rebuild Troy in all its former glory. When he marries an Eastern princess against her will, one of Ariadne's descendants waits in the wings to take revenge on the Trojan warrior whose ancestor destroyed hers.

Keywords: England—ancient/prehistoric; Princesses

Gods' Concubine. Tor, 2004. 557pp. Hardbound, 0765305410.

> It is now eleventh-century England, and the Labyrinth constructed by Brutus has turned into the city of London. Brutus has been reincarnated as William, Duke of Normandy, and the rivalry between him and Harold—the two heirs of Edward the Confessor—plays out.
>
> **Keywords:** England—high Middle Ages; Royalty

Darkwitch Rising. Tor, 2005. 607pp. Hardbound, 0765305429.

> Amid the tumult of the English Civil War in the early seventeenth century, all of the characters from the previous novels have been reincarnated once again.
>
> **Keywords:** England—Stuart era; English Civil War

Druid's Sword. Tor, 2006. 606pp. Hardbound, 0765305437.

> During the Blitz that nearly flattened London between late 1940 and early 1941, Brutus—reincarnated as Jack Skelton—tries to find a way of saving the world, thus completing the Troy Game for good.
>
> **Keywords:** Blitz; England—World War II

Radford, Irene.

Merlin's Descendants.

A loosely connected series of (mostly) stand-alone novels about mages, descendants of Merlin himself, who get involved in major historical events from Arthurian England onward. With their scenes of bloody violence, these historical fantasies are darker than most. The historical periods are noted.

Keywords: Arthurian themes; Magic and magicians

Guardian of the Balance. DAW, 1999. 529pp. Hardbound, 0886778263.

> Arthurian fantasy centering on Merlin's daughter Arylwren and the battle between Christianity and the Old Religion.

Guardian of the Trust. DAW, 2000. 462pp. Hardbound, 0886778743.

> Thirteenth-century England; King John and the secret, magical origins of the Magna Carta.

Guardian of the Vision. DAW, 2001. 519pp. Hardbound, 0886779944.

> The rivalry between Elizabeth I and Mary, Queen of Scots.

Guardian of the Promise. DAW, 2003. 544pp. Hardbound, 0756400783.

> A direct sequel to *Guardian of the Vision*, set in Stuart-era Scotland and Renaissance France.

Guardian of the Freedom. DAW, 2005. 532pp. Hardbound, 075640178X.

> George III's England and the American Revolution.

Yarbro, Chelsea Quinn.

Saint-Germain Cycle.

In this sensuous dark fantasy series, Yarbro chronicles the adventures of her vampire hero, the immortal, elegant, and articulate Count de Saint-Germain, during his travels throughout the world. The time period covered by the novels spans nearly two millennia. In creating this series, Yarbro deliberately subverts the traditional vampire stereotype; Saint-Germain is neither a frightening creature nor a force of evil, but a very human (if one can pardon the inherent paradox) creation, capable of deep emotion. The historical background of each novel is meticulously detailed, and even readers who don't normally touch vampire fiction may appreciate them. They are listed chronologically by publication date and can be read in any order. The historical settings are noted.

Keywords: Vampires

Hotel Transylvania. St. Martin's, 1978. 279pp. Hardbound, 0312392486.
 Paris circa 1743, during the reign of Louis XV.

The Palace. St. Martin's, 1978. 408pp. Hardbound, 0312594747.
 Renaissance Florence at the time of Lorenzo de Medici.

Blood Games. St. Martin's, 1979. 458pp. Hardbound, 0312084412.
 Nero's Rome.

Path of the Eclipse. St. Martin's, 1981. 447pp. Hardbound, 0312598025.
 China, Tibet, and India during the age of Genghis Khan.

Tempting Fate. St. Martin's, 1982. 662pp. Hardbound, 0312790872.
 The Russian Revolution and rise of the Nazi party.

The Saint-Germain Chronicles. Pocket, 1983. 206pp. Hardbound, 0671459031.
 A short story anthology about Saint-Germain's adventures in the nineteenth and twentieth centuries.

Darker Jewels. Tor, 1993. 398pp. Hardbound, 0312852967.
 The court of Tsar Ivan the Terrible.

Better in the Dark. Tor, 1993. 412pp. Hardbound, 0312855044.
 The Frankish kingdoms in the tenth century.

Mansions of Darkness. Tor, 1996. 430pp. Hardbound, 0312857594.
 The Incan Empire of Peru in the seventeenth century.

Writ in Blood. Tor, 1997. 543pp. Hardbound, 0312863187.
 Russia and England before the Bolshevik Revolution; a direct prequel to *Tempting Fate.*

Blood Roses. Tor, 1998. 382pp. Hardbound, 0312865295.
 The Black Death in fourteenth-century Provence.

Communion Blood. Tor, 1999. 477pp. Hardbound, 031286793X.
 Late seventeenth-century Rome.

Come Twilight. Tor, 2000. 479pp. Hardbound, 0312873301.
  Early seventh-century Moorish Spain.

A Feast in Exile. Tor, 2001. 469pp. Hardbound, 0312878435.
  India in the late fourteenth century, during the age of Tamerlane.

Night Blooming. Warner, 2002. 429pp. Hardbound, 0446529818.
  The Frankish Kingdoms (Tours and Aachen) during the reign of Charlemagne.

Midnight Harvest. Warner, 2003. 434pp. Hardbound, 0446532401.
  America in the 1930s.

Dark of the Sun. Tor, 2004. 460pp. Hardbound, 076531102X.
  Asia and central Europe during the sixth century.

States of Grace. Tor, 2005. 327pp. Hardbound, 0765313901.
  Sixteenth-century Venice and Amsterdam.

Roman Dusk. Tor, 2006. 352pp. Hardbound, 076531391X.
  Third-century Rome.

Borne in Blood. Tor, 2007. 367pp. Hardbound, 9780765317131.
  Switzerland circa 1817, after Napoleon's defeat.

9

10

11

12

13

14

15

Chapter 15

Resources for Librarians and Readers

There are a number of other resources available to help librarians and readers discover more information on historical fiction. Although some are geared toward readers' advisors, others target readers or authors in the genre. Many are fairly general; others are quite specialized or scholarly.

Bibliographies and Biographies

Librarians can consult these sources for lists of novels and/or biographical details on their authors. Only bibliographies generally listing novels for adults are given, though some contain titles of interest to young adults.

> **Adamson, Lynda M.** *American Historical Fiction: An Annotated Guide to Novels for Adults and Young Adults.* Oryx, 1999.
>
> A guide to more than 3,300 novels with American settings, mostly published since the 1980s, set in a time "earlier than readers are familiar with." This includes settings up through the 1970s. Arranged by time period, from "North America before 1600" to "The Late 20th Century." Each entry gives title, citation, number of pages, one-sentence annotation, and genre designation. Extensive indexes by author, title, genre, geography, and subject are provided. Appendixes list award winners and titles of possible interest to young adults. Both this and the following volume were written as updates to McGarry's and White's bibliography (see below).
>
> ——. *World Historical Fiction: An Annotated Guide to Novels for Adults and Young Adults.* Oryx, 1999.
>
> Similar in arrangement to *American Historical Fiction*, in this book Adamson annotates more than 6,000 novels set between prehistoric times and the late twentieth century. U.S. settings are excluded. Primary arrangement is by geographic area, then by time period.

Burgess, Michael, and Jill H. Vassilakos. *Murder in Retrospect: A Selective Guide to Historical Mystery Fiction.* Libraries Unlimited, 2005.

A single-volume guide to historical mystery fiction, with emphasis on popular, current titles and novels in series. Approximately seventy authors are represented. The books are listed alphabetically by author and grouped by series. The authors discuss each example in great detail, with critical commentary on the detective and series as well as plot summaries for each individual title.

Burt, Daniel S. *What Historical Novel Do I Read Next?* Gale Research, 1997–2003. 3 vols.

Nearly 7,000 titles by 3,000 authors are cited and annotated in volume 1, with historical accuracy evaluation and biographical details. The entries are arranged by author surname. Volume 2 provides eight different indexes to the books mentioned in volume 1. Volume 3 appeared in 2003, covering relevant novels through 2003 plus read-alike titles and review sources. Extensive, but pricey for public libraries.

Gerhardstein, Virginia Brokaw. *Dickinson's American Historical Fiction.* **5th ed.** Scarecrow, 1986.

The most recent edition of A. T. Dickinson's classic bibliography *American Historical Fiction*, this volume covers more than 3,000 historical novels set between European colonization and 1984.

Hartman, Donald K, and Gregg Sapp. *Historical Figures in Fiction.* Oryx, 1994.

A bibliographical guide to biographical historical fiction. Includes "4,200 novels in which almost 1,500 historical figures appear as significant characters." Included are English-language novels that were published since 1940, including some reissues. Young adult and juvenile titles are indicated. There are no annotations, but citations to reviews from major sources (*Booklist*, *Library Journal*, etc.) are provided. Quite comprehensive, but some of the books are not available in American libraries at all.

Hooper, Brad. *Read On . . . Historical Fiction: Reading Lists for Every Taste.* Libraries Unlimited, 2006.

Hooper, the adult books editor of *Booklist*, takes a new and creative approach to organizing historical novels, creating reading lists based on appeal factor, theme, and other topics of interest. Bibliographic details and lively plot annotations are included for more than 400 titles.

McGarry, Daniel D., and Sarah Harriman White. *World Historical Fiction Guide.* **2nd ed.** Scarecrow, 1973.

McGarry's and White's work was the first major modern bibliography for historical fiction, and it still has considerable value. Designed for use by both adults and high school students, this selective guide annotates historical novels published since 1900 and judged worthy of inclusion by the authors. Even with these guidelines, it's very comprehensive.

Mediavilla, Cindy. *Arthurian Fiction: An Annotated Bibliography.* Scarecrow, 1999.

Mediavilla's bibliography not only lists all of the major (and some minor) Arthurian historical fiction and fantasy novels, it also provides significant critical commentary that will aid librarians, teachers, and readers. Over 200 novels in total, divided into eight categories: Romance of Camelot; Arthur the Roman Leader; Women of Camelot; Merlin, Kingmaker and Mage; Unlikely Heroes of Camelot; the Holy Quest; Return of the King; The Legacy Continues.

Mort, John. *Read the High Country: A Guide to Western Books and Films.* Libraries Unlimited, 2006.

An annotated guide to traditional, historical, and contemporary Westerns, covering classics and new titles as well as Western films. More than 2,000 titles are grouped by subgenre and theme, with section introductions that detail the novels' historical background. Part of the Genreflecting Advisory Series.

Murph, Roxane C. *The English Civil War and the Restoration in Fiction: An Annotated Bibliography, 1625–1999.* Greenwood, 2000.

A comprehensive, scholarly guide to verse, novels, and short stories about the English Civil War in the seventeenth century. The annotations include detailed plot summaries, most of which give away the ending—potential readers beware! Murph knows her subject, and she always comments on a work's historical accuracy. However, she is contemptuous of romance novels, and her continual harping on their low quality will offend romance readers.

———. *The Wars of the Roses in Fiction: An Annotated Bibliography, 1440–1994.* Scarecrow, 1995.

Murph's first annotated bibliography looked at the Wars of the Roses, the fifteenth-century conflict when rival families Lancaster and York battled for England's crown. Includes novels, short stories, and verse, with commentary similar to her later book (above).

Pederson, James P, ed. *St. James Guide to Crime and Mystery Writers.* **4th ed.** St. James Press, 1996.

In the same series as *Twentieth Century Western Writers* and *Twentieth Century Romance and Historical Writers*, this volume includes biographical information on 650 crime and mystery writers of the twentieth century. Complete bibliographies (as of 1995) are provided for each.

Simone, Roberta. *The Immigrant Experience in American Fiction: An Annotated Bibliography.* Scarecrow, 1995.

A scholarly guide to novels about American immigrant groups (forty-one of them, in fact) as well as six "combined groups" (Asian, Hispanic, Jewish, Scandinavian, Slavic, and West Indian) from the nineteenth century through 1994. Not all are historical novels, but many are.

Sonnichsen, C. L., ed. *Twentieth Century Western Writers.* **2nd ed.** Gale, 1992.

In the same series as the two St. James Press titles on crime/mystery and romance writers, this title includes bio-bibliographical information on nearly 500 Western writers.

Van Meter, Vandelia L. *America in Historical Fiction: A Bibliographic Guide.* Libraries Unlimited, 1997.

Citations and summaries for more than1,100 historical novels with American settings, from 1492 through the late twentieth century. Additional titles are arranged by state. Geared toward secondary school history classes and selected with the *National Standards for United States History* in mind. Many of these titles were originally written for adults.

Vasudevan, Aruna, and Lesley Henderson, eds. *Twentieth-Century Romance and Historical Writers.* **3rd ed.** St. James Press, 1997.

A critical, bio-bibliographical guide to significant romantic and historical novelists, emphasizing British writers. The three editions (1990, 1994, 1997) overlap considerably but are not completely cumulative. Unfortunately, no updates are planned. Historical mystery and Western writers are omitted from this volume; they are covered instead in *St. James Guide to Crime and Mystery Writers* or *Twentieth Century Western Writers.*

History and Criticism

Interested in delving into the history and meaning of historical fiction? Investigate one of these stimulating volumes. Many of these works are fairly recent, signifying a renewed interest in how the past is portrayed in fiction.

Carnes, Mark C., ed. *Novel History: Historians and Novelists Confront America's Past (and Each Other).* Simon & Schuster, 2001.

An interesting concept: Carnes invited historians to contribute essays on how well historical novels with American settings represented the past. He then invited the authors of the novels to comment on those essays. Novels discussed include Gore Vidal's *Burr,* Larry McMurtry's *Lonesome Dove,* and Charles Frazier's *Cold Mountain,* among others.

Johnsen, Rosemary Erickson. *Contemporary Feminist Historical Crime Fiction.* Palgrave Macmillan, 2006.

This examination of historical mysteries featuring female sleuths analyzes the potential of these novels, and the genre as a whole, to advance feminist scholarship and political action. Men who write about women detectives are not included. Authors whose works are covered include Gillian Linscott, Sharan Newman, Miriam Grace Monfredo, and Laurie R. King.

Jordan, Margaret. *African-American Servitude and Historical Imaginings: Retrospective Fiction and Representation.* Palgrave Macmillan, 2004.

This collection of essays examines the representation of the African American servant in four works of historical fiction, including E. L. Doctorow's *Ragtime* and Charles Johnson's *Middle Passage.*

9

King, Jeannette. *The Victorian Woman Question in Contemporary Feminist Fiction.* Palgrave Macmillan, 2005.

A work of literary criticism that analyzes what it means to be a Victorian woman and presents examples taken from historical fiction written from a feminist perspective. Novels discussed include Sarah Waters's *Tipping the Velvet* and *Affinity*, Andrea Barrett's *The Voyage of the Narwhal*, Toni Morrison's *Beloved*, and Margaret Atwood's *Alias Grace*, among others.

10

Lukacs, Georg. *The Historical Novel.* Originally published in 1937; widely reprinted.

Although it is decades old and some of its definitions seem dated, this classical study remains the benchmark work about the genre. Lukacs describes the rise of the historical novel in the early nineteenth century and tells how practitioners like Walter Scott and Charles Dickens used the literary form to describe and effect social changes in their own time.

11

12

Rozett, Martha Tuck. *Constructing a World: Shakespeare's England and the New Historical Fiction.* Albany: State University of New York Press, 2002.

Analyzes the emergence of literary historical fiction in the mid- to late twentieth century, especially as seen through novels set in Shakespearean times.

13

Sachsman, David B., S. Kittrell Rushing, and Roy Morris, Jr., eds. *Memory and Myth: The Civil War in Fiction and Film from* Uncle Tom's Cabin *to* Cold Mountain. Purdue University Press, 2007.

Twenty-five essays on how the American Civil War and the past in general are represented in film and fiction.

14

Solander: The Magazine of the Historical Novel Society. 1997– . ISSN 1471-7484.

A semiannual literary magazine with critical articles, author interviews, and market reports on historical fiction. $50/year (includes subscription to the *Historical Novels Review*, below under Book Review Sources). Inquiries to richard@historicalnovelsociety.org.

15

Wallace, Diana. *The Woman's Historical Novel: British Women Writers, 1990–2000.* Palgrave Macmillan, 2005.

Wallace, a British academic specializing in women's literature, looks at the development of the genre as written by British women during the course of the twentieth century. A critical look at authors, from early notables such as Georgette Heyer, Margaret Irwin, and Mary Renault through Jean Plaidy, Pat Barker, and Philippa Gregory.

Writing Historical Fiction: A Virtual Conference Session. Albany: Department of History, University at Albany, State University of New York, 1998. Available online at http://www.albany.edu/history/hist_fict/home.htm.

In this online conference, the electronic version of a conference panel presentation, four novelists—Allen Ballard, Steven Leibo, Reed Mitchell, and William Rainbolt—contributed essays on writing historical fiction. Samples of their writing are provided.

Wyile, Herb. *Speaking in the Past Tense: Canadian Novelists on Writing Historical Fiction.* Wilfrid Laurier University Press, 2006.

Author Wyile talks to eleven Canadian novelists about their experiences writing historical novels, discussing not only why they chose their subjects but post-publication reaction as well. Interviewees include Guy Vanderhaeghe, Joseph Boyden, Michael Crummey, and Jane Urquhart.

Online Resources

Readers' advisory sources for historical fiction proliferate on the Internet, as do discussion groups and Web sites through which authors and fans can share their knowledge of the genre.

Subscription Databases

Booklist Online

The electronic version of *Booklist*, ALA's main readers' advisory publication, with a searchable archive of book reviews and feature articles dating back to 1992. Some content, including the blog Likely Stories, is free to everyone.

NoveList

Readers' advisory database from EBSCO Publishing. Includes a searchable interface (author, title, series, keyword) for its database of books, annotations, and full-text reviews. NoveList also offers feature articles, award lists, read-alikes for popular titles, quarterly columns by popular readers' advisors, book discussion guides, and staff resources for readers' advisory.

The Readers' Advisor Online

Based on the <u>Genreflecting</u> series of readers' advisory guides from Libraries Unlimited, this database includes searchable and browsable versions of books in the series. In addition, relevant titles may be retrieved by historical character name, location, series, time period, theme, author read-alikes, and more. A regularly updated blog authored by readers' advisory experts (http://www.readersadvisoronline.com/blog) is available free to all.

What Do I Read Next?

Thomson Gale's readers' advisory database includes the contents of books in their <u>What Do I Read Next?</u> reference book series. Includes historical fiction, romance, mystery, Westerns, general fiction, classic fiction, and others. Searchable by title, author, subject, genre, locale, and more.

Blogs

The historical fiction blogosphere is growing, with many authors and readers contributing their thoughts on historical fiction, history, and the intersection between the two. The following blogs provide book reviews, author interviews, industry updates, and other general commentary on historical fiction. In addition, many historical novelists have their own personal blogs, dealing with their own works and their experiences in the publishing business.

Carla Nayland Historical Fiction

http://carlanayland.blogspot.com

> Nayland, a UK-based author and reader with a special interest in Roman and early medieval Britain, writes critical reviews of novels set in the period.

Favorite PASTimes

http://favoritepastimes.blogspot.com

> Reviews, interviews, and commentary on historical novels, with a Christian focus.

Historical Boys

http://historicalboys.blogspot.com

> Features male (and some female) historical fiction writers who share their insights about their books, writing, publishing, and other news, compiled by historical novelist C. W. Gortner.

Historical Tapestry

http://historicaltapestry.blogspot.com

> Reviews and other comments on current historical novels, compiled by four avid readers in the genre.

History Buff's Author Interviews

http://historicalfictionauthorinterviews.blogspot.com

> Historical novelist Michelle Moran (*Nefertiti*) interviews her fellow authors. Updated at least monthly.

History Hoydens

http://historyhoydens.blogspot.com

> Observations on reading and writing historical fiction, from nine authors (Amanda Elyot, Lauren Willig, Tracy Grant, and more) who write romantic and traditional historical novels.

9

10

11

12

13

14

15

Loaded Questions

http://www.loaded-questions.com

> Historian Kelly Hewitt, who has a special interest in historical fiction, interviews authors in a variety of fiction and nonfiction genres.

Reading the Past

http://readingthepast.blogspot.com

> News, reviews, previews, and commentary on historical fiction, with occasional author interviews, compiled by the author of this book.

Unusual Historicals

http://unusualhistoricals.blogspot.com

> A group blog by novelists (mainly of romantic historical fiction) who incorporate less common historical settings in their work.

Word Wenches

http://wordwenches.typepad.com

> Novelists Jo Beverley, Edith Layton, Mary Jo Putney, Patricia Rice, Loretta Chase, Susan Fraser King, and Susan Holloway Scott discuss their current historical novels, the research process, and more.

Discussion Forums and Groups

In addition to the forums listed below, fans of the genre can find active discussions on historical fiction at many online bookstores and social networking sites, such as Amazon.com, BN.com, Facebook, LibraryThing (www.librarything.org), and Paperback Swap (www.paperbackswap.com). All of these groups require an account (free) to participate.

Fiction_L mailing list

http://www.webrary.org/rs/FLbklistmenu.html

> Sponsored by Morton Grove Public Library, Illinois, the Fiction_L discussion list serves as a resource for readers' advisory issues. Booklists, many of which are historical fiction–related, are compiled by subscribers and posted to the Web site. This list is essential for readers' advisors in libraries.

Historical Fiction Online

http://www.historicalfictiononline.com

> Active discussion forums on all types of historical fiction, with some book reviews mixed in.

Yahoo! Groups

http://groups.yahoo.com

> Most historical fiction lists on Yahoo! Groups are geared toward writers and readers, but readers' advisors may find them of use. Of particular note are CrimeThruTime (historical mysteries), histfict (historical fiction readers),

HistoricalNovelSociety (general group for historical fiction readers/writers), and RRA-L (Romance Readers Anonymous).

Web Sites

These sites offer a variety of resources: bibliographies, forthcoming books, reviews, short fiction, and more.

Ancient Egypt in Fiction

http://www.egyptomania.org/aef/Egyptfiction.html

An online bibliography of novels set in ancient Egypt, arranged by category: young adult, biblical, historical fiction, mysteries, romance, children's, etc.

Ancient Greece in Fiction

http://www.rhul.ac.uk/Classics/NJL/novels.html

A listing of novels and short stories set in ancient Greece.

CrimeThruTime

http://www.crimethrutime.com

A comprehensive historical mystery Web site, including forthcoming titles, mysteries by time period and locale, and booklists by author.

The Copperfield Review

http://www.copperfieldreview.com

Subtitled "a journal for readers and writers of historical fiction," this semiannual online publication offers short stories, author interviews, and book reviews.

Criminal History

http://www.criminal-history.co.uk

Web site for fans of historical crime fiction, with reviews, articles, bibliographies organized by time period, and more.

The Detective and the Toga

http://histmyst.org

A guide to Roman mysteries in many languages; updated frequently.

Fictional Rome

http://www.stockton.edu/~roman/fiction/

A database of historical novels set in Roman times, including book reviews. Housed at Richard Stockton College of New Jersey.

HistFiction.net

http://www.histfiction.net

> This staple in the field, maintained by historical fiction fan Soon-Yong Choi, serves as a meta-index to historical fiction on the Web. It also includes a master list of well-known historical fiction writers, with biographical details. Formerly known as "Soon's Historical Fiction Site."

HistoricalNovels.Info

http://www.historicalnovels.info

> An online bibliography of historical fiction, with more than 2,000 titles grouped by time and place, with brief annotations. Compiled by Margaret Donsbach.

Historical Mystery Fiction

http://members.tripod.com/~BrerFox/historicalmystery.html

> Comprehensive guide to historical mystery novels, arranged by author and time period.

The Historical Novel Society

http://www.historicalnovelsociety.org

> Besides describing the society itself, this site provides lists of forthcoming historical fiction by month, reviews of Editors' Choice titles from the *Historical Novels Review*, selected articles and interviews from the literary magazine *Solander*, and links to the Web sites of member authors.

Medieval Novels

http://www.medieval-novels.com

> Annotated lists of novels set in the Middle Ages, circa AD 500 to 1600, organized by country.

Modern Arthurian Fiction

http://www.triviumpublishing.com/articles/arthurian.html

> A straight bibliography (titles and authors only; no annotations) of Arthurian-themed historical fiction and fantasy.

The Nautical Fiction List

http://www.boat-links.com/books/nfl/nautfic-01.html

> The latest update is from 1999, but despite that flaw, this site offers a searchable database of nautical fiction, much of which is historical.

Prehistoric Fiction

http://www.trussel.com/f_prehis.htm

> Maintained by Steve Trussel, this is a comprehensive guide to prehistoric fiction titles, including definitions and a lengthy bibliography.

Reading Historical Fiction

http://www.squidoo.com/readinghistoricalfiction

> A meta-index to historical fiction sites on the Web, maintained by historical novelist Susan Higginbotham.

9

The Sibyl and Sleuth

http://personal.riverusers.com/~swanky/greece.htm

> Maintained by Kris Swank, this is an annotated guide to historical mystery fiction set in ancient Greece, with plot summaries, book cover images, and details on settings, with links to Amazon. Includes some author interviews.

10

Uchronia: The Alternate History List

http://www.uchronia.net

> A very comprehensive bibliography of alternate history novels, short stories, essays, and more. Alternate history fantasy novels are included, as are more strictly historically based works, such as those included in this book.

11

Publishers

12

Following are major publishers (and their imprints) as well as small presses that regularly publish historical novels. Addresses for main company offices, Web sites, and characteristics of the books they publish are listed. These companies publish fiction in a variety of genres, and most also publish nonfiction. The subgenres of historical fiction frequently published by each press are listed.

Only publishers of novels regularly found in American libraries and/or bookstores are included below. Relevant British publishers with considerable historical fiction output include Hodder Headline, Pan Macmillan, Penguin UK, Random House UK, Robert Hale, Simon & Schuster UK, and Transworld.

13

Major Publishers

14

All of the major trade presses publish historical fiction. Only imprints that offer relevant titles for the genre are included here.

Tom Doherty Associates, LLC

> 175 Fifth Avenue
> New York, NY 10010
> http://us.macmillan.com/TorForge.aspx

> Part of the Macmillan group of publishers. Imprints: Forge (traditional, literary, mystery, occasional romance); Tor (fantasy).

15

Farrar, Straus & Giroux

> 19 Union Square West
> New York, NY 10003
> http://us.macmillan.com/FSG.aspx

> Part of the Macmillan group of publishers. Literary historicals.

Five Star Press

295 Kennedy Memorial Drive
Waterville, ME 04901
http://www.galegroup.com/fivestar

Fiction imprint of Gale (a part of Cengage Learning), publishing hardcovers for the library market. Beginning in 2003 they also began printing paperbacks for the trade market. Romantic and traditional Westerns, mysteries, historical romances, and women's fiction.

Hachette Book Group USA

1271 Avenue of the Americas
New York, NY 10020
http://www.hachettebookgroupusa.com

Imprints: Back Bay (paperbacks); Forever (romance); Grand Central (traditional, literary, mystery); Little, Brown (literary); Miramax (traditional and literary).

Harlequin Enterprises Ltd.

225 Duncan Mill Road
Toronto, ON M3B 3K9, Canada
http://www.eharlequin.com

Mass-market paperbacks, trade paperbacks, and hardcover fiction for women. Nonseries imprints include Harlequin Historicals (romance), Mira (women's fiction), and Steeple Hill (Christian). Harlequin also offers many series romance imprints.

HarperCollins Publishers

10 E. 53rd Street
New York, NY 10022
http://www.harpercollins.com

Imprints: Amistad (African American interest), Avon (paperback romance and mystery), Avon A (women's fiction), Avon Inspire (Christian), Ecco (literary), Harper (traditional and literary), HarperSanFrancisco (spiritual fiction), Rayo (Hispanic interest), Perennial (paperback).

Henry Holt & Company

115 West 18th Street
New York, NY 10011
http://www.henryholt.com

Part of the Macmillan group of publishers. Literary historicals. Imprints: Henry Holt, Metropolitan Books.

Houghton Mifflin Harcourt

215 Park Avenue South
New York, NY 10003
http://www.houghtonmifflinbooks.com

Imprints: Houghton Mifflin (literary), Mariner (trade paperback).

Kensington Publishing Corporation

850 Third Avenue
New York, NY 10022
http://www.kensingtonbooks.com

Imprints: Kensington (mystery, romance), Zebra (romance, Westerns), Pinnacle (all types of genre fiction).

Penguin Group (USA)

375 Hudson Street
New York, NY 10014
http://us.penguingroup.com

Imprints and trademarks: Ace (fantasy), Berkley and Berkley Signature (traditional, romance, western), Berkley Prime Crime (mystery), Dutton (literary and traditional), G.P. Putnam's Sons (literary, mystery), Jove (romance), New American Library (traditional historicals, mysteries), Penguin (literary and traditional), Penguin Press (literary), Plume (trade paperback, literary), Riverhead (literary and traditional), ROC (fantasy), Signet (romance, mystery), Viking (literary and traditional).

Random House

1745 Broadway
New York, NY 10019
http://www.randomhouse.com

Publishers and imprints: Anchor (literary), Ballantine (traditional, romance, mystery), Bantam (traditional, mystery, romance), Crown (traditional and literary), Delacorte (literary, traditional, mystery), Dell (romance), Doubleday (literary and traditional), Ivy (romance), Knopf (literary), Pantheon (literary), Random House (literary), Schocken (Jewish influence), Three Rivers (traditional, paperback), Villard (literary).

Severn House Publishers

U.S. Office: 595 Madison Avenue, 15th Floor
New York, NY 10022
http://www.severnhouse.com

British publisher widely distributed in North America; hardcovers for the library market. Romance, mystery, sagas.

Simon & Schuster

1230 Avenue of the Americas
New York, NY 10020
http://www.simonsays.com

Imprints: Atria (traditional and literary), Free Press (political fiction), Pocket and Pocket Star (mass market paperback, mystery, Western), Simon & Schuster (traditional and literary), Scribner (traditional and literary hardcovers and trade paperbacks), Touchstone (hardcover and trade paperback), Washington Square Press.

St. Martin's Press

175 Fifth Avenue
New York, NY 10010
http://us.macmillan.com/SMP.aspx

Part of the Macmillan group of publishers. Imprints: St. Martin's Press (traditional and literary, including sagas, also some romance), Minotaur (mysteries), Picador USA (trade paperbacks).

Trafalgar Square Publishing

c/o Independent Publishers Group
814 North Franklin Street
Chicago, IL 60610
http://www.ipgbook.com/ipg_tsp.cfm

American distributor of British books. Mysteries, traditional, and literary fiction imported from the United Kingdom.

Small and Independent Presses

Historical fiction thrives in the small and independent press. The following publishers offer at least several new historical novels each year.

Algonquin Books of Chapel Hill

P.O. Box 2225
Chapel Hill, NC 27515-2225
http://www.algonquin.com

Literary historical fiction.

Arcade Publishing

116 John Street, No. 2810
New York, NY 10038
http://www.arcadepub.com

Traditional and literary historicals.

Dorchester Publishing

200 Madison Avenue, Suite 2000
New York, NY 10016
http://www.dorchesterpub.com

Mass-market paperbacks. Imprints: LoveSpell (romance), Leisure (romance and Westerns).

Grove/Atlantic

841 Broadway, 4th Floor
New York, NY 10003
http://www.groveatlantic.com

Literary historicals. Imprints: Grove Press, Atlantic Monthly Press.

Ingalls Publishing Group

197 New Market Center No. 135
Boone, NC 28607
http://www.ingallspublishinggroup.com

Traditional historicals and mysteries, often with Appalachian settings.

9

MacAdam/Cage Publishing

155 Sansome Street, Suite 550
San Francisco, CA 94104-3615
http://www.macadamcage.com

Traditional and literary historicals.

10

McBooks Press

ID Booth Building
520 North Meadow Street
Ithaca, NY 14850
http://www.mcbooks.com

Naval historical fiction and other military adventure novels, mainly in series.

11

Medallion Press

PO Box 48889
Tampa, FL 33647
http://www.medallionpress.com

Historical romance and traditional historicals, many with uncommon settings.

12

Poisoned Pen Press

6962 E. First Avenue, Suite 103
Scottsdale, AZ 85251
http://www.poisonedpenpress.com

Historical mystery.

13

Soho Press

853 Broadway
New York, NY 10003
http://www.sohopress.com

Mystery, traditional historicals, thrillers, and literary fiction. Imprints: Soho Constable and Soho Crime (both mystery).

14

15

The Toby Press, LLC

PO Box 8531
New Milford, CT 06776-8531
http://www.tobypress.com

English-language translations of popular European novels, both literary and traditional historicals; some original historical fiction as well.

W.W. Norton & Company

500 Fifth Avenue
New York, NY 10110
http://www.wwnorton.com

Literary and traditional historicals.

University Presses

University presses are good choices for regionally based historical fiction. Their works are suitable for both academic and public libraries. These publishers have the greatest output of historical novels.

Texas A&M University Press Consortium

http://www.tamu.edu/upress/

Member publishers with a combined catalog; includes Texas A&M University Press, Texas Tech University Press, Texas Christian University Press, and Southern Methodist University Press, among others. Individual publisher addresses listed at Web site. Western-themed historical fiction.

University of Nebraska Press

1111 Lincoln Mall
Lincoln, NE 68588-0630
http://www.nebraskapress.unl.edu

Reprints of classic literature; some literature in translation. No original fiction. Imprints: University of Nebraska Press, Bison Books.

University of New Mexico Press

1312 Basehart Road SE
Albuquerque, NM 87106-4363
http://www.unmpress.com

Literature of New Mexico and the American Southwest.

University of Oklahoma Press

4100 28th Avenue NW
Norman, OK 73069-8218
http://www.oupress.com

Literature of the American West.

Christian Publishers and Imprints

The following Christian publishers and imprints actively publish historical fiction. See also Steeple Hill, the Christian romance imprint of Harlequin.

B & H Publishing Group

127 Ninth Avenue North, MSN 114
Nashville, TN. 37234
http://www.bhpublishinggroup.com
Formerly Broadman & Holman.

Bethany House Publishers

11400 Hampshire Avenue South
Minneapolis, MN 55438
http://www.bethanyhouse.com

Part of the Baker Publishing Group.

David C. Cook

4050 Lee Vance View
Colorado Springs, CO 80918-7102
http://www.davidccook.com/Books/Fiction/

Imprint: RiverOak (literary Christian fiction).

Crossway Books

1300 Crescent Street
Wheaton, IL 60187
http://www.gnpcb.org/home/books/

Harvest House Publishers

990 Owen Loop North
Eugene, OR 97402-9173
http://www.harvesthousepublishers.com

Kregel Publishers

PO Box 2607
Grand Rapids, MI 49501-2607
http://kregel.gospelcom.net

Moody Publishers

820 N. LaSalle Boulevard
Chicago, IL 60610
http://www.moodypress.com

Thomas Nelson, Inc.

PO Box 141000
Nashville, TN 37214
http://www.thomasnelson.com

Revell Books

Baker Publishing Group
6030 East Fulton Road
Ada, MI 49301
http://www.revellbooks.com

Part of the Baker Publishing Group.

Tyndale House Publishers

351 Executive Drive
Carol Stream, IL 60188
http://www.tyndale.com

WaterBrook Press

2375 Telstar Drive, Suite 160
Colorado Springs, CO 80920
http://www.randomhouse.com/waterbrook/

The Christian division of Random House, Inc.

Zondervan

5300 Patterson SE
Grand Rapids, MI 49530
http://www.zondervan.com

The Christian imprint of HarperCollins Publishers.

Large Print

Many historical novels are offered in large print format, from the following specialized publishers. Some of the major U.S. trade publishers also have large-print divisions or imprints. Historical novels from Britain often make their way into American libraries via large print editions.

Severn House

See "Major Publishers" section above.

Thorndike Press

295 Kennedy Memorial Drive
Waterville, ME 04901
http://www.gale.com/thorndike/index.htm

An imprint of Gale (a part of Cengage Learning). Significant output, with selections in Christian fiction, historical romance, and Westerns, among others.

Ulverscroft Large Print USA

914 Union Road
West Seneca, NY 14224
http://www.ulverscroft.co.uk

British publisher, with emphasis on romance and family sagas.

Writer's Manuals

All books are written by authors in the genre. Both Martin and Oliver are British, and their works reflect publishing tastes in the United Kingdom, but many of the concepts are universal.

Emerson, Kathy Lynn. *How to Write Historical Mysteries.* Perseverance Press, 2008.

A guide to all of the stages for writing a historical mystery novel, from plotting to publication and publicity. Emerson (the author of the Face Down and Diana Spaulding mystery series) includes numerous examples, both from her own novels and those by other well-known writers.

Martin, Rhona. *Writing Historical Fiction.* St. Martin's Press, 1988.

A short guide to writing in the genre, written by a former winner of the Georgette Heyer Historical Novel Prize.

Oliver, Marina. *Writing Historical Fiction: Creating the Historical Blockbuster.* Studymates, 2005.

Another British handbook written by a former chairman of the Romantic Novelists' Association. Includes assignments that writers can complete while working on their novels.

Woolley, Persia. *How to Write and Sell Historical Fiction.* Writer's Digest Books, 1997.

Beyond creative writing techniques, Woolley describes how to market historical novels to publishers. Woolley has written an Arthurian trilogy about Guinevere.

Book Review Sources

The "big four" book review magazines—*Booklist*, *Kirkus Reviews*, *Library Journal*, and *Publishers Weekly*—all review historical fiction regularly. They provide considerable coverage, mainly in their general fiction sections. In addition, the following specialized publications include reviews of many worthwhile titles not mentioned elsewhere. Many relevant Web sites and blogs, cited earlier in this chapter, also publish book reviews.

All About Romance. Published online at http://www.likesbooks.com

Critical book reviews of novels in the romance genre, with considerable coverage of historical romance. Though the reviews are a highlight, AAR also offers reader forums, articles, interviews, and more, all written by enthusiasts who love the romance genre.

Civil War Book Review. ISSN 1528-6592

From the U.S. Civil War Center, *CWBR* reviews nonfiction and historical novels about the Civil War. Fifteen to twenty fiction reviews annually, with blurbs for many more, plus interviews with novelists. Formerly a print publication, *CWBR* is available free online at http://www.cwbr.com.

The Historical Novels Review. ISSN 1471-7492

Published quarterly by the Historical Novel Society since 1997, this magazine reviews new historical fiction from the United States and Great Britain. Reviews are written for readers by readers. 900 reviews annually. $50/year (2009); includes *Solander* subscription (see above, under "History and Criticism"). Inquiries to richard@historicalnovelsociety.org.

Paradox: The Magazine of Historical and Speculative Fiction. ISSN 1548-0119

A semiannual magazine with historical short fiction and speculative fiction with historical themes; lengthy, critical book and film reviews are included, as are feature articles and essays. Some material is online at www.paradoxmag.com. $25 for two-year subscription (four issues).

Rambles. Published online at http://www.rambles.net/fiction_ his.html

Short reviews of historical novels from *Rambles: A Cultural Arts Magazine* (an online publication covering folk music as well as literature).

Romantic Times BOOKreviews. ISSN 0747-3370

Formerly known as *Romantic Times*, this periodical boasts the subtitle "the magazine for fiction lovers," though it concentrates heavily on fiction for women. Although their coverage of historical romance and Regencies is considerable, they also cover inspirational fiction, mysteries, historical women's fiction, suspense, and, less frequently, traditional historical novels and sagas. $29.95/year (2008). Details at www.romantictimes.com.

Roundup Magazine. ISSN 1081-2229

Published bimonthly by Western Writers of America. Presents information on Western writing and publishing. Many book reviews per issue, some of which can be found online at the Web site. $30/year (2008); see http://www.westernwriters.org to subscribe.

Societies and Organizations

No general trade associations exist for historical novelists as they do for other genres. The Historical Novel Society, an organization welcoming both writers and readers of historical fiction, is the closest thing. Historical novelists often join one or more of the following groups to network with their fellow authors and share research and writing tips. The groups also publicize the literature of their genre/subgenre, including those works written by their author members. For specific information on awards granted by these groups, see Appendix A.

Historical Novel Society (HNS)

c/o Susan Higginbotham, Membership Secretary
405 Brierridge Drive
Apex, NC 27502
http://www.historicalnovelsociety.org

An international organization that actively promotes the genre. Open to all historical fiction enthusiasts—authors, agents, publishers, librarians, and general readers—with membership offices in Britain, the United States, and New Zealand. HNS publishes two magazines, the *Historical Novels Review* and *Solander*.

Mystery Writers of America

17 E. 47th Street, 6th floor
New York NY 10017
http://www.mysterywriters.org

"The leading association for professional crime writers in the United States" (Web site). Open to anyone interested in mysteries or crime writing. Presents the Edgar Allan Poe Award for excellence in crime fiction.

Novelists, Inc.

PO Box 2037
Manhattan, KS 66505
http://www.ninc.com

An organization for multi-published authors of popular fiction; to qualify for membership, authors must have published at least two print novels generally available to the American public.

Romance Writers of America (RWA)

16000 Stuebner Airline Road, Suite 140
Spring, TX 77379
http://www.rwanational.org

The major American association for published and aspiring romance writers. General membership is open to writers interested in pursuing a career in romance fiction; associate membership is for those in the publishing industry; affiliate memberships are open to librarians and booksellers. RWA's many local chapters offer networking opportunities. Presents the annual RITA Awards at the annual conference.

Romantic Novelists' Association (RNA)

See Web site for e-mail contact addresses for specific inquiries.
http://www.rna-uk.org

The British counterpart to Romance Writers of America. Published writers of romantic novels are eligible for membership; associate membership is available to those in the publishing industry. Aspiring writers must enter RNA's New Writers' Scheme to obtain probationary membership. Awards the Romantic Novel of the Year and the Category Romance Award.

Sisters in Crime (SinC)

PO Box 442124
Lawrence, KS 66044-8933
http://www.sistersincrime.org

An organization offering networking, advice, and support to mystery authors and seeking to combat discrimination against women who write mysteries. Open to everyone, including authors, publishers, librarians, booksellers, fans, and more.

Western Writers of America

> c/o Rod Miller
> 1665 East Julho Street
> Sandy, UT 84093
> http://www.westernwriters.org

> Promotes the literature of the American West, both fiction and nonfiction. Membership is open to published authors writing about the American West. Awards the Spur Awards in many categories.

Women Writing the West

> 8547 East Arapahoe Road, Box J-541
> Greenwood Village, CO 80112-1436
> http://www.womenwritingthewest.org

> A group dedicated to promoting literature about women's lives in the American West, both fiction and nonfiction. Open to all interested parties. Presents the annual WILLA Literary Awards.

Appendix A

Award-Winning Historical Novels

Although few awards for adult historical fiction currently exist, a number of historical novels have won national and international prizes in recent years. Relevant titles that have been awarded prizes since publication of the first volume of this book are listed below. Because historical novels have failed to win some major prizes (e.g., Booker Prize, Giller Prize) in recent years, they have been omitted. Complete lists of winners (and, occasionally, finalists) are often available at the sponsoring organization's Web site. Many lists can also be obtained via the "All Award Winners" section of NoveList.

Although young adult titles aren't the focus of this book, the Scott O'Dell Award for Historical Fiction is given annually to worthy children's or young adult novels in the genre. To be eligible, novels must be written by American authors and set in the New World, which includes North, South, and Central America. Winners are available online at http://www.scottodell.com.

Literary Fiction

ALA Notable Books

The ALA Notable Book distinction is given annually to twenty-five "very good, very readable, and at times very important" works of fiction, nonfiction, and poetry books for adults. The Notable Books Council, who judges this category, fits hierarchically within the Collection Development and Evaluation Section (CODES) of the Reference and User Services Association (RUSA) of ALA. Web site: http://www.ala.org/ala/rusa/protools/notablebooks/thelists/notablebooks.cfm

2008	*Away*, Amy Bloom
	Finn, Jon Clinch
2007	*Beautiful Dreamer*, Christopher Bigsby
	The Madonnas of Leningrad, Debra Dean
	The Whistling Season, Ivan Doig
	The Secret River, Kate Grenville
	The People's Act of Love, James Meek

2006   *Gilead*, Marilynne Robinson

        The Hummingbird's Daughter, Luis Alberto Urrea

2005   *Birds Without Wings*, Louis de Bernières

        The Plot Against America, Philip Roth

Betty Trask Prizes and Awards

These awards were originally funded starting in 1984 by British romance novelist Betty Trask for first novels in English, published or unpublished, written by Commonwealth authors under the age of thirty-five. Novels must be "of a romantic or traditional nature (not experimental)," but this definition has gotten broader over the years. The prize money, divided among all the winners, totals up to £25,000. The top awardee is granted the Betty Trask Prize; others receive the Betty Trask Award. Presented annually by the Society of Authors at their annual meeting. Web site: http://www.societyofauthors.org/prizes_grants_and_awards/

2006   *The Short Day Dying*, Peter Hobbs (Award)

James Fenimore Cooper Prize

Awarded biennially, in odd-numbered years, to literary historical novels with American settings that "make a significant contribution to historical understanding, portray authentically the people and events of the historical past, and display skills in narrative construction and prose style." Sponsored by the Society of American Historians. The winners are listed in full. Website: http://sah.columbia.edu/prizes/cooper.html

2007   *The Last Town on Earth*, Thomas Mullen

2005   *The Plot Against America,* Philip Roth

2003   *Paradise Alley*, Kevin Baker

2001   *Bone by Bone*, Peter Matthiessen

        A Dangerous Friend, Ward Just

1999   *Gain*, Richard Powers

1997   *The Cattle Killing*, John Edgar Wideman

1995   *In the Lake of the Woods*, Tim O'Brien

1993   *Shaman*, Noah Gordon

Costa Book Awards

Formerly entitled the Whitbread Book Award, the Costa honors the best in contemporary British literature.

Best Novel

2007   *Day*, A. L. Kennedy

2006   *Restless*, William Boyd

2004   *Small Island*, Andrea Levy

Best First Novel

2006   *The Tenderness of Wolves*, Stef Penney

2005   *The Harmony Silk Factory*, Tash Aw

Governor General's Literary Award: Fiction (English)

Presented annually by the Canadian Council for the Arts for the best novel in English by a Canadian writer. A separate award is given for French-language works. Web site: http://www.canadacouncil.ca/prizes/ggla/default.asp

2006   *The Law of Dreams*, Peter Behrens

National Book Award: Fiction

Sponsored by the National Book Foundation, this literary prize recognizes outstanding achievement in fiction. Web site: http://www.nationalbook.org/ nba.html

2005   *Europe Central*, William T. Vollman

National Book Critics' Circle Award: Fiction

Awarded annually by the National Book Critics' Circle, an organization for professional book reviewers and literary critics, for "the finest books published in English." Web site: http://www.bookcritics.org

2005   *The March*, E. L. Doctorow

2004   *Gilead*, Marilynne Robinson

Orange Prize for Fiction

Awarded to the best full-length, English-language novel written by a woman of any nationality, though only works published in the United Kingdom are eligible. Sponsored by the Orange Corporation (British). Web site: http://www.orange prize.co.uk

2004   *Small Island*, Andrea Levy

Pulitzer Prize for Literature

Chosen by the Pulitzer Prize Board, housed at Columbia University, for outstanding achievement in fiction. Web site: http://www.pulitzer.org

2006   *March*, Geraldine Brooks

2005   *Gilead*, Marilynne Robinson

General Fiction

Alex Awards

Awarded annually to novels for adults with special appeal to young adults, and sponsored by the by the Margaret Alexander Edwards Trust and *Booklist*. Web site: http://www.ala.org/ala/yalsa/booklistsawards/alexawards/alexawards.cfm

2008	*Genghis: Birth of an Empire*, Conn Iggulden
	The Night Birds, Thomas Maltman
2007	*The Whistling Season,* Ivan Doig
	Water for Elephants, Sara Gruen
	Color of the Sea, John Hamamura
2006	*My Jim*, Nancy Rawles
2004	*Maisie Dobbs*, Jacqueline Winspear

Book Sense Book of the Year: Adult Fiction

Prize winners are selected by American Booksellers Association member publishers as the novels they most enjoyed hand-selling to customers. Awarded annually at BookExpo America. Web site: http://bookweb.org/btw/awards/BSBY.html

2007	*Water for Elephants*, Sara Gruen
2006	*The Historian*, Elizabeth Kostova
2005	*Jonathan Strange and Mr. Norrell*, Susanna Clarke

Langum Prize for Historical Fiction

An annual prize given honoring American historical fiction for adult readers and across all geographic regions of America. For 2005 and 2006, this prize was limited to novels from small presses and university presses, and before 2005, to university press novels alone. As so few prizes for historical fiction exist, the winners are provided in full.

2007	*Heyday*, Kurt Andersen
2006	*Dreams to Dust*, Sheldon Russell
2005	*Madison House*, Peter Donohue
2004	*Seven Laurels*, Linda Busby Parker
2003	*Rebecca Wentworth's Distraction*, Robert J. Begiebing

Michael Shaara Award

Awarded annually by the Civil War Institute (at Gettysburg College) for excellence in Civil War fiction. Between 1997 and 2004, the award was sponsored by the United States Civil War Center. Web site: http://www.gettysburg.edu/civilwar/prizes_andscholarships/michael_shaaraprize/

2007	*The Judas Field*, Howard Bahr
2006	*The March*, E. L. Doctorow

2005   No award given

2004   *A Distant Flame*, Philip Lee Williams

Oprah's Book Club

Though not an award per se, the novels featured every month as part of Oprah Winfrey's televised Book Club received enormous publicity and became instant best sellers. Because of the demand for these books at public libraries, ALA's Web site lists past selections at http://www.ala.org/ala/ourassociation/membership/oprahbooks/oprahbookinfo.cfm

2007   *Middlesex*, Jeffrey Eugenides
        Love in the Time of Cholera, Gabriel Garcia Marquez
        Pillars of the Earth, Ken Follett

The Reading List

This new award, inaugurated in 2007 by the CODES section of RUSA within ALA, highlights outstanding genre fiction for adult readers in eight different categories.

2007   *The Second Objective*, Mark Frost (Adrenaline)
        The Religion, Tim Willocks (Historical Fiction)
        Mistress of the Art of Death, Ariana Franklin (Mystery)
        In War Times, Kathleen Ann Goonan (Science Fiction)

Mystery Fiction

Agatha Award

The Agatha Award, a fan-generated award named in honor of mystery writer Agatha Christie, is presented annually at the Malice Domestic convention. It is given annually to living authors of traditional mysteries of the type written by Christie (little gratuitous violence, and usually featuring an amateur detective). Web site: http://www.malicedomestic.org/agathaawards.html

2004   *Birds of a Feather*, Jacqueline Winspear (Best Novel)

Bruce Alexander Historical Award

This award, presented at the Left Coast Crime mystery convention between 2004 and 2006, honored historical mystery writer Bruce Alexander, who died in 2003.

2006   *Spectres in the Smoke*, Tony Broadbent

CWA Ellis Peters Historical Award

Named in honor of medieval mystery writer Ellis Peters (Edith Pargeter), this award for historical crime fiction has been given since 1999 by the Crime Writers' Association (United Kingdom). It is sponsored by British publishers Headline and Little

Brown as well as the estate of Ellis Peters. Formerly titled the Ellis Peters Historical Dagger. Web site: http://www.thecwa.co.uk

2007   *Mistress of the Art of Death*, Ariana Franklin
2006   *Red Sky Lament*, Edward Wright
2005   *Dark Fire*, C. J. Sansom

Edgar Award

The Edgars, short for the Edgar Allan Poe Awards, are given annually in several categories by the Mystery Writers of America. Includes mysteries of all types (not just historical). Web site: http://www.theedgars.com/

2007   *The Janissary Tree*, Jason Goodwin (Best Novel)
2006   *The Girl in the Glass*, Jeffrey Ford (Best Paperback Original)

Sue Feder Memorial Historical Mystery Award

This new award, established in 2006, is sponsored by Mystery Readers International, an organization for mystery fans and readers, and is presented annually at the Bouchercon mystery convention. It honors the late Sue Feder, founder of the Historical Mystery Appreciation Society (which had sponsored the Herodotus Awards) and publisher of the newsletter *Murder: Past Tense*. Web site: http://www.mysteryreaders.org/macavity.html

2008   *The Snake Stone*, Jason Goodwin
2007   *Oh Danny Boy*, Rhys Bowen
2006   *Pardonable Lies*, Jacqueline Winspear

Romantic Fiction

RITA Award

The RITA, the highest commendation in the American romance genre, is awarded annually by the Romance Writers of America in twelve different categories (which have changed slightly over the years). Relevant winners of the Best Inspirational Romance title are listed below under Christian Fiction. For a comprehensive guide to winners and finalists, see the Web site: http://www.rwanational.org/cs/contests_and_awards/rita_awards

Best Historical

2008   *Lessons of Desire*, Madeline Hunter

Best Regency Historical

2008   *The Secret Diaries of Miss Miranda Cheever*, Julia Quinn

Best Long Historical

2007   *On the Way to the Wedding*, Julia Quinn

2006   *The Devil to Pay*, Liz Carlyle

2005   *Shadowheart*, Laura Kinsale

Best Short Historical

2007   *The Book of True Desires*, Betina Krahn

2006   *The Texan's Reward*, Jodi Thomas

2005   *A Wanted Man*, Susan Kay Law

Best First Book

2007   *The Husband Trap*, Tracy Anne Warren

Best Novel with Strong Romantic Elements

2008   *Silent in the Grave*, Deanna Raybourn

2007   *A Lady Raised High*, Jennifer Ashley writing as Laurien Gardner

Best Regency

2006   *A Reputable Rake*, Diane Gaston

2005   *A Passionate Endeavor*, Sophia Nash

Romantic Novel of the Year Award

Awarded annually by the Romantic Novelists' Association (British organization). Open to both modern and historical novels, with entry limited to citizens of the United Kingdom. These novels may or may not be "historical romances" as defined in this book, but they do have romantic elements. Past winners include Valerie Fitzgerald's *Zemindar*, Rosamunde Pilcher's *Coming Home*, and Philippa Gregory's *The Other Boleyn Girl*. Web site: http://www.rna-uk.org

2007   *Iris and Ruby*, Rosie Thomas

Christian Fiction

Christy Award

Named in honor of Catherine Marshall's best-selling inspirational novel *Christy*, the annual Christy Awards recognize excellence in Christian fiction. The award has been organized by representatives from a dozen Christian fiction publishers since 1999; the first awards were given in 2000. The Historical categories include novels set before 1950, while Contemporary is meant to address time periods from 1950 to the present. Web site: http://www.christyawards.com

2008   *A Proper Pursuit*, Lynn Austin (Historical)

Remembered, Tamera Alexander (Romance)

2007   *Madman*, Tracy Groot (Historical)

The Measure of a Lady, Deeanne Gist (Romance)

William Henry is a Fine Name, Cathy Gohlke (Young Adult)

2006   *Whence Came a Prince*, Liz Curtis Higgs (Historical)

A Bride Most Begrudging, Deeanne Gist (Romance)

River Rising, Athol Dickson (Suspense)

2005   *King's Ransom*, Jan Beazely and Thom Lemmons (Historical)

RITA Award, Inspirational Category

Awarded annually by the Romance Writers of America for outstanding achievement in inspirational (i.e., Christian) fiction. Web site: http://www.rwanational.org/cs/contests_and_awards/rita_awards

2007   *Revealed*, Tamera Alexander

Western Fiction

Spur Award

The Spur Awards are given annually by Western Writers of America for distinguished writing about the American West. In 1997 the award was changed to reflect the year awarded rather than the year published. The distinction between Best Novel of the West and Best Western Novel now depends on length, but in the past it referred to historical and traditional Westerns. Between 1953 (inception of the Spurs) and 1981, separate awards were given to Novel and Historical Novel. See the Web site for detailed Spur award history: http://www.westernwriters.org/awards.htm

Best Western Long Novel

Western novels over 90,000 words in length are eligible for this award, which was formerly titled Best Novel of the West; shorter works are eligible instead for Best Short Western Novel, below.

2007   *The Night Journal*, Elizabeth Crook

2006   *High Country*, Willard Wyman

2005   *People of the Raven*, W. Michael and Kathleen O'Neal Gear

Best Original Mass Market Paperback

Includes Western historical novels as well as traditional Westerns, which are likely to appear in paperback.

2008   *Hellfire Canyon*, Max McCoy

2007   *The Horse Creek Incident*, Dusty Richards

2006   *Dakota*, Matt Braun

2005   *Vengeance Valley*, Richard S. Wheeler

Best Western Short Novel

At present, novels under 90,000 words are eligible for this award, which was formerly titled simply Best Western Novel. This wasn't always the case, however, as Larry McMurtry's epic Western *Lonesome Dove* took home the prize in 1985.

2008   *Tallgrass*, Sandra Dallas

2006   *Camp Ford*, Johnny D. Boggs (tie)

        The Undertaker's Wife, Loren D. Estleman (tie)

Best First Novel

Awarded for best first Western novel, formerly called the Medicine Pipe Bearers' Award; includes traditional Westerns.

2008   *The Night Birds*, Thomas Maltman

2007   *Broken Trail*, Alan Geoffrion

2006   *High Country*, Willard Wyman

Western Heritage Award: Outstanding Western Novel

Sponsored by the National Cowboy and Western Heritage Museum in Oklahoma City, these awards honor outstanding achievement in Western fiction. Web site: http://www.nationalcowboymuseum.org/

2008   *Harpsong*, Rilla Askew

2007   *Broken Trail*, Alan Geoffrion

2006   *Buffalo Calf Road Woman, The Story of a Warrior of the Little Bighorn*, Rosemary Agonito and Joseph Agonito

2005   *And Not to Yield*, Randy Lee Eickhoff

WILLA Literary Awards

Awarded annually by Women Writing the West since 1999 for literature featuring women's stories set in the American West. Selectors are librarians unaffiliated with the organization. Separate awards are given for contemporary fiction, historical fiction, and original paperbacks, as well as for children's/young adult fiction and nonfiction. Web site: http://www.womenwritingthewest.org/ willaaward.html

Historical Fiction

"Women's stories set in the west before contemporary times."

2007   *The Night Journal*, Elizabeth Crook

2006   *New Mercies*, Sandra Dallas

2005   *Tombstone Travesty: Allie Earp Remembers*, Jane Candia Coleman

Contemporary Fiction

"Women's stories set in the west during contemporary times."

2005   *The Real Minerva*, Mary Sharratt

Original Paperback

2005   *Echoes*, Erin Grady

Appendix B

Reading Lists by Plot Pattern or Theme

Following are selected lists of recommended titles in popular historical periods and subject areas, and on other commonly requested themes. These lists take a wide-ranging approach, covering authors and titles from a variety of historical fiction subgenres.

Core Authors by Period and Place

The following novelists have developed a significant repertoire of novels set in one or more historical periods and are generally reliable in presenting their subjects from a historical standpoint. Many important authors and titles from volume 1 of *Historical Fiction* are included here for the sake of completeness, along with new additions.

Multi-Period

These exceptional authors have mastered a number of historical periods.

Isabel Allende

Valerie Anand (also writes as Fiona Buckley)

Lynn Austin

Geraldine Brooks

Bernard Cornwell

Tracy Chevalier

Paul Doherty (many pseudonyms)

Karen Essex

Ken Follett

Margaret George

Cecelia Holland

Morgan Llywelyn

Norah Lofts

Edward Marston (Conrad Allen, David Garland—all pseudonyms of Keith Miles)

James Michener

Gilbert Morris

Diana Norman (Ariana Franklin)

Jean Plaidy (Philippa Carr, Victoria Holt)

Lucia St. Clair Robson

Edward Rutherfurd

Anya Seton

Jeff Shaara

Irving Stone

Reay Tannahill

Judith Tarr

Rose Tremain

Bodie and Brock Thoene

Harry Turtledove (H. N. Turteltaub)

Susan Vreeland

Barbara Wood

Prehistory

Jean Auel

W. Michael Gear and Kathleen O'Neal Gear

Sue Harrison

Linda Lay Shuler

Judith Tarr

Elizabeth Marshall Thomas

Biblical Times

India Edghill

Marek Halter

Angela Elwell Hunt

Francine Rivers

Ancient Egypt

Pauline Gedge

Christian Jacq

Lynda S. Robinson

Judith Tarr

Ancient Greece

Gillian Bradshaw

Steven Pressfield

Mary Renault

The Roman Empire

Gillian Bradshaw

Lindsey Davis

Michael Curtis Ford

Colleen McCullough

John Maddox Roberts

Steven Saylor

The British Isles

Early and High Middle Ages

Elizabeth Chadwick

Margaret Frazer

Roberta Gellis

Edith Pargeter/Ellis Peters

Sharon Kay Penman

Judith Merkle Riley

Rosemary Sutcliff

Nigel Tranter

Peter Tremayne

Jack Whyte

Tudor and Stuart Eras

Stephanie Cowell

George Garrett

Karen Harper

Patricia Finney (P.F. Chisholm)

Philippa Gregory

Karleen Koen

Robin Maxwell

C. J. Sansom

Susan Holloway Scott

Alison Weir

Georgian Era (includes Napoleonic Wars and Regency Era)

Mary Balogh

Jo Beverley

Bernard Cornwell

C. S. Forester

Diana Gabaldon

Georgette Heyer

Carla Kelly

David Liss

Patrick O'Brian

Victorian Era

Catherine Cookson

Michel Faber

Malcolm MacDonald

Anne Perry

Sarah Waters

Twentieth Century

Carola Dunn

Sebastian Faulks

Morgan Llywelyn

Charles Todd

Europe

The Middle Ages

Maurice Druon

Sharan Newman

Zoé Oldenbourg

Sigrid Undset

The Renaissance and Reformation

Dorothy Dunnett

Jeanne Kalogridis

Judith Merkle Riley

Samuel Shellabarger

Early Modern Era

Beryl Bainbridge

Sandra Gulland

Rosalind Laker

Twentieth Century

Robert Alexander

Sebastian Faulks

Alan Furst

Andrei Makine

The United States

Pre-Civil War

Max Byrd

Edward Cline

Sara Donati

Howard Fast

Thomas Fleming

Barbara Hambly

Margaret Lawrence

David Nevin

Mary Lee Settle

Beverly Swerling

James Alexander Thom

Civil War and After

Howard Fast

Charles Frazier

Dorothy Garlock

John Jakes

MacKinlay Kantor

Thomas Mallon

Margaret Mitchell

Eugenia Price

Jeff Shaara

Herman Wouk

American West

Win Blevins

Johnny D. Boggs

Willa Cather

Don Coldsmith

Jane Candia Coleman

Robert J. Conley

Sandra Dallas

Loren Estleman

Terry C. Johnston

Elmer Kelton

Jane Kirkpatrick

Louis L'Amour

Larry McMurtry

Lucia St. Clair Robson

Richard S. Wheeler

Jeanne Williams

Canada, Greenland, and the Arctic

Margaret Atwood

Andrea Barrett

Mazo de la Roche

Wayne Johnston

Janette Oke

The Middle East

Ann Chamberlin

Jason Goodwin

Elizabeth Peters

Bodie and Brock Thoene

Asia, Africa, and the Antipodes

Africa

Wilbur Smith

Australia

Colleen McCullough

Patricia Shaw

China

Pearl S. Buck

James Clavell

Eleanor Cooney and Daniel Altieri

Anchee Min

Lisa See

Amy Tan

Gail Tsukiyama

Robert Van Gulik

India

Valerie Fitzgerald

M.M. Kaye

Rebecca Ryman

John Speed

Japan

James Clavell

Arthur Golden

I. J. Parker

Laura Joh Rowland

Strong Women in History

These novels recount tales of women from history who persevered against overwhelming odds and triumphed in a man's world. They present a strong feminist message without necessarily being anachronistic (some authors do take literary license in this respect to make their heroines more appealing to today's readers). Many of the protagonists are based on historical figures. Many of these authors have written earlier works with the same themes.

Amirrezvani, Anita—*The Blood of Flowers*

Arruda, Suzanne—Jade del Cameron Series

Bradley, Marion Zimmer—Avalon Series, especially *The Mists of Avalon*

Coleman, Jane Candia—*Tombstone Travesty*

Cross, Donna Woolfolk—*Pope Joan*

Cunningham, Elizabeth—The Maeve Chronicles

Diamant, Anita—*The Red Tent*

Donati, Sara—Wilderness Series

Donnelly, Jennifer—*The Tea Rose, The Winter Rose*

Essex, Karen—*Leonardo's Swans; Stealing Athena*

Franklin, Ariana—Adelia Aguilar Series

Garrett, Ginger—*Chosen; Dark Hour*

Gillespie, Donna—*The Light Bearer; Lady of the Light*

Gist, Deeanne—Essie Spreckelmeyer Series

Gortner, C. W.—*The Last Queen*

Gulland, Sandra—*Mistress of the Sun*

Gunning, Sally—*The Widow's War*

Halter, Marek—Canaan Trilogy

Henderson, William Haywood—*Augusta Locke*

Kaufman, Pamela—Alix of Wanthwaite Trilogy

King, Susan Fraser—*Lady Macbeth*

Kingman, Peg—*Not Yet Drown'd*

Kirkpatrick, Jane—Change and Cherish Historical Series

Learner, Tobsha—*The Witch from Cologne*

Mitchell, Margaret—*Gone with the Wind*

Moran, Michelle—*Nefertiti*

Morgan, Jude—*Passion; Symphony*

Naslund, Sena Jeter—*Abundance*

O'Brien, Patricia—*Harriet and Isabella*

Orcutt, Jane—*All the Tea in China*

Paisley, Janet—*White Rose Rebel*

Peters, Elizabeth—Amelia Peabody Series

Peterson, Tracie—Ladies of Liberty Series

Raybourn, Deanna—Julia Grey Series

Riley, Judith Merkle—Margaret of Ashbury Trilogy

Robson, Lucia St. Clair—*Shadow Patriots*

Scott, Manda—Boudica Series

Scott, Susan Holloway—*Duchess*

Sharratt, Mary—*The Real Minerva; The Vanishing Point*

Shors, John—*Beneath a Marble Sky*

Steinke, René—*Holy Skirts*

Tipton, James—<u>Annette Vallon</u>

Turner, Nancy E.—<u>Sarah Agnes Prine Series</u>

Watson, Jules—<u>Dalriada Trilogy</u>

Willig, Lauren—<u>Pink Carnation series</u>

Revisionist Historical Novels

Authors of these novels recount well-known historical episodes from a new viewpoint, putting a different spin on what may have really happened in history. Revered historical figures are seen in a unique and sometimes unflattering light; in other cases, people who have gone down in history as villains are given the opportunity to explain their actions. Because of their subject matter, these works are often controversial.

Cunningham, Elizabeth—<u>The Maeve Chronicles</u>

Elyot, Amanda—*The Memoirs of Helen of Troy*

Gortner, C. W.—*The Last Queen*

Graham, Jo—*Black Ships*

Gregory, Philippa—*The Other Boleyn Girl*; *The Constant Princess*

Lawhead, Stephen R.—<u>King Raven trilogy</u>

Le Guin, Ursula K.—*Lavinia*

Lerner, Eric—*Pinkerton's Secret*

McGowan, Kathleen—*The Expected One*

Newman, Janis Cooke—*Mary*

Sierra, Javier—*The Secret Supper*

Literary Sequels and Reimaginings

Readers have a love-hate relationship with sequels to classic works of literature. Although they enjoy having the opportunity to visit well-loved places and characters once more, it can be disappointing for them when the sequels don't live up to the high literary standards of the originals, or when characters are portrayed in an inconsistent manner. The best literary sequels pay homage to the original works by keeping the style and tone believable. Other authors of sequels retell classic stories based on the point of view of minor characters, either in a straightforward manner or in the form of a parody. See also the listings for "Austen themes" and "Shakespearean themes" in the subject index, as well as the "Jane Austen sequels" category in Chapter 4.

Aston, Elizabeth—<u>Darcy series</u> (Jane Austen's *Pride and Prejudice*)

Berdoll, Linda—<u>Darcy series</u> (Jane Austen's *Pride and Prejudice*)

Blixt, David—*The Master of Verona* (William Shakespeare's *Romeo and Juliet*)

Brooks, Geraldine—*March* (Louisa May Alcott's *Little Women*)

Clinch, Jon—*Finn* (Mark Twain's *Huckleberry Finn*)

Gouge, Louise—Ahab's Legacy series (Herman Melville's *Moby-Dick*)

Hart, Lenore—*Becky* (Mark Twain's *Tom Sawyer*)

McCaig, Donald—*Rhett Butler's People* (Margaret Mitchell's *Gone With the Wind*)

Morris, R. N.—Porfiry Petrovich Series (Fyodor Dostoevsky's *Crime and Punishment*)

Noyes, Deborah—*Angel and Apostle* (Nathaniel Hawthorne's *The Scarlet Letter*)

Rawles, Nancy—*My Jim* (Mark Twain's *Huckleberry Finn*)

Tiffany, Grace—*The Turquoise Ring* (William Shakespeare's *The Merchant of Venice*)

Zimler, Richard—*Guardian of the Dawn* (William Shakespeare's *Othello*)

African American Interest

Many historical novels feature African American characters, but those in the following selected list are told from their own point of view. They show how members of this ethnic group played important roles in history. Additional examples of novels with prominent African American characters can be found in the subject index.

Baker, Calvin—*Dominion*

Baker, Kevin—*Strivers Row*

Cezair-Thompson, Margaret—*The Pirate's Daughter*

Foster, Sharon Ewell—*Abraham's Well*

Haley, Alex—*Roots*

Hill, Lawrence—*Someone Knows My Name*

Jenkins, Beverly—House of Le Veq series

McBride, James—*Song Yet Sung*

Miller, Judith—Freedom's Path Series

Morrison, Toni—*Beloved*

Neighbour, Mary E.—*Speak Right On*

Phillips, Caryl—*Dancing in the Dark*

Rawles, Nancy—*My Jim*

Tademy, Lalita—*Cane River* and *Red River*

Asian American Interest

These important novels portray the Asian and Asian American experience in historical fiction. See also relevant headings in the subject and place/time indexes.

Avery, Ellis—*The Teahouse Fire*

Epstein, Jennifer Cody—*The Painter from Shanghai*

Golden, Arthur—*Memoirs of a Geisha*

Hamumura, John—*Color of the Sea*

Min, Anchee—*Empress Orchid*, *The Last Empress*

Mukherjee, Bharati—*The Tree Bride*

Parker, I. J.—Sugawara Ikitada Series

Rowland, Laura Joh—Sano Ichiro Series

Shan, Sa—*Empress*

See, Lisa—*Peony in Love*; *Snow Flower and the Secret Fan*

Shors, John—*Beneath a Marble Sky*

Tsukiyama, Gail—*Street of a Thousand Blossoms*

Viswanathan, Padma—*The Toss of a Lemon*

Latin American Interest

Similar to the categories above, these novels portray the Latin American historical experience from the point of view of members of this ethnic group.

Allende, Isabel—*Daughter of Fortune, Portrait in Sepia, Inès of My Soul, Zorro*

Alvarez, Julia—*Saving the World*

Esquivel, Laura—*Malinche*

Gonzalez, Béa—*The Mapmaker's Opera*

Manrique, Jaime—*Our Lives Are the Rivers*

Rodriguez, Luis—*Music of the Mill*

Urrea, Luis Alberto—*The Hummingbird's Daughter*

Native American Interest

In these books the authors attempt to portray Native American characters sympathetically and/or from their own point of view.

Agonito, Rosemary, and Joseph Agonito—*Buffalo Calf Road Woman*

Coldsmith, Don—Spanish Bit Series

Conley, Robert J.—Real People Series

Gear, W. Michael and Kathleen O'Neal Gear—The First North Americans Series

Marshall, Joseph M., III—*Hundred in the Hand*

Robson, Lucia St. Clair—*Ride the Wind*

Wood, Barbara—*Daughter of the Sun*, *Woman of a Thousand Secrets*

Author/Title Index

Titles of books are in italic type; titles of series are underscored.

Subject Index

Historical Character Index

Place and Time Index

Under each main entry, subentries are listed in order by time period rather than alphabetically. In general, places are indexed using the terms by which they are most commonly known; for example, novels taking place in Montana Territory before it became a state (1889) are listed under Montana. As in the rest of this book, many novels are grouped by era, with specific years provided. For locales other than the British Isles, Europe and parts of the Middle East, and the United States, century designations are provided.

British Isles
    early Middle Ages refers roughly to
        449–1066 AD
    high Middle Ages, 1066–1485
    Tudor era, 1485–1603
    Stuart era, 1603–1714
    Georgian era, 1714–1837
    Regency era, 1811–1820
    Victorian era, 1837–1901
    20th century, 1901–1950
    World War I, 1914–1917
    World War II, 1939–1945
Europe and some Middle Eastern
    regions
    Middle Ages, 476–1492 AD

Renaissance/Reformation, roughly
    1492–1650
early modern era, 1650–1900
20th century, 1901–1950
World War I, 1914–1917
World War II, 1939–1945
United States
    colonial period, from first European
        settlement through 1775
    American Revolution, 1775–1783
    Early United States, 1783–1861
    Civil War, 1861–1865
    Reconstruction/Gilded Age, 1865–1900
    20th century, 1901–1950
    World War I, 1914–1917
        World War II, 1939–1945

Page numbers are provided in the following entries.